A Companion to American Religious History

WILEY BLACKWELL COMPANIONS TO AMERICAN HISTORY

This series provides essential and authoritative overviews of the scholarship that has shaped our present understanding of the American past. Edited by eminent historians, each volume tackles one of the major periods or themes of American history, with individual topics authored by key scholars who have spent considerable time in research on the questions and controversies that have sparked debate in their field of interest. The volumes are accessible for the non-specialist, while also engaging scholars seeking a reference to the historiography or future concerns.

A COMPANION TO AMERICAN RELIGIOUS HISTORY

Edited by

Benjamin E. Park

Sam Houston State University
Huntsville, Texas, USA

WILEY Blackwell

This edition first published 2021
© 2021 John Wiley & Sons, Inc.

The right of Benjamin E. Park to be identified as the author of the editorial material in this work has been asserted in accordance with law.

Registered Office
John Wiley & Sons, Inc., 111 River Street, Hoboken, NJ 07030, USA

Editorial Office
9600 Garsington Road, Oxford, OX4 2DQ, UK

For details of our global editorial offices, customer services, and more information about Wiley products visit us at www.wiley.com.

Wiley also publishes its books in a variety of electronic formats and by print-on-demand. Some content that appears in standard print versions of this book may not be available in other formats.

Library of Congress Cataloging-in-Publication Data
Names: Park, Benjamin E., editor.
Title: A companion to American religious history / edited by Benjamin E.
    Park, Sam Houston State University, Huntsville, Texas, USA.
Description: Hoboken, NJ, USA: John Wiley & Sons, Inc., 2021. | Series:
    Wiley Blackwell companions to American history | Includes
    bibliographical references and index.
Identifiers: LCCN 2020025382 (print) | LCCN 202002538 (ebook) | ISBN
    9781119583660 (hardback) | ISBN 9781119583677 (adobe pdf) | ISBN
    9781119583684 (epub)
Subjects: LCSH: United States–Religion–History.
Classification: LCC BL2525 .C647 2021 (print) | LCC BL2525 (ebook) | DDC
    200.973–dc23
LC record available at https://lccn.loc.gov/2020025382
LC ebook record available at https://lccn.loc.gov/2020025383

Cover Design: Wiley
Cover Image: © Devesh Tripathi/Getty Images

Set in 10/12pt Galliard by SPi Global, Pondicherry, India

10   9   8   7   6   5   4   3   2   1

Contents

List of Contributors

Carleigh Beriont
Harvard University
Cambridge
Massachusetts

Richard J. Boles
Oklahoma State University
Stillwater
Oklahoma

Vaughn A. Booker
Dartmouth College
Hanover
New Hampshire

Melissa May Borja
University of Michigan
Ann Arbor
Michigan

Christopher Cameron
University of North Carolina
Charlotte
North Carolina

Jennifer Caplan
Towson University
Towson
Maryland

Lori J. Daggar
Ursinus College
Collegeville
Pennsylvania

Sarah Dees
Iowa State University
Ames
Iowa

Jennifer H. Dorsey
Siena College
Loudonville
New York

Janine Giordano Drake
Indiana University
Bloomington
Indiana

Christian Gonzales
University of Rhode Island
Kingston
Rhode Island

Sarah Barringer Gordon
University of Pennsylvania
Philadelphia
Pennsylvania

Emily Suzanne Johnson
Ball State University
Muncie
Indiana

Christopher Cannon Jones
Brigham Young University
Provo
Utah

Nicole C. Kirk
Meadville Lombard Theological School
Chicago
Illinois

Joseph P. Laycock
Texas State University
San Marcos
Texas

Joseph L. Locke
University of Houston-Victoria
Victoria
Texas

Benjamin E. Park
Sam Houston State University
Huntsville
Texas

Brent M. Rogers
The Joseph Smith Papers
Salt Lake City
Utah

Arlene M. Sánchez-Walsh
Azusa Pacific University
Azusa
California

Jon F. Sensbach
University of Florida
Gainsville
Florida

Brent S. Sirota
North Carolina State University
Raleigh
North Carolina

Angela Tarango
Trinity University
San Antonio
Texas

Nicole Myers Turner
Yale University
New Haven
Connecticut

Peter W. Walker
University of Wyoming
Laramie
Wyoming

Rachel Wheeler
Indiana University-Purdue University
Indianapolis
Indiana

Cassandra L. Yacovazzi
University of South Florida
Sarasota-Manatee
Sarasota
Florida

Jason R. Young
University of Michigan
Ann Arbor
Michigan

Chapter One

The Centrality, Diversity, and Malleability of American Religion

Benjamin E. Park
Sam Houston State University, Huntsville, Texas

Every year in early spring, millions of Hindus across the globe gather to celebrate the end of winter and the blossoming of life. The day-and-a-half event, filled with distinct ceremonies, includes a series of rituals and prayers, yet it is best known for the festival of colors, the Rangwali Holi, in which participants smear themselves and each other with bright powder while accompanied by vibrant music. Large crowds dance, sing, and march as they spread their joyful colors and voices throughout the festival grounds and surrounding streets. And while the Holi Festival originated in India, it has spread outside of Asia and into many nations in the western hemisphere, including places where Hinduism makes up a small percentage of the population.

One of the largest Holi festivals takes place in Washington DC, where thousands of young Americans — most of whom are white, Christian, and know very little about Hinduism — gather at the Hare Krishna Temple to participate in this global Hindu celebration. While ignorant of the theological origins of the event, and not too interested in the rites that accompany the festival, they are mostly concerned with the joyous celebration. Social media accounts, newspaper editorials, and magazine features are then filled with these high school- and college-aged kids doused in vibrant colors and hailing the beauty of life.

That thousands of young, white, and Christian Americans could participate in an annual Hindu festival near the nation's capital would have seemed bizarre only a century earlier. In 1893, for instance, many prominent religious and political leaders worried that the Asian religions that were being featured at that year's Parliament of World Religions might corrupt the country's youth, and therefore did their best to ban "heretical" practices like yoga and belly dancing — let alone ornate ceremonies with thousands of attendees. For a nation still controlled by a Protestant majority that acted as a quasi-religious establishment, such measures could still be practiced.

But in the twenty-first century, the Holi Festival in DC captures many of the central elements of American religion: its embedded nature within the national culture, its diversity of sacred expression, as well as the porous nature of its spiritual boundaries. Previously marginalized practices that were seen as threatening are now embraced as a joyous embodiment of diverse cooperation. But to understand how this came to be, we must examine the many trajectories that culminated in the modern American religious marketplace.

A Companion to American Religious History, First Edition. Edited by Benjamin E. Park.
© 2021 John Wiley & Sons, Inc. Published 2021 by John Wiley & Sons, Inc.

* * *

Wherever one looks in modern America, they are confronted with the pervasive influence of religion. Most politicians are sworn in on the Bible, Qur'an, or Tanakh; "In God We Trust" is found on national currency; the Pledge of Allegiance beseeches the name of deity; and athletes frequently offer thanks to a higher power after their athletic achievements. This influence is even found in popular culture. In 2017, for instance, one of the most popular new songs was Kesha's "Praying" (drawing on the ritual of invocation), and one of the new hit television series was NBC's "The Good Place" (exploring competing ideas of the afterlife). Whether on the campaign trail, stage, athletic fields, or in shopping centers, then, religious ideas and language have become ubiquitous within American culture. Yet beyond this veneer of a shared culture is a complicated and evolving web of diverse expressions and conflicting values.

It has always been such. The earliest peoples who inhabited the land that eventually became America, thousands of Indigenous tribes with as many belief systems as languages, viewed society in a way that blended the material and spiritual; for many of them, there was little difference. Later, European settlers were as interested in spreading their religion as they were in colonizing land and building capital; to these newcomers, their particular form of Christianity was synonymous with civilized progress. And among those that were then expected to build these new societies were enslaved African laborers transported against their will; yet even these communities, many of whom were forced to leave their religious cultures behind, succeeded in developing spiritual practices that provided meaning to their lives and resistance to their oppressors. The North American colonies were founded upon these varied experiences.

By the time the United States was formed as an official polity, the landscape was littered with different — and often competing — religious cultures, so much so that it was impossible to identify and install a national, established religion. What resulted was therefore a spiritual marketplace that allowed all denominations — or at least those not deemed as a threat — to contend for converts under a broad, if not always consistent, umbrella of religious freedom. The vibrancy of this democratic experiment invited new innovations and radical interventions, as traditional churches now battled with upstart sects for the young nation's attention. Then, as the country evolved into an empire, religions were both martialed as part of that imperial pursuit as well as deployed to oppose those very aims; simultaneously, marginalized groups drew on religion in their efforts to oppose racial, economic, and gender oppression, and claim what they believed were constitutional, God-given, rights. In the twenty-first century, though religious affiliation has slightly decreased, the United States still polls much more religious than her European peers, in large part because of the traditions that built the country in the first place.

The story of America, then, can only be understood when taking into account the deep and divergent influences of religion. *A Companion to American Religious History*, designed as a primer for students of American history in general, exposes readers to the significance, variety, and malleability of the nation's religious past. The most recent generation of scholarship has produced a plethora of exciting and revisionist interpretations in the field, and this volume condenses and explains them for a new generation of students.

This *Companion* is unique, then, in its attempt to prove religion's centrality to broader historical narratives and themes. It is not just a story of religion *in* America, but a story of how religion *shaped* American history. It prioritizes chronological periods and larger contextual issues in order to introduce students of America's past to religion's role in the stories and events that already populate textbooks. The volume is a bridge between the robust field of American religion and the wider community — and especially the numerous classrooms — of American history writ large.

In a nation still struggling to define the parameters of pluralism, *A Companion to American Religious History* provides both a historical genealogy for the country's various religious traditions as well as meaning for its many cultural expressions.

* * *

This volume does not offer a comprehensive story, nor does it cover every single significant episode. Instead, it offers poignant case studies of distinct moments, movements, or themes that demonstrate the potency of America's religious past. Each chapter takes a theoretically small story and gleans much broader lessons, often framed through the lived experiences of those involved. These microhistories and thematic overviews are meant to give students of American history an entry point for understanding the legacies of the nation's religious traditions, as well as prompt further reflection and discussion related to the inchoate roles that belief and action have played in American culture.

Though a number of lessons could be prioritized, and while many chapters move in different directions and draw from divergent discourses, three themes hold this volume together. First, that religion has been *central* to American history, and that one cannot understand broader historical moments without investigating the religious actors and ideas that played a significant role. Whether it be European colonization, the American Revolution, slavery, territorial politics, imperialism, Gilded Age capitalism, the Civil Rights movement, or modern-day television, religion shaped how many citizens understood and challenged the world around them. Therefore, much of this volume is structured to augment courses focused on American history more broadly, proving religion's significance to the larger story.

A primary reason that religion is often downplayed in synthetic historical works is the cultural chasm between America's predominantly religious culture and the increasingly secular nature of the academy. Historians are hesitant to provide ammunition to cultural warriors hell-bent on proving the United States as a "Christian nation," and are instead mostly interested in deciphering the *real* motivations — social, cultural, economic, or political — beyond the religious rhetoric. Yet granting the depth of religious influence in America's past does not validate arguments for religious significance in the present; indeed, a better understanding of the variety, not just the gravity, of religious history often undercuts the type of cultural arguments that typically make academics blanche.

Second, chapters in this volume highlight the *diversity* of the nation's religious past. Though universalistic symbols and the common language of a "Christian Nation" seem to imply religious homogeneity, and while many Christians have envisioned a nation held together by shared beliefs, the reality is that America's story is filled with a vast array of different voices and distinct practices. At no point was there a shared creed, and all attempts for a joint identity were the result of an anxiety derived from entrenched pluralism. Individual case studies in this collection therefore highlight these diverse expressions, whether the variety is found in race, class, denomination, geography, or gender. Indeed, this volume eschews the typical discourse of an American religion in favor of American religion*s*.

Among the many forms of religious diversity this collection highlights are a sustained focus on Black and Indigenous religions. When it comes to African American religiosity, an explosion of recent scholarship has demonstrated its depth and variety, yet broader synthetic studies have still marginalized non-white experiences to the peripheries of the story, or, at the most, separated them into distinct frameworks. This volume, by contrast, attempts to integrate Black religious movements and ideas into mainstream trajectories of American life, ranging from the non-Christian religious practices of the enslaved, the Black prophetic tradition found among abolitionists, or the use of religion during the post-emancipation period to secure constitutional liberties. In every section of this volume, readers will be exposed to how Black religion was central to understanding its particular era.

These historiographic issues are even more complicated with Indigenous religions. Since traditional stories of America's religious past have been framed by white Protestant interests, the spirituality of Native Americans have typically been ignored or dismissed altogether. A theology of invisibility concerning Indigenous religiosity, not too dissimilar from the manifest destiny doctrine that dispossessed Native tribes, has erased a crucial part of the nation's story. Yet the variety and centrality of Indigenous religious practices and ideas can no longer be avoided. Whether it be the Wampanoag who challenged the Puritan's Godly settlement, the Lenape who tested the boundaries of Pennsylvania's inclusive vision, the Delaware who opposed Western expansion, the Haudenosaunees who appropriated their own form of spirituality, the Pueblo who pushed back against evolving federal policies, or the Mohawk who carved out a portion of Pentecostalism, every section in this volume contains at least one substantive example of Native American religiosity. This collection therefore aims to add to the reparation project of reintegrating these voices into America's past.

The third and final theme of this volume is the *malleability* that came with religious interaction. No religious tradition ever existed in a vacuum, but rather acted within a context of competing views and beliefs. This is especially true of the denominations and communities that have squeezed into America's boundaries as cultural contact and exchange became a consistent feature of American culture. Very few chapters in this volume examine one religion in isolation. Rather, most focus on how different communities reacted to their surrounding society, including other denominations and racial groups. Students will recognize that American religion was an evolving tradition with porous boundaries and interdependent trajectories. Only by highlighting the broader forest can the significance of each tree become clear.

* * *

A Companion to American Religious History is separated into five parts, each framed around a chronological period. Every section is based on the diversity of expressions within its own era. The first part, "Colonialism," briefly examines three different colonial projects that preceded the American Revolution. First, Richard Boles unpacks a typical New England town to show that religious diversity and contestation were always present, even in what was supposed to be a Puritan hamlet. Moving south, Rachel Wheeler exhibits how multiple communities — Moravian and Native — intersected within confined spaces. Both of these chapters give particular attention to the Indigenous tribes who were dispossessed by these religious colonization attempts. And finally, the section concludes with Jason Young's examination of enslaved religiosity throughout the colonial period.

The imperial crisis that rocked the North American continent during the late-eighteenth century and the creation of a new American nation each spurred novel and contested directions in religious life. Part Two, "Establishment," focuses on how new traditions were both established and disestablished during the American Revolution, as well as appropriated during the few decades that immediately followed. While nearly everyone in the formerly British colonies were forced to choose a side in the conflict, few faced such daunting choices as the clergy. Peter Walker's chapter zeroes in on the loyalist ministers who tried to stay faithful to the English crown, drawing upon a rich martyrdom legacy to do so; conversely, Christopher Jones's chapter follows a radical clergyman and his Methodist flock, including a number of free black believers, as they navigated numerous boundaries — both denominational and geographic — during an age of Atlantic rebellions. But what about the newly United States' creation of religious liberty that followed the political conflict? Sarah Barringer Gordon's study of the origins of disestablishment in Virginia reveals that one of the nation's most cherished ideals — religious freedom — was surprisingly tethered to one of its most controversial: a resurgence of pro-slavery arguments. But more than just political frameworks, Jon Sensbach's microhistory of one African-born man named Abraham unpacks the lived realities of enslavement and conversion. And finally, Lori Daggar's examination of the Delaware Tribe's witch hunt, and Jennifer Dorsey's chapter on the Shakers, demonstrate that the tensions of disestablishment and innovation crossed racial and denominational boundaries.

Once America was established as a new nation, with broadly accepted, if still challenged, religious traditions, a series of geographic and political transformations shifted the country and all the people who lived in it. The third part of this volume, "Expansion," provides examples of the many implications from this march of manifest destiny, as both the geographic and denominational boundaries remained undetermined. Christopher Cameron uses David Walker to display the foundations of a Black prophetic tradition destined to challenge both the legal practice of slavery as well as the theological institution of white supremacy. Yet African Americans were not the only individuals refused assimilation, as Cassandra Yacovazzi's chapter displays the potent risk that Catholicism, including the seemingly pacifist nuns, posed to the Protestant establishment. And among the new religious experiments introduced during the era, few challenged traditional theological parameters as much as those who attempted to appropriate new religious philosophies, like the Romantics as overviewed by Brent Sirota or the Haudenosaunees as traced by Christian Gonzales. But the major disruption of this era, of course, was the Civil War, which not only destroyed the South's bid for a slaveholding empire but also raised important questions regarding territorial politics and racial equality; Brent Rogers's chapter uses Mormonism to understand the former, while Nicole Turner's uses black denominations to understand the latter.

The decades that followed America's sectional crises witnessed America becoming an imposing power, with both domestic and global fissures reflected in various religious drives. This volume's fourth section, "Imperialism," details the battles that shaped the emerging nation's new world. A central conflict regarded the emerging capitalistic divide between poor and rich, and chapters by Janine Drake and Nicole Kirk depict the competing religious visions of a social gospel that improved the lives of the oppressed on the one hand, and a consumer culture that sanctified wealth and material goods on the other. Another deep division concerned the availability and consumption of alcohol, as Joseph Locke's examination of the prohibition movement exemplifies the potential — and pitfalls — of religious reform efforts. But once again, some of the most complicated questions regarded racial assimilation and acceptance, as Arlene Sanchez-Walsh's chapter on Hispanic believers among the Pentecostal movement, and Sarah Dees's chapter on federal policies over Indigenous tribes, show how the politics of religious recognition became even murkier as the "Christian nation" came into shape. Nor were these questions solely relegated to the continental United States: Carleigh Beriont's look at the Bikinian Islands in the Pacific during the World War II-era highlight the global dimensions of America's imperial and religious ambitions.

The final section, "Modernity," touches on the culmination of these disparate and interdependent trajectories and posits that they resulted in a number of competing, if related, modernities. Some of these divisions were found within groups that are typically lumped together, as Vaughn Booker's chapter digests two distinct brands of Black theology, each designed to gain civil liberties, in the post-war era. Joseph Laycock's contribution then details a more quixotic — yet still revealing — episode from the same period: an attempted exorcism of the Pentagon, which he uses as a lens through which to see what the "occult revival" of the 1960s tells us about popular religion. In another case of unexpected bedfellows, Angela Tarango examines how Native Americans, yearning for cultural assimilation, appropriated modern Pentecostalism to their own ends. Of course, the most famous coalition formed in the second half of the twentieth century, and one that remains a cultural touchstone, is the union of the Republican Party and Evangelicals; but while this political marriage is well-known, Emily Johnson's chapter unveils gender dimensions that are often overlooked. And as the volume began with an emphasis on diversity, so too will it end: Melissa Borja's overview of Asian-American immigration establishes the new demographic realities that shape the nation's present and future, and Jennifer Caplan's analysis of Judaism in modern television extends that reality to the streaming age.

Taken together, these chapters capture the vibrancy and variety of America's religious past. They serve as touchstones for understanding and engaging the broader themes and moments of United States history and give context to tensions that still exist in the present day. Americans have yet to fully comprehend the implications and potential of these diverse traditions — and indeed, some still tragically see it not as a "potential," but as a problem — but historians of American religion have provided a foundation for that important discussion. This volume hopes to only add to that vivacious chorus.

So when young Americans gather in springtime to participate in a sacred Hindu celebration, they are reenacting, either consciously or not, the fulfillment the nation's diverse religious heritage, a culture rooted in diversity as much as anything else.

Part I

COLONIALISMS

Chapter Two

NEMASKET/MIDDLEBOROUGH AND RELIGIOUS DIVERSITY IN COLONIAL NEW ENGLAND

Richard J. Boles
Oklahoma State University, Stillwater, Oklahoma

In popular memory and in many American history textbooks, colonial New England is depicted as remarkably homogenous in its religious culture. The traditional narrative stresses the Pilgrim and Puritan migration away from persecution in England and the attempted creation of an idealized "city upon a hill." From grade school forward, therefore, most Americans have been taught a basic story of these beleaguered groups. But much of this narrative focuses on homogeneity. Differences of opinion in early New England are sometimes acknowledged in the stories of Anne Hutchison and Roger Williams, who were outspoken critics of Boston's religious leaders, for example. But their 1630s exiles from Massachusetts imply the creation of a rigidly uniform Puritan colony that persisted rather statically until the Great Awakening or American Revolution.

The more complete history of religious beliefs and practices in New England is very dynamic. Colonial New England always featured a wide range of religious practices. This diversity included competing types of Christianity as well as the presence of non-Christian religions. Throughout the colonial era, the religious practices of the Wampanoag (Pokanoket), Narragansett, Pequot, Massachusett, Mohegan, Nipmuck, and other Indian communities were vibrant and varied. English colonists instituted congregation-based church governance that allowed for community control of religion as opposed to centrally controlled or top-down ways of governing churches. Differences in beliefs and practices among the clergy and laity were also occasionally significant. Furthermore, numerous colonists did not join a church at all and mixed Christian beliefs with other spiritual practices. Later, in the eighteenth century, religious revivals caused church schisms and produced competing churches in many towns. Europeans imported enslaved Africans to New England during the earliest decades of colonization, and some Africans and black Americans retained West African religious practices, including Islam, Catholicism, and polytheistic or nontheistic religious traditions. They preserved essential parts of these religious practices despite the oppression of slavery and legal prohibitions against publicly practicing these religions. Black and Indian peoples also participated in predominantly white churches, while Wampanoag, Narragansett, and other Indians maintained their own churches. Common depictions of colonial New England critically obscure and neglect much of this religious diversity.

A Companion to American Religious History, First Edition. Edited by Benjamin E. Park.
© 2021 John Wiley & Sons, Inc. Published 2021 by John Wiley & Sons, Inc.

Communities located in eastern Massachusetts, known consecutively as Nemasket, Middleberry, and Middleborough, provide a useful case study for examining the variety of religions in colonial New England. This chapter focuses on this one location because it is a good representation of the religious diversity that existed across the whole region. In many ways, Middleborough was quite typical and rarely was it exceptional. But while the focus remains mostly on Nemasket and Middleborough, this chapter occasionally broadens its coverage to understand how developments in nearby places influenced religious trends over time. Through examining this location and nearby communities, we can trace much of the religious history of the diverse peoples of southern New England before the nineteenth century.

* * *

In order to understand how religious diversity developed and changes, it is helpful first to outline how Europeans and Africans came to reside in this region, including the role that violence played in colonization. For thousands of years, Indigenous people inhabited this resource-abundant area in present-day eastern Massachusetts. Gradually, in the more recent past, English colonists, other Europeans, and enslaved Africans invaded the area and brought their religions. Europeans visited New England shores and Wampanoag communities sporadically after 1524 and regularly after 1602. Europeans not only traded with but also frequently attacked and kidnapped people from New England's Indigenous communities. In 1619, a small group of English migrants, including Pilgrims, arrived on the coast of Massachusetts and settled about twelve miles away from Nemasket. The Pilgrims' theft of food and desecration of Wampanoag graves almost led to the Pilgrims' demise, as some Wampanoag wanted to kill or drive them away. But Wampanoag paramount sachem Ousamequin (often known by his title "Massasoit") allowed the English colonists to stay, likely because he envisioned the English as a tributary community. Ousamequin resided west of Nemasket, so colonists and Wampanoags crossed this community when going to meet with each other and to trade.[1]

Beginning in 1630, English Puritans began arriving by the thousands, first settling north of Wampanoag territory and then later in present-day Rhode Island and Connecticut. The English population proliferated thereafter, and they occupied more and more Indian lands through means of purchase, theft, and war. Believing Christianity to be the only true form of worship and believing themselves "a chosen people," English colonists used their religion along with their understandings of "just war" and "property rights" and longstanding English legal traditions to justify dispossessing and fighting Indians.[2]

In the 1660s, descendants of Pilgrim immigrants made the first purchase of land in the area that would become Middleborough. English colonists routinely pressured sachems (community leaders) and other Indians to cede territory, often under the threat of violence. Colonists pushed some Wampanoags out of Nemasket and established the English town of Middleberry, which was incorporated in 1669. During King Philip's War of 1675–1676, a federation of Indians led by Wampanoag paramount sachem Pumetacom (called Metacom or Philip by the English), tried to regain their homeland and prevent colonists from extending jurisdictional control over sovereign Indian nations. Most of the English homes in Middleborough were destroyed by the Indian forces, who successfully eluded colonial troops until colonists convinced other Indians to fight with them against Pumetacom. Colonists eventually killed or enslaved thousands of Wampanoags and other Indians, and then took more land.[3] After the war, English residents returned to Middleborough and rebuilt. Wampanoags continued to live in the vicinity of Nemasket/Middleborough, especially the districts or communities of Titicut and Assawompset (Betty's Neck), into the late eighteenth century.[4]

Middleborough grew throughout the eighteenth century, and this site functioned as a crossroads for travelers moving between Plymouth (twelve miles east), Boston (forty miles north), Providence (thirty miles west), and Cape Cod. As was the case all over New England, enslaved Africans were crucial supplements to the labor provided by family members, and they helped make some Middleborough residents, including its ministers, relatively prosperous in the eighteenth century. Some of these enslaved black colonists participated in the town's churches, but others rejected Christianity.[5] The 1740s religious revivals, later known as the Great Awakening, led to the establishment of new churches in the region. Thereafter, residents could choose among multiple English ministers and houses of worship. As was the case for most of colonial New England, Nemasket/Middleborough was inhabited by a mix of Indian, African, and European peoples whose religious practices, beliefs, and institutions were multifaceted and diverse. Remarkably, the multiplicity of religions persisted and even expanded despite occasional institutional attempts, including violent warfare against Indians and slavery, to suppress religious differences.

Wampanoags of Nemasket

It is challenging to describe the religious lives of Wampanoags in Nemasket and surrounding areas before 1600 because Wampanoag communities and culture, of which religion was inseparable, were never static, and also because the Wampanoag did not yet produce the types of written records upon which historians heavily rely. Moreover, Native American religions were not homogeneous; religious beliefs varied at least as much as languages and the physical environment varied across New England. The stories and rituals diverged even between the Wampanoag who lived on the mainland and the Wampanoag on the island of Noepe (Martha's Vineyard). Nevertheless, we can speak in general terms about Wampanoag religious practices during this period because of archeological evidence and seventeenth-century written sources. Wampanoag also continued to hold many of these beliefs through recent centuries.[6]

In the Wampanoag's world, alive and inanimate objects pulsed with varying degrees of divine or spiritual power, known as manitou (or manit). Animals, plants, bodies of water, sacred objects, and environmental, meteorological, and celestial features contained manitou. Historian David Silverman writes that these things possessed "spirits capable of bestowing and withholding favor, of doing good and ill, depending on their whim." As a result, the place where they lived was inseparable from their religion. The Wampanoag at Nemasket depended upon Lake Assawompset and the Nemasket and Taunton rivers to provide freshwater, fish, and waterfowl. In nearby fields, they cultivated maize, beans, and squash, whose seeds and farming techniques originally developed in Mexico. Wampanoags also gathered berries and other plants and hunted animals. In summer months, inhabitants of Nemasket resided on the Atlantic coast, where clams and seafood abounded. For success in feeding themselves and their families, they depended upon the interventions and guidance of spiritual beings and power.[7]

The vital force of manitou was necessary to prosper and for health, but some objects and beings contained dangerous power that could be detrimental to human flourishing. Knowledge about and respectful engagement with objects that were richly infused with manitou determined communal and individual wellbeing. Pawwaws (religious specialists) were individuals, almost always men, whose understanding of and connections to manitou allowed them to assist people facing illness, important decisions, or the seasons of life.[8] Pawwaws made connections to manitou and spiritual beings through dreams, visions, induced trances, and rituals. They could "influence, tap, or control unseen powers of the world for the benefit or ill of mankind," writes scholar Kathleen Bragdon, by praying for aid or by placating dissatisfied spiritual beings.[9] Pawwaws provided "answers to questions about the cause of illness, the outcome of future actions, and choices in forthcoming decisions," noted ethnohistorian William Simmons, and they were trusted in identifying "thieves and murderers."[10] Because of the power that they wielded in these communities, when things went wrong, pawwaws were sometimes accused of doing harm.

Persons unseen by the naked eye and manitou filled the whole world, but some particular beings loomed larger in Wampanoag thinking and daily lives. In the seventeenth century, Wampanoags described a humanlike god named Kiehtan as the creator of their world and as the source of maize and beans (known as Cautantowwit among neighboring Narragansetts). The southwest was the direction of Kiehtan's house.[11] Often more important in the daily lives of Wampanoag was Cheepi, a powerful being associated with death, "the moon, night, cold, the horned winged serpent, and panthers." Water locations and the animals who dwelt therein were associated with Cheepi, especially swamps, springs, marshes, and whirlpools.[12] Pawwaws gained their standing in the community first by having a powerful, visionary encounter with Cheepi. They also turned to Cheepi when people were sick. Cheepi was sometimes the source of illnesses, which meant that it could also provide cures. However, if Cheepi was angry at an individual or a community and sought to punish them, no remedy would be possible.[13]

Dreams and visions, for anyone in these communities, served as a means of seeking aid from spiritual beings. Animals who appeared in their dreams carried different messages or warnings. Spiritual guardians, when respectfully sought in reciprocal relationships, might provide help in directing manitou toward people. When Wampanoag persons slept, one of their two souls departed the body to travel among spiritual beings in the upper world (sky) and underwater world, thereby communicating spiritual information through dreams.[14]

Pawwaws led the community in seasonal rituals, such as green corn festivals, and advised individuals and whole sachemships (distinct communities organized under a sachem, or leader) in preparing for war and in combatting sicknesses, drought, and other threats. They were knowledgeable about the rituals that accompanied births, deaths, and burials. Feasting, fasting, smoking tobacco, and giving away or destroying material objects were sacred activities associated with important moments in life.[15] English colonist Roger Williams, writing about the nearby Narragansetts, said that *Nickómmo* means "a feast or dance." He went on to explain that "of this feast they have publike and private and that of two sorts. First in sickness, or Drouth, or Warre or Famine. Secondly, After Harvest, after hunting, when they enjoy a calme of Peace, Health, Plenty, Property." For the Narragansett and the Wampanoag, these festivals, songs, and dances were of vital importance in times of distress and periods of plenty. They happened intermittently based on specific needs and seasonally, such as during spring plantings. Williams also noted that when a person was sick, the pawwaw "comes close to the sick person" and performs rituals to "threaten and conjures out the sickness."[16]

These beliefs and practices did not disappear, but neither were they static. When European-produced brass, glass beads, and other objects began trickling into Wampanoag communities, some of these objects were "incorporated into ritual and contributed to a continuation of Native ideas about health and well-being."[17] One or more epidemics, introduced by contacts with Europeans, killed between 70 percent and 90 percent of the Wampanoag on the mainland between 1616 and 1619. This catastrophe left people bereft of close relatives and led to the loss of community knowledge as the elderly were more susceptible to illness. Pawwaws and other individuals could do little to stem the staggering death rate, the cause of which was unknown, and catastrophes of this magnitude necessarily alter religious beliefs. To some Wampanoags, their confidence in the prevailing religious practices was deeply shaken. Others sought to reinvigorate and adapt their beliefs to the new reality. Over time, some communities slowly recovered, but others were left abandoned.

One of the sachems who joined Pumetacom in fighting the English in 1675 was known as Tispaquin or the "Black Sachem." He was sachem of Assawompset, and Plymouth officials forced him to cede land to the English, part of which became Middleborough. He was also respected as a powerful pawwaw. It was rare for a sachem also to be a pawwaw, but Tispaquin leveraged all his community's physical as well as spiritual resources in fighting for independence and survival.[18] Epidemics, English colonization, and wars altered but did not destroy the Wampanoag religion. It persisted throughout the colonial era, and even some English colonists turned to Wampanoag men and women for spiritual aid in their times of need throughout the eighteenth century.[19]

The Congregational Way

All English colonists in seventeenth-century New England did not practice identical rituals or ascribe to the same religious beliefs. Nemasket was proximate to three different manifestations of English Puritanism. English colonists were a heterogeneous group of Protestant Christians, most of whom sought to reform churches and create purer Christian communities in England and American colonies. Although the Wampanoags in Nemasket realized that English colonists were united during times of war, they also likely understood that there were differences and religious divisions among the English colonists located to the east, north, and west. While most of these English Christians fell within the broad Puritan reform movement and Reformed tradition, Puritans in Massachusetts Bay Colony, Pilgrims (Puritan Separatists) in Plymouth Colony, and the Baptists, Quakers, and other religious groups in the Colony of Rhode Island and Providence Plantations disagreed with one another on some religious and political subjects. Their system of locally controlled churches, a method of governing that they called "the Congregational way," protected local control of religion and enabled some variation of theological perspectives to co-exist in colonial New England. Quakers and Baptists made up small portions of the seventeenth-century population (around 1 percent of Christians). There were only twelve Baptist congregations in New England by 1700, but these groups were concentrated in Plymouth and Rhode Island colonies, and they expanded dramatically in the eighteenth century. By 1776, more than 15 percent of New England congregations were Baptist, and nearly 4 percent were Quaker.[20]

Puritan, Pilgrim, and Baptist colonists agreed on the vast majority of theological topics, but they separated from each other over a small number of doctrinal issues and ritual practices. New England Christians generally agreed with the foundational doctrines of Reformed-Protestant Christianity: the holiness and omnipotence of God, the three persons of this triune God (the Father, the Son, and the Holy Spirit), the literal death and resurrection of Jesus Christ, the absolute authority of the Bible, the deep sinfulness of humanity, salvation through faith alone, and the predetermined election of the saints. They all deeply opposed Roman Catholicism. Many New England Christians criticized the Church of England, the official form of Protestant Christianity in England. They criticized the Anglican Church's structure, especially its bishops, its interconnectedness with political power, and its relatively open access to the rituals of baptism and the Lord's Supper (also known as communion) for parish communities.[21]

Colonists, however, tended to disagree about how much English Protestantism required additional reforming. Most Puritans agreed that the Church of England was a legitimate and important part of Christ's visible church on earth, even though it needed further reformation. A large majority of Puritans remained in England and within Anglican parishes, and they hoped to purify their national church further. Only a minority of English Puritans migrated to American colonies. Pilgrims (Puritan Separatists), conversely, believed that the Church of England was too errant, and therefore, true Christians needed to fully separate from the state church and form new congregations made up of people who were faithful (as they defined it) to biblical requirements. Both Puritans and Pilgrims baptized infants and children of church members upon the basis of their parent's faith. Baptists, as their name implies, disagreed with Puritans and Pilgrims (and almost all other Christians) concerning how and when the ritual of baptism should be administered. Baptists believed that only people who made a personal public profession of faith should be baptized, thereby excluding infants and small children from the ritual. The Baptists were also Separatists because they formed independent congregations of professing believers who were distinct from the all-encompassing parishes of the Church of England.[22]

Plymouth Colony was founded by Pilgrims (Separatists) and other English colonists in 1619. Many of the Pilgrims had moved to the Netherlands between 1607 and 1609 before deciding to move to America because they faced legal penalties in England for establishing illegal churches.[23] They settled on Wampanoag territory nearby Nemasket. Not everyone in early Plymouth adhered to the same beliefs; in fact, people who were not dedicated Separatists outnumbered the religiously-committed Pilgrims, and economic, not religious reasons, motivated a good share of them.[24] The Massachusetts Bay Colony was founded in 1630, and Boston became the principal city in the region. Wealthier migrants brought indentured servants whose religious views varied. Moreover, the founding of churches in Boston did not keep up with the population growth; by 1650, the two meetinghouses used for worship in Boston could only accommodate at most one-third of the town's people. Non-puritan colonists included skilled wage workers, indentured servants, slaves, fishermen, and sailors who were important to the colony's prosperity but who did not frequently participate in Puritan churches. Some of these colonists were Anglicans. Even Puritans in Boston were divided amongst themselves over a variety of theological and political topics. Some Puritans left Massachusetts Bay to establish Connecticut colony; along with economic reasons for creating a new colony, leaders in Connecticut felt that the church admission requirements in Massachusetts churches were too strict, and they disagreed about parts of that colony's governing structures.[25]

Roger Williams and a few other families started the town of Providence and the colony that eventually became Rhode Island in 1636, and it became a refuge for people with dissenting opinions. Williams was a Puritan Separatist minister who disagreed with a number of religious and civil practices in the Massachusetts Bay and Plymouth colonies. His vocal criticism led to a court-ordered banishment from Massachusetts. Williams adopted Baptist beliefs and, in 1639, started the first Baptist church in North America. Similarly, after a protracted series of private meetings, debates, and trials, from 1636 to 1638, Anne Hutchinson and some followers were banished from Massachusetts for their publicly expressed dissent. Hutchinson claimed to receive direct revelation from God, criticized ministers' sermons publicly, and shared her religious views with dozens of people in her home. According to dominant Puritan (and Anglican) interpretations of the Bible, women were prohibited from teaching or preaching religious truths. Puritan religious and civil authorities were explicitly patriarchal. Anne, her husband William Hutchinson, and eighteen other families started the town of Portsmouth in Rhode Island.

From their beginnings, Providence and other Rhode Island towns instituted freedom of conscience, which fostered religious diversity. No one was compelled to pay taxes to support a church or minister (as was required in all other New England colonies), and there were no religious requirements for full political participation in Rhode Island. For years, Massachusetts and New Haven only allowed church members to vote in colony-level elections. Because of this unique religious liberty, a wide variety of religious dissenters settled in Rhode Island. It contained a much higher proportion of Baptists, Quakers (Religious Society of Friends), and the religiously unaffiliated than other colonies. In some ways, the religious views of many Rhode Island colonists were more individualistic and radical than the Puritans in Massachusetts or the Separatists in Plymouth. For instance, Quakers asserted that believers had direct access to God's revelations through the indwelling "inner light." They also practiced, for the time, radical equality by encouraging women to speak and share their testimonies in public meetings.[26] Because of these radical beliefs, Puritans in Massachusetts banished Quakers who preached in public and occasionally executed Quakers who returned after being banished more than once. A small number of Jewish families settled in Newport, Rhode Island, by the 1670s. In the early 1760s, they built a synagogue. In 1698 an Anglican Church was established in Newport, and Moravians came to Newport in 1758 (see Rachel Wheeler's chapter for more about Moravians).

The most significant public rituals for New England Christians (excepting Quakers) were baptism, the Lord's Supper, thanksgiving days, and fast days. For the Puritan communities, "fasting and confession were means of healing sickness in the body social."[27] In the early decades of colonization, baptism and the Lord's Supper were reserved only for members of Puritan churches, but after the 1660s, many churches in Massachusetts allowed people to "own the covenant" to be baptized or to have their children baptized. These "half-way" members (those who owned the covenant) could not partake in the Lord's Supper, which was reserved for full members.[28] Most Christians in colonial New England sought to have their infant children baptized very soon after birth, which suggests that they viewed this ritual as providing a measure of spiritual protection. In the case of the Lord's Supper, however, many English Christians avoided taking communion until facing a dangerous part of life, such as childbirth, or until they reached a more advanced age. Ministers warned congregants about the dangers of taking communion in an unworthy manner, and many introspective Puritans were cautious about approaching this ritual. "Half or more of all lay people never found the confidence to testify about the work of grace," which was a necessary part of joining and becoming a communicant in Puritan churches.[29] Baptism and communion were associated with the death and resurrection of Jesus Christ. The bread and wine represented the body and blood of the savior, and the water of baptism represented cleansing through burial in death and rebirth.

The central activities of public religious services were listening to sermons, praying, reading scripture, and singing psalms, but for some congregants, socializing and talking about business matters between the two Sunday services also motivated church attendance. In most of colonial New England, attending church services was nearly compulsory for town residents, but membership in a church was always voluntary. In Rhode Island, conversely, even attendance at worship services was voluntary. The residents of each town exercised complete control over their selection of a minister. No outside body — ecclesiastical or civil — could assign a minister to a town's church. Groups of ministers published guidelines for how "the congregational way" of organizing churches should function, but their recommendations were not binding on any independent congregation. Since towns and church members selected their ministers, the theological perspective of ministers varied slightly from town to town.[30]

Baptism and communion were infrequent rituals, so for many New England Christians, other weekly and daily devotional practices were central to their religious lives. The most frequent religious rituals for Christians in Middleborough and surrounded communities were individual and family prayers, fasting, confessions, and reading the Bible and other texts. Samuel Sewall, a Puritan merchant and judge, participated in nearly one hundred fast days during the years he kept a diary, and these "fasts were linked to a variety of troubles — drought and military defeat, sickness and death, politics at home and abroad, family troubles." New England Christians had high rates of literacy, and reading was a fundamental component of their religious experiences and identity. Most colonial households owned at least one Bible, printed in their native language; some households had psalms and other types of books written for devout laypeople. According to historian David Hall, "the uniqueness of the Bible was its status as the Word ... It was the living speech of God, the 'voice' of Christ, a text that people 'heard.'"[31] The Bible was so crucial to Puritans' religious practices that they translated the entire scriptures into the Wampanoag language and published it in 1663 as part of their missionary activities.

Both clergy and laypeople emphasized the importance of the Bible, but the theology and religious practices of college-educated clergy varied significantly from some of their congregants and community members. Nearly everybody in New England believed that they inhabited a "world of wonder," where nothing was an accident, and everything had a spiritual cause. According to Hall, for the Puritans, "God was immediately and actively present in the world, the ultimate force behind everything," so signs and wonders were indications of God's approval or displeasure. If manitou and spiritual beings lay behind everything good and ill that happened, according to the Wampanoags, then the Puritans likewise did not believe in accidents. Ultimately God, but in some cases Satan, caused everything that befell human beings. Puritans were continually watching for signs, such as comets, earthquakes, remarkable deliverances, and illness that suggested God's merciful generosity or angry wrath.[32] The clergy argued that prayer, repentance, fasting, and thanksgiving were the only proper ways to seek God's blessings, protection, or relief from troubles.

New Englanders generally engaged in these spiritual practices, but some of them also sought to influence the spiritual world by methods that were not rooted in Protestant Christianity. Some Puritans consulted fortune-tellers and "practiced magic to defend themselves from witchcraft." Puritans and later Christians in New England sought out Wampanoag and other Indigenous healing practices throughout the colonial era. Europeans, Indians, and West Africans all believed that witches could be threats to their families and communities because they all believed that some people could harness spiritual powers for ill purposes.[33] David Hall also describes how "lay people sometimes distanced themselves from the message of the clergy" in their beliefs and the religious books that they read. Books that diverged significantly from the dominant Puritan perspective in Massachusetts could be purchased in Boston bookshops in the seventeenth century, along with Bibles, psalm books, and Puritan devotionals. Baptist and Quaker books were available by the 1650s. According to Hall, what many New England farmers "guarded for themselves was the right of judgment. More exactly, they turned their familiarity with Scripture — their own capacities as readers — into criticism of the minister."[34]

From the last decades of the seventeenth century and into the eighteenth century, the number of church options and private religious practices increased in New England cities. An Anglican Church, King's Chapel, was organized in Boston in 1686. Baptists and the Religious Society of Friends (Quakers) began worshipping in Boston despite Puritan opposition. Puritan ministers and magistrates welcomed French Protestants (Huguenots), who they embraced as fellow Reformed Protestants. As the enslaved African population in New England grew rapidly in the eighteenth century, exceeding ten thousand enslaved black people by 1750, the variety of privately practiced religions increased as well. The religious backgrounds of slaves in New England rarely appears in the historical records, but some enslaved Africans held onto their religious beliefs, including Islam and Catholicism.[35] Occasionally, even people of different religious perspectives joined Boston churches. A free black man named John Vingus joined the Hollis Street Congregational Church of Boston in 1735 by "owning the covenant," professing to believe the church's teaching. He did so to have his seven-year-old daughter baptized. John Vingus was not baptized in 1735 because he had been "baptized in his own country by a Romish priest." Vingus had practiced Roman Catholicism either in West Africa, perhaps in the independent Kingdom of Kongo, or in the Portuguese or Spanish empires before arriving in Boston.[36] There was no Catholic Church in Boston at the time, so Vingus affiliated with a Protestant one in order to have his daughter baptized. The religious beliefs in the largest New England towns were varied, but diverse religions were also practiced in small communities too.

Christianities of Nemasket and Middleborough

Even within the area of Nemasket and Middleborough, people practiced multiple types of Christianity since the late seventeenth century. Some Wampanoags maintained their own churches there before English colonists officially established the Middleborough Congregational Church. By 1675, Wampanoag churches existed at Nemasket, Titicut, and Assawompset. In total, these churches included about 90 members. The number of members grew to about 110 by 1685.[37] These Wampanoag churches were the result of evangelical work by both English and Indian preachers. Several Puritans, especially John Eliot, John Cotton Jr., Thomas Mayhew Jr., and Richard Bourne, worked part-time to evangelize Indians. Some sachemships were amenable to Christian evangelists, while others resolutely refused missionaries. Massachusetts Bay Colony began organizing "praying towns" for Indians who were exploring Christianity; by 1674, about 2,300 Indians lived in these towns. These communities established their own churches, and colonists tried to equip Indian men to serve as ministers. Historian Edward Andrews has shown that Christianity among Native New Englanders mostly spread not by white missionaries but rather through the work of Indian evangelists.[38] Colonists stated that praying towns would protect and guarantee Indians' land possessions and independence. In reality, colonists bought or stole most of the land in these praying towns between King Philips' War and the 1750s.[39]

From the 1670s to the 1750s, a succession of Indian ministers served the churches at Nemasket, Titicut, and Assawompset. John Sassamon, who was a Massachusett Indian, attended Harvard and preached at Nemasket and Assawompset between 1673 and 1675. The complicated events surrounding his murder helped ignite King Philip's War. Other Indian ministers included Stephen, who preached at Nemasket in the late seventeenth century; Jocelin, who ministered at Assawompset from 1698 to 1711; Charles Aham, who preached at Titicut around 1698; John Hiacooomes, who preached at Assawompset from 1698 to 1718; Joseph Joshnin, who ministered at Titicut from 1710 to 1718; and John Symons (or Simons), who ministered there from 1747 to 1757.[40] John Symons, as was common for Indian men, served with English forces in colonial wars against France. Symons was wounded and disabled during military service, and the Massachusetts government granted him forty shillings a year as a pension. In Titicut, Symons served as the minister of the Indian church even as an English Baptist church developed in the same area. In 1753, Symons wrote a letter decrying the loss of more Indian land to English colonists, suggesting that Indian ministers also led the fight for community autonomy and protection.[41]

The Christianity practiced by Native Americans in colonial New England was not a simplified or partial copy of Puritan Christianity, and Indian Christians believed that maintaining a church could serve broader communities' goals of independence, self-governance, and retention of Indigenous cultures. In many ways, a new form of Christianity developed among Wampanoags in the seventeenth century. "Native people turned the missionaries' religion into a new way to express indigenous truths by melding Wampanoag religious concepts and spirits with their rough Christian equivalents," according to David Silverman. "To no small degree, this process was a natural result of using Wampanoag-language terms to communicate analogous Christian principles," a process not all that different from how Christianity changed as it spread from ancient Israel to Roman Europe. Some Native preachers and schoolteachers were paid salaries by the New England Company, a Puritan missionary organization.[42] Because of his education and bilingual abilities, John Sassamon was a cultural broker between Indians and colonists.

From the late seventeenth century until the 1740s, many of the English Christians in Middleborough sought to live out their faith as "godly walkers." They viewed their spiritual development as a life-long journey toward, hopefully by God's grace, final redemption and purification in heaven. They baptized their children when young, attended church services regularly, and engaged in family devotions. Many people, especially women, joined their church and took communion when the long-term pattern of their behavior reflected their Christian commitments. Church life was often orderly, predictable, and comfort-providing to many New Englanders. Basic knowledge of Christian theology, public behavior that conformed to society's expectations, and a desire to become a full communicant were usually the only requirements for church membership.[43] In other words, having and publicly sharing a dramatic experience of conversion was not necessarily a requirement for joining the church. The first English Congregational Church of Middleborough was constituted, and Samuel Fuller became the pastor in 1694, although Fuller had already resided in Middleborough for years and had probably led religious services in homes before that date. After Fuller's death in 1695, several ministers preached at the church for limited periods. Peter Thatcher served as pastor of this church from 1709 until his death in 1744.[44] Following the Great Awakening and Thatcher's death, however, the religious status quo was dramatically altered. The Congregational church divided as some people wanted to make churches purer by instituting more stringent requirements for membership. After the 1740s, Middleborough's residents could choose among several competing English congregations.

Great Awakening and Church Schisms

The 1740s was a period of tremendous religious change and divisions for New England communities, and Middleborough "experienced one of New England's most powerful revivals."[45] Religious revivals, periods of intense devotional practices and higher rates of church admissions, occurred periodically in earlier decades. Reverends Solomon Stoddard and Jonathan Edwards led the Congregational Church of Northampton, Massachusetts, through several revivals, and Edwards' revival of 1732–1733 became widely known because his account of it was published in London, England, in 1737. The revivals of the early 1740s, however, were different from previous revivals because of their broad impact and long-lasting consequences.

George Whitefield was an Anglican priest from England who pioneered new preaching and publication techniques that, along with many imitators, created a "Great Awakening" in New England. Whitefield traveled from town to town, drawing enormous crowds to hear him preach. He also used newspapers masterfully to share his message and prime his audiences. The effects were not identical or consistent from town to town, but a remarkably high number of people decided to join a church or be baptized in New England in 1741 and 1742. According to historian Douglas Winiarski, "perhaps as many as 60 percent of all New England churches admitted more than twice the yearly number of communicants" during these years. Middleborough was significantly affected by the preaching of Whitefield and other visiting colonial ministers such as Daniel Rogers, Gilbert Tennent, and Eleazar Wheelock.[46]

Not only did more people join the church, but the demographics of the church members changed during this revival. From 1741 to 1744, the average age of the people who joined the church dropped significantly. In the Congregational Church of Middleborough, "men admitted during the revival season were, on average, more than twelve years younger than their pre-awakening fathers, brothers, and neighbor; the mean age for women dropped by more than five years. More than one in five men and one in four women admitted to Middleborough church during the revival were under the age of twenty, compared to 3 and 9 percent, respectively before 1740." The youngest new members were ages seven and nine.[47] In earlier times, most people waited longer to join their church and take communion, but the revival preachers sternly warned listeners not to wait in committing their lives to the Lord. Those who waited too long might miss their chance and be called to God's judgment seat unprepared.

In addition to younger people joining, the Middleborough church baptized and admitted more black and Indian peoples in the 1740s than during the previous decades. One black child, a slave of the minister, was baptized in 1735, but six more African Americans and three Indians affiliated with the church between 1740 and 1744. These African American members, most likely all enslaved people, were named Prince, Sambo, Jenny, Peru, and Calli. The Indians were named Peggy, Thomas Felix, and Else Antony. Some of Peggy's children were also baptized.[48] African Americans participated in churches that opposed the revival preachers, including many of New England's Anglican parishes, but the revivals increased black people's participation levels in some New England congregations.[49] These people affiliated in churches even though the colonists used Christianity, on the whole, to defend the enslavement of Africans and the dispossession of Indians' lands (see Jon Sensbach's chapter). Other enslaved Africans rejected Christianity and resisted pressure to attend church services.

Middleborough minister Peter Thatcher specifically noted that black people and Indians participated in the revival services. In 1741, Thatcher stated that one of his children and two of his enslaved Africans were "under Awakening," and that the Indians who attended his church were "deeply wounded; and many I hope savingly and wonderfully wrought upon." After an evening service, Thatcher asked "an Indian Woman, 'Well how is it with your Soul.'" Apparently, she answered that "I am a sinful, impotent, odious, wretched Creature: but when I can get to a Promise, Christ helping me, I find Comfort and Rest."[50] While it is possible that Thatcher misquoted this woman, many eighteenth-century Christians used these sorts of demeaning descriptions for themselves, especially when emphasizing their sinfulness before the experience of God's forgiveness. For those who felt redeemed and pardoned, the revivals brought a deep comfort.

The visiting ministers' preaching and intensive devotional practices stimulated tremendous amounts of religious energy and imagination, which, according to contemporaries, changed peoples' hearts. Reverend Thatcher wrote that "Many secure and hard hearted Sinners" were altered by the revivals. Many of the people who experienced powerful conversions, "who were caught up in the revivals," were already church members, but the revivalists caused these "godly walkers" to question whether their previous religious professions had been genuine evidence of a redeemed soul. Sometimes people reacted to the preaching in dramatic ways. After one service in December 1741, according to Thatcher, some people began to make "Heart-affecting Crys!" People expressed a sense of dread and conviction, "One crying to another, 'O I am going to Hell! I have frolick'd with you and sinned with you! O what dismal Company shall we be one for another in Hell!'" Many of the people who felt convicted and powerfully moved by the preaching started to "screich, cry, condemn, and warn each other." As the congregants whipped one another into a frenzy, there was much "wringing of hands, and Floods of Tears."[51]

For some other people, conversely, these new religious practices seemed more inspired by delusional experiences than an outpouring of God's spirit. From its beginning, some ordinary Christians and ministers criticized the new preaching practices of Whitefield and others as inappropriate. To these critics, the revival participants' emotional responses and disorderly conduct seemed inconsistent with reason, Christianity, and the Bible. Indeed, during the revivals, some people made religious claims that would have been rare and widely condemned in previous decades. The people who were in favor of the revivals often sought to eliminate their most extreme manifestations and defended their own practices as scriptural. In 1743, Thatcher wrote that "This Revival of the Power of Godliness appears to be the genuine Work of the Holy Spirit ... We have not known Visions, nor Trances, nor Revelations. But brotherly exhorting with more Modesty and Affection than hath been represented."[52] That Thatcher felt the need to defend the revival by saying that it did not include eccentric visions or direct revelations from God suggests that others viewed it with suspicion or hostility. Ministers' attempts to control revivalism and prevent religious excesses, derogatorily termed "enthusiasms," did not work. A decade later, in 1753, Sarah Prentice, who lived in the neighboring town of Bridgewater and was the wife of a Congregational minister, audaciously declared herself to be sinless and immortal.[53]

Appalled by changes in church structures and the "excesses" of the revivals, some ministers and congregants voiced their criticism and sought to block pro-revival ministers from visiting their town. Numerous congregations in New England divided between anti-revival "Old Lights," moderate revivalists, and radical revivalists known as "New Lights." Following the 1744 death of Reverend Thatcher, the Middleborough church divided between a group that favored revival practices and those who did not. The pro-revival church members engaged Sylvanus Conant as the minister, but they lost control of the meetinghouse, which was controlled by the parish members who were more skeptical of revivalism. The parish, which made decisions about the community-owned meetinghouse, included a broader demographic than the church members because parish membership was based on pew rentals and not based on religious beliefs or religious experiences. Conant's church built a new meetinghouse for worship. The remaining church members and parish hired Thomas Weld. Thus, the Congregational church, where a majority of the town's residents had worshipped since the 1690s, split into two competing congregations in 1745. The two churches reunited a few years later under Conant's ministry.[54]

For some participants in Middleborough's revival, however, even the "New Light" congregation led by Conant was not pure enough. The Great Awakening promoted breakaway "separate" congregations to form across New England. These new churches were often founded by the most radical or outspoken revival converts, who felt that it was no longer possible for them to listen to "unconverted" ministers or take communion with worshippers who had not been "born again." One of these separate churches was founded in the northern part of Middleborough, the area called Titicut, and was led by Isaac Backus, who arrived there by December 1747.[55] Backus's congregation existed as a separate, independent Congregational church, but it also faced internal divisions over the issue of baptism.

Some members of Backus's church in Titicut adopted the position that baptizing children and infants was unscriptural. After a long, agonizing struggle with himself, Backus also became a Baptist. The first discussion of Baptist doctrines occurred in 1749, and the church debated this topic for roughly five years. For a while, Backus tried to accommodate both the Separates who affirmed infant baptisms and the Baptists in his congregation, but this compromise pleased no one. Some members returned to one of Middleborough's other Congregational churches, and "finally, in 1756, the Titicut congregation disbanded and was re-constituted as the First Baptist Church of Middleborough." Backus's Baptist church experienced a revival in 1762, and about sixty new members joined in six months. Church divisions and the formation of new churches were fostered by some peoples' insistence on the purity of the church membership, the empowerment of individual believers to interpret scripture for themselves, and the active evangelism by laypeople and ministers. By 1764, the Third Baptist Church of Middleborough had been established.[56]

After the revival's intensity diminished among some Christians, the two competing Congregational churches were reunited under the ministry of Reverend Conant, but the religious outlooks of church members were not entirely uniform or united. Many Middleborough Christians continued the longstanding patterns of how they participated in the church, but other congregants' testimonies now reflected revivalist or New Light emphases. In the second half of the eighteenth century, testimonies at this congregation reflected a mix of the older "godly walker" tradition and the newer revivalist focus on the experience of being born again. In a number of the relations (religious testimonies) for joining the church, people expressed their understanding of Protestant Christianity, their own experiences of sin and forgiveness, and their gratefulness for living in a community where churches proclaimed the gospel — they lived in a "land of gospel light." Some emphasized duty and knowledge of theology, while other people highlight the experiences they felt during revival meetings and private devotions.[57]

Eighty-six people joined the Middleborough Congregational Church during Conant's ministry, which lasted from 1745 to 1777, including Cuffee Wright. Cuffee was an enslaved man, owned by Reverend Conant, who was baptized and joined the church in March 1773 following a public profession of faith. Cuffee said that "Christ is presus [precious] to my Soule." He believed that he was unworthy of God's mercy, but he was grateful that God brought him "out of Land of Dearkness unto the Land of gloryous gosple Light." These sorts of statements about sin and unworthiness were typical of many Christian professions from this era. Without necessarily doubting the sincerity of the testimony that he wrote, it is important to note that Cuffee likely faced pressure from Conant and joined the church while he was not free. Numerous enslaved men and women rejected Christianity, but some enslaved African Americans sought to better their position within slavery by participating in a predominantly white church. Perhaps Cuffee's status as a church member helped convince Conant to free Cuffee in his will. Shortly after gaining freedom, he took the surname Wright and married a black woman named Anna.[58]

Anna Wright joined the Middleborough church in 1796. In her relation, Anna expressed gratitude that she "was born and brought up in the land of gospel light; and my parents gave me to god in baptism," but she lamented her long neglect to build faith upon this good foundation. Eventually, Anna came to be "concerned" about her soul and the spiritual "danger" she faced. She eventually found relief from her sense of sinfulness and described how "the lord in mercy has, I hope, apeard for me" and comforting biblical "words came to me."[59] The Congregational church of Middleborough did not include the full range of religious views of town residents, but its membership did extend widely enough to include divergent theological perspectives and some racial diversity.

Conclusion

In the nineteenth century, New England's religious landscape became more complex. Increasingly Unitarians, Universalists, Methodists, Shakers, Baptists, Catholics, Campbellites, Mormons, and others competed for religious adherents in New England. The unique characteristics of this later religious landscape, however, should not overshadow the longstanding religious diversity that preceded it. The region's many Indigenous peoples did not share identical beliefs or rituals, and despite the devastating consequences of European colonization for the Wampanoag, their spiritual practices did not disappear. Europeans and Africans brought a variety of religious traditions to New England. Devout colonists depended on the skills and economic activities of less-religious or non-Puritan colonists, and even within the Massachusetts Bay Colony, there were differences of opinion and theological divides. Pilgrims, Puritans, Anglicans, Baptists, unaffiliated-people, revivalists, anti-revivalists, Huguenots, Quakers, Moravians, Catholics, and Jews eventually all practiced their religion in colonial New England. The history of religious diversity matters because of the place that Pilgrims and Puritans have traditionally held in American memory and national identity. To the extent that Americans have thought and still think about colonial New England as an important part of their national, religious, or ethnic origins, it is important to trace the United States' religious diversity back to colonial New England as well as other colonial regions, including Dutch New York and Spanish North America.

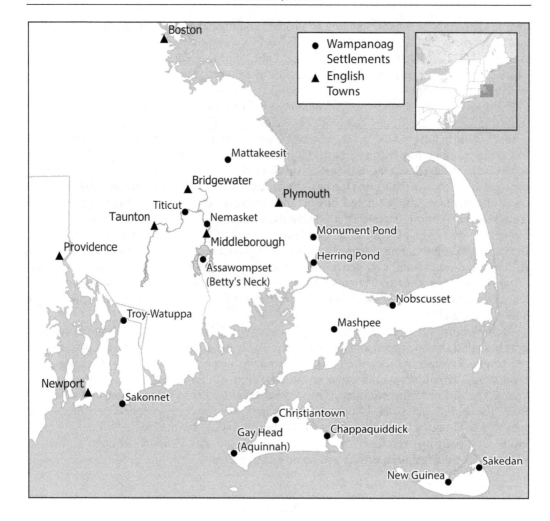

FURTHER READING

Brekus, Catherine A. *Sarah Osborn's World: The Rise of Evangelical Christianity in Early America*. New Haven: Yale University Press, 2013.

Conforti, Joseph A. *Saints and Strangers: New England in British North America*. Baltimore: Johns Hopkins University Press, 2006.

Hall, David. *Worlds of Wonder, Days of Judgment: Popular Religious Belief in Early New England*. Cambridge, MA: Harvard University Press, 1989.

Silverman, David J. *This Land Is Their Land: The Wampanoag Indians, Plymouth Colony, and the Troubled History of Thanksgiving*. New York: Bloomsbury, 2019.

Winiarski, Douglas L. *Darkness Falls on the Land of Light: Experiencing Religious Awakenings in Eighteenth-Century New England*. Chapel Hill: University of North Carolina Press, 2017.

NOTES

1   David J. Silverman, *This Land Is Their Land: The Wampanoag Indians, Plymouth Colony, and the Troubled History of Thanksgiving* (New York: Bloomsbury, 2019), 61–71, 156, 127–298.

2   Allan Greer, *Property and Dispossession: Natives, Empires and Land in Early Modern North America* (Cambridge University Press, 2018), 81–95, 191–237; For the complexity of Narragansetts land sales, see Julie A. Fisher and David J. Silverman, *Ninigret, Sachem of the Niantics and Narragansetts:*

Diplomacy, War, and the Balance of Power in Seventeenth-Century New England and Indian Country (Ithaca: Cornell University Press, 2014), 88–93.

3   Silverman, *This Land Is Their Land*, 294–355.

4   Daniel R. Mandell, *Behind the Frontier: Indians in Eighteenth-Century Eastern Massachusetts* (Lincoln: University of Nebraska Press, 1996); Silverman, *This Land Is Their Land*, 268–269.

5   Jared Ross Hardesty, *Unfreedom: Slavery and Dependence in Eighteenth-Century Boston* (New York: New York University Press, 2016).

6   Silverman, *This Land Is Their Land*.

7   Silverman, *This Land Is Their Land*, 30–52.

8   Kathleen J. Bragdon, *Native People of Southern New England 1500–1650* (Normal: University of Oklahoma Press, 1996), 184–230.

9   Bragdon, *Native People of Southern New England*, 203.

10 William S. Simmons, "Southern New England Shamanism: An Ethnographic Reconstruction," in *Papers of the Seventh Algonquian Conference*, edited by William Cowan (Ottawa: Carleton University, 1976), 235.

11 Simmons, "Southern New England Shamanism."

12 Silverman, *This Land Is Their Land*, 110–111, 433.

13 Simmons, "Southern New England Shamanism"; Silverman, *This Land Is Their Land*; Bragdon, *Native People of Southern New England*.

14 Simmons, "Southern New England Shamanism"; Bragdon, *Native People of Southern New England*.

15 Bragdon, *Native People of Southern New England*, 217–224.

16 Roger Williams, *A key into the language of America: or, An help to the language of the natives in that part of America, called New-England* (London: Printed by Gregory Dexter, 1643), 118–119; Simmons, "Southern New England Shamanism," 226–227, 241.

17 Bragdon, *Native People of Southern New England*, 246; Douglas L. Winiarski, "Native American Popular Religion in New England's Old Colony, 1670–1770," *Religion and American Culture: A Journal of Interpretation* 15, no. 2 (Summer 2005): 149.

18 Simmons, "Southern New England Shamanism," 223; Silverman, *This Land Is Their Land*, 265, 282, 287–288, 294, 316, 437.

19 Douglas L. Winiarski, *Darkness Falls on the Land of Light: Experiencing Religious Awakenings in Eighteenth-Century New England* (Chapel Hill: University of North Carolina Press, 2017), 487; Winiarski, "Native American Popular Religion," 147–186.

20 Robert G. Gardner, *Baptists in Early America: A Statistical History, 1639–1790* (Atlanta: Georgia Baptist Historical Society), 20–21; Rodney Stark and Roger Finke, "American Religion in 1776: A Statistical Portrait," *Sociological Analysis* 49, no. 1 (Spring, 1988): 47.

21 Edmund S. Morgan, *Visible Saints: The History of a Puritan Idea* (Ithaca: Cornell University Press, 1965); First Congregational Church (Middleborough, Mass.), *Book of the First Church of Christ, in Middleborough, Plymouth County, Mass.: with notices of other churches in that town* (Boston: C.C.P. Moody, 1852), 11–19.

22 Morgan, *Visible Saints*.

23 David Hall, *Worlds of Wonder, Days of Judgment: Popular Religious Belief in Early New England* (Cambridge, MA: Harvard University Press, 1989), 9.

24 Joseph A. Conforti, *Saints and Strangers: New England in British North America* (Baltimore: Johns Hopkins University Press, 2006), 38–39.

25 Hall, *Worlds of Wonder*, 17; Conforti, *Saints and Strangers*, 52, 69–77; David Hall, *A Reforming People: Puritanism and the Transformation of Public Life in New England* (New York: Alfred A. Knopf, 2011), 38–42.

26 Conforti, *Saints and Strangers*, 90–97.

27 Hall, *Worlds of Wonder*, 166, 196.

28 Morgan, *Visible Saints*.

29 Hall, *Worlds of Wonder*, 130, 152–160.

30 Hall, *Worlds of Wonder*; Hall, *A Reforming People*.

31 Hall, *Worlds of Wonder*, 7, 24, 32, 38, 233.

32 Hall, *Worlds of Wonder*, 77, 78, 225.

33 Hall, *Worlds of Wonder*, 7, 100; Winiarski, "Native American Popular Religion," 149.

34 Hall, *Worlds of Wonder*, 20, 54, 63, 69, 100.

35 Hardesty, *Unfreedom*.

36 Robert Dunke and Ann Smith Lainhart, ed., *Hollis Street Church Boston Records of Admissions, Baptisms, Marriages and Deaths 1732–1887* (Boston: The New England Historical Genealogical Society, 1998), 44, 229–230.

37 *Book of the First Church of Christ, in Middleborough*, 3; Mandell, *Behind the Frontier*, 50–51.

38 Silverman, *This Land Is Their Land*, 240–249, 360–363; Edward E. Andrews, *Native Apostles: Black and Indian Missionaries in the British Atlantic World* (Cambridge, MA: Harvard University Press, 2013); Winiarski, "Native American Popular Religion," 147–186.

39 Mandell, *Behind the Frontier*, 50–51, 75, 98–99, 172–173; Silverman, *This Land Is Their Land*, 250–255, 290–291.

40 Andrews, *Native Apostles*, 46, 235–236; Silverman, *This Land Is Their Land*, 292–298.

41 Mandell, *Behind the Frontier*, 129, 136.

42 Silverman, *This Land Is Their Land*, 243.

43 Winiarski, *Darkness Falls*, 23–130.

44 *Book of the First Church of Christ, in Middleborough*, 6–7.

45 Winiarski, *Darkness Falls*, 242.

46 Winiarski, *Darkness Falls*, 143, 144, 177; Thomas Prince, ed., *An account of the great revival: in Middleborough, Mass. A. D. 1741, 1742, during the ministry of Rev. Peter Thatcher; with a notice of his character* (Boston: Re-printed by T.R. Marvin, 1842), 9–10.

47 Winiarski, *Darkness Falls*, 179.

48 First Congregational Church (Middleborough, Mass.), First Church of Middleboro records, 1702–1925, RG4970, Congregational Library & Archives, Boston, MA, Digitized material available at: www.congregationallibrary.org/nehh/series1/MiddleboroMAFirst4970; *Book of the First Church of Christ, in Middleborough*, 90–94; Winiarski, *Darkness Falls*, 184.

49 Richard J. Boles, *Dividing the Faith: The Rise of Segregated Churches in the Early American North* (New York: New York University Press, 2020), 13–53.

50 Prince, *Account of the great revival*, 6, 8, 12.

51 Prince, *Account of the great revival*, 8, 10; Winiarski, *Darkness Falls*, 187.

52 Prince, *Account of the great revival*, 14.

53 Winiarski, *Darkness Falls*, 405–406.

54 *Book of the First Church of Christ, in Middleborough*, 8–10.

55 Winiarski, *Darkness Falls*, 388, 391; C.C. Goen, *Revivalism and Separatism in New England, 1740–1800* (Middletown: Wesleyan University Press, 1987), 215, 217–219.

56 Winiarski, *Darkness Falls*, 401; Goen, *Revivalism and Separatism*, 185, 215–221, 244, 260–261, 282–283.

57 Winiarski, *Darkness Falls*, 465, 473, 529–553, 499–500.

58 First Church of Middleboro records, 1702–1925; *Book of the First Church of Christ, in Middleborough*, 27, 97, 100; Richard J. Boles, "Documents Relating to African American Experiences of White Congregational Churches in Massachusetts, 1773–1832," *New England Quarterly* 86, no. 2 (June 2013): 293–323; Mary Blauss Edwards, "Communications," *New England Quarterly* 86, no. 4 (December 2013): 688–689; Winiarski, *Darkness Falls*, 499.

59 First Church of Middleboro records, 1702–1925; Winiarski, *Darkness Falls*, 499; *Book of the First Church of Christ, in Middleborough*, 27, 97, 100.

Chapter Three

A View from the Philadelphia Barracks: Religion in the Mid-Atlantic

Rachel Wheeler

Indiana University-Purdue University, Indianapolis, Indiana

The night of February 4th, 1764, was a sleepless one for the community of 140 Native Americans, mostly Lenape (Delaware), Munsee, and Mohican, huddled together in the Philadelphia Barracks, fearing attack by the vigilante group who came to be called the Paxton Boys. There was good reason to be afraid, as twenty Susquehannocks of Conestoga (near Lancaster) had been murdered by a mob of Scots Irish settlers from the backcountry just weeks earlier. Reports swirled that the same mob — now hundreds strong — was marching toward the city with murder on their minds, led by the "Fighting Parson" John Elder. It was the threat of such violence growing out of the Seven Years War and Pontiac's War that had forced the Native residents of the Moravian mission communities of Nain and Wequetank, near Bethlehem, Pennsylvania, from their homes and fields just two months earlier, into what was equal parts asylum and internment. With the Native community were two European couples[1] — the Grubes and the Schmicks who had lived and worked alongside the Native community for decades as members of the Renewed Unity of the Brethren, a largely German pietist group that burgeoned into a worldwide movement in the 1720s and 1730s. Also at the Barracks were three regiments of British regular soldiers under the direction of Captain J. Schlosser, a Palatine German who led the Royal American Regiment. Fearing the lower level living quarters would be too easily breached by the mob, Schlosser ordered the Native residents into the soldiers' second story quarters for safety and mounted eighteen-pound cannons outside the building while they awaited the mob.[2]

Although the soldiers and the Moravian community mixed uneasily, the Native Christians took heart from the additional protection offered by a force of two hundred citizens, including many Quakers, who pushed the limits of their pacifism to take up arms in defense of the Native Christians. Even the newly installed Governor, John Penn (grandson of Quaker founder William Penn), paid a midnight visit, doing his best to calm the frightened children as word reached the community that the rebels were just miles away in Germantown. The next day, the residents celebrated Sunday services in the cramped second floor sleeping quarters together with Moravians visiting from the city. No harm came to the Native community at the Barracks during those tense days, but it would be more than a year before the community was free to leave and the toll would be steep: smallpox and dysentery claimed fifty-six men, women, and children.[3]

A Companion to American Religious History, First Edition. Edited by Benjamin E. Park.

The colonial landscape had been dramatically transformed by the time the remaining members of the community set off in April 1765 toward the Susquehanna, where they would build a new community named Friedenshütten at the site of a destroyed Munsee village, Wyalusing. They quickly built a thriving new village, but the pattern of war and removal would be repeated again and again in subsequent decades, prompting moves to Ohio, Detroit, Indiana, and Ontario. With each move, the distance grew between the Native and European Moravian communities and the hopes of an interracial, interethnic community that selectively adapted elements of European culture and religion crumbled. Colonial, and later American, governments increasingly settled into the conviction that Native peoples and Europeans could not peaceably coexist and that removal, extermination or assimilation were the only options. Native professions of neutrality and pacifism offered little protection, as the 1782 massacre of ninety-six Native Moravians at Gnadenhütten, Ohio by an American militia made all too clear.[4] In the ensuing decades, many Native peoples, including former Moravians, came to similar conclusions and joined nativist movements like that of Tenskwatawa, the Shawnee Prophet, whose visionary encounters with the Great Spirit fueled a political and military movement for Native union against American forces, headed by the Prophet's brother, Tecumseh.[5] The events at the Barracks lay bare a discussion that continues to the present: who is perceived as a potential threat and who is counted as a potential or actual fellow citizen?

Exploring the backstory of that cold February night in the Barracks offers a window into the transformations of colonial society in this crucial era of American history. While the story of the Native Christian community at Philadelphia has appeared in many histories of Pennsylvania in this era, it has never taken center stage. Viewing the Native Christian community at the Barracks as the hub from which lines of connection can be traced outward across time and space provides a dramatically different view of early American religion than what we are accustomed to. The Mohican and Lenape Moravians at Philadelphia are directly connected to many well-known religious figures of the eighteenth century, including New England revivalist Jonathan Edwards, Anglican evangelist George Whitfield, incendiary pro-revival Presbyterian minister Gilbert Tennent, as well as lesser known or obscure figures like Presbyterian missionaries David and John Brainerd, Moravian missionary David Zeisberger, and Munsee preacher and prophet Johannes Papunhank. The Native Christians at the Barracks had significant interactions with the full spectrum of religious groups including traditionalist Native communities and Moravians, but also Quakers, Presbyterians, Congregationalists, and Lutherans. A host of prominent political leaders including Benjamin Franklin, the Pennsylvania Governor, and members of the Provincial Assembly were urgently concerned with the fate of Native Christians.

Placing this small community at the heart of a colonial American religious landscape might seem a strange move, since it is not especially representative of Native or Moravian communities more broadly considered. Yet because of the extraordinary breadth of their connections and the impassioned response — both positive and negative — their mere existence provoked, this focus on the Native Moravians proves immensely clarifying, revealing the complex intertwining of religious, ethnic, racial, and political identities in colonial British America. Two major conclusions come into focus: first, the transatlantic world was a very small world indeed, and second, community safety was almost always priority number one. This does not mean that professions of religious beliefs were disingenuous, but rather that the particular context and assessment of threats to community profoundly influenced the interpretation of inherited religious traditions. Tracing the connections outward from the Barracks requires a tour of the dizzyingly complex transatlantic world in the mid-eighteenth century. Accounting for the different responses to the Native community at the Barracks — while some had murder on their minds, others saw them as curiosities or objects of philanthropic endeavor — brings us through a wide swath of early American religious history and different visions for the future of the colonies, particularly concerning the interplay of religion, race, and civic identity.

The first part of this essay surveys the paths that brought the various groups together for those fraught days at the Philadelphia Barracks, while the second part takes a closer look at the lives of two Native residents of the Barracks during the year of confinement, and two Europeans with whom they were closely associated. The first pair includes Joshua, a Mohican man born in 1742 and John Antes, born in 1740. Both were students together at an inter-racial school founded by John's father, Henry Antes, where they both began their musical training, going on to lives as accomplished musicians and instrument builders. The other pair is a Native woman named Elizabeth, and a Moravian missionary named Margaretha Grube. Elizabeth was a Shawnee woman and sister of a Shawnee leader. She had been a parishioner in Jonathan Edwards's congregation in Stockbridge, Massachusetts, and married into a prominent Mohican family, many of whom left the Stockbridge community to join the Moravians. Margaretha was born into a Lutheran family in Reval, Livonia (now Talinn, Estonia). By the time she arrived in Philadelphia, she had joined the Moravian church; served as a missionary in St. Thomas, then Pachgatgoch (Kent), Connecticut, and then Wechquetank, Pennsylvania; and given birth to nine children! This microhistorical approach foregrounds the human experiences of ordinary people as they shaped and were shaped by global currents. It also calls attention to the intertwined lives of Native and European individuals, while highlighting the stark differences of their experiences.

Pathways to the Philadelphia Barracks

How is it that a community of Native Christians came to be interned at a military barracks alongside British Regular soldiers, whose job it was to defend the Native Christians against fellow British subjects? Answering that question brings us to two central themes of the eighteenth century and shows us just how tightly bound the one is to the other: religious revival and imperial war. In the colonies, this period of religious revivals and missionary activity occurred during a lull in imperial wars that lasted from 1713 until 1744, which helped to facilitate the movement of people as well as evangelical ideas and methods.[6] King George's War (1744–48), which pitted Protestant Britain against Catholic France, escalated an already heated anti-Catholic sentiment in British colonies, but failed to resolve territorial conflicts. Tensions festered until exploding into the Seven Years War (1755–1763), resulting in the ouster of France from its North American holdings.

The early eighteenth century saw a transatlantic Protestant evangelical awakening that spurred new forms of religious practice: itinerant ministers, an emphasis on religious experience over religious knowledge, and a renewed commitment to evangelism. In the northern British colonies, revivalism began among the Dutch Reformed (Calvinists) in New Jersey in the 1720s, followed by the spread among Presbyterians and Congregationalists in the 1730s and early 1740s, resulting in divisions into pro- and anti-revival factions. The revivalist movement fueled the growth of the Baptist movement and the newly formed Methodist offshoot of the Church of England. The Renewed Unity of the Brethren, as the Moravians were officially known, emerged in the 1720s when refugees from Catholic Bohemia (Czech Republic) were granted asylum on the Saxony estate of Nikolaus Ludwig, Count von Zinzendorf. The religious practices of this group soon drew in the Count and many new followers from the surrounding region, to the alarm of civil officials, who feared religious "enthusiasm" and the challenge to Lutheran orthodoxy. Zinzendorf and the newly formed Unity were exiled, lending further momentum to the group's already active missionary project. Within a matter of decades, Moravians had established missions from Greenland to Surinam, New York to St. Thomas.[7]

The Mohicans among the Native Christians at Philadelphia traced their roots to the first Moravian mission in North America, established in the 1740s at Shekomeko, a Mohican town of about 100 residents in the Taconic hills of New York. Most others present at the Barracks were Munsees who had joined or been born into the Moravian communities in Pennsylvania in the later 1740s and 1750s. The Moravian outreach to the Mohicans dates to a chance meeting in New York City, when two men from Shekomeko encountered a young Moravian, Christian Heinrich Rauch, whose dreams of preaching the word of the Savior to America's Native peoples had been sparked by Moravian leader Augustus Spangenberg's reporting from Georgia, propelling Rauch across the Atlantic from his home in Wetteravia.[8]

The Mohican men, Mammatsikan and Wasamapah, initially paid Rauch little mind, for they had good reason to be skeptical of the newly arrived Christians. Mohicans had had over a century of contact with European Christians since Henry Hudson sailed up the Muhheakantuck (Hudson) River in 1609, and most had presented a poor argument for their religion. Wasamapah later recounted their experience with missionaries:

> Once a preacher came and began to explain to us that there was a God. We answered, "Dost thou think us so ignorant as not to know that? Go back to the place from whence thou camest." Then again another preacher came and began to teach us, and to say, "You must not steal, nor lie, nor get drunk, etc." We answered "Thou fool, dost thou think that we don't know that? Learn first thyself, and then teach the people to whom thou belongest, to leave off these things. For who steal, or lie, or who are more drunken than thine own people?" And thus we dismissed him.[9]

Before the arrival of the Moravians, the only sustained mission effort to Mohicans was a Congregational mission forty miles from Shekomeko in western Massachusetts at a mission site named Stockbridge. A New England population boom in the early decades of the eighteenth century sent settlers westward seeking new lands, prompting some Congregational ministers to sound the alarm about the colony's failure to make good on their original charter's mandate to bring the gospel to the heathen. King Philip's War in the 1670s had ground missionary activity to a halt, but the decades of relative imperial peace and the desire for more lands added new impetus to mission efforts. The Massachusetts Assembly endorsed the mission on religious and political grounds: besides the promise of saving souls, a mission settlement would open up new lands when Native peoples exchanged hunting territories for secured town settlements. A 1734 meeting in Deerfield, Massachusetts laid the groundwork for the creation of the mission town of Stockbridge, incorporated in 1739 with Native representatives on the town council.[10]

Although both mission efforts to Mohican peoples—at Stockbridge and Shekomeko—were part of a larger transatlantic Protestant awakening, the Congregational and Moravian mission policies could scarcely have been more different. Mammatsikan and possibly other Shekomeko residents had considered joining their Mohican relatives at Stockbridge but deemed the cost too steep. The Stockbridge program was typical of Anglo-Protestant missions that emphasized "civilization before Christianization," demanding conformity to English forms of agriculture and husbandry as well as instruction in literacy and Christian doctrine. Admission to communion in Anglo Protestant churches was contingent on a persuasive conversion narrative drawing on a depth of biblical knowledge.

Moravian theology, by contrast, put little stock in "head" knowledge, emphasizing instead "heart" knowledge that came through ritual encounter with the blood of Christ. This message drew scores of converts to the new faith from all around Europe, often propelling them around the globe in the burgeoning mission program, bound more firmly to sect than to nation. The peripatetic religious and geographic experiences of the European Moravians and the tendency to de-emphasize European cultural forms as foundational to Christian experience created an opening for the indigenization of Christianity by the early Native affiliates. Moravian missionaries committed to preaching through their actions before they opened their mouths to preach. They contributed economically to Native communities laboring together in the fields and offering their services as craftsmen and women, healers, midwives, teachers, and advocates. Moravian missionaries also differed from their counterparts in other denominations in that they often worked as married pairs. European Moravian women provided essential labor: learning Native languages and forming close social bonds with Native women. Finally, the Moravian emphasis on spiritual empowerment through ritual contact with the blood of a powerful deity spoke to the spiritual and physical needs of the community at Shekomeko who keenly felt the press of colonialism: encroachment on Native lands and devastating disease, often exacerbated by alcohol. Mammatsikan and Wasamapah were among the first Mohicans to be baptized by the Moravians in 1742. By the year's end, dozens of others had joined them, including Tassawachamen, father to an infant son, both of whom would take the name Joshua, and both of whom were in the Barracks over twenty years later.

Moravian successes in gaining Native audiences in New York and Connecticut came at a time when much of the Northeast was reckoning with the flames of revivalism. The disagreements over the nature of true religion divided Presbyterians and Congregationalists into pro- and anti-revival camps. These fractures often tracked roughly along geographical and economic lines as well, with the wealthier favoring more sober, rational expressions of religion, and the more rural and less wealthy preferring "heart" religion and the spiritual promises of the New Birth offered in Christ. Pro- and anti-revivalists could agree on one thing however: no one liked the Moravians, especially their aversion to systematic theology, their seemingly "Papist" (Catholic) forms of worship, which included liberal use of litanies, music, and images, and their ability to outpace Anglo-Protestant mission efforts.

One might expect the Shekomekoans' embrace of Christianity to have eased tensions with neighboring Protestants, but instead, relations deteriorated even further, particularly as England and France hurtled toward war. The groundwork for hostility to the Native Moravians was laid by several anti-Moravian tracts published by leading colonial revivalists, including the Presbyterian minister, Gilbert Tennent. Tennent's attack, published in 1743, skillfully defined Moravians as outside the pale by charging them with enthusiasm, the very thing he was charged with by Old Side stalwarts. Tennent stoked fears by likening Moravian missionary practices to the tactics of Native warfare. The Moravians, according to Tennent, go "ravening after Souls, as Wolves, and use cunning like Foxes. They take sculking methods, creeping into Houses, and lead Captive silly Women." Tennent feared the consequences of a faith that empowered the socially disadvantaged, appealing as it did to "young Persons, Females, and ignorant People who are full of affection." Moravians leaned dangerously close to Catholicism by insisting, claimed Tennent, that "we must quit our Reason and turn real Fools; we must believe thro' thick and thin, Absurdities and Nonsense, and so turn Papists."[11]

These clerical attacks added further fuel to popular antipathy toward the Native Moravians. The Moravians' English neighbors grew increasingly nervous, and eventually both New York and Connecticut enacted legislation barring the Moravians from preaching to the Natives without a license.

These pressures led the community of several dozen members at Shekomeko to leave New York in 1746, first to the Moravian headquarters in Bethlehem, and then, following an outbreak of smallpox, to a new settlement named Gnadenhütten thirty miles away on the Lecha (Lehigh) River.[12] The community grew quickly as word spread, both through the travels of Native and European Moravians and the regular visitors who came to visit, drawn by curiosity and the desire to maintain ties with family and friends who resided there. For the new Lenape affiliates, there was an additional impulse: the desire to remain on secured Lenape lands, as Bethlehem and Gnadenhütten both stood on territory that had been alienated in the fraudulent 1737 Walking Purchase.

From the perspective of coastal Euro-American settlements, Gnadenhütten was a remote backcountry settlement. But looking East, it stood along an important highway that had long connected Native peoples as they engaged in trade and war. It was also a space for trading in religious beliefs and practices. Northeastern Native peoples lived in a world enlivened by *manitou*, or spirits, who could be enlisted to support human thriving, through proper maintenance of relationships and ceremonial practice. It is not too much of an exaggeration to say that Moravian modes of calling on the power of Christ's blood bore a greater resemblance to Native religious ceremony than to Anglo-Protestantism, at least as was commonly preached to Native peoples. The Gnadenhütten community adapted Moravian Christianity in ways that drew from distinctive Moravian "blood and wounds" theology, enlisting assistance of a powerful spirit to help in hunting, healing, and creating and maintaining community. Their Christian practice did not signal a renunciation of all ties with those who made different religious choices, a reflection of the non-exclusive and ecumenical nature of Native religious practice that carried over to the practice of Christianity.

For nine years, the community at Gnadenhütten thrived and grew. But one night in November of 1755, Native warriors protesting white intrusions set fire to the mission house, killing eleven European Moravians, an event that was one small part of the escalating war that would eventually come to be the Seven Years' War. This war was a global contest for empire that ultimately transformed the imperial landscape of North America and profoundly altered the prospects of Native communities by effectively ending French competition to Britain's imperial dominion in continental North America. The opening salvo of the war in North America came in 1754 when George Washington led a Virginia militia to Ohio Country (territory that encompassed what is now eastern Indiana, Ohio, western Pennsylvania, and northwestern West Virginia) in an effort to warn the French against the continued construction of forts in the backcountry. For the British, French, and the Haudenosaunee (Iroquois), the region was central to the maintenance of empire. For resident Ohio Country Native peoples, the region was home and they desperately wanted to keep out floods of white settlers.[13]

The larger imperial war moved eastward in 1755 with a series of attacks by Ohio Valley and western Pennsylvania Native warriors on white settlements in the Susquehanna Valley, which left many backcountry colonists terrified of all Native peoples. Western Lenape and Shawnee peoples were outraged that the Haudenosaunee had sold swaths of land that were not theirs to sell in the Susquehanna Valley to British interests in 1754 and they launched attacks on settlers in retaliation. Their attacks moved eastward, and in November 1755 they targeted the mission community at Gnadenhütten, attacking the mission house first, killing eleven European missionaries, and allowing time for the Native residents to escape harm.[14]

The destruction of Gnadenhütten made it clear the Native Moravian community could not return to their town, and so they decided to remain at Bethlehem, where round-the-clock guards were posted against further attacks. Initially, the community feared attack by English neighbors suspicious of the harboring of a large Native community, but the steady pace of attacks on frontier communities eventually led a stream of frightened settlers to take refuge at Moravian settlements and at least some recognized that the Native Moravian ties to hostile western Natives offered a degree of protection. Others, however, saw these ties not as a means of protection, but as a sign of collusion and a reason to distrust all Native peoples. Further, the response to the European Moravians was mixed as well, but the losses sustained by the Moravians generally bolstered the status of the German Moravians, as it challenged the long-held fears the Moravians were "Papists" who encouraged Native mission residents to collude with the French.[15]

In the years following the attack, the Lenape and Mohican Moravians found themselves being pulled in various directions. Some who had left the faith sought to persuade their family and friends remaining at Bethlehem to join the refugee communities along the Susquehanna, in keeping with Haudenosaunee efforts to maintain a buffer of dependent Native communities west of British settlements. In the intervening eight years between the destruction of Gnadenhütten and the flight to Philadelphia, the community rebuilt once again, founding a new town called Nain directly across the river from Bethlehem.[16] The town became a prosperous settlement sustained through agriculture, continued hunting, and trade in craftsmanship. Hymns were regularly sung in Mohican and Lenape as well as German. The construction of the town drew many who had fled to the Susquehanna in the wake of the Gnadenhütten attack.[17] Nain became another refugee community drawing new members from nearby Lenape villages such as Meniolagomekah and Wechquatank. Colonial treaties held in nearby Easton and Lancaster brought diverse populations of colonists and Native peoples through Moravian settlements.

On February 10, 1763 the Seven Years War officially came to an end with the signing of the Treaty of Paris, which essentially ousted France from North America, sparing only its lucrative Caribbean holdings. But the official peace unleashed a pent-up flood of British settlers into the backcountry, sparking further alarm among Native owners. Not surprisingly, these new incursions and affronts prompted outrage in Indian Country and created fertile ground for the emergence of prophetic religious and political movements. A Lenape visionary named Neolin received a message from the Master of Life, calling for rejection of European ways: "this land where ye dwell I have made for you and not for others. Whence comes it that ye permit the Whites upon your lands? Can ye not live without them?" Neolin exhorted followers to "live without any Trade or Connections with ye White people, Clothing & Supporting themselves as their forefathers did." An Ottawa leader named Pontiac took up the message and rallied like-minded communities from the Great Lakes, Illinois, and Ohio regions to war against the British. Allied warriors laid siege to Detroit in April 1763 and by late May, Fort Pitt was under siege. The attacks were moving eastward toward the Susquehanna, and settlers were terrified.[18]

While Fort Pitt was under siege, Moravian missionary David Zeisberger was visiting the town of Wyalusing, a relatively new settlement of several Munsee families led by a man named Papunhank, a visionary prophet of peace, who had preached his own message of temperance and pacifism before finding common cause with Quakers. Zeisberger hoped the Moravians might establish a new congregation at Wyalusing, but in the middle of his visit, Zeisberger was recalled to Bethlehem due to fears of imminent attack. These attacks thwarted the new Moravian settlement and heightened the fears of white settlers to a fever pitch. Not all colonial settlers shared the fear of Moravian-affiliated native communities, but growing numbers had come to view Pontiac's Rebellion as, in Moravian missionary and historian John Heckewelder's words, "a just punishment of God, because the Europeans, like the Israelites of old, had not destroyed the Canaanites, and therefore declared that all Indians, without exception ought to be put to the sword."[19]

Escalating tensions prompted a petition signed by more than two dozen residents of Nain to the Pennsylvania governor affirming they were "true Friends to the English, and that we love the great King and the government of this Province and that we will be faithfull to him and you" and that "we love our dear Savior." They declared they had nothing to do with attacks on white settlements, and instead that they stood in the same danger as whites of being killed. "Yet," wrote the petitioners, "some of the white People are jealous of us, and threaten to kill us. We remind you therefore of Your good Promises, to protect us for we are faithfull to you, as much as the white People."[20] The missionaries at Nain attempted to quell fears by issuing a document, titled, "Marks whereby Christian Indians may be distinguished from Wild Indians." Nain residents scarcely dared work their fields, let alone travel through the woods without a white person to vouch for them.[21]

By the fall, the Nain residents were effectively under house arrest, stripped of their hunting weapons, subjected to daily monitoring, and rightfully in fear of their neighbors.[22] In early October, the Irish settlement near Bethlehem was attacked by Lenape and Shawnee.[23] Soon after, a party of about fifty white men assembled on the banks of the Lehigh River opposite Nain and planned to ambush the community and kill all of the residents. The would-be murderers were dissuaded by a neighbor, however, who convinced them they would only be more vulnerable to attack. The next day, a group of "Irish freebooters" then descended on

Wechquetank, intent on murdering the Native residents. Missionary Bernard Grube attempted unsuccessfully to reason with the mob. When words failed, Grube resorted to offering food and drink and unspecified presents, and eventually the mob retreated. Despite the threats, the Moravian diarist noted that the Native residents maintained their courage, one proclaiming "wicked people are as weak as worms in the sight of our Savior, he can and will protect us, and cause fear to come upon them."[24] With the threats on their lives continuing, the Wechquetank community left their harvest and their cattle behind and removed to the largely European Moravian settlement at Nazareth.

Attacks by western Native peoples on frontier settlements continued, and thus, ironically, many white settlers fled to Bethlehem and Nazareth seeking protection. Some rightly believed that the Native Moravian presence ensured a degree of protection because Western Native peoples did not want to attack their kin. Others likened the Native Christians to wolves in sheep's clothing. This was the message that came from the pulpit and the pen of the Presbyterian "Fighting Pastor," John Elder, who headed a congregation of mostly Scots Irish in Paxton, 100 miles to the west of Bethlehem. In letters to the Provincial governor that fall, Elder advocated for the removal of all Native peoples from the region: "it is evident," he wrote, "that till that Branch of the [Susquehanna] River is cleared of the Savages, the frontier settlements will be in no safety."[25]

Communities like Paxton were divided by ethnicity, religious profession, language, and wealth. Besides Scots Irish Presbyterians, there were also Germans of various denominations including Lutheran, Reformed, and Moravian, as well as English Quakers. This diversity, combined with an extremely high rate of mobility, hindered the formation of strong social institutions. Elder's congregants, often called Ulster Scots, or Scotch-Irish, were Protestants of Scottish descent whose ancestors had migrated from Scotland to the Ulster region of Ireland as part of a colonization effort to subdue Irish Catholics and spread the Calvinist Protestantism of the Presbyterian Scottish Kirk, by more and less forceful methods. Those who migrated on to the American colonies were often too poor to buy land, especially at the escalating rates charged by wealthy proprietors and merchants like Edward Shippen, and were thus among those who chose to squat on Native lands, rendering themselves the most vulnerable to attack. Elder was a staunch Old Side (anti-revivalist) minister, who became a spokesperson for the Paxton community and their grievances against the wealthy and the remote.

By November, it had become unsustainable for the Native Moravian community to remain at Nain and Wechquetank. Gruesome details of the attacks on vulnerable communities spread like wildfire through these settlements and stoked anger toward several targets: toward the Quaker-dominated Assembly that refused to apportion sufficient funds for defense of the frontier, while benefiting from the buffering function these communities afforded; toward wealthy proprietors who charged such exorbitant prices for land that the poor often settled on un-ceded Native lands; and finally, toward Native peoples living within Provincial boundaries whom they suspected of collusion and complicity with hostile Natives to the West.[26] On the evening of November 5th, the order arrived from Philadelphia that all Native Moravians were to be sent to Philadelphia.

Two days later, a caravan of 121 men, women, and children made a tearful departure from Bethlehem. They were accompanied by the missionary couple, Bernhard and Margaretha Grube, and later joined by another, Johan and Johanna Schmick, who remained with the community for the duration of their confinement. A company of soldiers escorted the caravan, and as they passed through Germantown the townspeople gathered to watch the procession, hurling threats of burning and hanging the refugees. The harassment continued upon arrival in the city, as Grube reported, "the fury of the people in Philadelphia was indescribable, and we had to stand in front of the barracks for fully three hours and take all kinds of disgrace and scorn. We had many thousands accompanying us through the city, yet it came off without harm."[27]

The forlorn company travelled another four miles before arriving at Province Island, an island in the Schuylkill River near the confluence with the Lenape (at the site of the current

Philadelphia airport), which had served since 1741 as the site of a "pest house" for the quarantining of new arrivals. The Island was owned by the Province and overseen by Joseph Fox, a member of the Provincial Assembly and former Quaker, who had been disowned during the Seven Years War for violating the Quaker peace testimony and supporting defense spending. The refugees were lodged in two large brick buildings with twenty spacious rooms with fireplaces and were relieved to have a body of water between them and the crowds of angry and curious Philadelphians.[28]

In their new home, a sort of normalcy emerged: Native women were hired by a neighboring farmer to milk his cows, expeditions were made into the city to buy necessities, a nursing committee was formed of the Native Sisters to tend the sick, and the community welcomed the return of the Schmicks and their young daughter. Br. Grube noted in the diary, "it was very hard for us in the beginning to leave our nice homes, but now we are totally free of it, and we are happy that we can sleep peacefully again and eat our bread without fear."[29] Six weeks after they had left their homes, the community celebrated Christmas Eve with a children's Love Feast (a Moravian revival of the biblical feast celebrated by the disciples after Pentecost), at which Br. Schmick recounted the story of the Savior's birth. Services included the singing of hymns, most likely in Mohican, Lenape and German. Additional music was provided by the 24-year-old Mohican musician Joshua on the spinet, and a young Lenape man, Elias, on the cittern, a guitar-like instrument.

The hard-won sense of normalcy came to an abrupt end when at midnight on December 29, two boats arrived bearing a letter from Joseph Fox ordering the community to prepare to depart immediately, as the "Irish Rebels" were on their way from Lancaster County to kill them. Only after the community had packed up and boarded the three boats the government had sent for them did they discover the rumors were false. They then returned to the Island while officials debated their fate over the course of the next week. Arrangements were made for the community to be sent to the care of Sir William Johnson, the Superintendent of Indian Affairs, and an Irish-Catholic turned Protestant who came to America in 1739 to oversee his uncle's estate along the Mohawk River west of Albany. Johnson was prepared to serve as a cultural intermediary, as he had children by a German Palatinate common-law wife, as well as by a Mohawk woman, Molly Brant.[30] A regiment of seventy Scottish Highlanders was headed for Johnson's estate, and were enlisted to escort the Native Christians to their destination, where it was presumed Johnson could find a viable arrangement. The company consisted of "high and low ranking officers who came from Pittsburgh," who "acted quite wild and particularly harassed our young women folk." The Moravian missionaries reported with satisfaction, however, that the soldiers quickly reformed their lewd behavior toward the Native women.[31]

The soldiers and the company of Moravians made their way from Philadelphia, through New Jersey, stopping in Princeton, Trenton, and Amboy, and they were met with equal parts curiosity and hostility along the way. Just as they were about to be ferried across Arthur Kill from Amboy to Staten Island, they received word that the New York government did not want to take on the risk of harboring the Native Moravians, and so, having nowhere else to go, they retraced their journey back to Philadelphia.

They arrived back in Philadelphia on January 20 and had barely settled in when a new alarm was raised that the Paxton mob was on the march toward the city. This time, it proved to be well-founded. Quaker residents shed their pacifist convictions to take up arms, a stance that drew revulsion from the Paxtonites who charged race-betrayal. Alarmed officials then authorized a riot act and an ecumenical group of ministers set out to meet the mob. Among them were famed Presbyterian revivalist — and earlier strident critic of the Moravians — Gilbert Tennent, Francis Alison (another Presbyterian), two unnamed Anglicans, and a Swedish Lutheran minister, Paul Daniel Brycelius. This ministerial delegation was followed by Benjamin Franklin.[32] This alignment makes clear that denominational and doctrinal differences were now outweighed by political and social concerns.

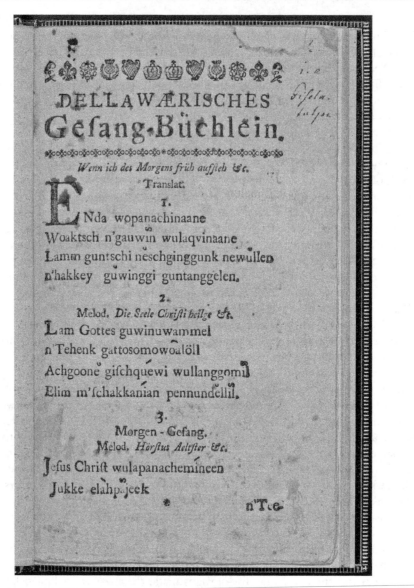

Bernhard Adam Grube, Dellawaerisches Gesang-Büchlein (Friedensthal bei Bethlehem: Johann Brandmueller, 1763).
Source: Reproduced with permission from Historical Society of Pennsylvania.

The Paxtonites were turned away from a physical attack on the Native Moravians, but the events marked a profound turning point and a significant shift in the political landscape in the colonies in the decade before the Revolution. Two decades earlier, English settlers feared Native Moravians because they were Moravian, which they equated with Catholicism. Now, Paxtonites objected not to the denominational affiliation of the Native peoples at the Barracks, but argued that Native peoples could not, by definition, be Christian. Benjamin Franklin objected to this logic, saying it made no more sense to kill all redheads if one red-head were found guilty of a murder than it did for the Paxtonites to attack British-allied and pacifist Christian Natives. But Franklin and the Quaker party lost this battle.

The Paxton mob failed in carrying out their attack, but the community of Native Moravians remained in animated suspension for more than a year before hostilities subsided and a path forward could be negotiated for this community. They would receive permission the following spring to leave Philadelphia to settle on the Susquehanna. After Philadelphia, the Native Moravian community would live far from the center of colonial Moravianism. The narrative so far, however, gives something of a false impression that people remained squarely rooted within their demographic categories. A closer look at four individuals—two white and two Native—demonstrates the complex tangle of religion and race in vast early America.

Part II

During the seventeen months in captivity, life — and death — continued. Bernhard Grube's summary at the end of 1764 provides a deadly reckoning: in addition to two marriages, seven "Abendmahl" (communion services), six births, and twelve baptisms, there were also fifty-six deaths: twenty-one children and thirty-five adults, felled by smallpox and dysentery.[33] But these numbers only tell the barest of stories. The days were full with surprisingly normal activities: English lessons, religious services, singing, milking cows, hauling firewood, digging for oysters, and shopping in the city for necessities.[34] The residents of the Barracks maintained longstanding connections, created and nurtured over generations and even centuries, with neighboring peoples and with the land. They welcomed some Native visitors but rebuffed those who carried rum with them to trade. They tolerated the gaze of strangers: visiting pastors, curious soldiers, visiting provincial officials observed the Native Christians' hymn-filled worship services, then lingered to place an order for "Indian shoes," boys from the city came with coins to purchase hickory bows from the Native youth. Scores of newly arrived immigrants filed by, eager to see for themselves America's Native peoples. On just one day in May, the Moravian diarist noted that 1,000 visitors descended on the community.[35]

Also during that year, a woman named Elizabeth gave birth to a daughter in the heat of the summer and a young man named Joshua regularly played the spinet to the astonishment of visitors. Shifting focus to some of the individuals who tried to carry on normal life during these extraordinary circumstances helps us to appreciate the very personal experiences of colonialism, and perhaps more surprisingly, the vast webs of relationships that the Native residents of Philadelphia had built and maintained across a wide span of Native and colonial societies.

The Native Christians had just settled into life at Province Island when word came on January 4, 1764 that they must pack up and leave immediately as the Paxton mob was on the way. They packed what they could carry and were hurried onto boats that carried them to a nearby farm. From there they would begin their journey to New York, hoping to find a secure route to settle along the Susquehanna, bypassing the Lancaster settlements where anti-Indian sentiment raged. The aged and infirm rode in wagons while the rest, including a company of one hundred Highland soldiers posted guard, walked alongside on what turned out to be a round trip of 160 miles to Amboy, New Jersey and back in frigid wintry conditions. Elizabeth was at least two months pregnant at the time, and she rode together with Sister Margaretha Elizabeth Grube, a 48-year-old missionary, wife, and mother of nine children, who been close to dying just one month earlier.[36]

Elizabeth and Margaretha had both journeyed far in their lifetimes. Margaretha was born in Reval (Tallinn, Estonia), a hotbed of Pietism (the evangelical movement within Lutheranism), in which Moravian ministers were active as early as 1729.[37] There, she met and married her first husband, Joachim Busse, in 1744. In September 1751, the Busses arrived in New York City on the Moravian ship, *The Irene*, with fellow passengers and future missionary co-workers, Johann Jacob Schmick and David Zeisberger.[38] The Busses worked as missionaries in St. Thomas until Joachim's death in 1754. Margaretha returned to Bethlehem with her eight children and soon married Bernhard Grube, a missionary then serving at Gnadenhütten. Together, the couple served at Pachgatgoch, Connecticut, as well as Shamokin, and Wechquetank, during which time Margaretha bore one more child, born in 1758, and suffered at least one miscarriage, and numerous ailments.[39] During her time among the Native Christians, Margaretha seems not to have developed the strong spiritual ties to the Native women as did her younger, healthier, and more linguistically accomplished missionary sister, Johanna Schmick.

Margaretha's companion in the wagon had not traveled as many miles, in arriving at that day, but had traversed as many different cultural boundaries. Elizabeth is mentioned by name just four times in the records of the Philadelphia exile. She was likely among the Native women who went every morning by boat from Province Island to the farm of Jacob Weiss to milk his cows. It was a more extraordinary incident, however, that led to her first named appearance in the journals. The caravan of Native Christians had been hoping to find refuge on Sir William Johnson's estate in New York only to be turned back at Amboy before crossing over to New York. The Highland soldiers who had accompanied them were continuing on to New York, and so the Moravian community was stuck at Amboy for a week as they awaited a new regiment to guard them on their return to Philadelphia. While housed at the Barracks, Margaretha's husband Bernhard held regular worship services outdoors, drawing curious onlookers among the soldiers and townspeople. Some were simply curious, some came to harass, and others were captivated by the beautiful singing, prompting one soldier to comment: "God would wish that all white people were as good Christians as these Indians are." Elizabeth may well have accompanied Anton, a Munsee man and prominent leader in the Native community, to gather oysters at the shore.[40]

Finally, after a week in Amboy, soldiers of the American Regiment arrived just back from service in Detroit to escort the Native Christians back to Philadelphia: 140 Native Christians, seven wagon loads of baggage, accompanied by 170 soldiers and their six wagon loads. Margaretha, Elizabeth and several other old and infirm Native Christians rode ahead of the long caravan in a stagecoach. Just one day into their return journey, Margaretha and Elizabeth waited in the carriage as the driver stepped in to an inn, and "a malicious man" approached and struck Elizabeth with a stick, leaving her unconscious.[41] She recovered, and two days later the Moravian party stopped for the night in Princeton. There, she likely found some comfort in speaking Mohican to a young college student named Jonathan who came out to greet them. The 19-year-old student would not have been a stranger to Elizabeth, for she had in fact known him since he was a boy of six years old, the youngest son of Jonathan Edwards's ten children when he arrived in 1750 as missionary in Elizabeth's home in Stockbridge, Massachusetts.[42]

Ironically, most information about Elizabeth's time in Stockbridge comes from the Moravian records. It is those records that identify her as a Shawnee woman, baptized in Stockbridge, with familial ties to Mohawk and Shawnee, and living with her Mohican husband Bartholomew, who was bound by family ties to the leaders of Stockbridge, Shekomeko, Pachgatgoch, and Wechquadnach.[43] The couple were living in Stockbridge in May 1751, when the Moravian missionaries from Shekomeko made the journey to pay their respects to the dying Mohican leader, Umpachenee. The first missionary at Stockbridge, John Sergeant, had made several trips in the 1740s guided by Mohicans to the "Great Island," a largely Shawnee village on the Susquehanna River, to invite newcomers to settle at Stockbridge. Perhaps Elizabeth's family had responded to the message from their "Older Brothers" the Mohicans. Or perhaps Elizabeth was the daughter of, Aunauwauneekheek, leader of the Mohican village, Kaunaumeek, near Stockbridge, and his unnamed Shawnee wife mentioned by John Sergeant in 1744.[44] By the early 1750s in Stockbridge, Edwards was locked in a battle with the prominent Williams family for control of the mission and mission school, which had recently welcomed Mohawk students. The school burned mysteriously in 1752, and not long after that, Elizabeth and her husband were accepted into the Gnadenhütten community.[45]

Elizabeth and her husband and his siblings travelled regularly between these communities, and their move to Gnadenhütten in 1753 may well have been in support of larger Mohican diplomatic aims, as former Shekomeko captain, Mammatsikan (now baptised Abraham), was appointed that year to be war captain of the larger Mohican confederacy, much to the chagrin of the pacifist Moravian ministers. Alternatively, or additionally, their move might have been prompted by the impending birth of a daughter, born two months after their arrival.[46] The couple had several other children, one born that summer in the Philadelphia Barracks, and another as late as 1771.[47]

Elizabeth lived out her life with the Moravian community, while clearly maintaining a wide range of ties to other Native communities, Christian and not. When they were finally allowed to leave Philadelphia, she moved with the community to Friedenshütten (Wyalusing) on the Susquehanna, and later to Gnadenhütten, Ohio. She regularly hosted visiting family, including her sister Tabea from Otsiningo,[48] her brother James who lived at a Lenape town on the Muskingum in Ohio, relatives from Stockbridge, as well as an unnamed relative identified as a Mohawk captain. When Shawnee leaders visited, Elizabeth served as interpreter. Her death is not recorded by the Moravians, the last mention of her dating to 1775, when she would have been in late 40s. Her companion on the coach, Margaretha, did not remain a missionary after the Philadelphia sojourn. She and her husband were called to serve at the European-Moravian community of Lititz, Pennsylvania, where they lived until her death in 1776, after another carriage ride in terrible weather, this time from Bethlehem to Lititz. Bernhard Grube's remembrance of his wife would serve as well for Elizabeth: "She was a woman of much experience."[49]

Also in the caravan that traveled to New Jersey and back to Philadelphia was a Mohican man named Joshua, and his childhood friend, John Antes, who came from Bethlehem to assist the community in securing housing and supplies along the way. The two young men were born within two years of each other and were students together at a Moravian school on John's family farm in Fredericktown, Pennsylvania, from the time Joshua was just five. Like Elizabeth and Margaretha, Joshua and John came from quite different backgrounds. But unlike Elizabeth and Margaretha, Joshua and John were born into their parent's religious experiments.

John Antes was the 9th child of Henry (Heinrich) Antes, a largely forgotten lynchpin of early Pennsylvania religion. The elder Antes had been one of many Palatine Germans from the Rhine region who fled the war-ravaged region. He had been born in Frensheim in 1701, just two years after the walled town was destroyed by fire. Antes emigrated to Pennsylvania in 1720, and quickly put to use skills he had no doubt acquired as he assisted his father and others who rebuilt Frensheim. Within fifteen years of his arrival, he was married, had built a house as well as grist, saw, oil, and paper mills, and was sought after for counsel by surrounding settlers. He was an active member of the Associated Brethren of Skippack, which tried to find common religious ground among the disparate German communities. In 1740, he hosted noted evangelist George Whitefield as he preached to a crowd of 2,000 from Antes's porch and was crucial to helping the Moravians purchase the land that gave rise to Bethlehem.[50] He was a leading force behind the Pennsylvania Synods in 1745, which brought together leaders of a dozen German Protestant Churches, including Lutherans, and Brethren, Quakers and Moravians.

Antes despised inter-denominational fighting and was drawn to the Moravians by their ecumenism and in 1745, offered up his homestead in Frederickstown for use as a Moravian school. He decamped to Bethlehem, leaving his sons behind to attend the school.[51] Two years after the school's founding, the Gnadenhütten diary recorded that young a Mohican boy named Joshua eagerly set off to school where he joined dozens of other students, mostly European, but also other Mohicans and at least one African, a boy named Anthony from St. Thomas.[52]

Joshua's family was part of the community of Mohicans recently arrived in Pennsylvania from Shekomeko, in New York, where Joshua had spent the first few years of his life. Joshua was born in February 1742 just months before the first members of the community were baptized by the newly arrived Moravian missionaries. His maternal grandfather, Gadrachseth, called the "old captain," had strong ties to the Mohican community still on the Hudson River homelands, took the name Cornelius. His mother was baptized Salome, and his father, Tassawachamen, became known as the name Joshua.[53] The Moravians were much lower impact than their Anglo-Protestant neighbors. Those who elected to be baptized found in the Moravian Heiland (Savior) a powerful man-god whose powers could be transferred through ritual action and deployed toward maintaining community and health. Men sang hymns in Mohican while hunting in hopes of calling the deer. Women sang those same hymns while tending the sick. Moravian successes in gaining a Native audience worried clergy like Gilbert Tennent, and when war erupted in 1744, those fears spread rapidly among neighboring colonists, like those at Reinbeck, who sought a warrant to kill the residents of Shekomeko.

Joshua and his family were among the several dozen Mohicans who left Shekomeko in the spring of 1746 and resettled at Bethlehem, which unfortunately proved catastrophic when smallpox ravaged the community that fall, claiming the lives of Joshua's father and two young brothers. When a new community was established at Gnadenhütten, Joshua, senior, took on a leading role as Ausseher in charge of economic affairs and assigning one- and two-acre plots to members for planting. Joshua helped tutor Moravian missionaries in the Mohican language, and together with his new wife, Bathsheba, composed a number of Mohican language hymns that remained in active use in the community throughout the rest of the century. His son would carry on his father's musical legacy.

Young Joshua remained at the school for nearly four years, when Antes broke his affiliation with the Moravians in 1750, outraged that Moravian bishop Spangenburg had begun to wear a special surplice.[54] Schooling for Joshua and John included a rigorous musical education with missionaries Johann Christopher Pyrlaeus (who had studied music in J. S. Bach's circles in Leipzig) and later, Johann Jacob Schmick, both of whom were accomplished linguists and musicians.[55] In the years before arriving at Philadelphia, Joshua, Jr. had become proficient at reading and writing in German, and could speak English, Mohican, and Munsee.[56] He often served as an interpreter, and helped missionaries write hymns in Munsee, following in his father's footsteps.[57] He was an able hunter and canoe builder. He could play the spinet and organ, and while living in Nain, might well have spent time with his childhood friend, John Antes, who was apprenticed to a wheelwright in Bethlehem and already building the first American-made violins and cellos.[58]

It was perhaps these ties forged in childhood that prompted John Antes to travel from Bethlehem to help Joshua and his fellow refugees. John was not surprised, of course, by Joshua's musical talents, but all others who heard him play during that year of confinement in Philadelphia seemed astonished at the novelty of a Native man playing European instruments. That it was so consistently surprising suggests that the hope of European and Native Moravians of creating a multiethnic community of Christians was becoming more and more elusive.

Soon after seeing his friend Joshua, and helping the community, John Antes returned to Bethlehem. From there, he traveled to Germany, where he learned watchmaking, before being posted as a Moravian missionary in Egypt. There he preached quietly in the Moravian way, plying his trade as a watchmaker and continuing his work as a composer, sending his chamber music compositions across the Atlantic to Benjamin Franklin. He was captured in 1779 by followers of Osman, leader of the Ottoman Empire, and spent several years recuperating in Egypt before moving to England, where he died in 1811. A decade before his death, Antes published his recollections of his time in Egypt. He was perhaps recalling his friend, Joshua, when he wrote of the Turks:

in this particular, they are no way different from some denominations of Christians, who, in former times, still more than at present, treated such as did not think exactly like themselves, not only no better, but really worse than the Turks treat us, and that often for the sake of principles, which, had the matter been candidly investigated, the persecutors as little believed as those whom they persecuted. Every body knows to what extent such persecutions have been carried, in spite of the injunctions of Scripture, not only to love each other, and to bear with the weaknesses of our friends, but even to love and serve our enemies.[59]

The years in Philadelphia represented a stark turning point, when such a vision was closed off; Native peoples like Joshua and Elizabeth's community continued to be harassed and driven off their lands, again and again.

Joshua died a few years before Antes, an ocean and half a continent away, along the White River in Indiana Territory. Joshua had married that year in Philadelphia, wedding the daughter of Johannes Papunhank, a Munsee prophet and visionary. When the community of Moravian Christians were allowed to leave Philadelphia in March 1765, Sophia was carrying their first child, who would be born that summer in the town of Friedenshütten, built on the ashes of Papunhank's former residence of Wyalusing. Joshua and his wife would have ten children in all, but not one outlived Joshua. They moved again and again, pushed westward, caught in the crosshairs of imperial wars. Joshua remained a Christian. He also continued to participate to some degree in non-Christian Native religious practices. This effort to bridge two worlds had become unacceptable not only to the Paxton Boys, but also to followers of the Shawnee Prophet, who accused Joshua of witchcraft, and in March of 1806, burned him on a pyre.

The stories of Joshua and John, Elizabeth and Margaretha, embody recurring themes of American religion: physical and spiritual movement and the quest for a secure home; insecurity sometimes fueled a narrowing definition of community as with the Paxton Boys, or a search for new forms of community as a means to weather the assaults of war and settler colonialism, as with the Moravians' Native affiliates.

FURTHER READING

Anderson, Fred. *The Crucible of War: The Seven Years' War and the Fate of Empire in British North America, 1754–1766.* New York: Alfred A. Knopf, 2000.

Calloway, Colin G. *The Scratch of a Pen: 1763 and the Transformation of North America.* New York: Oxford University Press, 2006.

Dowd, Gregory Evans. *War under Heaven: Pontiac, the Indian Nations, and the British Empire.* Baltimore: Johns Hopkins University Press, 2004.

Engel, Katherine Carté. *Religion and Profit: Moravians in Early America.* Philadelphia: University of Pennsylvania Press, 2009.

Fisher, Linford D. *The Indian Great Awakening: Religion and the Shaping of Native Cultures in Early America.* New York: Oxford University Press, 2012.

Kenny, Kevin. *Peaceable Kingdom Lost: The Paxton Boys and the Destruction of William Penn's Holy Experiment.* New York: Oxford University Press, 2011.

Merritt, Jane T. *At the Crossroads: Indians and Empires on a Mid-Atlantic Frontier, 1700–1763.* Raleigh: University of North Carolina Press, 2003.

Silver, Peter. *Our Savage Neighbors: How Indian War Transformed Early America.* New York: W. W. Norton, 2008.

Pointer, Richard W. *Pacifist Prophet: Papunhank and the Quest for Peace in Early America.* Lincoln: University of Nebraska Press, 2020.

NOTES

1   These four missionaries are apt representations of the diversity among the first generation of Moravians in North America, hailing from Erfurt and Königsburg (present day Germany), Reval (Talinn, Estonia), and Larvik (in Norway).

2   The Moravians kept extremely detailed records, many of which are preserved at the Moravian Archives in Bethlehem, Pennsylvania. The Records of the Moravian Missions to the Indians (cited here as MissInd) have been tremendously important to the study of eighteenth-century Native American history in recent decades. Katherine Carté has transcribed and translated the mission diaries related to the internment in Philadelphia. All citations to the missionary records are from these translations unless otherwise noted. Philadelphia diary, February 4, 5, 6, 1764,

http://bdhp.moravian.edu/community_records/christianindians/indiandiaryintro.html.   Early Moravian accounts of events can be found in George H. Loskiel, *History of the Mission of the United Brethren among the Indians of North America*, translation by Benjamin Latrobe (London: The Brethren's Society for the Furtherance of the Gospel, 1794), part 2, chapters 15 and 16 and John Heckewelder, *A Narrative of the Mission of the United Brethren among the Delaware and Mohegan Indians: From Its Commencement, in the Year 1740, to the Close of the Year 1808* (Philadelphia: M'Carthy & Davis, 1820). See also Alexander V. Campbell, *The Royal American Regiment: An Atlantic Microcosm, 1755–1772* (Norman: University of Oklahoma Press, 2010), 59, 167. The literature on the Paxton vigilantes is vast. The best single volume history is Kevin Kenny, *Peaceable Kingdom Lost: The Paxton Boys and the Destruction of William Penn's Holy Experiment* (New York: Oxford University Press, 2011). *Digital Paxton* is a digital humanities collaborative project involving the Historical Society of Pennsylvania, The Library Company of Pennsylvania, and many leading scholars in the field. The site makes available critical editions of primary sources, commentary, and instructional materials. See http://digitalpaxton.org/works/digital-paxton/index.

3   John Gilbert McCurdy, *Quarters: The Accommodation of the British Army and the Coming of the American Revolution* (Ithaca: Cornell University Press, 2019), 84–87. For a longer discussion of the community's journey and fate after leaving Philadelphia, see Rachel Wheeler and Thomas Hahn-Bruckart, "On an Eighteenth-Century Trail of Tears: The Travel Diary of Johann Jacob Schmick of the Moravian Indian Congregation's Journey to the Susquehanna, 1765," *Journal of Moravian History* 15, no. 1 (2015): 44–88.

4   Rob Harper, "Looking the Other Way: The Gnadenhutten Massacre and the Contextual Interpretation of Violence," *The William and Mary Quarterly*, 3rd ser., 64, no. 3 (July 1, 2007): 621–44.

5   For an overview of native prophetic movements, see Alfred A. Cave, *Prophets of the Great Spirit: Native American Revitalization Movements in Eastern North America* (Lincoln: University of Nebraska Press, 2006).

6   W. R. Ward, *The Protestant Evangelical Awakening* (Cambridge: Cambridge University Press, 1992).

7   For a one-volume history of the Moravian Church, see J. Taylor Hamilton and Kenneth G. Hamilton, *History of the Moravian Church: The Renewed Unitas Fratrum, 1722–1957* (Bethlehem: Interprovincial Board of Christian Education, Moravian Church in America, 1967).

8   A detailed account of this meeting can be found in Rachel Wheeler, *To Live upon Hope: Mohicans and Missionaries in the Eighteenth-Century Northeast* (Ithaca: Cornell University Press, 2008), chapter 4. Spangenberg also famously influenced the founders of Methodism, John and Charles Wesley, as they were shipmates on the journey to Georgia.

9   Tschoop/Wasamapah, quoted in Wheeler, *To Live upon Hope*, 69.

10 Solomon Stoddard, longtime minister at Northampton, Massachusetts, and both grandfather and predecessor to Jonathan Edwards, was among the most vociferous ministerial advocates for a renewal of missionary efforts. See for example, his 1723 sermon, *Question Whether God Is Not Angry with the Country for Doing so Little towards the Conversion of the Indians?* (Boston: B. Green, 1723). On the negotiations leading to the founding of Stockbridge, see Wheeler, *To Live upon Hope*, ch. 2, 3.

11 Gilbert Tennent, *Some Account of the Principles of the Moravians, Chiefly Collected from Several Conversations with Count Zinzendorf; and from Some Sermons Preached by Him at Berlin and Published in London* (London: S. Mason, 1743), 38, 45.

12 For an account of the Lenape peoples of the region, see: Amy C. Schutt, *Peoples of the River Valleys: The Odyssey of the Delaware Indians* (Philadelphia: Univ. of Pennsylvania Press, 2007); Gunlög Fur, *A Nation of Women: Gender and Colonial Encounters among the Delaware Indians* (Philadelphia: University of Pennsylvania Press, 2009). On the Munsee, see Robert S. Grumet, (*The Munsee Indians: A History*. University of Oklahoma Press, 2014.)

13 The literature on the Seven Years' War in North America is vast. The definitive account is Fred Anderson, *The Crucible of War: The Seven Years' War and the Fate of Empire in British North America, 1754–1766* (New York: Alfred A. Knopf, 2000). One of the most concise accounts of the impact of the war on Native peoples of North America is Colin G. Calloway, *The Scratch of a Pen: 1763 and the Transformation of North America* (New York: Oxford University Press, 2006); Matthew C. Ward, *Breaking the Backcountry: The Seven Years' War in Virginia and Pennsylvania,*

1754–1765 (Pittsburgh: University of Pittsburgh Press, 2004); Gregory Evans Dowd, *War under Heaven: Pontiac, the Indian Nations, and the British Empire* (Baltimore: Johns Hopkins University Press, 2004), 192–199. For an excellent collection of essays, see Warren R. Hofstra, ed., *Cultures in Conflict: The Seven Years' War in North America* (Lanham: Rowman & Littlefield Publishers, 2007).

14   Jane T. Merritt, *At the Crossroads: Indians and Empires on a Mid-Atlantic Frontier, 1700–1763* (Chapel Hill, NC: The University of North Carolina Press, 2003); Peter Silver, *Our Savage Neighbors: How Indian War Transformed Early America* (New York: W. W. Norton, 2008); Patrick Spero, *Frontier Country: The Politics of War in Early Pennsylvania* (Philadelphia, PA: University of Pennsylvania Press, 2016).

15   For an account of the attack and its aftermath, see Loskiel, *History of the Mission,* part II, 164–176.

16   The separate town was created in part to defend against rumors that the Native Moravians were being held captive at Bethlehem. For discussion of Nain, see Katie Faull, "The Nain Indian House, "The Nain Indian House," accessed July 15, 2019, http://storiesofthesusquehanna.blogs. bucknell.edu/2014/01/24/the-nain-indian-house/.

17   Loskiel, *History of the Mission,* part II, ch. 13, 14.

18   A short account of Pontiac's War can be found in Calloway, *Scratch of a Penn,* chapter 3 (quotation 70). The definitive account of the conflict is Dowd, *War under Heaven.*

19   Loskiel, *History of the Mission,* part II, 207.

20   Address by the Christian Indians of Nain (twenty-five names) and Wechquetank (twelve) signed by Schmick and Grube as witnesses, to Governor Hamilton, July 27, 1763, Records of the Moravian Mission among the Indians of North America (MissInd) 124.7.1, Moravian Archives, Bethlehem, PA (MAB).

21   They pleaded that they not be "upbraided with the Actions of other Indians, nor spitefully treated or threatened to be shot after, as so have already begun, they being as well under the Governments Protection as the white People." The document announced: "The wild Indians generally go only in a Shirt whereas these are always cloathed with something. A wild Indian is generally painted & weareth a Feather, or some other Indian Ornament, these are never painted & wear no feather, but they wear Hats or Caps. The wild Indians get their Heads shaved but these let the Hair grow naturally. The Nain & Wechquetanc Indians generally wear their Gun on the Shoulder with the Shaft upward, whereas others, that come with a bad Design, hide it" (August 1763, MissInd 127.7.4, MAB).

22   "Plan for Protecting and Supporting the Christian Indians at Nain … to ease the Inhabitants of that County from their Apprehensions and Fear" (October 1763, MissInd 127.7.4, MAB).

23   Also known as Craig's settlement, founded in 1728, now East Allen Township. See Levering, *History of Bethlehem,* 46.

24   Loskiel, *History of the Mission,* pt. II, 210.

25   Loskiel, *History of the Mission,* pt. II, ch. xv; Kevin Yeager, "Rev. John Elder and Identity in the Pennsylvania Backcountry," *The Pennsylvania Magazine of History and Biography* 136, no. 4 (2012): 470–71; William Buell Sprague, *Annals of the American Pulpit: Presbyterian* (New York: Robert Carter and Brothers, 1858), 77–79.

26   Spero, *Frontier Country,* 132–134. For in depth studies of European settlement in this region of Pennsylvania, see: Anthony L. Blair, "Schism on the Susquehanna: Community and Congregational Conflict on the Pennsylvania Frontier During the Era of the Great Awakening," *Pennsylvania History: A Journal of Mid-Atlantic Studies* 75, no. 1 (2008): 1–25; James T. Lemon, *The Best Poor Man's Country: A Geographical Study of Early Southeastern Pennsylvania* (Baltimore: Johns Hopkins Press, 1972); George William Franz, *Paxton, a Study of Community Structure and Mobility in the Colonial Pennsylvania Backcountry* (New York: Garland Pub, 1989); Ken Miller, *Dangerous Guests: Enemy Captives and Revolutionary Communities during the War for Independence* (Ithaca: Cornell University Press, 2014); Scott Paul Gordon, "The Paxton Boys and the Moravians: Terror and Faith in the Pennsylvania Backcountry" *Journal of Moravian History* 14, no. 2 (2014): 119–152.

27   Bethlehem Diary, Nov. 16, 1763.

28   Anne H. Cresson, "Biographical Sketch of Joseph Fox, Esq., of Philadelphia," *The Pennsylvania Magazine of History and Biography* 32, no. 2 (1908): 184–185, 188. Missionary Grube described the trustee of the Island, which must have been Fox: "The man who has the oversight of them is a nice man and will be very helpful to us" (Bethlehem Diary, November 16, 1763).

29   Philadelphia Diary, December 4, 1763.

30   On William Johnson, see Colin G. Calloway, "Sir William Johnson, Highland Scots, and American Indians," *New York History* 89, no. 2 (2008): 163–177 and Fintan O'Toole, *White Savage: William Johnson and the Invention of America* (New York: Farrar, Straus and Giroux, 2015).

31   Pilgrimage to Amboy, January 5, 1764. John Gilbert McCurdy, *Quarters: The Accommodation of the British Army and the Coming of the American Revolution* (Ithaca: Cornell University Press, 2019).

32   "Pennsylvania Assembly: Reply to the Governor, 11 February 1764," *The Papers of Benjamin Franklin*, vol. 11, *January 1, through December 31, 1764*, ed. Leonard W. Labaree (New Haven: Yale University Press, 1967), 69–76.

33   "Notable Events in the Year 1764," following December 1764.

34   Philadelphia Diary, May 15, 1764.

35   Philadelphia Diary, May 6, 1764.

36   The Philadelphia Diary, November 12, 1764, notes that Margaretha celebrated her 49th birthday on that day, which would mean she was born in 1715 (near death, Wechquetank Diary, November 25, 1763, MissInd 124/4 MAB).

37   On the Moravians in the Baltics, see Ward, *Transatlantic Protestant Awakening*, 149–159.

38   *Transactions of the Moravian Historical Society* 5 (1905): 75. On Margaretha's life, see *Transactions of the Moravian Historical Society* 7 (1905): 235.

39   Among her ailments, listed in Fliegel's *Index*: hemorrhage, fever, fainting spells, partial paralysis, and miscarriage. The Pachgatgoch diaries have been published in translation by Corinna Dally-Starna and William A. Starna, eds., *Gideon's People: Being a Chronicle of an American Indian Community in Colonial Connecticut and the Moravian Missionaries Who Served There* (Lincoln: University of Nebraska Press, 2009).

40   Pilgrimage to Amboy, January 16–17, 1764, http://bdhp.moravian.edu/community_records/christianindians/diaires/amboy/1764amboy.html. Anton's mother, Thamar, remembered the time when there were no Europeans and "many hundreds of Indians lived there," January 13, 1764.

41   "Travel Diary of the little Indian *Gemeine*," January 18, 1764.

42   Edwards is not mentioned by name, but the diary for January 7, 1764 identifies a student who could only be Jonathan Edwards, Jr., "We then returned to our road in the company of Mr. Epty and came in the evening to Princeton, a comfortable spot where there is pretty college, which 130 students attend. There was soon a big crowd of young people, yet they behaved very discreetly. … A student from the college made himself busy with our Indians, because he could speak Mahikan with them, which he had learned in Stockbridge." Edwards later published a treatise on the Mohican language: Jonathan Edwards, Jr., *Observations on the Language of the Muhhekaneew Indians* (New Haven: Printed by Josiah Meigs, 1788).

43   Bartholomew had grown up in the village of Wechquadnach (a town of forty-five men, women, and children near present day Sharon, Connecticut). His sister, Anna, married Jonathan, son of Abraham and Sarah of Shekomeko in January 1744. His brother Benjamin, also lived at Gnadenhütten.

44   Samuel Hopkins, *Historical Memoirs*, 63.

45   Edwards may have been influenced by the Moravian ministers in the message he delivered to the Stockbridges, preaching, for example, that "Christ died for some of all nations," and that "Christ stands at the door and knocks." For an account of the interaction of the Moravians with the Stockbridge community, see Wheeler, *To Live upon Hope*, ch. 10; and Wheeler, "'Friends to Your Souls': Jonathan Edwards' Indian Pastorate and the Doctrine of Original Sin" *Church History* 72, no. 4 (2003): 736–765.

46   Moravian archivist Carl John Fliegel created an extensive index of the Moravian mission records. It has been recreated in digital form and is available from Gale, Ind as "Records of the Moravian Mission Among the Indians of North America," at http://microformguides.gale.com/GuideLst.html.

47   Friedenshütten Diary, April 28, 1771, MissInd 131/8, MAB.

48   A multi-tribal town of Shawnee, Mohican, and Nanticokes at present day Binghamton, New York.

49   Transactions of the Moravian Historical Society, vol 7, 235.

50   Edwin MacMinn, *A German Hero of the Colonial Times of Pennsylvania; or, The Life and Times of Henry Antes* (Moorestown, N.J., 1886), 115.

51 Joseph Mortimer Levering, *A History of Bethlehem, Pennsylvania, 1741–1892* (Bethlehem: Times Publishing Company, 1903), 32, 40, 61, 75–76, 269. On German settlement in British North America, see Aaron Spencer Fogelman, *Hopeful Journeys: German Immigration, Settlement, and Political Culture in Colonial America, 1717–1775* (Philadelphia: University of Pennsylvania Press, 1996).

52 Gnadenhütten Diary, January 23, 1747, MissInd 116/1, MAB.

53 A list of single brothers in Nain dating to December 1759 lists Joshua as being seventeen years and ten months, which would date his birth to February 1742 ("Single Brothers in Nain," MissInd 125/4/11, MAB).

54 Gnadenhütten Diary, August 15, 16, 1750, MissInd 117/1, MAB.

55 Johann Jacob Schmick, Carl Masthay, ed. *Schmick's Mahican Dictionary* ([Philadelphia]: American Philosophical Society, 1991); Lawrence W. Hartzell, "Joshua, Jr.: Moravian Indian Musician." *Transactions of the Moravian Historical Society* 26 (1990): 1–19; Lawrence W. Hartzell, *Ohio Moravian Music* (Winston-Salem: Moravian Music Foundation Press, 1988); Friedenshütten Diary, December 24, 1767, MissInd. Box 131 MAB; Lawrence W. Hartzell, "Musical Moravian Missionaries: Johann Christopher Pyrlaeus," *Moravian Music Journal* 29, no. 4 (Winter 1984): 91–92; Lawrence Henry Gipson, Harry Emilius Stocker, Herman T. Frueauff, Samuel C. Zeller, John Peter Kluge, and Abraham Luckenbach, *The Moravian Indian Mission on White River; Diaries and Letters, May 5, 1799, to November 12, 1806*, Indiana Historical Collections 23 (Indianapolis: Indiana Historical Bureau, 1938).

56 In 1755, Joshua, then almost thirteen, was admired for his ability to write (Gnadenhütten Diary, January 18, 1755, MissInd., 118/4 MAB). Joshua makes cameo appearances in several works: John Heckewelder, *A Narrative of the Mission of the United Brethren among the Delaware and Mohegan Indians* (Philadelphia: McCarty & Davis, 1820); Lawrence Henry Gipson, ed., *The Moravian Indian Mission on White River; Diaries and Letters, May 5, 1799, to November 12, 1806*, Indiana Historical Collections 23 (Indianapolis: Indiana Historical Bureau, 1938).

57 Joshua, Sr. is credited with writing several hymns in the 1740s and 1750s, together with his wife, Bathsheba, and missionary Pyrlaeus. On the creation of the Mohican language hymns see Rachel Wheeler and Sarah Eyerly, "Singing Box 331: Re-Sounding Eighteenth-Century Mohican Hymns From The Moravian Archives," *The William and Mary Quarterly* 76, no. 4 (November 7, 2019): 649–696.

58 Rufus Grider, *Historical Notes on Music in Bethlehem, 1741–1871* (Philadelphia: John Pile, 1873), 5–6.

59 John Antes, *Observations on the Manners and Customs of the Egyptians: The Overflowing of the Nile and Its Effects* (J. Stockdale, 1800).

Chapter Four

Africana Religions in Early America

Jason R. Young
University of Michigan, Ann Arbor, Michigan

Introduction

Writing in *The Souls of Black Folk* in 1903, W. E. B. Du Bois described the Black Church as the social center of African American life in the United States. More than a mere house of worship, the Black Church was a universe unto itself, reproducing, in microcosm, all the worlds of political and social life from which African Americans were cut off by racism and discrimination.[1] From this central, stabilizing core, African American religiosity radiated outward, touching all aspects of American life. Indeed, Du Bois saw in black religiosity one of the principle gifts that African Americans had bestowed on America. Articulated in sermon and in song, this gift of the Spirit "has been neglected, it has been, and is, half despised, and above all it has been persistently mistaken and misunderstood; but notwithstanding, it still remains as the singular spiritual heritage of the nation."[2]

If *Souls* represents Du Bois's effort to translate the spiritual gifts of black people to a wider audience, *The Negro Church*, also published in 1903, is the first sociological approach to black religious life, focusing as it does on more mundane matters, including annual church budgets, seating capacities, and membership rolls. Like *Souls, The Negro Church* insisted on the centrality of the church to black life. According to Du Bois, the whole "Negro population of the United States is virtually divided into church congregations which are the real units of race life."[3]

In these twin publications, Du Bois situated the Church as both the spiritual as well as the institutional basis of black life in the country. Over the course of the twentieth century — *and even into the twenty-first* — this view has prevailed. For more than 100 years, prominent thinkers and writers — both scholarly and popular; religious and lay alike — have taken Black Christianity as the *sine qua non* of black religiosity in the United States. When followed to its furthest extent, this view has located in African American Christianity a compelling origin story not only for black religion, but also for black people more broadly. The conflation of black religiosity with black Christianity has the unfortunate effect of flattening much of the diversity that is at the heart of African American religion. Recent scholarship on African American religions not only challenges Du Bois's insistence on the centrality of the Black Church, but also calls into question some of the foundational tenets that lay at the heart of African American Religion. Revisionist views of the past along with speculative imaginings of the future are calling into question long-established periodizations of black life and religiosity. And novel cartographies of slavery are causing once stable notions of place and space to shuffle under our feet.

A Companion to American Religious History, First Edition. Edited by Benjamin E. Park.
© 2021 John Wiley & Sons, Inc. Published 2021 by John Wiley & Sons, Inc.

That Ole Time Religion

Writing in *African American Religious Thought*, Cornel West and Eddie Glaude divide African American religious history into five periods. The first, extending from the Great Revivals of the mid-eighteenth century to the Emancipation Proclamation, constitutes "African American Religion as the Problem of Slavery," a period when African Americans forged a distinctive Christian outlook in response to slavery. In this, West and Glaude see in the revival period the origin of African American religion; and they see in slavery, the central object of black religion's moral and ethical imperatives.[4] But, as Dianne Stewart and Tracey Hucks note, this periodization leaves the preceding 150 years — from 1619 to 1750 — simply outside the time-scale of African American religion.[5] What's more, this origin story presumes that black religion emerged as little more than a *response* to an external revival movement: a mere *reaction* to "the problem of slavery." It does not perceive of African American religion, in other words, as a body of belief and practice with its own animating logics and ethics. Published in 2003 — on the 100th anniversary of *The Souls of Black Folk* and *The Negro Church* — West and Glaude echo Du Bois's earlier elevation of the church as the central fact of black religiosity, supposing that when we say African American religion, what we really mean is African American Christianity. It is in this sense that Stewart and Hucks argue that African American religious studies in the twenty-first century "is still grappling with 20th century problems."[6]

In fact, the religious worlds of the African Diaspora — in Europe, the Americas and in Africa itself — were very much in flux between 1500–1800.[7] In Europe, the Protestant challenge encouraged the expansion and transfer of European conflicts *outre-mer* into emerging colonial zones, causing certain European theological and religious conflicts (not merely political and military ones) to be transplanted onto West African and American soils. In the Americas, this period was marked by a series of religious wars that pitted Europeans of various stripes against each other and that situated the gods of Christianity against those of Native Americans and Africans. In West Africa, the emergence of new and powerful imperial structures coincided with the rise of popular religious movements. This is true of the era of Islamic jihad in Senegambia, the disruptions of civil war in Kongo, and in the emergence of centralized empires along the Gold Coast in present-day Ghana. In this contested field, Africans in the diaspora did not merely react to forces foisted upon them, but instead created new and vibrant religious worlds of meaning and significance. Indeed, we have much to learn from the 150 years before the emergence of "African American Religion as the Problem of Slavery."

A prime lesson can be drawn from the historical relationship between West-Central Africa and the Lowcountry region of coastal South Carolina and Georgia from the seventeenth to the nineteenth centuries. During this period, the presence of European traders along the coast instigated a massive expansion of the slave trade and the subsequent destabilization of the Kingdom of Kongo. In this environment, Kongo witnessed a period of intense prophetic activity. Most notable was the eighteenth-century campaign of Dona Beatriz Kimpa Vita who, in 1704, was visited and subsequently possessed by St. Anthony. This event inaugurated Dona Beatriz's prophetic campaign based on a wholesale rejection of the theology espoused by European missionaries. She insisted that God had revealed to her a more accurate and thoroughly revised version of Christianity. Jesus was not born in Bethlehem but rather in the Kongo capital, Mbanza Kongo; Nazareth, the location of His baptism, was actually the northern Kongolese province of Nsundi. Beatriz maintained that takula wood, whose bark produced a red dye often used in weddings and rites of passage ceremonies, was the blood of Jesus Christ who was, himself, Kongolese. Though state authorities eventually captured and executed Dona Beatriz in 1706, her movement persisted. For years after her death, thousands of "little anthonys" devoted their lives to the movement, often paying a high price for their devotion as state authorities regularly rounded them up and delivered them to the ocean as so many slaves.[8]

Just a few years after Dona Beatriz's reform movement was quashed, sending unknown numbers of her supporters to the Americas in chains, Anglican missionary Francis Le Jau described a group of enslaved Africans in Carolina, writing in 1724:

> I have in this parish Negroe Slaves and were born and baptized among the Portuguese. They come to Church and are well instructed so as to express a desire to receive the H. communion. I proposed to them to declare openly their Abjuring the Errors of the Romish Church without which I cou'd not receive them.[9]

After an eighteen-month term of religious instruction, only two of the men remained under Le Jau's tutelage. The others were likely making other plans. Beginning in the late seventeenth century, small groups of enslaved men and women in South Carolina and Georgia began escaping their bondage in hopes of securing sanctuary with Catholic missionaries stationed in Spanish Florida. In response, Spanish officials adopted a general policy of manumission for all escaped slaves from British North America who made the journey and converted to Catholicism. Upon arrival in Florida, the refugees were interviewed by Catholic missionaries who regularly noted that some runaways were familiar with Catholicism due to their exposure to the faith in Kongo, though they "still prayed in their native tongue."[10]

The largest and most significant of these refugee bands formed in 1739 not far from the Stono River near Charleston, South Carolina. Many of the rebels were Kongolese and they hoped to cut a bloody path to the Catholic haven at St. Augustine. Writing in "African Dimensions of the Stono Rebellion," John Thornton argues that several leaders of the rebellion were likely Kongolese soldiers and that the rebellion was a fight for religious as much as political freedom.[11] Neither was South Carolina the only region that witnessed Kongo-inspired revolt. In Haiti, the fight for independence largely reflected martial techniques common in the Kingdom of Kongo.[12] More recently, James Sweet has documented the prophetic tradition of one ritual expert, Domingos Álvarez, who traveled as a captive from West-Central Africa to Brazil and subsequently to the Iberian peninsula where he was questioned and condemned as a "fetisher" during the Inquisition.[13] In each of these cases, prophetic traditions that began in West-Central Africa were transplanted onto American soils as a key feature of the religious experience of enslaved peoples. In this way, any full and robust history of African American religion must begin earlier than the eighteenth-century revival movement and must extend beyond the discrete borders of the United States.

But upon closer inspection, the revival movement itself is a questionable place to locate any sort of origin for black American religiosity. Albert Raboteau long ago recognized that despite the best efforts of eighteenth-century evangelicals, "the majority of slaves ... remained only minimally touched by Christianity by the second decade of the nineteenth century."[14] Indeed, many slaveholders expressed deep apathy, if not outright hostility, to the prospect of extending religious instruction to slaves on grounds that conversion would encourage slaves to rebel. As a result, religious authorities devised a theology that emphasized submission before authority and forbearance in face of oppression. In 1852, William Capers published *A Catechism for the Use of the Methodists Mission* that focused on the obligations of the enslaved to their enslavers:

> Let as many servants as are under your yoke count their own masters worthy of all honor ... and they that have believing masters, let them not despise them because they are brethren, but rather do them service because they are faithful and beloved.[15]

In addition, missionaries limited slaves' exposure to the Bible, preferring passages that emphasized obedience. Writing in *Twelve Years a Slave*, Solomon Northup recalls that Luke 12:47 was a favorite of the master class: "And that servant, which knew his Lord's will, and prepared not himself, neither did according to his will, shall be beaten with many stripes."[16] In 1807, the London-based Society for the Conversion of Negro Slaves produced a heavily abridged version of the Bible that excised scriptures deemed too likely to incite rebellion. While a typical Protestant edition of the Bible contains sixty-six books, the *Parts of the Holy Bible, selected for the use of the Negro Slaves, in the British West-India Islands* contained only parts of 14 books."[17] Excised from the "Slave Bible" was Jeremiah 22:13 — "Woe unto him that buildeth his house by unrighteousness, and his chambers by wrong; that useth his neighbor's service without wages and giveth him not for his work" — and Exodus 21:16 — "And he that stealeth a man, and selleth him, or if he be found in his hand, he shall surely be put to death." Instead, the "Slave Bible" focused on passages that encouraged submission, including Ephesians 6:5 — "Servants, be obedient to them that are your masters according to the flesh, with fear and trembling, in singleness of your heart, as unto Christ." Missionaries not only crafted a pro-slavery theology, but also became key slave owners. To take but one example, George Whitefield, one of the central figures in the eighteenth-century revival movement, initially embraced a staunchly anti-slavery theology, but soon relented on grounds that "[slavery] will be carried on whether we will [it] or not; I should think myself highly favored if I could purchase a good number of them."[18]

Some of black people's earliest engagements with Christianity were more rhetorical than religious. Christianity created for black people throughout the diaspora a legible language to articulate not only the morality of abolition, but also the model of an ideal society. This was certainly the case for Albert King, born Ukawsaw Gronniosaw. Initially captured in West Africa and sold as a slave, King subsequently won his freedom and traveled to England:

> I had for a great while entertained a desire to come to England. I imagined that all of the inhabitants of this island were *holy* ... [that] the people must be all *righteous* ... I had a vast inclination to visit England, and wished continually that it would please providence to make a clear way for me to see this island. I entertained a notion that if I could get to England I should never more experience either cruelty or ingratitude, so that I was very desirous to get among Christians.[19]

In these lines, King articulates a subtle, but pointed critique of England, in particular, and of the slave holding empires of Europe more broadly. Like many other early black Christians, King deployed Christianity politically and strategically. He used his faith as the basis for an insistence on the readiness of black people to be fully integrated not only into the body of Christ that was the Church, but also into the body politic and social of the West.

Writing of his own experience a century later, Frederick Douglass demonstrated the legacies of these tensions by making a sharp distinction between the Christianity of Christ and that of the slaveholder:

> Between the Christianity of this land, and the Christianity of Christ, I recognize the widest possible difference — so wide, that to receive the one as good, pure, and holy, is of necessity to reject the other as bad, corrupt, and wicked ... We have men-stealers for ministers, women-whippers for missionaries, and cradle-plunderers for church members. The man who wields the blood-clotted cow skin during the week fills the pulpit on Sunday, and claims to be a minister of the meek and lowly Jesus ... He who sells my sister, for purposes of prostitution, stands forth as the pious advocate of purity ... We have men sold to build churches, women sold to support the gospel, and babes sold to purchase Bibles for the poor heathen! All for the glory of God and the good of souls! ... The dealer gives his blood-stained gold to support the pulpit, and the pulpit, in return, covers his infernal business with the garb of Christianity. Here we have religion and robbery the allies of each other — devils dressed in angels' robes, and hell presenting the semblance of paradise.[20]

The revival period does not mark so much a point of origin for African American religion, but rather one in a long string of opportunities for black peoples around the Atlantic rim to take a rhetorical stab at slavery.

As an alternative to the pro-slavery theology adopted by some Christians, enslaved men and women developed a wholly different theology based not only on opposition to slavery in this world, but also on a belief in eternal justice in the next. While most white Christians identified the church as the central, organizing institution of the faith, African Americans preferred to worship in praise-houses: small, humble structures, that provided slaves an opportunity to gather and pray on plantation grounds, though outside the purview of the master class.

Slaveholders initially built praise-houses as mechanisms of social control in order to deprive slaves from different plantations the opportunity to gather and worship. Because they tended to be small, unimpressive structures located in the outer reaches of the plantation, praise-houses often failed to attract much attention from outsiders. Though unadorned, the praise-house cloaked within its walls the heart of slave spiritual and religious practice. Praise-houses were so ubiquitous on plantations that one observer noted that "on every one of the old plantations you will come across a tiny building furnished with rude backless benches and a leader's stand in front."[21] Inside, slaves engaged in a cathartic religious ecstasy. James Smith, a black preacher in antebellum Virginia admitted that "the way in which [slaves] worshipped is almost indescribable. The singing was accompanied by a certain ecstasy of motion, clapping of hands, tossing of heads ... the old house [itself] partook of the ecstasy; it rang with their jubilant shouts, and shook in all its joints."[22]

Enslaved men and women often reserved praise-house worship for their most prized religious practice — the ring shout. Historian Sterling Stuckey argues that the ring shout — which derived from a multitude of African-based circular dances common throughout West Africa — emerged in the slave South as "the means by which [slaves] achieved oneness in America."[23] That is, the ring shout helped combine some of the cultural and ethnic diversity of enslaved Africans into a coherent African American culture.

By the early decades of the nineteenth century, a once budding African American religious culture was in full bloom. Indeed, planters soon came to understand the rebellious potential of praise-houses. In Southampton, Virginia, Nat Turner was a preacher who lead his fellow slaves in worship before leading them in an armed rebellion against slavery in 1831. In the aftermath of that rebellion, many slaveholders in Virginia and beyond forbade praise-house worship, opting instead to use the back benches, balconies and galleries of their own churches for slaves' use. Writing of her own experience in North Carolina, Harriet Jacobs recalls that after Turner's rebellion, "visiting was strictly forbidden on the plantations. The slaves begged the privilege of again meeting at their little church in the woods ... Their request was denied, and the church was demolished. They were permitted to attend the white churches, a certain portion of the galleries being appropriated to their use."[24]

Given the close association between political and religious power in the slave South, Michael Gomez argues that "it is an unassailable fact that American Christianity is directly responsible for the psychological impairment of many within the African-based community. The white slaveholder's promotion of a white god aloft in white splendor, around whom stand the white heavenly host, was imagery sufficient to convey to the African a message of unmitigable disadvantage."[25] Writing in a similar context, philosopher V. Y. Mudimbe notes that "the missionary's objectives had to be co-extensive with his country's political and cultural perspectives ... With equal enthusiasm, he served as an agent of a political empire, a representative of a civilization, and an envoy of God ... All of these roles implied the conversion of African minds and space."[26] At the same time, enslaved men and women wove from the cloth of pro-slavery Christian theology, a new doctrine that helped them cope with the constraints of this world while anticipating a new Zion in the next.

Black Crescent

In marking the origins of African American Religion in the eighteenth-century revival movement, Glaude and West imagine black religion as always already Christian. But as many as fifty percent of the people who found themselves enslaved in the plantation Americas were from regions in West Africa where Islam was either the official state religion or the faith of sizable minority communities.[27] Islam first spread from the Arabian peninsula to North Africa in the early seventh century. Moving quickly across the continent; it was well established in West Africa by the tenth century. Al-Bakri, a Muslim traveler and writer described the central role that Islam played in the Kingdom of Ghana during the eleventh century:

> The King of Ghana ... led a praiseworthy life on account of his love of justice and friendship for the Muslims ... The city of Ghana consists of two towns situated on a plain. One of these towns, inhabited by Muslims, is large and possesses twelve mosques, in one of which they assemble for the Friday Prayer.[28]

Several centuries later, on the eve of the Trans-Atlantic Slave trade, African Muslims could be found living and moving between Europe, Africa and the Americas as sailors, merchants, and slaves. Writing in *Black Crescent*, Michael Gomez notes that the Muslim presence in the American South "antedates the arrival of English colonists." Prior to the establishment of British colonial outposts in Jamestown and Plymouth, Muslims were already being imported into Spanish-controlled Florida and French-controlled Louisiana.[29] As the volume of the slave trade increased in the seventeenth and eighteenth centuries, African Muslims found themselves increasingly ensnared in the complex net of war, trade, and slavery that linked military conflagrations in West Africa to budding plantation economies in the American South. Evidence for the Muslim presence in the Americas can be seen in runaway slave advertisements that often featured discernible Muslim names, African regions, and ethnic origins. In fact, the term "Mandigo" emerged in British North America as a trade name used to describe enslaved Africans taken from Senegambia, Sierra Leone and Nigeria — regions that all had sizable Muslim communities.[30]

Some evidence suggests that Muslim clerics, along with other types of religious leaders, might have been especially vulnerable to the Trans-Atlantic slave trade because their access to religious and spiritual authority posed an inherent challenge to the political authority of West African royals. As James Sweet notes, African religious leaders represented a clear challenge to African royal elites. The priestly class, much like the kingly court, held great sway over the populace. Like the courtly class, religious leaders often demanded payment for their services, which challenged African forms of political tribute and taxation. In effect, African royal authorities perceived the priestly classes as collecting money in the form of ritual offerings that might otherwise be placed in royal coffers.[31] As a result, political leaders throughout West Africa targeted ritual experts, selling them to European buyers who then sent them to the New World as slaves. Once enslaved in the Americas, many of these ritual experts, clerics and priests resumed their vocations once they arrived on the plantation.

In the United States, enslaved Muslims attempted to maintain the contours of their devotional lives even while under the constraints of slavery, effectively recreating "active, healthy and compelling" communities.[32] Enslaved Muslims attempted to maintain dietary restrictions and to perform ritual ablutions, daily prayers, and obligatory fasts consistent with Muslim practice. In particular, the lowcountry region of Georgia and South Carolina emerged as the region in the United States with the highest concentration of enslaved African Muslims, owing largely to planters' stated preference for Africans from the rice producing regions of West Africa, which tended to be areas with large numbers of Muslim adherents.

In this environment, enslaved Muslims often hid their faith in full view. "The Mohammedan Africans," one Christian missionary noted, "have been known to accommodate Christianity to Mohammedanism. 'God,' they say, "is Allah, and Jesus Christ is Mohammed — the religion is the same, but different countries have different names."[33] Some enslaved Muslims maintained their mastery of the Arabic language which they deployed strategically to support their struggle for freedom. Ibrahim Abd ar-Rahman, a Muslim enslaved in Mississippi, wrote copies of al-Fatiha, the opening chapter of the Qur'an, which he passed off as an Arabic translation of the Lord's prayer. Known as "The Prince," Abd ar-Rahman emerged as one of the most popular Africans in America and his capture and enslavement became a *cause-célèbre* due to a national humanitarian campaign that succeeded in securing Abd ar-Rahman's freedom and repatriation to Africa. If some Muslims hid their faith in full view, others may very well have practiced their faith openly, without fear of retribution as many Americans were generally ignorant of Islamic traditions. Added to this, planters often showed little interest, whatsoever, in the religious lives of their slaves. As one missionary makes clear:

> Provided that the slaves can multiply, and work hard for the benefit of their masters, most men are well satisfied, without the least thoughts of using their authority and endeavors to promote the good of the souls of those poor wretches.[34]

Islam persisted in African American communities even after the era of slavery. In the 1930s and 1940s, African Americans still recalled that Islamic ritual practices were part of the religious landscape of slavery. Rosa Grant, who was born into slavery in coastal Georgia, remembered the religious practices of her grandmother:

> Friday was the day she call her prayer day … I remember when I was a child seeing my gran Rayna pray. Every morning at sun-up she kneel on the floor in her room and bow over and touch her head to the floor three time.[35]

Similarly, Charles Wylly, grandson of the famed Georgia planter Thomas Spalding, remembered seeing "devout mussulmans, who prayed to Allah … morning, noon and evening."[36] It is highly probable that Muslims continued to be imported illegally into the United States between 1808–1860, a period marked by the illicit importation of enslaved Africans despite a ban on slave imports that became law in 1808. The continued and persistent practice of Islam throughout the nineteenth century may very well shed light on the subsequent emergence of several twentieth-century Islamic movements among African Americans, including the Moorish Science Temple and the Nation of Islam.[37]

Root Pow(d)ers

Alongside Muslim and Christian religious practices, enslaved men and women also devised alternate ritual and spiritual traditions. Commonly referred to as hoodoo, juju, conjure, or rootwork, these practices constituted separate realms of spiritual power and justice that were ubiquitous throughout the plantation Americas. In Brazilian Candomblé, Cuban Santería, Haitian Vodou, or the Hoodoo traditions of the American South, enslaved peoples merged African Traditional Religions (ATR) with European and Native American cultural elements toward the development of an independent body of ritual practices. Though not formally codified, these religious practices adhered to certain broadly held beliefs and methods. As art Historian Michael Harris notes in a related context, "here is the transplanted African learning to conjure with new roots, new herbs, and old meanings."[38]

Slave folk religion addressed not only religious, but also interpersonal, medicinal, romantic, and quasi-legalistic concerns. Practitioners often referred to ritual experts to help them determine the innocence or guilt of a suspected criminal, to heal a nagging ailment, or to secure the affections of a desired partner. Importantly, both blacks and whites acknowledged the efficacy of these slave derived remedies. As one observer noted, "many planters who have observed their tenants closely come to have a certain faith in the procedures themselves … they have seen the healing herb close wounds and the bitter tea allay fevers."[39] In one sense, slave folk religion was very much in line with the practice of spiritualism, divination, herbalism, and allopathy, which were all quite widespread in British North America throughout the era of slavery.

Indeed, the United States was home to a pronounced religious and spiritual pluralism during the eighteenth and nineteenth centuries. Despite the ubiquity of spiritualism in the larger landscape of American religion, slave folk religion was held up for especial scrutiny by members of the master class. That is, although slave folk religion included a broad set of widely diverse practices (including herbal remedies, divination, poisoning, cures, and curses), one of its principal cohesive elements was its political relationship to slavery. Slave folk religion constituted a form of spiritual resistance that not only challenged slavery, but also established an independent realm of criminality, justice, and punishment outside the immediate authority of whites. Conjure granted its practitioners and adherents an avenue to influence, power, health, and retribution over which the masterclass had very little influence.

In this way, slave folk religion was one of the principle means through which enslaved men and women resisted slavery. Root doctors, conjurers, and other ritual experts used their powers to protect slaves from the brutalities of slavery, creating in some slaves an obstinate culture of defiance. In 1822, Gullah Jack Pritchard encouraged slaves in South Carolina to rebel by providing them with ritual medicines that promised victory and invincibility in their fight against slave owners. The rebels firmly believed in Jack's powers and felt that if they "retained the charms which he had distributed they would themselves be invulnerable."[40] Frederick Douglass recalled that when he was a slave in Maryland, he sought the counsel of root doctor named Sandy, "a genuine African [who] had inherited some of the magical powers said to be possessed by the eastern nations."[41] Sandy prepared a ritual medicine for Douglass with the promise that as long as he kept it firmly in his possession, and always on the right side, no white man would ever cause him physical harm for as long as he lived.

The centrality of slave conjure in antebellum America created a figure of considerable influence in the person of the conjure doctor, known variously as a two-head, or root worker. So important were root doctors to the slave community that many of them enjoyed more status than preachers of the Gospel. Du Bois suggests the complexity and multiplicity of this ritual network when he described the conjure doctor as "the healer of the sick, the interpreter of the unknown, the comforter of the sorrowing, the supernatural avenger of wrong, and the one who rudely but picturesquely expressed the longing, disappointment, and resentment of a stolen and oppressed people."[42]

An Impossible People

Despite the rich religious heritage that Africans brought with them to the plantation Americas, the spiritual and devotional lives of slaves have more often been lampooned in facile stereotypes that all too often feature a well-worn cast of characters including fetish priests, witch doctors, and voodoo dolls. C.C. Jones, one of the leading Christian missionaries devoted to proselytizing slaves in the nineteenth century lamented that "the numbers of professors of religion, in proportion to the whole, is not large, that can present a correct view of the plan of salvation … *True religion* they are inclined to place in *profession…and in excited states of feeling. And true conversion, in dreams, visions, trances, voices.*"[43] Some have argued further that enslaved African Americans not only practiced inferior religions, but indeed had no religion at all. In the US, the early historiographical roots of this position can be found in U. B. Phillips's 1915 publication *American Negro Slavery*, in which captive Africans brought to the Americas were perceived as so many tabulae rasae.[44] In subsequent years, this presumption prevailed as when one historian noted, "there is no need to trace back to Africa the slave's … dread of witches, ghosts, and hobgoblins, his confidence in good-luck charms. These superstitions were all firmly rooted in Anglo-Saxon folklore."[45]

Others have argued for "an African *spiritual holocaust* that forever destroyed traditional African *religious systems* … and that left slaves remarkably bereft of traditional collective religious practice."[46] In this view, while some particular and discrete religious practices may have remained in the Americas, they lingered — as Saidiya Hartman suggests — in a manner "akin to a phantom limb, in that what is felt is no longer there."[47] Some of these dire conclusions can be traced back to Al Raboteau's magisterial *Slave Religion*; and, in particular, to that book's first chapter — *The Death of the Gods* — that proposed something of a whiggish history of African American religion in which the fading of traditional African religions led to inchoate slave beliefs and practices culminating in formal institutional African American religion based on evangelical Christianity.

More recently, black religious cultures in the Americas have come under attack from a novel angle. Writing in *The Cooking of History*, Stephan Palmié offers a trenchant rejection of Africa as a key cultural source for black cultural expression in the Americas.[48] Referring specifically to Afro-Cuban religion, Palmié suggests that there is, in fact, very little of Africa in it. Instead, that knotty network of practices that we have come to call "Afro-Cuban religion" first emerged when a group of eager and inquisitive scholars — anthropologists, archaeologists, linguists and others — descended on Cuba in service of a set of questions they had about the presumably primitive religious practices of black peoples. The product of those conversations and observations were subsequently lionized in academic monographs and ethnographies that became, in effect, the authoritative bibles that established the canon of Afro-Cuban religion. In subsequent years, local practitioners and devotees looked to these foundational texts in service of their own practice while, in the West, academic presses, university departments, fellowship granting institutions, conferences, and colloquia further cemented and defined the limits of "authentic" practice. In this way, Western traditions of academia were as much the founders of Afro-Cuban religion as were some distant African ancestors who bestowed upon their enslaved children some primordial cultural gift.

The idea that Africa might have played a significant role in the religious cultures of black people living in the plantation Americas tends to invite, as Michael Gomez notes, "a quality of critique unique in its level of elevated scrutiny, emphasizing distance and lacunae in the substance and circumstances separating Africa and the Americas."[49] Whether intended or not, the terms of this opposition result in the *"negrofication"* of African-descended peoples in the Americas, a process predicated on the alienation of black people in the diaspora from any generative relationship to African pasts.

Despite the dour debates that often attend the study of African religion and culture in the plantation Americas, I am just always so amazed at the subtlety, flexibility, and inventiveness of black people who imagine a place not here, a time not now, and a divine justice bigger than our jurists. I am thinking here of Yvonne Chireau who emphasizes play and enjoyment in black religiosity. "Delight," she writes, "What a word, what a concept ... We have possibilities for transcendence and play, delight ... in the movement, departure from sequence, leap away from linearity ... jump from order to disorder ... [in] ... the freedom of play."[50]

By the nineteenth century this long-standing tradition of flexibility and ingenuity was on full display. To take but one example, Frederick Douglass, writing in 1845, recalls the song of the slaves as, at once, dolefully plaintive and rapturously jaunty:

> They would make the dense old woods, for miles around, reverberate with their wild songs, revealing at once the highest joy and the deepest sadness. They would compose and sing as they went along, consulting neither time nor tune. The thought that came up, came out — if not in the word, in the sound — and as frequently in the one as in the other. They would sometimes sing the most pathetic sentiment in the most rapturous tone, and the most rapturous sentiment in the most pathetic tone.[51]

In Christianity, Islam, and folk religion, enslaved men and women created a set of broad-based rituals meant to be practiced — *in communion*. These religious practices comprised an unwieldy, disorderly discursive zone that nevertheless drew a diverse body of people and cultural practices into its embrace. And the communities that emerged from those devotions were, as Toni Morrison writes it, *"irrevocably black."*[52] Black, not because the devotees were black; neither because the subject matter, themes, or content conveyed some irreducible essence, "something intrinsic, indigenous, something in the way it was put together."[53] Instead, the irrevocable blackness of African American religiosity derived from what Tommie Shelby calls "the virtue associated with the steadfast pursuit of truth and justice *despite* being oppressed and/or from the promise that, through faith and collective struggle, blacks will ultimately be delivered from that oppression."[54] This, then, is the genealogy — *the obscure miracle of connection*[55] — that binds us one to the other. The subjectivity of black people is, as Lily Cho notes, "marked by the contingencies of long histories of displacements and genealogies of dispossession."[56] Black people living throughout the plantation Americas have only the hold of the ship to claim as their collective womb. We are *"the tribe of the middle passage."*[57] But when Gullah Jack walks along Stono's bloody path or Harriet Jacobs shuffles in the far pew of the praise-house; when Gran' Rayna prays to the east or Frederick Douglass carries a root on the right side — in those fleeting moments — *"we are Abraham's descendants, and have never been in bondage to anyone."*[58]

FURTHER READING

Brown, Ras Michael. *African-Atlantic Cultures and the South Carolina Lowcountry*. New York: Cambridge University Press, 2012.

Dorman, Jacob S. *Chosen People: The Rise of American Black Israelite Religions*. New York: Oxford University Press, 2013.

Gomez, Michael. *Black Crescent: The Experience and Legacy of Black Muslims in America*. New York: Cambridge University Press, 2005.

Manigault-Bryant, LeRhonda S. *Talking to the Dead: Religion, Music, and Lived Memory among Gullah/Geechee Women*. Durham: Duke University Press, 2014.

Raboteau, Albert. *Slave Religion: The "Invisible Institution" in the Antebellum South*. New York: Oxford University Press, 2004 [1978].

BIBLIOGRAPHY

Butler, Jon. *Awash in a Sea of Faith: Christianizing the American People*. Cambridge, MA: Harvard University Press, 1990.

Capers, William. *Catechism for the Use of the Methodist Missions*. Richmond: John Early, 1852.

Chireau, Yvonne. "Theorizing Africana Religions: A Journal of Africana Religions Inaugural Symposium." *Journal of Africana Religions* 2, no. 1 (2014): 125–160.

Diakité, Dianne M. Stewart and Tracey E. Hucks. "Africana Religious Studies: Toward a Transdisciplinary Agenda in an Emerging Field." *Journal of Africana Religions* 1, no. 1 (2013): 28–77.

Diouf, Sylviane. *Servants of Allah: African Muslims Enslaved in the Americas*. New York: New York University Press, 1998.

Douglass, Frederick. *Narrative of the Life of Frederick Douglass, an American Slave*. New York: Penguin Books, 1982 [1845].

Du Bois, W. E. B. The Negro *Church*. New York: Altamira Press, 2003 [1903].

Du Bois. *The Souls of Black Folk*. New York: Penguin, 1996 [1903].

Fage, J. D. ed. *The Cambridge History of Africa, volume 2, c. 500 B.C.–1500 A.D.* New York: Cambridge University Press, 1978.

Gallay, Alan. "Planters and Slaves in the Great Awakening." In *Masters & Slaves in the House of the Lord: Race and Religion in the American South, 1740–1870*, edited by John B. Boles, 19–36. Lexington: University Press of Kentucky, 1988.

Georgia Writers' Project. *Drums and Shadows: Survival Studies Among the Georgia Coastal Negroes*. Athens: University of Georgia Press, 1940.

Gilroy, Paul. "Living Memory: A Meeting with Toni Morrison." *Small Acts: Thoughts on the Politics of Black Cultures*. London: Serpent's Tail, 1993: 175–182.

Gomez, Michael. *Black Crescent: The Experience and Legacy of African Muslims in the Americas*. New York: Cambridge University Press, 2005.

_____. *Exchanging Their Country Marks: The Transformation of African Identities in the Colonial and Antebellum South*. Chapel Hill: University of North Carolina Press, 1998.

_____. *Exchanging Their Country Marks: The Transformation of African Identities in the Colonial.* "Muslims in Early America." *The Journal of Southern History* 60, no. 4 (November 1994): 671–710.

_____. *Reversing Sail: A History of the African Diaspora*. New York: Cambridge University Press, 2005.

Gronniosaw, James Albert Ukawsaw. *A Narrative of the Most Remarkable Particulars in the Life of James Albert Ukawsaw Gronniosaw, an African Prince, Related by Himself*. In Adam Potkay and Sandra Burr, eds., *Black Atlantic Writers of the 18th Century*. New York: St. Martin's Press, 1995.

Hair, P. E. H. et al. eds. *Barbot on Guinea: The Writings of Jean Barbot on West Africa, 1678–1712*. London: Haklyut Society, 1992.

Hartman, Saidiya. *Lose Your Mother: A Journey Along the Atlantic Slave Route*. New York: Farrar, Straus and Giroux, 2007

_____. *Scenes of Subjection: Terror, Slavery, and Self-Making in Nineteenth-Century America*. New York: Oxford University Press, 1997.

Jacobs, Harriet. *Incidents in the Life of a Slave Girl*. New York: Harcourt, Brace and Co., 1973 [1863].

Jones, C. C. Religious *Instruction of the Negroes in the United States*. New York: Kraus reprint co., 1969 [1842].

Laing, Annette. "'Heathens and Infidels'? African Christianization and Anglicanism in the South Carolina Low Country, 1700–1750." *Religion and American Culture: A Journal of Interpretation* 12, no. 2 (Summer 2012): 197–228.

Landers, Jane. *Black Society in Spanish Florida*. Urbana-Champaign: University of Illinois Press, 1999.

Le Jau, Francis. "Slave Conversion on the Carolina Frontier." In *African American Religious History: A Documentary Witness*, edited by Milton Sernett, 25–33. Durham: Duke University Press, 1999.

MacGaffey, Wyatt and Michael Harris. *Astonishment and Power: The Eyes of Understanding Kongo Minkisi*. Washington, DC: National Museum of African Art, 1993.

Martin, Michael. "Slave Bible From The 1800s Omitted Key Passages That Could Incite Rebellion." *All Things Considered*. Aired December 9, 2018 on National Public Radio. https://www.npr.org/2018/12/09/674995075/slave-bible-from-the-1800s-omitted-key-passages-that-could-incite-rebellion.

Mudimbe, V. Y. The *Invention of Africa: Gnosis, Philosophy, and the Order of Knowledge*. Bloomington: University of Indiana Press, 1988.

Northup, Solomon. *Twelve Years a Slave*. Mineola: Dover Publications, 1970 [1854].

Palmié, Stephan. *The Cooking of History: How Not to Study Afro-Cuban Religion*. Chicago: University of Chicago Press, 2013.

Phillips, U. B. *American Negro Slavery*. Baton Rouge: Louisiana State University Press, 1966 [1918].

Raboteau, Albert J. *Slave Religion: The "Invisible Institution" in the Antebellum South*. New York: Oxford University Press, 2004 [1978].

Scott, David. *Refashioning Futures: Criticism after Postcoloniality*. Princeton: Princeton University Press, 1999.

Shelby, Tommie. *We Who Are Dark*. Cambridge: Belknap Press of Harvard University Press, 2005.

Stampp, Kenneth. *The Peculiar Institution: Slavery in the Antebellum South*. New York: Vintage Books, 1989 [1956].

Starobin, Robert. ed. *Great Lives Observed: Denmark Vesey, The Slave Conspiracy of 1822*. Englewood Cliffs: Prentice Hall, 1970.

Stuckey, Sterling. *Slave Culture: Nationalist Theory and the Foundations of Black America*. New York: Oxford University Press, 1987.

Sweet, James. *Domingos Álvares, African Healing, and the Intellectual History of the Atlantic World*. Chapel Hill: University of North Carolina Press, 2013.

Thornton, John K. "African Dimensions of the Stono Rebellion." *The American Historical Review* 96, no. 4 (October 1991): 1101–1113.

_____. *A Cultural History of the Atlantic World, 1250–1820*. New York: Cambridge University Press, 2012.

_____. "'I Am the Subject of the King of Congo': African Political Ideology and the Haitian Revolution." *Journal of World History* 4, no. 2 (Fall 1993): 181–214.

West, Cornel and Eddie Glaude, Jr., eds. *African American Religious Thought: An Anthology.* Louisville: Westminster John Knox Press, 2003.

Woofter, T. J. Black *Yeomanry.* New York: H. Holt and Company, 1930.

Young, Jason. *Rituals of Resistance: African Atlantic Religion in Kongo and the Lowcountry South in the Era of Slavery.* Baton Rouge: LSU Press, 2007.

NOTES

1 W. E. B. Du Bois, *The Negro Church* (New York: Altamira Press, 2003 [1903]).
2 W. E. B. Du Bois, *The Souls of Black Folk* (New York: Penguin, 1996 [1903]), 157.
3 Du Bois, *Negro Church*, 208.
4 Cornel West and Eddie Glaude, Jr., eds., *African American Religious Thought: An Anthology* (Louisville: Westminster John Knox Press, 2003), xiii.
5 Dianne M. Stewart Diakité and Tracey E. Hucks, „Africana Religious Studies: Toward a Transdisciplinary Agenda in an Emerging Field," *Journal of Africana Religions* 1, no. 1 (2013): 54.
6 Stewart and Hucks, „Africana Religious Studies," 54.
7 John K. Thornton, *A Cultural History of the Atlantic World, 1250–1820* (New York: Cambridge University Press, 2012), 397.
8 Jason Young, *Rituals of Resistance: African Atlantic Religion in Kongo and the Lowcountry South in the Era of Slavery* (Baton Rouge: LSU Press, 2007), 64.
9 Francis Le Jau, „Slave Conversion on the Carolina Frontier," in. *African American Religious History: A Documentary Witness,* ed. Milton Sernett (Durham: Duke University Press, 1999), 27 (emphasis added). See also Annette Laing, „'Heathens and Infidels'? African Christianization and Anglicanism in the South Carolina Low Country, 1700–1750," *Religion and American Culture: A Journal of Interpretation* 12, no. 2 (Summer 2012): 197.
10 Jane Landers, *Black Society in Spanish Florida* (Urbana-Champaign, IL: University of Illinois Press, 1999), 48, 113.
11 John K. Thornton, „African Dimensions of the Stono Rebellion," *The American Historical Review* 96, no. 4 (October 1991): 1103.
12 See, for example, John K. Thornton, „'I Am the Subject of the King of Congo': African Political Ideology and the Haitian Revolution," *Journal of World History* 4, no. 2 (Fall 1993): 181–214.
13 James Sweet, *Domingos Álvares, African Healing, and the Intellectual History of the Atlantic World* (Chapel Hill: University of North Carolina Press, 2013).
14 Albert J. Raboteau, *Slave Religion: The „Invisible Institution" in the Antebellum South* (New York: Oxford University Press, 2004 [1978]), 149.
15 William Capers, *Catechism for the Use of the Methodist Missions* (Richmond: John Early 1852), 19; I Timothy 6:1– 2.
16 Solomon Northup, *Twelve Years a Slave* (Mineola, NY: Dover Publications, 1970 [1854]), 128.
17 Michel Martin, „Slave Bible From The 1800s Omitted Key Passages That Could Incite Rebellion," *All Things Considered,* aired December 9, 2018 on National Public Radio, https://www.npr.org/2018/12/09/674995075/slave-bible-from-the-1800s-omitted-key-passages-that-could-incite-rebellion.
18 Alan Gallay, „Planters and Slaves in the Great Awakening," in *Masters & Slaves in the House of the Lord: Race and Religion in the American South, 1740–1870,* ed. John B. Boles, (Lexington: University Press of Kentucky, 1988), 33.
19 James Albert Ukawsaw Gronniosaw, *A Narrative of the Most Remarkable Particulars in the Life of James Albert Ukawsaw Gronniosaw, an African Prince, Related by Himself,* in Adam Potkay and Sandra Burr, eds., *Black Atlantic Writers of the 18th Century* (New York: St. Martin's Press, 1995), 41, 43.
20 Frederick Douglass, *Narrative of the Life of Frederick Douglass, an American Slave* (New York: Penguin Books, 1982 [1845]), 154.
21 T. J. Woofter, *Black Yeomanry* (New York: H. Holt and Company, 1930), 148.
22 Raboteau, *Slave Religion*, 243–244.
23 Sterling Stuckey, *Slave Culture: Nationalist Theory and the Foundations of Black America* (New York: Oxford University Press, 1987), 12 and *passim*.
24 Harriet Jacobs (Linda Brent), *Incidents in the Life of a Slave Girl* (New York: Harcourt, Brace and Co., 1973 [1863]), 69.

25 Michael Gomez, *Exchanging Their Country Marks: The Transformation of African Identities in the Colonial and Antebellum South* (Chapel Hill: The University of North Carolina Press, 1998), 244–245.

26 V. Y. Mudimbe, *The Invention of Africa: Gnosis, Philosophy, and the Order of Knowledge* (Bloomington: University of Indiana Press, 1988), 47.

27 Michael Gomez, „Muslims in Early America" *The Journal of Southern History* 60, no. 4 (November 1994): 682.

28 J. D. Fage, ed., *The Cambridge History of Africa, volume 2, c. 500 B.C.–1500 A.D.* (New York: Cambridge University Press, 1978), 668.

29 Michael Gomez, *Black Crescent: The Experience and Legacy of African Muslims in the Americas* (New York: Cambridge University Press, 2005), 144.

30 Gomez, *Black Crescent*, 144–145.

31 James Sweet, *Domingos Álvares: African Healing, and the Intellectual History of the Atlantic World* (Chapel Hill, NC: University of North Carolina Press, 2011), 26, 40–41.

32 Gomez, „Muslims in Early America," 699.

33 C. C. Jones, *Religious Instruction of the Negroes in the United States* (New York: Kraus reprint co., 1969 [1842]), 125.

34 P. E. H. Hair et al. eds., *Barbot on Guinea: The Writings of Jean Barbot on West Africa, 1678–1712* (London: Haklyut Society, 1992), 552.

35 Georgia Writers' Project, *Drums and Shadows: Survival Studies Among the Georgia Coastal Negroes* (Athens: University of Georgia Press, 1940), 144.

36 Qtd. in Sylviane Diouf, *Servants of Allah: African Muslims Enslaved in the Americas* (New York: New York University Press, 1998), 62.

37 Gomez, *Black Crescent*, 143.

38 Wyatt MacGaffey and Michael Harris, *Astonishment and Power: The Eyes of Understanding Kongo Minkisi* (Washington, DC: National Museum of African Art, 1993), 134.

39 Woofter, *Black Yeomanry*, 104.

40 Robert Starobin, ed. *Great Lives Observed: Denmark Vesey, The Slave Conspiracy of 1822* (Englewood Cliffs: Prentice Hall, 1970), 10.

41 Douglass, *Narrative*, 111.

42 Du Bois, *Souls*, 159–160.

43 Jones, *Religious Instruction*, 125.

44 U. B. Phillips, *American Negro Slavery* (Baton Rouge: Louisiana State University Press, 1966 [1918]), 314.

45 Kenneth Stampp, *The Peculiar Institution: Slavery in the Antebellum South* (New York: Vintage Books, 1989 [1956]), 375.

46 Jon Butler, *Awash in a Sea of Faith: Christianizing the American People* (Cambridge: Harvard University Press, 1990), 153.

47 Saidiya Hartman, *Scenes of Subjection: Terror, Slavery, and Self-Making in Nineteenth-Century America* (New York: Oxford University Press: 1997), 87.

48 Stephan Palmié, *The Cooking of History: How Not to Study Afro-Cuban Religion* (Chicago, IL: University of Chicago Press, 2013), „Introduction" and *passim*.

49 Michael Gomez, *Reversing Sail: A History of the African Diaspora* (New York: Cambridge University Press, 2005), 2.

50 Yvonne Chireau, „Theorizing Africana Religions: A Journal of Africana Religions Inaugural Symposium," *Journal of Africana Religions* 2, no. 1 (2014): 133.

51 Douglass, *Narrative*, 57.

52 Paul Gilroy, „Living Memory: A Meeting with Toni Morrison," in *Small Acts: Thoughts on the Politics of Black Cultures* (London: Serpent's Tail, 1993), 181–182.

53 Ibid.

54 Tommie Shelby, *We Who Are Dark* (Cambridge: Belknap Press, 2005), 239.

55 David Scott, *Refashioning Futures: Criticism after Postcoloniality* (Princeton, NJ: Princeton University Press, 1999), 106; Kamau Braithwaite, „The African Presence in Caribbean Literature," in Kamau Braithwaite, *Roots* (Ann Arbor: University of Michigan Press, 1993), 190–258.

56 Lily Cho, „The Turn to Diaspora," *Topia* 17 (Spring 2007): 14.

57 Saidiya Hartman, *Lose Your Mother: A Journey Along the Atlantic Slave Route* (New York: Farrar, Straus and Giroux, 2007), 102.

58 John 8:33.

Part II

ESTABLISHMENT

Chapter Five

THE LOYALIST CHURCH OF ENGLAND CLERGY AND THE POLITICS OF MARTYRDOM IN THE AMERICAN REVOLUTION

Peter W. Walker

University of Wyoming, Laramie, Wyoming

When fighting broke out at Lexington and Concord, John Sayre was the Anglican clergyman for Fairfield, Connecticut.[1] His support for the British government was no secret, but he and his Patriot neighbors had nevertheless managed to live alongside one another in peace and quiet. Now, the newly formed Committees of Safety began disarming Loyalists, and two hundred armed men gathered outside his home, intent on searching for weapons. Finding his wife sick and heavily pregnant, they gave up. The Fairfield Committee instead ordered him to sign the Continental Association, the economic boycott of Britain. Sayre refused.

Sayre wrote to the Fairfield Committee, presenting himself as a conscientious objector to the Patriot movement. He told them that, as a clergyman, he could not countenance the armed resistance which they demanded. Nor could it matter whether he participated, since the clergy were concerned with the next world, not this one. "I am no politician," he explained, "and never will be either." He saw the war as "a judgement of God" which demanded "a sincere and immediate return to him." Citing Philippians 4:11 — "in whatever state I am in, therewith I must be content" — he insisted that submission, not resistance, was his Christian duty. Sayre sent his letter to the Committee to the *New-York Journal*, which published it. Then, an unlikely ally, the Quaker pacifist and slavery abolitionist Anthony Benezet, republished the letter in Philadelphia.

The Committee, however, was unimpressed. They banished Sayre from Fairfield. He recalled that he was permitted to return after seven months, but his mostly Loyalist congregation continued to be "oppressed merely on account of their attachment to their Church and King." Hostile townspeople shot bullets through his church, broke its windows, and carried away its wall hangings and roof tiles. Resolving "to remain with my people to see the end," he continued in Fairfield until July 7th, 1779, when British troops burned the entire town to the ground. Sayre then had little choice but to follow the British army to New York, where he, his wife, and their eight children joined the city's swelling population of Loyalist refugees.

Here, Sayre reflected on the spiritual meaning of his ordeal, and managed to strike a positive note. His congregation had been oppressed mightily, he wrote, yet had borne their sufferings with "patience and fortitude indicative of the power of religion." Indeed, they had

A Companion to American Religious History, First Edition. Edited by Benjamin E. Park.
© 2021 John Wiley & Sons, Inc. Published 2021 by John Wiley & Sons, Inc.

"considerably increased, not only in numbers, but also in attachment to the church [of England]." This was despite, or perhaps because of, the "persecution" they had endured. Sayre had lost his home and possessions, been ostracized by his neighbors, and suffered in body and health, yet retained something infinitely more valuable: "a conscience void of offence towards God." Drawing on a Christian tradition of martyrdom and virtuous suffering, Sayre claimed that the more he suffered in this world, the more he could look forward to salvation in the next one.[2]

This chapter will examine Loyalist Anglican clergymen such as John Sayre in order to consider a larger issue: the intertwined phenomena of religious and political martyrdom in the Revolutionary era. Martyrdom offered Loyalists a powerful means of dissent against the Patriot movement. Martyrdom provided forms of political subjectivity — ways of being political — which a wholly secular history of the Revolution would fail to recognize. Sayre represented himself as the unfortunate victim of persecution, but he actively fashioned himself as a martyr, and thereby offered a powerful moral critique of the Patriots. Yet martyrdom also provided forms of religious subjectivity — ways of being religious — which were at least as, or perhaps more important to Sayre than this political role. Martyrdom produced religious meaning out of the real hardship and trauma which many Americans experienced during the Revolutionary War. This chapter will consider both aspects of Loyalist martyrdom.

In considering Loyalist martyrdom from both religious and political angles, this chapter will also shed light on Americans' efforts to distinguish between "religion" and "politics." It was widely agreed that the clergy should stay away from political conflict. Of course, how to draw the boundary between "religion" and "politics" was both a political question and a religious one. Sayre accused the Fairfield Committee of religious persecution, a worse crime than political oppression. Patriots, meanwhile, accused the Anglican clergy of promoting loyalty "under pretense … of propagating religion"; that is, of preaching politics in the guise of religion.[3] Distinguishing between "religion" and "politics" was an inherently contested issue which the clergy had to confront directly.

Sayre's martyrdom was closely connected to his Anglican faith. The Anglican clergy were well positioned to play the role of Loyalist martyrs because they could draw on an American tradition of Anglican martyrdom. This claim might seem surprising, given that American Anglicans belonged to a powerful established church, and their American successors, the Episcopalians, were associated with the new nation's socioeconomic elite. Compared to Quakers such as Benezet, we are more likely to think of Anglicans as the wielders of power than its suffering victims. In fact, as we will see, colonial Anglicans thought of themselves as *both* members of the establishment *and* an oppressed minority, and this tension produced their peculiar aptitude for martyrdom.

This chapter seeks to explain why so many Anglican clergymen can be found playing the part of Loyalist martyrs during the Revolutionary War. It begins by surveying colonial Anglicans' longer history, showing how their conflicted and paradoxical identity produced a martyrological tradition. It will then consider their political allegiance during the Revolution, explaining why some (but not all) chose the Loyalist side. Finally, it will analyze the phenomenon of Loyalist martyrdom, asking what Loyalist martyrs hoped to achieve. It thereby addresses the relationship between religion and politics in the American Revolution, at the level of individual experience and in the larger political disputes.

Majority or Minority? Anglican Martyrdom before the American Revolution

Historians have not been particularly interested in colonial Anglicanism. It does not fit easily with the major themes of American religious history (pluralism, individualism, and revivalism), and scholars have instead concentrated on more "American" traditions such as

Puritanism or Evangelicalism. The colonial Church of England is often presented, in both academic scholarship and popular depictions, as an attempt to subjugate America to British political and ecclesiastical control, and something that never truly belonged there.[4] In fact, the experience of empire shaped colonial Anglicanism into something new and different from English Anglicanism. This was true, above all, in its embrace of martyrdom: a supremely American form of religiosity.

To understand their embrace of martyrdom, we must understand colonial Anglicans' conflicted identity: were they part of the Empire's religious "establishment," or one of its religious minorities? This identity crisis reflected the Church of England's ambiguous relationship with the British imperial state. Crucially, the nature of this relationship varied from one part of the Empire to the next. The Church of England was, of course, "established" in England itself. In England, the state funded the Church and excluded England's religious minorities (primarily Catholics and "Protestant Dissenters") from full civil rights. The monarch was the "supreme governor" of the Church, and the Anglican bishops sat in the House of Lords. In exchange, the clergy prayed for King and Parliament. In contemporaries' favorite metaphor, church and state were joined in marriage, at least in England.[5]

Beyond England, a messier situation prevailed. There was no single established church for the whole Empire. Instead, each colony had its own established church, or none. This was the result of accident rather than design. England's imperial expansion in the sixteenth and seventeenth centuries coincided with a period of protracted religious instability in the British Isles: a drawn-out reformation, a religious civil war, the creation of a republic, the restoration of the monarchy, and the revolutionary overthrow of the restored dynasty. Meanwhile, different colonies were settled by different groups of emigrants, and received different ecclesiastical arrangements according to the rapidly changing religious situation at home.[6]

The result was an empire comprising a patchwork of different established churches. The southern and Caribbean colonies generally received Anglican established churches, the New England colonies Congregationalist ("Puritan") ones, and the Mid-Atlantic colonies some form of disestablishment or partial establishment. Then, in 1707, England and Scotland were united into a new Kingdom of Great Britain with *two* established churches, Presbyterian in the north and Anglican in the south. The Empire's ecclesiastical pluralism was thereafter grounded in the mother country's.

In the absence of a unifying imperial church, the Empire's identity was derived from its shared Protestantism rather than a single Protestant denomination. Within the limits of Protestantism, then, the Empire was characterized by *religious pluralism* (the coexistence of different denominational communities) but also, more subtly, *ecclesiastical pluralism* (the coexistence of different established churches within a single polity).[7]

New England and Mid-Atlantic Anglicans thereby found themselves in a strange situation. They were a religious minority in their immediate vicinities, but they nevertheless thought of themselves as members of the mother country's national church and thus a majority by right. They therefore believed that they did not receive the privileges and recognition to which they were entitled. In 1759, for example, the Anglican clergyman Samuel Johnson complained that Connecticut's established Congregationalists (whom he called "Dissenters") had "pretended to establish themselves ... and make dissenters of us." It is easy to dismiss such complaints as whining or special pleading, but we should remember that Anglicans' "established" status meant more than just political privilege: it was part of their identity. Anglicans in New England and the Mid-Atlantic had to learn to live without it.[8]

This experience cut both ways. On the one hand, it could be humiliating. Northern Anglicans frequently complained of an unnatural world turned upside down, in which "Dissenters" subjugated members of the "national church." Their quarrels with their denominational rivals took on a peculiar rhetorical intensity, especially in their demands for Britain to send an Anglican bishop to America. The Empire's governors, reluctant to upset the *status quo*, repeatedly refused, and northern Anglicans complained that they were thereby condemned to a state of religious persecution.[9] On the other hand, their minority status made possible certain kinds of religious experience which were not available to their coreligionists in England: they could claim to have chosen the Church of England not for the rewards for establishment, but in spite of the challenges of persecution.

Martyrdom and virtuous suffering therefore emerged as central pillars of Anglican religiosity in New England and the Mid-Atlantic in a way that could not happen in England itself. John Sayre expounded on these themes in a sermon in May 1773, which prefigured the language of his confrontation with the Fairfield Patriots two years later. Sayre emphasized the suffering, persecuted condition of what he called "our established church": "In this new world, we behold the church in an unparalleled situation; like a system without a center," he lamented. These "present humiliating circumstances" could only be "a punishment on her children," demanding moral reform and spiritual renewal. Yet this was not necessarily a bad thing: after all, he reminded his audience, the Church England had been "sublimed in the flames of martyrdom" from its beginning.[10] For Sayre and his co-religionists, the experience of suffering and persecution was a source of moral authority and spiritual power.

Martyrdom, in short, provided Anglicans with two things as they struggled to come to terms with their status as a religious minority in this region. First, it allowed them to protest against the fact that the Church of England was not a true imperial church, established throughout the colonies. Simultaneously, it also gave meaning to their religious experience in the absence of that established status. Their identity as martyrs reflected both their privileges and their disadvantages, and the tension between the two.

The irony here is that these Anglicans thought of themselves as the true representatives of the Church of England, yet their identity as martyrs was something little known among Anglicans in England itself. In their embrace of martyrdom, they had far more in common with those they called "Dissenters."[11] As the historian Adrian Weimar has shown, Puritans and their descendants retained the identity of persecuted martyrs fleeing to the wilderness long after they had created powerful established churches there.[12] Anglicans in the region bought into this tradition by insisting that *they* were ones persecuted by Congregationalists, not the other way around. Anglican martyrdom was part of a distinctly American tradition.

Religion and Political Allegiance in the American Revolution

During the Revolution, Anglican clergymen supplied some of the most articulate Loyalist writers, intellectuals, ideologues, and lobbyists. The New Yorker Charles Inglis published one of the best-known responses to Thomas Paine's *Common Sense* in 1776, titled *The True Interest of America*. The same year, the British military authorities appointed him to take over *The New York Gazette* and turn it into an outlet for Loyalist propaganda. Inglis remained a prolific Loyalist writer throughout the war, fled with the British army at its end, and was rewarded with an appointment as the Bishop of Nova Scotia in 1787. How typical was he?[13]

Inglis's Loyalism was likely to be shared by Anglicans in the North. His southern brethren, conversely, were more likely to support the Patriot cause, or at least compromise with it. According to one estimate, the ninety-three Anglican clergy in the northern colonies comprised sixty-eight Loyalists, five Patriots, and twenty Neutrals; the 225 in the southern colonies comprised fifty-five Loyalists, eighty-three Patriots, and eighty-seven Neutrals.[14] American Anglicans' response to the Revolutionary War thus mapped onto a north-south divide. The un-established minorities in New England and the Mid-Atlantic generally became Loyalists, and the established majorities in the South did not.

There are three puzzles here which we must resolve. First, Anglicans in the northern colonies sided most forcefully with the British government in the revolutionary rupture, despite their long-standing complaints about the injustices of the British imperial state. Why did the most disaffected Anglicans become Loyalists? Second, southern Anglicanism, with its majoritarian established churches, looked a lot like Anglicanism in England, unlike the martyrdom-oriented minority in the North. Why were the more "English" southerners usually more willing to countenance independence than the more "American" northerners?

Third, Loyalist Anglicans claimed that their religious beliefs directed them to oppose American independence, but they formed a small minority in the colonial Church of England as a whole. Most American Anglicans were southerners. Not only did southerners supply most of the clergy, the southern clergy also ministered to vastly larger lay populations. Being an Anglican did not automatically make one a Loyalist: indeed, based on these geographic assumptions, most American Anglicans were not Loyalists. (Loyalist Anglicans claimed that Patriot Anglicans were evidently not good Anglicans, but this is a logical fallacy.) Why, then, did northern Anglicans become Loyalists, if they were more "American," unhappier with the *status quo*, and were not compelled to do so by their faith?[15]

Political considerations played a part. In the absence of large congregations, the Anglican clergy in the North depended on powerful patrons. Before he came to Fairfield, Sayre ministered to Newburgh in New York, where he was entirely dependent on Cadwallader Colden, governor of New York and a wealthy landowner. Colden's efforts to use the Church of England as an instrument of political control made Sayre unpopular with his parishioners, hence his move to Fairfield.[16] More generally, Loyalists were frequently members of "conscious minorities," as the historian William Nelson pointed out in 1961: "almost all the Loyalists were, in one way or another, more afraid of America than they were of Britain."[17] Put another way, northern Anglicans sought to use Loyalism to extract recognition, protection, or reward from the British imperial state. Southern Anglicans, with their larger numbers, did not need to do so.

Theological differences were also important. Northern Anglicans were more attached to a High Church theology, which considered the sacraments as a means of grace. This theology valued the clergy as dispensers of those sacraments. Southern Anglicans, on the other hand, were more attached to a Low Church theology. This theology considered faith in Christ, rather than participation in the sacraments, as necessary for salvation, and therefore emphasized the laity rather than the clergy. It is easy to see why High Church theology would be more appealing where Anglicans formed a demographic minority: it suggested that it did not matter for salvation if a church was full or empty as long as the officiating clergyman was properly ordained. Given its emphasis on the clergy, and thus on the continuity of the Church's institutions, High Church theology placed a higher premium on maintaining America's ecclesiastical connection to Britain. From a High Church perspective, if strict adherence to ecclesiastical forms alienated the laity, this was a price worth paying; a Low Church Anglican, however, might disagree. All around, High Church theology placed a greater emphasis on tradition, authority, and continuity.[18]

It must be emphasized, however, that religious belief did not determine political allegiance. As the rift between Britain and its colonies widened, Americans had to choose sides. A fantastic variety of factors influenced their decisions: high-minded principle; self-interest; institutional, communal, or familial networks; local power politics; contingency; and more. Two leading historians of Loyalism have noted that "every Protestant denominational community, and even Jewish synagogues and Roman Catholic parishes, harbored Patriots, Loyalists, and neutralists."[19] And as the historian of religion Kate Carté has written, "trying to map the organizational structure of British Protestantism onto the American Revolution is an exercise in futility."[20] Carté also makes a subtler point: it is important for historians to consider the impact of the American Revolution on the history of religion, and not just the impact of religion on the secular history of the American Revolution.[21] Without a doubt, Loyalists' religious beliefs shaped their political commitments and decisions, but this relationship went both ways. Loyalism also produced religious meaning.

Persecuting Patriots? Anglican Martyrdom in the American Revolution

The American Revolution gave colonial Anglicans new opportunities to become martyrs, new reasons for doing so, and new audiences for their martyrdom. Creating a new nation was a religious project as well as a political one. It meant tearing apart the old imperial religio-political community. This was a traumatic process, especially for Anglicans, for whom that community was sacred. There is a notable paradox here. American Anglicans' ties to the British imperial state put them in the firing line as Patriots came to declare independence, but during the colonial period Anglicans had complained mightily that they were not properly supported by that same imperial state, hence their well-established habit of thinking of themselves as martyrs. Had colonial Anglicans been either more powerful, or less powerful, they would not have made such good martyrs.

Loyalist martyrdom was a response to the Revolution's violence. Americans today imagine the Revolution as a founding moment of national unity. For a long time, scholars agreed. More recently, however, historians have begun to view the Revolution as America's first civil war, perhaps taking inspiration from the divisiveness of American public life today. These historians point to the popular violence, battlefield casualties, starvation, epidemics, and massive refugee crisis which accompanied the Revolutionary War. As a proportion of the population, more than five times as many Americans died in the Revolutionary War as in World War II. Moreover, Loyalists comprised between a fifth and a third of the colonists, and were often subject to various kinds of coercion, sometimes carried out by the people (for example, tarring and feathering) and sometimes by the state (for example, imprisonment or the confiscation of property). In response, one in forty Americans fled the Thirteen Colonies as Loyalist refugees.[22] Of the total Anglican clergy in the Thirteen Colonies, around a fifth died during the war, and a further quarter became refugees; these proportions were significantly higher in the mostly-Loyalist North.[23] Martyrdom made these difficult experiences spiritually meaningful.

American Anglicans suffered particularly as a result of their ecclesiastical ties to Britain. The process of declaring independence had a symbolic dimension, as when a crowd of New Yorkers pulled down a statue of George III three days after the Declaration of Independence and melted it into musket balls for the Continental Army.[24] Likewise, Americans had to declare ecclesiastical as well as political independence. In England, one of the Church of England's political duties was to sacralize the community by praying for the nation's leaders. To this end, the Anglican liturgy contained in the Book of Common Prayer included prayers for the King which were to be read in the weekly church service:

> Most heartily we beseech thee with thy favor to behold our most gracious sovereign Lord King George; and so replenish him with the grace of thy Holy Spirit, that he may always incline to thy will, and walk in thy way: Endue him plenteously with heavenly gifts; grant him in health and wealth long to live; strengthen him that he may vanquish and overcome all his enemies; and finally, after this life, he may attend everlasting joy and felicity, through Jesus Christ our Lord. *Amen* ...
>
> From all sedition, privy conspiracy, and rebellion; from all false doctrine, heresy, and schism; from hardness of heart, and contempt of thy Word and Commandment, *Good Lord, deliver us* ...
>
> That it may please thee to keep and strengthen in the true worshipping of thee, in righteousness and holiness of life, thy servant George, our most gracious King and Governor; *We beseech thee to hear us, good Lord* ...
>
> That it may please thee to be his defender and keeper, giving him the victory over all his enemies; *We beseech thee to hear us, good Lord.*[25]

These prayers suddenly became a point of conflict once the crisis commenced. After the Declaration of Independence, the new American states passed treason laws which made it illegal to aid, abet, or pray for the enemies of the United States. These were intended not only to identify and neutralize Loyalists, but also to complete the symbolic transfer of sovereignty to the new nation.[26] As a result, it became illegal to worship according to the Book of Common Prayer. American Anglicans found themselves in a position mirroring that of Roman Catholics in Britain, their religious practice prohibited due to their allegiance to a supranational church.

Throughout the new American states, the Anglican clergy had to decide how to respond to this situation. This was partly a political decision, a way to signal approval or disapproval of independence, but other considerations were also at play. How important was it to follow the letter of the Book of Common Prayer? Under what circumstances could changes be permitted, and by whose authority? What were the minister's duties to the congregation? Congregations were often at odds with the minister, or one another, and were usually more concerned with continuing worship than with the theological niceties that occupied the clergy. Last but not least, who wielded political power locally?

Individual clergy responded to the prohibition in various ways. Some chose to replace the prayers for the King with prayers for Americans' new political leaders. Others chose to omit the prayers altogether. Prayer books survive in which the offending prayers were either corrected by hand or physically cut from the page. Loyalists typically refused to officiate rather than do so with an incomplete or modified liturgy. In this way they could avoid breaking the letter of the treason laws. Refusing to adapt the liturgy was nevertheless interpreted as public disavowal of independence. It was often intended as such. Charles Inglis proudly wrote to Britain reporting that all the clergy in New York, New Jersey, and New England, "without excepting one … have proved themselves faithful, loyal subjects" to the King by closing their churches. For Inglis and others like him, Loyalism did not mean obedience to King or Parliament, but rather obedience to the Church of England and Book of Common Prayer.[27]

Anglican Loyalists therefore insisted that they were subject not just to political oppression but to religious persecution. When they were ordained, they had sworn allegiance to the King and to worship using the Book of Common Prayer. Breaking these oaths would endanger their souls, they explained, yet this is precisely what Patriots demanded. Of course, when they concluded that they could not modify the liturgy, they were grappling with a political question as well as a theological one. Anglican Patriots argued that the prayers should be for the nation's political leaders, whoever they happened to be. Loyalists retorted that only George III could release his subjects from their allegiance to him. When he eventually did so (with the Peace of Paris in 1783), they stopped praying for George III and prayed for Congress instead.[28] Evidently, then, their refusal to stop praying for the King during the Revolutionary War rested on a prior refusal to accept American independence. Nevertheless, they believed that political allegiance was a question affecting their salvation.

This is why the Loyalist clergy saw themselves as Christian martyrs. As far as they were concerned, they were suffering for the sake of conscience in the face of persecution, demonstrating that they cared more about their souls than their worldly interests. William Clark of Dedham, Massachusetts, explained to his congregation why he had chosen to close the church rather than worship without the outlawed liturgy. "You all know that in my preaching I have generally avoided these [political] matters," told them, but to deviate from the Book of Common Prayer "is against the present light of my own conscience." He hoped that his conduct would "convince both friends & enemies of the sincerity of our religious profession," thereby "promoting the revival and permanent stability of our Church." He concluded by quoting Revelation 2:10, which instructed Christians to undergo persecution gladly:

> Fear none of these things which thou shalt suffer; behold the devil shall cast some of you in prison, that ye may be tried, and ye shall have tribulation ten days; be thou faithful unto death, & I will give you the crown of life.[29]

In this declaration, Clark was deliberately situating himself in a longer tradition of Christian martyrdom stretching back to the early Church.

Moreover, when the Loyalist clergy described their sufferings, they followed the generic conventions of the martyrdom narrative. Martyrdom is a story with beginning, middle, and end, based on the template of Christ's crucifixion, resurrection, and ultimate triumph. Telling the story correctly is just as important as the original actions of the martyr. For example, Samuel Peters, an Anglican clergyman from Connecticut, published *A General History of Connecticut* in 1781 which praised Connecticut's Loyalist clergy. His account of his fellow clergyman John Beach is worth quoting at length:

> In July, 1776, the congress having declared the independency of America, and ordered the commonwealth to be prayed for instead of the King and royal family, all the loyal episcopal [Anglican] churches north of the Delaware were shut up, except those immediately under the protection of the British army, and one at Newtown, in Connecticut, of which last the Rev. Mr John Beach was the rector, whose grey hairs, adorned with loyal and christian virtues, overcame even the madness of the Sober Dissenters. This faithful disciple disregarded the congressional mandate, and praying for the King as usual, they pulled him out of his desk, put a rope around his neck, and drew him across Osootonoc river, at the tail of a boat, to cool his loyal zeal, as they called it; after which, the old Confessor was permitted to depart, though not without a prohibition to pray longer for the King. But his loyal zeal was insuperable. He went to church, and prayed again for the King; upon which the Sober Dissenters again seized him, and resolved upon cutting out his tongue; when the heroic veteran said, "If my blood must be shed, let it not be done in the house of God." The pious mob then dragged him out of the church, laid his neck on a block, and swore they would cut off his head; and insolently crying out, "Now, you old Devil! say your last prayer," he prayed thus, "God bless King George, and forgive all his and my enemies!" At this unexpected and exalted display of christian patience and charity, the mob so far relented as to discharge and never molest him afterwards for adhering to the liturgy of the church of England and his ordination oath; but they relaxed not in their severities towards the other clergymen, because, they said, younger consciences are more flexible.[30]

The details of this story are impossible to verify and may well be entirely untrue. Peters included egregiously false information elsewhere in the *General History*.[31] Yet what matters for our purposes here is the story. In this telling, Beach is given three opportunities to deny the faith (a Biblically significant number) but repeatedly holds firm. Thus, the mob's attempts to defeat him through violence backfire. They instead give him a platform from which to proclaim his faith, allowing him to triumph over them. Peters's storytelling transformed the Loyalist clergy from passive victims into triumphant martyrs.

Conclusion

What did these professions of Loyalist martyrdom achieve? Most obviously, they were politically useful, a way to advance the Loyalist cause. The battle for public opinion was a crucial part of the Revolutionary War. Both sides used violence against the other while publicizing atrocities committed against themselves.[32] Thus, suffering formed a central pillar of the identity and ideology of all Loyalists, notably in the public monuments to Loyalist refugees erected throughout Britain after the war.[33] Loyalists presented themselves as suffering victims in order to contest a competing tradition of Patriot martyrdom, of the kind which memorialized the five victims of the "Boston Massacre."[34] By publicizing their sufferings, Loyalists sought to reclaim the moral high ground from Patriots who insisted that *they* were the suffering victims of British tyranny. Patriot martyrdom is better known to us today, but Loyalists were just as capable of producing martyrs.

The Loyalist clergy played a key role in this moral contestation. The clergy were quite useless in military terms, but martyrdom transformed their uselessness into a source of moral authority. They could make a particularly convincing case that they were persecuted because of their religious beliefs. They were also particularly well-versed in the theology of martyrdom. They were not the only Americans to play the role of martyrs, but they were especially adept at doing so.

Of course, it is important not to exaggerate the extent of their sufferings. They were privileged, propertied white men with a ready audience among their coreligionists in England.

They were therefore more successful in publicizing their sufferings than other groups who suffered more. They are of interest not because they suffered most, but because of their role in a larger Anglo-American debate about suffering, persecution, and martyrdom.

All of this raises the question: what was so virtuous about suffering, anyway? When Loyalists condemned Patriots for outlawing Anglican worship, they implied that religious persecution was morally worse than simple political oppression. But why should this be the case? We can only account for the moral, political, and rhetorical power of martyrdom if we recognize its theological foundations. Martyrdom rests on a distinction between this world and the next one. It does not celebrate suffering for its own sake, but rather suffering in pursuit of salvation. It holds that persecution is worse than political oppression because it endangers the soul of the victim and not just their body. Without this theological logic, martyrdom simply does not make sense. Modern Americans remain drawn to the Revolution's secular "martyrs of liberty," such as Nathan Hale or Crispus Attucks.[35] However, they rarely confront martyrdom's underlying theology. These theological foundations are worth grappling with. Why did Americans in the Revolutionary era value martyrdom so highly? Why does martyrdom continue to be used by political dissidents? Why does sacrifice continue to figure so prominently in American civil religion?[36]

Martyrdom was politically powerful, but it was not just about politics. It was about salvation. John Sayre, Charles Inglis, Samuel Peters, and William Clark believed they were pursuing something more important than the secular debates over taxation and representation which historians often focus on. By insisting that they willingly suffered for their religious beliefs, they declared themselves sincere and conscientious Christians, refuting charges to the contrary levelled against them by their denominational competitors. They leveraged the political crisis into a call for Anglican revival and renewal. Most importantly, they found spiritual comfort at a time of undeniable hardship. Taking them seriously challenges the secular assumptions with which we tend to approach the subject of religion and politics in American history. We might be tempted to conclude that Loyalist martyrdom was nothing more than a cynical attempt to generate propaganda in service of the British war effort. That assumption, however, would do these people further violence.

FURTHER READING

Calhoon, Robert M. and Ruma Chopra. "Religion and the Loyalists." In *Faith and the Founders of the American Republic*, edited by Mark David Hall and Daniel L. Driesbach, 101–116. Oxford: Oxford University Press, 2014.

Charles Inglis to the Secretary of the Society for the Propagation of the Gospel, October 31, 1776. In *The Life and Letters of Charles Inglis*, edited by John Wolfe Lydekker, 156–172. London: SPCK, 1936.

McBride, Spencer. *Pulpit and Nation: Clergymen and the Politics of Revolutionary America*. Charlottesville: University of Virginia Press, 2016.

Rhoden, Nancy L. *Revolutionary Anglicanism: The Colonial Church of England Clergy during the American Revolution*. New York: New York University Press, 1999.

Weimer, Adrian Chastain. *Martyr's Mirror: Persecution and Holiness in Early New England*. Oxford: Oxford University Press, 2011.

BIBLIOGRAPHY

Unpublished Manuscripts

USPG Archive, Bodleian Library, University of Oxford.

Published Collections of Manuscripts

Historical Notices of the Missions of the Church of England in the North American Colonies. Edited by Ernest Hawkins. London: B. Fellowes, 1845.

Samuel Johnson: President of King's College. His Career and Writings. Edited by Herbert and Carol Schneider. New York: Columbia University Press, 1929.

The Life and Letters of Charles Inglis. Edited by John Wolfe Lydekker. London: SPCK, 1936.

Printed Primary Sources

Book of Common Prayer, 1762 edition.
Anthony Benezet. *Thoughts on the Nature of War, and its Repugnancy to the Christian Life.* [Philadelphia?], [1776?].
Charles Inglis. *The True Interest of America, Impartially Stated.* Philadelphia, 1776.
Samuel Peters. *A General History of Connecticut, from its First Settlement.* London, 1781.
John Sayre. *A Sermon Preached before the Convention.* New York, 1773.
John Sayre. *From the New-York Journal.* [Philadelphia?], [1775?].

Secondary Sources

Anderson, Virginia DeJohn. *The Martyr and The Traitor: Nathan Hale, Moses Dunbar, and the American Revolution.* Oxford: Oxford University Press, 2019.
Armitage, David. *Civil Wars: A History in Ideas.* New York: Vintage, 2017.
Bell, James B. "North America." In *The Oxford History of Anglicanism, Volume II: Establishment and Empire, 1662–1829,* edited by Jeremy Gregory, 160–88. Oxford: Oxford University Press, 2017.
Bellah, Robert N. "Civil Religion in America." *Daedalus* 96, no. 1 (1967): 1–21.
Boyarin, Daniel. *Dying for God: Martyrdom and the Making of Christianity and Judaism.* Stanford: Stanford University Press, 1999.
Bridenbaugh, Carl. *Mitre and Sceptre: Transatlantic Faiths, Ideas, Personalities, and Politics, 1689–1775.* Oxford: Oxford University Press, 1962.
Calhoon, Robert M. and Ruma Chopra. "Religion and the Loyalists." In *Faith and the Founders of the American Republic,* edited by Mark David Hall and Daniel L. Driesbach, 101–116. Oxford: Oxford University Press, 2014.
Chopra, Ruma. *Unnatural Rebellion: Loyalists in New York City During the Revolution.* Charlottesville: University of Virginia Press, 2011.
Engel, Katherine Carté. "Connecting Protestants in Britain's Eighteenth-Century Atlantic Empire." *William and Mary Quarterly* 75, no. 1 (2018): 37–70.
———. "Revisiting the Bishop Controversy." In *The American Revolution Reborn,* edited by Patrick Spero and Michael Zuckerman, 132–149. Philadelphia: University of Pennsylvania Press, 2016.
Gregory, Brad. *Salvation at Stake: Christian Martyrdom in Early Modern Europe.* Cambridge: Harvard University Press, 1999.
Gregory, Jeremy. "'Establishment' and 'Dissent' in British North America: Organizing Religion in the New World." In *British North America,* 136–169.
Haefeli, Evan. *Accidental Pluralism: America and the Religious Politics of English Expansion, 1497–1662.* Chicago: University of Chicago Press. 2021.
Hinderaker, Eric. *Boston's Massacre.* Cambridge, MA: Belknap Press, 2019.
Hoock, Holger. *Empires of the Imagination: Politics, War and the Arts in the British World, 1750–1850.* London: Profile, 2010.
Hoock, Holger. *Scars of Independence: America's Violent Birth.* New York: Broadway, 2017.
Irvin, Benjamin H. *Clothed in Robes of Sovereignty: The Continental Congress and the People Out of Doors.* Oxford: Oxford University Press, 2011.
Jacob, W. M. "England," In *The Oxford History of Anglicanism, Volume II: Establishment and Empire, 1662–1829,* edited by Jeremy Gregory, 91–119. Oxford: Oxford University Press, 2017.
Jasanoff, Maya. *Liberty's Exiles: American Loyalists in the Revolutionary World.* New York: Vintage, 2011.
Jones, T. Cole. *Captives of Liberty: Prisoners of War and the Politics of Vengeance in the American Revolution.* Philadelphia: University of Pennsylvania Press, 2019.
Kachun, Mitch. *First Martyr of Liberty: Crispus Attucks in American Memory.* Oxford: Oxford University Press, 2017.
Landsman, Ned C. "British Union and the American Revolution: Imperial Authority and the Multinational State" In *The American Revolution Reborn,* edited by Patrick Spero and Michael Zuckerman, 107–131. Philadelphia: University of Pennsylvania Press, 2016.
Maltby, Judith. "Suffering and Surviving: The Civil Wars, the Commonwealth and the Formation of 'Anglicanism.'" In *Religion in Revolutionary England,* edited by Christopher Durston and Judith Maltby, 158–180. Manchester, UK: Manchester University Press, 2006.

McBride, Spencer. *Pulpit and Nation: Clergymen and the Politics of Revolutionary America*. Charlottesville: University of Virginia Press, 2016.

Moss, Candida. *The Myth of Persecution: How Early Christians Invented a Story of Martyrdom*. New York: HarperCollins, 2013.

Nelson, William H. *The American Tory*. Oxford: Clarendon Press, 1961.

Pestana, Carla Gardina. *Protestant Empire: Religion and the Making of the British Atlantic World*. Philadelphia: University of Pennsylvania Press, 2009.

Rhoden, Nancy L. *Revolutionary Anglicanism: The Colonial Church of England Clergy during the American Revolution*. New York: New York University Press, 1999.

Sheehan, Jonathan. "Sacrifice Before the Secular." *Representations* 105, no. 1 (2009): 12–36.

Trumbull, J. Hammond. *The True-Blue Laws of Connecticut and New Haven and the False Blue Laws Forged by Peters*. Hartford, 1876.

Walker, Peter W. "The Bishop Controversy, the Imperial Crisis, and Religious Radicalism in New England, 1763–74." *New England Quarterly* 90, no. 3 (2017): 306–343.

Weimer, Adrian Chastain. *Martyr's Mirror: Persecution and Holiness in Early New England*. Oxford: Oxford University Press, 2011.

Notes

1   I would like to thank Adam Blackler, Zach Carmichael, Mary Freeman, Melissa Morris, Benjamin Park, and Matthew Wyman-McCarthy.

2   John Sayre to the Secretary of the Society for the Propagation of the Gospel (SPG), November 8, 1779, USPG Archive, B23 n. 233, Bodleian Library, University of Oxford; John Sayre, *From the New-York Journal* ([Philadelphia?], [1775?]); Anthony Benezet, *Thoughts on the Nature of War, and its Repugnancy to the Christian Life* ([Philadelphia?], [1776?]). Important studies of martyrdom include Daniel Boyarin, *Dying for God: Martyrdom and the Making of Christianity and Judaism* (Stanford: Stanford University Press, 1999); Candida Moss, *The Myth of Persecution: How Early Christians Invented a Story of Martyrdom* (New York: HarperCollins, 2013); Brad Gregory, *Salvation at Stake: Christian Martyrdom in Early Modern Europe* (Cambridge, MA: Harvard University Press, 1999). A distinction is sometimes drawn between "martyrs" who died for the faith and "confessors" who suffered for it without dying. The Loyalists discussed in this chapter were technically "confessors" rather than "martyrs."

3   John Peters to Samuel Peters, July 20, 1778, in *Historical Notices of the Missions of the Church of England in the North American Colonies*, ed. Ernest Hawkins (London: B. Fellowes, 1845), 252.

4   Carl Bridenbaugh, *Mitre and Sceptre: Transatlantic Faiths, Ideas, Personalities, and Politics, 1689–1775* (Oxford: Oxford University Press, 1962).

5   W. M. Jacob, "England," in *The Oxford History of Anglicanism, Volume II: Establishment and Empire, 1662–1829*, ed. Jeremy Gregory (Oxford: Oxford University Press, 2017), 91–119.

6   Evan Haefeli, *Accidental Pluralism: America and the Religious Politics of English Expansion, 1497–1662* (Chicago: University of Chicago Press, 2021); Carla Gardina Pestana, *Protestant Empire: Religion and the Making of the British Atlantic World* (Philadelphia: University of Pennsylvania Press, 2009).

7   Jeremy Gregory, " 'Establishment' and 'Dissent' in British North America: Organizing Religion in the New World," in *British North America in the Seventeenth and Eighteenth Centuries*, ed. Stephen Foster (Oxford: Oxford University Press, 2013), 136–169; Ned C. Landsman, "British Union and the American Revolution: Imperial Authority and the Multinational State," in *The American Revolution Reborn*, ed. Patrick Spero and Michael Zuckerman (Philadelphia: University of Pennsylvania Press, 2016), 107–131.

8   Samuel Johnson to Thomas Secker, March 1 1759, in *Samuel Johnson: President of King's College. His Career and Writings*, ed. Herbert and Carol Schneider (New York: Columbia University Press, 1929), i:286; James B. Bell, "North America," in *Oxford History of Anglicanism*, 160–188.

9   Peter W. Walker, "The Bishop Controversy, the Imperial Crisis, and Religious Radicalism in New England, 1763–74," *New England Quarterly* 90, no. 3 (2017): 306–343.

10 John Sayre, *A Sermon Preached before the Convention* (New York, 1773), 14–15. Also see *Oxford English Dictionary*, "sublime, *v*.": "To raise to an elevated sphere or exalted state; to elevate to a high degree of purity or excellence; to make (esp. morally or spiritually) sublime."

11 The exceptions to this rule are provided by the English Civil War, a rare instance in which English Anglicans found themselves as a minority: Judith Maltby, "Suffering and Surviving: The Civil Wars, the Commonwealth and the Formation of 'Anglicanism,'" in *Religion in Revolutionary England*, ed. Christopher Durston and Judith Maltby (Manchester, UK: Manchester University Press, 2006), 158–180.

12 Adrian Chastain Weimer, *Martyr's Mirror: Persecution and Holiness in Early New England* (Oxford: Oxford University Press, 2011).

13 Charles Inglis, *The True Interest of America, Impartially Stated* (Philadelphia, 1776); Ruma Chopra, *Unnatural Rebellion: Loyalists in New York City During the Revolution* (Charlottesville: University of Virginia Press, 2011), 44, 47, 81–86.

14 Nancy L. Rhoden, *Revolutionary Anglicanism: The Colonial Church of England Clergy during the American Revolution* (New York: New York University Press, 1999), 89.

15 *Ibid.*, 10–36.

16 Cadwallader Colden to the Secretary of the SPG, June 18, 1769, USPG Archive, B2 n. 120.

17 William H. Nelson, *The American Tory* (Oxford: Clarendon Press, 1961), 91.

18 Rhoden, *Revolutionary Anglicanism*, 37–87.

19 Robert M. Calhoon and Ruma Chopra, "Religion and the Loyalists," in *Faith and the Founders of the American Republic*, ed. Mark David Hall and Daniel L. Driesbach (Oxford: Oxford University Press, 2014), 101.

20 Katherine Carté Engel, "Connecting Protestants in Britain's Eighteenth-Century Atlantic Empire," *William and Mary Quarterly* 75, no. 1 (2018): 69.

21 Katherine Carté Engel, "Revisiting the Bishop Controversy," in *The American Revolution Reborn*, 135.

22 Holger Hoock, *Scars of Independence: America's Violent Birth* (New York: Broadway, 2017), figures p. 17; Maya Jasanoff, *Liberty's Exiles: American Loyalists in the Revolutionary World* (New York: Vintage, 2011), figures pp. 6, 8, 351–358; David Armitage, *Civil Wars: A History in Ideas* (New York: Vintage, 2017), 121–158.

23 Rhoden, *Revolutionary Anglicanism*, 103.

24 Benjamin H. Irvin, *Clothed in Robes of Sovereignty: The Continental Congress and the People Out of Doors* (Oxford: Oxford University Press, 2011), 140–141.

25 Book of Common Prayer, 1762 edition. Morning Prayer, Evening Prayer, and The Litany.

26 Hoock, *Scars of Independence*, 118.

27 Spencer McBride, *Pulpit and Nation: Clergymen and the Politics of Revolutionary America* (Charlottesville: University of Virginia Press, 2016), 68–101; Charles Inglis to the Secretary of the SPG, October 31, 1776, USPG Archive, B2 n. 68. The letter is printed in *The Life and Letters of Charles Inglis*, ed. John Wolfe Lydekker (London: SPCK, 1936), 156–172.

28 Rhoden, *Revolutionary Anglicanism*, 116–143.

29 [William Clark], "Address to the People of Dedham and Stoughton," March 1777, USPG Archive, B22 n. 339.

30 Samuel Peters, *A General History of Connecticut, from its First Settlement* (London, 1781), 419–421.

31 J. Hammond Trumbull, *The True-Blue Laws of Connecticut and New Haven and the False Blue Laws Forged by Peters* (Hartford, 1876).

32 Hoock, *Scars of Independence*; T. Cole Jones, *Captives of Liberty: Prisoners of War and the Politics of Vengeance in the American Revolution* (Philadelphia: University of Pennsylvania Press, 2019).

33 Holger Hoock, *Empires of the Imagination: Politics, War and the Arts in the British World, 1750–1850* (London: Profile, 2010), 75–81.

34 Eric Hinderaker, *Boston's Massacre* (Cambridge, MA: Belknap Press, 2019), 221–255.

35 Virginia DeJohn Anderson, *The Martyr and The Traitor: Nathan Hale, Moses Dunbar, and the American Revolution* (Oxford: Oxford University Press, 2019); Mitch Kachun, *First Martyr of Liberty: Crispus Attucks in American Memory* (Oxford: Oxford University Press, 2017); Hinderaker, *Boston's Massacre*, 257–284.

36 Robert N. Bellah, "Civil Religion in America," *Daedalus* 96, no. 1 (1967): 1–21; Jonathan Sheehan, "Sacrifice Before the Secular," *Representations* 105, no. 1 (2009): 12–36.

Chapter Six

FREEBORN GARRETTSON'S REVOLUTION: RELIGION AND THE AMERICAN WAR FOR INDEPENDENCE

Christopher Cannon Jones
Brigham Young University, Provo, Utah

In April 1785, Methodist preacher Freeborn Garrettson penned a letter to John Wesley, recounting his conversion and subsequent ministry. "I have been traveling in your connexion nine years," Garretson wrote. "My lot has mostly been cast in new places to form new circuits, which much exposed me to persecution." Garrettson had been "once … imprisoned; twice beaten; [and] left on the high way speechless and senseless." He was "once shot at; guns and pistols presented at my breast" before being "delivered from [the] armed mob."[1] Garrettson framed the persecution he faced as the timeless lot of true Christians and his deliverance an example of God's mercy. Left unspoken was the revolutionary context in which it occurred.

Freeborn Garrettson converted to Methodism in the summer of 1775 and soon after joined the Methodist ministry. As others his age enlisted in local militias to take up arms in support of the war against Great Britain, the twenty-three year-old Garrettson declared instead his own independence from his Anglican past. Over the course of the next decade, as American colonists and British regulars battled for control of the eastern seaboard, Garrettson traversed the newly independent states in search of lost souls. His travels took him to Virginia, Maryland, Pennsylvania, and Delaware, and then, once the war ended, to Nova Scotia, where he labored primarily among Loyalist exiles.

Garrettson's experiences as an itinerant preacher during and immediately after the Revolutionary War shed light on several aspects of religion and the American Revolution and speak to recent historiographical trends in scholarship on the subject.[2] This essay uses Garrettson to highlight three specific themes: First, Methodists like Garrettson occupied something of a precarious place in the religious landscape of Revolutionary America. Much of the opposition he encountered during his ministry in wartime America resulted from suspicions that Methodist preachers were Loyalists. But Garrettson was no Tory. He described himself as "a professed friend to the American cause," but refused to sign an oath of allegiance on religious principle. All such oaths, he insisted, were "too binding on my conscience" and inappropriate for "ministers of the gospel."[3] Garrettson, then, does not fit easily into the neat categories of "patriot" or "loyalist." Instead, he represents a third group to

A Companion to American Religious History, First Edition. Edited by Benjamin E. Park.
© 2021 John Wiley & Sons, Inc. Published 2021 by John Wiley & Sons, Inc.

whom historians of the American Revolution have recently turned renewed attention: those variously described as *disaffected*, *alienated*, or *neutral*.[4] But even those identifiers fail to capture Garrettson's specifically *religious* justifications for refusing to formally pledge allegiance to the United States.

Garrettson's objection to oaths of allegiance was hardly universal among Methodists during the war, even among Methodist preachers. In addition to revealing something about the nature of individual loyalty and identity during the American Revolution, his experience also points to the ways in which religious institutions adjusted to the new realities of revolutionary America. Following the war's conclusion in 1783, John Wesley reluctantly authorized Methodists in North America — until then a revival movement within the Church of England — to organize themselves into an independent church. Though occasioned by the "very uncommon train of providences" by which "many of the provinces of North America" were "totally disjoined from the British empire," the Methodist Episcopal Church's (MEC) ecclesiastical borders did not immediately align with the newly redrawn national boundaries of the United States. Bishops Francis Asbury and Thomas Coke assumed oversight also of Britain's remaining American colonies, and in 1785 sent Freeborn Garrettson as the first foreign missionary to Nova Scotia.

Garrettson spent two years in Nova Scotia. His time there reveals the difficulties of the arrangement. American preachers faced regular opposition from both rival Protestant clerics (some of whom accused them of preaching little more than republicanism) and Methodists who remained loyal to Great Britain. Garrettson's correspondence with both John Wesley and Francis Asbury while in Nova Scotia further reveals the uneasy alliance between British and American church leaders and foreshadowed the eventual transfer of ecclesiastical oversight for British North America from the MEC to the Wesleyan Methodist Missionary Society in England.

Thirdly, Freeborn Garrettson's ministry points to the religious experience of black Methodists during and after the Revolutionary war. Freeborn Garrettson's first act after converting to Methodism was manumitting the several slaves he inherited from his father, and he took an active interest in the welfare of both free and enslaved African Americans through his life. Over the next decade, he spent extended periods of time ministering to predominantly black audiences. While his role in the conversion of Richard Allen, who would later join Garrettson in the Methodist ministry and eventually found the African Methodist Episcopal Church in Philadelphia, is generally well-known, Garrettson's ministry among black Loyalists in Nova Scotia is less so. The experience of those black Methodists, most of whom would leave North America for Sierra Leone in 1792, provides an interesting comparison to Richard Allen and other free black Methodists in early America. In Sierra Leone, black Methodists asserted their own independence from white oversight, ultimately organizing themselves into the independent West African Methodist Society. The seeds of that independent spirit can be traced partly to Nova Scotia. There, Freeborn Garrettson both empowered black preachers to take charge of congregations across the Maritimes but also insisted on the racial segregation of the Methodist community.

Through the experience of Freeborn Garrettson, then, we see individual and institutional religious identities in flux. In much of the historiography on religion and the American Revolution, Methodists (and Baptists) are portrayed as the inheritors of the Revolution's legacy of disestablishment and religious freedom. Church membership in these evangelically oriented denominations surged in the early American republic, far outpacing their Episcopalian, Congregational, and Presbyterian counterparts. But, as Freeborn Garrettson's story shows, Methodism's rapid growth occurred alongside new divisions within the transatlantic Methodist movement. The Revolutionary War first separated American Methodists from the Church of England, and then, after the war, from British Methodists. Meanwhile, black Methodists throughout the English-speaking Atlantic World sought to lay claim to revolutionary promises of liberty and independence by separating themselves into independent African churches. While evangelical Protestants thus ascended in the wake of the American Revolution, their revolutionary experience was also marked by disruption and division. By the Civil War, Methodism was America's largest Protestant denomination, but also perhaps its least united. The seeds of both that growth and partition can be traced to its Revolutionary experience.

* * *

There was no unified Christian response to the announcement of war between England and several of her North American colonies in 1775. Like Anglicans, Baptists, Congregationalists, and others, Methodists debated the question of revolution. John Wesley's *Calm Address to Our American Colonies* (1775) defended the right of Parliament to tax the colonists and dismissed their claims that they lacked sufficient liberty. Several American Methodists followed Wesley's lead, and most of the preachers dispatched to the colonies in the years leading up to the war returned to England after the outbreak of violence. That group included George Shadford, who submitted a petition to Virginia's legislature in 1776 pledging Methodists' allegiance to the continued establishment of the Church of England in the state — an action viewed as treasonous by many patriots in the state.[5]

Others, including many American-born preachers, sided with the rebelling colonists. William Watters was shocked to hear an Anglican parson in Alexandria, Virginia rebuke Methodists as "a set of Tories, under the cloak of religion" in May 1776. To the parson's charge, Watters responded by demanding proof that Methodists were in any way guilty of activity "unbecoming good Citizens."[6] A year later, a meeting of preachers was interrupted by "a Magistrate" who "presented to us the oath of allegiance, (just published)." William Watters noted that the oath, passed by Virginia's General Assembly in May, "required ministers of every denomination belonging to another state, if they refused taking it, to give bond and security, to leave the state in a given time, or go to Jail." While Watters "had no hesitation in taking it," he noted that others were more hesitant. If the question of war was not necessarily a religious one, that of taking oaths was.

Hollis Hansen, appointed to the Sussex Circuit in southern Virginia, "had some scruples of conscience about taking the test oath" and returned to Maryland. Freeborn Garrettson was similarly reluctant to sign the required oath. Feeling that he "could by no means be subject to my rulers in this respect, as it touched my conscience toward God," Garrettson was left with the option of following Hansen and returning to Maryland or risk arrest in Virginia. "Many of my friends endeavoured to persuade me to comply" in order to avoid jailtime, he noted in his journal. But Garrettson, believing that his "appointment is approved of by my Heavenly Father," refused to leave the state and resigned himself to the threat of imprisonment.

Those threats emerged almost immediately, as Garrettson caught wind of rumors that "several of the rulers bound themselves to put me to gaol." Garrettson was saved by divine intervention. "The Lord laid his afflicting hand on some of those ruling men," he noted, "so that when I went there, several of them had already made their exit off the stage of human action: and another was lying on the point of death." Satisfied that there was none to lay the hand of violence upon me," he now rejoiced that "the persecution from this quarter entirely subsided during my stay in the state." In actuality, the persecution Garrettson courted by his refusal to either take the oath or leave the state was never particularly pronounced in Virginia, and those who took issue with the oath appear to have continued in their labors with little interference.

The relative peace enjoyed by Methodists in Virginia is brought into sharp relief when Garrettson's brief time there is compared with his subsequent travels in his native Maryland, where he returned in 1778, just after that state's "Act for the better security of the Government" went into effect. In contrast to William Watters, who reported that Methodists in Virginia "seldom suffered in either person or property," Garrettson faced near constant danger in neighboring Maryland, where he was threatened with imprisonment twice within a month of his arrival and only barely escaped the efforts of a mob to hang him. Leaving the state in September, Garrettson traveled to Delaware, where he was "also accused of being a friend to King George" and again threatened with violence. Returning to Maryland in November, Garrettson was greeted in Somerset by local authorities "with a writ to take me to goal." Narrowly escaping yet again, the constantly harassed itinerant again left the state, traveling to Philadelphia at Francis Asbury's request to help reorganize the societies there. Upon his return to Maryland in the late fall, Garrettson's hopes for a more peaceful sojourn were quickly dashed.

In early February 1780, Freeborn Garrettson was informed that the county court in Dorchester County had "charged me with toryism." Opting to "withdraw to Mr. A's" for "two days," Garrettson was compelled to return after "a most remarkable vision of the night ... revealed to me what I was to suffer; and that the Lord would stand by me, so that my enemies should not injure me." On Saturday, February 25, after "preach[ing] with freedom to a weeping flock," Garrettson and fellow itinerant preacher Joseph Hartley found themselves surrounded by a large group of men. "They beat my horse, cursed and swore, but did not strike me," recounted Garrettson in his journal. Forcefully taken before James Shaw, a local magistrate Garrettson characterized as "as much my enemy as any of [the mob]," the two men were "committed to goal." In the published edition of his journal, Garrettson claimed their only offense was "the crime ... of preaching the gospel," but court documents make clear that the charges were in response to their refusal to take the test-oath. "By a Certificate transmitted to this Board by James Shaw one of the Justices of the Peace of Dorchester County in the State of Maryland," reads a deposition concerning the arrest, "it appears that F. Garrettson was carried before him as a Disaffected Fugitive from the State of Delaware." "On Examination" by Shaw, Garrettson "acknowledged he had not taken the Oath prescribed by the Act of the General Assembly of Maryland entitled an Act for the better Security of the Government," and on February 27, he was "thrust into prison," where he remained two weeks with "a dirty floor for my bed, my saddle bags for my pillow, and two large windows" left open to let in the cold, late winter winds. Garrettson passed the time reading, corresponding with friends, and preaching to a steady stream of curious visitors.

On March 13, Thomas Hill Airey, the wealthy son of an Anglican cleric, co-signed Garrettson's 20,000£ bond and personally "went to the governor of Maryland" to plead Garrettson's innocence on the grounds that "his residence was in the Dellaware State generally," and that he was not "a Disaffected Fugitive." Airey was successful, and Garrettson was given twenty days to "make his Personal Appearance before the Executive Council of the State of Delaware," and ten additional days to then return to Maryland and present his new credentials. Airey and Thomas White, a respected Delaware judge and Francis Asbury's benefactor and friend, arranged Garrettson's meeting with Delaware officials, and on March 20, he secured a signed statement from Governor Caesar Rodney that "the said Freeborn Garrettson" was "a Preacher among the People called Methodists, who hath a considerable time past resided chiefly in this state, and under its Protection." On April 5, the charges were finally dropped and Garrettson resumed his itinerant duties, though more circumspectly than before.

When Freeborn Garrettson rehearsed his conversion and wartime preaching career to John Wesley in 1785, he downplayed the backdrop of the American Revolution. The persecution he encountered (and his deliverance from it) was an opportunity to emphasize the goodness of God. His short stay in prison was evidence that sometimes believers were called upon to suffer. But Garrettson's experience cannot be understood apart from the Revolution. It speaks to the experiences of those who refused to explicitly align themselves with either side, the men and women whose loyalties over the course of the war remained uncertain. Unlike others, who "found themselves pulled in multiple directions as the war affected their own families, households, and communities," Freeborn Garrettson's refusal to swear an oath of allegiance was based on his unique interpretation of his Christian conversion and his duties and rights as preacher of the gospel.[7] In both Virginia and Maryland, Garrettson refused to sign oaths of allegiance. But the reception his refusal met differed across regions. That reception was shaped by the wartime exigencies of a particular state, but also by Methodism's relative strength in each locale.

* * *

Following the conclusion of the war in 1783, Freeborn Garrettson may have hoped that demands he sign an oath of allegiance were behind him. But he would be called upon once more to do so in 1785. The letter Garrettson wrote Wesley in April that year was sent from Halifax, Nova Scotia, where Garrettson had been assigned at the inaugural conference of the newly formed Methodist Episcopal Church in December 1784. With John Wesley's initially reluctant blessing, Francis Asbury was ordained to superintend the new church with Thomas Coke on Christmas Day. The American itinerants who emerged as important leaders during the war, including Freeborn Garrettson and William Watters, were formally ordained to the ministry and dispatched to preach, organize new societies, and administer church sacraments.

As part of the formal founding of the Methodist Episcopal Church, Coke and Asbury published the first *Discipline* of the new church, an abridgement and revision of John Wesley's "Large Minutes" that established the rules and regulations governing all Methodists. A seemingly small but significant alteration to the minutes came in response to the question, "What may we reasonably believe to be God's Design in raising up the Preachers called *Methodists*?" Where Wesley's *Minutes* answered, "To reform the Nation, particularly the Church; and to spread scriptural holiness over the land," Coke and Asbury's Discipline replied: "To reform the *Continent*, and to spread scriptural Holiness over these *Lands*."[8] Deleted was any reference to the Church of England. Methodists in America were now independent of Anglican oversight. Their responsibility to spread scriptural holiness was aimed not at the English *Nation* and its *land*, but rather the *lands* of the American *Continent*.

The lands that Asbury and Coke set out to reform included not only the thirteen United States, but also those territories along the western frontier and regions of North America further north still controlled by Great Britain, including Nova Scotia, New Brunswick, and Quebec (divided into Upper and Lower Canada in 1791). At the Christmas Conference of 1784, two itinerant preachers were assigned to Nova Scotia: Jesse Cromwell and Freeborn Garrettson, whose tireless preaching during the war had won the trust and admiration of Francis Asbury. Garrettson and Cromwell, assisted by local preachers William Black and John Mann, set out to organize the influx of several hundred Methodists who had arrived as part of the loyalist diaspora. "There seems to be a loud call for the gospel in Halifax, Shelburne, and many other places in Nova Scotia," wrote Garrettson to a friend. "I am willing, and want to go in the power of the blessed Spirit."[9] Their efforts were met with some success, and official membership in Nova Scotia grew to over one thousand by the early 1790s, with thousands more regularly attending Methodist meetings, making the region an unexpected stronghold in the Methodist Episcopal Church's early years.

The growth of Methodism in Nova Scotia occurred as Methodist leaders on both sides of the Atlantic adjusted to the newly independent status of the Methodist Episcopal Church in the United States. Indeed, what occurred in the Maritime (and later, Canadian) provinces of British North America in the decades following the 1784 formation of the MEC was crucial to the development of institutional Methodism and the relationship of Methodists in Britain and America. In Nova Scotia, New Brunswick, and Quebec, Methodists were not "totally disentangled" from either the state or the Church of England, as they now were in the United States. Furthermore, in spite of Wesley's urging American leaders to send preachers to those provinces, it does not appear that he understood those preachers (or those they ministered to) to be outside of his own immediate oversight.

In 1785, shortly after Freeborn Garrettson's arrival in Nova Scotia, Wesley wrote to the American preacher-turned-foreign missionary, expressing his desire that "God may find out a way for you to visit England," which he expected would "be the means of receiving more strength … [and] light." In a later letter, Wesley advised Garrettson to work with Anglicans in the colony. "Wherever there is any church service, I do not approve of any appointment the same hour," he wrote, "because I love the Church of England, and would assist, not oppose it, all I can."[10] Garrettson's responses to Wesley do not reveal his own less-than-enthusiastic feelings about the Church of England (that he regarded Anglicanism as largely a dead form of religion he wisely kept quiet to Wesley). They do, however, reveal a lack of communication and simmering tensions between British and American Methodist leaders. After his petitions for financial assistance from the MEC toward to erection of church buildings in Nova Scotia were rebuffed, Garrettson asked Wesley. He and Methodist merchant Philip Marchington requested 500–600 pounds "to build houses in America." But Wesley likewise demurred, using the opportunity to rib Americans, who he viewed as materialistic and insufficiently attuned to the things of the Spirit. "English Methodists," Wesley wrote, "do not roll in money like many of the American Methodists."[11]

Not content with the rejection, Garrettson appealed further to Wesley for books, tracts, and hymnals. But most pressingly, he requested English preachers be sent. "It is impossible for us to supply half the places where [the people] want us," he wrote to Wesley in April 1786. "I have written to Mr. Asbury for help, but with no certainty of obtaining it, as the work seems to be spreading among them."[12] While Garrettson's request for preachers came in response to the demand for Methodist preaching in the Maritimes, his specific appeal for English preachers came in response to the demands of the Methodist community there. In a letter to Francis Asbury, Garrettson explained that "a number of people would prefer an Englishman to an American," revealing that "many have refused hearing me on this account." While he expressed confidence that "this prejudice would soon wear away," Garrettson and the other Methodist preachers encountered increasing opposition.[13]

Upon his initial arrival in Nova Scotia, Garrettson was summoned to meet with colonial officials and informed it might "be expedient for me to take the oath of allegiance to his majesty." Upon meeting the colony's governor, Garrettson was relieved to learn that "there was not the least necessity" of such a step, and secured promises that "if there should happen any disorders in our meeting, to apply to a magistrate, and I should find favour."[14] As he soon learned, however, not all Nova Scotians agreed with the governor and his secretary.

Much of the opposition Methodists encountered in the Maritimes was theological in nature. While Nova Scotians were largely united politically, they disagreed religiously, competing for converts among the newly-exiled Loyalist population. As in the United States, Baptists, Congregationalists, and Methodists ridiculed and reviled one another's theological particulars. Anglican leaders, meanwhile, sought to secure the region as a Church of England stronghold. In their published and private writings, Methodists were portrayed as not only a religious, but also a political threat. Taking aim at Freeborn Garrettson and his colleagues, they alleged that Methodist missionaries were seeking to spread revolutionary ideals further north.

Leading the charge in leveling those accusations was Jacob Bailey, an Anglican minister in Cornwallis and a Loyalist refugee who had been forced from his home in Maine in 1779. Bitter over his expulsion and the war's outcome and horrified at the success of religious dissenters in Nova Scotia, he launched a number of rhetorical assaults on their legitimacy. Bailey's preferred mode of expression was poetry — biting, satiric verse in the Hudibrastic tradition. Shortly after the arrival of Garrettson and Cromwell in 1785, Bailey began work on an extended narrative poem entitled, "The Adventures of Jack Ramble, the Methodist Preacher." Adding to the poem periodically over the next decade, the result was a thirty-one-book long rhetorical assault on the sect. The poem chronicled the life and misadventures of Jack Ramble, a Revolutionary War drummer-turned-itinerant preach sent to Nova Scotia. Bailey mocked the fictional preacher's humble origins and lack of theological training, as well as Methodism's supposedly unrestrained enthusiasm and rejection of common sense morality and tradition.

Lurking beneath this rather common anti-Methodist polemic, though, were concerns about the political aims of the American preachers in British territories. In one verse, Bailey imagined Methodist leaders telling Jack Ramble their belief that the US "congress ought to reign / O're Britains proud usurped domain. / And, to extend its mighty power / Thro' all the vast Columbian shore." Acting as unsuspecting agents of American empire, the Methodists would "drive the Britons forth / From the cast regions of the north, and "make our states wide as our souls / To grasp in all between the poles." Bailey saw in the MEC's ministerial conferences and councils echoes of earlier Committees of Correspondence used to "muster schism and sedition." And Bailey believed the Maritime colonies served as the front lines of their initial efforts. As one church leader explains to the excited Ramble:

> "With Britons let us then engage
> "And make them feel our vengeful rage;
> "To work their downfall and perdition
> "Arouse them up to mad sedition.
> "Tis our intent first to command
> "New Brunswic and the Acadian land.

In the minds of Jacob Bailey and his fellow Anglican clergy, Methodism's religious and political aims were two sides of the same coin, and the currency was American republicanism.

"The Adventures of Jack Ramble" is both unfinished and undated. A close reading of the text suggests that Bailey began writing in 1786 and penned the last entries approximately a decade later. That timeline coincides almost exactly with the rise and gradual decline of Methodist strength in the Maritimes. Freeborn Garrettson's left Nova Scotia in 1787, and was replaced by William Black in 1789, a local preacher newly ordained and set apart as the general superintendent of eastern British North America. Black's ecclesiastical title points to the unclear place Nova Scotia occupied in the larger Methodist community. Ministers in charge in conferences within the United States were called Presiding Elders. In spite of the fact that Black was ordained by Francis Asbury, he received a title that echoed that initially assumed by Asbury: superintendent.

The title might have been intended to ward off civil and religious leaders in Nova Scotia suspicious of Black's subordination to American Methodists. In 1792, he wrote to Asbury that "put[ting] ourselves under the direction of the American bishops ... would excite the jealousies of our Civil Governors." But with Wesley's continued refusal to send English preachers to North America, Black remained reliant upon the Methodist Episcopal Church for missionaries. At the 1792 MEC Annual Conference in Baltimore, "it was mentioned ... that preachers were wanting as misaneries for several places," including "espesialy" Nova Scotia. Black "spacke very pressive to Conference for preachers," and succeeded in recruiting a few, though "with great reluctance." Nova Scotia's harsh climate and remote location discouraged American preachers from volunteering for the station. So, too, did ongoing international conflict.

As early as 1786, John Wesley expressed his fears of "another American revolution," wondering in a letter to Freeborn Garrettson how it might affect Methodists in Nova Scotia. Those worries accelerated with the outbreak of war between Britain and France in 1793. Isaac Lunsford, one of the American preachers who ("after a fiew Hours consideration & deliberation") agreed to go to Nova Scotia, wrote in his journal on April 19 of that year of "certin news today by a packit from Urope, that war is declared between France & Ingland." He was especially concerned with rumors of a potential "war, between Great Britain and The United States." If that occurred, he confided to his diary, "I cannot stay heare unless They put me like

The People of old, did Jeramiah in Prison." Worse still in Lunsford's mind was the threat of being impressed into the British Navy. "Some friends advised me to be carful in how I walked The streats," he wrote, "for Thare was avery hot press gang going about town."

Lunsford safely return to the US in 1795, avoiding both imprisonment and impressment. He was one of the last American Methodist preachers to undertake an assignment to Nova Scotia. The scarcity of preachers willing to follow in his footsteps led William Black to appeal to British church leaders once more for assistance. This time he was successful, and in 1799 the first English preachers arrived, bringing Nova Scotian Methodism under the umbrella of the British Methodist Church and ending its formal ties with the MEC and American Methodism.

The arrival of Wesleyan missionaries from England did not end the Methodist Episcopal Church's presence in British North America. The Methodist Episcopal Church continued to supply preachers to Upper and Lower Canada into the nineteenth century. But the breakdown of relations between American and English Methodists in Nova Scotia foreshadowed what would also eventually occur further west in Canada. American preachers were expelled from British North America during the War of 1812, and after a brief return following the conclusion of hostilities in 1815, eventually withdrew altogether. The Methodist experience in North America, then, further severed Methodism from its Anglican roots. It also extended tensions between American and British Methodists initiated by the American Revolution.

* * *

At the same time that civil and religious authorities in Nova Scotia accused Methodist missionaries of being agents of American republicanism, Methodists in Virginia faced renewed charges of being "Tools of the British Administration." In several petitions submitted to the Virginia legislature, more than 1,200 Virginians signed their names to documents claiming that Methodists were "Enemies of our Country" and "contemptible Emissaries and Hirelings of Britain." The basis for the charges was an effort by Methodist bishops Francis Asbury and Thomas Coke to introduce gradual emancipation of slaves in the state.[15]

Though the extent of Methodist antislavery efforts in early America are often overstated, there were several Methodists who, motivated by religious principles, manumitted their slaves. Indeed, at the time of his conversion, Freeborn Garrettson's heard a heavenly voice tell him "It is not right for you to keep your fellow creatures in bondage; you must let the oppressed go free." Garrettson's first act following his 1775 conversion was to set free the enslaved women and men he had inherited from his father. Garrettson remained committed to opposing slavery for the remainder of his life, and took a special interest in both the spiritual and temporal welfare of enslaved and free people of color throughout North America.[16]

During his time in both the United States and Nova Scotia, Freeborn Garrettson spent extended periods of time ministering to predominantly black audiences, and played an indirect role in the future formation of not one, but two, independent African Methodist churches. Just months before his 1780 arrest in Maryland, Garrettson preached to several enslaved men and women in the Delaware River Valley, including a recent convert known at the time as "Negro Richard." The enslaved man convinced Methodist preachers to visit his owner, Stokely Sturgis, in the hopes of provoking his own conversion and awakening him to the sin of slaveholding. After "some months" of visiting preachers, Freeborn Garrettson arrived in the fall of 1779, and according to Richard's later account, "preached from these words, 'Thou are weighed in the balance, and art found wanting.'" It was a powerful sermon, likely imbued with the conviction of Garrettson's own history of slave ownership. According to Richard, "after that [Sturgis] could not be satisfied to hold slaves, believing it to be wrong." Rather than immediately manumitting his slaves, however, Sturgis offered to allow them to purchase their freedom for "60£ gold and silver, or $2000 Continental money."[17] After paying off the last installment of the purchase price in 1783, Richard adopted the surname Allen and embarked on his own career as an itinerant preacher. In the years that followed, Richard Allen emerged as the leader of black Methodism and one of the most important black leaders in early America.[18]

Allen and Garrettson's friendship persisted for years to come. In fact, Garrettson played a crucial role in convincing Allen to remain with the Methodist Episcopal Church while serving as Presiding Elder of the church's Philadelphia Conference in 1793, during a period of heightened tensions between black and white Methodists in the city. In an 1805 antislavery pamphlet, Garrettson recalled his relationship with Allen, celebrating him as "a man of note and fortune, and a minister in the African church, in Philadelphia."[19] Though Garrettson worked hard to nurture ties with black Methodists in Philadelphia and elsewhere, Richard Allen and others eventually had enough of unequal treatment in the MEC and white interference with their ecclesiastical affairs. In 1816, they legally incorporated the African Methodist Episcopal (AME) Church, with Allen elected bishop.[20]

Freeborn Garrettson's ministry among black Methodists, though, extended beyond his ties with Allen. When he was appointed to labor in Nova Scotia in 1785, Freeborn Garrettson was surprised to find a thriving black Methodist community in Shelburne and nearby Birchtown, already organized into congregations and classes. The black Methodists had arrived as part of the larger Loyalist diaspora from New York City, where they had sustained Methodism there during Britain's wartime occupation of the city. Most were former slaves from the American South, including a large contingent from Tidewater Virginia who were among the earliest Methodist converts following the arrival of preachers to that region in the early 1770s. Many of Virginia's black Methodists took advantage of Lord Dunmore's 1775 proclamation offering freedom to those "indentured Servants, Negroes, or others" who fled their rebel masters and joined "His Majesty's Troops."[21] A group of more than 100 Tidewater Methodists successfully escaped between 1776 and 1779, eventually ending up in New York, where they were joined by additional black converts from coastal Carolina and the mid-Atlantic states. Most then secured passage to Nova Scotia, where they arrived in August 1784.

The majority of the black Methodists settled in Birchtown, the community set apart for black settlement near Shelburne. Over the next several years, the black Loyalists expanded beyond Nova Scotia's southern shore. When William Black returned in April 1785, he was delighted to find a thriving community of both black and white Methodists. "I preached three times and met two classes," he recorded in his journal on April 17. "The blacks are very lively. O that they might provoke the whites to jealousy, to love and to good works!" The following day in Birchtown, Black "preached to about two hundred negroes" and was pleased to find some "deeply affected, and others greatly comforted." He noted with satisfaction that the black Methodists had appointed among themselves several lay preachers, including Moses Wilkinson, a former Virginia slave left blind and lame after surviving smallpox while enlisted in the British military during the Revolutionary War. "The principal instrument God has employed in this work," Black recorded with surprise, "is a poor negro, who can neither see, walk, nor stand." Wilkinson, assisted by fellow black preachers Luke Jordan and Joseph Brown, had organized fourteen classes in the community, all, according to Black, "in a prosperous state."[22]

None of the black Methodist preachers in Nova Scotia had been ordained. Their standing within the community came rather from a personal sense of divine calling and the consent of their fellow black Methodists. Freeborn Garrettson's introduction to Shelburne and Birchtown's black Methodists in August was noteworthy for two reasons. First, Garrettson lent some institutional legitimacy to the black preachers' authority, recognizing some as class leaders and dispatching others to attend to black settlements elsewhere. Though he stopped short of ordination, Garrettson recognized the benefits of black leaders continuing to lead black classes and congregations. In a letter to Francis Asbury, he acknowledged that the number of black Methodists was so large that "brother Cromwell [the white preacher] was not able to attend them constantly," and enquired with Asbury about the possibility of "sending Harry here this spring."

Harry Hosier, known among white Methodist leaders as "Black Harry," was a free black man and Francis Asbury's longtime traveling companion in the middle Atlantic states. Asbury was reluctant to let him go and declined Garrettson's proposal. Garrettson wisely opted instead to empower those black Methodists already acting as preachers in Nova Scotia.[23]

The decision proved crucial in strengthening and expanding the black Methodist community in Nova Scotia. The 1786 *Minutes* of the Methodist Episcopal Church reported 510 members throughout the colony. Four years later, the number had grown to more than 700. The British Minutes for 1791 recorded 730, including 200 black Methodists. Both figures are much too low, especially the estimated number of black church members. Moses Wilkinson's Birchtown congregation alone numbered at least 200 (and according to Garrettson, "about five hundred in the town" attended his preaching in 1785), to which need to be added more than 60 in the black settlement of Brindleytown and 34 in the "tolerable congregation" in Preston. Several hundred additional black Methodists worshiped in congregations in Shelburne, Halifax, Liverpool, and Saint John, New Brunswick.[24] Moreover, there was significant crossover between black Anglican and Methodist communities in Nova Scotia. In Brindleytown, Anglican Bishop Charles Ingliss accused the black preacher Joseph Leonard of "lean[ing] toward Methodism" in 1791, a move Leonard would later make official. Ingliss was shocked and dismayed to learn that Leonard had begun baptizing prospective converts and administering the sacrament, and rejected the lay preacher's requests for ordination and authorization to form "an entirely independent" congregation "separate from the whites," on the Methodist model.[25]

It was not only in appointing black preachers to leadership roles in their congregations that Freeborn Garrettson encouraged the independence of black Methodists. The very act of segregating Methodist congregations by race was Garrettson's idea. When he arrived in Shelburne in the summer of 1785, black Methodists were initially relegated to gallery seating, much as Richard Allen and black Methodists in Philadelphia were. Garrettson's efforts "to regulate the society," however, included the recommendation that "the blacks of Shelburne buil[d] themselves a little house at the north end of town," where he could preach "to them separately, in order to have more room for the whites."[26] As historians Russell Richey, Kenneth Rowe, and Jean Schmidt concluded, "even the antislavery zealots, like Garrettson, played their part in the qualification of Methodism's tentative egalitarianism."[27] If this policy represented a missed opportunity to racially integrate black and white Methodists, segregated worship services were a resumption of independent meetings held by black Methodists, going back to their time as slaves in Tidewater Virginia and coastal Carolina.

At the same time that American Methodist preachers began to withdraw from Nova Scotia, black Methodists departed the colony en masse, joining more than 1,200 free black Nova Scotians who volunteered to help settle the abolitionist colony of Sierra Leone. Black Methodist independence was further nurtured in their new West African home, as they resented the increasing control white civil and ecclesiastical leaders attempted to exert there. In July 1796, just a few years after Richard Allen and Absalom Jones staged a walkout of St. George's Methodist Episcopal Church in Philadelphia and organized themselves into an independent African Methodist congregation, 128 of their black counterparts in Sierra Leone signed their names to a letter announcing the formation of "The Independent Methodist Church of Freetown." Writing to colonial governor Zachary Macaulay, they declared themselves to be "Dissenters" and, in their own estimation, "a perfect Church" with "no need of the assistance of any worldly power to appoint or perform religious ceremonies for us."[28] It was a radical move, and one with immediate consequences.

The church was short-lived. Most signatories withdrew their names when threatened with treason by governor Macaulay, and the church as an independent entity quickly receded. It nevertheless marks the first attempt by black Methodists anywhere in the world to legally establish a church entirely independent of white oversight. One month later, across the Atlantic Ocean, nine trustees in Philadelphia signed the "Articles of Association of the African

Methodist Episcopal Church." While the Articles provided "that none but coloured persons shall be chosen as trustees of" the AME Bethel Church, it also made clear "that the trustees and members of the African Methodist Episcopal Church do acquiesce in, and accord with the rules of the Methodist Episcopal Church ... and that they and their successors will continue forever in union with the 'Methodist Episcopal Church of Philadelphia.'"[29] As it turned out, that union did not continue forever. After prolonged legal battles, Richard Allen's African Methodist Episcopal Church won its independence from the MEC in 1816. For black Methodists on both sides of the Atlantic, the events of 1796 were only the first efforts in a twenty-plus year struggle for full autonomy.

After retreating from their initial efforts to separate themselves, black believers in Sierra Leone ultimately persisted in their move toward independence. In the immediate wake of Governor Macaulay's threats, Freetown's Methodist community debated how best to proceed. By 1807, they had split into three main factions, with some resuming attendance at Anglican services and relying on those clergymen for marriage, burial, and baptism, even as they regarded "the church of England as bad for them" and refused to "confess its faith." Others reached out to Methodist leaders in London to request missionaries be sent to take charge. A portion of the community, meanwhile, maintained ecclesiastical independence as the preferred path forward. Events came to a head with the back-to-back appointments to Sierra Leone of English Methodist missionary William Davies in 1815 and John Huddleston in 1820. Independent-minded black Methodists were joined by some of their peers who previously pushed for cooperation but now balked under the missionaries' heavy hand. Huddleston attempted to dissolve the society and readmit only those black congregants who recognized his authority. In response, black Methodists physically occupied the local chapel, once more announced their independence from white rule, and eventually won a legal battle granting them control of the chapel. In 1822, just six years after the formation of the AME Church in the United States, Methodists in Sierra Leone organized the West African Methodist Society, a fully independent black Methodist church.[30]

The parallel timelines of the push for institutional independence among black Methodists in North America and Africa is striking, especially in light of the fact that leaders on either side of the Atlantic were almost certainly unfamiliar with the other's specific circumstances. It speaks to the resonances of religious freedom for African-descended peoples throughout the Atlantic world, wrought in part by the American Revolution. It also reveals additional divisions within the transatlantic Methodist community.

* * *

In the spring of 1787, Freeborn Garrettson made his way from Halifax, Nova Scotia to Baltimore, Maryland for the annual Conference of the Methodist Episcopal Church. It was a long journey — nearly a month — undertaken by boat, stage coach, and on horseback. When Garrettson arrived in Baltimore, he expected to "be set apart for the superintendency of the work in Nova Scotia" and the West Indies, a position John Wesley had lobbied for on Garrettson's behalf. But Bishops Asbury and Coke had other plans, and Garrettson's own doubts about his fitness for the position helped persuade him to remain in the United States.

In the published edition of his journal, Garrettson noted that though his "mind was divided," he "concluded not to leave the states." Perhaps because he knew Wesley would read this printed version, Garrettson mentioned nothing of Asbury's involvement in rejecting the appointment. His manuscript diary, however, reveals a more complicated picture. "My mind was under very deep exercises," he confided that evening, "and I was not willing to take that office." Garrettson listed several reasons for his decision, including not being "acquainted with all the preachers especially those who were lately from England" and, tellingly, the admission that "I was not clear that I had a call wholly to leave the states." As if trying to convince himself, Garrettson then wrote: "The Methodists in every part of the world are one. I am not ashamed to own Mr. Wesley under God, as the head and founder of the Methodist Church. I want to do all the good I can. I resign. ... Oh God, stand by thy people." What Garrettson likely realized — indeed, what his time in Nova Scotia had taught him — was that Methodists throughout the world were not *one*. The ideal of a unified, transnational Methodist community led by John Wesley was giving way to divergent Methodist churches in different nations. Though neither Wesley, Garrettson, nor Asbury realized it yet, the movement would also soon divide over racial segregation and strife.

As other recent works have shown, individual lives can illuminate much about religion and the American Revolution, breaking down sweeping generalizations and demonstrating regional differences.[31] Freeborn Garrettson is often held up as the embodiment of early American Methodist ideals: a tireless preacher whose extensive travels helped grow the MEC and symbolized a rejection of traditional forms of religious authority. But his experience also reveals the divisions that accompanied the movement's exponential growth. Those divisions, so often ignored by historians of Methodism, come into clearer focus when we study the movement throughout the Atlantic world and privilege the perspectives of black Methodists. Viewed in this light, the impact of the American Revolution on religion is seen less in the democratization of American Christianity and more in the divisions that followed. Nationalism strained, and in some instances severed, the ties uniting Christians across borders, while racism pushed black believers to separate themselves into independent churches.

Methodism was far from the only religious movement to witness divisions of this sort during the Revolutionary era. The Society for Promoting Christian Knowledge imagined itself as a voluntary organization that could unite Protestants across both geographical and denominational lines, but the American Revolution laid bare the limits of those ideals.[32] White and black Baptists, as well as Anglicans and members of the Countess of Huntingdon's Connexion, likewise migrated as part of the broader Loyalist diaspora and confronted many of the same difficulties as Methodists — something to which recent scholarly reassessments of Loyalism nod.[33] But much more remains to be done analyzing the relationship between the American Revolution and religion. That research can demonstrate not just the Revolution's political and legal impact on the category of religion in the United States, but also the political and religious institutions and individual lives it changed in the British Empire and broader Atlantic World.

FURTHER READING

Andrews, Dee. *The Methodists and Revolutionary America, 1760–1800: The Shaping of an Evangelical Culture*. Princeton: Princeton University Press, 2000.

Byrd, James P. *Sacred Scripture, Sacred War: The Bible and the American Revolution*. New York: Oxford University Press, 2013.

Frey, Sylvia R. and Betty Wood. *Come Shouting to Zion: African American Protestantism in the American South and British Caribbean to 1830*. Chapel Hill: University of North Carolina Press, 1998.

Kidd, Thomas S. *God of Liberty: A Religious History of the American Revolution*. New York: Basic Books, 2010.

Pybus, Cassandra. *Epic Journeys of Freedom: Runaway Slaves of the American Revolutions and Their Global Quest for Liberty*. Boston: Beacon Books, 2006.

Rohrer, R. Scott. *Jacob Green's Revolution: Radical Religion and Reform in a Revolutionary Age*. University Park: Pennsylvania State University Press, 2014.

BIBLIOGRAPHY

Allen, Richard. *The Life, Experience, and Gospel Labours of the Rt. Rev. Richard Allen. To Which is Annexed the Rise and Progress of the African Methodist Episcopal Church in the United States of America*. Philadelphia: Martin & Boden, 1833.

Andrews, Dee. *The Methodists and Revolutionary America, 1760–1800: The Shaping of an Evangelical Culture*. Princeton: Princeton University Press, 2000.

Articles of Assocsiation of the African Methodist Episcopal Church, of the City of Philadelphia, in the Commonwealth of Pennsylvania. Philadelphia: John Ormrol, 1799.

Byrd, James P. *Sacred Scripture, Sacred War: The Bible and the American Revolution.* New York: Oxford University Press, 2013.

David, James Corbett. *Dunmore's New World: The Extraordinary Life of a Royal Governor in Revolutionary America — with Jacobites, Counterfeiters, Land Schemes, Shipwrecks, Scalping, Indian Politics, Runaway Slaves, and Two Illegal Royal Weddings.* Charlottesville: University of Virginia Press, 2013.

Emory, Robert. *History of the Discipline of the Methodist Episcopal Church.* New York: G. Lane and C.B. Tippett, 1845.

Engel, Katherine Carté. "The SPCK and the American Revolution: The Limits of International Protestantism." *Church History* 8, no. 1 (March 2012): 77–103.

Frey, Sylvia R. and Betty Wood. *Come Shouting to Zion: African American Protestantism in the American South and British Caribbean to 1830.* Chapel Hill: University of North Carolina Press, 1998.

Garrettson Family Papers, Methodist Collection — Drew University, Madison, New Jersey.

Garrettson, Freeborn. *A Dialogue Between Do-Justice and Professing Christian.* Wilmington, Delaware: Peter Brynerg, 1805.

Garrettson, Freeborn. *American Methodist Pioneer: The Life and Journals of the Rev. Freeborn Garrettson, 1752–1827.* Edited by Robert Drew Simpson. Rutland: Academy Books, 1984.

Glasson, Travis. "The Intimacies of Occupation: Loyalties, Compromise, and Betrayal in Revolutionary-Era Newport." In *The American Revolution Reborn*, edited by Patrick Spero and Michael Zuckerman, 29–47. Philadelphia: University of Pennsylvania Press, 2016.

Gordon, Sarah Barringer. "The African Supplement: Religion, Race, and Corporate Law in Early National America," *William and Mary Quarterly* 72, no. 3 (July 2015): 385–422.

Grasso, Christopher. *Skepticism and American Faith: From the Revolution to the Civil War.* New York: Oxford University Press, 2018.

Haselby, Sam. *The Origins of American Religious Nationalism.* New York: Oxford University Press, 2015.

Jasanoff, Maya. *Liberty's Exiles: American Loyalists in the Revolutionary Atlantic World.* New York: Alfred A. Knopf, 2011.

Jones, Christopher Cannon. "Methodism, Slavery, and Freedom in the Revolutionary Atlantic, 1770–1820." PhD diss., College of William and Mary, 2016.

Kidd, Thomas S. *God of Liberty: A Religious History of the American Revolution.* New York: Basic Books, 2010.

Knutsford, Viscountess. *Life and Letters of Zachary Macaulay.* London: Edward Arnold, 1900.

Lyerly, Cynthia Lynn. *Methodism and the Southern Mind, 1770–1810.* New York: Oxford University Press, 1998.

Minutes of the Annual Conferences of the Methodist Episcopal Church, for the Years 1773–1828. New York: T. Mason and G. Lane, 1840.

Minutes of the Methodist Conferences. London: John Mason, 1862.

Nelson, John K. *A Blessed Company: Parishes, Parsons, and Parishioners in Anglican Virginia, 1690–1776.* Chapel Hill: University of North Carolina Press, 2001.

Newman, Richard S. *Freedom's Prophet: Bishop Richard Allen, the AME Church, and the Black Founding Fathers.* New York: New York University Press, 2008.

O'Brien, Glen. "John Wesley's Rebuke to the Rebels of British America: Revisiting the Calm Address." *Methodist Review: A Journal of Wesleyan and Methodist Studies* 4 (2012): 31–55.

Pybus, Cassandra. *Epic Journeys of Freedom: Runaway Slaves of the American Revolutions and Their Global Quest for Liberty.* Boston: Beacon Books, 2006.

Richey, Matthew. *A Memoir of the Late Rev. William Black, Wesleyan Minister, Including an Account of the Rise and Progress of Methodism in Nova Scotia.* Halifax: William Cunnabell, 1839.

Richey, Russell E., Kenneth E. Rowe, and Jean Miller Schmidt. *The Methodist Experience in America: A History, Volume 1.* Nashville: Abingdon Press, 2010.

Rohrer, R. Scott. *Jacob Green's Revolution: Radical Religion and Reform in a Revolutionary Age.* University Park: Pennsylvania State University Press, 2014.

Schama, Simon. *Rough Crossings: Britain, the Slaves, and the American Revolution.* New York: Ecco, 2006.

Schmidt, Frederika Teute and Barbara Ripel Wilhelm. "Early Proslavery Petitions in Virginia." *William and Mary Quarterly* 30, no. 1 (January 1973): 133–146.

Straker, Ian B. "Black and White and Gray All Over: Freeborn Garrettson and African Methodism." *Methodist History* 37, no. 1 (October 1998): 18–27.

Sullivan, Aaron. "Uncommon Cause: The Challenges of Disaffection in Revolutionary Pennsylvania." In *The American Revolution Reborn*, edited by Patrick Spero and Michael Zuckerman, 48–67. Philadelphia: University of Pennsylvania Press, 2016.

Walker, James W. St. G. *The Black Loyalists: The Search for a Promised Land in Nova Scotia and Sierra Leone.* Toronto: University of Toronto Press, 1992.

Watters, William. *A Short Account of the Christian Experience and Ministerial Labours, of William Watters, Drawn up by Himself.* Alexandria: S. Snowden, 1805.

Wesley, John. *The Works of John Wesley.* Oxford: Clarendon Press, 1975–1983; Nashville: Abingdon Press, 1984–.

Wigger, John W. *American Saint: Francis Asbury and the Methodists.* New York: Oxford University Press, 2009.

Williams, Jeffrey. *Religion and Violence in Early American Methodism: Taking the Kingdom by Force.* Bloomington: Indiana University Press, 2010.

Wood, Gordon S. "Religion and the American Revolution." In *New Directions in American Religious History*, edited by Harry S. Stout and D.G. Hart, 173–205. New York: Oxford University Press, 1997.

NOTES

1   Freeborn Garrettson to John Wesley, April 20, 1785, Garrettson Family Papers, Methodist Collection — Drew University, Madison, New Jersey (hereafter DUL).

2   Much of the historical literature on religion and the American Revolution has focused on either the religious contributions (or lack thereof) to revolutionary ideology and organizing or the legacies of the Revolution on disestablishment and religious freedom. For a helpful overview of those interpretations, see Gordon S. Wood, "Religion and the American Revolution," in *New Directions in American Religious History*, ed. by Harry S. Stout and D.G. Hart (New York: Oxford University Press, 1997), 173–205. This essay follows more recent work in considering what a single individual or institution's experience in Revolutionary American can tell us about religion. It focuses less on the religious causes of revolution and more on the ways in which the revolution shaped religious experience.

3   Garrettson, *Experience and Travels*, 25, 67, 82, 144; "Thomas White Kent Co. Delaware State Deposition — 19 Feb. 1780;" "Freeborn Garretson's Bond to the State of Maryland — 13 March 1780;" "Cesar Rodney, Dover, Delaware State Certificate — 20 March 1780, 5 Apr. 1780," Appendix One in Garrettson, *American Methodist Pioneer*, 404–405.

4   See, for example, Travis Glasson, "The Intimacies of Occupation: Loyalties, Compromise, and Betrayal in Revolutionary-Era Newport" and Aaron Sullivan, "Uncommon Cause: The Challenges of Disaffection in Revolutionary Pennsylvania," in *The American Revolution Reborn*, ed. Patrick Spero and Michael Zuckerman (Philadelphia: University of Pennsylvania Press, 2016), 29–47, 48–67.

5   On Wesley's *Calm Address*, see Glen O'Brien, "John Wesley's Rebuke to the Rebels of British America: Revisiting the Calm Address," *Methodist Review: A Journal of Wesleyan and Methodist Studies* 4 (2012): 31–55 and Jeffrey Williams, *Religion and Violence in Early American Methodism: Taking the Kingdom by Force* (Bloomington: Indiana University Press, 2010), 43–55.

6   William Watters, *A Short Account of the Christian Experience, and Ministereal Labours, of William Watters, Drawn up by Himself* (Alexandria: S. Snowden, 1806), 48–52. Anglican Parson Townshend Dade served in Fairfax Parish in Alexandria from 1765–1778. He also served on the Fairfax Committee of Safety. See John K. Nelson, *A Blessed Company: Parishes, Parsons, and Parishioners in Anglican Virginia, 1690–1776* (Chapel Hill: University of North Carolina Press, 2001), 307. For more on Methodist responses to the Revolutionary War, see Dee E. Andrews, *The Methodists and Revolutionary America, 1760–1800: The Shaping of an Evangelical Culture* (Princeton: Princeton University Press, 2000) and Christopher Cannon Jones, "Methodism,

Slavery, and Freedom in the Revolutionary Atlantic, 1770–1820," PhD Diss. (College of William and Mary, 2016), 23–28.

7 Glasson, "The Intimacies of Occupation," 31.

8 Robert Emory, *History of the Discipline of the Methodist Episcopal Church* (New York: G. Lane and C.B. Tippett, 1845), 27. See also Sam Haselby, *The Origins of American Religious Nationalism* (New York: Oxford University Press, 2015), 126–127.

9 Freeborn Garrettson to "Dear Brother," undated, in Garrettson, *American Methodist Pioneer*, 243–244. On Garrettson's time in Nova Scotia, see Robert Drew Simpson, "Biographical Essay," in Garrettson, *American Methodist Pioneer*, 7–9.

10 Wesley to Garrettson, 26 June 1785; Wesley to Garrettson, 30 November 1786, in Telford, *Letters*, 7:276, 354.

11 Wesley to Garrettson, 26 June 1785, in Telford, *Letters*, 7:276. Garrettson to Wesley, 25 April 1786, Garrettson Family Papers, DUL. Transcriptions of both letters are included in *American Methodist Pioneer*, 245–247.

12 Garrettson to Wesley, 25 April 1786, Garrettson Family Papers, DUL.

13 Garrettson to Asbury, 1786, Garrettson Family Papers, DUL. Reprinted in Garrettson, *American Methodist Pioneer*, 251.

14 Garrettson to Coke, Halifax, 1785, Garrettson Family Papers, DUL. Reprinted in Garrettson, *American Methodist Pioneer*, 243. See also Garrettson to Coke, undated, Garrettson Papers, DUL.

15 Amelia County Petition, 10 November 1785; Lunenberg County Petition, 29 November 1785, both in Legislative Petitions of the General Assembly, Library of Virginia, Richmond, Virginia. See also Frederika Teute Schmidt and Barbara Ripel Wilhelm, "Early Proslavery Petitions in Virginia," *William and Mary Quarterly* 30, no. 1 (January 1973): 133–146.

16 Garrettson, *American Methodist Pioneer*, 48. On early Methodist antislavery, see Cynthia Lynn Lyerly, *Methodism and the Southern Mind, 1770–1810* (New York: Oxford University Press, 1998), 119–145 and Jones, "Methodism, Slavery, and Freedom," 61–161.

17 Richard Allen, *The Life, Experience, and Gospel Labours of the Rt. Rev. Richard Allen. To Which is Annexed the Rise and Progress of the African Methodist Episcopal Church in the United States of America* (Philadelphia: Martin & Boden, 1833), 7.

18 Richard S. Newman, *Freedom's Prophet: Bishop Richard Allen, the AME Church, and the Black Founding Fathers* (New York: New York University Press, 2008).

19 Freeborn Garrettson, *A Dialogue Between Do-Justice and Professing Christian* (Wilmington, Delaware: Peter Brynerg, 1805), 35–36. On Garrettson as Presiding Elder in Philadelphia, see John Wigger, *American Saint: Francis Asbury and the Methodists* (New York: Oxford University Press, 2009), 250. See also Ian B. Straker, "Black and White and Gray All Over: Freeborn Garrettson and African Methodism," *Methodist History* 37, no. 1 (October 1998): 18–27.

20 Newman, *Freedom's Prophet*. See also Sarah Barringer Gordon, "The African Supplement: Religion, Race, and Corporate Law in Early National America," *William and Mary Quarterly* 72, no. 3 (July 2015): 385–422.

21 *Virginia Gazette*, 24 November 1775. On the background of Dunmore's Proclamation, see James Corbett David, *Dunmore's New World: The Extraordinary Life of a Royal Governor in Revolutionary America—with Jacobites, Counterfeiters, Land Schemes, Shipwrecks, Scalping, Indian Politics, Runaway Slaves, and Two Illegal Royal Weddings* (Charlottesville: University of Virginia Press, 2013), 94–110.

22 Matthew Richey, *A Memoir of the Late Rev. William Black, Wesleyan Minister, Including an Account of the Rise and Progress of Methodism in Nova Scotia* (Halifax: William Cunnabell, 1839), 128–129.

23 Garrettson to Asbury, 1786, Garrettson Family Papers, DUL. Reprinted in Garrettson, *American Methodist Pioneer*, 251. On Harry Hosier, See Wigger, *American Saint*, 149–150.

24 Garrettson, *American Methodist Pioneer*, 128. *Minutes of the Annual Conferences of the Methodist Episcopal Church, for the Years 1773–1828* (New York: T. Mason and G. Lane, 1840), 26, 43; *Minutes of the Methodist Conferences* (London: John Mason, 1862), 1:252. A conservative estimate of 350 for Nova Scotia Methodism's total black membership during the late 1780s would still place it among the largest black Methodist communities in the MEC at the time. The Birchtown congregation alone was larger than the total black membership of Methodist churches in

Philadelphia and New York, and roughly equal to that of Baltimore. See *Minutes of the Annual Conferences*, 47.

25   Charles Ingliss Journal, September 1791, as cited in James W. St. G. Walker, *The Black Loyalists: The Search for a Promised Land in Nova Scotia and Sierra Leone* (Toronto: University of Toronto Press, 1992), 68–69.

26   Garrettson, *Experience and Travels*, 206.

27   Russell E. Richey, Kenneth E. Rowe, and Jean Miller Schmidt, *The Methodist Experience in America: A History, Volume 1* (Nashville, Tennessee: Abingdon Press, 2010), 60.

28   "The Independent Methodist Church in Freetown to the Governor and Council (11 July 1796)," in Viscountess Knutsford, *Life and Letters of Zachary Macaulay* (London: Edward Arnold, 1900), 145–146.

29   *Articles of Assocsiation of the African Methodist Episcopal Church, of the City of Philadelphia, in the Commonwealth of Pennsylvania* (Philadelphia: John Ormrol, 1799), 6, 8.

30   Walker, *The Black Loyalists*, 293–95; Jones, "Methodism, Slavery, and Freedom," 202–259.

31   See, for example, R. Scott Rohrer, *Jacob Green's Revolution: Radical Religion and Reform in a Revolutionary Age* (University Park: Pennsylvania State University Press, 2014) and Christopher Grasso, *Skepticism and American Faith: From the Revolution to the Civil War* (New York: Oxford University Press, 2018), 25–158. In addition to biographies and microhistories, scholars have recently devoted attention to the contested nature of religious texts during the American Revolution, to fruitful effect. See James P. Byrd, *Sacred Scripture, Sacred War: The Bible and the American Revolution* (New York: Oxford University Press 2013) and *Eran Shalev, American Zion: The Old Testament as a Political Text from the Revolution to the Civil War* (New Haven, Connecticut: Yale University Press, 2014), 15–49.

32   See Katherine Carté Engel, "The SPCK and the American Revolution: The Limits of International Protestantism," *Church History* 81:1 (March 2012): 77–103. The 2012 article is part of Carté's forthcoming book, *Religion and the American Revolution: An Imperial History* (Chapel Hill and Williamsburg: University of North Carolina Press for the Omohundro Institute of Early American History and Culture, forthcoming).

33   See, for example, Maya Jasanoff, *Liberty's Exiles: American Loyalists in the Revolutionary Atlantic World* (New York: Alfred A. Knopf, 2011), Cassandra Pybus, *Epic Journeys of Freedom: Runaway Slaves of the American Revolutions and Their Global Quest for Liberty* (Boston: Beacon Books, 2006), and Simon Schama, *Rough Crossings: Britain, the Slaves, and the American Revolution* (New York: Ecco, 2006).

Chapter Seven

THE FIRST WALL OF SEPARATION BETWEEN CHURCH AND STATE: SLAVERY AND DISESTABLISHMENT IN LATE-EIGHTEENTH-CENTURY VIRGINIA

Sarah Barringer Gordon
University of Pennsylvania, Philadelphia, Pennsylvania

In the spring of 1785, a traveling Methodist minister preached against slavery in the Virginia countryside. It was a momentous occasion, pitting British native and newly minted Methodist bishop Dr. Thomas Coke against a group of lay Virginians gathered to hear the Gospel. Coke condemned slaveholding as unchristian and urged his audience to manumit their slaves. Many stalked out of Brother Martin's barn, vowing to "flog" Coke as soon as he emerged. "A high-headed Lady" egged them on, Coke reported, promising "fifty pounds, if they would give that little Doctor one hundred lashes." The threat came to naught finally, but the danger was palpable. The crowd dispersed only after Martin, who was the local justice of the peace as well as a Methodist convert, cornered the ringleader and talked him down. Yet neither Coke nor his opponents were willing to back down. As Coke's reputation for antislavery preaching spread, doors were shut against him, he was formally indicted for sedition, and at least one plot to murder him got underway.[1]

Coke's campaign in Virginia had consequences that change our understanding of religious liberty. We are used to thinking of separation of church and state as a great stride forward. And it certainly protected freedom of conscience. But there was a heavy price attached to such liberty: it protected slavery. By separating religion from politics, Virginians silenced antislavery preaching. The story is full of twists and turns, but the connection of spiritual freedom to physical bondage emerges clearly from the record. This was not only an aspect of American freedoms limited to white people, it was a means of maintaining and strengthening slavery.

Widespread resistance to Coke's antislavery message emerged just as the more elite political movement for disestablishment gained steam. Methodism was traditionally a branch of the Church of England. Coke, an ordained minister in the King's Church, may have thought of himself as representing a new faith. But to most Virginians, he was suspect. They connected both Coke and antislavery to a British plot to steal American property and recolonize the new United States. We have long known of James Madison's 1785 "Memorial and Remonstrance" against religious establishment.[2] And some scholars of early national Virginia

A Companion to American Religious History, First Edition. Edited by Benjamin E. Park.
© 2021 John Wiley & Sons, Inc. Published 2021 by John Wiley & Sons, Inc.

have studied the petitions that poured in from religious groups in favor of disestablishment in late 1785, while others have read the proslavery petitions from the same period. But we have not yet connected proslavery to support for separation of church and state and to the charge that both antislavery and religious establishment were fundamentally British in nature. For the most part, this story has lain just outside the historian's gaze.

Thomas Jefferson, whose Bill for Establishing Religious Freedom was enacted in early 1786, later described disestablishment in Virginia as erecting "a wall of separation between Church & State." Precisely what lived on either side of the wall he left unsaid, but it bears scrutiny, especially because the wall that white Virginians built became iconic. Separation of church and state has become a central pillar of American freedoms, first proposed in Congress by James Madison in 1789 and memorialized in the First Amendment to the national Constitution. Virginia's role in setting the example for how to do church and state has figured large in Supreme Court jurisprudence as well as historical scholarship. The roots of disestablishment in Virginia thus deserve our attention, because they are still important elements of American constitutional, political, and religious life.

The groundswell of popular reaction against Coke is documented in more than a hundred petitions submitted to the Virginia General Assembly, which record the convergence of proslavery attitudes and support for disestablishment.[3] The story is bracketed by the work of two clerics: one, the British Methodist Thomas Coke, and the other, William Graham, a Presbyterian minister who became Coke's nemesis. Both men shifted their positions in response to the outcry over slavery. They learned that popular sentiment among white Virginians overwhelmingly supported slavery, and that religious leaders — if they wanted to succeed — would do well to adjust their perspective to suit their congregants. Separation of church and state became politically popular among everyday Virginians, especially proslavery evangelicals, who were convinced in the 1780s that slavery and disestablishment were both mandated by their Christian faith.

* * *

By the time he toured Virginia in 1785, Coke was no stranger to controversy (Figure 1). Born into a wealthy family in 1747, Coke attended Oxford at age sixteen, where he earned a doctorate in law. This legal training proved useful, especially but not only in America. In appearance, Coke was "cherubic": small of stature and round of form, with waving hair and chubby cheeks. Despite his innocent appearance, Coke was ambitious: he dreamed of a bishop's mitre and was willing to betray his friends to get it.

When he was exposed to Methodism in his early twenties, Coke became Methodist founder John Wesley's trusted confidant. In September 1784, Wesley secretly ordained Coke as superintendent (a title later changed at Coke's urging to bishop, a move that horrified Wesley) of the rapidly growing church in America. Wesley was apparently persuaded by Coke that the new United States deserved a separate church. Coke seized the day and was rewarded with a plum post. A firestorm of protest followed. His enemies charged Coke with using undue influence over the senile Wesley.

Coke sailed for North America only two weeks after his ordination. He arrived in time to join fellow Englishman and longtime American resident Francis Asbury in Baltimore in late December for the Christmas Conference. There Coke consecrated Asbury as a second superintendent, and they began the work that established the new American Methodist Church. Then Coke left with Asbury for the preaching tour that caused so much strife.[4]

Unfortunately for him, Coke embodied much of what made Americans suspicious of British interlopers in the affairs of the new nation. His journals from his travels through Virginia are sprinkled with stories of mobs that "came to meet me with staves and clubs." He described deciding (when he learned of the staves and clubs) that he did not need to address slavery that day.

But Coke also found support for his anti-slavery crusade. The newly formed Methodist Episcopal Church formally submitted his petition against slavery to the Virginia General Assembly in November 1785, at the same time that pro-disestablishment and proslavery petitioning also were at their most intense. Coke's petition called for emancipation in dramatic terms: "the Interest of Religion, the honour & real Interests of the State, and the Welfare of Mankind do unanswerably, incontroulably plead for the Removal of this grand Abomination." With Coke's petition, the Methodists demonstrated that evangelical preachers could be expert at legal maneuvering. Coke was an old hand at petitioning for Methodist causes in Britain.[5]

Indeed, Coke brought powerful arguments based in Christian evangelism to Virginia. In early May 1785, he drafted the antislavery petition. Copies were carried around the commonwealth that spring and summer by itinerant Methodist preachers. The petition emphasized Coke's claim that those who kept slaves denied them access to the Gospel. The effect of slavery, Coke claimed, was contrary to the fundamental work of Christianity, because it prevented conversion among enslaved persons.[6] In this view, slaveholders were not true Christians. This argument was more biting than the familiar debate over whether conversion to Christianity should alter a slave's civil status. He argued instead that slaveholding altered the master's religious status, transforming him into an enemy of the Gospel.

Coke's boldness infuriated his proslavery opponents. If such convictions were spread as religious truth in the fast-growing Methodist faith in America, then the threat was dire. Further, Coke's manners added insult to injury. His petition argued that emancipation was justified in part because "the Oppression exercised over [slaves] exceeds the Oppression formerly exercised by Great Britain over these States."[7]

Coke mistook his ground and stirred up a hornet's nest. But he learned this lesson only after designing an emancipation regime for his charges in the New World. Among the denomination's first acts after its formation was to craft a governing Book of Discipline. Included were provisions that built on Virginia's manumission law of 1782. The discipline specified the age at which slaves must be manumitted as well as formal procedures for doing so. In effect, Coke translated a permissive Virginia law into mandatory rules for Methodists, who must free their slaves or be denied communion and eventually expelled. Members in Virginia were given two years to comply. But any Methodist buying or selling a slave was to be excluded immediately, no matter where he was located.[8]

Coke's attack on slavery unsettled Christians in ways that Enlightenment principles could not. Brother Martin, for example, emancipated fifteen slaves, and another congregant who had attended the sermon in Martin's barn was "so affected … that he came to Brother Martin and desired him to draw up a proper instrument for the emancipation of his eight slaves." And a few days earlier, "a dying friend" had asked Coke to draw up his will, which manumitted eight slaves. After the uproar at Martin's barn, Coke noted that "Brother Ragland" had also freed his slave (a Reuben Ragland freed Cain in 1785).[9]

Slaveholding elites condemned Coke, of course, but the little Doctor also ran into resistance from Methodist preachers, many of whom dreaded the reaction of the laity. Even Coke's fellow superintendent Francis Asbury was worried. But Coke would not bend. Both clergy and laity eventually moved against him, and Coke acknowledged the wisdom of suspending the rule against slaveholding in the summer of 1785, "on account of the great opposition that had been given it."[10]

But the effects of Coke's antislavery tour were unstoppable. On a return voyage to America in 1787, he conceded that it had been "ill-judged of me to deliver [antislavery views] from the pulpit." This position, of course, was the key — he had used his standing as a preacher to lecture free Virginians on what (they were coming to believe) was a civil, political matter only. Religion, especially worship, was to be directed elsewhere, he was instructed. Coke internalized this lesson so completely that he soon assured Caribbean planters that Methodist

Figure 7.1 *Thomas Coke* (1799), by Henry Edridge. Thomas Coke (1747–1814) is known today as the founder of the Methodist missionary movement. Less well known is the reaction to his antislavery preaching tour around Virginia in 1785, which earned him an indictment for sedition and violent threats from his hearers on many occasions. Courtesy of the National Portrait Gallery, London.

missionaries would induce docility among enslaved converts. Then he praised the treatment of slaves on Grenada, and — even more shocking — in 1791, he purchased slaves (between six and ten, according to an exposé published by a vocal opponent) to work fields donated to the church on St. Vincent. Coke claimed that he had been assured that slaves on the Methodist plantation "would certainly be treated by us in the tenderest manner." As soon as he left the island, however, Coke said he regretted the purchase and arranged for the slaves' emancipation. But excuses did not save him from charges of rank hypocrisy.[11]

Coke's most powerful opponent was the Presbyterian divine William Graham, a hatchet-faced man, thin, and taller than Coke. His temper was dictatorial and resentful, his "choleric disposition" explained as a consequence of (or, one wonders, perhaps the cause of) an unhappy marriage. His Scotch-Irish parents had migrated to Pennsylvania, and Graham grew up on a farm near Paxton. His family were lettered just enough to read the Bible, making Graham's education at Princeton a notable attainment. Graham's lifelong hatred of the British and distrust of secular government reflected his family roots. His support of vigilante movements, including the Paxton Boys in the 1760s (and their successors in the Whiskey Rebellion of the mid-1790s), demonstrated his sympathy for populist politics. Graham joined the flood of Pennsylvania Presbyterians who migrated to Virginia. Thanks to Princeton president John Witherspoon's courting of elite southern and Caribbean families, slaveholding students became a majority under his leadership, and the college forged deep ties to white southern culture. A significant number of Graham's fellow Princetonians from Pennsylvania migrated to Virginia and the Carolinas, where many adapted to southern ways. Graham followed suit and came to the Valley of Virginia at the invitation of Princeton classmates in 1774. There he undertook to minister to two churches, but his sermons were dull and monotonous. Instead, Graham's efforts as a schoolmaster were lasting. He also became a slaveholder.[12]

Like Coke, William Graham shifted in response to the laity. Graham's Presbyterians also created an American branch in the mid-1780s. Virginia Presbyterians opposed claims that Christian doctrine or scripture could be "perverted" to an antislavery mandate. They led the twin movements in favor of slavery and against establishment.[13] The end of the story is well known. In early 1786, the Virginia General Assembly passed a statute introduced years earlier by Thomas Jefferson. The change in support for the measure was rapid. Enactment of Jefferson's Bill for Establishing Religious Freedom, complete with soaring invocations of liberty from coercion of the mind and a mandate for complete separation of church and state, would have been surprising even a year earlier. The shift of opinion in 1785 makes sense when it is situated in a broader perspective of Virginia's dense politics of religion and slavery. We turn now to the political arena, where religious freedom had been raised before, but had a checkered history.

* * *

In 1784, postwar crises prompted the General Assembly to address lingering questions of church and state that had been raised during the Revolution but only partially answered. A widely noted decline in religious life — amid other worries such as the bankruptcy of great estates, the falling price of tobacco, the manumission of slaves, and renewed (often virulent) anti-British sentiment — concerned many Virginians. Action on support for religion seemed more plausible in such troubled times.[14]

This was a renewed effort. Its roots lay in the late colonial and Revolutionary periods. Virginia's establishment had been powerful, but it was also localized and controlled by lay-men. Religious governance was in the hands of each parish's vestrymen, the elite men who ran the colony's religious as well as political and economic life. At the inaugural session of the House of Delegates in 1776, patriotic vestrymen struggled to cut the cord to the Church of England without killing the church in Virginia. They compromised, protecting dissenters but eliding the issue of establishment. The Virginia Declaration of Rights stated boldly that "all men are equally entitled to the free exercise of religion."[15]

Freedom of practice was a significant advance. Before the Revolution, the gentry prohib-ited preaching -- especially to slaves -- by dangerous dissenters, including both Baptists and Presbyterians. But by 1776, dissenters could point to their patriotism in spite of the treat-ment they had received. They were rewarded not only with the Declaration of Rights but also with statutory protection against forced taxation to support the "church as by law estab-lished" (but only on a year-to-year basis).[16]

Dissenters were not the only problem for the Mother Church. The 1772 *Somerset* case involved the freedom suit of a slave, James Somerset, who was brought by his owner from Virginia to Britain. The case inaugurated a pitched battle among Anglican churchmen over the legitimacy of slavery. In America, planters worried that slavery would be endangered by British judges and bishops. A bitter Thomas Jefferson complained that the British king was the true villain because he had imposed slavery on Virginia and now was "now exciting those very people [slaves] to rise in arms among us, and to purchase that liberty of which *he* has deprived them, by murdering the people upon whom *he* also obtruded them."[17]

The long War for Independence further undermined the desirability of protecting the king's church and suppressing dissenters in Virginia. Presbyterians' support for the Revolution allowed them to indulge long-standing Scotch-Irish hatred of the king and his church. William Graham, for example, rashly volunteered for military service, declaring that the war was as much religious as political. He was censured by the presbytery and never saw action, but he always bragged about being a warrior for Christ in the Revolution.[18] Methodists were surprising winners, too. The storied Methodist itinerants surged into newly opened ground for evangelizing. Virginia saw enormous growth among Methodists, from just 291 in 1774 to over 3,400 in 1777, and then from about 6,100 in 1778 to 13,740 in 1783. Throughout that period, more than half of American Methodists, and often 60 percent of ministers, were in Virginia.[19] The spectacular Methodist growth in Revolutionary and early national Virginia just deepened the crisis of the established church.[20]

By the mid-1780s, the old suspicions of evangelicals had eased, but anti-British sentiment revived notably after the end of the Revolutionary war in 1783. In 1785, the new American Methodist Church entered a confused and uncertain climate for religious institutions, especially those (like the Methodists) descended from the Church of England. Neither the 1776 state constitution nor the Virginia General Assembly had addressed the establishment. The legislature did not cede the power to govern the established church, including times and places of worship, the content of liturgy, and the licensing of clergy. In other words, the grant of free exercise did not extend to the Mother Church. Adding to the pain, the General Assembly at every session through 1779 quietly extended the suspension of tax support for established clergy but did nothing more.[21]

The Mother Church suffered mightily throughout the Revolutionary era. Vulnerable clerics fled, died, or whined about their poverty. In 1774 there were ninety-five primary parishes in Virginia as well as the seminary at William and Mary. After the Revolution, active parishes had fallen by more than half. Jefferson eliminated the theological faculty at the college in 1779, so that the church had no place to train replacements. Only twenty-eight of ninety-one parish priests in 1776 were still in Virginia in 1784. Buildings suffered as well. Twenty-three parishes were destroyed entirely, and many others were damaged and looted.

Antislavery forces within the Church of England also grew louder in the 1780s.[22] This was already a sore point: the British army's recruitment of runaway slaves had outraged Patriots. In 1786 Jefferson estimated that in Virginia 30,000 slaves had escaped to the British during the Revolution. He exaggerated, but he did so strategically. Like other Virginians, Jefferson was in debt to British creditors and claimed that he should not have to repay. He had suffered financially from slave escapes, he stressed, and the British refused to return fugitive slaves.[23]

In the early years of the Revolution, Methodists had stood by their more orthodox Anglican brethren, arguing in favor of the establishment. By 1785, however, the worm had turned. Now, Coke claimed the Revolution had "broken the antichristian union which before subsisted between Church and State." Beleaguered Anglican churchmen claimed that Methodists were conspiring to steal their congregants and churches. The General Assembly, however, showed signs of sympathy in late 1784. In addition to the elite's economic woes, the reduction in ministers meant that learned clergy (many of whom had run schools) were scarce on the ground, and the decay in moral life seemed to many leading Virginians to be traceable to the decline in Christian observance. Looting of churches also made for an embarrassing spectacle. The House of Delegates resolved in November 1784 that there ought to be a "moderate tax or contribution annually for the support of the Christian religion." Memorials in support poured in from around the commonwealth. Patrick Henry followed up with a general assessment bill in December. This proposal promised peace and stability, because individual taxpayers could choose which church to support.[24]

In this atmosphere, William Graham and several other Presbyterian leaders in Virginia were drawn to the general assessment bill. Like Henry, Graham was dismayed by deism among the elite. When the Presbytery of Hanover met in October 1784, Graham and a fellow minister were charged with preparing a memorial to represent the views of Presbyterian churchmen. The result was approval of the assessment bill, if "done on the most *liberal plan*" — that is, without dictating times and modes of worship or articles of faith (all features of the pre-Revolutionary establishment). It is worth noting, moreover, that Graham's income had suffered drastically during the war, and he longed for a respectable living. Presbyterian churchmen abhorred both the Anglicans and the "ignorant ... Sectaries" in equal measure, but some among them were also concerned with guaranteeing their salaries.[25]

Unexpectedly, Henry's bill unleashed a torrent of opposition starting in the spring of 1785. For one thing, thanks particularly to Methodists' efforts, it became evident on a careful reading of the proposal that Henry's law could result in taxes flowing to antislavery preachers. Taxpayers could direct their funds to a Christian minister of their choice, so that opponents of slavery would have the option of designating an abolitionist preacher. Because many churchmen had shown themselves unreliable on slavery, moreover, a recipient of tax funds might thereafter embrace abolition, in defiance of his congregation (perhaps, as with the Methodists, at the behest of denominational superiors). Preachers, it seemed by the mid-1780s, could not be trusted on this crucial question.[26]

Coke's antislavery petition and his sermons cemented the connection. Although his petition was not submitted formally to the legislature until the late fall, reaction against the Methodists began soon after Coke sent it out in May. Over the summer, the preparation of proslavery petitions outpaced the itinerants. These new petitions rested on religious justifications for slavery and drew on claims that the Revolution was fought to vindicate slaveholding property rights in the eyes of God. When Methodists called for emancipation in religious as well as political language, therefore, their proslavery opponents answered them in the same register.[27]

Equally important, by the spring of 1785, Presbyterian laymen and some ministers had begun to oppose their leaders. Critics of the pro-assessment petition aired their grievances in the press and on the floor the legislature. James Madison reflected with satisfaction that the Presbyterian clergy now went in "*fear of their laity.*" Graham and others who supported assessment, Madison wrote to Jefferson, had been schooled by "fermentation below the Mountains & a violent [explosion] beyond them." On the ground, where Virginians lived, support for separation and support for slavery traveled hand in glove.

The Hanover Presbytery unanimously rejected any measure that would free the clergy from the oversight of laity in May 1785, only six months after their ministers' memorial in favor of the general assessment. Graham promptly changed in response and was once again chosen to write to the General Assembly. Now he composed a full-throated call for disestablishment. In August 1785 at Bethel Church, assembled delegates approved Graham's draft, which complained that Henry's bill would oppress Presbyterians by asserting "Supremacy in Spirituals as well as Temporals." Submission to taxation in favor of religion, "would be a fatal symptom of abject slavery in us, were we to submit to the usurpation." Presbyterians thus drew the line between religion and politics (and spiritual and secular realms) that also emerged in debates over slavery in 1785.

Graham's new petition produced an outpouring of support among Presbyterians. Twenty-two separate petitions, all of which endorsed the Bethel petition, were filed shortly after Graham's petition was submitted in early November. The size of this effort has rested out of sight, likely because many of the petitions were misfiled. Twelve petitions, the largest of which had 146 signatories, are simply included with other files for November 12 and 18, 1785, and have apparently escaped notice. Including them brings the total of religious petitions to 101 and clarifies the importance of Presbyterian efforts. Among religious groups Presbyterians accounted for more than 75 percent of all memorials to the legislature.[28] Graham himself signed a petition in support of the petition he had drafted, dated August 25, 1785, and submitted to the legislature on November 12.[29]

The petitions' religious arguments in favor of slavery were the mirror image of those for disestablishment. They argued that the Bible dictated that slavery was a political (not religious) status and that religious arguments against slavery thus violated the boundaries between secular and spiritual realms that God intended for His creation. These arguments were remarkable because they were included in political documents, and because they presented the flip side of the argument for disestablishment. Pro-disestablishment petitions argued that government should not interfere in spiritual life; proslavery petitions that religious actors must stay out of politics. Together, they placed slavery solely within the purview of secular government and emphasized that enslavement had nothing to do with spiritual freedom.[30]

When Coke argued that slavery violated God's law, his proslavery opponents replied with their own biblical verses, as Graham became the leading spokesman for the biblical justifications for slavery. The proslavery petitions followed the same pattern as Graham's disestablishment petition for the Bethel convention. They, too, were laced with patriotism, anti-British sentiment, and evangelical theories of Christian history. And even though the biblical references used in the petitions were well known, they did new work for those who deployed them in 1785. The proslavery petitions were written to draw a line between religious freedom (for white men) and political subordination (for slaves). The former was the precious result of the Revolution — the latter survived the tumult unchanged. Freedom and bondage were separated into clearly delineated religious and secular categories.[31]

"When the British Parliament usurped a Right to dispose of our Property without our Consent," declared one petition, "we risked our Lives and Fortunes, and waded through Seas of Blood. Divine Providence smiled on our Enterprize, and crowned it with Success." But now a plot to reverse the victory was underway. "Tools of the British Administration" (Coke and his supporters) had persuaded a "Number of deluded Men among us" to support a "general Emancipation" of Virginia's slaves, "an Attempt," as another petition added, that was "unsupported by Scripture or sound Policy." These traitors hid their strategy behind a "Veil of Piety and Liberality of Sentiment." But, the petitions countered, the "Word of God" contradicted the Methodists. Leviticus established the legitimacy of slavery in the Old Testament, and Paul's First Letter to the Corinthians made it clear that the freedom associated with Christianity was internal liberty from sin and the devil rather than any change in a believer's civil status. A Christian believer's "Outward Condition, whatever that was before they embraced Christianity, whether Bond or Free, it remained the same afterwards." The outward condition, of course, was the proper subject of legislative governance, while conscience was none of its business.[32]

In some senses, the debate was as familiar to the faithful as wrangling over taxes was to legislators. British and colonial statutes denied any connection between conversion to Christianity and emancipation from slavery. Traditionally, the rule facilitated slaves' conversion without stoking resentment from masters, and new Christians in turn helped support claims that slavery also civilized its unhappy victims.[33] But the Methodists changed the rules of the game, when Coke charged slaveholders with anti-Christian acts at the same time as the relationship between religious and civil law was at issue in the debate over disestablishment.

William Graham's public defense of slavery was a first, both for a clergyman and for a professor who trained candidates for the clergy. Yet his role in the turbulent politics of 1785 makes sense. For one thing, Graham's impulsive nature made him more likely to sympathize with a popular cause than many of his fellow churchmen. In addition, Graham's substantial investment in slaves meant that he had a financial interest in the matter. The speed and power of Graham's response to Coke reflected the depth of the reaction among proslavery evangelicals and marked Graham as their leader. His post at Liberty Hall gave Graham gravitas, and his inclination gave him passion.[34]

Many Presbyterians followed Graham in both ventures. Five of the six counties that memorialized in favor of slavery in 1785 also submitted petitions in support of the Bethel disestablishment petition. The overlap among them in tone, language, and structure makes Graham's influence visible, especially in light of his place at the forefront of proslavery religion. His Bethel petition declared that protecting property and guaranteeing the free exercise of religion were the only goals of a legitimate government.[35] And as Presbyterians made clear across the summer of 1785, slavery fell on the secular side: indeed, the security of slavery was the central goal of government — the protection of property. From the perspective of religion, the proslavery petitions were written to establish that Christianity directed all slaves to remain loyal and obedient to their masters. As one petition put it: "the Freedom which the Followers of Jesus were taught to expect was a Freedom from the Bondage of Sin and Satan, ... but [their civil status] remain[ed] the same.... "[36]

In other words, the proslavery petitions of 1785 and the pro-disestablishment petitions of the same year rested on a shared basic foundation: religious conscience was private and distinct from the political realm, whereas protection of (slave) property was the essential role of government. This division was supported, even institutionalized, by separation of church and state.

Both sets of petitions put the pieces in place in religious life as well as government. The consignment of slavery to secular government settled in, as the solution to the issue for religious bodies and the partner to disestablishment. In 1793, the Baptist General Committee debated whether to revive discussions about the legitimacy of slavery, and the minsters did exactly what disestablishment dictated: they directed "that the subject be dismissed from this committee, as believing it *belongs to the legislative body*."[37] Others followed suit, invoking secular law as the justification for eliding the great moral sinkhole of slavery. Rules about marriage between enslaved persons are especially pertinent. In 1791, the Hanover Presbytery decided that enslaved persons might be married "in the sight of God," even though the civil law would not recognize the relationship. But if one spouse was sold away from the other, then the marriage was considered dissolved "as if the other was dead." Local Baptist congregations also endorsed a "death or removal" standard for slave marriages. Any other policy would yield "unpleasant things," according to the Dover Baptist Association. Such separations were an enormous issue: one study concludes that one-third of all slave marriages were terminated by the internal slave trade.[38]

Acceptance of the distinction between freedom of the spirit and the coercion of slavery also spread among Methodists. By the mid-1790s, Bishop Asbury traded away abolitionist principles in the hope that Christianity would "sweeten the bitter cup" of bondage. The Reverend Edward Dromgoole (a Methodist) openly acknowledged that he owned slaves who labored on his plantation.[39] Some objected to this compromise. "When," asked minister Samuel Mitchell, "did [human] laws wash away the guilt of an act prohibited by the word of God?" But Mitchell's son (also a Methodist minister) became a slaveholder and eventually a colonel in the Confederate army.[40]

This post-Revolutionary settlement imposed a regime of silence on slavery among clergy. Acceptance of the new order reflected popular acceptance of the divide between spirituals and temporals, even among many of those who earlier had fought tenaciously to deny it.[41] Focusing on the debates of 1785 reveals that protection of the status quo was built into disestablishment.

* * *

Viewed through the lens of debates over slavery, a different picture of Jefferson's statute emerges. This story is less heroic but more grounded in local religious history and political reality. In 1815, Jefferson received a book of sermons delivered by a minister who called for preaching directly on politics, especially slavery. Jefferson wrote to thank his correspondent for the book, although he noted that the author had "breach[ed] [the] contract" that underlay disestablishment in America by "discussing public affairs *in the pulpit*."[42]

But Jefferson's contract was vulnerable, because Virginia eventually could not control how other jurisdictions interpreted separation of church and state on their own turf. By 1815, Jefferson had been attacked for his religious skepticism and his relationship with his slave Sally Hemings, often in ways that blended the two. The wall of separation, in other words, never eliminated religious arguments against slavery in the ways that Virginia's elite secular thinkers and proslavery Christians had hoped it would.

In the end, the vigor and creativity of religious life in America defied attempts to confine religion to the realm of "opinion," even in Virginia. Those who could not stand the constraint often left, and many who had no choice were sold away. Once out of the state, they were no longer bound by the Virginia model. Some found their way to freedom, and those who had left voluntarily resented the strictures of the divide between spiritual freedom and bodily coercion. Cracks in the wall and the fissures that they became reveal that while the first wall of separation was all about power, it was not — finally — all powerful.

Further Reading

Andrews, Dee E. *The Methodists and Revolutionary America, 1760–1800*. Princeton: Princeton University Press, 2000.

Buckley, Thomas E. *Church and State in Revolutionary Virginia, 1776–1787*. Charlottesville: University of Virginia Press, 1977.

Carte, Kate. "Revisiting the Bishop Controversy." In *The American Revolution Reborn*, edited by Patrick Spero and Michael Zuckerman, 132–139. Philadelphia: University of Pennsylvania Press, 2016.

Gerbner, Katherine. *Christian Slavery: Conversion and Race in the Protestant Atlantic World*. Philadelphia: University of Pennsylvania Press, 2018.

Irons, Charles F. *The Origins of Proslavery Christianity: White and Black Evangelicals in Colonial and Antebellum Virginia*. Chapel Hill: University of North Carolina Press, 2008.

Isaac, Rhys. *The Transformation of Virginia, 1740–1790*. Chapel Hill: University of North Carolina Press, 1982.

Taylor, Alan. *The Internal Enemy: Slavery and War in Virginia, 1772–1832*. New York: W.W. Norton, 2013.

Bibliography

Andrews, Dee E. *The Methodists and Revolutionary America, 1760–1800: The Shaping of an Evangelical Culture*. Princeton: Princeton University Press, 2000.

Beeman, Richard R. *The Old Dominion and the New Nation, 1788–1801*. Lexington: University of Kentucky Press, 1972.

Buckley, Thomas E. *Church and State in Revolutionary Virginia, 1776–1787*. Charlottesville: University of Virginia Press, 1977.

Carey, Bryccham, Markman Ellis, and Sara Salih, eds. *Discourses of Slavery and Abolition: Britain and Its Colonies, 1760–1838*. New York: Palgrave MacMillan, 2004.

Coke, Thomas. *An Address to the Preachers, Lately in Connexion with the Rev. John Wesley: Containing Strictures on a Pamphlet Published by Mr. William Hammet* ... London, 1793.

_____. *Extracts of the Journals of the Rev. Dr. Coke's Three Visits to America*. London, 1790.

_____. *Extracts of the Journals of the Rev. Dr. Coke's Five Visits to America*. London, 1793.

_____. *A History of the West Indies* ... 3 vols. Liverpool, England, 1808–1811.

_____. *The Substance of a Sermon, Preached at Baltimore, in the State of Maryland, Before the General Conference of the Methodist Episcopal Church, on the 27th of December, 178[4], at the Ordination of the Rev. Francis Asbury to the Office of a Superintendent*. Baltimore, 1785.

Daniel, W. Harrison. "Southern Presbyterians and the Negro in the Early National Period." *Journal of Negro History* 58 (July 1973): 291–312.

Drescher, Seymour. *Capitalism and Antislavery: British Mobilization in Comparative Perspective*. New York: Oxford University Press, 1987.

Drew, Samuel. *Life of the Rev. Thomas Coke*. New York, 1818.

Dyer, Justin Buckley. "After the Revolution: *Somerset* and the Antislavery Tradition in Anglo-American Constitutional Development." *Journal of Politics* 71 (October 2009): 1422–1434.

Goetz, Rebecca Anne. *The Baptism of Early Virginia: How Christianity Created Race*. Baltimore: Johns Hopkins University Press, 2012.

Gudmestad, Robert H. *A Troublesome Commerce: The Transformation of the Interstate Slave Trade*. Baton Rouge: Louisiana State University Press, 2003.

Hammet, William. *An Impartial Statement of the Known Inconsistencies of the Reverend Dr. Coke, in His Official Station, as Superintendent of the Methodist Missionaries in the West-Indies.* Charleston, South Carolina, 1792.

Hempton, David. *Methodism and Politics in British Society, 1750–1850.* Palo Alto: Stanford University Press, 1984.

Isaac, Rhys. *The Transformation of Virginia, 1740–1790.* Chapel Hill: University of North Carolina Press, 1982.

Kulikoff, Allan. *Tobacco and Slaves: The Development of Southern Cultures in the Chesapeake, 1680–1800.* Chapel Hill: University of North Carolina Press, 1986.

Lewis, Jan. *The Pursuit of Happiness: Family and Values in Jefferson's Virginia.* New York: Cambridge University Press, 1983.

Lyerly, Cynthia Lynn. *Methodism and the Southern Mind, 1770–1810.* New York: Oxford University Press, 2006.

MacMaster, Richard K. "Liberty or Property?: The Methodists Petition for Emancipation in Virginia, 1785." *Methodist History,* 10 (October, 1971): 44–55.

Madison, James. "Memorial and Remonstrance against Religious Assessments," [ca. June 20,] 1785. In *The Papers of James Madison,* vol. 8, *10 Founders Online,* edited by Robert A. Rutland and William M. E. Rachal. National Archives and Records Administration, Washington, DC https://founders.archives.gov/documents/Madison/01-08-02-0163.

Mann, Bruce H. *Republic of Debtors: Bankruptcy in the Age of American Independence.* Cambridge, MA: Harvard University Press, 2002.

Mathews, David G. *Slavery and Methodism: A Chapter in American Morality, 1780–1845.* Princeton: Princeton University Press, 1965.

Minutes of Several Conversations between the Rev. Thomas Coke, LL.D., and Rev. Francis Asbury and Others ...: Composing a Form of Discipline for the Ministers, Preachers and Other Members of the Methodist Episcopal Church. Philadelphia, 1785.

Najar, Monica. *Evangelizing the South: A Social History of Church and State in Early America.* New York: Oxford University Press, 2008.

Oast, Jennifer. *Institutional Slavery: Slaveholding Churches, Schools, Colleges, and Businesses in Virginia, 1680–1860.* New York: Cambridge University Press, 2016.

Porteus, Beilby. *A Sermon Preached before the Incorporated Society for the Propagation of the Gospel in Foreign Parts ... on Friday, February 21, 1783.* London, 1783.

Pybus, Cassandra. "Jefferson's Faulty Math: The Question of Slave Defections in the American Revolution." *William and Mary Quarterly, 3rd ser.,* 62 (April 2005): 243–264.

Robson, David W. "'An Important Question Answered': William Graham's Defense of Slavery in Post-Revolutionary Virginia." *William and Mary Quarterly, 3rd ser.,* 37 (October 1980): 644–652.

Smith, Warren Thomas. "The Christmas Conference." *Methodist History,* 6 (July 1968): 3–27.

Spangler, Jewel L. "Proslavery Presbyterians: Virginia's Conservative Dissenters in the Age of Revolution." *Journal of Presbyterian History* 78 (Summer 2000): 111–123.

_____. *Virginians Reborn: Anglican Monopoly, Evangelical Dissent, and the Rise of the Baptists in the Late Eighteenth Century.* Charlottesville: University of Virginia Press, 2008.

Thrift, Minton. *Memoir of the Rev. Jesse Lee, with Extracts from His Journals.* New York, 1823.

Vickers, John A. *Thomas Coke: Apostle of Methodism.* New York: Wipf and Stock, 2013.

Weiner, Mark S. "New Biographical Evidence on *Somerset's Case.*" *Slavery and Abolition* 23 (April 2002): 121–136.

White, Henry Alexander. *Southern Presbyterian Leaders.* New York, 1911.

Wiecek, William M. "*Somerset*: Lord Mansfield and the Legitimacy of Slavery in the Anglo-American World." *University of Chicago Law Review* 42 (Autumn 1974): 86–146.

Wigger, John. *American Saint: Francis Asbury and the Methodists.* New York: Oxford University Press, 2009.

Wilder, Craig Steven. *Ebony and Ivy: Race, Slavery, and the Troubled History of America's Universities.* New York: Bloomsbury Press, 2013.

Wolf, Eva Sheppard. *Race and Liberty in the New Nation: Emancipation in Virginia from the Revolution to Nat Turner's Rebellion.* Baton Rouge: Louisiana State University Press, 2009.

Wood, Betty. *Come Shouting to Zion: African American Protestantism in the American South and British Caribbean to 1830.* Chapel Hill: University of North Carolina Press: 1998.

NOTES

1   *Extracts of the Journals of the Rev. Dr. Coke's Five Visits to America* (London, 1793), 35; hereinafter cited as *Coke's Five Visits to America*.

2   James Madison, "Memorial and Remonstrance against Religious Assessments," [ca. June 20,] 1785, in *The Papers of James Madison*, Vol. 8: *10 March 1784–28 March 1786*, ed. Robert A. Rutland and William M. E. Rachal (Chicago: University of Chicago Press, 1973), 295–306, and in *Founders Online* (National Archives and Records Administration, Washington, D.C.), https://founders.archives.gov/documents/Madison/01-08-02-0163.

3   The petitions in favor of and against disestablishment were first digitized by the Library of Congress, in a project called "Early Virginia Religious Petitions." The collection has now been transferred to the Library of Virginia in Richmond, which has folded the religious petitions into its much larger Legislative Petitions Digital Collection, http://www.virginiamemory.com/collections/petitions.

4   John A. Vickers, *Thomas Coke: Apostle of Methodism* (New York: Wipf and Stock, 2013), 79–99. Thomas Coke, *The Substance of a Sermon, Preached at Baltimore, in the State of Maryland, Before the General Conference of the Methodist Episcopal Church, on the 27th of December, 178[4], at the Ordination of the Rev. Francis Asbury to the Office of a Superintendent* (Baltimore, 1785), 6 (quotation); Dee E. Andrews, *The Methodists and Revolutionary America, 1760–1800: The Shaping of an Evangelical Culture* (Princeton: Princeton University Press, 2000), 55–72; David Hempton, *Methodism and Politics in British Society, 1750–1850* (New York: Routledge, 2013), 92–94.

5   Petition, Frederick County, November 8, 1785, #000333248, Legislative Petitions Digital Collection (quotation); Richard K. MacMaster, "Liberty or Property?: The Methodists Petition for Emancipation in Virginia, 1785," *Methodist History* 10 (October 1971): 44–55 (a version of the petition is reprinted in full on pp. 48–49); Samuel Drew, *Life of the Rev. Thomas Coke* (New York, 1818), 59–84; Vickers, *Thomas Coke*, 41–67; David Hempton, *Methodism and Politics in British Society, 1750–1850* (Palo Alto: Stanford University Press, 1984).

6   Richard K. MacMaster, "Liberty or Property?: The Methodists Petition for Emancipation in Virginia, 1785," *Methodist History* 10 (October 1971): 48–50 (quotation on 49). For Coke's authorship of the petition at a church conference in Brunswick County, as well as a description of the "great many principal friends" who attended the conference and "insist[ed] on a Repeal of the Slave-Rules" (Coke refused categorically), see Vickers, ed., *Journals of Dr. Thomas Coke*, 58. Multiple copies of the Methodist petition were submitted, the first on November 8, 1785, from Frederick County with eighteen signatories. Altogether the Methodists collected 260 additional signatures on seven separate petitions. Petition, Frederick County, November 8, 1785, #000333248; and Petitions "of Sundry Persons respecting Emancipation of Slaves," November 8, 1785, #000305302, both in Legislative Petitions Digital Collection.

7   Petition, Frederick County, November 8, 1785, #000333248, Legislative Petitions Digital Collection. Pennsylvania's 1780 "Act for the Gradual Abolition of Slavery" also spoke of the tyranny exercised by Britain over the colonies as generating a deep appreciation for freedom in ways that translated into support for emancipation. "Pennsylvania — An Act for the Gradual Abolition of Slavery, 1780," Avalon Project (Lillian Goldman Law Library, Yale Law School, New Haven, Connecticut), http://avalon.law.yale.edu/18th_century/pennst01.asp.

8   Warren Thomas Smith, "The Christmas Conference," *Methodist History*, 6 (July 1968): 3–27, esp. 15–17; Robert Emory, *History of the Discipline of the Methodist Episcopal Church* (New York, 1844), 43–44; "An act to authorize the manumission of slaves," May 6, 1782, in William Waller Hening, comp., *Statutes at Large: Being a Collection of All the Laws of Virginia, from the First Session of the Legislature, in the Year 1619* (13 vols.; Richmond, Virginia, 1809–1823), 11:39–40.

9   *Coke's Five Visits to America*, 34–35 (first quotation on 35; second quotation on 34); on Ragland, see "Virginia's Slaves Freed After 1782," http://www.freeafricanamericans.com/virginiafreeafter1782.htm.

10 Minton Thrift, *Memoir of the Rev. Jesse Lee, with Extracts from His Journals* (New York, 1823), 78–79; *Extracts of the Journals of the Rev. Dr. Coke's Three Visits to America* (London, 1790), 46 (quotation).

11 *Coke's Five Visits to America*, 69 (first quotation); Seymour Drescher, *Capitalism and Antislavery: British Mobilization in Comparative Perspective* (New York: Oxford University Press, 1987), 119–20; Thomas Coke, *A History of the West Indies ...* 3 vols. (Liverpool: Nuttall, Fisher, and Dixon,

1808–1811), 2:61; William Hammet, *An Impartial Statement of the Known Inconsistencies of the Reverend Dr. Coke, in His Official Station, as Superintendent of the Methodist Missionaries in the West-Indies* (Charleston: W.P. Young, South Carolina, 1792), 13–16; Thomas Coke, *An Address to the Preachers, Lately in Connexion with the Rev. John Wesley: Containing Strictures on a Pamphlet Published by Mr. William Hammet* ... (London, 1793), 17–19 (second quotation on 18–19).

12   For Princeton graduates and proslavery in the early republic and beyond, see Craig Steven Wilder, *Ebony and Ivy: Race, Slavery, and the Troubled History of America's Universities* (New York: Bloomsbury Press, 2013), 101–12. Henry Alexander White, *Southern Presbyterian Leaders* (New York, 1911), 124–39; Washington and Lee University, "A Brief History," https://www.wlu.edu/about-wandl/history-and-traditions/a-brief-history. One has to dig to find Graham on the Washington and Lee website; see "William Graham: Principal, Liberty Hall Academy, 1776–1796," https://www.wlu.edu/presidents-office/history-and-governance/past-presidents/william-graham.

13   William Graham, "An Important Question Answered," reprinted in David W. Robson, "'An Important Question Answered': William Graham's Defense of Slavery in Post-Revolutionary Virginia," *William and Mary Quarterly*, 3rd ser., 37 (October 1980): 644–52, esp. 649–52 (quotation on 649); hereinafter cited as Graham, "An Important Question Answered," with the page references to the Robson reprint.

14   Bruce H. Mann, *Republic of Debtors: Bankruptcy in the Age of American Independence* (Cambridge, MA: Harvard University Press, 2002); Allan Kulikoff, *Tobacco and Slaves: The Development of Southern Cultures in the Chesapeake, 1680–1800* (Chapel Hill: University of North Carolina Press, 1986); Eva Sheppard Wolf, *Race and Liberty in the New Nation: Emancipation in Virginia from the Revolution to Nat Turner's Rebellion* (Baton Rouge: Louisiana State University Press, 2009); Richard R. Beeman, *The Old Dominion and the New Nation, 1788–1801* (Lexington: University of Kentucky Press, 1972), xi–xii, 122; John A. George, "Virginia Loyalists, 1775–1783," *Richmond College Historical Papers* 1 (June, 1916): 174–221, esp. 219.

15   Virginia Declaration of Rights, June 12, 1776, Section 16 (quotation), *America's Founding Documents* (National Archives), https://www.archives.gov/founding-docs/virginia-declaration-of-rights; George MacLaren Brydon, *Virginia's Mother Church and the Political Conditions Under Which It Grew*, 2 vols. (Richmond: Virginia Historical Society, 1947), 1:98–102, 2:334–35; Thomas E. Buckley, *Church and State in Revolutionary Virginia, 1776–1787* (Charlottesville: University of Virginia Press, 1977), 8–12.

16   "A Bill for extending the Benefit of the Several Acts of Toleration to his Majesty's Protestant Subjects, in this Colony, dissenting from the Church of England," Williamsburg *Virginia Gazette* (Rind), March 26, 1772, p. 1 (quotation); Brydon, *Virginia's Mother Church and the Political Conditions Under Which It Grew*, 2:378–79; Rhys Isaac, *The Transformation of Virginia, 1740–1790* (Chapel Hill: University of North Carolina Press, 1982), 198–201; Paul K. Longmore, "'All Matters and Things Relating to Religion and Morality': The Virginia Burgesses' Committee for Religion, 1769 to 1775," *Journal of Church and State* 38 (August 1996): 775–97; Robert B. Semple, *A History of the Rise and Progress of the Baptists in Virginia*, edited by G. W. Beale (rev. ed.; Richmond, Virginia, 1894), 29–54; Jewel L. Spangler, *Virginians Reborn: Anglican Monopoly, Evangelical Dissent, and the Rise of the Baptists in the Late Eighteenth Century* (Charlottesville: University of Virginia Press, 2008), 119–66; William Henry Foote, *Sketches of Virginia: Historical and Biographical* (Philadelphia: J.B. Lippincott, 1856), 319–48.

17   Mark S. Weiner, "New Biographical Evidence on *Somerset's Case*," *Slavery and Abolition* 23 (April 2002): 121–36; Justin Buckley Dyer, "After the Revolution: *Somerset* and the Antislavery Tradition in Anglo-American Constitutional Development," *Journal of Politics* 71 (October 2009): 1422–34; William M. Wiecek, "*Somerset*: Lord Mansfield and the Legitimacy of Slavery in the Anglo-American World," *University of Chicago Law Review* 42 (Autumn 1974): 86–146; "Jefferson's 'Original Rough draught' of the Declaration of Independence," in *The Papers of Thomas Jefferson*, vol. 1: *1760–1776*, edited by Julian P. Boyd et al., 423–27 (Princeton: Princeton University Press, 1950), (quotation on 426).

18   Edward Graham, "A Memoir of Rev. William Graham [Part 3]," *Evangelical and Literary Magazine, and Missionary Chronicle* 4 (May 1821): 253–63, esp. 256–57.

19   Numbers drawn from *Minutes of the Methodist Conferences, Annually Held in America: From 1773 to 1813, Inclusive* (New York, 1813), 16–41, esp. 8, 14, 17, 41; hereinafter cited as *Minutes of the Methodist Conferences, 1773–1813*.

20 Hempton, *Methodism and Politics in British Society*, 92–94; Andrews, *Methodists and Revolutionary America*, 60–62; John Wigger, *American Saint: Francis Asbury and the Methodists* (New York: Oxford University Press, 2009), 111–26.

21 "An act for exempting the different societies of Dissenters from contributing to the support and maintenance of the church as by law established," October 1776, in Hening, comp., *Statutes at Large*, 9:164–67; Buckley, *Church and State in Revolutionary Virginia*, 37, 61; Petition, Cumberland County, November 6, 1778, #000147396, Legislative Petitions Digital Collection (first quotation); Petition, King William County, November 21, 1778, #000215846, Legislative Petitions Digital Collection; "To the Publick," Williamsburg *Virginia Gazette* (Dixon and Nicolson), August 14, 1779, p. 1; Petition, Lancaster County, October 20, 1779, #000273553, Legislative Petitions Digital Collection; Petition, Essex County, October 22, 1779, #000389307, Legislative Petitions Digital Collection (second and third quotations); Curry, *First Freedoms*, 138–39.

22 Beilby Porteus, *A Sermon Preached before the Incorporated Society for the Propagation of the Gospel in Foreign Parts ... on Friday, February 21, 1783* (London, 1783); Bob Tennant, "Sentiment, Politics, and Empire: A Study of Beilby Porteus's Anti-Slavery Sermon," in *Discourses of Slavery and Abolition: Britain and Its Colonies, 1760–1838*, edited by Bryccham Carey, Markman Ellis, and Sara Salih, 158–74 (New York: Palgrave MacMillan, 2004).

23 Cassandra Pybus, "Jefferson's Faulty Math: The Question of Slave Defections in the American Revolution," *William and Mary Quarterly*, 3rd ser., 62 (April 2005): 243–64; Jan Lewis, *The Pursuit of Happiness: Family and Values in Jefferson's Virginia* (New York: Cambridge University Press, 1983), 48–50.

24 Charles F. James, *Documentary History of the Struggle for Religious Liberty in Virginia* (Lynchburg, Virginia, 1900), 126 (first quotation), 129 (second quotation). For the entire text of the bill, styled as "A Bill 'Establishing a Provision for Teachers of the Christian Religion,'" see Buckley, *Church and State in Revolutionary Virginia*, 188–89.

25 Foote, *Sketches of Virginia*, 336–338 (first quotation on 337); Minutes of Hanover Presbytery, October 26, 1784, quoted in Buckley, *Church and State in Revolutionary Virginia*, 92 (second quotation). On Graham's lifelong pursuit of wealth, see Edward Graham, "A Memoir of Rev. William Graham [Part 4]," *Evangelical and Literary Magazine, and Missionary Chronicle* 4 (August 1821): 397–412, esp. 406–07.

26 The bill specified that the sheriff or tax collector would send a taxpayer's designated funds "to what society of Christians ... [the taxpayer] shall direct the money to be paid," thus allowing broad latitude among the potential beneficiaries of the collected revenue. "Bill 'Establishing a Provision for Teachers of the Christian Religion,'" in Buckley, *Church and State in Revolutionary Virginia*, 188–89.

27 *Minutes of Several Conversations between the Rev. Thomas Coke, LL.D., and Rev. Francis Asbury and Others ...: Composing a Form of Discipline for the Ministers, Preachers and Other Members of the Methodist Episcopal Church* (Philadelphia, 1785), 15–17; David G. Mathews, *Slavery and Methodism: A Chapter in American Morality, 1780–1845* (Princeton: Princeton University Press, 1965), 3–29; Andrews, *Methodists and Revolutionary America*, 124–32, esp. 126–27.

28 These twelve petitions are buried in folders marked as though they contain a single petition but in fact include multiple documents, some of which are marked with a date but no place of origin (on several, an apparent county of origin is noted on a back fold). Several simply say that they write in support of the Bethel petition, without further elaboration.

29 Petition, Augusta and Rockbridge Counties, November 12, 1785, #000390252, Legislative Petitions Digital Collection. Graham's Princeton classmate and coauthor on the earlier pro- assessment petition, the Reverend John Blair Smith, president of Hampden-Sydney College, also changed from a supporter to an opponent of Henry's bill and presented the Presbyterian argument in the legislature before the committee of the whole in December. According to William Henry Foote, with the Hanover petition and Smith's verbal defense of it, Smith "represented the whole Presbyterian population in the State" (Foote, *Sketches of Virginia*, 345–46 [quotation on 346]).

30 The proslavery petitions are collected and reprinted in Schmidt and Wilhelm, "Early Pro-slavery Petitions in Virginia."

31 Two proslavery petitions submitted in November 1784 by Henrico and Hanover Counties were entirely secular, calling for the repeal of the manumission law because manumitted slaves had become thieves, and some masters had freed slaves to defraud their creditors, while other former slaves who had fled to the British army were now "passing in this country as free men." Petitions

"of freeholders and inhabitants" of Henrico County and Hanover County, November 16, 1784, #000215139 and #000214124, Legislative Petitions Digital Collection (quotation). Contrast with petitions submitted just one year later, and the difference is plain. After the encounter with Methodist abolitionism, proslavery petitions were deeply religious and far more broad-ranging, fiercely deploying scripture to argue that slavery was not prohibited by Christianity. The 1784 petitions had a total of 247 signatories; the 1785 petitions had a total of 1,072 signatories.

32 Petition, Halifax County, November 10, 1785, #000217710, Legislative Petitions Digital Collection (first through fifth, eighth, and ninth quotations); Petition, Amelia County, November 10, 1785, #000042393, Legislative Petitions Digital Collection (sixth and seventh quotations); Petition, Pittsylvania County, November 10, 1785, #000249243, Legislative Petitions Digital Collection (tenth quotation).

33 "An act declaring that baptisme of slaves doth not exempt them from bondage," September 1667, in Hening, comp., *Statutes at Large*, 2:260; Rebecca Anne Goetz, *The Baptism of Early Virginia: How Christianity Created Race* (Baltimore: Johns Hopkins University Press, 2012), 112–37.

34 For widespread slaveholding among Presbyterian churches and ministers, see Jennifer Oast, "'The Worst Kind of Slavery': Slave-Owning Presbyterian Churches in Prince Edward County, Virginia," *Journal of Southern History* 76 (November 2010): 867–900; Jennifer Oast, *Institutional Slavery: Slaveholding Churches, Schools, Colleges, and Businesses in Virginia, 1680–1860* (New York: Cambridge University Press, 2016), 87–125; and Jewel L. Spangler, "Proslavery Presbyterians: Virginia's Conservative Dissenters in the Age of Revolution," *Journal of Presbyterian History* 78 (Summer 2000): 111–23.

35 Petition of "the Ministers and Lay representatives of the Presbyterian Church in Virginia," Augusta County, November 2, 1785, #000305300, Legislative Petitions Digital Collection.

36 "An Important Question Answered," 649; Petition of Presbytery of Hanover, Hanover County, November 18, 1785, #000305310, Legislative Petitions Digital Collection; see also Petition, Halifax County, November 10, 1785, #000217710, Legislative Petitions Digital Collection (first quotation); Petition, Brunswick County, November 10, 1785, #000145334, Legislative Petitions Digital Collection (second quotation).

37 Quoted in Monica Najar, *Evangelizing the South: A Social History of Church and State in Early America* (New York: Oxford University Press, 2008), 147.

38 W. Harrison Daniel, "Southern Presbyterians and the Negro in the Early National Period," *Journal of Negro History* 58 (July 1973): 291–312; Spangler, "Proslavery Presbyterians," 116; Sylvia R. Frey and Betty Wood, *Come Shouting to Zion: African American Protestantism in the American South and British Caribbean to 1830* (Chapel Hill: University of North Carolina Press, 1998), 185; *Minutes of the Dover Baptist Association, Held at Upper King and Queen Meeting-House in King and Queen County, Virginia* ... (Richmond, Virginia, 1817), 14; W. Harrison Daniel, "Virginia Baptists and the Negro in the Early Republic," *Virginia Magazine of History and Biography* 80 (January 1972): 60–69; Robert H. Gudmestad, *A Troublesome Commerce: The Transformation of the Interstate Slave Trade* (Baton Rouge: Louisiana University Press, 2003), 8.

39 Francis Asbury to George Roberts, February 11, 1797, in Clark, Potts, and Payton, eds., *Journal and Letters of Francis Asbury*, 3:160 (first quotation); Mathews, *Slavery and Methodism*, 22–23 (second quotation on 23; third quotation on 22); Wigger, *American Saint*, 153. On Dromgoole's complex and varied approach to slaveholding across his life, see Christopher C. Jones, "Methodism, Slavery, and Freedom in the Revolutionary Atlantic," Ph.D. diss., (William & Mary, 2016), 98–107.

40 Mitchell quoted in Mathews, *Slavery and Methodism*, 27. On the Methodist turn away from antislavery activism in the 1790s and beyond, see Cynthia Lynn Lyerly, *Methodism and the Southern Mind, 1770–1810* (New York: Oxford University Press, 2006), 119–45.

41 Charles Irons cautions that the silence of the 1780s and 1790s was not the full-throated proslavery religion of later decades, indirectly bolstering the contemporary theory that silence was actually a compromise (Irons, *Origins of Proslavery Christianity*, 66–69). For the language of compromise, see, for example, Mathews, *Slavery and Methodism*, 266.

42 Thomas Jefferson to Peter H. Wendover (unsent draft), March 13, 1815, *The Papers of Thomas Jefferson: Retirement Series*, Vol. 8: *1 October 1814 to 31 August 1815*, ed. J. Jefferson Looney et al. (Princeton: Princeton University Press, 2011), 340–43 (first quotation on 342; second quotation on 341). The book in question was Alexander McLeod, *A Scriptural View of the Character, Cause, and Ends of the Present War* (New York: Eastburn, Kirk & Co., 1815).

Chapter Eight

ABRAHAM REMEMBERED: AN AFRICAN CAPTIVITY TALE IN EARLY AMERICA

Jon F. Sensbach
University of Florida, Gainsville, Florida

Slavery lay at the heart of the early American experience. Between 1500 and the end of the nineteenth century, slave traders sent more than 12 million African captives across the Atlantic to the Caribbean, North America and Latin America. Slave labor on plantations, docks and cattle ranches and in forests, mines and kitchens supported colonial economic development, at frightful human cost to the enslaved. One of those costs was historical anonymity. Among the millions, we know the names of thousands but the life stories of just a few. A plantation owner might record his slaves' names in a ledger but ignore details he considered insignificant, such as their African ethnic identities, personalities, religious beliefs, and emotions. Enslavers scrubbed the record of all the things that made their victims human.[1]

And so when, in 1797, an African-born man named Abraham died in Salem, North Carolina, he probably would have been forgotten like most, except that a minister of the Moravian congregation in which Abraham worshiped wrote down his *Lebenslauf*, a German word meaning "life course," a hybrid genre of memoir and short biography. The Moravians were German-speaking immigrants who, in the mid-eighteenth century, settled in tightly knit communities in Pennsylvania and North Carolina to practice their pietistic faith, which emphasized a heartfelt spiritual rebirth in Christ. They did not oppose slavery, and they bought and owned slaves. Believing in the universality of Christian salvation, however, they baptized enslaved people into their congregations. Abraham was one such "Brother" in the fellowship of Christ, giving him the right, like all church members, to record his *Lebenslauf*, to tell his life story. Abraham narrated that account to a minister, providing a rare glimpse into the journey of one African sold into American slavery and his conversion to Christianity. The document forces us to consider the unholy bond between religion and slavery in early America. How could an African be a respected member of a church that enslaved him? And what was the lived experience of an African Christian within that fellowship?[2]

The opening sentence of Abraham's *Lebenslauf* contains vital clues about his African origins. "Our dear Brother Abraham, otherwise called Sambo, a Negro from the Mandingo Nation on the coast of African Guinea, was born in about the year 1730." The Mandingo, or Mandinka, people lived in the region of West Africa comprised of present-day Senegal, Gambia, Guinea and Sierra Leone. Along with groups of related people known collectively as Mande, they had comprised the kingdom of Mali on the upper Niger River, founded by

A Companion to American Religious History, First Edition. Edited by Benjamin E. Park.
© 2021 John Wiley & Sons, Inc. Published 2021 by John Wiley & Sons, Inc.

a powerful general, Sundiata, in the thirteenth century. As the empire of Mali declined during the fifteenth century, the Mandingos became masters of state-building who created provinces throughout the Upper Guinea Coast, especially on the coast and inland along the Gambia River.[3]

In Mandingo society, as in West Africa generally, there was no line dividing sacred and secular; the African universe was spiritual. Religion dominated every aspect of life, for God's will was believed to lie behind every event. Sambo's *Lebenslauf* tell us that "through diligent praying he established a religious way of thinking himself, though this was mixed with heathen superstition." The nature of his beliefs is unclear from this description. It is likely he was Muslim, since Islam had taken hold in Senegambia by the twelfth century via Muslim traders from northern Africa, many of whom received positions of honor at the courts of such empires as Ghana and Mali. In Mandingo society, a prestigious class of Muslim teachers, traders, and medical practitioners called Marabouts spread literacy in Arabic. Abraham's pre-Christian name, Sambo, further suggests a Muslim identity. Though the name later gained racist connotations in nineteenth-century America, Sambo is in fact an African name meaning "second son" in some West African languages, including among the predominantly Muslim Hausa and Fulbe peoples.[4]

For Sambo and his people, religion was an expression of communal identity and history. In African religions broadly, including Islam but also "traditional" or non-monotheistic faiths, the individual could not exist separately from the larger spiritual community that included living kin as well as ancestors, whose memories were preserved in oral tradition and who watched the community closely to safeguard tradition and ethics. It was this partnership of multiple interlocking spirits that was shattered forever for Sambo and millions of Africans sold into American slavery.

By the eighteenth century, the slave trade had become the dominant economic force in West Africa. African nations constantly raided and fought each other to secure captives. Many of these campaigns were wars of *jihad* between Muslim and non-Muslim peoples. In the Upper Guinea region, Mandingo warriors took thousands of slaves annually from the African hinterlands for sale to European traders on the coast. "The unhappy captives," wrote an Englishman, "many of whom are people of distinction, such as princes, priests and persons high in office, are conducted by Mandingos in droves of twenty, thirty and forty, chained together" to slaving depots. The Mandingos fought a debilitating cycle of wars with their neighbors that raged back and forth for many years. In one such campaign, Sambo was captured. The year must have been sometime between 1760 and 1770 when he would have been about thirty to forty years old. As his life account explains, he was already an adult with several children when "he went to war like others in the frequent hostilities with the neighboring tribes. In one of those wars he was wounded severely in head and face and was taken prisoner, and then sent back to his father with mutilated ears."[5]

Sambo's father, "a respected man among his countrymen," continued the narrative, was angered and "stirred the inhabitants of the community to another war to get revenge. They started at once, and Abraham, wounded though he was, followed them." The Mandingo forces apparently were defeated in this campaign, for Sambo "was taken prisoner for a second time." This time, his captors sold him to European slave traders, probably either French or English, who were bitterly contesting the Senegambian trade at the time. As another African recalled years after his capture, he first thought white people were "devils who wanted to take us, because we had never before seen a white man and never in our lives heard that such men existed."[6]

Through descriptions by white traders and the testimony of other Africans sold into slavery, what undoubtedly happened next to Sambo, as to so many others, has become a familiar story. He would have been among scores of prisoners manacled together on the long march to the sea, which many inlanders had never seen. On the coast, he and other captives would have huddled in barracks, sometimes for weeks or months, before being hustled on board a slave ship to be chained in a cramped, stinking hold. The traumatizing voyage to America in what have been called "floating tombs" could last months. But beyond the images of suffering and despair, the Middle Passage raised fundamental questions for all captive Africans. When they last gazed at the African coast, the prisoners were about to embark on a forced journey into a frightening abyss. What part of their former selves remained, and what part died? How much of the inner spirit world lived on through the rupture?[7]

Sambo's subsequent life thrust him headlong into a search for answers. He was first shipped to a French colony in the West Indies to help feed the French sugar industry's voracious appetite for slave labor. But he stayed there just long enough to pick up some knowledge of French before being taken a few years later to Virginia, perhaps via illicit trade links between the French Caribbean and British North America. In Virginia, a man named Edmund Lyne bought him, and then, in 1771, took him to the Moravian settlement in the western Piedmont section of North Carolina. The Moravians bought him and another African named Jupiter, whom they described as "by nature a very proud man ... a true heathen, a king's son from Guinea." Like Sambo, Jupiter, whose African name was unrecorded, "had taken part in various battles in his homeland, from which his face was still noticeably marked with cuts and scars."[8]

In contrast to the huge rice plantations of colonial South Carolina or the tobacco fields of Virginia, Sambo's new home was a different place altogether. Founded in 1766, the Moravian town of Salem was a religious community defined by congregational cohesion and a desire to keep outsiders out. Moravian church leaders who regulated the town wanted to promote craft apprenticeship and an industrious livelihood among young people, so they forbade individuals from owning slaves. Instead, to bolster their workforce as needed, the church itself bought slaves and rented them to white Moravians in certain crafts and industries. In the 1770s, the town's enslaved population was quite small, numbering perhaps ten out of just a few hundred residents. The church leaders who bought Sambo assigned him to work with master tanner Heinrich Herbst, who had trouble finding steady laborers to operate the community-owned tannery. Sambo quickly became immersed in the long, labor-intensive process of turning raw hides into leather.[9]

During his first years in Salem, he struggled to confront his new, and often hostile, surroundings. The solitude of life and labor among strangers must have been overwhelming. "For quite a while he stayed in his former heathen ways and mores," noted the *Lebenslauf*. "We could not give him the right instruction, because he understood only his native language and a little French." His apparent unwillingness to learn German signaled his resistance to the alien culture around him. In addition, like thousands of other people of African descent in the mid-1770s, he expressed his hostility in more overt ways. On the eve of the American Revolution, one-sixth of the colonial population, or about 450,000 people, were enslaved, the highest proportion at any time in American history. Many sought to assert their own claims to freedom by exploiting the political fracture between the colonies and Britain. Arson, escape, work stoppage, and even armed slave insurrection increased. In November 1774, town leaders in Salem noted "all sorts of excesses" by Sambo and considered selling him, "the sooner the better." Though the Moravians were pacifist by doctrine and sought to remain neutral in the independence struggle, they quietly stockpiled arms and powder in the event of slave revolt.[10]

No rebellion broke out in Salem, but at the height of the tense summer of 1775, Sambo tried to run away. The royal governor of Virginia, Lord Dunmore, issued a proclamation granting freedom to any slave belonging to a revolutionary who would join him in suppressing the colonial uprising. Hundreds of enslaved workers throughout the southern colonies tried to run away and reach Dunmore, and Sambo may have been trying to do likewise. But after three weeks on the run, he was recaptured and brought back to Salem "very miserable and hungry, [he] has lived most of the time on berries he found in the woods and will probably not be so eager to run away again." The Moravians whipped him for his insubordination and again a few months later for being "impudent." He persisted, receiving for his "freshness" yet another beating so severe he had to be treated by a doctor.[11]

In the late 1770s, after several years of fighting the Moravians, Sambo changed course—he sought to join them. While we will never know his precise reasons for doing so, he may have concluded that further direct resistance was futile and that church membership offered certain advantages, chiefly an immediate improvement in his status. As he had no doubt observed, the church already had several African American members who worshiped side by side with white Moravians, attended Moravian school, and learned to read and write. A few black congregants even bunked together with white "Brethren" in sex-segregated dormitories for single men and women. Enslaved members gained respect, a sense of belonging, and protection from abuse, especially preservation of their families from arbitrary sale and separation as was so often the case among enslaved people. Above all, they gained recognition that they were more than chattel — they were humans with souls, spiritually equal to white people, if equality meant spiritual freedom in Christ.

For this mix of pragmatic and spiritual reasons, Sambo "started to think about the status of his soul, attended diligently the Congregation meetings, and was eager to learn German and verses." A period of such preparation passed before "he learned to see himself as the poorest sinner and to realize this evil." Eventually, "he came to the thorough perception of his lost condition, and admitted openheartedly and repentantly to a Brother what a slave of sin he had been up to now and how much he would like to be saved and become happy." In December 1779, the Board of Elders reported that "Sambo has already expressed at various times his desire for baptism. Although he cannot express himself very understandably in either German or English, we nevertheless have noted meaningful signs of grace working in his heart." Aspirants to Moravian fellowship could gain baptism only after giving lasting evidence of godliness and after gaining diving permission, which church leaders determined by drawing a positive "lot," which indicated God's approval. After drawing a negative lot several times, which they interpreted as meaning Sambo was not ready for baptism, the Elders finally drew a positive lot, clearing Sambo for baptism in December 1780. At the age of about fifty, the African warrior received a new, Biblical name: Abraham.[12]

Baptism symbolized the erasure of the initiate's former self and a "new birth" into Christian fellowship. For Abraham, who had led the marginalized life of an enslaved, non-Christian outsider for the past decade, incorporation into the Moravian community heralded a transition from what the sociologist Orlando Patterson has called the "social death" of slavery to social resurrection. Congregational membership could never replace or duplicate the circle of gods, ancestors, and kin that Abraham had left behind. But it was like being welcomed into a new kind of spiritual family in which black and white Moravians addressed each other as "Brother" and "Sister" and shared ancient Biblical rituals like foot washing and the kiss of peace.[13]

Of course, it was a family with free and enslaved members. Baptism, as a minister told one African American who inquired about Moravian worship in 1776, "does not mean that he becomes free and the equal of his master." Spiritual equality did not equal legal equality. Enslaved Brothers and Sisters served in no official church capacity and were still regarded as property. Though they gained an anchor of security in an uncertain world, they were expected to resign themselves to enslavement. Disobeying congregational rules risked the threat of banishment and sale out of the community.

These contradictions embodied the relationship between Christianity and slavery that had prevailed since the earliest days of the colonies. The Catholic Church permitted the enslavement of Africans in Spain and Portugal as early as the mid-fifteenth century and in those nations' Caribbean and Latin American colonies by the early sixteenth. Thousands of Africans joined the church despite being told that baptism would not set them free. Many disputed this view on the grounds that the church sanctioned slave marriages, interpreting that recognition to mean "they are free and have obtained liberty." Indeed, church membership sometimes provided pathways to legal freedom, and the fusion of African and Catholic spirituality and ritual produced vibrant new forms of worship in Brazil, Cuba, Haiti, and elsewhere.[14]

Protestant English and Dutch colonists, too, propped up slavery with the crutch of Christianity and some legal sleight of hand. Under English law, one Christian could not enslave another. Some Africans in English colonies exploited this legal loophole by converting to Christianity and gaining freedom. In Virginia, the legislature closed the loophole in 1666 with a new law that "the conferring of baptisme doth not alter the condition of the person as to his bondage or freedom." In other words, a slave who became Christian would remain enslaved. Other colonies passed similar statutes legalizing the enslavement of African, and in some cases, Native American, Christians. These laws, which produced a legal revolution in colonial America, helped create the modern fiction of race on the basis of differences in skin pigmentation that justified the oppression of one group by another. The English and other European colonists claimed that slavery was part of God's law, pointing as evidence to frequent Biblical passages such as "Servants, obey your masters" (Col. 3:22). They contended that Africans, in particular, could be enslaved because their dark hue was a divine curse for their sinfulness.[15]

From North America to the Caribbean, African slavery accelerated swiftly in the late seventeenth- and early eighteenth-century colonies. The words "*Negro* and *Slave*" grew "by custom Homogeneous and Convertible," according to Morgan Godwyn, a minister who, against the opposition of planters, supported African Christianization. Some white people protested the rapid spread of slavery. Quakers in Pennsylvania drafted the first formal antislavery petition, in 1688, insisting that it was unchristian to enslave others. In a pamphlet from 1700 called *The Selling of Joseph,* Massachusetts minister Samuel Sewall similarly protested that "all Men, as they are the Sons of *Adam,* are Coheirs; and have equal Right unto Liberty." Slave owners mostly ignored such logic. Worried that slaves would still try to seek freedom through baptism, they tried to keep them away from Christianity, since it was easier to justify enslaving "heathens." For them, Africans were manifestly not the earthly or spiritual equal of whites. Many enslaved people already shunned the religion that was complicit in their captivity.[16]

In the mid-eighteenth century, during and after the intercolonial religious revivals known as the Great Awakening, spearheaded by the famous itinerant preacher George Whitefield, many churches made a more concerted effort to reach out to Africans. The Moravians invested enormous energy in mission work on Caribbean sugar colonies, baptizing thousands into the faith. Evangelical denominations in North America drew in hundreds, and eventually thousands, of hitherto excluded African American worshipers. Many of these early black Christians were attracted by the promise of redemption through baptism and the egalitarianism fostered by Baptists, Methodists, and others. During the 1760s and 1770s, that message dovetailed with both longstanding African protests against slavery and the revolutionary rhetoric of liberty. "We have in common with all other men a natural right to our freedoms without Being deprived of them by our fellow men as we are freeborn Pepel," a group of slaves in Massachusetts petitioned the governor in 1774. "There is a great number of sincere members of the Church of Christ, how can the master be said to bear my Burden when he bears me down with the chains of slavery?" Influenced by these ideas, some white people began to liberate their slaves.[17]

The Moravians did not go that far, but their fellowship probed many of the searching questions of the era. They still clung to the language of race that justified African slavery. For a Brother like Abraham, though, the embrace of spiritual equality was at least something to build on. Baptism brought the enslaved into the intricate social world of Moravian congregational life. The church sought to instill a sense of group solidarity through a succession of church services, prayer meetings, and festivities. The means for doing so was the so-called choir system, which divided congregants into "choirs," or groups according to age, sex, and life stage. Single men worshiped together, as did single women, married men, and so on. Abraham, the Mandingo with facial markings and clipped ears, participated with the Single Brothers' Choir, praying on the same bench alongside immigrants from Germany and Denmark. The choir concept might even have seemed familiar to him. In many West African cultures, sex-segregated secret societies provided a similar nurturing environment by steering adolescent boys and girls into adulthood through initiation rituals and mediating their place in the spirit world. Moravian choirs served much the same purpose. For a survivor of the Middle Passage, stolen from his wife and children in Africa, the Moravian brothers became his new family.

Abraham developed other layers of kinship through baptismal sponsorship. When adults and children were baptized, they were accompanied by *Taufzeugen*, baptismal witnesses or sponsors who, like godparents, served as extended family and helped socialize them into the Unity. To enslaved brothers and sisters, these connections could provide an important extra web of support, or "fictive kin." When the African-born slave named Jupiter, who had arrived in 1771 with Abraham, was baptized and christened Paul in 1783, his sponsors were Abraham and two other black Moravians, Johann Samuel and Christian. Together they formed a small black sub-family united by spiritual kinship within the congregation. Abraham also served as godfather to one of Paul's children named, significantly, Abraham. Because naming a child after a grandparent or other relative or respected person was common in Africa, Paul and Abraham seemed to be adapting that custom to Christian practice in America, reflecting their affinity through what historians call the "idiom of kinship."[18]

When Abraham expressed the desire to marry, the Elders arranged that, too, as they did for everyone, white or black. To keep individual free will at bay, no one was at liberty to court potential mates; all co-religionists had to wait for the elders to broker matches in accordance with God's perceived preference. In Abraham's case, the Elders scouted around, identified an enslaved woman named Sarah in a nearby community, and asked her whether she would be willing to marry him, even giving her "an opportunity to get to know Abraham" before deciding. Both prospective partners had the right to agree to or decline the match. The records do not say, but it seems at least possible the Elders chose Sarah as a counterpart to her Biblical namesake, completing the symmetrical couple from Genesis, Abraham and Sarah. In any case, she agreed, they purchased her, and the two were married. In the midst of a slave society wantonly indifferent to the formation or sanctity of enslaved families, Abraham's and Sarah's marriage was an odd mixture of control and consent that both limited and preserved a degree of personal choice.[19]

Little further information about the couple's marriage has survived. They had no children. But there was this: Abraham left Sarah money in his will. When he died in 1797, the Elders explained, he "left a sort of testament concerning his own estate, in which he makes his widow Sarah heir of his cash money, with the condition that one Brother should keep it and give it to her from time to time as she needs it." The idea of an enslaved person leaving an estate, a will, and an heir is rare, to say the least. But if a will is a documentary bridge between the past and the future, Abraham's legacy suggests that he thought it vital to remember Sarah by improving her remaining years in servitude. It also indicates that, like some enslaved Moravians who were paid for their work, Abraham earned wages at the tannery, or that he had some source of income by which to accumulate savings and property. That in itself was not unusual, since many enslaved people earned money by raising and selling garden produce or by hiring themselves out for all kinds of extra work. In fact, Abraham had received his own small plot of land years earlier, though whether he earned money from it is unknown. But the ability to store his savings and to trust white people to disburse them to his wife was a function of his respected place in the congregation. In his will, he also left belongings to his co-workers in the tannery, a sign that he might have felt a sense of camaraderie toward them, in contrast to his early years of resentment and resistance. Christian fellowship blurred the boundaries between slavery and freedom.[20]

What, then, are we to make of one displaced African's experience with enslavement and with religion in early America? Historians have long debated the extent to which African religions and cultures, or aspects of them, survived the dislocation and alienation of the slave trade. Some have argued that, as cultural systems dependent on a panoply of deities, kinship networks, and ancestor spirits, African religions could not be preserved intact under slavery and were essentially destroyed. Others contend that in regions with a high ratio of Africans in the population, continually renewed through the slave trade, as in lowcountry South Carolina and Georgia or, especially, in the Caribbean and Brazil, African religious practices and beliefs persisted, even thrived, in American exile and were passed on to successive generations. Still others suggest a fusion of these positions: African religions were neither extinguished nor preserved entirely but changed and adapted to different situations as African-descended people melded elements from several traditions, infusing them into Christianity and creating new kinds of religious formats. It is possible that, depending on location and circumstance, any and all of these might happen at once in any given population or region.[21]

It is difficult to judge where Abraham fit on this spectrum of religious continuity and change. It is possible, perhaps likely, that he, too, experienced all those variations at different times, or simultaneously. We do not have his own words describing the emotions and thoughts behind his turn to Christianity — whether he thought the African spirits had deserted him, or that he might regenerate his flagging spirituality in the Moravian Church, or that it was purely a practical decision. Did he still honor African deities behind a Christian mask, as many Africans probably did? The records do not say. His cohort of fellow black Moravians was too small to sustain vigorous observance of African religiosity, at least outwardly; privately, perhaps.

Thinking of him as a Muslim-turned-Christian offers few helpful clues either. Both monotheistic religions, Islam and Christianity shared the original patriarch, his namesake Abraham, and the first five books of the Bible. If he had been raised and educated in Islam, which recognized Jesus as a prophet (though not as God's son or as a savior), he would have been familiar with some of the tenets of Christianity by the time he arrived in North Carolina. Perhaps that familiarity and those shared texts eased the way into Christianity. On the other hand, slave owners and missionaries sometimes described enslaved Muslims as so resistant to, even contemptuous of, any religion other than Islam, that they held themselves aloof from non-Muslims, including fellow Africans. Some wrote documents in Arabic testifying to the faith that survived the slave trade to endure in America, though one of the best-known of these, Omar ibn Said, converted to Presbyterianism late in life. Moravian records, including the *Lebenslauf*, make no mention of Abraham observing Muslim prayer before he became a Christian, and there is no other indication of his steadfast adherence to Islam other than his overall disdain for the Moravians until he became one. The surviving evidence is ambiguous enough that, if we try to conclude much about the durability or flexibility of African beliefs in America based on the case of this one man, we reach a dead end.

But what we do have is the *Lebenslauf*, the rare manuscript, written in archaic German script and tucked away in a church archive, that tells the life story of one survivor of the slave trade. How did it come into being, and what further clues might it hold? Every Moravian left a *Lebenslauf*. Most people wrote their own as a first-person autobiography or memoir, which, after their death, the minister would finish in the third person and read aloud at the funeral. It was meant to be an instructive document that illustrated the stony path from spiritual deadness to resurrection in Jesus' loving embrace. Many conversion narratives in other

Christian traditions followed a similar format. While providing some details about the outer circumstances of life — birthplace, occupation, marriage, and family — memoirists typically recounted a sinful life of abandon that gave way to doubt, spiritual crisis, and eventually a last-ditch, and life-saving, resolution to turn their corrupt selves over to Christ. In this vein, Abraham "came to the thorough perception of his lost condition and admitted openheartedly and repentantly to a Brother what a slave of sin he had been up to now and how much he would like to be saved and become happy. It was a comfort for him that Jesus Christ had come into this world to make sinner happy. He prayed to the Lord for mercy and pardon."

No one who embraced the Christian life was expected to be perfect, and the documents often refer obliquely to waywardness overcome through prayer and faith. And so it was with Abraham, who, the *Lebenslauf* recounts, "had some weaknesses in his character that required the patience of his master and all those who were around him." Smoothing life's rough edges, the *Lebenslauf* was a lesson imparted and learned. On his deathbed, Abraham "prayed like a child the verse: The blood and righteousness of Christ are my adornment and dress of honor."[22]

The style of the genre had a tendency to stifle the individual voice, making it difficult to peer behind the formulaic language for the qualities that made the narrator singular. In Abraham's case, because he was unable to write himself, a minister wrote his life story in the third person, taking details of Abraham's life, filtering and shaping them into a narrative that suited the convention, likely omitting things that did not fit. Abraham's heathenish experiences in Africa serve as a prelude to Christian redemption, thereby almost justifying his enslavement as necessary to God's plan. Reserving the right to appropriate an enslaved Brother's life for a larger purpose, the minister spun his own interpretation of Abraham's actions and motivations. Mediated by such editorship, the *Lebenslauf* seems to contain little of the subject's own voice, his distinctive Africanness. Nor can we glean what he really thought about Christianity.

But stamp his mark on the document he did. At some point, the minister must have explained the idea of the *Lebenslauf* and asked to interview him about his life. Or perhaps Abraham approached the minister and offered to tell his story. Either way, here was an extraordinarily unusual opportunity for an African to preserve some record of his existence. We can imagine a conversation, or several, in a church, perhaps, or in Abraham's home, in which he unspooled the details as the minister scribbled. Mandingo; early religiosity; wife and children; warfare and captivity; French West Indies; arrival in North Carolina. Only he would know those things; only he could explain why his ears got clipped or how he fell into enemy hands, never to see home again. The narration must have lasted hours. The life details that, in most Moravian *Lebensläufe*, sketch out an ordinary backdrop to a life in Christ, here govern the story, demanding attention. No doubt he struggled to explain some things in German, and it is impossible to know what the minister misunderstood, misrepresented, did not ask, or left out. No one who survived the Middle Passage, for instance, could have forgotten it — a description of two months on a slave ship, his forced odyssey from one life to another, might have proven cathartic for him and priceless for historians. Yet, the memoir makes no mention of it.

Still, Abraham remembered. In the African storytelling tradition, he became something like a griot, an oral historian, a keeper of the past, a witness, a remembrancer. To orate a chronicle was a venerated act: it condensed time, it connected history to the present, it told of gods and ancestors working in human affairs. In recounting his own story, Abraham kept alive his people's memory, for himself and for anyone who would hear it or read it. To be sure, it was a saga of loss and subjugation, of captivity, enslavement, and lifelong displacement in another world across the sea. If a minister reworked it into a parable of Christian triumph, then so be it. It was also a survivor's deposition, a record of fortitude, a link to generations past and future, a chant of outlasting. Perhaps this testimony best expressed an undying African spirit, a form of sacred knowledge adapted to American exile. Abraham claimed the right to tell his own story. His memory, and his appropriation of the memoir format, worked as a type of spirit travel, of transport to another dimension, a "cosmic crossing," as the historian of religion, Thomas Tweed, calls it, "between the most distant horizon and the most intimate domain." And from at least one perspective, his memory excavation worked: more than two hundred years later, we now know how one captive African transcended affliction to make a life in America.[23]

As black Brothers and Sisters intersected with white Moravians in life, so they did in death. Moravians believed that death leveled social distinctions, a view shared by enslaved Africans and African Americans who looked forward to liberty in the afterlife and, perhaps, the soul's return to Africa. Following an illness, Abraham died in 1797 and was buried in the interracial church graveyard, or "God's Acre," a few feet from Heinrich Herbst, his master in the tannery for nearly thirty years. Within a few years, such burials would cease. In the early nineteenth century, white Moravians, like many evangelicals and others, recoiled from including black co-religionists because the implied equality of that practice threatened their increasing use of slave labor. They assigned black worshipers to separate benches at the back of the church; then banned them from rituals like the kiss of peace; then allotted their burials to a separate graveyard; then excluded them from fellowship altogether, setting up a new all-black congregation in 1822. In the Moravian community, as elsewhere throughout the young nation, prospects for a just society faded as Christianity's complicity with slavery intensified in the American South.

Finding a sort of refuge in the church, Abraham lived in the seam between slavery and freedom. In some ways, he was atypical of most enslaved Africans in America, few of whom assimilated into a German religious fellowship. In other ways, his experience was representative of all survivors of the transatlantic slave trade. Though they faced a harsh new environment as best they could with few resources, perhaps their greatest asset was the power of the devotional embedded in the power of recall. To remember was to live.

FURTHER READING

Berlin, Ira. *Many Thousands Gone: The First Two Centuries of Slavery in North America*. Cambridge, MA: Belknap Press, 1998.

Horne, Gerald. *The Counter-Revolution of 1776: Slave Resistance and the Origins of the United States of America*. New York: New York University Press, 2014.

Raboteau, Albert. *Slave Religion: The "Invisible Institution" in the Antebellum South*. New York: Oxford University Press, 1978.

Sobel, Mechal. *The World They Made Together: Black and White Values in Eighteenth-Century Virginia*. Princeton: Princeton University Press, 1987.

Sommer, Elisabeth. *Serving Two Masters: Moravian Brethren in Germany and North Carolina, 1727–1801*. Lexington: University Press of Kentucky, 2000.

Tweed, Thomas A. *Crossing and Dwelling: A Theory of Religion*. Cambridge, MA: Harvard University Press, 2006.

BIBLIOGRAPHY

Bennett, Herman. *Africans in Colonial Mexico: Absolutism, Christianity, and Afro-Creole Consciousness*. (Bloomington: Indiana University Press, 2003).

Brown, Vincent. "Social Death and Political Life in the Study of Slavery." *American Historical Review* 114 (2009): 1231–1249.

Carretta, Vincent, ed. *Unchained Voices: An Anthology of Black Authors in the English-Speaking World of the Eighteenth Century*. Lexington: University Press of Kentucky, 2003.

Davis, David Brion. *The Problem of Slavery in Western Culture*. New York: NCROL, 1967.

Donnan, Elizabeth, ed. *Documents Illustrative of the History of the Slave Trade to America*. 4 vols. Washington D.C.: Willian S. Hein, 1930–1935.

Faull, Katherine. *Moravian Women's Memoirs: Related Lives, 1750–1820*. Syracuse: Syracuse University Press, 1997.

Frey, Sylvia. *Water from the Rock: Black Resistance in a Revolutionary Age*. Princeton: Princeton University Press, 1992.

_____. "The Visible Church: Historiography of African-American Religion Since Raboteau." *Slavery and Abolition* 29 (2008): 83–110.

_____. "The Visible Church: Historiography of African-American Religion Since Raboteau." *Slavery and Betty Wood. Come Shouting to Zion: African American Protestantism in the American South and British Caribbean through* 1830. Chapel Hill: University of North Carolina Press, 1998.

Fries, Adelaide, et al., eds. *Records of the Moravians in North Carolina*. 11 vols. Raleigh: 1922–1969.

Gerbner, Katharine. *Christian Slavery: Conversion and Race in the Protestant Atlantic World*. Philadelphia: University of Pennsylvania Press, 2018.

Goetz, Rebecca Anne. *The Baptism of Early Virginia: How Christianity Created Race*. Baltimore: Johns Hopkins University Press, 2012.

Gomez, Michael A. "Africans, Culture, and Islam in the Lowcountry." In *African American Life in the Georgia Lowcountry: The Atlantic World and the Gullah Geechee*, edited by Philip Morgan, 103–130. Athens: University of Georgia Press, 2010.

_____. *Exchanging Our Country Marks: The Transformation of African Identities in the Colonial and Antebellum South*. Chapel Hill: University of North Carolina Press, 1998.

Kaplan, Sidney and Emma Nogrady Kaplan. *The Black Presence in the Era of the American Revolution*. 2nd ed. Amherst: University of Massachusetts Press, 1989.

Lindsay, Lisa A. and John Wood Sweet, eds. *Biography and the Black Atlantic*. Philadelphia: University of Pennsylvania Press, 2014.

Lovejoy, Paul E. *Transformation in Slavery: A History of Slavery in Africa*. 3rd ed. New York: Cambridge University Press, 2011.

Moglen, Seth. "Enslaved in the City on a Hill: The Archive of Moravian Slavery and the Practical Past." *History and the Present* 6 (2016): 155–183.

Patterson, Orlando. *Slavery and Social Death: A Comparative Study*. Cambridge, MA: Harvard University Press, 1982.

Rediker, Marcus. *The Slave Ship: A Human History*. New York: Penguin Books, 2008.

Rodney, Walter. *History of the Upper Guinea Coast, 1545–1800*. New York: Monthly Review Press, 1970.

Schwartz, Stuart B. "Cleansing Original Sin: Godparenthood and the Baptism of Slaves in Eighteenth-Century Bahia." In *Kinship Ideology and Practice in Latin America*, edited by Raymond T. Smith, 35–56. Chapel Hill: University of North Carolina Press, 1984.

Scott, Rebecca J. and Jean M. Hébrard. *Freedom Papers: An Atlantic Odyssey in the Age of Emancipation*. Cambridge, MA: Harvard University Press, 2014.

Sensbach, Jon F. *A Separate Canaan: The Making of an Afro-Moravian World in North Carolina, 1763–1840*. Chapel Hill: Omohundro Institute and University of North Carolina Press, 1998.

_____. *Rebecca's Revival: Creating Black Christianity in the Atlantic World*. Cambridge, MA: Harvard University Press, 2005.

Smallwood, Stephanie. *Saltwater Slavery: A Middle Passage from Africa to American Diaspora*. Cambridge, MA: Harvard University Press, 2008

Sparks, Randy J. *Africans in the Old South: Mapping Exceptional Lives across the Atlantic World*. Cambridge, MA: Harvard University Press, 2016.

Sweet, James. *Domingos Álvares, African Healing, and the Intellectual History of the Atlantic World*. Chapel Hill: University of North Carolina Press, 2013.

Thornton, John K. *Africa and Africans in the Making of the Atlantic World, 1400–1680*. 2nd ed. New York: Cambridge University Press, 1998.

Thorp, Daniel B. "Chattel with a Soul: The Autobiography of a Moravian Slave." *Pennsylvania Magazine of History and Biography* (1988): 433–451.

Tweed, Thomas A. *Crossing and Dwelling: A Theory of Religion*. Cambridge, MA: Harvard University Press, 2006.

Wheat, David. *Atlantic Africa and the Spanish Caribbean, 1570–1640*. Chapel Hill: University of North Carolina Press, 2016.

NOTES

1   The exceptions to these generalizations are growing. A collection of autobiographical accounts of enslaved Africans and African Americans in the eighteenth-century Anglophone world is Vincent Carretta, ed., *Unchained Voices: An Anthology of Black Authors in the English-Speaking World of the Eighteenth Century* (Lexington: University Press of Kentucky, 2003.) Through patient archival research, historians have also begun to trace the outlines of other African lives in the Atlantic world. Recent examples include Lisa A. Lindsay and John Wood Sweet, eds., *Biography and the Black Atlantic* (Philadelphia: University of Pennsylvania Press, 2014); Randy J. Sparks, *Africans in the Old South: Mapping Exceptional Lives across the Atlantic World* (Cambridge, MA: Harvard University Press, 2016); James Sweet, *Domingos Alvares, African Healing, and the Intellectual History of the Atlantic World* (Chapel Hill: University of North Carolina Press, 2013); Rebecca J. Scott and Jean M. Hébrard, *Freedom Papers: An Atlantic Odyssey in the Age of Emancipation* (Cambridge, MA: Harvard University Press, 2014).

2   Abraham's *Lebenslauf,* along with those of thousands of other church members, including several black congregants, is housed in the Moravian Church Archives, Southern Province, in Winston-Salem, North Carolina. The full document can be read in Jon F. Sensbach, *A Separate Canaan: The Making of an Afro-Moravian World in North Carolina, 1763–1840* (Chapel Hill: Omohundro Institute and North Carolina University Press, 1998), 309–311, from which this essay is adapted.

3   *Lebenslauf* of Abraham; Walter Rodney, *History of the Upper Guinea Coast, 1545–1800* (New York: Monthly Review Press, 1970); David Wheat, *Atlantic Africa and the Spanish Caribbean, 1570–1640* (Chapel Hill: University of North Carolina Press, 2016), 34–42.

4   *Lebenslauf* of Abraham; Michael A. Gomez, "Africans, Culture, and Islam in the Lowcountry," in Philip Morgan, ed., *African American Life in the Georgia Lowcountry: The Atlantic World and the Gullah Geechee* (Athens: University of Georgia Press, 2010), 103–130, esp. 103–104.

5   Elizabeth Donnan, ed., *Documents Illustrative of the History of the Slave Trade to America,* 4 vols. (Washington DC: William S. Hein, 1930–1935), vol. 4, 599; *Lebenslauf* of Abraham. On the course of the West African slave trade during these years, see Paul E. Lovejoy, *Transformation in Slavery: A History of Slavery in Africa,* 3rd ed. (New York: Cambridge University Press, 2011).

6   *Lebenslauf* of Abraham; Daniel B. Thorp, "Chattel with a Soul: The Autobiography of a Moravian Slave," *Pennsylvania Magazine of History and Biography* (1988): 448.

7   Marcus Rediker, *The Slave Ship: A Human History* (New York: Penguin Books, 2008); Stephanie Smallwood, *Saltwater Slavery: A Middle Passage from Africa to American Diaspora* (Cambridge, MA: Harvard University Press, 2008).

8   *Lebenslauf* of Abraham; Minutes of the Society for the Propagation of the Gospel to the Heathen, Nov. 1802, Section B1, Moravian Archives.

9   *Lebenslauf* of Abraham.

10 Provincial Helpers' Conference, Nov. 21, 1774; *Aufseher Collegium* (Board of Overseers), June 28, 1775, both in Moravian Archives. On the American Revolution as a period of heightened resistance and window of opportunity for freedom among African Americans, see Sylvia R. Frey, *Water from the Rock: Black Resistance in a Revolutionary Age* (Princeton: Princeton University Press, 1992).

11 Adelaide Fries, ed., *Records of the Moravians in North Carolina,* 11 vols. (Raleigh: 1922–69), Vol. 2:876–877; *Aufseher Collegium,* April 19, 1776.

12 *Lebenslauf* of Abraham; *Aeltesten Conferenz* (Elders' Conference), Dec. 13 and 20, 1780, Moravian Archives.

13 Orlando Patterson, *Slavery and Social Death: A Comparative Study* (Cambridge, MA: Harvard University Press, 1982). For a recent reassessment of Patterson's thesis, see Vincent Brown, "Social Death and Political Life in the Study of Slavery," *American Historical Review* 114 (2009): 1231–1249.

14 Herman Bennett, *Africans in Colonial Mexico: Absolutism, Christianity, and Afro-Creole Consciousness* (Bloomington: Indiana University Press, 2003); John K. Thornton, *Africa and Africans in the Making of the Atlantic World, 1400–1680,* 2nd ed. (New York: Cambridge University Press, 1998).

15 Rebecca Anne Goetz, *The Baptism of Early Virginia: How Christianity Created Race* (Baltimore: Johns Hopkins University Press, 2012); Katharine Gerbner, *Christian Slavery: Conversion and Race in the Protestant Atlantic World* (Philadelphia: University of Pennsylvania Pres, 2018).

16 Goetz, *Baptism of Early Virginia,* 1; Katharine Gerbner, "'We are against the traffick of Men-Body': The Germantown Quaker Protest of 1688 and the Origins of American Abolitionism," *Pennsylvania History* 74 (2007): 149–172; David Brion Davis, *The Problem of Slavery in Western Culture* (New York: NCROL, 1967), 344.

17 Sylvia R. Frey and Betty Wood, *Come Shouting to Zion: African American Protestantism in the American South and British Caribbean through 1830* (Chapel Hill: University of North Carolina Press, 1998); Jon Sensbach, *Rebecca's Revival: Creating Black Christianity in the Atlantic World* (Cambridge, MA: Harvard University Press, 2005); Sidney Kaplan and Emma Nogrady Kaplan, *The Black Presence in the Era of the American Revolution,* 2nd ed. (Amherst: University of Massachusetts Press, 1989), 13.

18 Stuart B. Schwartz, "Cleansing Original Sin: Godparenthood and the Baptism of Slaves in Eighteenth-Century Bahia" in Raymond T. Smith, ed., *Kinship Ideology and Practice in Latin America* (Chapel Hill: University of North Carolina Press, 1984), 35–56.

19 *Aeltesten Conferenz,* June 22, July 20, and 27, 1785.

20 *Aufseher Collegium,* April. 18, 25, 1797; *Aeltesten Conferenz,* Nov. 5, 1783.

21 For an overview of these debates, see Sylvia R. Frey, "The Visible Church: Historiography of African-American Religion Since Raboteau," *Slavery and Abolition* 29 (2008): 83–110; Michael A. Gomez, *Exchanging Our Country Marks: The Transformation of African Identities in the Colonial and Antebellum South* (Chapel Hill: University of North Carolina Press, 1998), esp. 244–290.

22 Katherine Faull, *Moravian Women's Memoirs: Related Lives, 1750–1820* (Syracuse: Syracuse University Press, 1997); Seth Moglen, "Enslaved in the City on a Hill: The Archive of Moravian Slavery and the Practical Past," *History and the Present* 6 (2016): 155–183.

23 Thomas A. Tweed, *Crossing and Dwelling: A Theory of Religion* (Cambridge, MA: Harvard University Press, 2006), 123, 158.

Chapter Nine

THE WHITE RIVER WITCH-HUNT AND INDIGENOUS PEOPLES' NEGOTIATIONS WITH MISSIONARIES IN THE ERA OF THE EARLY REPUBLIC

Lori J. Daggar
Ursinus College, Collegeville, Pennsylvania

On April 1, 1806, John Peter Kluge, Moravian missionary, had had enough. He wrote from his mission post to Brother Loskiel, a fellow Moravian who was then residing in Bethlehem, Pennsylvania, that he would "most earnestly and at the same time most humbly beg you to call us away from this post." He continued to assure Loskiel that "we are ready and willing to be used further in the service of the dear Saviour, *only not here.*"[1] Kluge wrote his letter from his mission near the White River in Indian Country and what was then, to Euro-Americans, known as Indiana Territory. He had been working there among the Delawares along with his colleague, Abraham Luckenbach, for several years. The two men had been joined by a small group of individuals who had, according to them, converted to the Christian faith. One was Joshua, a Mohican man who had experienced numerous hardships throughout his life and who served as the missionaries' interpreter. Another was Caritas, baptized Ann Charity, a Delaware woman who, from all appearances, had aimed to live her life according to her adopted religion. Both individuals had chosen to associate with the Moravians, and by the time of Kluge's letter, both were dead.

Just days prior, area Delawares embraced the leadership of the Shawnee Prophet Tenskwatawa and conducted a witch-hunt. Tenskwatawa claimed that the Great Spirit visited him in a dream and told him of a paradise open to those who lived correctly by abstaining from alcohol, lasciviousness and adultery, excessive violence, and witchcraft.[2] He then spread his message against witchcraft and other vices among Shawnees, Delawares, and Wyandots alike, providing words that proved foundational to renewed pan-indigenous unity. Such spiritual messages supported his brother Tecumseh's famed resistance to the United States in the years prior to and during the War of 1812, and it proved meaningful for Native peoples besieged by US imperialism.[3] At the heart of Tenskwatawa and Tecumseh's movement were two interconnected concerns — maintaining Indigenous identity and culture and remaining unmolested on their lands. Delawares who conducted and supported the witch-hunt aligned themselves with this vision: the 1806 witch-hunt was part of a broader effort to counter

A Companion to American Religious History, First Edition. Edited by Benjamin E. Park.

Euro-American cultural and territorial encroachments, and it was intricately connected with ideas of Indigenous identity and land.

While the number of witch-hunt victims is unknown, several are explicitly named by the Moravian missionaries who recorded the ordeal in their mission diary. Two were Ann Charity and Joshua, while three others — Tetapatchsit, Billy Patterson, and Hockingpompsga — were recent signatories to a land treaty that threatened to obliterate Delawares' land claims in the region. As the list suggests, each was connected with the mission, Euro-Americans, or Euro-American culture in some way. As such, the witch-hunt was a dramatic event that struck terror into the hearts of the Moravian diarists, and the Moravians' diary thus offers a great deal of insights into the event and the mission itself as well as the peoples and politics of the region.[4]

The witch-hunt that took place in 1806 near the White River was not an occurrence that proved commonplace. Missions among Native Americans during the era of the early republic were not always associated with such dramatically deadly affairs — though the political, social, and cultural violence that they could bring to Indigenous communities of North America was potent enough. Nonetheless, the intense conflagration of suspicions, animosities, and politics, showcases in stark relief the importance of studying mission spaces in the early nineteenth century due to the negotiations of power and authority that took place within and near them as well as among the peoples who inhabited them. Missions could and did serve as outposts of Americans' empire — places where Euro-Americans brought and endeavored to convert Native peoples to their notions of religion and economy. Yet, far from being places where Euro-Americans wielded complete control, missionaries were there met by Indigenous peoples who strategically chose to engage with the missions or refuse them. In the case of the White River Delawares, the Moravians proved to be unsuccessful; their mission failed. In many cases, however, missions could combine with US policies and settlers to facilitate Native peoples' dispossession and removals, even while they offered some Native peoples additional opportunities to negotiate or combat those policies.[5]

In light of the complex history of missions in the early republic, the failed mission at White River is instructive. The Moravians undertook their mission as others — members of the Society of Friends (Quakers), Baptists, Methodists, and the American Board of Commissioners for Foreign Missions (ABCFM) — began or would soon begin to spearhead the US civilization plan that was premised upon offering agricultural education to agriculturally-proficient Native peoples. Those missions that were aligned with the civilization plan, as they were increasingly as time wore on, were products and producers of a shifting geopolitical reality on the North American continent. They were crucial nodes in the development of a changing economy — an economy marked by the growth of markets and profits — and they were also physical spaces that facilitated changes to landscapes, economies, and local politics. The Moravians' failed mission was, on the other hand, more driven by the quest to proselytize, and it did not enjoy the same degree of federal financial and diplomatic support that other contemporary missions did.[6] Despite these general differences, however, Euro-Americans' missions did share the common goal of changing Native peoples' societies. Both were also places where Native peoples could use missionaries as diplomatic connections between themselves and the federal government, or where they could send a clear message that their politics was of the distinctly anti-settler-encroachment variety. Mission spaces in the early republic thus operated as zones of contact and negotiation, just as they did during earlier eras and with other imperial powers in North America. They reveal the ways in which nineteenth-century Euro-Americans both borrowed and diverged from other imperial precedents as well as how Native peoples continued to assert authority and pursue a politics of their own in ways that had lasting consequences for themselves and for the US imperial state. Analyzing the history of the White River mission and the violent event that took place there offers a means to trace the myriad politics and worldviews that could meet in and near mission spaces and that met in Delaware Country in 1806.

* * *

Abraham Luckenbach and John Peter Kluge traversed the same roads and crossed the same rivers as many of their fellow settlers did in the early nineteenth century. Their journey from present-day Pennsylvania to present-day Indiana took them through settler towns such as Marietta, Ohio, and it led them to rub elbows with myriad Euro-Americans and Native peoples alike. Their White River diary, meant to document their mission work on Indiana's White River among the Delawares living there, captures their profound uncertainty, unabashed biases, and sometimes-harsh judgments of those whose paths they encountered, and it captures, too, their observations of a world-in-flux.

The Moravians liked Marietta, Ohio, in particular, and noted that it was "a pretty little town, with an especially fine situation, in a pleasing neighborhood."[7] Much of that fine situation was the result of the town's position on the Ohio River, the primary route from the eastern coast to the heart of the continent and the waters of the Mississippi that there awaited westward travelers and their wares. In 1805, the town possessed "a large trade," a consequence of its river access. The missionaries observed that a ship was "ready to be loaded with flour and go down the Mississippi, and then sail from there to Havana."[8] The grain bounties of the Ohio Country traveled from this small town upon the Ohio and then the Mississippi, where it flowed from New Orleans to the oceanic ports of a number of Atlantic empires. Such commerce rendered places like Marietta an obvious way point for travelers, and such migration and the services supporting it only fueled further the town's growing market economy.

While the two men enjoyed their time among the settlers of Marietta, Luckenbach and Kluge did not smile quite so kindly upon all whom they encountered during their travels, and they chose to indicate as much, in particular, by noting that some did not live up to their own ideas of cleanliness. In the fall of 1805, for example, they noted that some "white people living in this neighborhood ... did not look much cleaner than the Indians."[9] At another location they observed that "In our room there was a barrel of honey in which a child was wading about, and an old man, the grandfather of the child, would every now and then scrape the honey off the child's legs." They then expressed their disgust when they observed that "Some of this honey was put on the table for the evening meal."[10] Similarly, when the two men stayed with hosts in Pennsylvania who offered them beds "infested with bugs" and meals pertaining of "sickly looking mutton," they were unhappy.[11] The passages reveal their condescension and scorn for others, and suggest that they compared what they considered to be a lack of hygiene among Euro-American settlers with the status of Native peoples.

In contrast, the men expressed comfort and admiration when they encountered fellow Germans; their observations reveal a bit about settler life and the varied peoples who inhabited and squatted upon lands towards the heart of the continent, but they also offer a glimpse into the many culturally-based biases that these men carried with them on their mission ventures. The two men were overjoyed, for example, when they found themselves in the company of fellow Germans. Everything among those folk, they claimed, "was very neat and clean, and we had good meals which compensated for the poor quarters of the night before."[12] Euro-Americans often used cleanliness as a barometer of one's supposed civilized status, and these men clearly had a preference for individuals of German heritage.[13] They were German and felt most at home among their fellow Germans. Their judgments offer, like other missionaries' writings, both a window into the social world of North America, as well as a cautionary reminder of the men's own perspectives and worldviews.

Other missionaries in the early republic likewise shared in the practice of evaluating others based upon their notions of civilization, similarity, and difference. Such notions were, of course, not new to the early nineteenth century. Since the earliest days of Euro-American missionary projects in North America and the Atlantic world, traveling religious individuals offered their assessments of Indigenous peoples, fellow Europeans, and African and African-descended peoples alike. Ideas of savagery and civilization produced notions of a hierarchy of peoples who, according to missionaries, required saving from their own ways.

In the early years of the republic, such ideas of a hierarchy of civilized and barbaric peoples offered one reasoning behind the United States' plan to "civilize" the Native peoples of North America.[14] These missions emphasized agricultural education and labor. While Euro-Americans' own biases, assumptions, and ideas of race certainly lurked behind such mission efforts, economic considerations too were at the heart of such civilizing schemes.[15] The early republic's *mission complex* combined ideas of civilization and "benevolence" with material economic development efforts: both missions and the US factory stores that supplied agricultural implements to regional settlers and Native peoples served as nodes in a network that linked manufacturers and shippers on the urban coast with lands in the heart of the continent. Manufactured axes and ploughs made Euro-American style agricultural education possible, while mission spaces contributed to Euro-Americans' visions of material changes and development on the land — fences and mills, for example. Like missions of the Spanish empire in North America before them, civilizing missions in the early imperial United States thus operated as spaces where religious, individual, and state interests converged. Like the Spanish too, such missions nonetheless offered spaces for Native peoples to negotiate the terms of American imperialism: they could employ missionary labor for their own investments in their land, and they could use missionaries as diplomatic envoys between themselves and the US federal government. Unlike the Spanish, however, these missions were part and parcel of an emerging market capitalist political economy.[16]

For their part, Kluge and Luckenbach did not seem quite so invested in such economic and agricultural projects. Rather, they focused their efforts on the "saving" of Native souls and proselytizing. Theirs was a mission that likewise borrowed from earlier imperial precedents. Most notoriously, both Spanish and French missionaries in the heart of the continent emphasized the importance of baptism and "saving" Native peoples from what these Europeans feared would be certain damnation. The Spanish missions in Pueblo Country and in what is now California were notoriously abusive, while the French seemingly pursued a somewhat more accommodating approach to proselytizing, though produced ample violence of their own. Underlying each approach was — as it was with Moravians — a culturally-grounded sense of difference, barbarism, and increasingly as time wore on, race.[17]

The Moravians were also familiar with mission work in the eastern woodlands. In 1741, the Moravians founded Bethlehem in eastern Pennsylvania. The town served as missionaries' base; from there, men and women could travel freely outward, toward Native and European villages alike.[18] As Katherine Carté Engel makes clear, Bethlehem's primary aim was to facilitate Moravians' proselytizing work. The town was set up communally: each individual inhabitant of Bethlehem performed functions supportive of Moravian missionary endeavors and were identified as members of either the "pilgrim congregation" or the "house congregation." "Pilgrims" traveled to mission outposts, while members of the "house congregation" ensured that such travelers had a home upon their return.[19] Kluge and Luckenbach operated very much on their brethren's eighteenth-century model of missionary work: they left their homes behind in order to proselytize and would return once their mission was complete.

* * *

Events did not, however, unfold quite as the Moravian men had imagined upon their departure for Indian Country. Rather, Kluge and Luckenbach's mission on the White River exacerbated political divisions among the Delawares who already lived there. The first decade of the nineteenth century was one of intense tension, particularly among Native peoples in the Ohio Country. British and Americans settled in the area and competed for Indigenous loyalties, while Native peoples, in turn, worked to carve out space for themselves, courted both sides for political and economic favor, as well as listened to the politics of Indigenous leaders like the Shawnee brothers Tenskwatawa and Tecumseh. The Shawnee men's efforts to create a pan-Indigenous alliance in the region and as far south as Cherokee Country appealed to those Delawares who hoped to combat Euro-American presence and influence in the region. Such politics added to local concerns to foster intense debate among Delawares, Shawnees, and their neighbors.[20]

In the midst of this debate arrived Luckenbach and Kluge. Ideas of difference between and among Native peoples and Euro-Americans came to the fore as Delawares adjusted to the mission's presence. Such was often the case with missions in the early republic. Shawnees and Miamis in the Ohio Country, too, debated the extent to which they should ally with members of the Society of Friends and their mission outposts — and with Euro-Americans more generally — in what is now Ohio and Indiana; they too, received visits from the Shawnee Prophet Tenskwatawa. Missions often heightened political debate among Native peoples as some, like Shawnees at Wapakoneta, endeavored to use missions and missionaries to their benefit, while others saw them as additional evidence of Euro-Americans' ever-creeping presence. Mission spaces were thus places where indigenous leaders and individuals construed and negotiated their stances regarding Euro-Americans as well as the extent to which they would adopt settlers' ideas and practices. The White River mission was no different, and Delawares' political divides and notions of difference made the Moravians' theological work increasingly difficult as the months wore on.

Complicating the Moravians' work was the fact that many Delawares were not particularly interested in joining the ranks of the converted. Instead, they evoked ideas of "separate creations" and race in their dismissals of the Moravians' proselytizing.[21] One brother wrote, for example, that the Delaware Chief Pachgantschihillas, told them that "We have another skin, therefore our teaching must be different, too." The Moravians also recorded the chief as indicating that "the Indians had to hold fast to their customs and not believe that which we were teaching, for this was meant only for the white people."[22] Here, the sentiments recorded by the Moravians offered Pachgantschihillas's particular worldview, yet one that others undoubtedly shared. Indeed, such ideas were not new among Delawares. The Presbyterian missionary David Brainerd recorded similar sentiments in the mid-eighteenth century. Brainerd recorded that "[The Delawares] told me that the great God first made three men and three women, viz.: the Indian, the negro, and the white man. That the white man was the youngest brother, and therefore the white people ought not to think themselves better than the Indians." According to Brainerd's records, the Delawares also indicated "That God gave the white man a book, and told him that he must worship him by that; but gave none either to the Indian or negro, and therefore it could not be right for them to have a book, or be any way concerned with that way of worship."[23] Both ideas of racial difference old and new and religious difference mapped onto one another to lead Delawares to harbor great suspicion of the Moravians' teachings by 1806.

The Moravians' presence among Delawares also stirred painful memories of past traumas. In 1782, settlers massacred nearly 100 Delawares at a Moravian mission post, many of whom had adopted Christianity, on the Tuscarawas River in Ohio. In discussing their lack of success in 1803, Brother Kluge noted that the Delawares "advance as an excuse, the murder of the believing Indians in Gnadenhütten, and say: 'The white teachers were to blame that our friends were murdered, therefore we will take heed that we are not made tame, too; otherwise we will fare likewise.' "[24] Such fears of being "made tame" were also linked with land treaties and US overtures of benevolence. The language of treaties often involved rhetoric of protection and civilization, and were likewise often premised upon Native peoples offering their promises of peace and friendship with the United States. One treaty with the Wyandots and their neighbors (including the Delawares) in 1805 proclaimed, for example, that "the said Indian nations do again acknowledge themselves and all their tribes, to be in friendship with, and under the protection of the United States."[25] Here, the United States presupposed that the various tribes required "the protection of the United States."

White River Delawares thus carried with them memories of not only violence but of political subjugation as well. During the eighteenth century, the Haudenosaunee, who live in what is now New York, endeavored to assert dominance over the Delawares, labeling them as "women." As scholars such as Amy Schutt and Gunlog Fur note, however, in many Indigenous societies, including the Delawares, women were hailed as peacemakers, and this notion, coupled with the Delawares' other title of "Grandfather" nation, makes the use of the term "women" in one sense indicative of respect and diplomatic power.[26] Nonetheless, the memory of the Gnadenhütten massacre combined with memories of past experiences as well as the ongoing threat of subjugation to heighten animosities against Euro-Americans — animosities that had been long brewing among the Delawares. Such experiences shaped Delawares' politics and views of missionaries and Euro-Americans in general.

With news circulating on the White River that the United States and neighboring Miamis each, in turn, laid claim to lands near Vincennes in 1804 and 1805, respectively — lands upon which Delawares made their homes — Delawares' suspicions of Euro-Americans, missionaries, and those who associated with each, grew.[27] The witch-hunt thus represented Delawares' attempt to define and enforce communal boundaries that revolved around a shared sense of history, culture, and identity. One woman descended from Ann Charity illuminated as much when she explained that the presence of Nanticokes (who were recognized by Delawares as practitioners of the supernatural), along with a series of infant deaths, encouraged the witchcraft accusations along the White River. Such suspicions, combined with the quest to preserve their lands, encouraged Delawares to view outsiders negatively. Indeed, one scholar concludes that Delawares' witch-hunt was a logical response to the crimes of the accused from Delawares' perspectives: the accused did not meet the standards and norms of Delawares' desired community.[28] The witch-hunt was, therefore, a consequence of a meeting of worldviews, suspicions, and community politics, and the mission on White River exacerbated these tensions.

* * *

Uncertainty, frustration, and the prevalent ideas of difference meant that the Moravian missionaries were not particularly welcome members of the White River Delawares' community — and Delawares did not shy from making their sentiments known. Throughout 1805 and 1806, Delawares and several of their Cherokee neighbors confronted Moravians' occupation of nearby lands by employing a number of tactics. They attacked mission livestock — prominent symbols of US efforts to "civilize" Native peoples as well as ecologically destructive by-products of Euro-American occupation of Indigenous lands.[29] In 1805, moreover, the Moravians reported that a "Cherokee family who, under false pretense, settled here against our will, prepared a sacrificial feast right in our own village, and invited to it all the young Indians of the town four miles away."[30] Using physical space to make a bold symbolic statement stripped the missionaries of autonomous authority in the same way that the recent land treaty obliterated Delaware land claims nearby. During this same episode, the missionaries noted that inhabitants of the town four miles away were rumored to "leave their place, in order that they may build nearer us."[31] Again, the gesture was one of great symbolism that had everything to do with land and power. The Delawares and their neighbors endeavored to reclaim what was once theirs. Delawares, Cherokees, and others along the White River combined space with the symbolic to assert their vision of indigenous power and unity — a vision grounded in both old and new ideas of territoriality. A similar, larger scale effort was later realized, albeit temporarily, when Tenskwatawa established "Prophetstown" in Indiana.[32] Such efforts reveal the centrality of land in Delawares' politics.

Such symbolic efforts paid psychological and, in turn, political dividends for Delawares. The Moravians' mission diary displays their manifest fear, and indeed, as soon as Cherokees and Delawares made their territorial claims, the Moravian Brothers attempted to send strands of white wampum — shell beads that were the cornerstone of Indigenous diplomacy. Such a move suggests both their familiarity with Indigenous diplomatic protocols, and that the missionaries played by Native rules of diplomatic exchange.[33] The Delawares' efforts were intelligible to the Moravians and thus effective: the missionaries understood the political symbolism of the Delawares' efforts, and they understood that they would need to engage in diplomacy if they hoped to ameliorate their situation.

Delawares confronted Moravians through territorial gestures, and they simultaneously endeavored to ensure political cohesion by excluding particular persons from within their community. Such exclusions were part of a broader contestation over meanings of community and the future of independent Native authority in North America. Beata, a female prophet who spoke among the Delawares in 1805 and 1806, played a key role in Delawares' efforts to define their community. As part of her efforts to define the parameters to which community members should adhere, she chose particular individuals to undergo what Moravians described as an examination. The examination both borrowed Christian imagery and practices — those of the Catholic Eucharist — and drew upon ideas of cleanliness and purification. According to the Moravians' diary, the prophet Beata claimed that the Great Spirit had tested her in a similar manner through a ritual examination in January 1806. According to the Moravians, Beata reported that:

> [He] asked her if she was clean and when she answered in the affirmative, he said, "We shall see if you are clean. If you are clean the good spirit will enter into you." He then showed her a small white thing, which came to her. Thereupon God said: "Hold up your hands! this is the good spirit. Take it and swallow it." … she gently put it into her mouth and swallowed. The good spirit was therefore inside of her and consequently she spoke only the Word of God.[34]

Beata's ordeal highlights the care with which we must approach historical sources that describe Native rituals. The described ritual recalls the Catholic ritual of the Eucharist, and the diarists may have invoked such a reference for a number of reasons. Beata may have relayed her experience in such a fashion — a distinct possibility given the region's history of French Catholic presence. The Moravians also may have been making a conscious or unconscious rhetorical flourish in an effort to further connect the witch-hunters and their prophets with their own ideas of — and contempt for — Catholic "superstitions." Given the detail of the entry, however, it is reasonable to assume that the Moravians did hear of some sort of "examination" taking place among the White River Delawares, and that the test did not ultimately bar Beata from power. Such an examination further suggests that in 1806, Delawares endeavored to find a method by which they could proclaim an individual — and her politics — acceptable or not. After she passed her examination, Beata, continued to craft and maintain new ideas of belonging and deviancy, though the The Shawnee Prophet, newly arrived to the White River towns, would eventually assume leadership of the witch-hunt.[35]

While many Delawares clearly understood the mission as an intrusion, by 1806, many younger Delawares regarded with contempt any individual who worked alongside the Moravians and Euro-Americans. This included those individuals associated with the mission. The missionaries' interpreter, a Mohican named Joshua, was particularly noticed by those White River Delawares who regarded the settlers with hostility. According to the Moravian diarists, Delawares targeted him for an examination similar to that of Beata on February 21, 1806. Joshua traveled with the Moravians from Pennsylvania and had, according to Kluge and Luckenbach, converted to Christianity. The Moravians' own notes regarding the man suggest, however, that rather than convert to Christianity wholesale, Joshua instead practiced his religion in a manner akin to numerous people before him; he engaged in a religious translation wherein he understood Christian concepts within his own worldview and engaged with his religion in a profoundly Mohican manner.[36]

On a number of occasions during their travels, the Moravians expressed their disappointment in Joshua. At one point they noted, for example, that "Joshua had fallen into his old sins in that he had secretly taken his son to a witch doctor in order to have him cured."[37] While the statement reveals much about the Moravians' view of the Mohican's religion and culture, it also betrays their expectation that individuals should convert to Christianity completely — an expectation that was, as a number of scholars have shown, unrealistic. What is more, the sentence offers a faint glimpse of Joshua himself and the ways in which he may have practiced his religion. As scholars such as David Silverman and Allan Greer note, Indigenous individuals tended to adopt aspects of Christianity that most made sense for their lives and that complemented their own ideas regarding the world and the supernatural.[38] Sometimes individuals made such decisions in the face of disease and trauma, other times they did so due to another inherently personal calculus. Based on the missionaries' observations it appears that Joshua likely saw some value in his association with the Moravians and their religion, yet he also maintained his own ideas regarding the spiritual. He did not, it seems, hesitate to turn to an Indigenous healer when he felt that it would benefit his son.

Joshua occupied a precarious position as a result of his status as a Mohican who associated with the missionaries and their faith. Such was particularly the case in the time and place wherein he found himself in the decade before the War of 1812. Joshua, like others who served as mediators and cultural brokers between Native peoples and Euro-Americans in early America, was, at once, a part of Native and Euro-American worlds.[39] In this time and place, such a position was a dangerous one, and it rendered Joshua susceptible to some Delawares' distrust and disdain. He became a primary target of Delawares' eventual witch-hunt.

That event began when a small group of Delawares arrived at the mission seeking Joshua. Kluge and Luckenbach informed them, however, that he was off "making raccoon traps."[40] According to the diarists, the Delawares responded "that all Indians had to assemble because the examination to determine who had poison or who practiced sorcery from which so many Indians die, would soon take place; that they were anxious to get rid entirely of such a bad thing among them."[41] Joshua and his possible "sorcery," then, were explicitly labeled as a thing to expel from their midst.

Joshua was not, however, alone among those targeted. The Delawares also accused the leader Tetapatchsit of possessing a dangerous "poison" with which he had "already destroyed many Indians."[42] The accused chief, no doubt in fear for his life, soon claimed that "he had stored poison in our Indian Br. Joshua's house."[43] As one historian argues for the European context, such "confessions" often appealed to the victim's perceptions of what the interrogators wanted to hear.[44] Tetapatchsit knew that his fellow Delawares feared dangerous "poisons" and he knew that the "poison" was a tangible object that could be found in one's house — particularly in a Christian man's cabin. In this case, the "poison" in question was associated with a witch bundle — an item that could contain elements of objects associated with evil and impurity. Those of the 1806 accused were rumored to house pieces of the Great Serpent, a creature associated both with great power and Euro-Americans' arrival in North America.[45] For White River Delawares, such associations were potent and political, and they provided ample evidence for the suspected witches' crimes.

For many Delawares, such associations with Moravians and with Euro-Americans more generally was enough to consider them enemies and guilty of the crimes for which they were accused.[46] The conflagration of politics, suspicion, fear, and anger of settler encroachments facilitated the violent affair that resulted in the deaths of Joshua, Tetapatchsit, and several others. On March 15, the Moravians recorded Anne Charity's death. Tetapatchsit's death, recorded by Moravians as occurring on March 17, quite significantly took place in fiery, dramatic fashion on mission grounds. The Delawares' motivations were likely multi-fold: they likely aimed to expel deviant individuals from their midst, instill fear in both Moravians and fellow Delawares who disagreed with their politics, as well as make a clear gesture that was grounded in the land and territory by killing Tetapatchsit where Moravians located their mission. Not long after Tetapatchsit's death, Delawares killed Joshua, again near the Moravians' mission site.[47]

* * *

Such witch-hunts were not commonplace when missionaries and Native peoples met in the early republic. Yet, the deaths that occurred in 1806 on the White River were full of meaning. The Delawares who led the hunt opposed the presence of the mission, missionaries, and Euro-Americans more generally, and they made those politics clear when Kluge and Luckenbach added their controversial presence to the already-tense situation on the White River. While an extreme case study of the ways in which politics, agendas, and cultures met and interacted in mission spaces, the Moravians' mission is yet instructive. These episodes reveal the precarious positions that missions in the heart of the continent occupied in the era of the early republic. While US officials employed missionary outposts during these decades in ways similar to those ways in which the government wielded the army in frontier spaces, they were anything but spaces of unabashed US power.[48] Rather, intense negotiations of power took place near and within mission spaces. Sometimes these negotiations were subtle, sometimes they were less so as was the case on the White River. Conflicts over land, religion, and culture could make some mission spaces volatile.

The Moravians' mission on the White River and the events that took place there reveals that not all missions during the era of the early republic were alike. The witch-hunt that took place in 1806 was the result of combination of politics, Delawares' particular experiences and history, suspicion, land treaties, the influence of individuals such as Tenskwatawa, Beata, and the missionary men themselves, and numerous other contingencies. Missions did, nonetheless, share similarities, and they often intersected with Native peoples' politics as the White River mission did in 1806. Missions could provoke conversations among Native individuals regarding whether particular Euro-Americans — missionaries and Indian agents, for example — would make useful allies and partners or whether they were better kept at arms-length. They could offer an additional means by which Indigenous individuals, leaders, and communities could work to secure political or economic advantage, and they could also work to facilitate the political, cultural, and economic violence that settlers' presence and the government's policies sought to produce. These complexities, differences, and similarities, the dramatic events and the subtler forms of violence that they produced, together make missions in the early republic important for scholars' consideration. They reveal much regarding the ways in which settlers, US government officials, missionaries, and Indigenous peoples together advocated for and pushed against myriad worldviews and visions for the future of the North American continent, Indian Country, and the American empire.

FURTHER READING

Edmunds, R. David. *The Shawnee Prophet.* Lincoln: University of Nebraska Press, 1985.

Fur, Gunlog. *A Nation of Women: Gender and Colonial Encounters Among the Delaware Indians.* Philadelphia: University of Pennsylvania Press, 2009.

Lakomaki, Sami. *Gathering Together: The Shawnee People Through Diaspora and Nationhood, 1600– 1870.* New Haven: Yale University Press, 2014.

Schutt, Amy C. *Peoples of the River Valleys: The Odyssey of the Delaware Indians.* Philadelphia: University of Pennsylvania Press, 2007.

Snyder, Christina. *Great Crossings: Indians, Settlers, and Slaves in the Age of Jackson.* New York: Oxford University Press, 2017.

BIBLIOGRAPHY

Berkhofer Jr., Robert F. *Salvation and the Savage: An Analysis of Protestant Missions and American Indian Response, 1787–1862.* Lexington: University of Kentucky Press, 1965.

Blackburn, Carole. *Harvest of Souls: The Jesuit Missions and Colonialism in North America, 1632–1650.* Montreal: McGill-Queens University Press, 2000.

Bottinger, Patrick. "Prophetstown for Their Own Purposes: The French, Miamis, and Cultural Identities in the Wabash-Maumee Valley." *Journal of the Early Republic* 33, no. 1 (Spring 2013): 29–60.

Brainerd, Thomas. *The Life of John Brainerd, the Brother of David Brainerd, and his Successor as Missionary to the Indians of New Jersey.* Philadelphia: Presbyterian Publication Committee, 1865.

Brown, Kathleen M. *Foul Bodies: Cleanliness in Early America.* New Haven: Yale University Press, 2009.

Carté Engel, Katherine. *Religion and Profit: Moravians in Early America.* Philadelphia, University of Pennsylvania Press, 2009.

Cave, Alfred. "The Failure of the Shawnee Prophet's Witch-Hunt." *Ethnohistory* 42, no. 3 (Summer 1995): 445–475.

Cave, Alfred. *Prophets of the Great Spirit: Native American Revitalization Movements in Eastern North America.* Lincoln: University of Nebraska Press, 2006.

Cayton, Andrew R. L. " 'Separate Interests' and the Nation-State: The Washington Administration and the Origins of Regionalism in the Trans-Appalachian West." *The Journal of American History* 79, no. 1 (Jun. 1992): 39–67.

Cronon, William. *Changes in the Land: Indians, Colonists, and the Ecology of New England.* New York: Hill & Wang, 1983.

Daggar, Lori J. " 'A Damnd Rebelious Race': The U.S. Civilization Plan and Native Authority." In *Quakers and American Indians,* edited by Ignacio Gallup-Diaz and Geoffrey Plank, 197–217. Leiden: Brill Academic Press, 2019.

_____. "The Mission Complex: Economic Development, 'Civilization,'" and Empire in the Early Republic." *Journal of the Early Republic* 36, no. 3 (Fall 2016): 467–491.

Demos, John. *The Heathen School: A Story of Hope and Betrayal in the Age of the Early Republic.* New York: Alfred A. Knopf, 2014.

Dennis, Matthew. *Seneca Possessed: Indians, Witchcraft, and Power in the Early American Republic.* Philadelphia: University of Pennsylvania Press, 2010.

Dowd, Gregory Evans. *A Spirited Resistance: The North American Indian Struggle for Unity, 1745–1815.* Baltimore: Johns Hopkins University Press, 1993.

Edmunds, R. David. *The Shawnee Prophet.* Lincoln: University of Nebraska Press, 1985.

Fur, Gunlög. *A Nation of Women: Gender and Colonial Encounters among the Delaware Indians.* Philadelphia: University of Pennsylvania Press, 2009.

Gollin, Gillian Lindt. *Moravians in Two Worlds: A Study of Changing Communities.* New York and London: Columbia University Press, 1967.

Greer, Allan. *Mohawk Saint: Catherine Tekakwitha and the Jesuits.* Oxford: Oxford University Press, 2005.

Horsman, Reginald. *Race and Manifest Destiny: Origins of American Racial Anglo-Saxonism.* Cambridge, MA: Harvard University Press, 1981.

_____. *Expansion and American Indian Policy, 1783–1812.* East Lansing: Michigan State University Press, 1967.

Jortner, Adam. *The Gods of Prophetstown: The Battle of Tippecanoe and the Holy War for the American Frontier.* Oxford: Oxford University Press, 2011.

Kappler, Charles J., ed. *Indian Affairs: Laws and Treaties.* 7 vols. Washington, DC: Government Printing Office, [1903–1971]. https://purl.fdlp.gov/GPO/gpo90901.

Knaut, Andrew L. *The Pueblo Revolt of 1680: Conquest and Resistance in Seventeenth-Century New Mexico.* Norman: University of Oklahoma Press, 1995.

McLoughlin, William. *Cherokees and Missionaries, 1789–1839*. New Haven: Yale University Press, 1984.

Merritt, Jane T. "Dreaming of the Savior's Blood: Moravians and the Indian Great Awakening in Pennsylvania." *The William and Mary Quarterly* 54, no. 4 (Oct. 1997): 723–746.

Merrell, James H. *Into the American Woods: Negotiators on the Pennsylvania Frontier*. New York: W. W. Norton & Company, 2000.

Miller, Jay. "The 1806 Purge among the Indiana Delaware: Sorcery, Gender, Boundaries, and Legitimacy." *Ethnohistory* 41, no. 2 (1994): 245–266.

Olmstead, Earl P. *Blackcoats among the Delaware: David Zeisberger on the Ohio Frontier*. Kent: Kent State University Press, 1991.

Porterfield, Amanda. "Witchcraft and the Colonization of Algonquian and Iroquois Cultures." *Religion and American Culture* 2, no. 1 (Winter 1992): 103–124.

Roeber, A. G., ed. *Ethnographies and Exchanges: Native Americans, Moravians, and Catholics in Early North America*. University Park: Pennsylvania State University Press, 2008.

Roper, Lyndal. *Witch Craze: Terror and Fantasy in Baroque Germany*. New Haven and London: Yale University Press, 2004.

Schutt, Amy C. "Tribal Identity in the Moravian Missions on the Susquehanna." *Pennsylvania History* 66, no. 3 (Summer 1999): 378–398.

Sheehan, Bernard. *Seeds of Extinction: Jeffersonian Philanthropy and the American Indian*. New York: W. W. Norton & Company, 1973.

Silverman, David. J. "Indians, Missionaries, and Religious Translation: Creating Wampanoag Christianity in Seventeenth-Century Martha's Vineyard." *The William and Mary Quarterly Third Series*, 62, no. 2 (Apr. 2005): 141–174.

Stocker, Harry Emilius. *A History of the Moravian Mission among the Indians of the White River in Indiana*. Bethlehem: Times Publishing Co., Printers, 1917.

Tantaquidgeon, Gladys. *A Study of Delaware Indian Medicine Practice and Folk Beliefs*. New York: AMS Press, 1942.

The Moravian Indian mission on White River; diaries and letters, May 5, 1799, to November 12, 1806. Edited by Lawrence Henry Gipson. Translated by Harry Emilius Stocker, Herman T. Frueauff, Samuel C. Zeller. Indianapolis: Indiana Historical Bureau, 1938.

Tinker, George E. *Missionary Conquest: The Gospel and Native American Cultural Genocide*. Minneapolis: Fortress Press, 1993.

Trowbridge, C.C. *Shawnese Traditions: C.C. Trowbridge's Account*. Edited by W. Vernon Kinietz and Erminie Wheeler-Voegelin. Ann Arbor: University of Michigan Press, 1939.

Wheeler, Rachel. "An Imagined Mohican-Moravian 'Lebenslauf': Joshua Sr., d. 1775." *Journal of Moravian History* 11 (Fall 2011): 29–44.

Witchcraft and Sorcery of the American Native Peoples. Edited by Deward E. Walker, Jr. Moscow: University of Idaho Press, 1989.

NOTES

1   *The Moravian Indian mission on White River; diaries and letters, May 5, 1799, to November 12, 1806*, ed. Lawrence Henry Gipson, trans. Harry Emilius Stocker, Herman T. Frueauff, Samuel C Zeller (Indianapolis: Indiana Historical Bureau, 1938), mission letters, April 1, 1806, 563, italics in the original.

2   R. David Edmunds, *The Shawnee Prophet* (Lincoln: University of Nebraska Press, 1985), 28–41. See also Gregory Evans Dowd, *A Spirited Resistance: The North American Indian Struggle for Unity, 1745–1815* (Baltimore: Johns Hopkins University Press, 1993).

3   See Edmunds, *The Shawnee Prophet*; Dowd, *A Spirited Resistance*.

4   This essay is indebted to a number of scholars and their work. Gladys Tantaquidgeon's work, for example, offers crucial insights regarding Delaware Indians' conceptions of medicine and witchcraft. See Gladys Tantaquidgeon, *A Study of Delaware Indian Medicine Practice and Folk Beliefs* (New York: AMS Press, 1942). A number of other scholars, meanwhile, have examined the mission and the 1806 witch-hunt and noted victims' connections with Euro-Americans and/or Euro-American ideas and culture. See Harry Emilius Stocker, *A History of the Moravian Mission among*

the Indians of the White River in Indiana (Bethlehem: Times Publishing Co., Printers, 1917); R. David Edmunds, *The Shawnee Prophet* (Lincoln: University of Nebraska Press, 1983); Alfred Cave, "The Failure of the Shawnee Prophet's Witch-Hunt," *Ethnohistory* 42, no. 3 (Summer 1995): 445–475; Alfred Cave, *Prophets of the Great Spirit: Native American Revitalization Movements in Eastern North America* (Lincoln: University of Nebraska Press, 2006); Jay Miller, "The 1806 Purge among the Indiana Delaware: Sorcery, Gender, Boundaries, and Legitimacy," *Ethnohistory* 41, no. 2 (1994): 245–266; Adam Jortner, *The Gods of Prophetstown: The Battle of Tippecanoe and the Holy War for the American Frontier* (Oxford: Oxford University Press, 2011). Others' works offer overviews of witchcraft among myriad Native peoples. See, for example, Amanda Porterfield, "Witchcraft and the Colonization of Algonquian and Iroquois Cultures," *Religion and American Culture* 2, no. 1 (Winter 1992): 109–114; Matthew Dennis, *Seneca Possessed: Indians, Witchcraft, and Power in the Early American Republic* (Philadelphia: University of Pennsylvania Press, 2010); *Witchcraft and Sorcery of the American Native Peoples*, ed. Deward E. Walker, Jr. (Moscow: University of Idaho Press, 1989).

5   Shawnees at Wapakoneta, for example, worked with members of the Society of Friends to build economic infrastructure on their lands in an effort to remain. While such efforts did not prevent their forced removal, they represent the fact that some Native peoples hoped to take advantage of Euro-American labor and money to remain and fulfill their own visions for the future. See Lori J. Daggar, "'A Damnd Rebelious Race': The U.S. Civilization Plan and Native Authority," in *Quakers and American Indians*, ed. Ignacio Gallup-Diaz and Geoffrey Plank, 197–217 (Leiden: Brill Academic Press, 2019).

6   Robert Berkhofer delineates between the two forms of missions as part of a "Christianity first" versus civilization first debate in the early republic. Both forms of missions sought to change Native peoples yet disagreed over whether education in "civilization" or the Bible first would yield the best results. See Robert F. Berkhofer Jr., *Salvation and the Savage: An Analysis of Protestant Missions and American Indian Response, 1787–1862* (Lexington: University of Kentucky Press, 1965), 2–6.

7   *The Moravian Indian mission on White River*, 74.

8   Ibid.

9   Ibid., 71.

10   Ibid., 46.

11   Ibid., 44.

12   Ibid.

13   Kathleen M. Brown, *Foul Bodies: Cleanliness in Early America* (New Haven: Yale University Press, 2009).

14   Reginald Horsman, *Race and Manifest Destiny: Origins of American Racial Anglo-Saxonism* (Cambridge, MA: Harvard University Press, 1981); Reginald Horsman, *Expansion and American Indian Policy, 1783–1812* (East Lansing: Michigan State University Press, 1967); Berkhofer Jr., *Salvation and the Savage*; Bernard Sheehan, *Seeds of Extinction: Jeffersonian Philanthropy and the American Indian* (W. W. Norton & Company, 1973).

15   A number of scholars examine civilizing missions in Cherokee Country, Seneca Country, and elsewhere, and they have also endeavored to understand Euro-Americans' motivations behind such missions as well as their policy implications. See, for example, Berkhofer Jr., *Salvation and the Savage*; Sheehan, *Seeds of Extinction*; Dennis, *Seneca Possessed*; John Demos, *The Heathen School: A Story of Hope and Betrayal in the Age of the Early Republic* (New York: Alfred A. Knopf, 2014); William McLoughlin, *Cherokees and Missionaries, 1789–1839* (New Haven: Yale University Press, 1984).

16   Lori J. Daggar, "The Mission Complex: Economic Development, 'Civilization,'" and Empire in the Early Republic," *Journal of the Early Republic* 36, no. 3 (Fall 2016): 467–491.

17   The scholarship on missionaries and the Spanish and French imperial projects is vast and reveals missions as sites of interaction and violence. Allan Greer, *Mohawk Saint: Catherine Tekakwitha and the Jesuits* (Oxford: Oxford University Press, 2005); Andrew L. Knaut, *The Pueblo Revolt of 1680: Conquest and Resistance in Seventeenth-Century New Mexico* (Norman: University of Oklahoma Press, 1995); Carole Blackburn, *Harvest of Souls: The Jesuit Missions and Colonialism in North America, 1632–1650* (Montreal: McGill-Queens University Press, 2000); George E. Tinker, *Missionary Conquest: The Gospel and Native American Cultural Genocide* (Minneapolis: Fortress Press, 1993).

18   Katherine Carté Engel, *Religion and Profit: Moravians in Early America* (Philadelphia: University of Pennsylvania Press, 2009), 31.

19 Ibid., 30; See also 32–38 for a discussion of Bethlehem's "Oeconomy." Engel argues that missionary work was the primary reason for Bethlehem's existence: "The needs of missionary work, and not the spiritual lives of the residents, dictated the town's organization and economy, and missionary work led directly to communalism." (35).

   For further reading on the Moravians and Moravian-Indian relations in early America, see See also Jane T. Merritt, "Dreaming of the Savior's Blood: Moravians and the Indian Great Awakening in Pennsylvania," *The William and Mary Quarterly* 54, no. 4 (Oct. 1997): 723–746; Amy C. Schutt, "Tribal Identity in the Moravian Missions on the Susquehanna," *Pennsylvania History* 66, no. 3 (Summer 1999); Gillian Lindt Gollin, *Moravians in Two Worlds: A Study of Changing Communities* (New York and London: Columbia University Press, 1967); A. G. Roeber, ed. *Ethnographies and Exchanges: Native Americans, Moravians, and Catholics in Early North America* (University Park: The Pennsylvania State University Press, 2008); Earl P. Olmstead, *Blackcoats among the Delaware: David Zeisberger on the Ohio Frontier* (Kent: The Kent State University Press, 1991); Harry Emilius Stocker, *A History of the Moravian Mission among the Indians on the White River in Indiana* (Bethlehem, PA: Times Publishing Co., 1917).

20 R. David Edmunds, *The Shawnee Prophet*; Gregory Evans Dowd, *A Spirited Resistance: The North American Indian Struggle for Unity, 1745–1815* (Baltimore: Johns Hopkins University Press, 1993).

21 On theories of "separate creations," see Dowd, *A Spirited Resistance.*

22 *The Moravian Indian mission on White River*, October 26, 1803, 509. Since the Moravians recorded such sentiments, not the Delawares themselves, the mission diary also offers insights into the intellectual constructs of difference that shaped missionaries' understanding of Native peoples and their ideas. It is clear from the passages that both Moravians and Delawares harbored suspicions of one another.

23 Thomas Brainerd, *The Life of John Brainerd, the Brother of David Brainerd, and his Successor as Missionary to the Indians of New Jersey*, (Philadelphia: Presbyterian Publication Committee, 1865), 234–235.

24 *The Moravian Indian mission on White River*, October 26, 1803, 508–509.

25 Treaty with the Wyandot, Etc., 1805. July 4, 1805, in Kapper, ed., *Indian Affairs, Laws and Treaties*, vol. 2, 77.

26 Amy C. Schutt, *People of the River Valleys: The Odyssey of the Delaware Indians* (Philadelphia: University of Pennsylvania Press, 2007), 89–93, 123; Gunlög Fur, *A Nation of Women: Gender and Colonial Encounters among the Delaware Indians* (Philadelphia: University of Pennsylvania Press, 2009) 160–198.

27 Treaty with the Delaware Indians, 1804. Aug. 18, 1804, in Charles J. Kappler, ed., *Indian Affairs, Laws and Treaties*, vol. 2, 70; Treaty with the Wyandot, Etc., 1805 in Kappler.

28 Miller, "The 1806 Purge among the Indiana Delaware."

29 Bill Cronon's seminal work details the environmental consequences of European colonialism in North America. William Cronon, *Changes in the Land: Indians, Colonists, and the Ecology of New England* (New York: Hill & Wang, 1983).

30 *The Moravian Mission on White River*, August 6, 1805, 539.

31 Ibid., 541.

32 For Prophetstown's importance in relation to Tenskwatawa's leadership and goals, see Jortner, *The Gods of Prophetstown*; for the many "purposes" for Prophetstown, see Patrick Bottinger, "Prophetstown for Their Own Purposes: The French, Miamis, and Cultural Identities in the Wabash-Maumee Valley," *Journal of the Early Republic* 33, no. 1 (Spring 2013): 29–60.

33 *The Moravian Mission on White River*, September 24, 1805, 547.

34 Ibid., 402–403.

35 On Beata, see Miller, "The 1806 Purge among the Indiana Delaware," 251–254.

36 Miller, The 1806 Purge among the Indiana Delaware," 256–258. Joshua was also the son of a well-known Mohican man who likewise engaged with Christianity in the eighteenth-century. See Rachel Wheeler, "An Imagined Mohican-Moravian 'Lebenslauf': Joshua Sr., d. 1775," *Journal of Moravian History* no. 11 (Fall 2011): 29–44; Schutt, "Tribal Identity in the Moravian Missions on the Susquehanna."

37 *The Moravian Mission on White River*, 113–114.

38 David J. Silverman, "Indians, Missionaries, and Religious Translation: Creating Wampanoag Christianity in Seventeenth-Century Martha's Vineyard," *The William and Mary Quarterly*, Third Series, 62, no. 2 (Apr. 2005): 141–174; Greer, *Mohawk Saint*.

39 James Merrell's work captures the complexities of go-betweens' positions in early America. James H. Merrell, *Into the American Woods: Negotiators on the Pennsylvania Frontier* (W. W. Norton & Company, 2000).

40 *The Moravian Mission on White River*, February 1806, 408.

41 Ibid., 409.

42 Ibid., 557.

43 Ibid., 557–558.

44 Lyndal Roper, *Witch Craze: Terror and Fantasy in Baroque Germany* (New Haven and London: Yale University Press, 2004), 44–66. While Roper writes about the German context, the idea that torture could solicit confessions designed to please torturers is likely applicable to other contexts.

45 C. C. Trowbridge, *Shawnese Traditions: C.C. Trowbridge's Account*, W. Vernon Kinietz and Erminie Wheeler-Voegelin eds. (Ann Arbor: University of Michigan Press, 1939), 43–46. On serpents and witch bundles, see also Porterfield, "Witchcraft and the Colonization of Algonquian and Iroquois Cultures," 113–114; Tantaquidgeon, *A Study of Delaware Indian Medicine, Practice, and Folk Beliefs*, 40. While most bundles contained various sacred objects such as "a bird claw, a feather, a piece of bone or horn, or an animal tooth," the witch's bundle often contained elements of objects associated with evil and impurity, in the case of the 1806 witches, pieces of the Great Serpent. Years after the Delawares' witch-hunt, the Shawnee prophet Tenskwatawa revealed that the serpent's "body was cut into small pieces and ... carefully preserved ... and forms the medecine which the witches use." He also detailed how the Great Serpent rose out of the sea — a clear metaphor for European arrival — and how Native peoples then fought the serpent.

46 Miller, "The 1806 Purge among the Indiana Delaware."

47 *The Moravian Indian mission on White River*, March 17, 1806, 415.

48 Andrew R. L. Cayton, " 'Separate Interests' and the Nation-State: The Washington Administration and the Origins of Regionalism in the Trans-Appalachian West," *The Journal of American History* 79, no. 1 (Jun. 1992): 39–67.

Chapter Ten

THE SHAKERS AND THE PERFECTING SPIRIT IN EARLY AMERICA

Jennifer H. Dorsey
Siena College, Loudonville, New York

The Shaker song "Simple Gifts" is among the most recognizable tunes in American music:

> 'Tis the gift to be simple
> 'Tis the gift to be free
> 'Tis the gift to be free,
> 'Tis the gift to come down where we ought to be,
> And when we find ourselves in the place just right,
> 'Twill be the valley of love and delight.
>
> When true simplicity is gain'd,
> To bow and bend we shan't be asham'd,
> To turn, turn, will be our delight
> 'Till by turning, turning we come around right.

The song's charming message and appealing melody have made it a staple in the American songbook. School children across America learn "Simple Gifts" in elementary music classes. Folk singers, opera singers, and a bluegrass artist have all recorded and performed variations of this classic. In 2008, John Williams, the Academy Award winning composer best known for the *Star Wars* soundtrack revived American interest in the tune by reworking it as a classical quartet to be performed at President Barack Obama's first inauguration.

Although popularly recognized as a Shaker song, "Simple Gifts" actually tells us nothing about the history or the faith of the Shakers. By comparison, the lyrics of the hymn "The Son and Daughter" help us to appreciate what made the Shakers exceptional among early American Christians. These lyrics serve as a primer to Shaker theology. The hymn describes God as having sent into the world a "blessed Son and Daughter, Completely join'd in one." God sent the Son and the Daughter "To visit the creation and teach us what to do." The hymn designated these divine siblings as the "heavenly Parents" of humanity. Moreover, this blessed Daughter sits alongside Jesus "Upon the Judgment seat," where with the Son of God she forgives the sins of humankind. Faithful Christians who confess their sins to the blessed Daughter will have the power to "bid all sin adieu." They will possess divine strength to live "beyond temptation's line." In other words, this Shaker hymn argues that only those Christians who recognize the "blessed Two" can live without sin in the present and experience eternal life in the future.[1]

A Companion to American Religious History, First Edition. Edited by Benjamin E. Park.

This chapter examines the early history of the Shakers as a model for understanding the interconnectivity of religion, culture, and economics in the early Republic. It traces the origins of the movement from England to America, explains key tenets of their faith, and describes the function of Shaker communal settlements. It argues that the Shakers offered early republican Americans a radically different religious order grounded in charismatic worship, gender equality, and communalism. Although the appeal of Shakerism declined in the 1830s, Shaker values persisted in antebellum America, gaining a second life in new religions, social reform movements, and utopian communities.

Shakerism originated in England in the context of the Industrial Revolution and Protestant revivalism. Textile manufacturing had radically changed the lives of working people, and in response, the Church of England had organized The Society for the Promotion of Christian Knowledge, a missionary society focused on evangelism among the laboring classes of emerging wool and cotton mill-towns. This new ministry opportunity attracted younger clergymen with an affinity for adventure and distinctive gifts for teaching, preaching, and pastoral care. John Wesley and George Whitefield, two of the most celebrated English evangelists of the era, were among those who heeded this call to evangelize to the poor and disenfranchised. Both men offered religious instruction to populations that had largely been ignored by the established Church. They preached in public spaces, on street corners and in open fields, and their sermons urged Christians to develop a personal, spiritual connection with God. Wesley and Whitefield urged their listeners to pray regularly, to avoid all kinds of sinful indulgences, to practice charity with one another, and most important, to form small prayer groups and clubs with other Christians in order to support one another in their spiritual development. Wesley also advanced the doctrine of Christian Perfection, insisting that at the moment that penitent men and women publicly renounced their sins God would bestow upon them the "perfecting" Spirit of God. This Spirit, now dwelling within the Christian, would enable faithful believers to live holy lives, devoted to the service of God.[2]

This evangelism gave rise to Shakerism.[3] Mother Ann Lee (1736–1784), the religion's founder and chief evangelist, was among those who yearned for a meaningful religious life and relief from worldly discomfort. As a child, she would have attended the Church of England, but as a teenager laboring in a mill town, she gravitated to the street preachers. It is likely that Lee encountered Anglican evangelist like John Wesley, but in her twenties, she was drawn to the charismatic ministry of two lay preachers, James and Jane Wardley. Like others who embraced Christian Perfection, the Wardleys believed the Holy Spirit could purify and perfect believers from within. But the Wardleys also insisted the same perfecting Spirit poured out divine gifts and revelations on the Christian faithful. Such special gifts, or charismata, might include the gift of healing, the capacity to speak in unfamiliar languages, and even prophecy. Charismatic worship services were emotional events. Ecstatic congregants confessed their sins, cried out for salvation by the Spirit, and at times exhibited signs of receiving divine gifts. This style of worship was not new in England, or even unique to the Wardleys. Even so, mainstream Anglicans ridiculed charismatic Christians as zealots and radicals. They derogatorily referred to them as "Shaking Quakers" or "Shakers."

Soon after Ann Lee began worshiping with the Wardleys, she began preaching. Nearly everything we know about her ministry in England and then America comes from a single work, *Testimonies of the Life, Character, Revelations, and Doctrines of Mother Ann Lee, and the Elders with Her*, a retrospective published by her disciples nearly twenty-five years after her death.[4] The *Testimonies* describe Lee as a fearless woman who, from a young age, possessed remarkable spiritual gifts. She spoke in tongues, communicated with the dead, and claimed prophetic powers. She could see and "hear the angels sing, and converse with them daily." She exhibited remarkable Christian frugality, patience, and charity with others. She believed that the indwelling Spirit of God strengthened her to deny "everything which my appetite craved in order that my soul might hunger for nothing but God." Above all else, Lee abstained from sex, which she called "the sin which is the root of all evil." She insisted "no soul could follow Christ in the [spiritual] regeneration, while living in the works of natural regeneration [sex] and wallowing in their lust."[5]

According to the *Testimonies*, Lee's divine gifts attracted the ire of Satan, who tormented her for nearly nine years. Her followers noted that in a particular episode "blood perspired through the pores of her skin," a description that would have drawn comparison to the stigmata in Christian tradition. In due time, however, God rescued Lee from this spiritual warfare and revealed that the suffering had served a divine purpose. Lee believed that God had called her to be "the first Mother of all souls in the regeneration." She was "God in Mother," possessing divine power to reconcile humanity to God. While her claim may seem strange, it rested on certain theological and scientific truths that made sense to many eighteenth-century people. First, Lee shared with other Christians a belief that God contains both a male and female nature and that by divine design, all earthly creation is categorized as either male or female. Second, it was evident to anyone with eyes to see that the creation of new life requires both male and female (father and mother). Therefore, Lee concluded, a spiritual rebirth similarly requires both a father and mother.[6]

Lee, or Mother Ann, identified as co-head of the "family of Christ," and as such, she had the same authority over Christians as a wife or a mother had over an eighteenth-century household. According to Lee, when a "man [e.g. husband, father] is gone, the right of government belongs to the woman." Accordingly, Mother Ann assumed authority over the spiritual care of Christians in the present. Like Jesus of the New Testament, Mother Ann claimed disciples who were divinely chosen witnesses to the imminent second appearance of God in human history. These disciples also claimed charismatic gifts and asserted the Spirit of God had similarly empowered them to live lives without sin and "in daily obedience to the will of God." Finally, Lee insisted that others could also achieve spiritual purity or spiritual perfection by confessing their sins directly to her or one of her apostles.[7]

Ann Lee counted several family members, including her husband, among her first disciples. But other family members and some of her neighbors viewed her as an embarrassment and a public nuisance. She was subject to mob violence and imprisoned more than once for disturbing the peace outside an Anglican Church. Still, she persisted in her street evangelism expressly because the Church of England and the English government had officially prohibited the persecution of nonconforming or dissenting Protestants with the 1689 Act of Toleration. In other words, English law protected her right to preach, and Lee knew her rights. According to *Testimonies*, Lee said the judges "gave me liberty to speak my faith without being posted; and I did not spare them."[8]

These English Shakers continued preaching in the streets until Mother Ann discerned a prophecy that she should go to the colonies in America. The *Testimonies* document Lee as saying, "God is about to raise up a people here in America, who will serve Him and honor the gospel" of Christ's second appearing. In 1774, Lee and eight of her apostles boarded a vessel for the City of New York. According to the *Testimonies*, Lee evangelized across the Atlantic to the great annoyance of other passengers and crew, who "threatened to throw [her]" overboard. Although they arrived safely, the Shakers struggled in New York. They scraped by as domestics and day laborers. Within a year, Ann and her husband Abraham had separated. By 1779, the Shakers had relocated northwest of Albany, New York, where they had purchased a parcel of undeveloped land from Philip Van Rensselaer, one of the richest men in colonial America. The Shakers persisted in their charismatic worship and soon attracted the attention of local authorities, who were understandably curious about, and often suspicious of, these English newcomers who lived marginally at their new settlement and persisted in their ecstatic worship.[9]

Because Mother Ann believed that the Revolutionary War was the "work of God" intended "to open the way for the gospel," she and two of her English apostles, William Lee and James

Whittaker, began evangelizing in America. They directed their attention to a region labeled by historians as the Yankee Zone. Situated between Albany, New York and Pittsfield, Massachusetts, this underdeveloped region was densely populated with yeoman farmers, including a number of Revolutionary War veterans. The Yankee Zone claimed few formally organized churches, but in the decades leading up to the American Revolution, they had received a number of itinerant preachers, including George Whitefield, who passed through the region in 1770. The English Shakers, therefore, were not the first charismatic Christians to evangelize in this region.[10]

The Shakers, however, enjoyed remarkable and lasting success among these rugged frontier families. She attracted some high profile converts, including Joseph Meachem, a New Light Baptist preacher, who brought many of his parishioners into the Shaker-fold. Many Yankees found Shaker worship, with its singing and dancing, familiar and engaging. They related to the Shakers as fellow settlers and frontiersmen, determined to make a home in America. Nearly all were mainline Protestants (Congregationalists, Presbyterians), who knew the plot and the timeline of the Christian Bible, and Lee's millenarian message had credibility in the post-Revolutionary War era. The blessed Daughter of God prophesized the imminent return of Christ and so appealed to her audience to ready themselves for the judgment day by confessing their sins to her. These rugged frontiersmen found Lee a credible prophet. She was remarkably frugal, virtuous, and industrious; the very embodiment of Christian Perfection. These same qualities would endear her to New Englanders, and her message of the imminent Second Coming of Christ would have resonated with a people rebuilding their lives in the aftermath of war. It is no wonder that Lee, a prophet who professed to have direct access to the divine, was warmly welcomed in an age of uncertainty.[11]

As in England, Mother Ann also experienced physical violence and harassment. She ended her itinerant ministry in the spring of 1784 and died soon after returning to Albany. The Shaker movement, so clearly defined and driven by Lee, would have likely died with her were it not for James Whittaker (1751–1787), an English disciple who led the Shaker's early transformation from a Spirit-led religious movement to an organized religion.

Whittaker established several precedents that had lasting consequences for the growth and development of American Shakerism.[12] First, he established a decidedly undemocratic system of governance for this Spirit-led religious movement. The Shakers had not elected Whittaker to lead them. Instead, he had assumed leadership of the movement by virtue of his close association with Mother Ann. Until now, the Shakers had insisted they were a people led and moved by divine revelation, but now, Shakers acknowledged a hierarchy of believers that was determined not by charismata but by a kind of apostolic succession. Second, Whittaker's understanding of the Shakers in America as a spiritual family, divinely knit together by the Spirit of God, led him to experiment with communalism. Whittaker articulated this view in a 1785 letter to his English family that was subsequently published as an appendix in the Shakers' first religious treatise: *A Concise Statement of the Principles of the Only True Church, According to the Gospel of the Present Appearance of Christ* (1790). In it, Whittaker boasted that the indwelling Spirit of God had not only empowered him to abstain from sin (namely, sex), but rewarded him with a fruitful ministry that had increased his spiritual family. He characterized these new believers as a family "begotten" by God and divinely formed for him. Whittaker described the Shakers in America as "one community," divinely delivered and redeemed from the evils of the world and "able to help many in a temporal sense."[13]

The Shakers had been a semi-nomadic evangelical movement under the leadership of Mother Ann, but now, Father James urged fellow believers to live in community so they could better support each other in their spiritual development.[14] He oversaw the construction of the first Shaker meeting house in Lebanon, New York and established the first Shaker rituals and rules for Shaker conduct. When Whittaker died, leadership passed to the

American-born convert Father Joseph Meachem (1787–1796), who also prioritized this work of building community. He incorporated the Shakers as a religious society, legally empowered to own and manage real estate for the benefit of its members. He directed Shakers to put their worldly assets, and especially land, in a trust to be managed by the Society's leadership. In short time, the Shakers acquired substantial acreage from converts following this direction, and then Meachem directed the wholesale "ingathering" of Shakers into newly organized communes. Early American census data suggests that a majority of Shakers fell into line, leaving their parents or spouses and relocating to these newly organized Shaker "villages" in order to live among their fellow coreligionists. By 1800, the Shaker leadership had incorporated nine such villages across New England and resettled nearly 1,000 Shaker men, women, and children into "family" units within these villages.[15]

Communal living provided obvious economic, social, and spiritual advantages in post-Revolutionary America. At a time when many farm families struggled to make ends meet from year to year, Shakers of all ages and abilities could expect to enjoy some material comfort and economic security within their commune. The Shakers themselves characterized the villages as "heaven on earth," sacred spaces where faithful men and women lived without conflict, possessiveness, vanity, personal property, individual ambition or social distinctions based on race, class or gender.[16] From the beginning the Shakers welcomed visitors to their meeting houses to observe their charismatic worship, inclusive of singing and dancing. If visitors found the worship strange, they were inevitably impressed by the layout of the village, its single sex dwelling houses, single sex workshops, and well-tended farmlands and pasturage.

In these communes the Shakers also developed a distinctive system of labor based on their guiding principle of spiritual union. The Shakers had always believed themselves bound together as spiritual siblings within the family of Christ, but now, Father Joseph Meachem extended the concept of spiritual union to organize work routines on the principal of mutuality and reciprocity. Union was integral to the Shaker model of Christian communalism and their understanding of family. Shakers appreciated and insisted that social harmony required a good working partnership between family members or sisters and brethren. Work and workplaces were gendered, but the Shakers valued the contributions of men and women as equally necessary to achieve material comfort (ample food, clothing, shelter) and maintain social harmony within the village. Sisters kept their male brethren fed and clothed; and in return, brothers planted crops, tended to livestock, and maintained the buildings. The Shakers affirmed men and women as equal partners in the enterprise of community building. It was this attention to reciprocity that contributed to Shaker union.[17]

Father Joseph also applied this spiritual equality of men and women to Shaker governance. In 1788, he made Sister Lucy Wright (1760–1821) co-administrator of the Shaker society. By all accounts, Meachem and Wright respected each other's expertise and gifts, and their partnership led Mother Lucy to muse, "you cannot get to heaven alone, but you can be lost alone."[18] Undoubtedly, other Shaker men valued their sisters as spiritual leaders, but not all agreed that women should govern the affairs of the society. In the 1790s, as many as twenty Shaker men and boys left New Lebanon rather than submit to the authority of a woman. Before his death, Meachem named Wright as his successor. In 1796, she assumed the title of Mother-in-Chief of the Shaker society. She held this position until her own death in 1821, but not without occasional objection by Shaker men. Still, New Lebanon never wavered in its support of Mother Lucy, insisting as they did in a letter to the Shaker village in Maine: "It is not man, nor woman, that is to govern the Church, but it is Christ: and whether Christ governs us through the medium of man, or woman, it is the same unction from the Holy One, and we are equally satisfied."[19]

In 1805, Wright learned of a religious revival on the American frontier. She interpreted this news as proof that the Spirit of God was calling the Shakers "to spread the Shaker gospel to a Worldly audience." She supported missionary efforts to Kentucky, Indiana, and Ohio and sanctioned the publication and distribution of treatises and hymnals for the instruction of new believers. In 1816, the Society published *Testimonies of the Life, Character, Revelations and Doctrines of Mother Ann Lee*. In the preface, the Shakers declared they had a "duty" to document the early history of the Society and especially the life and revelations of Mother Ann in order that "those who come after us may know and understand more fully, concerning the truth of those things wherein they may be instructed." Next, the Society published *Millennial Praises* (1813).[20]

True to their charismatic tradition, the Shaker leadership insisted that published treatises and hymnody should never supplant the authority of Spirit revelations. They affirmed: "It is not expected that the people of God will ever be confined, in their mode of worship to any particular set of hymns, or any other regular system of words — for words are but the signs of our ideas, and of course, must vary as the ideas increase with the increasing work of God."[21] Still, the hymns proved effective tools for evangelism. They explained the history of Lee's ministry and Shaker theology, including the principle of union. The hymns "The Son and Daughter" and "The heavenly Bridegroom & Bride" explained to potential converts how Mother Ann Lee had continued the redemptive work initiated by Jesus Christ. The hymn "Union" describes the Shaker principle of spiritual union with God as the foundation for all social harmony. Moreover, these hymns had greater meaning and power as Shakerism expanded geographically. At the height of its expansion in 1826, Shaker men, women and children lived in eighteen villages stretching from Maine to Kentucky. East and West, Shakers sang hopefully that divinely inspired hymnody would guide the enlarged Shaker family to "Beauty, Union, and Love."

But this image of cheerful, singing Shakers belies the evidence that the movement was losing momentum in the 1820s. Evangelism had depleted the central ministry of money and capable leaders who had been appointed to lead the villages at Pleasant Hill, Kentucky; Whitewater, Ohio; and West Union, Indiana. Back East, the villages continued to welcome visitors to their Sunday worship services, but the membership was not growing in tandem. More troubling, the Panic of 1819 and other economic recessions led to a rising population of seasonal or "winter Shakers," men and women who temporarily joined the Society to weather economic hardship. At about the same time the Shakers began receiving indentured and orphaned children. According to one historian, Shaker villages had become "havens for the homeless, widows, orphans, the unemployed, and the handicapped" in times of economic crisis."[22]

In 1821, a few months after Mother Lucy Wright's death, the Shaker central ministry published *Millennial Laws, or Gospel Statues & Ordinances, Adapted to the Day of Christ's Second Appearing* (1821), a manual of laws and ordinances "for the moral and religious government of Believers." The *Laws* asserted New Lebanon's authority over all Shaker villages and the hierarchical governance structure within villages. It declared "the gospel of Christ's second appearing strictly forbids all private union between the two sexes" and included precise rules for how to maintain separation. As an example, men and women could not be alone with one another or share gifts with one another or even "pass each other on the stairs." With an eye toward maintaining social harmony within villages, the *Laws* listed unacceptable behaviors, such as "all tattling, talebearing & backbiting." Still more rules regulated the conduct of Shakers when they went into the world. They were prohibited from leaving the village without permission and from taking excursions "for the sake of curiosity." The *Laws* also directed Shakers to report any violations of these ordinances to the village leadership, "or to some other one in whom he or she can place the greatest confidence for salvation."[23]

New Lebanon anticipated that centralized authority and strict regulation of Shaker conduct would fortify the Society, but this attention to self-preservation left the Shakers unprepared to adapt to the changes around them. Since Albany became the capital of New York State in 1797, the city's population had swelled nearly fourfold. Aggressive public and private investments in new roads, bridges, and the opening of the Erie Canal in 1825 had made the city the undisputed hub for commerce between Western New York and New York City. These same transportation networks facilitated a mass migration of New England farmers to westward territories where they grew grains for international markets. More immigrants came from Europe to work in construction, shipping, and manufacturing. In many ways, life in New York in the 1830s now mirrored life in England in the 1760s. Commercialization, industrialization, urbanization, and migration had radically changed the working lives of Americans. Protestant evangelism flourished and the same doctrines of Christian Perfection that had informed Shaker theology fifty years earlier now swept through New York State, and a new generation of ordained and lay itinerant preachers brought Christianity to the unchurched communities along the Erie Canal.

But the Shakers were no longer at the vanguard of change. In the 1780s and 1790s, they had pioneered charismatic worship, gender equity, and communalism in the early American Republic. The Shakers had rejected the religious conventions of the day and offered their members a new order based on new religious principles. They established Shaker villages as an example of how Americans could achieve "heaven on earth" and practice an alternative model of family. They used hymns and songs to teach Shaker theology and create a shared collective culture across American Shakerdom.

But in the 1830s, the Shakers failed to complete with new distinctly American faiths such as the Millerites (Seventh Day Adventist) and the Mormons (Church of Jesus Christ of Latter-day Saints) for worshipers and adherents. Even communitarianism was no longer unique to the Shakers. Communalism enjoyed a surge in 1840s America, offering the curious and the disillusioned with ample opportunity to experiment with alternative models for governance, domestic life, and economy. In a similar vein, the authority Shaker women had experienced uniquely in a village was now more broadly available to American women, who engaged in public life by participating in reform movements for abolition, temperance, education reform, and civil rights. Within this changing religious and social landscape, Americans viewed the Shakers not as radicals but as relics of another age.

FURTHER READING

Humez, Jean McMahon, ed. *Mother's First-Born Daughters: Early Shaker Writings on Women and Religion*. Religion in North America. Bloomington: Indiana University Press, 1993.
Medlicott, Carol. *Issachar Bates: A Shaker's Journey*. Hanover: University Press of New England, 2013.
Shaker Museum Mount Lebanon. "Shaker Museum Mount Lebanon." https://shakerml.org/.
Wergland, Glendyne R., ed. *Visiting the Shakers, 1778–1849: Watervliet, Hancock, Tyringham, New Lebanon*. American Communal Societies Series, no. 1. Clinton: Richard W. Couper Press, 2007.

BIBLIOGRAPHY

Bishop, Rufus, Seth Y. Wells, Giles B. Avery, J. P. MacLean, and Shaker Collection (Library of Congress), eds. *Testimonies of the Life, Character, Revelations, and Doctrines of Mother Ann Lee, and the Elders with Her: Through Whom the Word of Eternal Life Was Opened in This day of Christ's Second Appearing*. 2nd ed. Albany: Weed, Parsons & Co., printers, 1888.
Brewer, Priscilla J. "The Demographic Features of the Shaker Decline, 1787–1900." *Journal of Interdisciplinary History* 15, no. 1 (1984): 31–52.
Brewer, Priscilla J. *Shaker Communities, Shaker Lives*. Hanover: University Press of New England, 1986.
Goodwillie, Christian, and Jane F. Crosthwaite, eds. *Millennial Praises: A Shaker Hymnal*. Amherst: University of Massachusetts Press, 2009.

Humez, Jean M. "Weary of Petticoat Government: The Specter of Female Rule in Early Nineteenth-Century Shaker Politics." *Communal Societies* 11 (1991): 1–17.

_____, ed. *Mother's First-Born Daughters: Early Shaker Writings on Women and Religion.* Religion in North America. Bloomington: Indiana University Press, 1993.

Letourneau, Marcus Reginald. "Holy Mount: Identity, Place, Religion and Narrative at New Lebanon Shaker Village, 1759–1861." PhD diss. Queen's University at Kingston, 2009. http://hdl.handle.net/1974/1882.

Marini, Stephen A. *Radical Sects of Revolutionary New England.* Cambridge, MA: Harvard University Press, 1982.

Morgan, John H. (John Henry). "Experience as Knowledge: A Study in Shaker Theology." *The Shaker Quarterly* 14, no. 2 (1974): 43–55.

Paterwic, Stephen. *The A to Z of the Shakers.* The A to Z Guide Series. Lanham: Scarecrow Press, 2009.

Shaker Collection Highlights: Williams Digital Collection. "A Concise Statement of the Principles of the Only True Church, According to the Gospel of the Present Appearance of Christ," 1790. https://unbound.williams.edu/williamsarchives/islandora/object/shakers%3A73.

Stein, Stephen J. *The Shaker Experience in America: A History of the United Society of Believers.* New Haven: Yale University Press, 1992.

Taysom, Stephen C. *Shakers, Mormons, and Religious Worlds: Conflicting Visions, Contested Boundaries.* Religion in North America. Bloomington: Indiana University Press, 2011.

Thurman, Suzanne Ruth. *"O Sisters Ain't You Happy?": Gender, Family, and Community among the Harvard and Shirley Shakers, 1781–1918.* 1st ed. Women and Gender in North American Religions. Syracuse: Syracuse University Press, 2002.

Wergland, Glendyne R. *Sisters in the Faith: Shaker Women and Equality of the Sexes.* Amherst and Boston: University of Massachusetts Press, 2011.

NOTES

1   Christian Goodwillie and Jane F. Crosthwaite, eds., "The Son and Daughter," in *Millennial Praises: A Shaker Hymnal* (Amherst: University of Massachusetts Press, 2009), 58.

2   Jeremy Gregory, "The Long Eighteenth Century," in *The Cambridge Companion to John Wesley,* ed. Randy L. Maddox and Jason E. Vickers, Cambridge Companions to Religion, 13–39 (Cambridge and New York: Cambridge University Press, 2010), 32.

3   For a comprehensive history of the Shaker movement in England and America from the eighteenth through the twentieth century, see Stephen J. Stein, *The Shaker Experience in America: A History of the United Society of Believers* (New Haven: Yale University Press, 1992).

4   As an historical account of Lee's life and ministry, *Testimonies* should be read critically. It was compiled and published decades after her death and was published with an eye toward promoting the Shaker Gospel. It offers valuable insights for understanding how Lee's followers experienced her ministry, but *Testimonies* is as much a spiritual autobiography and a work of hagiography as it is a work of history.

5   Rufus Bishop et al., eds., *Testimonies of the Life, Character, Revelations, and Doctrines of Mother Ann Lee, and the Elders with Her: Through Whom the Word of Eternal Life Was Opened in This day of Christ's Second Appearing,* 2nd ed. (Albany: Weed, Parsons & Co., printers, 1888), 51, 36 and 5.

6   Bishop et al., *Testimonies of the Life, Character, Revelations, and Doctrines of Mother Ann Lee, and the Elders with Her,* 4.

7   Bishop et al., *Testimonies of the Life, Character, Revelations, and Doctrines of Mother Ann Lee, and the Elders with Her,* 17 and 14.

8   Bishop et al., *Testimonies of the Life, Character, Revelations, and Doctrines of Mother Ann Lee, and the Elders with Her,* 45.

9   On Lee's arrival in New York, see Stein, *The Shaker Experience in America, 10–14.* Bishop et al., *Testimonies of the Life, Character, Revelations, and Doctrines of Mother Ann Lee, and the Elders with Her,* 10 and 52.

10   On the ministry that provided the foundation for the Shaker village at New Lebanon, New York, see Marcus Reginald Letourneau, "Holy Mount: Identity, Place, Religion and Narrative at

New Lebanon Shaker Village, 1759–1861" (PhD diss., Queen's University at Kingston, 2009), http://hdl.handle.net/1974/1882. See also Bishop et al., *Testimonies of the Life, Character, Revelations, and Doctrines of Mother Ann Lee, and the Elders with Her*, 28.

11   On the appeal of Lee among New England yeomen, see Suzanne Ruth Thurman, "Gathering the Believers," in *"O Sisters Ain't You Happy?": Gender, Family, and Community among the Harvard and Shirley Shakers, 1781–1918*, 1st ed., Women and Gender in North American Religions (Syracuse: Syracuse University Press, 2002), 24–40.

12   Stephen Paterwic, "Whittaker, James (1751–1787)," in *The A to Z of the Shakers*, The A to Z Guide Series (Lanham: Scarecrow Press, 2009), 244.

13   "A Concise Statement of the Principles of the Only True Church, According to the Gospel of the Present Appearance of Christ," Shaker Collection Highlights: Williams Digital Collection, 1790, https://unbound.williams.edu/williamsarchives/islandora/object/shakers%3A73, 23.

14   Stephen C. Taysom, *Shakers, Mormons, and Religious Worlds: Conflicting Visions, Contested Boundaries*, Religion in North America (Bloomington: Indiana University Press, 2011), 4–11.

15   Brewer, *Shaker Communities, Shaker Lives*, 27.

16   Taysom, *Shakers, Mormons, and Religious Worlds*, 9.

17   For a fuller description of Shaker gender relations, see Glendyne R. Wergland, "Work, Reciprocity, Equality and Union," *Sisters in the Faith: Shaker Women and Equality of the Sexes* (Amherst: University of Massachusetts Press, 2011), 102–113.

18   Brewer, *Shaker Communities, Shaker Lives*, 20–21.

19   Humez, "Weary of Petticoat Government: The Specter of Female Rule in Early Nineteenth-Century Shaker Politics," 9.

20   Bishop et al., *Testimonies of the Life, Character, Revelations, and Doctrines of Mother Ann Lee, and the Elders with Her*, v. Seth Y. Wells, *Millennial Praises, Containing a Collection of Gospel Hymns, in Four Parts; Adapted to the Day of Christ's Second Appearing* (Hancock: Printed by Josiah Tallcott, Jr., 1813), https://catalog.hathitrust.org/Record/001400752.

21   *Millennial Praises*, 45.

22   On the Shaker's Children Order, see Judith A. Graham, "The New Lebanon Shaker Children's Order," *Winterthur Portfolio* 26, no. 4 (1991): 215–229. On the rise and fall of the Shaker population see, Priscilla J. Brewer, "The Demographic Features of the Shaker Decline, 1787–1900," *Journal of Interdisciplinary History* 15, no. 1 (1984): 31–52, 40, and 42.

23   "The 'Millennial Laws' of 1821," *The Shaker Quarterly* 7, no. 2 (Summer 1967): 35–58.

Part III

EXPANSION

Chapter Eleven

DAVID WALKER AND BLACK PROPHETIC RELIGION

Christopher Cameron
University of North Carolina, Charlotte, North Carolina

In his 1829 *Appeal to the Coloured Citizens of the World*, David Walker stated that "the Lord has a suffering people, whose moans and groans at his feet for deliverance from oppression and wretchedness, pierce the very throne of Heaven, and call loudly on the God of Justice, to be revenged."[1] This theme of divine justice and God's vengeance on his enemies would be a central one in the pamphlet and established Walker as a key figure in the black prophetic tradition. According to the philosopher Cornel West, the black prophetic Christian tradition, which includes figures such as Walker, Frederick Douglass, Fannie Lou Hamer, and Martin Luther King, Jr., has been one of the central streams in black intellectual life from the nineteenth century to the present. Thinkers in this tradition exemplify, according to West, "a courage to hope in the face of undeniably desperate circumstances rooted in a love that refuses to lose contact with the humanity of others or one's self."[2] But while West explores this tradition among a wide variety of thinkers, he devotes less than one page to David Walker and does not fully flesh out just what makes him a black prophetic thinker.

This essay argues that Walker was the central figure in propagating the black prophetic tradition during the antebellum period. While many scholars have argued for Walker's significance as an antislavery advocate and political thinker, I argue that his key intellectual contribution was as a religious thinker whose ideas and rhetorical strategies would inform black activists in his own time as well as in the twentieth and twenty-first centuries. With regards to the former, Walker influenced both the pioneering black feminist thinker Maria Stewart along with black religious radicals such as Henry Highland Garnet during the 1830s and 1840s. And in the long run, Walker's prophetic voice and rhetorical style became standard among activists and thinkers ranging from Fannie Lou Hamer to Malcolm X.

Early Proponents of Black Prophetic Religion

While David Walker emerged as one of the strongest proponents of the black prophetic tradition, other black religious thinkers voiced aspects of this tradition as early as the 1770s. These individuals include Phillis Wheatley, Caesar Sarter, and Prince Hall, all of whom lived in Massachusetts. The theme of divine retribution for the sin of slavery appeared in all of their

A Companion to American Religious History, First Edition. Edited by Benjamin E. Park.
© 2021 John Wiley & Sons, Inc. Published 2021 by John Wiley & Sons, Inc.

writings. What differentiated them from Walker, however, was the milder tone of their writings as well as the lack of an extended treatment of divine wrath. Wheatley, Sarter, and Hall all published shorter pieces that mentioned or alluded to the possibility of divine judgment, yet none of them explored the topic to the length that Walker did, and none were nearly as abrasive as he was in his *Appeal*. Nevertheless, they were all important predecessors to Walker and foundational thinkers in African American religious history.

Phillis Wheatley, born in Africa and brought to Boston as a slave around 1761, published multiple works influenced by the Puritan jeremiad. For white Puritan ministers in the colonial era, the jeremiad relied on notions of providentialism and articulated a worldview whereby God was intimately involved in earthly affairs. This outlook that would have accorded well with traditional African cosmology, as scholars have noted a similar lack of distinction between sacred and secular realms in African thought.[3] Wheatley employed this rhetorical device in both her poetry and correspondence. In her 1774 letter to Samson Occom, for instance, she wrote that the love of freedom implanted by God lives in the hearts of blacks, and is "impatient of Oppression, and pants for Deliverance. Because of this disdain for oppression, Wheatley believed God would "get him honor upon all whose Avarice compels them to countenance and help forward the Calamities of the Fellow Creatures. This I desire not for their Hurt, but to Convince them of the strange Absurdity of their Conduct whose Words and Actions are so diametrically opposite."[4] By writing that God would "get him honor," Wheatley contended that if American colonists continued their hypocritical practice of holding slaves, God would take revenge upon them, an interpretation supported by her next sentence, where she said she does not desire God's getting "him honor" to hurt the colonists, but to teach them a lesson. She takes a similar approach in her 1778 poem "On the Death of General Wooster," where she asks the colonists "how presumptuous shall we hope to find/Divine acceptance with th' Almighty mind/While yet (O deed Ungenerous!) they disgrace/And hold in bondage Afric's blameless race?"[5] Linking the success of the American Revolution to the abolition of slavery, Wheatley subtly threatens the colonists with divine punishment should they continue in their sinful ways.

Caesar Sarter was another former slave in Massachusetts who published an antislavery essay that articulated elements of what would become the black prophetic tradition. Born in Africa, Sarter was forcefully captured and transported to Massachusetts, likely sometime in the 1740s. He spent twenty years enslaved, but by 1774 he was a free man living in Massachusetts, likely somewhere on the North Shore. That year he published an antislavery essay in the *Essex Journal and Merrimack Packet*, located in Newburyport, that articulated similar themes as Wheatley.

Sarter began his piece by speaking to the broader context of the American Revolution, stating "as this is a time of great anxiety and distress among you, on account of the infringement, not only of your Charter rights; but of the natural rights and privileges of freeborn men," the colonists should understand the emphasis that all people, white and black, place on their liberty.[6] He then built on this point by stating that God was a God of the oppressed, and that He would have vengeance on the colonists for enslaving Africans. "Why, in the name of Heaven," he thundered, "will you suffer such a gross violation of that rule by which your conduct must be tried, in that day, in which you must be held accountable for all your actions, to, that impartial Judge, who hears the groans of the oppressed and who will sooner or later, avenge them of their oppressors!"[7] His reference to the impartiality of God was an idea that would recur often in the writings and sermons of black prophetic thinkers, as was his statement that God would destroy those who perpetuated slavery. Speaking once more to the context of the Revolution, Sarter asked the colonists: "Would you desire the preservation of your own liberty? As the first step let the oppressed Africans be liberated; then, and not till then, may you with confidence and consistency of conduct, look to Heaven for a blessing on your endeavors."[8] If the colonists hoped to be successful in their political struggle against

Great Britain, they needed to repent for their sins, especially that of holding blacks in bondage.

Prince Hall was the foremost black activist in revolutionary Massachusetts, and spoke to similar themes as Wheatley and Sarter in a speech he delivered in 1797. Hall was born enslaved in Barbados in 1748, transported to Massachusetts, and purchased his freedom there in 1770. Within a few short years, Hall had become one of Boston's most well known and respected black citizens. He established the African Masonic Lodge there in 1775, the first formal all-black institution in the United States, and led multiple petition drives to the Massachusetts General Court calling for the end of slavery and a ban on slave trading.[9] Over the next couple decades, Hall focused on building Boston's black community and continually combating racial injustice. He did this in large part through his work with black Masons in the city. Each year, Masons held a celebration during the festival of St. John the Baptist and two of Hall's speeches on these occasions have survived.

In the second of these speeches, Hall implied that African Americans were God's new chosen people, similar to the ancient Israelites, when he posited that blacks had been "dragg'd from their native country, by the iron hand of tyranny and oppression ... to a strange land and a strange people."[10] In this brief line Hall alluded to Psalm 137:4: "How shall we sing the Lord's song in a strange land?" By making this comparison, Hall implied that God might take the same vengeance on blacks' enslavers and oppressors as he did on the enemies of the Israelites in the Old Testament. He went on to make a much less subtle threat, noting that his audience should "remember what a dark day it was with our African brethren six years ago in the French West-Indies. Nothing but the snap of the whip was heard from morning to evening ... but blessed be God, the scene is changed; they now confess that God hath no respect of persons."[11] In referencing the Haitian Revolution, which began in 1791 and was still ongoing at the time of his speech, Hall, like Sarter, claimed that an impartial God was on the side of blacks and would deliver them from their enemies, forcibly if necessary.

As a member of Boston's African Masonic Lodge, David Walker may have been familiar with Hall's "Charge," although the speech was given nearly thirty years before he arrived in Boston. And while it is unlikely that Walker was familiar with Sarter's essay, he almost certainly encountered Phillis Wheatley's writings in the pages of *Freedom's Journal*, the first black newspaper in the United States and a publication that he helped to distribute in Boston. But whether or not he read or was familiar these authors, Walker built on their ideas and fully fleshed out their implications. In doing so, he became a leading thinker in the tradition of black prophetic witness, a tradition with its roots in the revolutionary period.

David Walker's Early Life and Activism

David Walker was born in Wilmington, North Carolina, likely sometime between 1795–1797, to an enslaved father and a free mother, which meant that he was free. Wilmington had a majority African American population in the years immediately preceding Walker's birth and lasting until the 1820 census, and nearly all local businesses and trades were dominated by blacks, including rice cultivation, metalworking, selling goods at the market, masonry, carpentry, and other construction jobs. Growing up in Wilmington, therefore, Walker would have seen the critical importance of black labor to the southern economy, while also witnessing the degradation of these same blacks under the system of bondage. While Wilmington did have a large black population, most of these were enslaved and it was thus difficult for individuals such as Walker to compete with slave labor and secure gainful employment. Walker thus decided to move to Charleston, South Carolina sometime after 1816 to secure better employment and be part of a larger community of free blacks, whose population nearly quadrupled in the years between 1790–1820, from 950 to 3,615. Walker was probably also attracted to the prospect of the black controlled Methodist Church in Charleston, as an African Methodist Episcopal church was founded there in 1816.[12]

This church represented the flowering of the group consciousness building among Charleston's black residents since the late eighteenth century, and likely imbued Walker with many of the revolutionary ideas he would later publish in Boston. Free blacks in Charleston, including refugees from Saint Domingue, established mutual aid societies, burial societies, and other institutions that demonstrate an increasing level of organization within the black community, even if some of these societies were built around color distinctions. Both slaves and free black Methodists began meeting together and holding religious services around 1815 and they established the AME Church the following year. In doing so, the congregants faced many difficulties, chief of which was harassment from whites who did not like the prospect of large groups of black people meeting together for any purpose. Members of the church were charged with disorderly conduct and unlawful assembly on multiple occasions, yet they nevertheless continued to meet, even after being forced to change locations. The church was finally burned down after the Denmark Vesey conspiracy in 1822, as local whites believed that the plot to rebel had been hatched in the church and discussed there. Indeed, three of the five leaders charged in the conspiracy were class leaders in the congregation. It is likely that David Walker knew Vesey and others charged in the conspiracy, a situation that may have shaped his emerging views on the necessity and practicality of slave rebellions.[13]

Walker likely left Charleston shortly after the Vesey conspiracy was uncovered and traveled around the eastern seaboard for the next few years. He may have spent some time in Philadelphia, as his *Appeal* suggests he met Richard Allen, founder and bishop of the AME Church, at some point. By 1825, Walker appeared for the first time in Boston's city directory as a used clothes dealer. In short order, he established a full life in his new home. On February 23, 1826, he was married to Eliza Butler, a member of Boston's black middle class. In August of that year, Walker joined the African Masonic Lodge that was founded by Prince Hall, which provided him with connections to Boston's leading black citizens, including Thomas Paul, minister of the African Baptist Church, Walker Lewis, a militant black abolitionist, and James G. Barbadoes, a political organizer. While many of Boston's most prominent black citizens attended Paul's African Baptist Church, founded in 1805, Walker joined the smaller and less well-known Methodist May Street Church, led by Samuel Snowden, himself a black émigré from the South. Snowden was an ardent abolitionist and was likely far more radical than the moderate Thomas Paul. It was likely that combination of religion and political critique that drew Walker to Snowden's church, as well as Walker's historical ties to Methodism.[14]

Walker's staunch commitment to Methodism was replicated across the United States, as the denomination quickly became the largest in the country, reflecting the success of what has come to be known as the Second Great Awakening. This string of revivals began with revivals in Kentucky during the late eighteenth century and soon spread throughout the nation. It was characterized by the massive growth of evangelical sects such as the Methodists and Baptists, who achieved success through the use of itinerant preachers, many of whom were common people without the formal education of their Congregationalist or Presbyterian peers. Many preachers of the Second Great Awakening mounted an attack on the prevailing doctrine of predestination, arguing that anybody could achieve salvation through accepting Jesus as their Lord and Savior. Preachers such as Charles Grandison Finney, a former lawyer who became a leading voice in American revivalism during the 1820s and 1830s, expounded the doctrine of perfectionism, whereby individuals could not only achieve spiritual perfection for themselves but could help to perfect American society. It was in this religious context that Walker developed his theology and political philosophy. While African American religion has sometimes been criticized for its perceived otherworldliness, for Walker, religion was all about improving human life in the here and now.[15]

Walker quickly put his religious views into practice in Boston by becoming one of the foremost political organizers and antislavery voices in the city. He was an early supporter of the black newspaper *Freedom's Journal*, launched by Samuel Cornish and John Russwurm in 1827, and served as a Boston agent for the paper along with Thomas Paul. In this role, Walker helped to raise subscriptions for the paper and collected funds. *Freedom's Journal* published articles on a host of topics important to African Americans, including the effects of racial discrimination, the colonization movement, and abolitionism. More importantly, it was a venue where black voices could be heard and helped tie together disparate black communities throughout the North. In addition to this role, Walker in 1826 became one of the founders of the Massachusetts General Colored Association. This was an antislavery organization that gained a national reputation for advocating the immediate emancipation of southern slaves, opposing the colonization movement that aimed to send free blacks to Africa, and working to create a unified political consciousness among northern free blacks.[16]

Black unity was the key theme of Walker's speech to the Massachusetts General Colored Association, published in *Freedom's Journal* on December 19, 1828. At the semi-annual meeting of the organization, Walker, by now one of the most prominent black abolitionists in Boston, said that "the primary object of this institution, is, to unite the colored population, so far, through the United States of America, as may be practicable and expedient; forming societies, opening, extending, and keeping up correspondences, and not withholding any thing which may have the least tendency to meliorate *our* miserable condition."[17] Building upon the work of Massachusetts activists such as Prince Hall and Paul Cuffe to organize African Masonic Lodges and African Institutions throughout the country, Walker called for blacks to build institutions to foster greater connections among free blacks in order to more effectively coordinate strategies and goals. He also argued in this speech that disunity among blacks is what kept them from "rising to the scale of reasonable and thinking beings," and it was in keeping blacks ignorant that masters were able to keep them enslaved.[18]

Walker's speech to the Massachusetts General Colored Association also contained hints of arguments he would make more forcefully in his *Appeal to the Coloured Citizens of the World*. He argued that blacks have an obligation to help their brethren suffering under slavery, but also that God will assist them. "It is indispensably our duty," he wrote, "to try every scheme that we think will have a tendency to facilitate our salvation, and leave the final result to that God, who holds the destinies of people in the hollow of his hand, and who ever has, and will, repay every nation according to its works."[19] Here he implied that America has sinned against God for holding blacks in slavery and that the nation would be judged for this crime. This argument was one in a long line of jeremiads by Massachusetts' black activists, ranging from Phillis Wheatley to Prince Hall. And like these earlier activists, Walker argued that black America represented God's new covenanted nation, writing that "I verily believe that God has something in reserve for us, which, when he shall have poured it upon us, will repay us for all our suffering and miseries."[20] Walker's God was one that was intimately involved in earthly affairs and interested in the cause of American blacks, who must also work to help themselves to achieve freedom from slavery and racial discrimination.

Appeal to the Coloured Citizens of the World

Walker developed these ideas in his most well-known text, *Appeal to the Coloured Citizens of the World*, first published in Boston in 1829. According to historian Peter Hinks, Walker's *Appeal* "embodied the positive activism required by the evangelicalism fueling the Second Great Awakening of the 1830s: the individual must enthusiastically assent to receiving God's free offer of grace and must make that receipt manifest through acts of goodwill in the world."[21] While Walker's text was key in the ties it made between black religion and politics, it was not just the fact that Walker argued religion must serve a political function that make the *Appeal* a foundational text in black religious history. Rather, it was the arguments he made and the rhetorical style he adopted that would make this text such an influential one for black religious and political thinkers in both his own time and as far forward as the twentieth century US civil rights movement. These arguments and rhetorical style constitute the tradition of black prophetic witness.

Walker began the pamphlet by claiming that African Americans were "the most degraded, wretched, and abject set of beings that ever lived," and stated that his desire was "to awaken in the breast of my afflicted, degraded, and slumbering brethren, a spirit of inquiry and investigation respecting our miseries and wretchedness in this Republican Land of Liberty."[22] He saw himself as a prophet sent by God to educate fellow blacks and knew that he could face prison or even death for printing the book. Slavery was the chief source of blacks' degradation in the United States, he argued, and this degradation took a number of forms, including ignorance, obsequiousness, and a resignation to their fate. Walker built his case through historical examples, arguing that slaves in the ancient world had enjoyed far greater privileges and rights than African Americans. And he likewise spoke to contemporary politics, noting that the colonization plan, whereby free blacks would be removed from the United States to strengthen slavery, was another aspect of blacks' wretchedness in the country.

From the earliest pages of the text, Walker also articulated elements of the black prophetic tradition in a way that built on but also extended the ideas and rhetoric of predecessors such as Sarter and Wheatley. He argued that slave masters are happy to keep blacks in ignorance, but these individuals "forget that God rules in the armies of heaven and among the inhabitants of the earth, having his ears continually open to the cries, tears and groans of his oppressed people."[23] Since God is a just deity, it is likely the case that he "will at one day appear fully in behalf of the oppressed, and arrest the progress of the avaricious oppressors."[24] It was unclear just how that would happen, however. God could destroy slaveholders through a slave rebellion, or he could use other means, such as a civil war. In perhaps the most prescient statement of the *Appeal*, Walker stated of God, "not unfrequently will he cause them to rise up one against another, to be split and divided, and to oppress each other, and sometimes to open hostilities with sword in hand."[25] A righteous God would find some way to ensure that justice reigned in the world, Walker argued.

While these ideas were similar to those that earlier black activists and intellectuals had articulated, Walker went even further in offering recommendations to slaves for actions they should take with the knowledge that God was on their side. He counseled patience and noted slaves should wait until an opportune time to rebel against their masters. When that times comes, he counseled slaves to "be not afraid or dismayed; for be you assured that Jesus Christ the King of heaven and of earth who is the God of Justice and of armies, will surely go before you. And those enemies who have for hundreds of years stolen our *rights*, and kept us ignorant of Him and His divine worship, he will remove."[26] Walker claimed here that God would support a slave revolt not only because of slavery itself, but also because the institution hindered the progress of Christianity. This religion, far from being a peaceable one, actually enjoined blacks to fight for their freedom, as Walker also argued that blacks should recognize no master but God so staying in bondage voluntarily was actually a form of blasphemy.[27]

Walker built on this latter idea in Article II of the pamphlet. He noted there that God would raise up a Hannibal, or a black military leader, among them to lead a nationwide slave rebellion, as had occurred in Haiti. He likewise claimed that slave kidnappers and slave traders are God's enemies who deserve to be destroyed. Since whites think nothing of murdering blacks to enslave them, "therefore, if there is an attempt made by us, kill or be killed. Now I ask you, had you not rather be killed than be a slave to a tyrant, who takes the life of your mother, wife, and dear little children?"[28] Some might think this is going to far, but Walker states again that it is just and right for slaves to kill those who are trying to keep them in bondage. Indeed, this is something they have an obligation to do if they want to call themselves Christians.

The heart of Walker's *Appeal* predicted the destruction of the United States. Earlier, he had confined these predictions to those who held slaves, but later in the pamphlet he noted that the entire country was at risk if it permitted the institution to continue. "I tell you Americans," he proclaimed, "that unless you speedily alter your course, you and your country are gone ... For God Almighty will tear up the very face of the earth."[29] Like the biblical prophet Jeremiah, whom the prophetic sermon the jeremiad was named after, Walker predicted the destruction of the nation for its offenses against God. "O Americans! Americans!," he continued, "I call God — I call angels — I call men, to witness, that your destruction is at hand, and will be speedily consummated unless you REPENT."[30] Here Walker reaffirmed his status as a prophet with the power to call on both God and angels as witnesses to the veracity of his words. Just as Moses warned Pharaoh of his impending destruction should he fail to free the Israelites, Walker now warned the United States of a similar fate should the nation persist in its course.

Walker aimed to distribute his pamphlet as widely as possible to achieve his goal of fomenting a slave rebellion and empowering free blacks. To do so, he relied partially on networks of sailors, both black and white, who traveled between the northern and southern states. He published the first edition of the text in September 1829, and by December of that year, at least sixty copies had surfaced in Savannah, Georgia, where a local black Baptist preacher was briefly detained on suspicion of distributing seditious literature. In response to the pamphlet's arrival there, legislators quickly passed laws aimed at regulating the movement of black seamen and preventing sedition. The mayor of Savannah also wrote to Boston mayor Harrison Gray Otis, demanding some action be taken to stop Walker, to which Otis replied there was nothing he could do. Copies of Walker's *Appeal* likewise surfaced in Richmond (Virginia), New Bern (North Carolina), New Orleans (Louisiana), and Charleston (South Carolina).[31] In this latter city, a white man named Edward Smith was actually arrested and charged with seditious libel for distributing copies of the text. He testified that in Boston "a colored man of decent appearance & very genteelly dressed called on board of the vessel and asked him if he would do a favor for him." This black man, presumably David Walker, then stated that he wanted Smith to bring a packet of pamphlets to Charleston "and to give them to any negroes he had a mind to, or that he met, that he must do it privately and not let any white person know any thing about it."[32] It was actions such as these and the *Appeal*'s presence in a number of southern cities that led some contemporaries and future historians to link the text with Nat Turner's revolt in 1831, although there is no evidence indicating Turner read Walker.[33]

Influence on Maria Stewart and Frederick Douglass

One activist whom David Walker almost certainly influenced was his neighbor Maria Stewart. Born free in Hartford, Connecticut in 1803, Stewart found herself in Boston in the mid-1820s, where she joined Thomas Paul's African Baptist Church and made the acquaintance of antislavery activists such as Walker. Stewart's first publication, *Religion and the Pure Principles of Morality*, appeared shortly after Walker's death in 1831 and built on many of the themes from his *Appeal to the Coloured Citizens of the World*. Here she argued most forcefully for black unity and a focus on education, noting that "the day on which we unite, heart and soul, and turn our attention to knowledge and improvement, that day the hissing and reproach among the nations of the earth against us will cease."[34] Her argument here was certainly not a novel one. African American intellectuals in the revolutionary and early national periods, including Thomas Paul and Primus Hall, had called for increased access to education as a means of racial uplift. What was new about Stewart was the fact that she said these things in public, before audiences of men and women, becoming the first American woman, white or black, to do so.

In taking her stand against slavery and racism and in favor of black unity, Stewart saw herself as an instrument of God sent to aid in the reformation of the black community. "It was God alone who inspired my heart to publish the meditations thereof," she proclaimed in a speech before the African-American Female Intelligence Society. "And it was done with pure motives of love to your souls, in the hope that Christians might examine themselves, and sinners become pricked in their hearts."[35] Unlike Phillis Wheatley or David Walker, Stewart's jeremiads do not predict the destruction of the United States, but they do predict that of the black community should African Americans fail to heed her warnings.

Stewart also became the first woman in the United States to lecture on women's rights. She despised the fact that black girls and women could generally attain to no higher employment than being domestic servants, a job which she had done for twenty years. And she argued that the future of the race lay in the hands of black women: "O woman, woman! Upon you I call; for upon your exertions almost entirely depends whether the rising generation shall be any thing more than we have been or not."[36] Her reasoning behind this was that black men had failed in their obligations to the race. In a bold speech before the African Masonic Lodge of Boston she asked the assembled men, "Where can we find among ourselves the man of science, or a philosopher, or an able statesman, or a counsellor at law?" If the black Masons truly are men, she noted, they need to convince others that they "possess the spirit of men."[37] This statement did not go over very well, of course, and Stewart had relocated to New York City within two years, where she became an educator and journalist. Despite this fact, Stewart's brief career in Boston, spanning the years 1831–1835, made her the first black feminist in the country and continued the important black prophetic tradition that David Walker strengthened with his work.

David Walker's prophetic version of Christianity likewise informed the rhetoric of another leading antebellum black activist, namely Frederick Douglass. Douglass, born enslaved in Maryland around 1817, was only twelve years old when the first edition of Walker's *Appeal* was published. Yet Douglass's denunciations of American Christianity and writing style display the influence of Walker's work. In his 1845 *Narrative*, Douglass implicitly agrees with Walker's belief that violence against slave masters is justified when he notes that his own path to freedom began after he physically bested Mr. Covey, the man whom his master hired as a "slave breaker." Covey attacked Douglass one morning after Douglass had run away from the plantation, and when Douglass prevailed in a fight that lasted hours, he noted that "however long I might remain a slave in form, the day had passed forever when I could be a slave in fact."[38] For Douglass, as for Walker, the assertion of his masculinity and strength was the key to his freedom and the only thing that gained him the respect that was his due as a human being.

Douglass's denunciations of American Christianity also fall within the tradition of the black jeremiad that David Walker helped initiate. Throughout his first autobiography, Douglass notes again and again that religious slaveholders "are the worst. I have ever found them the meanest and basest, the most cruel and cowardly, of all others." Statements such as these are part of his broader critiques of American Christianity and found their fullest expression in his 1852 speech "What to the Slave is the Fourth of July?" Here Douglass states in no uncertain terms that American republicanism and American Christianity are hypocritical. And it is not just southern Christians whom Douglass denounces, as northern churches have also made themselves "the bulwark of American slavery, and the shield of American slave-hunters."[39] They did this by refusing to expel slaveholders from their congregations and by actively opposing the efforts of abolitionists to combat the institution. Like David Walker, Douglass argued that the nation might soon be destroyed should it persist in its course. "Oh!

be warned! Be warned!," he proclaimed. "A horrible reptile is coiled up in your nation's bosom; the venomous creature is nursing at the tender breast of your youthful republic."[40] Unless Americans repent of the sin of slavery, the nation was likely to see a large scale slave rebellion or race war, Douglass claimed.

Conclusion

David Walker was a key religious thinker who significantly impacted the antislavery movement as well as African American theology, both in his time and throughout the nineteenth and twentieth centuries. His influence on American abolitionism has been well recognized. The pamphlet helped contribute to unified southern opposition to abolition, which in turn strengthened the resolve of northerners, especially those on the fence, to fight for the end of slavery.[41] But Walker's influence on African American religion was perhaps even greater. His willingness to speak truth to power, his uncompromising and abrasive style, and his argument that slavery and racism were sins for which God would punish America all informed the theological and political perspectives of thinkers ranging from Stewart to Henry Highland Garnet to Frederick Douglass during the antebellum period. Garnet, a black Presbyterian minister in New York City, admired Walker's work so much that he reprinted an edition of the *Appeal* in 1848. Walker's contempt for racist whites and images of the apocalypse would likewise resonate in the speeches of Malcolm X during the 1950s and 1960s, while his hope for democracy and staunch attachment to the power of Christianity would be present in the sermons and writings of Martin Luther King, Jr.[42] And since the civil rights movement of the 1960s, countless students and scholars have read updated editions of the text. Its arguments and rhetorical strategies hold particular resonance for activists in the contemporary Black Lives Matter movement, a proposition that Walker never explicitly articulated himself, but one with which he would have certainly agreed.

FURTHER READING

Blight, David W. *Frederick Douglass, Prophet of Freedom.* New York: Simon and Schuster, 2018.
Howard-Pitney, David. *The Afro-American Jeremiad: Appeals for Justice in America.* Philadelphia: Temple University Press, 1990.
Jackson, Kellie Carter. *Force and Freedom: Black Abolitionists and the Politics of Violence* Philadelphia: University of Pennsylvania Press, 2019.
Jarrett, Gene Andrew. "'To Refute Mr. Jefferson's Arguments Respecting Us': Thomas Jefferson, David Walker, and the Politics of Early African American Literature." *Early American Literature* 46, no. 2 (2011): 291–318.
Rogers, Melvin L. "David Walker and the Political Power of the Appeal." *Political Theory* 43, no. 2 (April 2015): 208–233.

BIBLIOGRAPHY

Primary Sources

Blight, David W., ed. *Narrative of the Life of Frederick Douglass, An American Slave: Written by Himself, with Related Documents.* 2nd ed. Boston and New York: Bedford/St. Martin's, 2003.
Brooks, Joanna and John Saillant, eds. *"Face Zion Forward": First Writers of the Black Atlantic, 1785–1798.* Boston: Northeastern University Press, 2002.
Douglass, Frederick. *Narrative of the Life of Frederick Douglass, An American Slave: Written by Himself.* Boston: American Anti-Slavery Society. https://www.docsouth.unc.edu/neh/douglass/douglass.html.

Essex Journal and Merrimack Packet (Newburyport, MA).

Freedom's Journal (New York, NY).

Richardson, Marilyn, ed. *Maria Stewart: America's First Black Woman Political Writer*. Bloomington: Indiana University Press, 1987.

Walker, David. *David Walker's Appeal to the Coloured Citizens of the World, but in particular, and very expressly, to those of the United States of America*. Edited by Sean Wilentz. New York: Hill and Wang, 1995.

Wheatley, Phillis. *Complete Writings*. Edited by Vincent Carretta. New York: Penguin Books, 2001.

Secondary Sources

Bercovitch, Sacvan. *The American Jeremiad*. Madison: The University of Wisconsin Press, 1978.

Cameron, Christopher. *To Plead Our Own Cause: African Americans in Massachusetts and the Making of the Antislavery Movement*. Kent: The Kent State University Press, 2014.

Hinks, Peter P. *To Awaken My Afflicted Brethren: David Walker and the Problem of Antebellum Slave Resistance*. University Park: The Pennsylvania State University Press, 1997.

Horton, James Oliver. "Generations of Protest: Black Families and Social Reform in Ante-Bellum Boston." *New England Quarterly* 49, no. 2 (1976): 242–256.

Howard-Pitney, David. *The Afro-American Jeremiad: Appeals for Justice in America*. Philadelphia: Temple University Press, 1990.

West, Cornel. *Prophesy Deliverance!: An Afro-American Revolutionary Christianity*. Anniversary Edition. Louisville: Westminster John Knox Press, 2002.

Wilentz, Sean. *The Rise of American Democracy: Jefferson to Lincoln*. New York: W. W. Norton, 2005.

NOTES

1 Sean Wilentz, ed., *David Walker's Appeal to the Coloured Citizens of the World, but in particular, and very expressly, to those of the United States of America* (1829; New York: Hill and Wang, 1995), xii; Peter P. Hinks, *To Awaken My Afflicted Brethren: David Walker and the Problem of Antebellum Slave Resistance* (University Park: Pennsylvania State University Press, 1997), 48–49.

2 Cornel West, *Prophesy Deliverance!: An Afro-American Revolutionary Christianity* Anniversary Edition (1982; Louisville: Westminster John Knox Press, 2002), 7.

3 For the jeremiad as it applies to white Puritans see Sacvan Bercovitch, *The American Jeremiad* (Madison: University of Wisconsin Press, 1978), xi; Historian David Howard-Pitney's study of the black jeremiad begins with an analysis of the ideology of Frederick Douglass. See *The Afro-American Jeremiad: Appeals for Justice in America* (Philadelphia: Temple University Press, 1990).

4 "Phillis Wheatley to Samson Occom, 11 February 1774," *Complete Writings*, ed. Vincent Carretta (New York: Penguin Books, 2001), 153.

5 Wheatley, "On the Death of General Wooster," *Complete Writings*, 92.

6 Caesar Sarter, "Address, To Those Who are Advocates for holding the Africans in Slavery," *Essex Journal and Merrimack Packet* (Newburyport, MA), August 17, 1774, 1.

7 Sarter, "Address, To Those Who are Advocates for holding the Africans in Slavery," 1.

8 Sarter, "Address, To Those Who are Advocates for holding the Africans in Slavery," 1.

9 James Oliver Horton, "Generations of Protest: Black Families and Social Reform in Ante-Bellum Boston" *New England Quarterly* 49, no. 2 (1976): 243–245.

10 Prince Hall, "A Charge Delivered to the African Lodge June 24, 1797," in *"Face Zion Forward": First Writers of the Black Atlantic, 1785–1798*, ed. Joanna Brooks and John Saillant (Boston: Northeastern University Press, 2002), 200.

11 Hall, "A Charge Delivered to the African Lodge June 24, 1797," 204.

12 Hinks, *To Awaken My Afflicted Brethren*, xii–xiii, 8–29.

13 Hinks, *To Awaken My Afflicted Brethren*, 26–38; There is some controversy among historians regarding whether or not the Vesey conspiracy was a real one. For the argument that the conspiracy was not a real one see Michael P. Johnson, "Denmark Vesey and His Co-Conspirators," *William and Mary Quarterly* 58 (2001): 915–976. James O'Neil Spady has in turn questioned Johnson's argument, showing, for example, that the first two witnesses for the state came forward

of their own accord. See his "Power and Confession: On the Credibility of the Earliest Reports of the Denmark Vesey Slave Conspiracy," *William and Mary Quarterly* 68 (2011): 287–304.

14 Hinks, *To Awaken My Afflicted Brethren*, 63–79.

15 Charles Sellers, *The Market Revolution: Jacksonian America, 1815–1846* (New York: Oxford University Press, 1991), 202–236; Nathan Hatch, *The Democratization of American Christianity* (New Haven: Yale University Press, 1989), 8, 87–89.

16 *David Walker's Appeal to the Coloured Citizens of the World*, 75–78.

17 David Walker, "Address, Delivered before the General Colored Association of Boston" *Freedom's Journal*, December 19, 1828, 2.

18 Walker, "Address, Delivered before the General Colored Association of Boston," 2.

19 Walker, "Address, Delivered before the General Colored Association of Boston," 2.

20 Walker, "Address, Delivered before the General Colored Association of Boston," 2.

21 Hinks, *To Awaken My Afflicted Brethren*, 33.

22 *David Walker's Appeal to the Coloured Citizens of the World*, 1, 2.

23 *David Walker's Appeal to the Coloured Citizens of the World*, 3.

24 *David Walker's Appeal to the Coloured Citizens of the World*, 3.

25 *David Walker's Appeal to the Coloured Citizens of the World*, 3.

26 *David Walker's Appeal to the Coloured Citizens of the World*, 12.

27 *David Walker's Appeal to the Coloured Citizens of the World*, 16.

28 *David Walker's Appeal to the Coloured Citizens of the World*, 25–26.

29 *David Walker's Appeal to the Coloured Citizens of the World*, 39.

30 *David Walker's Appeal to the Coloured Citizens of the World*, 43.

31 Hinks, *To Awaken My Afflicted Brethren*, 116–119, 128–148.

32 "Testimony and Confession of Edward Smith" in Wilentz, ed., *David Walker's Appeal to the Coloured Citizens of the World*, 86.

33 Sean Wilentz notes that by his own testimony, Nat Turner began receiving divine instruction a decade before Walker's *Appeal* was published. See Sean Wilentz, *The Rise of American Democracy: Jefferson to Lincoln* (New York: W. W. Norton, 2005), 340.

34 Maria Stewart, "Religion and the Pure Principles of Morality," in Marilyn Richardson, ed., *Maria Stewart: America's First Black Woman Political Writer* (Bloomington: Indiana University Press, 1987), 37.

35 Maria Stewart, "Address Delivered before the African-American Female Intelligence Society," Richardson, ed., *Maria Stewart*, 52.

36 Stewart, "Address Delivered before the African-American Female Intelligence Society," 55.

37 Maria Stewart, "An Address Delivered at the African Masonic Hall," Richardson, ed., *Maria Stewart*, 57.

38 Frederick Douglass, *Narrative of the Life of Frederick Douglass, An American Slave: Written by Himself* (Boston: American Anti-Slavery Society), 73. https://www.docsouth.unc.edu/neh/douglass/douglass.html.

39 Frederick Douglass, "What to the Slave is the Fourth of July?" in *Narrative of the Life of Frederick Douglass, An American Slave: Written by Himself, with Related Documents*, ed. David W. Blight, 2nd ed. (Boston and New York: Bedford/St. Martin's, 2003), 164.

40 Douglass, "What to the Slave is the Fourth of July?," 168.

41 Wilentz, ed. *David Walker's Appeal to the Coloured Citizens of the World*, xx.

42 Wilentz, ed. *David Walker's Appeal to the Coloured Citizens of the World*, xxii.

Chapter Twelve

"DOWN WITH THE CONVENT!": ANTI-CATHOLICISM AND OPPOSITION TO NUNS IN ANTEBELLUM AMERICA

Cassandra L. Yacovazzi

University of South Florida, Sarasota-Manatee, Sarasota, Florida

The antebellum era was a time of religious awakening, known for towering revivalists such as Charles Grandison Finney, Lyman Beecher, and "Crazy" Lorenzo Dow. By this time, Methodist itinerate ministers had crisscrossed the American frontier on horseback to deliver the gospel, remaking the landscape into one dotted with church steeples in their wake. Women were often at the forefront of what historians call the Second Great Awakening, attending revivals in greater numbers than men, prompting husbands and sons to join them, and spearheading religiously-inspired reforms, such as the temperance movement, that would alter American history. But the period from 1830 to 1860 was also a time of bitter religious in-fighting among established traditions and a myriad of new religious off-shoots, each contending for influence in what was becoming a very noisy religious marketplace. The fiercest religious competition was fought between old enemies: Protestants and Catholics. Their battles played out in verbal attacks in the press and physical violence in the streets. They were waged in classrooms and in legislative chambers.

Anti-Catholicism in America, of course, dated back to the colonial era. Children of Puritan New Englanders played a game called "Break the Pope's Neck," while Anglican Virginians prohibited "papists" from carrying fire arms or holding public office. Yet because the Catholic population was a mere minority in a few cities during the colonial era and Early Republic, Protestants and Catholics lived mostly peaceably together, sometimes even cooperating toward common cause, such as Independence.[1]

The country transformed during the antebellum era through industrialization, western expansion, and sectionalism. It also became profoundly more Catholic. In 1815, there was a meagre Catholic population of around 150,000 (in a US population of about 8.3 million) scattered throughout the country. But by 1830, a quarter of a million immigrants, largely Irish and German and mostly Catholic, entered the US. Three times that number came to America in 1840. The growing American Catholic Church, led by bishops but also operating on the ground with a growing number of priests and nuns, was good at recruiting and keeping many of these newcomers. By 1860, the Catholic population in the US reached 3.1 million, making Catholicism the single largest religious group in the nation. As if overnight, Protestant Anglo-Americans watched their nation transformed ethnically and religiously.

A Companion to American Religious History, First Edition. Edited by Benjamin E. Park.
© 2021 John Wiley & Sons, Inc. Published 2021 by John Wiley & Sons, Inc.

Non-Catholics had long ridiculed Catholicism as being undemocratic with its religious hierarchy and ornate rituals. These traditions chafed against the sensibilities of Congregationalists, Baptists, Methodists, and other decidedly "Low-Church" denominations, which made up the most popular sects of the Second Great Awakening. The "High-Church" trappings of Catholicism were also seen as decidedly "Old World" and un-American. Such castigations gained new lifeblood by the 1830s, prompting an array of anti-Catholic conspiracy theories. Samuel F. B. Morse, more popularly known for the telegraph, penned one of the most famous of these: *Foreign Conspiracy against the Liberties of the United States*, tracing what he saw as a vast Catholic conspiracy throughout Europe to transform and dominate the US.[2]

Among the growing number of Catholics, nuns particularly stood out. With their distinct dress or habit, unmarried state, and communal lifestyle, the nun appeared as an aberration from the growing vision of what many Americans were coming to see as the ideal or "true" woman — the gentle wife and mother. The presense of nuns — or women religious as they are known officially within Catholicism ("religious" here being used as a noun rather than an adjective) — raised important questions in the US about a woman's role in society. At a time when it was understood that young women would venture down the path of marriage and motherhood, could a woman choose to remain single? What was the role of unwed women in society? When men often relied on the domestic labor of women so that they could fulfil their responsibilities outside the home, what would happen if female domestic labor was not a given? For the most part, non-Catholic Americans saw the nun as a serious threat to traditional gender roles and single women as a waste of womanhood if not a threat to the cosmic order of things.

Nuns also stood as a conspicuous representatives of a largely despised religion. While anti-Catholicism defined one of the most significant religious developments of the antebellum era, the nun was at the center of what historian Ray Allen Billington dubbed "the Protestant crusade." One of the worst acts of nativist anti-Catholic violence of this period was the burning of a convent. The most popular anti-Catholic book before the Civil War was about an "escaped nun." One of the defining reforms from the era, the establishment of common schools, was launched in part to combat the influence of convent schools. And the most popular third political party in the US before the Civil War, the Know Nothings, defined themselves by their opposition to immigrants and Catholics, reserving special contempt for convents, which they attempted to ban from the US. Thus, just as much as the Second Great Awakening and other religious developments at this time shaped people and society in America, so too did opposition to certain religious traditions, like Catholicism, that were deemed un-American, un-Christian, or threatening to traditional gender roles.[3]

An Escaped Nun

In order to understand this context, it is helpful to examine how one book became a national sensation. The text unveiled the supposedly horrific life of nuns and the secret machinations of Catholic clergy. It was full of falsehoods, but it's popularity and the degree to which non-Catholic Americans regarded it as factual reveal the deep roots of anti-Catholicism and especially aversion to nuns in antebellum America. The most infamous nun in American history was at the center of this book, but she was never really a nun. Her story, which was not her real story, profoundly shaped the American imagination concerning nuns. *Awful Disclosures of the Hotel Dieu Nunnery of Montreal*, by the poetically named Maria Monk, was published in New York in January, 1836. As first-hand narrator, Monk led readers behind convent walls, through closed doors, into secret chambers, and along underground tunnels. What they read confirmed their worst fears and fantasies about convent life: nuns held against their will and tortured for their disobedience (including "flesh burned off their bones with hot irons"); a tyrannical Mother Superior (with "quite a beard on her face"); lust-driven priests; illicit sexual affairs between nuns and priests; babies born of these affairs who were quickly baptized, strangled, and discarded into a giant pit covered with lime in the cellar floor; elaborate plots among the nuns and priests to keep their misdeeds hidden from the public and to lure more unsuspecting women within their walls. Maria Monk claimed that she naïvely joined the convent before being exposed to these corruptions. After being impregnated by one of the priests, she narrowly escaped and barely survived. Making her way to New York, she met a group of prominent ministers (subsequently known as her "Protestant protectors") who nursed her back to health and encouraged her to publish her story so that the world could know the truth about convents.[4]

Awful Disclosures became an immediate success, selling over 20,000 copies in the first five weeks. Book sales surpassed 300,000 by 1860, making *Awful Disclosures* second only to *Uncle Tom's Cabin* on the eve of the Civil War, and to this day, it has never gone out of print. But its popularity was instantly matched by controversy. No sooner had the book been published than critics cried foul. Maria Monk's own mother testified that her daughter had never been a nun and in fact had a major lying problem after a slate pencil was smashed into her skull as a child. She also claimed that one of Monk's Protestant protectors offered her a large sum of money if she would go along with the story. But Monk's supporters dismissed her mother as "unreliable" due to "an extreme backwardness" common among Canadian Catholics, and they quickly matched letter for letter rebutting detractors. Her critics, they claimed, were simply part of a larger, more sinister "Jesuitical hoax," referring to a male monastic order whom many Protestants regarded as Catholic spies.[5]

The book received so much attention that several people launched formal investigations of the convent. After John Jones, a Montreal journalist, led a group of investigators through the convent, they found that Monk's description of the convent looked nothing like the Hotel Dieu, but rather matched the neighboring Magdalen Asylum for the restoration of prostitutes. The administrator of the Magdalen Asylum confirmed Monk's enrollment there. Jones subsequently dismissed Monk as "the prostitute" and went on to publish his own book-length denunciation entitled *Awful Exposure of the Atrocious Plot*. Colonel William L. Stone, a respected editor of the *New York Commercial Advertiser* and Protestant with admitted "prejudices against the Catholic faith," conducted his own search of the convent with Monk's book in hand. He concluded that Monk was an "errant impostor ... and that the nuns and priests were innocent in this matter." Meanwhile, a copyright dispute over the book revealed that Monk was not even the author of *Awful Disclosures*; rather it was the work of her Protestant protectors, most likely famed minister, abolitionist, and anti-Catholic author, George Bourne. Yet belief in Maria Monk as the famed escaped nun from Montreal prevailed. Her supporters simply dismissed any evidence against her as what might be termed in the twenty-first century as "fake news." They responded with lengthy responses to critics, complete with illustrations as further "proof." Her book inspired a host of escaped-nun spin-offs, many of which became best-sellers in their own right, including: *The Escaped Nun*, *The Haunted Convent*, *The Convent's Doom*, and *The Beautiful Nun*.[6]

In 1838, just two years after its publication, Maria Monk gave birth to a child whose father was nowhere to be found. This time, no Protestant protectors came to her aid. Her name faded slowly from the press. She died in 1849 at age thirty-two while serving a prison sentence for "grand larceny" in Sing-Sing, a New York state prison in Auburn. She never saw a penny from the book that bore her name. A short newspaper notice announced her death even as readers continued to pour over the pages of *Awful Disclosures*. "Maria Monkism," as one commentator put it, mattered more than the real Maria Monk. *Awful Disclosures* confirmed the anti-Catholic biases of many Americans as Catholicism was growing in the US. The book served as a bulwark against the changing religious, ethnic, and cultural

Bring me before a Court
Maria Monk

Figure 12.1 Maria Monk, "Bring Me Before a Court," printed as inside cover image in *Awful Disclosures of the Hotel Dieu*. Courtesy of HathiTrust.

demographics of the country and as a warning against the single, celibate, communal life for women. The image of the convent as a scary place where unsuspecting women were tortured, abused, and even murdered, suggested not only that Catholicism was a false religion, but also that happiness and indeed safety lie not in a convent but in a home, that the best life for women was not that of Sister but rather wife and mother.[7]

Published at the time of the "printing revolution," when new machinery like the revolving cylinder press allowed for mass publishing, books like *Awful Disclosures* circulated easily and widely. Evangelical organizations such as the American Home Missionary Society and American Tract Society took advantage of the innovations in printing, churning out millions of tracts, Bibles, periodicals, and religious books, many flagrantly anti-Catholic. Romances, city mysteries, and sentimental novels were also part of the growing paperback craze, most reinforcing a happily-ever-after-in-marriage trope. This literary outpouring at once widened the scope of the reading public beyond elite circles while spreading anti-Catholicism and reinforcing a particular brand of middle-class domesticity with prescribed roles for women that did not include convents.[8]

Nuns in America and True Womanhood

Before 1800, there were only two convents in the United States — houses of the Carmelites and the Poor Clares — and both of them were in Maryland, a former Catholic stronghold in the colonial era. After the Louisiana Purchase, the Ursulines of New Orleans, a long estab-lished religious house and a pillar of the community there, entered the US. Soon after the number of women's religious houses grew rapidly. Between 1803 and 1830, ten additional orders were founded throughout the country. This included the Sisters of a Charity, an order dedicated to the children of the poor and one that would essentially start the Catholic parochial school system in America, founded by the first native-born citizen of the US to be canonized by the Catholic Church, Elizabeth Ann Seton. The Sisters of Charity ran free schools, academies, and orphanages in Maryland, Cincinnati, New York, and New Orleans and opened the first hospital west of the Mississippi by 1846. Most of the new American convents adopted the French model of the Ursulines, embracing active (rather than monastic or cloistered) missions such as teaching, nursing, and other engagements in the community. By that time nuns lived and worked in the North and South, in eastern cities and throughout the growing frontier. The Mississippi River Valley, a haven for French Catholics before the land was acquired by the US, and a place where scores of German immigrants settled, became home to a number of thriving orders of women religious. The School Sisters of Notre Dame, the Sisters of St. Joseph of Carondelet, and the Sisters of the Sacred Heart, all European orders, were established there. They offered schools that included German-language classes, catechism, along with reading, writing, arithmetic, and geography, allowing immigrant communities the opportunity to preserve their culture, faith, and dignity and secure an education that would allow them to flourish in their new environments. In 1850 thirty-one coventual houses operated by 1,941 Sisters existed in the US.[9]

In 1836, the same year *Awful Disclosures* was published, Philippine Duchesne, founder of the American Society of the Sisters of the Sacred Heart, wrote a letter to her cousin back in France about the challenges her order faced in the US. "Sects tirelessly try to make all the Nunneries crumble," she explained, "since to them, they are houses of the Devil and idolatry." She described a "war" against the Catholic Church "evident in newspapers that repeat the absurdities they copy from each other." When Mary Hardy, vicar general of the Sacred Heart Sisters, traveled to the various Sacred Heart convents throughout the States, she always wore "secular attire" and used the title "Mrs." instead of "Mother" to avoid harassment. Women religious in the US at this time all knew about the burning of the Ursuline convent, Mount Benedict, in Massachusetts, and other attacks on convents and at times feared for their lives. These statements and measures speak to the hostile environment in which nuns found themselves in antebellum America. Despite the work they did within their communities, in the eyes of many non-Catholics, nuns were an affront to womanhood and a target of scorn. In *Female Convents, Secrets of Nunneries Disclosed*, another popular convent narrative of the time, the author referred to nuns as "useless," asking "what woman can be justified for abandoning all the obligations which she owes society?"[10]

The most important roles of a woman in colonial New England was procreation and being a "helpmeet" to her husband. In fact, one of the reasons that middle-aged and old women women were more likely than younger ones to be accused of witchcraft in seventeenth-century New England colonies, argue some historians, is because they were beyond childbearing and childcare years. Single women were also overrepresented among the accused. Not having children and being unwed made women vulnerable to accusations of deviance. In the late eighteenth century, leading Americans began placing new importance on the role of mothers. By raising virtuous children, they argued, especially sons who would grow up to be public-spirited citizens, mothers offered a vital contribution to the republic. To this end, many promoted greater educational opportunity for women. While this ideology of "republican motherhood" placed new currency on maternity, opening new avenues of opportunity for women, it also narrowly defined a woman's place within society. Such views were heightened and revamped in the antebellum era. As more men moved outside the home to work in a quickly industrializing world, women were more often associated with the home and all that the home represented. This led to the formation of what historians call the "cult of true womanhood." Within this ideology, mostly espoused by northern Protestants, the ideal woman was religious, pure, submissive, and domestic.[11]

While not all women necessarily fit this bill — more women were venturing outside of the home to work in textile mills and some forewent marriage — the theoretical ideal was seen everywhere. Ladies' magazines, sermons, prescriptive literature, novels, and religious tracts all heralded matrimony as the happiest and surest vocation for women and motherhood as an angelic undertaking that would not only sustain the republic but also sanctify the world. So closely associated was true womanhood with the "private sphere" or the home, that "public women" or "women of the street" became synonymous with prostitution. Moreover, in salacious convent narratives and even more sober middle-class literature, nuns often figured as pseudo-prostitute figures, as women allegedly at the disposal of the sexual pleasures of priests, in a brothel-like convent, outside the safe confines of the home. There was therefore, a long tradition in colonial British North America and the early United States of female domesticity. Some women used assumptions about womanhood to justify their involvement in reforms such as teaching, claiming that their domestic sensibilities rendered them better suited to weigh in on social issues that effected children and the home. Even though nuns engaged in such charitable ventures as well, they simply did not conform to this middle-class domestic ideal. Their rejection of the dependent conditions of marriage, of childbearing, and their withholding of domestic labor in family homes rendered them dangerous ideological outlaws in the eyes of many Americans.[12]

Two years before the caricatures of nuns and convent life became solidified in sensational anti-Catholic literature, like *Awful Disclosures*, the rising tide of anti-Catholicism and the campaign against convents was inaugurated with one of the most violent nativist attacks in American history. The story revealed the lengths to which some Americans were willing to go to maintain dominance, and how convents were at the center of this fight.

The Burning of Mount Benedict

On the night of August 11, 1834, a group of mostly working-class men marched toward Mount Benedict, a girls' boarding school run by Ursuline nuns in Charlestown, Massachusetts. They covered their faces in war paint and carried torches. "Down with the Pope! Down with the Convent!" they drunkenly shouted. The mob had special contempt for Mary Anne Moffatt, the Mother Superior of Mount Benedict, whom one of the rioters called "the sauciest woman I ever heard talk." They called out her name that night and demanded she show herself and release her "innocent victims." After the men fired gun shots into the air and threw bricks through the convent windows, the fifty girls in residence at the Academy startled awake. Under the instruction of their teachers they began to hurriedly dress and file out of the building through a back door. They watched from a neighboring lawn as shadowy figures, outlined by the light of their flaming torches, flooded into their school and home. The men ransacked the convent, going from room to room, piling furniture, instruments, personal belongings, and altar decorations before burning them all. Donning the girls' uniforms, they merrily turned to the cemetery, where they broke into coffins, taking teeth from corpses as souvenirs. They stormed the bishop's cottage and ransacked the gardens. After seven hours of mayhem, at the light of dawn, the mob finally dispersed. Hundreds of townspeople who had gathered watched in shock. The firemen went home. No one had made an effort to stop the destruction of Mount Benedict. The damage inflicted that night came to a monetary total of $50,000 (over $100,000 today). It would never be repaid.[13]

A few weeks before the burning of Mount Benedict, Elizabeth Harrison, who took the name of Sister Mary John as a professed nun, ran away from the convent. Harrison, an overbooked music teacher had had enough after her duties were doubled during the Academy's annual summer fête. In a state of anxious delirium on that hot August night, she wandered to a neighbor's home vowing never to return to Mount Benedict. Although doctors

Destruction of the Charlestown Nunnery, August 24th, 1834.

Figure 12.2 "Burning of the Convent".
Source: Image courtesy of the American Antiquarian Society.

diagnosed her with "a nervous excitement or fever," and she returned to the convent, rumors began to circulate around town that Harrison had gone mad under the Mother Superior's harsh rule. People whispered that she was chained up in the convent basement, and even that she might have been murdered. Days before the mob attacked Mount Benedict, handbills appeared throughout town stating, "It is currently reported that a *Mysterious* affair had lately happened in Charlestown; now it is your duty, gentlemen, to have this affair investigated immediately, if not, the truckmen of Boston will demolish the nunnery."[14]

Before Harrison's "mysterious" retreat, Rebecca Reed, a former novice at Mount Benedict, who had hoped to become a nun there, left when she became disillusioned with the religious life. No one chased after her. Reed discussed her experience with an Episcopal priest who helped her write what would become, *Six Months in a Convent*, the first anti-Catholic bestseller in the US. Although the book appeared months after the burning of Mount Benedict, news of the story spread throughout Charlestown before the attack. Reed claimed she narrowly escaped from her "prison" after seeing other nuns starved and caged and that she overheard the bishop pray for a "bushel of gold" to be sent down from heaven so that he might build another convent on Bunker Hill (a place considered sacred ground for many Americans and off limits to "foreign" Catholics). After the burning of Mount Benedict, Mary Anne Moffatt dismissed Reed's book as an obvious "tissue of lies," and credited it with inciting the attack.[15]

A third event contributed to the burning of Mount Benedict. Just days before the attack, Lyman Beecher, famed Congregationalist minister, firebrand of the Second Great Awakening, and patriarch of the Beecher clan, gave a fiery sermon in Charlestown in which he warned of a Catholic conspiracy. If the Catholics were not designing against us, he asked, then why would they "empty upon our shores such floods of pauper immigrants?" The "Romish influence" was especially spread through schools, like the academy at Mount Benedict. Beecher raged against "reckless parents" who sent their daughters to such schools and demanded his listeners "wake up!" Beecher's audiences took him seriously and surely pictured Mount Benedict as he warned against the encroaching dangers of a foreign faith and the threat this posed to American daughters.[16]

These three incidences reinforced deeply-seated biases about Catholicism generally and nuns in particular, leading to the burning of Mount Benedict. Harrison's "mysterious disappearance" confirmed many non-Catholic Americans' belief that nuns were held against their will in convents and that women would not willingly reject a life of marriage and motherhood. The suspicion that the Mother Superior aided in torturing or possibly murdering her suggested the common conviction in the Early Republic and antebellum era that women in positions of public authority lost their feminine sensibilities and transformed into tyrannical monsters. Many non-Catholic Americans simply could not accept the idea that these women, living in households without fathers or husbands were okay on their own. They either needed rescuing (as in Harrison's case) or punished (as with the Mother Superior). Rebecca Reed fit into this paradigm well. When a committee investigating the burning of Mount Benedict turned a critical eye toward Reed, local residents rallied to her defense, describing her as a "defenseless female" and an "American daughter" who needed saving from "foreign institutions." This rhetoric not only demarcated Catholics as foreigners but also stressed the importance of keeping women within certain prescribed boundaries. The men who stormed the convent that night claimed they were responding to their "gentlemanly duty" of protecting women, but they endangered women and children with the attack and robbed them of their home. This was an act of retribution against women who lived counter-cultural lives.[17]

While opposition to nuns was rooted in theological differences between Catholics and Protestants, the burning of Mount Benedict and some of the major religious clashes of the antebellum era revealed underlying gendered concerns. At stake was the role of women in the new republic. What happened when women opted out of the prescribed role to raise virtuous sons who would be contributing citizens? What would happen without their domestic labor? Rebecca Reed's *Six Months in a Convent*, in a line likely not written by herself, put it succinctly: "It is not a question of sects and creeds, but it is a grave question of how the future ornaments of our refined society, the future accomplished mothers of American citizens, are to be educated." As Lyman Beecher warned, convent education could not be considered sitting down.[18]

The Bible Wars

The tensions between Protestants and Catholics in antebellum America erupted again in the 1840s over the question of children's education in what became known as the Bible Wars. Partially to compete with the growing number of academies and free schools operated by nuns, reformer Horace Mann spearheaded the common school movement, which would become the basis for the vast public education system in the US. He championed common schools as a way to train up American youth to be virtuous citizens whose values reflected those of the nation. In addition to offering reading, writing, and arithmetic, Mann believed common schools should extend a moral education, and he looked to women as the best instructors of morals and sentiments. Indeed teaching became the first acceptable vocation outside of the home for women in America. To justify this, Mann and others stressed that the school was simply an extension of the home and that teaching would prepare women to be better wives and mothers.[19]

Although there was no official national church, many antebellum reformers saw religious instruction as essential to education and saw no conflict assigning the Bible in public schools. Mann and other reformers insisted on the use of the King James Bible, a Protestant version, which they assumed all Christian denominations could support. Starting with Philadelphia, cities began passing Free School Acts, making the King James Bible a compulsory textbook. This appeased most Protestants, but some Catholics objected. In addition to using a Protestant Bible, public schools assigned McDuffy readers with frequent anti-Catholic slurs, such as "priestcraft" and "papists," along with references to John Huss a "zealous reformer of Popery" who "trusted himself to deceitful Catholics." Indeed common school advocates had an "interventionist mission," as one historian put it, directed at the growing number of Catholic immigrant children to rid them of their "religious and cultural foreignness." "We have a mill, of which the common school is the nether, and the Bible ... the upper stone," explained one reformer. "Into the mill let us cast the people of all countries and all forms of religion that come here, and they will come out in the grist Americans and Protestants."[20]

Convent schools were not always available to the growing number of Catholics in America's eastern cities where common schools first appeared. The prospect of sending children of Catholic families to these public schools prompted New York's bishop, John Hughes, to speak out. Hughes opposed taxing Catholics to fund common schools and requested government money for alternative Catholic education. His debates with school boards and reformers drew a lot of attention from the press and convinced many Americans that Hughes opposed the Bible in general, confirming their view of Catholic irreligion. Seeing his request for government support of Catholic schools as a blatant violation of the separation of church and state and just another example of a Catholic conspiracy for influence, the New York School Board dismissed Hughes' complaints. But the debate was only getting started and would soon turn violent in Philadelphia.[21]

Philadelphia's bishop, Francis Patrick Kenrick appealed to the Philadelphia School Board in 1843 to allow Catholic children to be excused from reading the King James Bible. Philadelphia was already a city rife with tension between the growing Irish immigrant population and native-born Americans. After much debate, the Board ruled that Catholic children could read a different version, given that the translation was without commentary, but this actually disqualified Catholic Bibles. The ruling only stoked the anger of the city's Protestants and Catholics, as the former considered it a violation of American values and evidence that Catholics wanted to keep Bibles out of the hands of the people, and the latter still felt ostracized in American schools.

On the afternoon of May 3, 1844, the Native American Republican Association, a group that would merge into the Know Nothing Party, a major nativist third party, met in Kensington, an Irish-Catholic neighborhood in northeast Philadelphia. Tensions between the city's native-born Americans and Catholic newcomers were already heightened as the two groups competed for jobs and influence. As members of the Association gave loud speeches lambasting Catholics for objecting to the common school curriculum, Irish onlookers heckled the speakers before trying to chase them from their neighborhood. Soon violence broke out in the streets, and more men joined the ranks on both sides. Nativists set fire to homes as Irish immigrants shot guns from their windows. From there, the nativists attacked the Sisters of Charity School, setting fire to the fence and throwing stones in the windows before burning the building to the ground. The fighting continued for days until a local militia established peace. By that time, two Catholic churches had been destroyed, the schoolhouse and multiple homes torched, and thirty people left dead while hundreds emerged wounded.[22]

Two months after the Philadelphia Bible Riots, a grand jury blamed the violence on poor law enforcement and the city's Irish Catholics' attempt to remove the Bible from common schools. In celebration of their victory, the Native American Republicans threw an extravagant parade in the streets of Philadelphia. Marchers held up a banner of Columbia, goddess of Liberty, donned by the inscription: "Beware of Foreign Influence." An American flag lay draped around her shoulder and she held an open Bible, symbolizing the school debate. She crushed a serpent beneath her feet, echoing popular Catholic images of Mary with the Satan serpent underfoot. But this time the snake symbolized the defeat of Rome. Another banner displayed the figure of George Washington's mother and read "To Mary, Mother of Washington." Columbia and Mary Washington rose in opposition to the elevation of the Catholic vision of the Virgin Mary, "Mother of God," to represent a new, American Mary. Her heirs were patriots, not papists; they were wives and mothers, not nuns.[23]

The Philadelphia Bible Riots reflected ethnic, social, and personal conflicts. But they were also the result of religious and gendered debates. The insistence on Protestant Bibles in public schools showed the deep-seated belief in the intrinsic connections between American values and Protsetant Christianity. The fiery reaction against Catholic opposition to this curriculum and the lack of recognition of its sectarian nature reflected entrenched opposition to Catholic influence and the view of Catholicism as foreign and anti-American. When the Sisters of Charity School became a focus of the attack during the riots, this was a statement against Catholic schools in general and against certain kinds of women in particular. Although reformers were turning increasingly to women as the ideal teachers for the new common schools, nuns were not seen as the right kind of female teachers. Their instruction was not an extension of domestic ideals. How could they raise young girls to be wives and mothers, not being so themselves? The Bible Wars was a race for influence of the nation's children, and the stakes were high. Fearing a growing Catholic presence that reflected a different way of life, nativist, non-Catholic Americans joined forces to oppose such influence, violently at times, and the question was becoming more political, focusing on who was a "real" American and who was not.

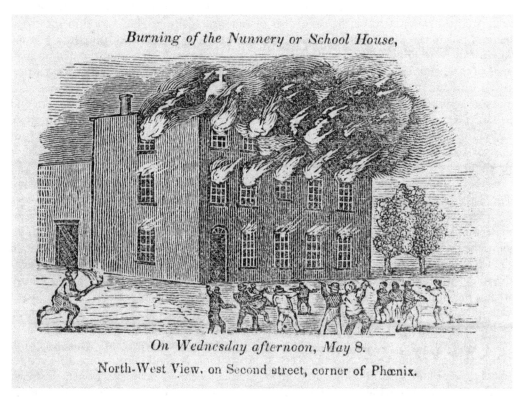

Burning of the Nunnery or School House,

On Wednesday afternoon, May 8.

North-West View, on Second street, corner of Phœnix.

Figure 12.3 "Burning of the Nunnery or Schoolhouse," Philadelphia Bible Riots, 1844.
Source: Courtesy of HathiTrust.

Conclusion

By 1854 the campaign against convents had become formally politicized. That year various nativist third parties coalesced to form the American Party (referred to as "Know Nothings" by their detractors because of their secretive meetings and membership). The Party platform rested on immigration restriction, limiting the rights of Catholic citizens, mandating Protestant Bibles in schools, and deporting immigrant dependents. They won major mid-term victories in Massachusetts, New York, Maryland, and other states. In the Bay State, Know Nothing legislators wasted no time before forming a "Nunnery Committee" to investigate convents. Although they had no incriminating evidence, the search committee and a group of their curious friends descended on local convents, pushing their way through every room and cornering women with questions. They found nothing suspicious. Instead the Committee members found themselves the objects of investigation when word spread of their late-night carousing on the public dime. A cartoon mocked them as the "Smelling Committee," picturing the men as dogs sniffing aimlessly around every corner. But the general public seemed none too concerned with the grave incursions of the state government into private homes and religious institutions. Indeed, the Committee was only giving many of their constituents what they had been demanding for decades. In Massachusetts and throughout the US, the American Party declined in the face of the increasingly contentious slavery question. But the fact that legislative attention was given to the investigation of convents even as the slavery debate loomed large, shows how entrenched opposition to nuns had become in antebellum America.[24]

The Massachusetts Nunnery Committee, the Bible Wars, the burning of Mount Benedict, and the popularity of Maria Monk's *Awful Disclosures* illustrate the centrality of nuns within the larger religious contests in antebellum America. As the Catholic Church grew in the US and as the number of women religious increased, they faced a fierce backlash by those who understood themselves to be the vanguards of American culture. Nuns stood in the crosshairs of religious, ethnic, and gender debates, appearing as a threat not only to a broadly Anglo-American Protestant cultural dominance, but also to the home and the delicate balance of male and female gender roles. By their very ways of living, nuns challenged patriarchal norms and the ideals of the "true woman," whose virtue — achieved through marriage and motherhood — promised to keep the nation pure of corruption. While it may seem odd to target women who devoted their lives to God and service, during the antebellum era, many non-Catholics perceived nuns through a one-dimensional lens, as dupes or ambassadors of a false religion and backward way of living, who were either in need of rescue or retribution.

Catholicism both challenged and shaped religion in America and American society generally. The fierce reaction against the growing number of Catholics and Catholic cultural influence brought into relief the depth and breadth of Protesant traditions in America. As many Americans understood national political values and familiar networks to be supported by Protestant religion, the presence of Catholics seemed to threaten the American way. And yet, Catholicism in the US expanded, shaping immigrant communities, schools, benevolent associations, and gender roles. Although it would be a long time before Catholics were folded into the notions of what it meant to be an American. The story of Catholicism in America cannot be understood without appreciating the role of nuns, many of whom provided education, medical assistance, and community connections to a rapidly growing immigrant population, allowing them to retain their cultural and religious identity while integrating into their new home. Far from peripheral figures, nuns were also an object of anti-Catholicism and debates of female gender roles in antebellum America. Although women religious separated themselves from mainstream culture as part of their vocation, their lives and the reactions to them reveal a lot about America at a pivotal time in the shaping of the nation.[25]

FURTHER READING

Clark, Emily. *Masterless Mistresses: The New Orleans Ursulines and the Development of a New World Society, 1727–1834.* Chapel Hill: University of North Carolina Press, 2007.

Franchot, Jenny. *Roads to Rome: The Antebellum Protestant Encounter with Catholicism.* Berkeley: University of California Press, 1994.

Schultz, Nancy Lusignan. *Fire and Roses: The Burning of the Charlestown Convent, 1834.* Boston: Northeastern University Press, 2000.

Yacovazzi, Cassandra L. Escaped Nuns: *True Womanhood and the Campaign Against Convents in Antebellum America.* New York: Oxford University Press, 2018.

BIBLIOGRAPHY

Beecher, Lyman. *Plea for the West.* New York: Leavitt, Lord, & Co., 1835.

Billington, Ray Allen. "Maria Monk and Her Influence." *Catholic Historical Review* 22, no. 3 (October 1936): 283–296.

Billington, Ray Allen. *The Protestant Crusade, 1800–1860: A Study in the Origins of American Nativism.* Chicago: Quadrangle Books, 1938.

Billington, Ray Allen. "Tentative Bibliography of Anti-Catholic Propaganda in the United States (1800–1860)." *Catholic Historical Review* 18, no. 4 (January 1933): 492–513.

Bunkley, Josephine. *The Escaped Nun; or, The Disclosures of Convent Life.* New York: DeWitt & Davenport, 1850.

Buntline, Ned. *The Beautiful Nun.* Philadelphia: T. B. Peterson & Brothers, 1866.

Butler, Jon. *Awash in a Sea of Faith: Christianizing the American People.* Cambridge, MA: Harvard University Press, 1990.

Clark, Emily. *Masterless Mistresses: The New Orleans Ursulines and the Development of a New World Society, 1727–1834.* Chapel Hill: University of North Carolina Press, 2007.

Dolan, Jay P. *Catholic Revivalism: The American Experience, 1830–1860.* Notre Dame: University of Notre Dame Press, 1978.

Ewens, Mary. *The Role of the Nun in Nineteenth Century America: Variations on the International Theme.* Thiensville: Caritas, 2014.

Feldberg, Michael. *The Philadelphia Riots of 1844: A Study in Ethnic Conflict.* Westport: Greenwood Press, 1975.

Fessenden, Tracy. "The Convent, the Brothel, and the Protestant Woman's Sphere." *Signs* 25, no. 2 (Winter 2000): 451–478.

Fessenden, Tracy. *Culture and Redemption: Religion, the Secular, and American Literature.* Princeton: Princeton University Press, 2013.

Franchot, Jenny. *Roads to Rome: The Antebellum Protestant Encounter with Catholicism.* Berkeley: University of California Press, 1994.

Frink, Sandra. "Women, the Family, and the Fate of the Nation in American Anti-Catholic Narratives, 1830–1860." *Journal of the History of Sexuality* 18, no. 2 (May 2009): 242–243.

Frothingham, Charles. *The Convent's Doom, A Tale of Charlestown in 1834.* Boston: Graves & Weston, 1854.

_____. *The Haunted Convent.* Boston: Graves & Weston, 1854.

Gaustad Edwin Scott. *Historical Atlas of Religion in America.* New York: Harper & Row, 1962.

Hatch, Nathan O. *The Democratization of American Christianity.* New Haven: Yale University Press, 1989.

Hewitt, Nancy. *Women's Activism and Social Change: Rochester, New York, 1822–1872.* Ithaca: Cornell University Press, 1978.

Johnson, Paul E. *A Shopkeeper's Millennium: Society and Revivals in Rochester, New York, 1815–1837.* New York: Hill & Wang, 1978.

Jones, J. *Awful Exposure of the Atrocious Plot Formed by Certain Individuals Against the Clergy and Nuns of Lower Canada Through the Intervention of Maria Monk.* New York: Jones & Co. of Montreal, 1836.

Kerber, Linda. *Women of the Republic: Intellect and Ideology in Revolutionary America.* Chapel Hill: University of North Carolina Press, 1980.

Krugler, John D. "Lord Baltimore, Roman Catholics, and Toleration: Religious Policy in Maryland during the Early Catholic Years, 1634–1649." *The Catholic Historical Review* 65, no. 1 (Jan. 1979): 49–75.

Mann, Thomas. Tenth Annual Report of the Secretary of the Board of Education 1846.

McCadden, Joseph J. "Bishop Hughes Versus the Public School Society of New York." *Catholic Historical Review* 50, no. 2 (July 1964): 188–207.

McCrindell, Rachel. *The Protestant Girl in a French Nunnery; or, The Snares of Popery: A Warning to Protestants Against Education in Catholic Seminaries.* 10ᵗʰ ed. New York: Wellman, 1846.

McDannell, Colleen. *The Christian Home in Victorian America, 1840–1900.* Bloomington: Indiana University Press, 1994.

Moffatt, Mary Anne Ursula. *An Answer to Six Months in a Convent, Exposing its Falsehoods and Manifold Absurdities.* Boston: J. H. Eastburn, 1835.

Monk, Maria. *Awful Disclosures of the Hotel Dieu Nunnery of Montreal.* New York: Howe & Bates, 1836.

Morse, Samuel F. B. *Imminent Dangers to the Free Institutions of the United States and Foreign Conspiracy Against the Liberties of the United States.* New York: E. B. Clayton, 1835.

Mulkern, John R. "Scandal Behind Convent Walls: The Know-Nothing Nunnery Committee of 1855." *Historical Journal of Massachusetts* 11, no. 1 (1983): 22–34.

Nord, Paul. *Faith in Reading: Religious Publishing and the Birth of Mass Media in America.* New York: Oxford University Press, 2004.

O'Donnell, Catherine. *Elizabeth Seton: American Saint.* Ithaca: Cornell University Press, 2018.

Oxx, Katie. *The Nativist Movement in America: Religious Conflict in the Nineteenth Century.* New York: Routledge, 2013.

Pagliarini, Marie Anne. "The Pure American Woman and the Wicked Catholic Priest: An Analysis of Anti-Catholic Literature in Antebellum America." *Religion and American Culture: A Journal of Interpretation* 9, no. 1 (Winter 1999): 97–128.

Pierson, Michael D. *Free Hearts and Free Homes: Gender and American Antislavery Politics.* Chapel Hill: University of North Carolina Press, 2003.

Preston, Jo Anne. "Domestic Ideology, School Reformers, and Female Teachers: School Teaching Becomes Women's Work in Nineteenth Century New England." *New England Quarterly* 66, no. 4 (Dec. 1993): 531–551.

Reed, Rebecca. *Six Months in a Convent.* Boston: Russell, Odiorne & Metcalf, 1835.

Schultz, Nancy Lusignan. *Fire and Roses: The Burning of the Charlestown Convent, 1834.* Boston: Northeastern University Press, 2000.

Stone, William L. *A Complete Refutation of Maria Monk's Atrocious Plot Concerning the Hotel Dieu Convent.* Nottingham, England: s.n., 1837.

Welter, Barbara. "The Cult of True Womanhood: 1820–1860." *American Quarterly* 18, no. 2 (Summer 1966): 151–174.

Whitney, Louisa Goddard. *The Burning of the Convent.* Cambridge: Welch, Bigelow, and Company, 1877.

Yacovazzi, Cassandra L. *Escaped Nuns: True Womanhood and the Campaign Against Convents in Antebellum America.* New York: Oxford University Press, 2018.

NOTES

1   For more on the Second Great Awakening, see Nathan O. Hatch, *The Democratization of the American Christianity* (New Haven: Yale University Press, 1989); for more on sectarianism during this time, see Jon Butler, *Awash in a Sea of Faith: Christianizing the American People* (Cambridge, MA: Harvard University Press, 1990); for women and reform in the Second Great Awakening, see Nancy Hewitt, *Women's Activism and Social Change: Rochester, New York, 1822–1872* (Ithaca: Cornell University Press, 1988) and Paul E. Johnson, *A Shopkeeper's Millennium: Society and Revivals in Rochester, New York, 1815–1837* (New York: Hill & Wang, 1978). Despite the relative low tenor of anti-Catholicism in the colonial era, there were some violent episodes, such as the Protestant-led raid against Maryland Catholics in 1644. For more on this, see John D. Krugler, "Lord Baltimore, Roman Catholics, and Toleration: Religious Policy in Maryland during the Early

Catholic Years, 1634–1649," *The Catholic Historical Review* 65, no. 1 (Jan. 1979): 49–75. During the War for Independence and the Early Republic, anti-Catholicism was less volatile, as evidenced by the signing of the Declaration of Independence by prominent Catholic of Maryland, Charles Carroll.

2 For the growth of Catholicism in America, see Jay P. Dolan, *Catholic Revivalism: The American Experience, 1830–1860* (Notre Dame: University of Notre Dame Press, 1978); Edwin Scott Gaustad, *Historical Atlas of Religion in America* (New York: Harper & Row, 1962), 101–110; Samuel F. B. Morse, *Imminent Dangers to the Free Institutions of the United States and Foreign Conspiracy Against the Liberties of the United States* (New York: E. B. Clayton, 1835).

3 Ray Allen Billington, *The Protestant Crusade, 1800–1860: A Study of the Origins of American Nativism* (Chicago: Quadrangle Books, 1938); for a more on the opposition to nuns in antebellum America, see Cassandra L. Yacovazzi, *Escaped Nuns: True Womanhood and the Campaign Against Convents in Antebellum America* (New York: Oxford University Press, 2018).

4 Maria Monk, *Awful Disclosures of the Hotel Dieu Nunnery of Montreal* (New York: Howe & Bates, 1836); see also Yacovazzi, *Escaped Nuns*, 1–6.

5 Figures in Billington, *Protestant Crusade*, 108; "Affidavit of my Mother," in "Appendix," in Monk, *Awful Disclosures*, 215–217; One Who Knows, "Maria Monk and Her Awful Disclosures," *New York Evangelist* 7, no. 15 (April 9, 1836); "The Hotel Dieu Nunnery in Labor Hath Brought Forth a Jesuitical Hoax," *American Protestant Vindicator* (New York, July 27, 1837); for more on this, see Yacovazzi, 12–15.

6 J. Jones, *Awful Exposure of the Atrocious Plot Formed by Certain Individuals Against the Clergy and Nuns of Lower Canada Through the Intervention of Maria Monk* (New York: Jones & Co. of Montreal, 1836); William L. Stone, *A Complete Refutation of Maria Monk's Atrocious Plot Concerning the Hotel Dieu Convent* (1837); Yacovazzi, 16–22; Josephine Bunkley, *The Escaped Nun; or, The Disclosures of Convent Life* (New York: DeWitt & Davenport, 1850); Charles Frothingham, *The Haunted Convent* (Boston: Graves & Weston, 1854); Frothingham, *The Convent's Doom, A Tale of Charlestown in 1834* (Boston: Graves & Weston, 1854); Ned Buntline, *The Beautiful Nun* (Philadelphia: T. B. Peterson & Brothers, 1866).

7 New York *Observer* (October 6, 1838); Ray Allen Billington, "Maria Monk and her Influence," *Catholic Historical Review* 22, no. 3 (October 1936): 283–296; Yacovazzi, 24–25.

8 For more on the printing revolution and the influence of religious literature in particular, see David Paul Nord, *Faith in Reading: Religious Publishing and the Birth of Mass Media in America* (New York: Oxford University Press, 2004).

9 Geroge C. Stewart Jr., "Women Religious in America, Demographic Overview," in *The Encyclopedia of American Catholic History*, ed. Michael Glazier and Thomas J. Shelley (Collegeville: Liturgical Press, 1997), 1496–1497; for more on the Ursulines of New Orleans, see Emily Clark, *Masterless Mistresses: The New Orleans Ursulines and the Development of a New World Society, 1727–1834* (Chapel Hill: University of North Carolina Press, 2007); for more on Elizabeth Seton and the Sisters of Charity, see Catherine O'Donnell, *Elizabeth Seton: American Saint* (Ithaca: Cornell University Press, 2018); for a general overview, see Mary Ewens, O. P., *The Role of the Nun in Nineteenth-Century America: Variations on the International Theme* (Thiensville: Caritas, 2014).

10 Letter from Philippine Duchesne to Madame de Rollin, May 1836, "Duchesne to Her Family and Lay People," Box 5, Society of the Sacred Heart, US Province Archives, translation from the French provided by Antoine Matondo; Letter from Mary Hardy, March 15, 1884, cited in Ruth Cunningham, *First American Daughter: Mary Aloysia Hardy, 1809–1886* (Accra: Kenwood, 1981), 12–13.

11 Carol F. Karlsen, *The Devil in the Shape of a Woman: Witchcraft in Colonial New England* (New York: W. W. Norton, 1998), 71; Linda K. Kerber, *Women of the Republic: Intellect and Ideology in Revolutionary America* (Chapel Hill: The University of North Carolina Press, 1980); Barbara Welter, "The Cult of True Womanhood: 1820–1860," *American Quarterly* 18, no. 2 (Summer 1966): 151–174.

12 For more on the nun as prostitute trope in nineteenth century discourse, see Tracy Fessenden, "The Convent, the Brothel, and the Prostestant Woman's Sphere," *Signs* 25, no. 2 (Winter 2000): 451–478; for more on true womanhood and women's involvement in reform movements, see Michael D. Pierson, *Free Hearts and Free Homes: Gender and American Antislavery Politics* (Chapel Hill: University of North Carolina Press, 2003); Clark, *Masterless Mistresses*, 5.

13 For a first-hand account of the attack on Mount Benedict, see Louisa Goddard Whitney, *The Burning of the Convent* (Cambridge: Welch, Bigelow, and Company, 1877); for a more recent narrative history of the event, see Nancy Lusignan Schultz, *Fire and Roses: The Buring of the Charlestown Convent, 1834* (Boston: Northeastern University Press, 2000); "Report," in *Documents Relating to the Ursuline Convent in Charlestown* (Boston: Reprinted by Samuel N. Dickinson, 1842).

14 "Mysterious," *Mercantile Journal* (August, 1834); "Report," 8; Whitney, *The Burning of the Convent*, 55–57; Yacovazzi, 32–33.

15 Rebecca Reed, *Six Months in a Convent* (Boston: Russell, Odiorne & Metcalf, 1835); Mary Anne Ursula Moffatt, *An Answer to* Six Months in a Convent, *Exposing its Falsehoods and Manifold Absurdities* (Boston: J. H. Eastburn, 1835), iii, vii.

16 Lyman Beecher's sermon was reprinted in Beecher, *Plea for the West* (New York: Leavitt, Lord, & Co., 1835); Yacovazzi, 34–40.

17 Boston *Daily Advocate* (October 10, 1834).

18 Reed, *Six Months in a Convent*, 6.

19 Horace Mann, *First Annual Report of the Massachusetts Board of Education* (Washington DC: National Education Association, 1847), 58, 66; for more on the feminization of teaching, see Jo Anne Preston, "Domestic Ideology, School Reformers, and Female Teachers: School Teaching Becomes Women's Work in Nineteenth-Century New England," *New England Quarterly* 66, no. 4 (December 1993): 531–551.

20 Mann, *Tenth Annual Report of the Sectary of the Board of Education* (1846); Tracy Fessenden, *Culture and Redemption: Religion, the Secular, and American Literature* (Princeton: Princeton University Press, 2007), 67; Kirwin [Nicholas Murray], *Romanism at Home: Letters to the Hon. Roger B. Taney* (New York: Harper & Brothers, 1852), 249–250.

21 Joseph J. McCadden, "Bishop Hughes Versus the Public School Society of New York," *Catholic Historical Review* 50, no. 2 (July 1964): 188–207; see also Yacovazzi, 75–76.

22 Katie Oxx, *The Nativist Movement in America: Religious Conflict in the Nineteenth Century* (New York: Routledge, 2013), 54, 63–65; see also Michael Feldberg, *The Philadelphia Riots of 1844: A Study in Ethnic Conflict* (Westport: Greenwood Press, 1975).

23 Feldberg, *The Philadelphia Riots of 1844*, 136–38; Yacovazzi, 77–78.

24 For more on this, see John R. Mulkern, "Scandal Behind Convent Walls: The Know-Nothing Nunnery Committee of 1855," *Historical Journal of Massachusetts* 11, no. 1 (1983): 22–34; Yacovazzi, 124–142.

25 While not all women religious were immigrants or served immigrant communities alone, the Catholic Church at this time in America was still largely an immigrant Church and seen as foreign.

Chapter Thirteen

ECCLESIOLOGY AND THE VARIETIES OF ROMANTICISM IN AMERICAN CHRISTIANITY, 1825–1850

Brent S. Sirota
North Carolina State University, Raleigh, North Carolina

In a September 1843 review in *The Christian Examiner*, the Unitarian minister Samuel Osgood remarked upon the "peculiar poetical capabilities" of what had come to be known as the "Oxford Movement," then unfolding in England. The Oxford Movement was an intellectual and theological insurgency of young high-church Anglican clergymen and fellows associated with the university, who sought to call the Church of England to a greater sense of itself as a divine institution, and to reconcile Anglicanism, in some measure, with its Catholic heritage. Osgood's subject was the poetry of one of the leading figures associated with that movement, the English divine Isaac Williams, whose great work *The Cathedral, or The Catholic and Apostolic Church in England,* depicted the physical structures and spaces of a gothic church as symbolic embodiments of Anglican theology and worship. Osgood was duly impressed. "The Churchman," — that is, the Anglican — "loves to connect outward beauty with religion," he noted. By contrast, the Protestantism of Osgood's native New England, born of dissent from the Church of England, starved the imagination. The Anglican churchmen succeeded in "throwing romantic beauty round their doctrines and ritual," in ways unavailable to the austere Calvinist or the rationalistic Unitarian in the United States.[1]

Interestingly, the only American analogue to this romantic Anglicanism was the movement with which Osgood himself had been loosely associated: New England transcendentalism.[2] Despite the vast theological gulf that divided them, Osgood sensed between the Anglican high churchmen and the American transcendentalists a common spiritual regard for the imaginative life that was otherwise alien to the Protestant outlook. The aesthetic sensibility of the Oxford divines was, Osgood suggested, simply "transcendentalism carried beyond nature and connected with glorious buildings and ancient rites, instead of blue skies and holy instincts."[3] Osgood intuitively apprehended something that subsequent historians and literary scholars have not sufficiently appreciated: that New England transcendentalism and what we might call *ecclesiology* in America, this intensifying regard for ecclesiastical life and worship, were rival claimants to the bequest of European romanticism.

A Companion to American Religious History, First Edition. Edited by Benjamin E. Park.
© 2021 John Wiley & Sons, Inc. Published 2021 by John Wiley & Sons, Inc.

The late eighteenth- and early nineteenth-century international cultural and intellectual movement known as romanticism has proven notoriously difficult to define. It has been nearly one hundred years since the intellectual historian Arthur Lovejoy, surveying the wildly disparate and contradictory applications of the term, suggested it be jettisoned altogether.[4] And the ensuing century has seen numerous scholars and critics responding to Lovejoy's challenge by affirming the thematic coherence of the romantic movement.[5] This debate cannot be surveyed here.[6] For our purposes, it is sufficient to point out the centrality to romanticism of the idea of what we might call, following the literary scholar J. Robert Barth, "symbolic experience."[7] In romantic art and literature, the imaginative encounter with reality, whether the natural world or the artifacts of the human past, is held to disclose the presence of a higher, unseen reality. Barth goes so far as to consider romanticism a restoration of the "sacramental" sense of the world eroded by the mechanistic philosophy of the enlightenment — that is, the sense of the world as a material symbol of the spiritual life above and beyond it.[8] The English romantic poet William Wordsworth, for instance, embodied this sensibility when he discerned in the wild landscape of the Swiss Alps what he described as "Characters of the great Apocalypse,/The types and symbols of Eternity,/Of first and last, and midst, and without end."[9]

From this perspective, Samuel Osgood's dichotomy between the ecclesiological and the transcendentalist sensibility in American divinity was not far off the mark. Both tendencies in antebellum American religion accorded aesthetic and imaginative fulfilment a spiritual value.[10] The transcendentalist, of course, sought to restore the visionary sensibility by which the individual mind might once again apprehend the spiritual dimension of the natural world. The ecclesiologist, meanwhile, partook of the historicist dimension of romantic thought.[11] Spiritual encounter was to be mediated through traditional, even archaic, symbols and rituals. The transcendentalist Ralph Waldo Emerson's celebrated demand for "an original relation to the universe" was therefore anathema to the ecclesiological outlook.[12] For the latter, religion was a matter of participation in the consecrated and historical forms, a fluency in the symbolic language of ecclesiastical tradition. Opposing the "ancient rites" of the high-church Anglican to the "blue skies" of the transcendentalist, Osgood rightly sensed that a common regard for symbolic experience underpinned what were, in effect, divergent programs of religious reform.

The historian Perry Miller affirmed the indisputably religious character of New England transcendentalism. It was, indeed, what Miller called a "religious demonstration." But as such, it was also an emancipatory project.[13] It channeled the literary and philosophical energies of European romanticism into the project of liberating spiritual encounter from the ritual and institutional confines of the church. The extent of transcendentalism's actual discontinuity with the prevailing liberalism of Unitarian Boston has been extensively litigated by historians and literary scholars, but the movement undoubtedly intensified the trend toward a more individualistic spirituality liberated from traditional modes and sites of Christian worship.[14] As Emerson preached in his incendiary July 1838 commencement address before the students and faculty of Harvard Divinity College, "In the soul, then, let the redemption be sought." Emerson's address had scandalized Unitarian Boston with its radical reconfiguration of the content of Christian revelation. The gospel of Jesus, Emerson had claimed, disclosed not the central fact of Christ's own divinity, but the divinity of all human beings. The true Christianity, then, did not consist of faith in Christ, but, Emerson explained, "a faith like Christ's in the infinitude of man." And the rites and formularies that comprised what Emerson dismissively referred to as "historical Christianity" has merely compounded over the centuries this fundamental misunderstanding of the gospel.[15] Emerson's friend Theodore Parker, minister of the Unitarian Second Church in Roxbury, continued in this vein in his controversial May 1841 ordination sermon *On the Transient and Permanent in Christianity*. Parker there sought to excavate the solid kernel of what he called "absolute, pure religion," which was no more than the undisturbed love of God and man, from the infinitely mutable and variegated forms and creeds in which the history of Christianity had embedded it.[16] The fruits of this emancipatory program, in the making not only of the liberal strain in American Protestantism, but also in the syncretistic and expressly post-Christian set of new age religious impulses known simply as "spirituality" or "metaphysical religion" is quite well known.[17] These antipathies toward formal and historical Christianity impelled the literary scholar Leon Chai to describe the impact of European romanticism on American divinity as nothing less than "the secularization of religion."[18] Religion, in other words, might be thought of as a state of mind, rather than as formal participation in a traditional institution and worship.

Emerging alongside the religious radicalism of the New England transcendentalists in the second quarter of the nineteenth century, ecclesiology represented a wholly countervailing movement in American Christianity.[19] Ecclesiology, or "the church question" as it was often more colloquially known, sought to more firmly embed spiritual experience within the institutional life of the church. The term "ecclesiology" was of somewhat limited currency in the United States during the period under consideration, but it may be employed here to comprehend the emergent set of historical, theological, and cultural discourses regarding the nature and organization of the Christian church and its relation to the other institutions of this world. Channeling many of the same European romantic influences as transcendentalism, ecclesiological thought in various denominations eschewed the de-institutionalizing impulses of Emerson and his confreres in New England. Rather than emancipating spiritual encounter from the institutional confines of historical Christianity, ecclesiology sought to more deeply embed religion in its church setting. This problematizes considerably the long-standing characterization of American romanticism as "fundamentally individualistic."[20] Religious romanticism in America clearly fostered both individualistic and what we might call corporatistic impulses at the same time, a more interiorized and solitary religious sensibility alongside a more exteriorized and historically minded one. The unmediated spiritual experience prized by transcendentalists was rejected by the devotees of ecclesiology, who prescribed the enhanced aesthetic and ritual forms of ecclesiastical life precisely as a remedy to the atomism of antebellum American civil society. It was not enough to merely affirm the indispensability of the historical church and its offices to the Christian economy of salvation. The church had to be rendered visibly and palpably manifest, unmistakably set apart from the profane commerce of everyday life.

This chapter will consider the various manifestations of the ecclesiological tendency in American Christianity during the second quarter of the nineteenth century as an alternative romanticism in religious and cultural life. Ecclesiology shared with New England transcendentalism, and indeed the romantic movement as a whole, a core disaffection with the commercial and utilitarian values of the emergent bourgeois world of the late eighteenth- and early nineteenth-century northern Atlantic.[21] Indeed, its devotees would not have disagreed with Ralph Waldo Emerson's declaration, "There is nothing more important in the culture of man than to resist the dangers of commerce."[22] But ecclesiology's response to the materialism and commercialism of American social life was not the idealization of self-reliance, but a heightened sense of religious communion and what it called "the beauty of holiness." The cultivation of both the historical and the aesthetic aspect of religious worship were ultimately designed to restore a putatively lost collective dimension to Christian life in America, the sense of the church not simply as another voluntary association in civil society but as the actual body of Christ. In its own way, this enhanced religious institutionalism was as radically dissident as anything advocated by the transcendentalists, at least in its rebuke of the Protestant mainstream of American life.[23] Like transcendentalism, ecclesiology protested against an America that had grown acquisitive, materialistic and socially fragmented. It is no wonder that observers like Samuel Osgood considered them as parallel efforts at re-enchanting American life.[24]

* * *

Notwithstanding a few scattered earlier references, the term *ecclesiology* really only entered the English language through a January 1837 issue of the London-based high-church Anglican periodical *The British Critic*. By this time, *The British Critic* had become an unofficial organ of the Oxford Movement.[25] The Oxford Movement had formally commenced in 1833 as a protest against British state interference in the established Church of England and quickly evolved into a broader call to awaken the Church to an enhanced consciousness of its own divine constitution.[26] And it was under these auspices that the editors had called for a new department of religious knowledge to sit alongside the traditional sciences of theology and ethics. "It is not often that we like the coinage of new terms," the article apologized, "but there are cases which require it." Where theology addressed the doctrines of faith and ethics (the conduct of life), what the editors called "ecclesialogy" — a spelling which did not catch on — was to address the institutional life of a Christian society. "We mean, then, by Ecclesialogy," the article explained, "a science which may treat of the proper construction and operations of a Church, or Communion, or Society of Christians; and which may regard men as they are members of that society."[27]

The call of *The British Critic* may well have gone unheeded (and the original spelling unaltered) but for a group of Anglican undergraduates at Trinity College, Cambridge, who began meeting in March 1839 under the name 'The Ecclesiological Society.'[28] This "high church club," as one of its founders casually described it, became the nucleus of the Cambridge Camden Society, founded later that year, and devoted to the study of ecclesiastical antiquities and the advocacy of traditional — mostly, medieval — modes of church architecture, ornamentation and worship.[29] The Cambridge Camden commenced the publication of its journal, *The Ecclesiologist*, in November 1841, the first issue of which declared its devotion to "the feeling of the beautiful and the Catholick" in ecclesiastical design and furnishing.[30] The Cambridge Camden Society would go on to be one of the primary engines of the gothic revival in ecclesiastical architecture throughout the English speaking world; and its publications on liturgy and the use and ornamentation of sacred space would become foundational to the mid-nineteenth century movement in Anglicanism known as ritualism.[31]

The streams that coalesced into ecclesiology in Great Britain were nursed by tributaries from abroad. Across Europe in the first half of the nineteenth century, disparate political, religious and intellectual movements were attempting to apprehend the autonomous life of the Christian church as both a historical and a theological reality. The figures behind the Oxford and Cambridge Movements in Britain drew from the emergent Berlin school in ecclesiastical history for a new sensibility regarding the historical life of the Christian church and the organic development of its doctrines and rituals.[32] Others looked to the contemporaneous movement in French Catholicism surrounding the renegade priest Hugues-Félicité Robert de Lamennais and his newspaper *L'Avenir*, which pressed for a complete emancipation of the Church from the French state in the hopes that a politically free and unimpeded Roman Catholic Church would superintend a more robust christianization of social life in France.[33] All of these movements were rooted in a situation peculiar to European Christendom, or, at any rate, alien to the religious ecology of the United States. They tended to emerge not from religious minorities, but rather from within national or privileged churches. And when they cried for religious liberty, they did not mean freedom for the conscience of the individual believer, but rather the institutional autonomy of established churches from interference by secular governments.[34] Such a situation had no real analogue in the United States, where the separation of church from state legally consigned all religious entities to a pluralistic and competitive denominational order largely unimpeded by political interference.

Ecclesiology, then, did not answer any obvious need in the United States for a sharper sense of the independence of the church from the state. Interestingly, it was almost precisely the opposite. Ecclesiology was imported into America as a means of differentiating the church from the myriad voluntary associations, clubs and charities that make up what we call 'civil society.' American denominationalism had largely separated church from state, but only by consigning religion to a competitive marketplace of rival sects, bible societies, revivals and interdenominational groups. Proponents of ecclesiological thought worried about the seeming interchangeability of denominations in American religious life, the sense that one church was just as good as another and that the grounds of selection between them were little more than habit, convenience, or, worse, entertainment. The practice of pulpit exchanges between ministers of different denominations, the expanding infrastructure of interdenominational associations and philanthropic endeavors, and the waves of religious revivalism all conspired to render confessional distinctions among Protestant Christians seemingly inconsequential. The lines between one religious tradition and another faded; worse, the demarcations between worship, revival and new-fangled associations of benevolence such as temperance meetings were no longer obviously discernible. While American churches were in little danger of being devoured by the leviathan of the state, they were nevertheless adrift amidst a civil society which made little distinction between the variety of moral and religious associations. "Even if it be taken for granted that the various sects are only so many ways to the same place, yet there must be a ground of selection among them. One must needs be the best," said John Henry Hopkins, the first episcopal bishop of Vermont in his 1835 lectures on *The Primitive Church*. The celebrated ecumenism of Protestant life in the antebellum United States struck some observers as indifference to all sense of religious authority and tradition, a lack of distinction between the doctrines and practices that were sanctioned and universal, and those — Hopkins singled out prayer meetings and temperance societies — that were but unwarranted innovations and fads.[35]

Given the Anglican roots of the term, it is perhaps not surprising that it was the post-revolutionary American successor to the Church of England, the Protestant Episcopal Church, which first championed ecclesiology in the United States. With its formal liturgy based on the English Book of Common Prayer and its insistence on the indispensability of the three-fold ministry of bishops, priests, and deacons, the Episcopal Church had long held itself aloof from the mainstream of American Protestantism, which possessed neither.[36] But where its mother church in Great Britain availed itself of its legal establishment to maintain its ascendancy over sectarian rivals, the Episcopal Church in America possessed no such advantage. Instead, it could only manifest its distinctiveness, one critic put it, "by the effect of a solemn and imposing exterior."[37] This aesthetic dimension to Episcopalian identity, the notion that its religious spaces and formal worship were intended to visually communicate its difference from other Protestant denominations, accounts, in no small part, for its receptivity toward English romanticism.

Beginning in the late 1820s, figures such as the New England clergymen and poets William Croswell and George Washington Doane channeled the poetry and thought of William Wordsworth and Samuel Taylor Coleridge into an expressly devotional idiom. Against "the cold and naked barrenness of worship" in American Protestantism, the New England newspapers they co-edited championed the Anglican service not simply as orthodox, but as tangibly and sensually fulfilling.[38] It was, we might say, a symbolic experience. In their first newspaper, *The Episcopal Watchman* from Hartford, Connecticut, Doane penned a regular column entitled "The Ritualist," examining the procession of fasts and festivals that make up the Anglican liturgical year. The column began each week with an excerpt from the Anglican William Wordsworth's *Ecclesiastical Sonnets:* "in fixed career/As through a zodiac, moves the ritual year/Of England's Church — stupendous mysteries."[39] The aesthetic dimensions of liturgical worship became, for Episcopalians like Croswell and Doane, the warranty of their spiritual efficacy. "There is nothing," wrote one contributor to *The Episcopal Watchman*, "like the electric sympathy of kindred minds in one common form of devotion, to kindle the ecstatic fervor of gratitude — to exalt and agitate the laboring soul of the worshipper — to purge and purify it from its native degradation — to lift it higher in its heavenward aspirings."[40]

The church was to be affirmed not simply as a gathering of pious individuals, but as a time and a space separate from the course of everyday life. To this end, Doane and Croswell began publishing in their Boston newspaper *The Banner of the Church* excerpts from the work of an English divine who would become one of the leading figures of the Oxford Movement. John Keble's deeply Wordsworthian cycle of devotional poems *The Christian Year,* which had appeared in England in 1827, comprised a series of meditations keyed to the liturgical calendar of the Book of Common Prayer.[41] Doane and Croswell were immediately transfixed by the ways Keble's poems used the traditional fasts and festivals of the Church of England as a framework to structure spiritual encounter. Each holy day, each liturgical season, provided some fresh opportunity for symbolic experience, by which the material world disclosed the divine presence above and around it. As the historian Sheridan Gilley argues, Keble's *Christian Year* represented nothing less than the "churching" of English romanticism, resituating the imaginative encounter with the natural world cherished by the romantic poets (and within a few years, the American transcendentalists) within the daily and seasonal ministrations of the Anglican liturgy.[42] The excerpts proved so popular that Doane prepared in late 1833 an American edition of *The Christian Year,* complete with annotations to rectify what he imagined was the general unfamiliarity in the United States with the liturgical arrangements of the prayer book.[43] It was a general principle of philosophy, Doane explained in his introduction, "that whatever is to make the strongest impression on men, must be made *visible,* either to the bodily, or to the 'mind's eye.'" Christ exemplified this principle in the institution of his "few simple, beautiful, visible sacraments." And his Church, following suit, "applied this principle to the commemoration of the great facts of Christianity" by instituting the fasts and festivals of the liturgical year.[44] And, with both the audacity and insecurity with which many writers in the nascent "American renaissance" engaged with the fruits of British romanticism, Doane brazenly interlaid the devotional poems of his friend William Croswell throughout his edition of Keble's work.[45] Even the heirs of the Puritans took notice. In a review of the work, the congregationalist *Religious Magazine* was forced to admire the "excellent contrivances of the Episcopal church for extending and deepening the impression of religious truth, by means of her external arrangements."[46]

As the celebration of the liturgical calendar would demarcate the seasons of devotion from the course of ordinary time, a new regard for sacred space and architecture would physically distinguish ecclesiastical life. High-church Episcopalians routinely complained that churches built in the neoclassical style made them virtually indistinguishable from any other edifice in the civic landscape. "And tell me why, to human eyes/No outward signs declare," versed Croswell, "If it be house of merchandize,/Or holy house of prayer."[47] While still serving as Doane's assistant minister at Trinity Church, Boston, John Henry Hopkins commenced research in the Athenaeum's holdings in architectural history. In 1836, some years after he had left the city for Vermont, Hopkins published the fruits of his research as an *Essay on Gothic Architecture,* the first such study to appear in the United States. The rehabilitation of medieval architecture would provide a visual language by which the site of our "spiritual interests" would be unmistakably set off from those of secular business and politics. Hopkins advocated a sumptuousness and ornament to Christian churches befitting what he called "the most precious of all earthly edifices," by which they would be visibly differentiated from the manifold institutions of civic life. He insisted that the cushions and drapery be "old fashioned crimson" and that windows be kept to a minimum and of stained glass wherever possible — too much natural light being, in his words, "unfriendly to devotion." He confessed his preference for a cross above the altar, though "many pious people are afraid of this figure" because of its association with the Church of Rome. Indeed, much of Hopkins's *Essay* was devoted — fairly unsuccessfully, it must be admitted — to liberating gothic from its association with the theological errors of medieval Catholicism.[48] Unsurprisingly, when the New York Ecclesiological Society was founded in April 1848 for the explicit promotion of the gothic style in American church building, John Henry Hopkins was invited to serve as its patron.[49]

It is one of the ironies of American religious history that the Oxford Movement unfolding within the Church of England arrived in the United States when it was substantially unnecessary. With its political autonomy, influential high-church wing, and an increasingly aestheticized culture of liturgical and architectural traditionalism, American Episcopalianism felt itself already well equipped with much of what constituted the agenda of the Oxford divines. As we have already seen, there was initially more interest in the poetic fruits of the Oxford Movement — Keble's *The Christian Year*, Williams's *The Cathedral*, and the collection of devotional poems known as the *Lyra Apostolica* — than the movement's incendiary series of numbered theological manifestos, the *Tracts for the Times*, published between 1833 and 1841.[50] While the literary face of the movement helped foster a popular new idiom of romantic Anglican poetry in the United States, which the literary scholar Kristie Blair calls "transatlantic Tractarianism," its controversial divinity simply proved obstreperous and divisive.[51]

Indeed, the *Tracts for the Times* went substantially unnoticed and unread in the United States until the later 1830s. The leading high-church Episcopalian journal, *The Churchman* of New York, made no mention of the *Tracts* before 1837, and thereafter treated them as merely forceful and elegant reaffirmations of the catholic tradition in Anglicanism, perfectly congruent with the high churchmanship then prevalent in the Protestant Episcopal Church.[52] It was only after the forces of American evangelicalism began to assail the so-called "Oxford divinity" as fundamentally irreconcilable with the basic tenets of Protestantism that the *Tracts for the Times* were embraced as a totem of ecclesiastical partisanship.[53] In early 1838, the self-appointed custodians of Calvinist orthodoxy at *The Princeton Review* proclaimed *The Tracts* incompatible with "the great doctrine of the Reformation," justification by faith. In the place of faith, the *Review* charged, were substituted the ritual works of the Church. "The Oxford *Tract* writers make the church the main point; the church as an ordinance for conveying life to all its members by means of the sacraments. The church, with them, is the great mediator between God and man, the only authorized channel of divine communication."[54]

Beginning with a charge to the clergy of his diocese in September 1839, the leading evangelical Episcopalian, Charles Pettit McIlvaine, bishop of Ohio, inaugurated a campaign against Tractarian error, culminating in his monumental *Oxford Divinity Compared with that of the Romish and Anglican Churches* in 1841.[55] The Tractarians' "systematic abandonment of the vital and distinguishing principles of the Protestant faith," above all, justification by faith alone, opened Reformed Christianity to the travesties of purgatory, indulgences, invocation of the saints, the sacrament of penance, and ultimately, the elevation of tradition and papal infallibility above the authority of Scripture.[56] The bitter controversy over the Oxford Movement polarized the Episcopal Church for virtually the entirety of the 1840s and jeopardized its identity as a Protestant denomination.[57] Ironically, the transcendentalist journal *The Western Messenger* was one of the few Protestant newspapers to review the *Tracts for the Times* with anything approaching sympathy. The Tractarians, the reviewer confessed, affirmed something that the puritans and their Unitarian descendants had forgotten: that religion requires an aesthetic dimension. "Man is still to be often reached through eye and ear," he argued, "and by means of music, pictures, symbolic acts and ceremonies we would approach him.[58]" There was a quiet, perhaps grudging affinity, among these rival schools of American romanticism.

Perhaps the most illuminating engagement with the Oxford Movement's *Tracts for the Times* was that of the renegade transcendentalist Orestes A. Brownson. Brownson encountered the *Tracts* relatively late in his long spiritual pilgrimage from Protestant orthodoxy through radical transcendentalism to the Roman Catholic Church.[59] Brownson's 1836 book

New Views of Christianity, Society and the Church, appearing within a few months Emerson's seminal essay *Nature,* helped establish transcendentalism as a force in American culture. His exposition of the inadequacies of historical Christianity, which he presented as a dialectic between an otherworldly spiritualism and a profane materialism, was a good deal more complex than Emerson's casual dismissals in the Divinity School address. But unlike Emerson, Brownson was profoundly uninterested in seeing spirituality de-institutionalized. Instead, his *New Views* made a powerful plea for a new church, a "future religion," which would embody "a new synthesis of the elements of the life of Humanity."[60] This corporate sensibility, influenced in no small part by the French socialism of Henri de Saint-Simon and Pierre Leroux, tended to alienate Brownson from the ardent individualism of the transcendentalist milieu. Brownson's 1842 work *The Mediatorial Life of Jesus* vigorously argued for the necessity of religion as communion, as collective life. Repudiating the transcendentalist deification of the human soul he associated with Emerson and Theodore Parker, Brownson adorned his notion of communion with overtly catholic (if not yet Roman Catholic) elements such as the apostolic succession, the authority of ecclesiastical tradition and a profound regard for the sacraments of baptism and the eucharist.[61] Brownson encountered the *Tracts for the Times* precisely as his own Christianity was taking on an increasingly ecclesiological dimension.

Brownson reviewed the American edition of the *Tracts for the Times* in the very first issue of his newly re-established *Brownson's Quarterly Review* in January 1844. The review, tellingly entitled "The Church Question," formed a natural complement to the "Introduction" with which Brownson recommenced his journal. There, Brownson dispelled the rumors that he had converted to Roman Catholicism but affirmed his new ecclesiological consciousness. In something of a palinode to his *New Views,* Brownson confessed his newfound traditionalism, "I find in the old Church, theoretically considered, all that I hoped from a new Church."[62]

This new commitment primed Brownson to treat the "Oxford divinity" with considerable sympathy, as evidence of the "great movement, already commenced throughout Christendom, towards unity and catholicity." Brownson did not, it must be stressed, accept the Tractarians' claims on behalf of the catholicity of the Church of England; it remained to him, an irreducibly Protestant church which stood on no better footing than any of the other sects of the Reformation. But he was willing to consider the Oxford Movement as at least grappling with what he had come to see as the fundamental religious problem of the age. "The truth is, the church — we speak generally — has lost the clear sense of the profound significance of her own organization, doctrines, sacraments and symbols." Christians, he lamented, had lost the sense of the church as a divine institution. It had become instead merely "a voluntary association of believers for religious purposes," whose organization was fungible and whose sacraments were mostly decorative. "No wonder, then," Brownson exclaimed, "that the great mass marvel why the church is here; are puzzled to make out what business it has to be here at all." Absent a theology in which the church and its worship was indispensable to the economy of salvation, the institution would be regarded as utterly superfluous to Christian life. The physical edifice, he remarked sardonically, was simply taking up space that might be better occupied by a cotton-mill or a residence, "or at best by a lyceum, a school-house, an anatomical, or chemical laboratory." Unfortunately, the Oxford divines offered nothing more than a *historical* account of their church, a narrative of the imagined continuity between the primitive institution of the apostolic age and modern Anglicanism. They could not supply what Brownson called a *philosophy of the church,* that is, a sense of the church as communion, as shared life. When they did so, Brownson predicted, they would discern the limits of their insular tradition. Brownson, of course, could not have known of the wave of Tractarian conversions from Anglicanism to Roman Catholicism in late 1845 — most prominently, that of the leading Oxford divine, John Henry Newman. But he believed that the movement was indeed, "possessed by a sentiment which will be found too big and too expansive for the Church of England."[63]

Significantly, Brownson's review of the *Tracts* immediately prompted a letter from none other than John Henry Hopkins, bishop of Vermont, defending the catholicity of the Anglican communion.[64] By the time of Brownson's own admission to the Roman Catholic Church in October 1844, he retained precious little sympathy for the claims of Anglican ecclesiology.[65] Still, Brownson after his conversion became one of the foremost American exponents of what Patrick Carey has called "Catholic romanticism," and remained committed to the notion of the Church as an embodiment of "supernatural communion" transcendent of individual belief.[66]

A mere five days after Orestes Brownson's reception into the Roman Catholic Church, the Swiss-born émigré Philip Schaff delivered his inaugural address as professor of church history at the Mecersburg Seminary before the general synod of the German Reformed Church in Reading, Pennsylvania. An expanded version of this address was translated into English by Schaff's Mercersburg colleague John Williamson Nevin, who added a lengthy introduction and appended his own August 1844 sermon "On Catholic Unity." Like Brownson's writings in this period, Schaff and Nevin's *The Principle of Protestantism* was positively haunted by the "Oxford divinity" emanating from the Anglican communion on both sides of the Atlantic.[67] And like Brownson, the Mercersburg theologians considered the Oxford Movement a promising but ultimately inadequate answer to the so-called "church question." Schaff proclaimed the Oxford Movement "an entirely legitimate and necessary reaction" to the individualism and sectarianism that had become the distinguishing mark of the Protestant denominational order in the United States. Such an awakening was to be welcomed in an American Protestantism in which, as Schaff explained, "the significance of the Church has been forgotten, or at least practically undervalued, in favor of personal individual piety." And he could not but admire the Oxford Movement's reverence for history, rich sacramental life, observation of fasts and festivals, and the aesthetic sensibility which delighted in "beautifying sanctuaries and altars."[68] The Oxford Movement was, in Nevin's words, "the grand rebounding movement of the Reformation," in which the Protestant tendency toward inwardness and individual subjectivity had finally catalyzed a reaction which stressed the external and sensuous life of the Church and its offices.[69] With all this, Schaff announced, "we go with the young Oxford hand in hand."[70] But beyond this the Mercersburg divines would not go.

While Orestes Brownson came to consider Anglican ecclesiology, for all its pretensions to catholicity, irremediably Protestant and schismatic, the Mercersburg theology held it insufficiently devoted to the spirit of the Reformation. An ecclesiological movement emanating from within the Reformed tradition, the Mercersburg divines could not abide the Anglican insistence upon episcopacy as the indispensable element of church life. They considered the Anglican doctrine of the apostolic succession, the notion that the bishops were the direct successors of the apostles, as a crude and "mechanical" device for ensuring ecclesiastical continuity.[71] And as heirs to the Protestant Reformation, they forcefully rejected the narrow antiquarianism of high-church Anglicanism, which revered the first four centuries of Christian church history as a pristine and unsurpassable model of Christian polity and worship. The Anglican reverence for history was ultimately undermined by its utter disregard for the principle of *development*. Christianity, Schaff wrote, "is itself the absolute religion, and in this view unsusceptible of improvement." But this must not be confused, he insisted, with "the apprehension and appropriation of Christianity in the consciousness of mankind," which indeed unfolded in "a progressive process of development."[72] The Mercersburg theologians, drawing upon the Berlin school of ecclesiastical history in which Schaff had been educated, thus posited a dynamic ecclesiology, *evangelical catholicity*, which considered the successive epochs of the church as part of "an ever deepening appropriation of Christianity as the power of a divine life, which is destined to make all things new."[73] From this perspective, the divided state of Protestantism, particularly in the American denominational order, was a necessary, but impermanent state of affairs. Ultimately, the genuine disagreements in human understanding of Christian revelation embodied in the division of sects were to be and overcome and reconciled in Church unity.[74]

* * *

"The great theological question of the present century will be the Church Question," proclaimed the transcendentalist minister James Freeman Clarke at the March 15, 1848, dedication of his congregation's new chapel in Boston's South End. Borrowing a recent formulation from the German Lutheran church historian and pastor Theodor Klieforth, Clarke explained that the earliest centuries of the Christian Church had been oriented around questions of *theology* — the nature of Christ and of the Trinity; and the immediately succeeding ages, the questions of *anthropology*, that is, the needs and nature of a sinful humanity. To the era of the Protestant Reformation then fell the central problems of *soteriology*, the matter of man's justification and salvation by God. And thus, there remained for the present age the question of what he called *ecclesiology*, the nature and organization of the Christian Church. "The tendency of the age draws our minds toward it," Clarke preached, "for in all things the present century tends toward union, harmony [and] synthesis." The preoccupations of the European enlightenment, which "tended to division, individualism, analysis," had given way to a romantic era transfixed by the questions of institutions and solidarities, the contours of our shared lives and experiences. Clarke proceeded to outline for the congregation his vision of a syncretistic and comprehensive "church of the future," which he believed might stand athwart the two countervailing forces acting upon antebellum American Protestantism: the lure of Roman Catholicism, on the one hand, and the tendency toward what he called "Individualism and No-Churchism," on the other.[75]

That New England transcendentalism in its second decade was openly speaking the language of ecclesiology testifies to the inescapability of the church question in American Christianity before the Civil War. Indeed, it was the in the discourse of ecclesiology that American culture first confronted the putative weakness of institutional life in antebellum civil society.[76] The questions posed by European romanticism about the obligations of history and community, and the necessary embeddedness of the self in social institutions, were, if anything, more discomfiting that those it posed about individual subjectivity. And the vaunted "imperial self" of American literary romanticism would long be shadowed by the ineluctable moral and spiritual claims of community life.[77] The most apparent fruit of ecclesiology in the United States was the gothic revival in ecclesiastical architecture, which rapidly outstripped the confines of denominations invested in reconciliation with the Catholic middle ages.[78] The gothic style provided a symbolic language by which civic life might be newly demarcated: the ostentatious medievalism of church buildings projected a physical distinction from secular edifices. Implicit in this visual demarcation, however, was the ecclesiological critique of bourgeois society in America: that religion must sensibly embody a time and a space distinct from that of everyday life.

And, indeed, ecclesiology in the second half of the nineteenth century would provide one of the major discourses of dissent from Gilded Age materialism.[79] These critical resources, as this essay has suggested, were present from its inception. A theological and cultural language designed to more forcefully affirm ecclesiastical independence from the confessional states of Europe was imported into the United States to sustain the separation of church from civil society.

FURTHER READING

Conser, Jr., Walter. *Church and Confession: Conservative Theologians in Germany, England and America, 1815–1866.* Macon: Mercer University Press, 1984.

Franchot, Jenny. *Roads to Rome: The Antebellum Protestant Encounter with Catholicism.* Berkeley: University of California Press, 1994.

Gura, Philip F. *American Transcendentalism: A History.* New York: Hill and Wang, 2007.

Harvey, Samantha C. *Transatlantic Transcendentalism: Coleridge, Emerson & Nature.* Edinburgh: Edinburgh University Press, 2013.

Mullin, Robert Bruce. *Episcopal Vision/American Reality: High Church Theology and Social Thought in Evangelical America.* New Haven: Yale University Press, 1986.

Prickett, Stephen. *Religion and Romanticism: The Tradition of Coleridge and Wordsworth in the Victorian Church.* Cambridge: Cambridge University Press, 1976.

NOTES

1 [Samuel Osgood] "The Poet of Puseyism" (Sept 1843), *Christian Examiner,* vol. 35, third series, vol. 17 (Boston: James Munroe & Co, 1843), 45–54.

2 Judith Kent Green, "A Tentative Transcendentalist: Samuel Osgood and the *Western Messenger,*" *Studies in the American Renaissance* (1984): 79–92.

3 [Osgood,] "Poet of Puseyism," 54.

4 Arthur O. Lovejoy, "On the Discrimination of Romanticisms," *PMLA* 39, no. 2 (June 1924): 229–253.

5 The most important being those of René Wellek, "The Concept of 'Romanticism' in Literary History I. The Term 'Romantic' and Its Derivatives," *Comparative Literature* 1, no. 1 (Winter 1949): 1–23; and "The Concept of 'Romanticism' in Literary History II. The Unity of European Romanticism," *Comparative Literature* 1, no. 2 (Spring 1949): 147–172.

6 Much of this debate, including Lovejoy and Wellek, has been anthologized in *Romanticism: Points of View,* ed. Robert F. Gleckner and Gerald E. Enscoe, 2nd ed. (Detroit: Wayne State University Press, 1975).

7 J. Robert Barth, *The Symbolic Imagination: Coleridge and the Romantic Tradition* (Princeton: Princeton University Press, 1977), 127.

8 Barth, *Symbolic Imagination,* 130–137.

9 William Wordsworth, *The Prelude,* ed. Basil Worsfold (London: A. Moring Ltd., 1904), 161.

10 Lawrence Buell, *Literary Transcendentalism: Style and Vision in the American Renaissance* (Ithaca: Cornell University Press, 1973), 23–54; Robert Bruce Mullin, *Episcopal Vision/American Reality: High Church Theology and Social Thought in Evangelical America* (New Haven: Yale University Press, 1986), 75–77.

11 Sidney E. Ahlstrom, "The Romantic Religious Revolution and the Dilemmas of Religious History," *Church History* 46, no. 2 (June 1977): 149–170.

12 Ralph Waldo Emerson, *Nature* (Boston: James Munroe & Co, 1849), 1.

13 Perry Miller, ed., *The Transcendentalists.* (Cambridge, MA: Harvard University Press, 1967), 3–15.

14 See William R. Hutchison, *The Transcendentalist Ministers: Church Reform in the New England Renaissance.* (Hamden: Archon Books, 1972); Buell, *Literary Transcendentalism.*

15 Ralph Waldo Emerson, *An Address Delivered Before the Senior Class in Divinity College, Cambridge. Sunday Evening, 15 July, 1838* (Boston: James Munroe and Company, 1838), 11–13, 25.

16 Theodore Parker, *A Discourse on the Transient and Permanent in Christianity* (Boston: Freeman and Bolles, 1841), 23–25.

17 See Gary Dorrien, *The Making of American Liberal Theology: Imagining Progressive Religion, 1805–1900.* (Louisville: Westminster John Knox Press, 2001), 58–110. On metaphysical religion, see Leigh Eric Schmidt, *Restless Souls: The Making of American Spirituality* (New York: Harper Collins, 2005); and Catherine L. Albanese, *A Republic of Mind and Spirit: A Cultural History of American Metaphysical Religion* (New Haven: Yale University Press, 2007).

18 Leon Chai, *The Romantic Foundations of the American Renaissance* (Ithaca: Cornell University Press, 1987), 169–243.

19 For an alternative reading of this development, see Jonathan G. Koefoed, "Cautious Romantics: Trinitarian Transcendentalists and the Emergence of a Conservative Religious Tradition in America," (PhD diss., Boston University, 2014).

20 Duane E. Smith, "Romanticism in America: The Transcendentalists," *The Review of Politics* 35, no. 3 (July 1973): 302–325.

21   Robert Sayre and Michael Löwy, "Figures of Romantic Anti-Capitalism," *New German Critique* 32 (Spring-Summer 1984): 42–92; Michael Löwy and Robert Sayre, *Romanticism Against the Tide of Modernity,* trans. Catherine Porter (Durham: Duke University Press, 2001). Philip Connell, *Romanticism, Economics and the Question of 'Culture'* (Oxford: Oxford University Press, 2001).

22   Ralph Waldo Emerson, intro "The Present Age," in *The Early Lectures,* vol. 3, 190; and see Michael T. Gilmore, *American Romanticism and the Marketplace* (Chicago: University of Chicago, 1985).

23   On transcendentalism as a program of social reform, see Anne C. Rose, *Transcendentalism as a Social Movement, 1830–1850* (New Haven: Yale University Press, 1981).

24   And here it is worth noting that Osgood eventually abandoned Unitarianism for the Episcopal Church. See Kent, "A Tentative Transcendentalist," 91.

25   Esther Rhoads Houghton, "'The British Critic' and the Oxford Movement," *Studies in Bibliography* 16 (1963): 119–137; S. A. Skinner, "Newman, the Tractarians and the *British Critic,*" *Journal of Ecclesiastical History* 50, no. 4 (Oct. 1999): 716–759.

26   For an overview, see George Herring, *What Was the Oxford Movement?* (London: Continuum, 2002).

27   "Ecclesialogy," *The British Critic* 21 (Jan. 1837): 218–248.

28   Extracts for the Diary of Benjamin Webb, Lambeth Palace Library, MS 3595.

29   James F. White, *The Cambridge Movement: The Ecclesiologists and the Gothic Revival* (Cambridge: Cambridge University Press, 1979).

30   "New Churches," *The Ecclesiologist* 1 (Nov. 1841).

31   See Nigel Yates, *The Oxford Movement and Anglican Ritualism* (London: Historical Association, 1983).

32   Geoffrey Rowell, "Europe and the Oxford Movement," *The Oxford Movement: Europe and the Wider World 1830–1930,* ed. S. J. Brown and P. B. Nockles (Cambridge: Cambridge University Press, 2012), 153–167.

33   Peter N. Stearns, "The Nature of the Avenir Movement (1830–1831)," *American Historical Review* 65, no. 4 (July 1960): 837–847; W. G. Roe, *Lammenais and England: The Reception of Lamennais's Religious Ideas in England in the Nineteenth Century* (Oxford: Oxford University Press, 1966).

34   Walter Conser, Jr., *Church and Confession: Conservative Theologians in Germany, England and America, 1815–1866* (Macon: Mercer University Press, 1984); J. N. Figgis, *Churches in the Modern State,* 2nd ed. (London: Longmans Green & Co., 1914).

35   John Henry Hopkins, *The Primitive Church Compared with the Protestant Episcopal Church of the Present Day* (Burlington: Smith and Harrington, 1835), 6.

36   See Robert Bruce Mullin, *Episcopal Vision/American Reality: High Church Theology and Social Thought in Evangelical America* (New Haven: Yale University Press, 1986).

37   A. H. Everett, *America, or a General Survey of the Political Situation of the Several Powers of the Western Continent* (Philadelphia: Carey & Lea, 1827), 355.

38   The Beauty of Holiness," *The Banner of the Church* 1, no. 25 (18 Feb. 1832): 99–100.

39   "The Ritualist," *The Episcopal Watchman* 1, no. 1 (26 March 1827): 2–3.

40   "Responsive Worship," *The Episcopal Watchman* 1, no. 43 (14 Jan. 1828): 337–339.

41   For an overview, see Kristie Blair, "Keble and *The Christian Year,*" in *The Oxford Handbook of English Literature and Theology,* ed. Andrew Hass, David Jasper, and Elisabeth Jay (Oxford: Oxford University Press, 2009), 607–623; G. B. Tennyson, *Victorian Devotional Poetry: The Tractarian Mode* (Cambridge, MA: Harvard University Press, 1981).

42   Sheridan Gilley, "John Keble and the Victorian Churching of Romanticism," in *An Infinite Complexity: Essays in Romanticism,* ed. J. R. Watson (Edinburgh: Edinburgh University Press, 1983), 226–239. On the romanticism of the Oxford movement, see Stephen Prickett, *Religion and Romanticism: The Tradition of Coleridge and Wordsworth in the Victorian Church* (Cambridge: Cambridge University Press, 1976); Michael H. Bright, "English Literary Romanticism and the Oxford Movement," *Journal of the History of Ideas* 40, no. 3 (July–Sept. 1979): 385–404.

43   Doane to Croswell, 10 June 1833, Doane Family Papers, Box 13, Folder 14, New York State Library; Doane to Samuel Seabury, Philadelphia, 1 Feb. 1834, Dr. Samuel Seabury (1801–1872) Papers, MSS. SeLL62, Box 1, General Theological Seminary.

44 John Keble, *The Christian Year, Thoughts in Verse for the Sundays and Holydays throughout the Year*, 1st American ed. (Philadelphia: Cary, Lea & Blanchard, 1834), 9–11.

45 Robert Weisbuch, *Atlantic Double-Cross: American Literature and British Influence in the Age of Emerson* (Chicago: University of Chicago Press, 1986); Richard Gravil, *Romantic Dialogues: Anglo-American Continuities, 1776–1862* (New York, St. Martin's Press, 2000).

46 "The Episcopal Ritual," *The Religious Magazine* 2, no. 1 (15 Oct. 1834): 34–40.

47 William Croswell, *Poems, Sacred and Secular* (Boston: Ticknor & Fields, 1861), 166–168.

48 John Henry Hopkins, *Essay on Gothic Architecture* (Burlington: Smith & Harrington, 1836), 2, 12, 18–20, 36.

49 John Henry Hopkins, Jr., *The Life of the Right Reverend John Henry Hopkins, First Bishop of Vermont* (New York: F. J. Huntington, 1873), 269; and see Phoebe B. Stanton, *The Gothic Revival & American Church Architecture: An Episode in Taste, 1850–1856* (Baltimore: Johns Hopkins Press, 1968), 159–211.

50 Austin Cooper, "The *Tracts for the Times*," in *The Oxford Handbook of the Oxford Movement*, ed. S. J. Brown, P. Nockles, and J. Pereiro (Oxford: Oxford University Press, 2017), 137–150.

51 Kristie Blair, "Transatlantic Tractarians: Victorian Poetry and the Church of England in America," *Victorian Studies* 55, no. 2 (Winter 2013): 286–299.

52 Thomas Williams, "Early Hobartian Reaction to the Oxford Movement: Assessments of The *Tracts for the Times* in *The Churchman*, 1835–1841," *Anglican and Episcopal History* 81, no. 4 (Dec. 2012): 390–412

53 Kenneth M. Peck, "The Oxford Controversy in America: 1839," *Historical Magazine of the Protestant Episcopal Church* 33, no. 1 (Mar. 1964): 49–63.

54 "Tracts for the Times," *Princeton Review* 10 (Jan. 1838), 84–119.

55 Diana Hochstedt Butler, *Standing Against the Whirlwind: Evangelical Episcopalians in Nineteenth-Century America* (New York: Oxford University Press, 1993), 93–135.

56 Charles Petit McIlvaine, *Oxford Divinity Compared with that of the Romish and Anglican Churches* (Philadelphia: Joseph Wetham & Son, 1841), 14.

57 George E. DeMille, *The Catholic Movement in the American Episcopal Church* (Philadelphia: Church Historical Society, 1941), 40–73.

58 J. H. Perkins, "The Oxford Tracts, or Old Episcopacy Revived," *The Western Messenger* 7, no. 1 (May 1839): 287–288.

59 On Brownson's religious development, see Patrick W. Carey, *Orestes A. Brownson, American Religious Weathervane* (Grand Rapids: Eerdmans, 1997).

60 Orestes A. Brownson, *New Views of Christianity, Society and the Church* (Boston: James Munroe, 1836), 88–113.

61 Orestes A. Brownson, *The Mediatorial Life of Jesus. A Letter to Rev. William Ellery Channing, D. D.* (Boston: Charles C. Little and James Brown, 1842).

62 [Orestes A. Brownson,] "Introduction," *Brownson's Quarterly Review* 1, no. 1 (Jan. 1844): 14–15.

63 [Orestes A. Brownson,] "The Church Question," *Brownson's Quarterly Review* 1, no. 1 (Jan. 1844): 57–84.

64 Hopkins to Brownson, [Jan. 1844], *Orestes Augustus Brownson Papers at the University of Notre Dame Archives* (microfilm), §11322.

65 See Orestes A. Brownson, "The Anglican Church Schismatic," *Brownson's Quarterly Review* 1, no. 4 (Oct. 1844): 487–514.

66 Patrick W. Carey, "American Catholic Romanticism, 1830–1888," *The Catholic Historical Review* 74, no. 4 (Oct. 1988): 590–606.

67 James Hastings Nichols, *Romanticism in American Theology: Nevin and Schaff at Mercersburg* (Chicago: University of Chicago Press, 1961) 45, 74, 77–83; W. Bradford Littlejohn, *The Mercersburg and The Quest for Reformed Catholicity* (Eugene: Pickwick, 2009), 88–123.

68 Philip Schaff, *The Principle of Protestantism As Related to the Present State of the Church*, trans. John W. Nevin (Chambersburg: Publication Office of the German Reformed Church, 1845), 122–124.

69 John W. Nevin, "Catholic Unity" in Schaff, *Principle of Protestantism*, 213.

70 Schaff, *Principle of Protestantism*, 124.

71   Schaff, *Principle of Protestantism*, 125.

72   Schaff, *Principle of Protestantism*, 179.

73   Schaff, *Principle of Protestantism*, 160–161.

74   John W. Nevin, *Antichrist; or the spirit of sect and schism* (New York: John S. Taylor, 1848).

75   James Freeman Clarke, *A Discourse Delivered at the Dedication of the Chapel, Built by the Church of the Disciples, Wednesday, March 15, 1848* (Boston: Benjamin H. Greene, 1848), 3–4, 18, 19–23, 25–26.

76   George M. Frederickson, *The Inner Civil War: Northern Intellectuals and the Crisis of the Union* (New York: Harper & Row, 1965), 7–35.

77   Quentin Anderson, *The Imperial Self: An Essay in American Literary and Cultural History* (New York: Knopf, 1971).

78   Agnes Addison, *Romanticism and the Gothic Revival* (New York: Gordian, 1967), 133–144.

79   T. Jackson Lears, *No Place of Grace: Antimodernism and the Transformation of American Culture, 1880–1920* (New York: Pantheon, 1981), 183–215; Peter W. Williams, *Religion, Art, and Money: Episcopalians and American Culture from the Civil War to the Great Depression* (Chapel Hill: University of North Carolina Press, 2016).

Chapter Fourteen

BEING HAUDENOSAUNEE: SEEING INDIGENOUS ONTOLOGY UNDER AMERICAN SETTLER COLONIALISM

Christian Gonzales
University of Rhode Island, Kingston, Rhode Island

In 1851 the Quaker missionary Solomon Lukens reported how impressed he was by changes he had witnessed among the Haudenosaunees.[1] Commenting on Native homes, he explained that they now contained many of the same items as were to be found in American households. He reported that "there has been a decided improvement ... in their manner of living, they have tables, dishes, knives & forks."[2] Beyond these material changes, Lukens explained that the Senecas had also embraced American notions of cleanliness and order. "I was agreeably surprised to see ... that they had divided their cabin with a rough partition ... things looked neat & clean & in comparative good order."[3] Another Quaker missionary, Joseph Elkinton, noticed what he perceived to be a significant shift among the younger generation of Senecas. To him, they too seemed to have become keenly aware of the connotations between cleanliness and order on the one hand, and social respectability on the other. Writing to his son in 1853, Elkinton reported "I have frequently observed when visiting families in which there were any children that had been with Friends, they seem distressed when their parents houses are found in disorder, and go immediately at work cleaning up and setting things to rights."[4]

Lukens and Elkinton perceived these material and social transformations as evidence of Seneca "improvement." In other words, they saw changes that demonstrated the Senecas' "progress" precisely because they had adopted some of the behaviors defined as normative by the dominant American settler society.[5] The conceptual paradigm through which they processed these ideas, moreover, assumed that as Native peoples "improved," they would concomitantly embark upon a process of the gradual abandonment of Indigenous culture. Looking back from the perspective of the early twenty first century, it is easy for students of history to make a similar assumption: that Native adoption of the practices of American society that Lukens and Elkinton noted also signaled the loss of Indigeneity. That assumption needs to be disrupted.

Since the publication of Anthony Wallace's *The Death and Rebirth of the Seneca*, cultural transformations have served as key sites of historical and anthropological investigations into both Native religious experience and what those experiences reveal about how Natives were

A Companion to American Religious History, First Edition. Edited by Benjamin E. Park.
© 2021 John Wiley & Sons, Inc. Published 2021 by John Wiley & Sons, Inc.

affected by the settler society. Wallace for instance concluded that the Handsome Lake Religion was a driving factor for a renaissance of the Haudenosaunees. The religion was an amalgam of Native and Christian practices that provided meaning for a people decimated and demoralized by the ravages of colonialism in the post-Revolutionary War and Early National periods. The religion was also vital to the persistence of the Senecas as it both promoted Seneca identity and culture while simultaneously facilitating their coexistence with the United States through shared understandings of Christian doctrine.[6]

Others have built on Wallace's insights. Linford Fisher for instance has explained how southern New England Natives used the Great Awakening to navigate colonialism, and then to ultimately reassert degrees of Native autonomy through building their own churches and congregations.[7] Most recently, scholars have moved away from binary models of Native religious practice built on poles like "traditional" and "Christian," recognizing that such models were too simple and restrictive. In their place, scholars have adopted a paradigm in which mutual cultural transformations help explain the ramifications of Native and white inter-relations. Such relationships particularly affected religious practice. For example, Tracy Neal Leavelle in *The Catholic Calumet* has used the amalgamation of Christian and Algonquin practices involved in ceremony surrounding the singing of hymns and the presentation of the Calumet as an exemplar of this dynamic.[8] Finally, others have investigated the ambivalence consequent to Native/white inter-relations. For example, in their relations with Native communities, missionaries could serve both as agents of colonialism and allies who acted to thwart colonialism. Likewise, Native Christians were both abettors of American imperialism and also key to Native communities' capacity to exercise agency in the face of settler colonialism.[9]

These excellent studies share a foundational focus on culture to understand persistence and transformation among Native peoples. Cultures are of course always subject to varying degrees of continuity and change. Within the colonial contexts of the Early National United States, Indigenous cultures were indeed in flux. To understand Indigenous identities in such circumstances can be tricky because of the complex linkages between culture and identity. To navigate this problem, this essay uses a different analytical lens in comparison to those scholars discussed above. It bases its analysis on Indigenous thought, rather than on culture. It does so in order to demonstrate that Haudenosaunee ideological understandings of the universe remained stable despite the massive degree of cultural changes they experienced in the early nineteenth century. In this way, a core element of Haudenosaunee identity remained unchanged through the experience of colonialism. More specifically, this essay asserts that central tenets of Haudenosaunee *ontology* persisted despite the fundamental cultural transformations experienced by Haudenosaunee communities located inside the United States settler civilization.

I understand ontology in accordance with its most basic definition as the science of being. How the Haudenosaunees comprehended the basic values that structured the universe is what I mean by ontology.[10] The first half of the nineteenth century witnessed significant developments in Haudenosaunee religious history. Christianity made inroads into Seneca society, evidenced in part by the political split between the Christian and Pagan political parties; and it was in the early nineteenth century that the Handsome Lake Religion (with elements of both Haudenosaunee and Christian beliefs) arose. Nonetheless, Seneca understandings of the fundamental nature of the universe persisted. For example, central to the Handsome Lake Religion is the reciting of the Gai'wiio. This recitation is a religious (cultural) practice. The use of storytelling as pedagogy, which is an underlying ideological structure of the recitation of the Gai'wiio, is an example of ontology. The belief in the validity of storytelling as teaching, in other words, represents a way of being that remains unchanged even amongst the creation of something — the Handsome Lake Religion — that is new. Therefore, examining how ontology manifested in Seneca behavior allows us to trace Haudenosaunee religious history in a way that is not dominated by a focus on the Haudenosaunees' adoption of Christianity. It permits us to *see* Haudenosaunee Indigeneity because we do not get bogged down in a construct in which cultural change can be read as a direct corollary to the either the loss of, or the radical transformation of, Indigeneity itself. In the case of the Senecas' embrace of the Handsome Lake Religion, the fact that this religion was infused with Christianity did not mean the end of longstanding Haudenosaunee beliefs about the basic structure of the world.

Working from this foundation, this essay asks how the Haudenosaunees lived in accordance with their ontological beliefs in an environment of profound cultural change. The answer, and the essay's argument, is that the Haudenosaunees expressed their ontological values *inside of* the cultural institutions they adopted as they negotiated living with an American settler society. Therefore, despite the fact that that American settler society generally sought to use "assimilation" as a tool to eradicate Indigenous cultures, the Haudenosaunees understood and used cultural change in a way that promoted the persistence of, rather than the disappearance of, Seneca Indigeneity, and consequently, of the Senecas themselves. When we work from this foundation, the history in question looks different. For example, the desire noted by Elkinton of Seneca youth to clean and arrange their homes when a Quaker visitor arrived was not indicative of an obsequious effort to gain social respectability, or by a desire on the part of the Senecas to be more "American." Rather, the youths' actions were motived by an effort to fulfill their obligations to their Quaker friends and allies. The Seneca youths sought to meet the expectations of the Quakers not because they wanted to prove that they had "improved," but because meeting the needs of one's friends was the behavior ethically required by Haudenosaunee conceptions of friendship, kinship, and alliance. The Seneca youth were showing first that they understood that the Quakers valued cleanliness and order and second that they would respect and assume these values when the Friends visited. Even though the material goods inside Seneca homes, and at times the behavior of the Seneca occupants of those homes, may have resembled those that were to be found in homes of white Americans, the Seneca youths Elkinton described were in reality enacting what it meant to be Haudenosaunee. The missionary simply misconstrued what he saw.

* * *

Perhaps the most salient example of this chapter's central argument is the Haudenosaunees' longstanding relationship with the Quakers. This relationship began in the late eighteenth century and persisted throughout the nineteenth. On the surface, the Haudenosaunee/Quaker partnership can appear as Seneca capitulation to, and cooperation with, Quaker "assimilation" efforts designed to promote Native adoption of American culture and the Christian religion. However, from Haudenosaunee perspectives, relations with the Quakers constituted an alliance based on Seneca understandings of *reciprocity*. This meant that the relationship was maintained by ongoing efforts of the allied partners to meet each other's needs and to work for each other's interests. In addition, allies were ritualized kin who supported each other precisely because they had become "family." The Haudenosaunees befriended the Quakers not because they sought to mimic American cultural practices but because they wanted non-Indigenous ritual kin allies who were bound by reciprocal obligation to aid the Natives, particularly as they navigated pressures brought on by the expanding United States. Indeed, throughout the 1830s and 1840s, the Haudenosaunees would repeatedly call upon the Quakers to support their attempts to resist forced Removal.[11] Most famously, the Quakers were pivotal allies of the Senecas in their efforts to stop enforcement of the First and Second Treaties of Buffalo Creek, which provided for Seneca relocation to the West. In these cases, the gestures the Haudenosaunees made toward cooperating with Quaker efforts to promote cultural change were repaid by the pivotal roles Quakers played in lobbying the US to forego acting on Removal.

In addition to leveraging reciprocity in response to the existential threat of Removal, the Haudenosaunees lived by its ethos in more quotidian interactions with the Quakers. For example, reciprocity was at play when some Senecas decided to hire out their children as workers to Quaker missionary families. It appears that these children did not receive any type of compensation and that they generally worked only for short periods of time. Both of these conditions would make sense given Haudenosaunee reasons for making available the labor of their children. Missionaries John and Susannah Wood hired Seneca children after arriving to Allegheny, but were disappointed that these little workers soon left them. "I have tried two boys & neither has stayed much more than a week. ... Susan ... has had one or two Indian girls ... but they were not contented to stay any length of time."[12] The children did not stay long because their primary reason for working was not wages. Rather, the Senecas used their children's labor as "gifts" in order to maintain good relations with the missionaries. The children's work represented an offering from the Haudenosaunees to the missionaries and was meant to bond the Natives and the Quakers in a reciprocal relationship. More deeply, it established a precedent for a system of mutual aid in which the Haudenosaunees and Quakers could call on one another for help. So while the hiring of the children may have had for the Quakers an important economic component — work — it was for the Senecas mostly a social phenomenon governed by Haudenosaunee efforts to act as allies. They used their children to meet — to a small degree — the labor demands of their Quaker allies so that those allies would be obligated to reciprocate to the Haudenosaunees whenever they needed the assistance of the missionaries.

These types of efforts, moreover, extended beyond day to day interactions within Seneca reservations. For instance, many tribal leaders wanted young Haudenosaunee men to learn trades and explicitly used the concept of reciprocity to achieve this goal. They developed a plan to provide apprentice workers to their Quaker allies, who in return would acquire laborers (whom they could also evangelize). The Haudenosaunees hoped these apprenticeships would create a cadre of skilled laborers who could provide needed services to the Seneca Nation so that those services would not need to be purchased from white Americans. The work to develop a class of Haudenosaunee artisans began in the early 1820s when a few chiefs sent their children to live with Quakers in Philadelphia. James Robinson, for example, sent his son to a Quaker family in order that he learn the "shoe making business."[13] Two decades later, artisan crafts and Haudenosaunee youths were still key to fulfilling the reciprocal obligations between Natives and Quakers under this apprenticeship plan. When Quakers visited the Allegheny Seneca in 1845, the Indians asked them if they would approve of "their men learning blacksmithing, carpentry, and cobbler [sic]."[14] The decades-long attempt to produce skilled Haudenosaunee craftsmen evinced a calculated strategy to preserve a measure of Seneca power and self-sufficiency through labor activities afforded by Seneca participation in the American economy. In return, the Quakers acquired a small, but ongoing, supply of workers and potential converts.

Beyond the pivotal role reciprocity played in the Haudenosaunee/Quaker alliance, other elements of Haudenosaunee ontology governed their relationship. For instance, the Haudenosaunee concept of *ritual kinship* was ever present in Quaker/Seneca interactions. The centrality of kinship to the alliance, for example, as well as the failure of the Senecas to embrace the cultural changes the Quakers peddled, is evident from a speech the aforementioned Joseph Eklinton gave to the Seneca National Council in 1827. He stated

Brothers, you are few in number surrounded by many white people and it is probable you will become more closely so. How do you expect to get your living in years to come? Do you calculate to continue where you now are?. ... If you calculate to continue where you now are, is it not high time that you looked around you and endeavored to understand how you are getting along? You have enlarged your fields some, you have better houses, and some of you have better barns, but brothers we think you are yet very deficient in these things; you might generally have better houses, you might have more barns, and you might have larger fields.[15]

Elkinton spoke as kin to his Seneca "brothers" whom he called upon to redouble their efforts to transform their communities to resemble those of white Americans. Yet, he and his Quaker brethren had so far been disappointed in the pace of change precisely because the alliance was, for the Senecas, not chiefly about cultural change. Haudenosaunee values, not "assimilation," governed the Seneca/Quaker partnership. Elkinton's pleas reflected this reality as he urged the Natives to "have better houses" and "larger fields."

Missionaries other than Elkinton noted Haudenosaunee efforts to tie themselves and the Quakers together. Again, we should understand such efforts as motivated by the Senecas' desire that the two groups see each other as kin. For example, missionary Susannah Wood noted that some Seneca had purposefully explained to her significant commonalities between Haudenosaunee spiritual (i.e. ontological) beliefs and Christianity. This was an effort to strengthen the bond between themselves and the Quakers.[16] She wrote "they believe in future rewards and punishments." She also reported that the same phenomenon had occurred between Senecas and the missionary Ebenezer Worth, explaining that the Natives had told him that "they believed just as he did." Making the point more forcibly, she shared that from the perspectives of many Haudenosaunees, the similarities in Indigenous and Quaker beliefs implied that they and the Quakers could be considered as the same people. "They have said," wrote Wood, that "they ought to be called the 'Old Quaker Party.' "[17] Such pointed verbal reminders on the part of Haudenosaunees to their Quaker guests served to reinforce the kinship bonds shared by the alliance partners.

This was particularly important and necessary because the Haudenosaunees knew that from the Quakers' perspectives, the Natives' adoption of Christianity was woefully lacking. And since evangelism was the main motivation behind Quaker presence in the Seneca Nation, some Haudenosaunees worried that the lack of widespread Native conversion to the Christianity peddled by the Quakers would imperil the bonds between the Natives and the preachers. The verbal notations of similar beliefs between the groups was consequently meant to foreclose upon disruptions to their alliance through highlighting the values they shared, even when shared beliefs applied only to a minority of Senecas. Thus, the Haudenosaunee Solomon Lane urged the missionaries to "Be guardians to my people ... though it is true that but very few of us are Christian." Lane continued "many of us are pagans, and also many Christian pagans." Lane classified the Senecas into a tripartite structure of religious belief — Christian, pagan, and Christian pagan — to show that the exact nature of ostensive religious belief was less important than the obligations the Senecas and the Quakers had to each other. Reinforcing his point Lane continued "Our dear guardians we hope you will not withdraw from us in our infancy to perish."[18] The hyperbole of his sentence served to emphasize Lane's point that the foundation of the Natives' relationship with the Quakers was an alliance between "kin" groups who were bound to support one another. This vision ran back straight to the heart of Haudenosaunee ontology.

Just as they had used seminal concepts of Haudenosaunee ontology to shape their alliance with the Quakers, the Senecas did the same with their employment of another borrowed socio-cultural institution — the written constitution.[19] In the late 1840s a dispute arose over Seneca governance and ended up splitting the Senecas into two parties — one that supported a political system predicated on the power of chiefs, and one that advocated for a more democratic diffusion of power to the people, or to the "warriors." The party of the warriors briefly gained power and instituted a new constitution. A few years later though the warrior party was ousted and another constitution was drafted. The new document re-empowered the chiefs and set up a government that more closely mirrored older Haudenosaunee political practice by centering the Council as the main instrument for political discussion.

What is important for our purposes is to recognize that the new Seneca constitution codified and embedded within it concepts significant to Haudenosaunee ontology. I will discuss two of those concepts here. First, the Senecas enshrined ideas about *peace and the arbitration of disputes* into the constitution through the office of the "peacemaker." The peacemaker was a judge who mediated disputes and made rulings to resolve them. The notion of a peacemaker reached back to the Deganawida narrative in which the hero Deganawida used arbitration to put an end to incessant intra-Iroquois warfare. The story was fundamental to the twelfth century founding of the Iroquois Confederacy under the Great League of Peace. The Seneca constitution's office of peacemaker reflected the long-standing value the Senecas placed on non-violent resolution of disagreement and thereby re-articulated, albeit in changed form, this value that had always been so central to Haudenosaunee governance. Second, the constitution codified the power that Haudenosaunee women had always wielded in relation to the control of material resources. Such power had been conceptually linked to the power of women to take raw resources and convert them into more refined finished products. This included the ability to process raw foods into meals, raw building materials into clothes and longhouses, and even semen into babies. The new constitution reflected, protected, and perpetuated this conceptualization of women's power. Specifically, the constitution reserved to women the right to keep their property after divorce. This provision replicated and maintained the idea that women should exercise control over natural resources by protecting women's ownership of one of the most important natural resources, land. In addition, by supporting women's access to material resources, the constitution made strides towards shielding Haudenosaunee women from the dominant gendered power relations of mid-nineteenth century American civilization, which generally placed control of material resources into the hands of men. In sum, the new constitution contained within it important Haudenosaunee ontological values concerning dispute resolution and gender roles.[20]

Though the notion that anyone could "own" land was a concept borrowed from the American settler society, the Senecas nonetheless continued to live in accordance with older, indigenous understandings of land. More to the point, they continued to perceive the *land as a system of relationships* that interlinked the various peoples (both human and non-human i.e. fauna and flora) that inhabited it. Indeed, "indigenous" fundamentally meant to be part of, and in relationship with, the land and its other inhabitants. These relationships, moreover, flowed multi-directionally through time; from the present through the past and into the future. The Haudenosaunees' protestations against efforts early in the nineteenth century to coercively "encourage" them to leave their lands and emigrate evince this indigenous conceptualization of "the land." For example, in 1818 a Council address to the President argued "Father, We have confidence in you; you cannot see your red children with their little bones driven off of their land … leaving the sepulchers of their fathers, their farms, their farming tools and cattle, dying by families on the road through hardship and privation … without house or friend."[21] The references to "bones" and "sepulchers of their fathers" emphasized relationships with ancestors, and those to "their farms" highlighted relations to the land itself. Finally, the picture painted of "dying families" who were "driven off of their land" and were consequently "without house or friend" exposed the dire consequences of the dislocation of, or the ripping of, the Haudenosaunees from their larger "body" — the land.

Scholars have explained that such an understanding of land is present in its basic form in all Indigenous North American peoples, both in the past and in the present. Glen Sean Coulthard has called this view of land "grounded normativity," while Leanne Betamosake Simpson has used the 'Nishnaabeg term *Aki* to describe it. Likewise, Wabanaki scholar Lisa Brooks has used the metaphor of "the common pot" to discuss how Algonquin speaking groups in colonial New England understood land. Brooks has explained that groups of people on the land were obligated to fulfill their duties to each and to the land, and in so doing would ensure the reproduction and healthy management of the land, its inhabitants, and its resources. By meeting these obligations, denizens of the land were rewarded with sharing in the consumption of the land's resources. In simple terms, shared responsibilities led to mutual health and shared consumption.[22]

The insights of Coulthard, Simpson, and Brooks apply to the Haudenosaunees. Indeed, the understandings of land that these scholars have explicated, fundamentally shaped early nineteenth century Haudenosaunee behavior with regards to their land. When we acknowledge this point, we gain deeper insight into how the Senecas used their land. More importantly, we can see that how they leveraged the economic value of their lands was not solely a consequence of their simply having adopted the economic values of the settler society that saw land as an inert "natural" resource to be exploited for monetary gain. While the economic value that their lands "held" was not unimportant, the understanding that the land comprised relationships between different groups of people who were responsible for caring for and sharing the land, were arguably more consequential to how the Haudenosaunees lived on their lands in the early nineteenth century.

One important ramification of this conception of the land was that it meant that the Haudenosaunees had to take into account the presence of white Americans who lived on or near their land. More particularly, they had to consider how the land and its produce would mediate relationships between the Haudenosaunees and white Americans. For example, the chiefs at Allegheny used the Nation's property in order to acquire cash by renting the reservation's sawmill to "whites" as well as to the Haudenosaunees' "common people."[23] The sawmill was a shared resource that benefited and could be used by the groups who inhabited or lived upon the land. The rental of the mill of course generated economic benefits, but the practice of local leaders delineating who could "use" the land and its resources replicated a long-standing paradigm of Haudenosaunee land utilization practice. This paradigm was based on a reciprocal exchange in which groups who were granted access to the land repaid this benefit by sharing the gains accrued from it. In this case, the repayment came in the form of rental payment making the use of the sawmill beneficial to all involved including the "chiefs," white Americans residing on the reservation, and Seneca "commoners."

A similar pattern was at play when the Haudenosaunees rented out parcels of land owned by the tribe. In the early 1850s the Allegheny chiefs agreed, for instance, to lease a pair of two acre parcels to a railroad company that they had allowed to run a line through the reservation.[24] In addition to Seneca leaders, it was also common practice for Seneca families to rent or lease their privately owned farms to white Americans. The Quakers bristled at this practice because they wanted the Senecas to work the land themselves as they believed that farm labor developed "habits of industry." In 1845 the Philadelphia Indian Committee expressly told the Senecas to stop renting land to white families,[25] and in 1852 missionary Solomon Lukens attended a council and made "a few remarks ... on the subject of their having so many white families residing on their lands, and employing them to cultivate."[26] By renting out their farms the Haudenosaunees were on the one hand determining how they participated in the larger agricultural economy and reaping money without actually having to become farmers themselves. Yet on the other, this practice was not governed by economics alone as it was also a reinterpreted expression of Native conceptualization of the relationship amongst land and its inhabitants. In this case, the land supported both its Haudenosaunee owners, and the white tenants who rented it. In other words, the land supported all human groups who lived upon it. The economic realities of the mid-nineteenth century worked in tandem with Haudenosaunee understandings of land, it did not supplant them. Thus, Haudenosaunee conceptualizations of land as a relational system comprised of itself and its inhabitants were embedded within how the Senecas enacted their ownership of land and other pieces of real property like sawmills.

The same is true of how the Haudenosaunees utilized the produce of their lands. Simply put, they used it to facilitate and reinforce connections and relationships between the denizens of the land, thereby working to benefit all of those who inhabited it. This is most clear in the various ways the Haudenosaunees traded with those white Americans residing on or adjacent to Seneca reservations. For example, the Allegheny Senecas often engaged with the growing market economy through trading goods produced from their lands. One way they accomplished this was through harvesting the reservation's natural resources and then trading these resources for basic foodstuffs. Quaker missionary Ebenezer Worth noted that the Senecas had decided to "harvest sugar," by which he meant maple sap, for trade. The Haudenosaunees traded other goods as well in exchange for food. Worth reported that many Seneca men built and traded rafts to whites who worked for lumbering operations on lands bordering Seneca reservations. Worth explained that sugar and rafts were often given in exchange for "meat, meal, and potatoes."[27] The Senecas also worked their own lumbering operations, cutting and selling timber. The Allegheny Reservation was particularly well suited to lumbering as it was rich in hemlock trees. The Haudenosaunees would cut timber, build rafts, and float logs down the Allegheny River to be sold at mills. The Quakers were dismayed by Seneca involvement in the lumber business and reported that the Natives often drank aboard their rafts as they transported timber loads.[28] They repeatedly tried to dissuade Seneca men from lumbering by warning them that lumbering was unsustainable since timber was a limited resource. They argued that farming provided the only renewable source of support for the Haudenosaunees and advised them to focus attention on it.[29] Nonetheless, Seneca men ignored these arguments and continued to lumber because it was a productive source of income. Yet again, it would be a mistake to see these practices as only about monetary gain. They were also about connection. The shared labor Haudenosaunee men experienced working timber, for instance, also allowed for bonding, especially during down time. As male timber workers floated down river on log rafts, for instance, they used the time to drink and talk. And the broader trade of goods between the Haudenosaunees and white Americans was surely understood by the Natives as reciprocal exchanges in which groups mutually benefited. Again, engagement with the market economy did not displace older Haudenosaunee understandings of the profound social meanings contained within the exchange of material goods.

One way that we know the Haudenosaunees continued to see themselves as connected to those white Americans who lived near them is because they explicitly drew upon their connections to them during the repeated removal crises of the mid-nineteenth century. In so doing, the Haudenosaunees rejected the dominant social assumptions that guided the American government's Removal policy and instead behaved in accordance with their belief that linkages between the various peoples on the land produced power. In other words, while the US government envisioned Natives as impediments to American "progress," the remedy for which was either the extirpation of Natives from their lands or "assimilation," the Haudenosaunees combated Removal by drawing on an ontology that saw power and benefit in the relationships between groups who lived in the same place. In this case, such power was to be found in relations with the white Americans who lived adjacent to Seneca reservations. The Haudenosaunees specifically argued that their proximity to white Americans was beneficial. Writing to President Jackson they explained "we are now surrounded on every side by the white people. We love them and suffer no inconvenience from them, but on the contrary, We desire from them great and permanent assistance." The Natives inverted the logic that proponents of Removal used to justify emigration by insisting that their well-being lay in continued proximity to white Americans. Though it was in part a calculated, political argument, the Haudenosaunees nonetheless made the case for a multiracial occupation of the land, and consequently expressed a vision of social relations governed by the idea that interconnected groups benefited rather than lost through their links to each other. "We believe we can continue at home and be at peace with our neighbors," they concluded.[30]

Indeed, the Senecas actively put to the test the idea that their relationship with white neighbors was an asset by directly enlisting their aid in the Haudenosaunees' fight against the Treaty of Buffalo Creek. They used white neighbors to substantiate their argument that a corrupt and relentless abuse of power had been used to pressure the Natives to support the Treaty. In concert with their Quaker allies, they asked several citizens of Chattaqua County, New York to draft a petition against the Buffalo Creek Treaty. The signatories included important officers such as the sheriff, officers of the court, the district attorney, fourteen other attorneys, and all twenty members of the grand jury. Eighty-nine other white citizens also signed the document. The petitioners explained that they were not against Removal as a general policy. "We admit the benefits that would result to the white population from their [the Senecas] removal, & concede to the proper authorities the right to adopt such measure." This notwithstanding, the citizens of Chattaqua were nonetheless upset because the Indian Commissioners had used pressure and subterfuge to coerce the Haudenosaunees to sign the treaty. As they put it "we have been desirous that our Indian neighbors might judge it for their interest to emigrate; but no motives of interest can induce us to approve of that result, if effected [sic] by deception, fraud, or violence." The petition then confirmed that the Senecas had rejected the treaty in Council and it detailed the "iniquitous" methods the Indian Commissioners had used after the Council to obtain Seneca signatures, including "intoxication" and "large rewards." The petitioners continued that they wanted the government to act "in good faith" and to "protect the rights of the feeble." What had happened surrounding the signing of the Buffalo Creek Treaty had proved sufficiently odious to the citizens of Chattaqua to motivate them to come to the aid of the Senecas. Most importantly though, this aid was forthcoming because the Haudenosaunees had drawn upon their ethical sensibilities in order to involve a group of white neighbors in efforts to resist Removal.[31]

* * *

By the turn of the nineteenth century, American settler civilization was well on its way to overlaying itself upon the Haudenosaunees. Through the first half of the century, the Haudenosaunees would consistently face the twin existential threats of Removal and assimilation. In such an environment, the Senecas experienced profound cultural changes. These changes were apparent on the land itself as the Haudenosaunees increasingly took up family farming, allowed the construction of railroads, built sawmills and taverns, and opened schools for their children. In addition, forms of Christianity took root within Seneca communities.

Despite these changes, the Haudenosaunees remained an Indigenous people. One reason why is because they continued to see and live in the world as such. When examining Haudenosaunee religiosity, it is perhaps more useful to investigate Seneca ontology rather than religion itself. This is because ontology's focus on structure, rather than religion's concern with faith or belief, is most helpful in analyzing the thought processes of Native peoples, including the Haudenosauness. The Haudenosaunees understood the world as comprised of systems of interconnected relationships. This formed the base of their ontology and did not require "faith" that the world was indeed arranged in this manner. One important way that the Haudenosaunees reproduced themselves as Indigenous people then, especially in an environment in which they continually had to contend with an expanding settler civilization, was by living in accordance with a world that they understood as relational in its foundation.

In practice this meant continuing to enact values that had long been used to align Indigenous peoples and societies with the relational and interconnected world they perceived. Values like *alliance building, ritual kinship, peaceful dispute resolution*, and *reciprocity* were meant to tap into the power of the universe so as to produce good and healthy lives. This is what we can see happening with the Haudenosaunees of the early nineteenth century. Despite the substantive cultural changes brought on by living with an ever present settler state, the Haudenosaunees were able to reproduce themselves as Native people by embedding their ontological values inside of the cultural structures adopted in response to the extreme pressures brought on by the political and socio-economic power wielded by American civilization. There were of course practical benefits to be had from some degree of cooperation with cultural transformation, including the generation of fiscal income and the ability on the part of the Senecas to cite cultural change as a reason why they should not be forcibly removed from their homelands. But these pragmatic benefits should not elide our ability to see that the Haudenosaunees nonetheless lived as Indigenous people despite the cultural changes they experienced. If we look closely, we can clearly see that they enacted the central values of their long-standing ontological conceptualization of the universe. We see the Haudenosaunees living by this ontology and its associated values in their alliance building with the Quaker missionaries who lived on their lands, and in the relationships they established with their white neighbors who resided adjacent to them. We also see it in how they crafted their written constitution and in the ways that they used their lands vis-à-vis the expanding market economy. The significance of Haudenosaunee adherence to their Native ontology was that it served as one vital avenue through which the Haudenosaunees were able to regenerate themselves as Indigenous peoples despite the fact that they were beset by a colonizing entity that envisioned the eventual erasure of Indigeneity itself.

FURTHER READING

Brooks, Lisa. *Our Beloved Kin: A New History of King Philip's War*. New Haven: Yale University Press, 2018.

Byrd, Jodi. *The Transit of Empire: Indigenous Critiques of Colonialism*. Minneapolis: University of Minnesota Press, 2011.

Coulthard, Glen Sean. *Red Skin, White Masks: Rejecting the Colonial Politics of Recognition*. Minneapolis: University of Minnesota Press, 2014.

Hauptman, Laurence. *In the Shadow of Kinzua: The Seneca Nation of Indians Since World War II*. Syracuse: Syracuse University Press, 2016.

Simpson, Audra. *Mohawk Interruptus: Political Life Across the Borders of Settler States*. Durham: Duke University Press, 2014.

Simpson, Leanne Betasamosake. As We Have *Always Done: Indigenous Freedom through Radical Resistance*. Minneapolis: University of Minnesota Press, 2017.

BIBLIOGRAPHY

Bowes, John P. *Land Too Good for Indians: Northern Indian Removal*. Norman: University of Oklahoma Press, 2016.

Brooks, Lisa. *The Common Pot: The Recovery of Native Space in the Northeast*. Minneapolis: University of Minnesota Press, 2008.

Coulthard, Glen Sean. *Red Skin, White Masks: Rejecting the Colonial Politics of Recognition*. Minneapolis: University of Minnesota Press, 2014.

Dowd, Gregory. *A Spirited Resistance: The North American Indian Struggle for Unity, 1745–1815*. Baltimore: Johns Hopkins University Press, 1992.

Fisher, Linford. *The Indian Great Awakening: Religion and the Shaping of Native Cultures in Early America*. New York: Oxford University Press, 2012.

Martin, Joel W., Mark A. Nicholas, and Michelene E. Pesantubbee, eds. *Native Americans, Christianity, and the Reshaping of the American Religious Landscape*. Chapel Hill: University of North Carolina Press, 2010.

Leavelle, Tracy Neal. *The Catholic Calumet: Colonial Conversion in French and Indian North America*. Philadelphia: The University of Philadelphia Press, 2012.

Simpson, Leanne Betamosake. As We Have *Always Done: Indigenous Freedom Through Radical Resistance*. Minneapolis: University of Minnesota Press, 2017.

Wallace, Anthony. *The Death and Rebirth of the Seneca*. New York: Vintage, 1972.

Wolfe, Patrick. *Settler Colonialism and the Transformation of Anthropology: The Politics and Poetics of an Ethnographic Event*. London: Cassell, 1998.

NOTES

1   I am using "Haudenosaunees" to mean only the tribe of Iroquois who are often referred to as the Senecas. Many use "Haudenosaunees" to refer to the entire Iroquois Confederacy. I will use the terms Haudenosaunees and Senecas interchangeably throughout this essay.

2 Solomon Lukens to Thomas Evans, April 7, 1851, AA41, Box 3, # 232, PYMIC Correspondence, Records of PYMIC, Quaker Collection, Special Collections, Haverford College.

3 Solomon Lukens to Philadelphia Yearly Meeting Indian Committee, January 14, 1850, AA41, Box 3, #177, PYMIC Correspondence, Records of PYMIC, Quaker Collection, Special Collections, Haverford College.

4 Joseph Elkinton to his son, 1853, Indian Records Vol. 1–10, AB 31, 1851–1860, Records of PYMIC, Quaker Collection, Special Collections, Haverford College.

5 A settler society is one which arises from a process that scholars generally call settler colonialism. Settler colonialism is defined by two main characteristics. First, it is a colony in which the colonizing group seeks permanent settlement for themselves and for their posterity. Second, the settler colony works for the displacement, erasure, or subordination of the people indigenous to the place in which the colony is planted. For a study of settler colonialism see Patrick Wolfe, *Settler Colonialism and the Transformation of Anthropology: The Politics and Poetics of an Ethnographic Event* (London: Cassell, 1998).

6 Anthony Wallace, *The Death and Rebirth of the Seneca* (New York: Vintage, 1972).

7 Linford Fisher, *The Indian Great Awakening: Religion and the Shaping of Native Cultures in Early America* (New York: Oxford University Press, 2012).

8 Tracy Neal Leavelle, *The Catholic Calumet: Colonial Conversion in French and Indian North America* (Philadelphia: The University of Philadelphia Press, 2012).

9 Joel W. Martin, Mark A. Nicholas, and Michelene E. Pesantubbee, eds., *Native Americans, Christianity, and the Reshaping of the American Religious Landscape* (Chapel Hill: University of North Carolina Press, 2010).

10 More precisely, I am using ontology in accordance with its two main meanings. Thus by ontology I mean "the nature of being" and also the relationships and values that structure that nature.

11 Removal refers to the US government policy that sought to relocate Indigenous peoples who lived east of the Mississippi River. Such groups were to be moved onto lands west of the Mississippi. This policy became law with President Andrew Jackson's signing of the Indian Removal Act in May 1830. For a discussion of Removal in the northern United States see John P. Bowes, *Land Too Good for Indians: Northern Indian Removal* (Norman: University of Oklahoma Press, 2016).

12 Solomon Lukens to Philadelphia Yearly Meeting Indian Committee, January 14, 1850, AA41, Box 3, PYMIC Correspondence, Records of PYMIC, Quaker Collection, Special Collections, Haverford College.

13 Blue Eyes, James Robinson, John Pierce, and John Long to Philadelphia Yearly Meeting Indian Committee, April 27, 1821, AA41, Box 1, #109, PYMIC Correspondence, Records of PYMIC, Quaker Collection, Special Collections, Haverford College.

14 Report of the Committee to visit the Indians on the Allegheny, December 12, 1845, Indian Records Vol. 1–10, AB 30, 1841–1850, Records of PYMIC, Quaker Collection, Special Collections, Haverford College.

15 Journal entry on April 21, 1827, AB 39, Journal of Joseph Elkinton, Records of PYMIC, Quaker Collection, Special Collections, Haverford College.

16 Such a strategy was not uncommon among Northeastern Indigenous peoples. See for example Gregory Dowd, *A Spirited Resistance: The North American Indian Struggle for Unity, 1745–1815* (Baltimore: Johns Hopkins University Press, 1992).

17 Susannah Wood to Rebecca, March 3, 1853 in Notebook of Susannah Wood, copied by Margaret Lightfoot, April 19, 1883, in AA41, Box 5, PYMIC Correspondence, Records of PYMIC, Quaker Collection, Special Collections, Haverford College.

18 Solomon Lane to Philadelphia Yearly Meeting, March 30, 1849, AA41, Box 1, #156, PYMIC Correspondence, Records of PYMIC, Quaker Collection, Special Collections, Haverford College.

19 The Iroquois of course had an indigenous variant of a constitution, only it was not in written form. Rather it was enacted ceremonially. Their constitution had governed the Iroquois Confederacy since the twelfth century.

20 To see the constitution I am discussing see, "Laws of the Seneca Nation, January 28, 1854, Indian Records Vol. 1–10, AB 31, 1850–1861, Records of PYMIC, Quaker Collection, Special Collections, Haverford College.

21 "Seneca Indians No. 1" in the *New York Daily Advertiser, Vol. II, Issue 489*, November 4, 1818.

22 See Glen Sean Coulthard, *Red Skin, White Masks: Rejecting the Colonial Politics of Recognition* (Minneapolis: University of Minnesota Press, 2014); Leanne Betamosake Simpson, *As We Have Always Done: Indigenous Freedom Through Radical Resistance* (Minneapolis: University of Minnesota Press, 2017); and Lisa Brooks, *The Common Pot: the Recovery of Native Space in the Northeast* (Minneapolis: University of Minnesota Press, 2008).

23 Ebenezer Worth to Philadelphia Yearly Meeting Indian Committee, June 22, 1846, Indian Records Vol. 1–10, AB 30, 1841–1850, Records of PYMIC, Quaker Collection, Special Collections, Haverford College.

24 John and Susanna Wood to Philadelphia Yearly Meeting Indian Committee, no date, Indian Records Vol. 1–10, AB 31, 1850–1861, Records of PYMIC, Quaker Collection, Special Collections, Haverford College.

25 Report of the Committee to visit the Indians on the Allegheny, December 12, 1845, Indian Records Vol. 1–10, AB 30, 1841–1850, Records of PYMIC, Quaker Collection, Special Collections, Haverford College.

26 Solomon Lukens to the Philadelphia Yearly Meeting Indian Committee, March 2, 1852, Indian Records Vol. 1–10, AB 31, 1850–1861, Records of PYMIC, Quaker Collection, Special Collections, Haverford College.

27 Ebenezer Worth to Philadelphia Yearly Meeting Indian Committee, April 3, 1844, Indian Records Vol. 1–10, AB 30, 1841–1850, Records of PYMIC, Quaker Collection, Special Collections, Haverford College.

28 Ebenezer Worth to Philadelphia Yearly Meeting Indian Committee, February 1, 1845, Indian Records Vol. 1–10, AB 30, 1841–1850, Records of PYMIC, Quaker Collection, Special Collections, Haverford College.

29 Solomon Lukens to Philadelphia Yearly Meeting Indian Committee, January 14, 1850, AA41, Box 3, PYMIC Correspondence, Records of PYMIC, Quaker Collection, Special Collections, Haverford College.

30 "Address of the Seneca to the President," unknown date between 1838 and 1842, AA44 Folder, 5, #57, Records of PYMIC, Quaker Collection, Special Collections, Haverford College.

31 "Citizens of the County of Chatauque to the Honourable the Senate of the United States," February 1838, AA44, Folder 5, #28, Records of PYMIC, Quaker Collection, Special Collections, Haverford College.

Chapter Fifteen

MORMONS AND TERRITORIAL POLITICS IN THE AMERICAN CIVIL WAR ERA

Brent M. Rogers
The Joseph Smith Papers, Salt Lake City, Utah

While territorial politics can often appear boring and irrelevant to the larger story, learning more about the intersections of religion and politics in Civil War-era territories is crucial to understand the period. The debate over Utah Territory, especially, reveals much about western expansion, popular sovereignty, and slavery's future. Indeed, viewing the era through the lens of the Church of Jesus Christ of Latter-day Saints — whose members, more commonly known as Mormons,[1] moved from New York to Ohio to Missouri to Illinois before eventually settling near the Great Salt Lake in the late 1840s — provides a unique perspective on local authority, territorial politics, and federal sovereignty, key phrases in the era's sectional conflict that led to the American Civil War.

Perhaps the best place to begin is by looking at a point of departure in the political ideologies of Americans and Latter-day Saints. American republicanism established a representative form of government. In this system, political power is held by the people who exercise their collective will to elect representatives. A successfully run republican government, then and now, depended on independent voters selecting principled representatives to run a government that privileged societal needs over individual self-interest. Contradicting this political culture saturated with republican ideas, the political principles embodied in Latter-day Saint scripture were not republican, but rather featured governments run by prophet-kings. The locus of power for Latter-day Saints was their prophet, whom they believed had direct communion with deity. Flowing downward from the prophet was a leadership structure of men enriched with priesthood authority, or the believed power to act for God. The concepts of prophets and priesthood are certainly religious in nature, but, in the antebellum era and beyond, these concepts have had significant ramifications for Latter-day Saint political behavior. In other words, American republican government privileges the democratic voice of the people. Latter-day Saints privilege priesthood authority and prophetic voice.

Joseph Smith was recognized as the first prophet and president of the Latter-day Saint Church, which he organized in 1830. In America at that time the majority in national politics, particularly those affiliated with the Democratic Party, promoted states' rights or local autonomy. Fearing that use or abuse of federal power would upset the precarious balance in the union, especially as it related to the omnipresent slavery issue, Democratic political figures leaned increasingly toward majority rule and local will.[2] An illustration of this localized

A Companion to American Religious History, First Edition. Edited by Benjamin E. Park.
© 2021 John Wiley & Sons, Inc. Published 2021 by John Wiley & Sons, Inc.

political power is seen in the Mormon experience in Missouri. Confrontations with neighbors in Jackson County, Missouri forced Latter-day Saints from their homes in fall 1833 and after the Missouri state legislature created a "Mormon county" in 1836, the state governor, Lilburn W. Boggs eventually issued an executive extermination order in 1838 that called for the removal of or death for all Mormons. That faith group therefore faced state-sanctioned violence. First at the county level then at the state, local majority power was used to subvert their constitutional rights. This tactic of employing states' rights rhetoric and local power was used in other places, particularly against enslaved blacks in the South, as well as against other minority groups for decades to come. Minority rights were not protected under the prevalent idea of states' rights.[3]

When they appealed to legislators and government officials in the nation's capital, Latter-day Saints were consistently directed back to state or local authorities because, they were told, their complaints revealed violations of state, and not federal, law.[4] Among the proponents of this localist philosophy was Martin Van Buren. While serving as president of the United States in the winter of 1839–1840, Van Buren told Mormon petitioners, including Joseph Smith, that the federal government could provide no redress for their expulsion from the state of Missouri because the persecution incidents were a matter to be handled at the state level.[5] Van Buren, a staunch Jackson Democrat, waxed political when he told Smith that his cause was just but that he could do nothing for fear that he would "come in contact with the whole State of Missouri."[6] The president would not intervene on the Mormons behalf, especially if Missouri officials had not invited his arbitration.

Van Buren's sentiment rankled Joseph Smith. The Mormon leader felt betrayed that the president would yield to the power, and votes, of a state when American citizens' First Amendment right to exercise religious freedom was being violated. The president and federal government, Smith thought, had the power to protect citizens, but in the Mormons' case chose not to act. Yet Smith was wrong in this assumption. The First Amendment did not protect the freedom of religion from state or municipal governments, as those entities could, according to one historian, "constrain religious belief in any way they saw fit."[7] Despite Smith's thinking and hope, the federal government had incredibly limited power to protect religious belief and practice at this time because the Bill of Rights did not apply to the state or local level. Smith and the American president therefore had differing concepts of the free exercise of religion and the role the government had in providing for it. And while Smith emerged from his meeting with the president as part of a vanguard advocating for the federal protection of religious rights, this would not be the last time that a Mormon and American government official would see the First Amendment differently.[8] In fact, the differences and disagreements only intensified, even if their perspectives later flipped.

The Latter-day Saints made several appeals to Congress over the next few years, all of which met with almost identical replies. The federal government's denial of their appeals based on the states' rights philosophy signaled to members and leaders of the sect that no level of government would ensure to them their Constitutional rights. That Latter-day Saints received no justice for their Missouri encounters from any level of government left them dismayed at American republican governance in practice.

Latter-day Saints really wanted to have it both ways. They wanted to be protected by American political institutions and republicanism when it suited them, but they also wanted to be governed by the dictates of their prophet and priesthood leaders. In late 1840, as Latter-day Saints were building a new settlement on the east bank of the Mississippi River, the Illinois legislature granted the religious community a charter to legally organize Nauvoo as a city with expanded municipal powers. The Nauvoo charter allowed Latter-day Saints the privilege to form a city council, a municipal court with jurisdiction over local cases and the power to issue writs of habeas corpus, and a local militia unit, which was known as the Nauvoo Legion and was led by Joseph Smith.[9] The combination of powers in the charter and the exercise of those powers in Nauvoo effectively made the Mormon community a self-governing and self-protecting entity.[10] But that growing power generated in nonbelieving neighbors fears of Mormon despotism. Based on the power of the Nauvoo city charter they witnessed Latter-day Saints use the city's laws and militia to shield their prophet from arrest. Those outside the Latter-day Saint faith also believed that all church members would vote only according to the dictates of ecclesiastical leaders.

The Mormons, particularly their leaders, did not observe a strict separation between church and state.[11] In 1844, when Joseph Smith campaigned for the nation's executive office he offered up a theodemocratic model, or a blend of American republicanism and divine authority, as the ideal form of republican government. Smith wanted to reform what he viewed as a corrupt governing system in the United States. He believed that only "theodemocracy" could guarantee and protect individual liberties and rights, regardless of race or religious minority status.[12] As a part of his efforts to become president he established a secret organization, the Council of Fifty, designed to protect the religious rights and worship practices of the Latter-day Saints.[13] At a 18 April 1844 meeting of the Council of Fifty, Joseph Smith closed his remarks by saying that the only difficulty with the Constitution of the United States was that it lacked "the power to carry the laws into effect," and that it needed to be altered "so as to make it imperative on the officers to enforce the protection of all men in their rights."[14] Smith understood theodemocracy as an opportunity for "the people to get the voice of God and then acknowledge it, and see it executed."[15] Brigham Young, a member of the council and a leader in the church, similarly stated "No line can be drawn between the church and other governments, of the spiritual and temporal affairs of the church. Revelations must govern. The voice of God, shall be the voice of the people."[16] Only by God's direction, these men thought, could the United States be properly governed; this sentiment, however, flew in the face of the American ideal separating church and state.

Whisperings of the secret council, Smith's plans for the presidency, and the Mormon consolidation of power in Nauvoo drew the ire of other Americans. Critics called Joseph Smith the "Mormon King" and non-Mormons generally viewed his religious community as a mighty and independent empire governed by an ecclesiastical dictator who sought "after monarchal power and authority."[17] Non-Mormons in western Illinois struck back at the empire, which culminated in a mob killing Smith in Carthage, Illinois on 27 June 1844. Brigham Young then assumed the role of leading the church and eventually the mantle of prophet. Having experienced a series of violent encounters that they cast as religious persecutions, Young and the Latter-day Saints decided to physically leave the United States in early 1846. They were willing to go to great lengths to achieve the twin goals of security and self-rule. Rather than immigrate to another state in the Union and have the trauma of Missouri and Illinois repeat, they instead left the nation's borders in search of a new place to make *their* country where they could govern themselves without interference.[18]

As the religious group prepared to leave the United States, many speculated that they would become a subversive threat to the expanding American nation. A *New York Sun* article claimed that the refugees would establish a mighty and independent "Mormon empire" on the Pacific coast.[19] However, while in Iowa heading west in 1846, the religious exiles accepted President James K. Polk's call to create a Mormon Battalion to serve in the US-Mexico War then taking place. Polk had been elected on a platform to enlarge the American empire to the Pacific Ocean. In creating a Mormon military contingent, Polk specifically wanted to conciliate the Mormons after their tumultuous first fifteen years and "prevent them from assuming a hostile attitude towards the United States" after their arrival in the West. Polk feared that disgruntled Latter-day Saints would side with Mexicans or the British against the United States in the war. He, like the press, believed they would create a sovereign protectorate in Upper California, thereby potentially jeopardizing American expansionist designs.[20] That failed to materialize, as the United States acquired the far west from Mexico as a result of the war. The federal government and the empire it represented now faced a new challenge to colonize, organize, and integrate new peoples and lands into the body politic even as it attempted to hold together a nation that was being torn apart by the politics and practice of slavery.

Meanwhile, Latter-day Saints under Brigham Young's direction settled near the shore of the Great Salt Lake in the Great Basin of the Intermountain West, a place that put them once again in the boundaries of the United States of America. They had not escaped the nation's clutches, but they still wanted to establish and exercise political, legal, and cultural power for the fullest measure of self-rule in their new location.[21] They also wanted to protect the exercise of their religious practices, which by this time included polygamy, or the marriage of one man to more than one woman. The Latter-day Saints, based in their previous experiences, understood the power of local autonomy and they wanted to have it in their own sovereign space.

They did so initially by forming their own provisional government structured similarly to the church with the prophet at the head and other ecclesiastical leading men in civil governing positions. The Latter-day Saints believed these men of God could run Christ's church. They also considered their church leaders capable to run the civil government.[22] The saints did not want their society governed by strangers who opposed their will and their desire to protect their religious rights and practices. Rather than wait for Congress to act, Latter-day Saint leaders set up a provisional civil government to suit their "present necessities" and satisfy their local needs. They also hoped their initiative would convince the federal government that they were capable of being a "sovereign and Independent state into the Union upon an equal footing with the original states."[23]

Mormon leaders soon petitioned Congress again. This time, however, they wanted to receive protection in the form of statehood. They drew up a grand proposal that sought a large, sprawling geographic space for their community ranging from present-day San Diego, California, to Denver, Colorado. They called this space the State of Deseret. The proposed constitution of Deseret outlined a republican form of government where all political power came from the people.[24] Brigham Young, though, differed in his understanding of a republican form of government. "A Republican Government consists in letting the people rule by their united voice," Young declared, "without a dissension; in learning what is for the best and unitedly doing it. This is true Republicanism."[25] The Latter-day Saint prophet described why he believed theocracy was the ideal form of republican government. To know God's will, he explained, meant to do and choose right. The will of the people, then, would choose to exercise God's will. Young, and by extension the Mormon people, saw no apparent contradiction between republicanism and theocracy. Young even suggested that a theocratic government was in every sense of the word "a republican government, and differs but little in form from our National, State, and Territorial Governments."[26]

These terms were crucial. Republicanism was the common ideology of the American people, and individualism the hallmark of American character. Mormonism was neither republican nor individual. It was characterized by a centralized authority, a hierarchy leading a highly unified people that extended religious and familial ideologies into temporal and governmental affairs. The Mormons' combining of church and state, which was inherent in its operation of a theocratic form of government, made it impossible for the federal government to trust their loyalty.[27]

What was true republicanism to Mormons was tyrannical to other Americans who were suffused in the political culture of democracy. Like reactions to Mormon Nauvoo, public rhetoric about Latter-day Saints in the Great Basin underscored the nation's collective angst that the religious group had already established a "quasi-independent" government that would resist the authority of the federal government. One newspaper declared that "there is a principle involved in the Mormon organization which is hostile to the republican principle on which all our institutions rest — something hostile even to the republic itself, which in the eyes of the Latter Day Saints, is only a part of the 'Gentile' earth, destined, in the fullness of time, to be brought under the Mormon sway."[28] Though just one example, this editorial and others like it indicate that the American public worried that American republican expansion was unsafe in the hands of the Latter-day Saints.

The fear of Brigham Young's power over the civil government came from a similar nativist strain in antebellum America that voiced ardent opposition to immigrants and Catholics, whose perceived social practices placed loyalty to the church and Pope above allegiance to republican notions of civic governance. Protestants feared Catholics and viewed them as unfit for citizenship. Such alarm intensified in the antebellum era alongside misgivings about Mormon theocracy and hierarchy. Americans believed Catholics were a threat to and possessed the potential to subvert American republicanism, in the same way that they viewed Mormons. When Americans differed with each other politically, it was often over their perceptions of what most threatened the survival of republicanism, and Americans almost universally viewed Brigham Young and his followers as a dire threat to republicanism in the West.[29]

What made these concerns about Latter-day Saints more pressing was national politics, as the proposal for the State of Deseret was rejected during the intense debate over how to organize the Mexican war cession into geopolitical entities. The larger political context, of course, centered on territory and slavery. As one delegate wrote, "The exciting and distract-ing subject of slavery, in connection with the California and Territorial questions, has been the standing topic of discussion."[30] Prior to this point, the nation's politicians had continu-ally compromised when it came to slavery. Yet the desire for compromise was now waning, as northerners were increasingly concerned with the growth of slavery into western spaces. Americans agreed that the Constitution left to the States the issue of slavery. However, the Constitution also gave Congress the power to "make all needful rules and regulations respect-ing the territory," thereby making the federal government responsible for slavery in new territories. Such was the case in antebellum America.

With a vast expanse of new land being actively organized by the federal government, pro-slavery interests wanted to ensure that its peculiar institution was able to grow with the American empire. Not everyone agreed. In fact, even before the nation acquired the lands from Mexico, a congressman from Pennsylvania named David Wilmot proposed that Congress prohibit slavery from all lands acquired from the war with Mexico. Southerners threatened, as early as 1846, that if such a proposition was ever enacted, they would secede from the Union. What was becoming clearer was that there were competing visions for American expansion and empire.

Congress finally settled on another compromise in 1850 that brought California into the Union as a free state and, thanks in large part to the tireless efforts of Illinois Senator Stephen A. Douglas, organized New Mexico and Utah into territories fashioned out of the land remaining from the Mexican cession. Utah Territory, named after the Utes, one of the larger Native American groups of the Great Basin, replaced the proposed State of Deseret. The federal government did not recognize Utah's settler population as capable or loyal enough to bestow upon them the autonomy they craved. It also denied their statehood request. Instead, Latter-day Saints became subject to federal purview in the territorial system.[31] Utah and New Mexico were organized based on popular sovereignty, a political doctrine that ena-bled the inhabitants of each territory to determine whether they would permit slavery and certain domestic institutions within their geopolitical boundaries. As Congress agreed to the Compromise of 1850, popular sovereignty emerged as the guiding principle. It was meant to take the federal government out of the equation on the slavery question. Popular Sovereignty made territorial politics critical to the nation moving forward.

Talk of popular sovereignty, or local self-government with freedom from Congressional interference in determining domestic institutions, particularly the expansion of slavery, pervaded antebellum political discourse. Many Americans, primarily those affiliated with the Democratic Party, believed that the territories were entitled to local self-government, like the position of the states in the United States' system of dual sovereignty. Democrats had long advocated the limitation of federal powers and the extension of local autonomy. Southern Democrats especially feared federal aggression and authority. In the 1850s, therefore, the focus shifted to the territories, particularly the power of territorial populations to make legislative decisions outside of Congressional interference. This strategy, the Democrats hoped, would resolve the national tension as it related to slavery extension and United States geographic expansion. The solution appeared to once again favor local self-government.

Despite the rhetoric of popular sovereignty, in the American system of federalism, territories were not sovereign in themselves, but under federal jurisdiction. As a by-product of expansion, the federal government, vested with sovereignty over the territories by the Constitution and other foundational national laws, sought to extend its power to control new territories in the West and ensure that the peoples in those lands conformed to American political traditions.[32] In the process to prepare territories for statehood, the President appointed federal officers including governors, prosecutors, judges, Indian agents, surveyors, and others, to supervise a territory's population, elections, and passage of territorial laws. Federal officers were constitutionally mandated to ensure that a properly functioning republican form of government operated within the bounds of each territory.[33] In addition, the president oversaw military operations and gave orders for any US troops stationed in the territories.[34]

When the federal government organized the territories of Kansas and Nebraska in 1854, the issue of slavery and popular sovereignty arose again. The final legislation creating those territories declared, "It being the true intent and meaning of this act not to legislate slavery into any Territory or State, nor to exclude it therefore, but to leave the people thereof perfectly free to form and regulate their domestic institutions." A literal fight then occurred in Kansas over the ensuing years as pro-slavery and free-soil advocates poured into the boundaries of the new territory.[35] Each side organized rival governments and vigilantes sought to coerce the people through violence.

Even as the watchful nation monitored "bleeding Kansas," the Mormons in Utah hoped the vague language of domestic institutions meant popular sovereignty was adaptive. But it was designed solely as a placation for slavery interests, a one size approach for a singular issue. It was not adaptive, or at least not adaptive enough to encompass the Mormons' appeals. Popular sovereignty was a means to keep slavery alive and growing. But, they argued, and others (primarily those in the emerging Republican Party) thought it ought to include, among other matters, family affairs and marriage. Mormons believed in, practiced, and supported plural marriage. Though seen as immoral by Protestant America, Latter-day Saints claimed the right to practice polygamy because of local will and popular sovereignty. There was, at this point, no federal law on marriage, and Mormons touted the idea of local determination. Latter-day Saints, like slaveholders, opportunistically embraced popular sovereignty in hope that it would provide them cover and protection for the practice of their own "peculiar institution." They simultaneously feared that a territorial government would result in federal control exercised by non-Mormons, which would reverse the autonomy they were trying to build with their colony in the Great Basin. They hoped that their version of "true republicanism" would prevail and that they would be allowed to elect their own civil leaders. After all, states' rights, congressional compromises, and early 1850s legislation had emphasized local autonomy. In this context, Utah Territory once again became a key battleground and hotbed of antebellum American political debate and discourse. Utah Territory and its Mormon population were an unintended wrinkle in popular sovereignty drawn into national conversations about government authority.

The pivotal 1856 presidential election placed territorial politics on the center stage, situating popular sovereignty and Utah in the cross hairs. James Buchanan, the Democratic candidate, campaigned on a platform that recognized and adopted "the principles contained in the organic laws establishing the Territories of Kansas and Nebraska." The platform emphasized that popular sovereignty in the territories embodied "the only sound and safe solution of the 'slavery question.'" Buchanan's candidacy and the Democrat's platform reinforced decades of party politics, and they maintained that local choice triumphed in American republican governance.

John C. Frémont, the Republican candidate, conversely campaigned on a platform that put popular sovereignty and local choice in the territories to the test. The 1856 election was the first for the Republican Party and it quickly put the nation on notice that it had a new vision for the expanding American empire. Frémont's platform stated, "That the Constitution confers upon Congress sovereign powers over the Territories of the United States for their government; and that in the exercise of this power, it is both the right and the imperative duty of Congress to prohibit in the Territories those twin relics of barbarism — Polygamy, and Slavery." Polygamy, of course, referred directly to Utah Territory, as it was the only territory where citizens practiced plural marriage. Mormons therefore challenged the assumption of local autonomy in the territories, an assumption that Mormons wanted to maintain and now enjoy despite a long history of local power being used against them.[36]

The Republicans further made morality and moral policing a national issue (though typically left to state jurisdiction) by inextricably linking the immoral and generally reviled practice of polygamy with the deeply controversial institution of slavery. The twin relics connection generally offended southern slave owners who considered themselves morally superior to the western religionists who practiced a truly peculiar institution of plural marriage. These individuals clung to the Democratic promise of local choice when it came to their peculiar institution. To Republicans, on the other hand, the growth of either institution was deemed unacceptable in their new vision of the emerging American empire. Buchanan nevertheless won the critical 1856 election, only to preside over a nation teetering precariously on the brink of war over the issue of slavery expansion into the western territories.

The problem of Utah and its Mormon population did not disappear after the election. Since the early days of the Church of Jesus Christ of Latter-day Saints, those outside the faith perpetuated an image of them as embracing separation from the United States and attempting to take the west coast by conquest for their new and independent empire.[37] The Buchanan Administration bought into this belief and agreed that the Mormons' singular society led by the faith's leader Brigham Young was a threat to civil republicanism and federal interests in the West. Strong federal action was needed in Utah. Secretary of War John B. Floyd wrote of the Mormons: "This people have claimed the right to detach themselves from the binding obligations of the laws which governed the communities where they chanced to live. They have substituted for the laws of the land a theocracy." Utah Territory chief justice John F. Kinney similarly advised the White House that the "Mormons are inimical to the Government of the U.S."[38] Kinney declared that federal officers in Utah could only do their jobs if sustained by a military force. Jacob Thompson, the secretary of the interior, also advocated using military force in Utah Territory to uphold the Constitution and federal laws.

In late May 1857, just over two months after his inauguration, President James Buchanan made the decision to send about one quarter of the standing US Army, approximately 2500 troops, to Utah Territory in what has become known as the Utah War. In his first public remarks about this decision, Buchanan stated that Brigham Young had a dictatorial thirst for power and that he led his followers as a despot.[39] Federal authority was under attack and the government needed to renew its sovereign supremacy in this western territory and over this minority people. This was a decisive move that demonstrated federal jurisdiction over the territories.

This was not the only influential federal action taken in early 1857. Just as James Buchanan took office, the US Supreme Court ruled in the case *Dred Scott v. Sandford*. The *Dred Scott* ruling upheld the right of an American citizen to hold slaves in any federal territory and asserted that territories could not exclude slavery.[40] While the decision appeared to overrule the doctrine of popular sovereignty, the political and rhetorical battle over the territories continued unrelentingly. The rightful and legal obligation of the federal government to manage the territories and ensure that a republican form of government was established and maintained within them still applied and Utah remained at the crux of western territorial supervision.[41] Because of this constitutional responsibility, Buchanan defended his action to send an army to Utah Territory as legitimate.

Other major political figures also supported the president's decision. Though he pushed back on the federal power embedded in the *Dred Scott* decision, Democratic Senator and popular sovereignty promoter Stephen A. Douglas paradoxically argued in favor of the federal offensive in Utah. He declared that the "Mormon government" was not a republican form of government based on their religious practice of polygamy and subversive alliances with American Indian tribes. Congress, he thought, had the right to repeal the territory's organic act, remove it as a geopolitical entity, and assert greater federal sovereignty over that jurisdiction. Douglas further articulated a position that the Mormons disavowed their allegiance to the United States, and they were "alien enemies and outlaws, unfit to exercise the right of self-government." The Illinois senator and chairperson of the Senate Committee on Territories emphasized that Mormons were incapable of exercising popular sovereignty in the territory and that they only sought political autonomy to "protect them in their treason and crime, debauchery and infamy." Furthermore, he argued that to protect them in their "treasonable" and "bestial" practices by allowing them to govern themselves would be a disgrace to humanity and civilization and potentially fatal to American interests in the West. Douglas advocated no temporary policy or halfway measures, but rather decisiveness on the Utah question. When it came to Latter-day Saints in Utah, he was now promoting strong federal power over local popular will.[42]

However, the president's military action in Utah and Senator Douglas's harsh rhetoric came with a cost. Many Americans soon perceived that federal military action in Utah contradicted the longstanding Democratic Party principle of popular sovereignty and local authority. Republicans did not disagree with the government's power over the territory, as their 1856 party platform had demonstrated, but made a direct connection to the overarching issue of local self-government and slavery. The most important critique came from Republican up-and-comer Abraham Lincoln.

Lincoln offered a strong rebuttal to the Democratic direction in Utah. Popular sovereignty supposedly secured to the people of the territories the right to live with and legislate domestic institutions as they pleased, but the Democrats had moved to regulate the popular will of Latter-day Saints and force federal sovereignty onto them. "This thing of Squatter Sovereignty was never anything but a humbug," Lincoln asserted, because it was designed to extend slavery to the West. And it was. Lincoln used an opportunity presented to him by Douglas's renunciation of the Mormon version of popular sovereignty to attack the expansion of slavery by the same principle.[43] Lincoln proclaimed: "To be sure, it would be a considerable backing down by Judge Douglas from his much vaunted doctrine of self government for the territories; but this is only additional proof of what was very plain from the beginning, that that doctrine was a mere deceitful pretence for the benefit of Slavery." Popular sovereignty was never intended to ensure the will of the people, Lincoln emphasized, and he used the Latter-day Saint institution of plural marriage to hammer home the point. "Those who could not see that much in the Nebraska Act itself, with forced Governors, and Secretaries, and Judges on the people of the Territories, without their choice or consent," Lincoln stated before reminding his audience, "There is nothing in the United States Constitution or law against polygamy? And why is it not a part of the Judge's 'sacred right of self government' for that people to have it, or rather to *keep* it, if they choose?"[44] Lincoln explained that the

Mormons simply had not used popular sovereignty according to the Democratic Party's plan to protect slavery interests.

With this speech, Lincoln articulated a stark quandary facing the Democrats and the nation. If Congress could enact laws, or the President could send an army to eliminate plural marriage, the same federal power used to regulate one domestic institution in a western territory could be used against another, like slavery. Assertive and explicit legislative and military action to crush Utah's domestic institutions violated the Democratic Party's doctrine of popular sovereignty and aggravated southern fears about restrictions on future slavery expansion and threats to its very existence. This was the logical extension of the 1856 Republican Party platform, which sought to prohibit polygamy and slavery in the territories. President Buchanan may have hoped to unite a nation fracturing over slavery expansion, but his Utah operation and the support of it by other Democrats such as Stephen A. Douglas illustrated the potential for federal aggression in the territories. It did not take long for the nation to understand that, by virtue of its responsibility over the territorial system, the federal government could indeed act to prohibit slavery expansion in the West.

While it is important to note that President Buchanan was very careful not to mention polygamy as a cause of his sending the troops to Utah, likely hoping to maintain the distance between slavery and polygamy so adeptly connected by the Republican Party, the public and politicians alike understood the action as a measure to eradicate polygamy. It also was a move to interrupt local autonomy with federal force. The doctrine of local self-government had dominated political discourse for decades. The Democrats acted in defense of popular sovereignty and local choice as it related to slavery but were quick to assert control over an undesirable religious population in the West. At that politically contested time, however, such a trend toward federal authority did nothing to alleviate Southern concerns about the future of slavery. And Republicans like Abraham Lincoln highlighted this inconsistency.[45]

The Mormons, too, chafed at the discrepancy. They defended their believed right to local sovereignty and domestic arrangements with the argument that if they could be punished for their private institutions, so too could slaveholders. Church leader Orson Pratt declared, "Undertake to deprive the people of this one domestic institution," polygamy, and "you can, upon the same principle, deprive them of all others."[46] The Mormons found themselves on the wrong end of the political pendulum again. For years they were told the federal government had no power, but that local and state governments did. But now the federal government exercised its sway over local choice. Doing so further undermined the Democratic policy of popular sovereignty; it demonstrated the fundamental flaw of a localist philosophy in the territorial system.

Southerners watched the Utah War with some interest. Though initially supportive of the federal march against a reviled religious group, the popular sovereignty debates that followed reminded them of their lingering fears of national authority. Southern Democrats soon understood that popular sovereignty could not provide the protection for slavery that they coveted. It could just as easily be an antislavery as a proslavery doctrine. A fracture emerged between Northern and Southern Democrats that helped widen the gulf of sectionalism in the late 1850s. Southern Democrats, long afraid of federal power, reversed course on their long cherished local autonomy. Local choice was not enough. They needed the federal government to step in and Southern legislators went so far as to demand a federal slave code from Congress in 1860 to guarantee the sanctity of slave property. The future president of the Confederacy, Jefferson Davis, likewise sought to gain a constitutional guarantee for slavery in the territories. Such efforts proved the death knell for the popular sovereignty ideology.[47]

When the federal government demonstrated its unwillingness to protect slavery's expansion and after the nation elected a Republican president in 1860, Southerners eventually made good on the promise articulated in the debates over the Wilmot Proviso: with slavery all but prohibited in the western territories they seceded from the Union. Later, in mid-1862, with the nation entangled in civil war, Abraham Lincoln signed legislation that officially barred slavery from United States territories. About the same time, he also passed an act outlawing plural marriage in the territories. Lincoln thus fulfilled the 1856 Republican Party platform plank to "prohibit in the Territories those twin relics of barbarism — Polygamy, and Slavery."[48] The president and federal government no longer compromised on slavery's growth. For more than a decade legislators and presidents had tried to placate slavery interests and stave off the ultimatum Southerners had given David Wilmot in 1846. But Americans could no longer delude themselves. Federal authority could be and had been used in the territories. It was employed in Utah against an outcast religious population. That strong federal action added a large crack to the weakening dam holding back the raging flood waters of civil war. After the dam broke and the flood waters eventually receded, the federal government emerged dominant and with a singular vision for the American empire.

Mormons were often at the center of politics of the West. Their experience helps explain how and why territorial politics mattered in the American Civil War era and beyond. Moreover, when placed in a broader context, the history of the Latter-day Saints provides a multifaceted example of the complexities of religious and minority difference and power dynamics in American history.

FURTHER READING

Childers, Christopher. *The Failure of Popular Sovereignty: Slavery, Manifest Destiny, and the Radicalization of Southern Politics.* Lawrence: University Press of Kansas, 2012.

Etcheson, Nicole. *Bleeding Kansas: Contested Liberty in the Civil War Era.* Lawrence: University Press of Kansas, 2004.

Mason, Patrick Q. "God and the People: Theodemocracy in Nineteenth-Century Mormonism." *Journal of Church and State* 53, no. 3 (Summer 2011): 349–375.

Morrison, Michael A. *Slavery and the American West: The Eclipse of Manifest Destiny and the Coming of the Civil War.* Chapel Hill: University of North Carolina Press, 1997.

Park, Benjamin E. *Kingdom of Nauvoo: The Rise and Fall of a Religious Empire on the American Frontier.* New York: Liveright, 2020.

Rogers, Brent M. *Unpopular Sovereignty: Mormons and the Federal Management of Early Utah Territory.* Lincoln: University of Nebraska Press, 2017.

BIBLIOGRAPHY

"Affairs in Utah," *North American and United States Gazette*, 13 June 1853.

Baugh, Alexander L. "A Call to Arms: The 1838 Mormon Defense of Northern Missouri." PhD diss., Brigham Young University, 2000.

Berkhofer Jr., Robert F. "The Northwest Ordinance and the Principle of Territorial Evolution" in John Porter Bloom, ed., *The American Territorial System.* Athens: Ohio University Press, 1973.

Bigler, David L. and Will Bagley. *The Mormon Rebellion: America's First Civil War.* Norman: University of Oklahoma Press, 2011.

Bloom, John Porter, ed. *The American Territorial System.* Athens: Ohio University Press, 1973.

Boritt, Gabor S. ed. *Why the Civil War Came.* New York: Oxford University Press, 1996.

Buchanan, James. "First Annual Message to Congress on the State of the Union." 8 December 1857. Online at Gerhard Peters and John T. Woolley, *The American Presidency Project*, https://www. presidency.ucsb.edu/node/202407.

Bushman, Richard Lyman. *Joseph Smith: Rough Stone Rolling.* New York: Vintage, 2007.

_____. *Believing History: Latter-day Saint Essays.* Edited by Reid L. Neilson and Jed Woodworth. New York: Columbia University Press, 2004.

_____. "The Book of Mormon and the American Revolution." *Brigham Young University Studies* 17 (Autumn 1976): 3–20.

Cartwright, James F. "John M. Bernhisel Letter to Brigham Young." *Brigham Young University Studies* 22 (Summer 1982): 358–362.

Childers, Christopher. *The Failure of Popular Sovereignty: Slavery, Manifest Destiny, and the Radicalization of Southern Politics.* Lawrence: University Press of Kansas, 2012.

Collection of Missouri Documents, Church History Library of the Church of Jesus Christ of Latter-day Saints, Salt Lake City, UT.

Dirkmaat, Gerrit J. "Enemies Foreign and Domestic: US Relations with the Mormons in the US Empire in North America, 1844–1854." PhD diss., University of Colorado, 2010.

Etcheson, Nicole. *Bleeding Kansas: Contested Liberty in the Civil War Era.* Lawrence: University of Kansas Press, 2004.

Flanders, Robert Bruce. *Nauvoo: Kingdom on the Mississippi.* Urbana and Chicago: University of Illinois Press, 1975.

Fluhman, J. Spencer. *"A Peculiar People": Anti-Mormonism and the Making of Religion in Nineteenth-Century America.* Chapel Hill: University of North Carolina Press, 2012.

Gienapp, William E. "The Crisis of American Democracy: The Political System and the Coming of the Civil War." In *Why the Civil War Came*, edited by Gabor S. Boritt, 79–124. New York: Oxford University Press, 1996.

Godfrey, Matthew C. "'Seeking after Monarchal Power and Authority': Joseph Smith and Leadership in the Church of Christ, 1831–1832." *Mormon Historical Studies* 13 no. 1–2 (Spring/Fall 2012): 15–37.

Godfrey, Matthew C., Spencer W. McBride, Alex D. Smith, and Christopher James Blythe, eds. *The Joseph Smith Papers: Documents, Volume 7: September 1839–January 1841.* Salt Lake City: Church Historian's Press, 2018.

Grow, Matthew J. *"Liberty to the Downtrodden": Thomas L. Kane, Romantic Reformer.* New Haven and London: Yale University Press, 2009.

_____, Ronald K. Esplin, Mark Ashurst-McGee, Gerrit J. Dirkmaat, and Jeffrey D. Mahas, eds. *The Joseph Smith Papers: Administrative Records: Council of Fifty, Minutes, March 1844–January 1846.* Salt Lake City: The Church Historian's Press, 2016.

Hedges, Andrew H., Alex D. Smith, and Brent M. Rogers, eds. *The Joseph Smith Papers: Journals, Volume 3: May 1843–June 1844.* Salt Lake City: The Church Historian's Press, 2015.

Hicks, Edward L. "Republican Religion and Republican Institutions: Alexander Campbell and the Anti-Catholic Movement." In *The Stone-Campbell Movement: An International Religious Tradition*, edited by Michael W. Casey and Douglas A. Foster. Knoxville: University of Tennessee Press, 2002.

"Highly Important from the Mormon Empire on the Mississippi." *New York Herald*, 21 May 1842.

Holt, Michael F. *The Political Crisis of the 1850s.* New York: W. W. Norton & Co., 1983.

Johnson, Clark V., ed. *Mormon Redress Petitions: Documents of the 1833–1838 Missouri Conflict.* Provo: Religious Studies Center, Brigham Young University 1992.

"Kansas — The Mormons — Slavery: Speech of Senator Douglas: Delivered at Springfield, Ill, 12 June 1857." *New York Daily Times*, 23 June 1857.

Kimball, Jr., James L. "A Wall to Defend Zion: The Nauvoo Charter." *BYU Studies* 15, no. 4 (1975): 491–497.

_____. "The Nauvoo Charter: A Reinterpretation." *Journal of the Illinois State Historical Society* 64 (Spring 1971): 66–78.

Lamar, Howard R. *The Far Southwest, 1846–1912: A Territorial History*, revised ed. Albuquerque: University of New Mexico Press, 2000.

Leonard, Glen M. *Nauvoo: A Place of Peace, A People of Promise.* Salt Lake City and Provo: Deseret Book Co. and Brigham Young University Press, 2002.

LeSueur, Stephen C. *The 1838 Mormon War in Missouri.* Columbia: University of Missouri Press, 1987.

"Life in Nauvoo." *New York Daily Tribune*, 28 May 1844.

"Lincoln's Springfield Speech." *Chicago Tribune*, 29 June 1857.

MacKinnon, William P., ed. *At Sword's Point, Part I: A Documentary History of the Utah War to 1858.* Norman: The Arthur H. Clark Company, an imprint of the University of Oklahoma Press, 2008.

McBride, Spencer W. "When Joseph Smith Met Martin Van Buren: Mormonism and the Politics of Religious Liberty in Nineteenth-Century America." *Church History* 85, no. 1 (March 2016): 150–158.

McDonald, Forrest. *States' Rights and the Union: Imperium in Imperio, 1776–1876.* Lawrence: University Press of Kansas, 2000.

Message from the President of the United States. January 9, 1852. 32d Cong., 1st Sess., House of Representatives, Ex. Doc. 25.

Morgan, Dale L. *The State of Deseret.* Logan: Utah State University Press, 1987.

Mason, Patrick Q. "God and the People: Theodemocracy in Nineteenth-Century Mormonism." *Journal of Church and State* 53, no. 3 (Summer 2011): 349–375.

Neilson, Reid L. and Nathan N. Waite, eds. *Settling the Valley, Proclaiming the Gospel: The General Epistles of the Mormon First Presidency.* New York: Oxford University Press, 2017.

Onuf, Peter S. *Statehood and Union: A History of the Northwest Ordinance.* Bloomington: Indiana University Press, 1987.

Peters, Gerhard and John T. Woolley. The American Presidency Project. https://www.presidency.ucsb.edu/.

Potter, David M. *The Impending Crisis: America Before the Civil War, 1848–1861.* New York: Harper Perennial, reprint ed., 2011.

Quaife, Milo Milton ed. *The Diary of James K. Polk, During his Presidency.* Vol. 1. Chicago: A. C. McClurg & Co., 1910.

"Remarks, by President Brigham Young, Bowery, Sunday Morning, September 13, 1857." *Deseret News,* 23 September 1857.

"Reply to Senator Douglas: Speech of Hon. A. Lincoln, of Indiana." *New York Daily Times,* 4 July 1857.

"Report of Gov. Ford." *The Ottawa (Illinois) Free Trader,* 10 January 1845.

Rogers, Brent M. *Unpopular Sovereignty: Mormons and the Federal Management of Early Utah Territory.* Lincoln: University of Nebraska Press, 2017.

Sehat, David. *The Myth of American Religious Freedom.* New York: Oxford University Press, 2011.

Smith, Joseph. *General Smith's Views on the Powers and Policy of the Government of the United States.* Nauvoo: John Taylor, 1844.

_____. "The Globe." *Times and Seasons (Nauvoo, Illinois),* 15 April 1844.

State of Deseret, Constitution, Church History Library of the Church of Jesus Christ of Latter-day Saints, Salt Lake City, UT.

"The Mormons." *The Raleigh (North Carolina) Register,* 23 November 1853.

"The Mormons." *Times and Seasons (Nauvoo, Illinois),* 1 December 1845.

Walker, Ronald W. "The Affairs of the 'Runaways': Utah's First Encounter with the Federal Officers, Part 1." *Journal of Mormon History* 39, no. 4 (Fall 2013): 1–43.

Watson, Harry L. *Liberty and Power: The Politics of Jacksonian America.* New York: Hill and Wang, 1990.

Watt, G. D., J. V. Long, *and others. Journal of Discourses.* 26 vols. London: Latter-Day Saints' Book Depot, 1854–1886.

Wilentz, Sean. *The Rise of American Democracy: Jefferson to Lincoln.* New York: Norton, 2005.

NOTES

1   In this essay, I use "Mormons" and "Latter-day Saints" interchangeably to refer to members of the Church of Jesus Christ of Latter-day Saints. I recognize that there are other individuals, institutions, and practices that trace their religious origin back to Joseph Smith during the timeframe covered by this essay and that they are part of the umbrella of Mormonism. Nevertheless, this essay focuses solely on the history of the Church of Jesus Christ of Latter-day Saints.

2   Sean Wilentz, *The Rise of American Democracy: Jefferson to Lincoln* (New York: Norton, 2005), 320–360; Harry L. Watson, *Liberty and Power: The Politics of Jacksonian America* (New York: Hill and Wang, 1990), 117–131. For more on states' rights issues and the division of power at various government levels, see, for instance, Forrest McDonald, *States' Rights and the Union: Imperium in Imperio, 1776–1876* (Lawrence: University Press of Kansas, 2000).

3   These ideas culminated with and are encapsulated in Joseph Smith's 1844 presidential platform, see Joseph Smith, *General Smith's Views on the Powers and Policy of the Government of the United States* (Nauvoo: John Taylor, 1844).

4   See Lewis Cass to A. S. Gilbert, et. al., 2 May 1834, Collection of Missouri Documents, folder 4, CHL.

5   Letter to Hyrum Smith and Nauvoo High Council, 5 December 1839, in Matthew C. Godfrey, et al., eds., *The Joseph Smith Papers: Documents, Volume 7: September 1839–January 1841* (Salt Lake City: Church Historian's Press, 2018), 66–73.

6   Letter to Hyrum Smith and Nauvoo High Council, 5 December 1839, 69.

7   David Sehat, *The Myth of American Religious Freedom* (New York: Oxford University Press, 2011), 4.

8   Spencer W. McBride, "When Joseph Smith Met Martin Van Buren: Mormonism and the Politics of Religious Liberty in Nineteenth-Century America," *Church History* 85, no. 1 (March 2016): 150–158.

9   James L. Kimball, Jr., "A Wall to Defend Zion: The Nauvoo Charter," *BYU Studies* 15, no. 4 (1975): 491–497. James L. Kimball, Jr., "The Nauvoo Charter: A Reinterpretation," *Journal of the Illinois State Historical Society* 64 (Spring 1971): 66–78; Richard Lyman Bushman, *Joseph Smith: Rough Stone Rolling* (New York: Vintage, 2007), 412–416; Glen M. Leonard, *Nauvoo: A Place of Peace, A People of Promise* (Salt Lake City and Provo: Deseret Book Co. and Brigham Young University Press, 2002), 91–92, 101–119.

10 J. Spencer Fluhman, *"A Peculiar People": Anti-Mormonism and the Making of Religion in Nineteenth-Century America* (Chapel Hill: The University of North Carolina Press, 2012), 96; and Robert Bruce Flanders, *Nauvoo: Kingdom on the Mississippi* (Urbana and Chicago: University of Illinois Press, 1975), 284.

11 Patrick Q. Mason, "God and the People: Theodemocracy in Nineteenth-Century Mormonism," *Journal of Church and State* 53, no. 3 (Summer 2011): 353.

12 Joseph Smith, "The Globe," *Times and Seasons*, 15 April 1844. As early as 27 August 1843, Smith publicly declared his belief that the perfect law and form of government came through God giving the law to the people and the people abiding by that law. Joseph Smith, Journal, 27 August 1843, in Andrew H. Hedges, Alex D. Smith, and Brent M. Rogers, eds., *The Joseph Smith Papers: Journals, Volume 3: May 1843–June 1844* (Salt Lake City: The Church Historian's Press, 2015), 85–87.

13 Matthew J. Grow, et al., eds., *The Joseph Smith Papers: Administrative Records: Council of Fifty, Minutes, March 1844–January 1846* (Salt Lake City: The Church Historian's Press, 2016), xiii (hereafter cited as Council of Fifty, Minutes.)

14 Council of Fifty, Minutes, 18 April 1844, 129.

15 Council of Fifty, Minutes, xxxvi.

16 Council of Fifty, Minutes, 5 April 1844, 82–84.

17 "Life in Nauvoo," *New York Daily Tribune*, 28 May 1844; "Highly Important from the Mormon Empire on the Mississippi," *New York Herald*, 21 May 1842; see Richard Lyman Bushman, *Believing History: Latter-day Saint Essays*, ed. Reid L. Neilson and Jed Woodworth (New York: Columbia University Press, 2004), 25, 47; see also Richard L. Bushman, "The Book of Mormon and the American Revolution," *BYU Studies* 17 (Autumn 1976): 3–20; and Matthew C. Godfrey, " 'Seeking after Monarchal Power and Authority': Joseph Smith and Leadership in the Church of Christ, 1831–1832," *Mormon Historical Studies* 13, no. 1–2 (Spring/Fall 2012): 15–37.

18 For more on the history of Mormon conflicts in Missouri and Illinois see Clark V. Johnson, ed. *Mormon Redress Petitions: Documents of the 1833–1838 Missouri Conflict* (Provo: Religious Studies Center, Brigham Young University 1992); Stephen C. LeSueur, *The 1838 Mormon War in Missouri* (Columbia: University of Missouri Press, 1987); Alexander L. Baugh, "A Call to Arms: The 1838 Mormon Defense of Northern Missouri," (PhD diss., Brigham Young University, 2000); and Bushman, *Joseph Smith: Rough Stone Rolling*.

19 "The Mormons," *Times and Seasons*, 1 December 1845. This was not the first time that the Mormons had been accused of establishing an independent empire, and it would not be the last. Many of the earlier newspaper articles focused on Joseph Smith being crowned as the "Mormon King." See "Life in Nauvoo," *New York Daily Tribune*, 28 May 1844, [4]; Journal of the Senate

of the Fourteenth General Assembly of the State of Illinois, 94; "Report of Gov. Ford," *The Ottawa Free Trader*, 10 January 1845.

20 James K. Polk, Diary, 5 June 1846, in Milo Milton Quaife, ed., *The Diary of James K. Polk, During his Presidency*, vol. 1 (Chicago: A. C. McClurg & Co., 1910), 131–132; Gerrit J. Dirkmaat, "Enemies Foreign and Domestic: US Relations with the Mormons in the US Empire in North America, 1844–1854," (PhD diss., University of Colorado, 2010), 141.

21 Dale L. Morgan, *The State of Deseret* (Logan: Utah State University Press, 1987), 23.

22 Catholics in New Mexico believed similarly about their religious leaders. See Howard R. Lamar, *The Far Southwest, 1846–1912: A Territorial History*, revised ed. (Albuquerque: University of New Mexico Press, 2000), 77–87.

23 "Memorial signed by members of the Legislative Assembly of Utah to the President of the United States," 29 September 1851 in Message of the President, 9 January 1852, 32nd Congress, 1st Session, Ex. Doc. No. 25, p. 33.

24 State of Deseret, Constitution, art. II, sec. 1 & 2, available at Church History Library of the Church of Jesus Christ of Latter-day Saints, Salt Lake City, UT.

25 "Remarks, by President Brigham Young, Bowery, Sunday Morning, September 13, 1857," *Deseret News*, 23 September 1857.

26 Brigham Young, "Human and Divine Government," in *Journal of Discourses*, 6:342; see also Mason, "God and the People," 359.

27 See David L. Bigler and Will Bagley, *The Mormon Rebellion: America's First Civil War* (Norman: University of Oklahoma Press, 2011), 8–9.

28 "Affairs in Utah," *North American and United States Gazette*, 13 June 1853. An article, "The Mormons," *The Raleigh Register*, 23 November 1853, stated that Brigham Young's imperious rule over both church and state in Utah Territory was the "law of its life."

29 Michael F. Holt, *The Political Crisis of the 1850s* (New York: W. W. Norton & Co., 1983), 4–5, 161–164, 176–180; Edward L. Hicks, "Republican Religion and Republican Institutions: Alexander Campbell and the Anti-Catholic Movement," in Michael W. Casey and Douglas A. Foster, eds., *The Stone-Campbell Movement: An International Religious Tradition* (Knoxville: University of Tennessee Press, 2002), 204–205.

30 John M. Bernhisel to Brigham Young, 23 April 1850, available in James F. Cartwright, "John M. Bernhisel Letter to Brigham Young," *Brigham Young University Studies* 22, no. 3 (Summer 1982): 361.

31 See, for example, Matthew J. Grow, *"Liberty to the Downtrodden": Thomas L. Kane, Romantic Reformer* (New Haven and London: Yale University Press, 2009); Ronald W. Walker, "The Affairs of the 'Runaways': Utah's First Encounter with the Federal Officers, Part 1," *Journal of Mormon History* 39, no. 4 (Fall 2013): 1–43.

32 The 1787 Northwest Ordinance and later the Compromise of 1850 and the 1854 Kansas-Nebraska Act maintained that the federal government held the ultimate sovereignty over the territories and the people therein by controlling appointments to various offices and veto power over legislation.

33 The Constitution authorized the acquisition of new territory and permitted the development of new states out of these lands, if the people within those geopolitical boundaries operated a republican form of government. US Const. art. IV, secs. 3, 4. For the founding generation and Americans that followed, republicanism meant a promise that a collection of self-governing communities would exercise their sovereignty to inhibit consolidated power and the threat of control by the few. (Watson, *Liberty and Power*, 6, 44.)

34 William E. Gienapp, "The Crisis of American Democracy: The Political System and the Coming of the Civil War," in Gabor S. Boritt, ed., *Why the Civil War Came* (New York: Oxford University Press, 1996), 113.

35 See Nicole Etcheson, *Bleeding Kansas: Contested Liberty in the Civil War Era* (Lawrence: University of Kansas Press, 2004).

36 See Brent M. Rogers, *Unpopular Sovereignty: Mormons and the Federal Management of Early Utah Territory* (Lincoln: University of Nebraska Press, 2017), 135–145.

37 Sixth General Epistle of the First Presidency, 22 September 1851, in Reid L. Neilson and Nathan N. Waite, eds., *Settling the Valley, Proclaiming the Gospel: The General Epistles of the Mormon First Presidency* (New York: Oxford University Press, 2017), 136–155; "Extract of a Letter from a

Judicial Officer of the Government," at Great Salt Lake City, 20 September 1851, in *Message from the President of the United States*, 32d Cong., 1ˢᵗ Sess., House of Representatives, Ex. Doc. 25, p. 6; *New York Herald*, 18 October 1851; *New York Herald*, 8 November 1851.

38   John F. Kinney to Jeremiah S. Black, 20 March 1857, in William P. MacKinnon, ed., *At Sword's Point, Part I: A Documentary History of the Utah War to 1858* (Norman: The Arthur H. Clark Company, an imprint of the University of Oklahoma Press, 2008), 110.

39   James Buchanan, "First Annual Message to Congress on the State of the Union," 8 December 1857, online by Gerhard Peters and John T. Woolley, *The American Presidency Project*, https://www.presidency.ucsb.edu/node/202407 accessed 8 August 2019.

40   For more on the *Dred Scott* case and decision and its importance, see, for example, David M. Potter, *The Impending Crisis: America Before the Civil War, 1848–1861* (New York: Harper Perennial, reprint ed., 2011); Christopher Childers, *The Failure of Popular Sovereignty: Slavery, Manifest Destiny, and the Radicalization of Southern Politics* (Lawrence: University Press of Kansas, 2012.)

41   The Constitution authorized the acquisition of new territory and permitted the development and addition of new states out of these lands, if the people in those geopolitical entities operated a republican form of government. US Const. art. IV, secs. 3, 4. For the founding generation and Americans that followed, republicanism meant a promise that a collection of self-governing communities would exercise their sovereignty to inhibit consolidated power and the threat of control by the few. (Watson, *Liberty and Power*, 6, 44; see also Robert F. Berkhofer Jr., "The Northwest Ordinance and the Principle of Territorial Evolution" in John Porter Bloom, ed., *The American Territorial System* (Athens: Ohio University Press, 1973), 45; Peter S. Onuf, *Statehood and Union: A History of the Northwest Ordinance* (Bloomington: Indiana University Press, 1987), xiii.)

42   "Kansas — The Mormons — Slavery: Speech of Senator Douglas: Delivered at Springfield, Ill, 12 June 1857," *New York Daily Times*, 23 June 1857; Rogers, *Unpopular Sovereignty*, 164–168.

43   "Reply to Senator Douglas: Speech of Hon. A. Lincoln, of Indiana," *New York Daily Times*, 4 July 1857.

44   "Lincoln's Springfield Speech," *Chicago Tribune*, 29 June 1857.

45   Rogers, *Unpopular Sovereignty*, 170–177.

46   Orson Pratt, "Theocracy," in G. D. Watt, J. V. Long, and others, *Journal of Discourses*, vol. 7 (London: Latter-Day Saints' Book Depot, 1860), 226.

47   Childers, *The Failure of Popular Sovereignty*, 235–282.

48   Rogers, *Unpopular Sovereignty*, 285.

Chapter Sixteen

BLACK CHRISTIANITY AFTER EMANCIPATION

Nicole Myers Turner
Yale University, New Haven, Connecticut

According to family history, in 1869, Caroline Bragg, a formerly enslaved woman, played a central role in the establishment of St. Stephen's Episcopal Church, an all-black parish in Petersburg, Virginia. Bragg, who migrated with her family from Warrenton, North Carolina, to Petersburg after the Civil War, collaborated with the white rector of Grace Episcopal Church to found St. Stephen's. Listed among the first eight vestrymen were two of Caroline's sons — George F. and Peter — and three grandsons, David, John, and Thomas Cain. The church had a black rector, and initially housed a parish school with three black teachers including Thomas W. Cain.[1] But when the Diocese of Virginia refused to recognize the Church, the rector left in disgust and was replaced by a white priest who was a former Confederate soldier. Despite the complex racial marginalization that this turn of events reflected, the school was an important facet of community life, eventually becoming a divinity school for training black ministers and many black Episcopal priests, including noted historian, Rev. George Freeman Bragg, Jr. — Caroline's grandson — and Archdeacon James Solomon Russell.

Most histories of black churches do not begin with women or the Episcopal Church, and yet the themes of gender and race relations reflected in the story of St. Stephen's were at the heart of Reconstruction-era politics. If Reconstruction was a moment where the nation was reordered to include black men as political actors, and racism was reformulated on the basis of free labor, land, and rights definition, black churches were key sites that shaped that change. Inside black churches, enslaved communities were reconstituted in freedom and cultivated new dynamics influenced by church doctrine and political demands placed on freedpeople and their families. Black communities were rebuilt on communal church property, and patriarchy and religion conjoined to codify gender roles. Outside the church, the political landscape was complicated by these gendered ideas as well as by how freedpeople navigated with white folks who were, like Grace Episcopal Church's rector, allies in the struggle despite lingering racism. Whether and how ministers were going to wield power and engage the political landscape was also a prominent concern.

This essay focuses on the post-emancipation political activism of black church people and the racial politics of black churches after emancipation, as both are intertwined and yet distinct. It describes how black churches made the transition from slavery to freedom, as well as the ways church members and leaders participated both to secure lives for themselves and to transform the landscape of the United States' political system. Black churches, in

A Companion to American Religious History, First Edition. Edited by Benjamin E. Park.
© 2021 John Wiley & Sons, Inc. Published 2021 by John Wiley & Sons, Inc.

summary, were important sites for the formation of black post-emancipation political culture. As African Methodist Episcopal (AME) Minister Wesley J. Gaines testified before a congressional committee, "there would have been no political movement without the black church."[2] Churches were primary sites of organizing that the physical space of church buildings promoted.[3] And they were sites of spiritual and moral guidance through which black folks made sense of their struggle. Through these churches, free black and freedpeople found resources for resilience in what was still a mean world of violence and labor exploitation. They built community networks of accountability and support, raised funds to support themselves and others, defined proper relations, resolved conflicts between themselves, and interacted with white missionaries and fellow believers in a constant battle to recognize black humanity.

Religion Before Emancipation

Before emancipation and the restructuring of the United States to incorporate a racialized slave caste into government, enslaved and free black people practiced Christianity in a variety of settings that were political and spiritual at the same time. Some worshiped in the hush harbors far away from the paternalist prying eyes of enslavers but not outside of the reach of patrollers they attempted to evade with the use of upturned pots.[4] The religious practices in these clandestine places are not definitively known but are understood to be mixtures of Christianity and African Traditional Religions.[5] Others worshipped under the watchful eye of masters who sought to make a more docile enslaved population. Missionary work among enslaved people began with the Society for the Propagation of the Gospel in Foreign Parts in the 1700s and expanded with the Second Great Awakening in the 1820s–1830s as the evangelical sense that all people were created equal and each individual could approach God on their own took hold.[6] This gave rise to independent black churches and black-white interracial churches where there were many permutations of leadership. The first such churches like George Liele's Silver Bluff Church in South Carolina, established in 1773, and Andrew Bryan's First African Baptist Church in Savannah, Georgia established in 1788, had black leaders under the supervision of white preachers and trustees.[7] Sometimes the result of evangelical awakening was black and white people worshipping together, but not always on equal footing.[8] In other instances, black people had to fight for self-governance. For example, in 1816 the AME Church legally secured its independence by order of the State Supreme Court when a white minister pressed his claim to be able to preach at an AME church.[9] Sometimes segregation, and sometimes separation, was the result of these communities because, despite the initial espousal of equality, the threat to slavery was too great and white folks succumbed to pro-slavery ideology over the doctrines of faith and equality.[10]

In the antebellum era, the existence of interracial worship and racism clarified free and enslaved people's spiritual choices of denominational affiliation and reinforced black Christians' struggle for the recognition of black humanity. The religious aims of black people often transcended the racial boundaries that white supremacy tried to establish. In this regard, they joined with white folks in religious institutions because of shared doctrinal and ecclesiastical beliefs. This was true before and after the Civil War.[11] Episcopal priest and church historian, George Freeman Bragg, Jr. reinforced this idea in his account of Absalom Jones's choice to remain within the Episcopal Church after the dramatic separation of black worshippers from St. George's Episcopal Church of Philadelphia as an act of resistance against racial segregation in the house of God and its reinforcement in the midst of holy worship. While Allen chose to join a different denomination — the Methodists — Jones remained in the Episcopal Church and was ordained a priest with charge over what became the African Episcopal Church of St. Thomas, a black parish within the denomination.

In pursuing this route, Jones reaffirmed black humanity and equality and established a foothold for future black parishoners and priests to continue the struggle for the recognition of the full and equal humanity of black folks within the church.[12] For black Christians like Richard Allen, who chose separation into an independent black church and then denomination, this assertion of black humanity included the effort to compel other black people to take similar action.[13] Both staying in and separating from white churches were aimed at establishing black humanity, freedom and equality.

In addition to the resistance that staying in fellowship represented, enslaved and free black people also cultivated a theology that sustained their struggle and helped them to resist slavery. In the antebellum period, enslaved folks believed that God was on their side and that they would play a role in their own liberation.[14] Moreover, they cultivated a racial identity along with "a revolutionary sense of nationhood as both a secular and sacred priority."[15] The organization of independent black worship spaces was joined with a burgeoning set of ideas that affirmed black humanity and the pursuit of political freedoms.

There were at least two emancipations in United States history. The first round of manumissions that occurred after the First Great Awakening and the American Revolution largely made ending slavery an individual act motivated by a conscience pricked by the inconsistencies of the arguments for evangelicalism, revolution and slavery. Several northern states adopted some form of gradual abolition of slavery, allowing some people to remain enslaved until at least the 1830s. Thus, there was no bright line demarcating the pre-emancipation and post-emancipation landscapes of black religious institutions in the North. Instead, if one wanted to mark these transformations, it would be based on individual lives like Sojourner Truth and Elizabeth Manning James, the first Black Mormon. These remarkable women floated in and out of a number of the different religious communities of their time, including the AME Church, Millerites, Mormons, and the Kingdom of Matthias.

By the time federal emancipation happened, black folks in the North and South had a variety of worship experiences that reinforced their challenges to slavery. The greatest of these was the emancipation event itself, which they likened to the liberation of Israel in the book of Exodus or to Jubilee.[16] From this foundation of spiritual vindication, black Christians approached the political transformation with critiques of democracy and ambitions for themselves.[17] Their faith positioned them to critique and engage the political and social changes that reconstruction brought about. Not only did they have particular organizational and oratorical leadership skills cultivated through their church work and worship at their disposal, but they also had a sense of the way democratic society should run and a belief in their rights that translated into the way they organized and the way they participated in democracy.[18]

The cultural differences between northern and southern black people, however, meant that there were clashes between northern missionaries and the southern freedpeople they sought to aid. After the the Civil War ended, many northern black churches sent missionaries to the South because they believed they had the requisite skill and knowledge to best serve the freedpeople and that the freedpeople would be absorbed into these predominantly black churches. Those who went to the South also experienced and fostered cultural conflicts between black northerners who viewed themselves as more evolved socially and culturally than black southerners[19] Bishop Daniel Alexander Payne of the AME Church criticized black southerners for the persistence of the ring shout and extemporaneous preaching. Rev. Peter Randolph, who left from Boston, Massachusetts to become the pastor of Ebenezer Baptist Church in Richmond, Virginia, criticized the churches for the ways that they marginalized women. He sought to correct this by requiring families to sit together rather than in sex-segregated seating patterns. Randolph explained that he had been trained in the North and his ideas were influenced by that context.[20] Many of the northern and western abolitionist associations dissolved into the denominational and state associations whose missions shifted focus to establishing networks of religious community. Other black missionaries like Charlotte Forten went South under the auspices of white northern organizations. Forten went to South Carolina with a contingent of northern missionaries. Unlike some of the more critical northerners, Forten found the enslaved children to be eager to learn and as skilled and studious as northern white children, and in some instances even better, when one considered the more numerous opportunities and resources northern white children had.

Inside Black Churches

Emancipation set the stage for a new expression of black religion. The black church of Reconstruction was not just an extension of the institutional church of the pre-emancipation period or an evolution of the hush harbor traditions, however. Black churches of emancipation were a new creation. The institutional church merged with the separate black religious worship spaces established under slavery.[21] These new churches, built on the institution of the family and cultivated alongside the fledgling black press, rose to political prominence both within and outside the black community. No longer under the legalized supervision of white people, freedpeople established new churches, new denominations, new patterns of internal and external relations, even as they retained familiar practices like the discipline meeting, the annual association meeting or even their membership in predominantly white denominations. Within these new churches, liberation entailed a spiritual eschatology and changes in the literal landscape of religious life where property ownership accrued to former property, black political representation was real, democratically selected representatives, and independence from white leadership and open critique were possible.

Even as black churches made these important advancements toward meaningful freedom, they did not create an uncomplicated sense of black community regarding gender roles. Black churches grappled with how freedom changed gender roles and responsibilities while the vestiges of the slave institution that wreaked havoc on domestic ideals, concepts of family and gendered responsibilities continued to affect relations between black men and women. In this context, black women's place was circumscribed in relation to their roles in the community.

From Enslaved Religion to Independent Black Churches

Freedpeople's choices about where to worship after emancipation were influenced by many factors. Most freedpeople separated themselves into independent black churches and denominations after emancipation. Though white racism was a provocation for black separation from white churches, the desire for freedom also was an important motivator.[22] Some black ministers saw the formation of independent black churches as an eschatological moment, or as a development in the long story of the return of Christ. While the great majority left the denominations and churches of their enslavers in search of freedom from racial discrimination in the Lord's house, others sought positive religious freedom — the freedom to worship where, how and under what doctrinal decrees they chose.

Forming separate black churches was as much a fulfillment of first amendment rights to religious freedom as to biblical claims of independence reflected in the verse from the prophet Micah that "they shall sit every man under his vine and under his fig tree."[23] Some did so immediately, others after a period of seeking a way forward with white fellow believers. Black Christians did not just choose from what was already on offer; they created their own denominations. For some this process involved a tour through different denominations in search of what felt right to them.[24] In one instance in Mecklenburg County, Virginia, black Baptists and Episcopalians worshipped together as they carved out their path to what religious community looked like. This gathering eventually formed its own denomination, the Zion Union Apostolic Church in 1869.[25]

In other instances, freedpeople chose to remain in white denominations because they believed the doctrine and liturgy, even if mishandled by humans. Whatever the pathway, most ended up in separate black Baptist and Methodist churches, and in a few instances, separate denominations altogether. Black Methodists, in separate denominations like the AME Church, started with a small contingent of 20,000, but had grown to 400,000 by the 1880s. The AMEZ Church experienced similar growth, going from 4,600 members in 1860 to 300,000 by 1884.[26] Notably, by 1877 black people had withdrawn almost completely from white churches; only Catholic churches managed to retain some black members, likely because they did not have the same practices of segregation that other Protestant denominations did.[27]

The pathway to these independent churches often began with pursuit of property ownership, as enslaved people participated in purchasing property despite the legal impossibility of the act. The formation of independent black churches was yet another expression of freedom and black church members often had to establish this independence through purchasing their own buildings and getting their own ministers. Reports from the Freedman's Bureau indicate that they had contributed funds to purchasing property and after emancipation sought control of the same. In some instances, white fellow believers willingly yielded the property to the freedpeople in gestures of good will and in support of their transition to freedom. In other instances, like the Immanuel Methodist Episcopal Church in Portsmouth, Virginia, white fellow believers were unwilling to yield the property and therefore self-determination to the freedpeople and refused to relinquish the property to the people who had paid for it. Purchasing church property was an important part of the freedom movement that tutored freedpeople in the operations of the legal system and allowed them to exercise the rights of citizenship — of being able to testify in courts and bring cases.[28]

Beyond the pursuit of property, which had important consequences for black political development, churches were also important sites of community development and identity formation. Churches fostered a sense of belonging and responsibility. For example, six individuals were selected to represent freedpeople of Richmond as a delegation to President Andrew Johnson to inform him of the challenges they were facing under the leadership of the Union soldiers who were overseeing the city in the transitions after the war. The delegation of six men was selected from a gathering of all of the churches of Richmond, and each church nominated one man to represent their interests. Not only were delegates selected from the churches, but the churches also served as sites for communal development through the various associations that often had roots in the churches — the benevolent and literary societies and masonic orders.[29]

Engendering Church: Black Manhood and Black Womanhood

After emancipation, black churches differentiated the roles of women and men within the churches. Though women had held significant roles in enslaved religion, after emancipation, their roles in the churches became more institutionalized and circumscribed.[30] Black women in churches faced challenges being recognized as equal partners. In the AME Church, women were appointed to the role of stewardess, but they were not granted any control over the male stewards, even though male stewards had the authority to remove stewardesses.[31] Similarly, in the Gilfield Baptist church, women could participate in the discipline meeting decision making, but they could not bring discipline cases before the church. This work was limited to the deacons.[32]

Anna Julia Cooper attested to the lack of equitable access to education black women experienced in the Episcopal Church. Reflecting on her own experience at Episcopal Church sponsored St. Augustine Normal School and Collegiate Institute in Raleigh, North Carolina, she argued that women's intellectual goals were marginalized. Cooper was a precocious child. At the age of nine she enrolled in St. Augustine and began teaching adult literacy classes soon thereafter. She studied through the normal school level before going on for additional study at Oberlin College. Cooper, who went on to become the principal of the prestigious M Street School in Washington, DC, in 1925, became the fourth black woman to earn her doctorate.

Cooper's successful trajectory began while she was at St. Augustine's and enrolled in advanced language classes that had been designated for the men going on to the ministry. This opportunity came by chance rather than by design, a fact that Cooper critiqued. In an address to black Episcopal clergy, Cooper accused the Episcopal Church of hampering black women's advancement. She said,"while yearly numerous men have been kept and trained for the ministry by the charities of the Church, the number of indigent females who have here been supported, sheltered and trained, is phenomenally small. Indeed, to my mind, the attitude of the Church toward this feature of her work, is as if the solution of the problem of Negro missions depended solely on sending a quota of deacons and priests into the field, girls being a sort of *tertium quid* whose development may be promoted if they can pay their way and fall in with their plans mapped out for the training of the other sex."[33]

In her estimation, the church's poor record of educating black women — graduating only five women in twenty years — underscored the limitations of the church's mission strategy: focusing on educating black ministers meant treating black girls and women as a indefinite, undefined, degraded or unknown element in the alchemy of educational opportunities. Indeed, Cooper's own experience bore this out.[34]

Denominational difference seemed to carry little weight in differentiating women's experiences. Whether in the African Methodist Episcopal (AME), African Methodist Episcopal Zion (AMEZ), Zion Union Apostolic, Episcopal, or Baptist churches, black women were not easily recognized as leaders. In the Baptist church, the more flexible polity and church-based leadership may have meant that the experiences differed from congregation to congregation, but there was no overarching reprieve from male domination.[35]

One way that gender roles were established was through the participation of women in decision-making. Women did participate in the discussions in the discipline meetings, and in a select few instances of unwed pregnancy. In these meetings, deacons presented members before the congregation for social, religious, and political infractions. The community then decided on the reasonable punishments — usually expulsion or censorship. However, women were most often the *disciplined* rather than disciplinarians. In the case of unwed pregnancy, women were the ones disciplined, even though, for a brief moment in one particular church, men were also held accountable. This moment of equitable practice was foreshortened, however, because the pastor argued that it caused disorder among members and was not biblically sound. The process, in other words, was not the action of holding men accountable. But in holding up so-called scriptural issues, the protection of males against charges was also reinforced.[36] In this way, the discipline meetings of the churches became tools of gender hierarchy, and they became spaces where ministers could exert a fair amount of power, though it is notable that not all ministers participated in these meetings. In Richmond, Rev. Anthony Binga, Jr. did not participate in the discipline meetings, and according to Carter G. Woodson, the first academically trained historian of black churches, only the more conservative ministers participated in the meetings, while the more progressive ones stayed out of the community fray.[37]

In the black churches after freedom, gender roles reinforced patriarchal black male leadership. Still, black women were able to exert control and influence by being the individuals who controlled the finances.[38] This authority was not simply the power of the purse where one gets to decide what happens by being able to choose what gets funded or not. The financial power black women wielded was also a spiritual power. Women became central figures in the churches through the conventions where their donations were initially and then repeatedly recognized as exemplars of sacrificial giving.[39] Not only was their sacrificial giving publicly recognized, but also black women viewed their fiscal donations as key parts of their contribution to racial uplift.[40]

Beyond the spiritual and political significance of black women's financial contributions to churches garnering them authority, gendered ideas about fundraising also bolstered their fiscal role in the churches. Women were also the ones who were able to go about asking for money. Men who were missionaries were initially the ones who were supposed to do the fundraising for the church, but most did not. Once women became missionaries, however, fundraising became an important component of their work. This idea that women were able to solicit funds and support for the church is another way that women became the financiers of black progress. This gendered idea of who could and should ask for money was a double-edged sword that opened up opportunities for black women in church leadership while also denigrating their work as "woman's work" and further limiting their horizons.[41] It should not be lost that some women resented being charged with raising money and even called attention to this exploitation, taking particular aim at the familiar chicken dinner fundraiser.[42]

Gender dynamics within black religious community seemed to track along the lines of the complicated negotiations of family and responsibility that the Freedman's Bureau espoused. Black churches, like Bureau agents, promoted nuclear black families, and women in subordinate positions. The churches were not completely consistent, though; they also wanted women to have equal political opportunity. AME ministers like Reverends Henry McNeal Turner and Richard H. Cain of Georgia and South Carolina, respectively, both advocated for black women to have the right to vote.[43] In Richmond, Virginia, women actively participated in political meetings and went to the polls with black men.[44] Notably, Turner ordained Sarah Ann Hughes, the first black woman deacon in the AME Church, an act which drew the ire of his fellow churchmen for going against the General Convention of 1884 that decided to allow women to be ordained evangelists but not preachers.[45] Despite the genderless aims for black political participation in the public sphere, within the black churches black women were viewed as women and were kept from exercising voting authority in some aspects of church life.[46]

Just as the new terrain of emancipation religious freedom created opportunity to define black women's roles in church communities, so too did black men undergo a transformation in the definition of manhood and men's roles. Now placed as heads of household and pf organizations, black men had more space to lay claim to the patriarchal qualities associated with Victorian manhood.

Again, with churches as the main institution that came under black people's control, the pulpits were an important representation of freedom. Black people explicitly wanted and pursued black preachers for their churches. At one post-emancipation Negro Convention in North Carolina, attendees voted for a resolution articulating their preference for black ministers even when they did not pass a similar resolution about black teachers.[47] These churches were places where black men and women who were disrespected and called by their first names by white children and everyone else, became Mister and Miss and held places of esteem. Pulpits were one of the most immediately available outlets for black leadership that were controlled by black people. Black men were certainly able to hold elected office in the constitutional conventions, state legislatures and local governments, but these and other positions of influence could also be determined by white people who decided who they thought the leaders of the black community should be.[48] Church leadership reflected the will of the people; the leadership that they empaneled and to which they assented. Thus, it was a position of respect and responsibility.

As a position held primarily by men, the pulpit also became a site for the construction of black manhood. For black men, it affirmed their own manhood to see another black man wielding the authority of a leadership position and being held in esteem and respected in a way that was uncommon in broader society. AME Bishop William Heard reported how much hearing William J. White speak on politics and religion inspired in him the desire to "be a MAN."[49] The ministry, when carried out by itinerant preachers, as was the case in the AME Church, was an opportunity to demonstrate the rugged strength of black ministers. Being able to withstand the rigors and physical demands of regular travel over varied terrains in changing weather conditions was a badge of honor and strength.[50] Though principal of Hampton Normal Institute, Samuel Chapman Armstrong, derided black ministers as "effete" because they did not work with their hands,[51] committing to and surviving rigorous travel challenged such an assertion. This was necessary and helpful because, with limited political and financial power, black men had little else upon which to base their claims to manhood. Black ministers were visible representations of black manhood who countered claims of black male degeneracy.

As the figures most closely related to the will of the people, black ministers also wielded political influence that allowed black manhood to become tied to political efficacy and leadership in the freedom struggle. In large measure, this was because they could argue for the protection of black women. Black manhood was predicated on the ability to protect and defend black women, and thus was reinforced after emancipation even if the reign of domestic terror and economic inequality made that role difficult to realize.[52]

They exerted this role through arguing for the establishment of schools for black women so that women could become educated and self-sufficient. Arguing to extend the franchise to black women placed black men in the role of patron. Protecting black women by withdrawing their labor to the household and using the political power of the pulpit or the priest's collar became a means of claiming black manhood.

Outside Black Churches: Political Engagement from the Pulpits to the Pews

Black churches played an important role in facilitating freedpeople's transition to freedom. As the primary institution that they controlled and a key site where black folks came together, churches shaped new gender ideas and relations between black men and women. These roles had important bearings on the political lives of the freedpeople — securing resources for development and support, clarifying shared values, ideas and accountabilities, and defining the parameters of leadership. While these configurations carried important implications for life within the communities, it also affected the landscape of political engagement by shaping ministerial leadership, debates about engaging in politics, negotiating with white people, and ultimately cultivating politically effective networks.

The political context of the immediate post-emancipation period was both tumultuous and violent. Southern states were plunged into the work of reconstructing states, communities, and eventually the political structures once the Radical Republicans of the United States Congress stepped in to ensure that the abolition of slavery would be more meaningful. The presence of federal military governors to enforce the transition by supervising the political transformation — overseeing registration of black male voters and ensuring political representation in the constitutional conventions that had to abolish slavery — reinforced southern white people's fears about the social and political transformation that was going on and that was expressed through violent domestic terrorism.

Black churches were one prime target of such violence, and this reinforces the idea that black churches were key sites of political contest during Reconstruction. These buildings were markers of the reversal of racial organization of distribution of resources and rights.

Burning them to the ground or attempting to do so was a denial of that new reality as well as an attempt to intimidate black folks from pursuing the freest expression of their existence — religious worship.[53] In Petersburg and other places, churches were sites of violence because they were not just churches but also schools, and because they marked black freedom on the landscape in a way that almost no other institutions did. Though black churches and black education were key political flashpoints after emancipation, black folks gathered to pursue freedom and contest any curtailments. They established that they wanted black leaders in their churches and black teachers in their schools, even if they were politically cowed from demanding black teachers in their schools.[54]

Ministers were among the most salient black leaders during Reconstruction. Easily recognizable because of the deferential titles they bore, they held a position of prominence within black communities. A meeting called in the final year of the Civil War by US Secretary of War Edwin M. Stanton and Union General William T. Sherman illustrates the central role ministers played. In January 1865, Stanton and Union General Sherman conducted a focus group with twenty preachers, pastors and lay church leaders in Savannah, Georgia to find out what were their attitudes toward the war, the Union and General Sherman. The group of men represented nearly 4,500 church members and shared their understandings of black people's expectations of their post-emancipation relations with white people.[55] Garrison Frazier was the elected spokesman for the collection of black men pulled together to represent the community of enslaved people. They were free born and enslaved, church leaders and lay people. Frazier was sixty-seven years old, born in Granville, North Carolina as a slave, and had been a Baptist pastor for thirty-five years. Older than most of the men who were present at the meeting, Frazier represented the various positions of the community. When asked what they understood slavery meant he said that it was taking someone's labor without paying them. When asked if they wanted to live among white people or separately, all but one preferred to live separately. This moment gave rise to Sherman's issuance of Field Order No. 15, which set apart land in South Carolina and Georgia for the use of the formerly enslaved people. This gathering was an important moment in the development and definition of freedom and it was brokered by church leaders and laity. Notably there were no women present in this discussion.

Many of the political leaders during reconstruction came from the ranks of ministerial leadership.[56] Whether this status came from their calling, or they pursued the status of the minister because of their leadership skills, varied from person to person. Ministers' calling was a topic of consideration with one visitor to South Carolina who opined that ministers "are rather preachers because they are leaders than leaders because they are preachers."[57] Added to leadership potential, ministers' qualifications included a range of expertise. Carter G. Woodson, for instance, pointed out that the black minister was able to address every situation.[58] He had to provide succor for the social and political affronts black people faced, guide and direct their spiritual lives, and even be able to recommend the best tonic for any physical malady a person might suffer. While others posited that because spiritual leadership was so valued among black people, ministers were naturally the political leaders selected to represent the community. From these places of esteem, minsters also shaped the moral culture of the people they served.

However, when it came to the political realm, preachers did not direct the community from positions at the helm, but rather reflected the views and concerns of the people they served. This was evidenced in the ways that ministers were reported to have participated in political activities around the congressional campaign of black activist John Mercer Langston. While ministers did not figure prominently in the media coverage of this signal event, they were important supporters of Langston's because their members were.[59]

Despite the inherent politics of black religion, black Christians debated whether and how black ministers and church people should engage in politics. Black Christians struggled over what role black ministers should play in politics and their positions changed over time and varied within the denominations. By the end of Reconstruction, AME ministers arrived at the position that staying out of politics was best.[60] Some black Baptists chose not to participate, while others took a much more nuanced approach suggesting that political engagement outside should not affect the dynamics within churches. By the latter part of the nineteenth century, however, it became clear that folks were using their churches to reinforce political ideology among their leaders, running ministers out of their pulpits if they supported politicians that their members did not.[61] Black church people also took positions on the political parties. For example, AME ministers critiqued Republicans for being weak supporters of black people's rights.[62] Similarly, the Hasadiah Baptist Association questioned the tactics of political party operatives. They decried the use of alcohol to ply the voters' support and cautioned members against engaging in politics, not because of the political failures of the party, but rather the morally questionable tactics they deployed.[63]

The extent to which ministers participated in politics through office-holding varied considerably across geography. The percentage of black men who served in political office who were ministers varied by state and by region. About sixteen percent (237 of 1465) of black office holders were ministers.[64] As much as 85 percent (sixteen out of nineteen) of the constitutional convention delegates in Georgia were ministers.[65] In the Upper South states, like Virginia, by contrast, the percentage was much lower — only about 25 percent of the Constitutional Convention delegates were black and a smaller percentage of those were ministers. Political leadership by black church ministers was powerful, but also diverse.

Even as ministers held political office at varying levels, the political ideology of black Christians varied and was very much influenced by their theology and racial ideology.

When ministers chose their political allies, sometimes they aligned with the landed aristocracy — former plantation owners — and did not push education or land issues. These positions have been attributed to master-slave dynamics, in which black people became accustomed to accommodating white folks. These alliances were particularly prevalent in the Deep South.[66]

Political conservatism among black religious folks and their leaders was not only explained by their social status before emancipation but rather by their beliefs. The conservatism of black ministers that historian William Montgomery identifies was less a reflection of their prior conditions of servitude, as many were not enslaved or came from the North to pastor congregations, but rather came from their faith and their sense of right moral practice. This was evident in the evangelical uses of the bible to which they subscribed and how they used the bible to articulate values around temperance and land.[67]

However, this is perhaps a too facile explanation of how black church ministers or black people in general navigated the complicated racial dynamics of emancipation. After emancipation, freedpeople immediately dropped the deferential behaviors enforced upon enslaved people, which caused considerable concern among white southerners.[68] Some church people adopted a gradualist approach to racial equality because they believed it would work. Changing social and political dynamics too quickly, they argued, might incite more violence and resistance from white people. And freedpeople who had little access to the resources that could sustain them needed time to develop the skills, education, and finances to secure freedom in the new political and economic landscape. Nevertheless, the intractable nature of racism ensured that, speed notwithstanding, black progress was to be impeded at all costs.

Other black church people, standing on their theological interpretations of a liberating god and a universal church, pursued political equality immediately, even if they demurred at the notion of pursuing social equality.[69] These interpretations led them to pursue equality inside the churches and they might have refused to yield the sidewalk to white women or demanded that they be called by their honorifics-Reverend, Elder, Mister and Miss. The landscape of resistance within religious faith and community was more complicated than binaries of accommodation or protest suggest.

There were also moments of collaboration or combination as the freedpeople sought to carve out the meaning of freedom for themselves. Sometimes this resulted in conversations where they tried to preserve their autonomy and sense of freedom but also sought to remain religiously affiliated with co-religionists of shared beliefs. This was not, however, easily achieved in the face of white supremacy that required black subservience and that overrode the dictates of faith that called for human equality, dignity, freedom and respect.

In the church associations, the full scope of black religious politics — engagement of leadership and laity, radicalism and conservatism, comes into focus. Additionally, these sites illuminate how black religious organizations supported and sustained black political engagement. Black Christians participated in the political landscape of freedom by building strong spiritual and social networks that were the basis of political claims. Immediately after emancipation, black Christians met in associations of churches as a means to foster greater dialogue and support for the fledgling independent churches that dotted the landscape of freedom. These annual meetings began as regional associations, and in the case of Virginia even became a state convention. As the years passed, these associations' aspiration to unite black Baptists in the state and in the nation grew stronger and the associations achieved these goals by sending delegates to association meetings in the state and throughout the country. These delegates represented the tendrils that connected the ideas and experiences of the association members and carried with them messages that filled in the details of what connected them — the development of the churches, their financial status, leadership, and growth, messages of greeting and empowerment.

The messengers and missives connected black folks across political and geographical boundaries and fostered the foundations of a black religious political culture. These networks formed the basis of patronage political claims. This is one of the ways churches became sites of political organizing, but it is also important to note that the political networks extended beyond individual churches and ministers as politicians' efforts to organize using these broader networks of churches in associations and state convention meetings reveal.[70]

Conclusion

Black church politics during Reconstruction was a new kind of politics. The changed landscape of freedom and inclusion changed the ways black churches and leaders engaged the political landscape, and even what black churches meant. They added to their status as spiritual sustainer and as a central site for independent development of community. And just as the independence of black church communities was taking shape, so too were ideas about gender roles in free and freed black communities. Thus, black womanhood and manhood were constructed in the churches of freedom. Churches that once facilitated the development of home grown and at times clandestine leadership now promoted public leaders that stood outside of the clutches of white politics and thus could be fully accountable to black people and developed networks that not only sustained and fostered community development but also became agents of political change.

The arrival of the gendered political black church reinforced the political changes of Reconstruction in defining black freedom and supporting political change, but it did not break the racism that mutated and permeated the political landscape and even the churches. By the closing decades of the nineteenth century, black political alliances were weakened, gendered dynamics within churches were more pronounced and black churches engendered a new phase of political development. Once churches became agents in the political sphere, decisions about whether to engage politics became more pronounced and the disappointments like segregation, and disfranchisement were responses to the powers that they had amassed.

Women forged their own venues for leadership that played important roles in supporting and sustaining black community. Black hope rooted in an emancipationist theology that God delivered black folks from slavery persisted through the networks and associations that had been established. These were the foundations that supported later generations' efforts to mobilize for rights in the twentieth century.

FURTHER READING

Angell, Stephen W. *Bishop Henry McNeal Turner and African-American Religion in the South.* Knoxville: The University of Tennessee Press, 1992.

Bailey, Julius H. *Around the Family Altar: Domesticity in the African Methodist Episcopal Church, 1865–1900.* The History of African-American Religions Series. Edited by Stephen W. Angell and Anthony B. Pinn. Gainesville: University Press of Florida, 2005.

Brown, Elsa Barkley. "Negotiating and Transforming the Public Sphere: African American Political Life in the Transition from Slavery to Freedom." In *The Black Public Sphere: A Public Culture Book,* edited by Houston Baker, Jr. Black Literature and Culture. Chicago and London: The University of Chicago Press, 1995.

Harper, Matthew. *The End of Days: African American Religion and Politics in the Age of Emancipation.* Chapel Hill: The University of North Carolina Press, 2016.

Turner, Nicole Myers. *Soul Liberty: The Evolution of Black Religious Politics in Postemancipation Virginia.* Chapel Hill: The University of North Carolina Press, 2020.

BIBLIOGRAPHY

Angell, Stephen W. *Bishop Henry McNeal Turner and African-American Religion in the South.* Knoxville: The University of Tennessee Press, 1992.

Bailey, Julius H. *Around the Family Altar: Domesticity in the African Methodist Episcopal Church, 1865–1900.* The History of African-American Religions Series. Edited by Stephen W. Angell and Anthony B. Pinn. Gainesville: University Press of Florida, 2005.

_____. *Down in the Valley: An Introduction to African American Religious History.* Minneapolis: Fortress Press, 2016.

Bragg, George F. *The Story of the First of the Blacks, the Pathfinder Absalom Jones, 1746–1818.* Baltimore, MD, 1929.

Brown, Elsa Barkley. "Negotiating and Transforming the Public Sphere: African American Political Life in the Transition from Slavery to Freedom." In *The Black Public Sphere: A Public Culture Book,* edited by Houston A. Baker Jr. Black Literature and Culture. Chicago and London: The University of Chicago Press, 1995.

_____. "To Catch the Vision of Freedom: Reconstructing Southern Black Women's Political History, 1865–1880." In *African American Women and the Vote, 1837–1965,* edited by Ann D. Gordon, 66–99. Amherst: University of Massachusetts, 1997.

Butchart, Ronald E. *Schooling the Freed People: Teaching, Learning, and the Struggle for Black Freedom, 1861–1876.* Chapel Hill: The University of North Carolina Press, 2010.

Camp, Stephanie M. H. Closer to Freedom: Enslaved Women and Everyday Resistance in the Plantation South. Gender and American Culture. Edited by Thadious Davis and Linda K. Kerber. Chapel Hill: University of North Carolina Press, 2004.http://www.loc.gov/catdir/toc/ecip0411/2003024975.html

Carrie Bragg Campbell Papers. Special Collections/Archives, Johnston Memorial Library, Virginia State University Library, Petersburg, Virginia.

Chireau, Yvonne. "The Uses of the Supernatural: Toward a History of Black Women's Magical Practices." In *A Mighty Baptist: Race, Gender, and the Creation of American Protestantism,* edited by Susan Juster and Lisa MacFarlane, 171–188. Ithaca: Cornell University Press, 1996.

Church, General Education Board of the R.Z.U.A. *History of the Reformed Zion Union Apostolic Churches of America.* Lawrenceville: Brunswick Publishing, 1998.

Collier-Thomas, Bettye. *Jesus, Jobs and Justice: African American Women and Religion.* New York: Alfred A. Knopf, 2010.

Cooper, Anna Julia. *A Voice from the South.* The Schomburg Library of Nineteenth-Century Black Women Writers. Edited by Henry Louis GatesJr. New York: Oxford University Press, [1892] 1988. [Xenia Ohio, The Aldine Printing House, 1892].

Cooper, Melissa L. *Making Gullah: A History of Sapelo Islanders, Race, and the American Imagination.* The John Hope Franklin Series in African American History and Culture. Edited by Waldo E. MartinJr. and Patricia Sullivan. Chapel Hill: University of North Carolina Press, 2017.

Dailey, Jane. *Before Jim Crow: The Politics of Race in Postemancipation Virginia.* Gender and American Culture. Chapel Hill: University of North Carolina Press, 2000.

Dinnella-Borrego, Luis-Alejandro. *The Risen Phoenix: Black Politics in the Post-Civil War South.* The American South Series. Edited by Elizabeth R. Varon and Orville Vernon Burton. Charlottesville: University of Virginia Press, 2016.

Du Bois, W. E. B. *The Negro Church: Report of a Social Study Made under the Direction of Atlanta University; Together with the Proceedings of the Eighth Conference for the Study of Negro Problems, Held at Atlanta University, May 26th, 1903. Reprint ed.* Walnut Creek, Lanham, New York, and Oxford: Altamira Press, [1903] 2003.

Du Bois. *The Souls of Black Folk.* Dover Thrift ed. New York: Dover Publications, Inc., [1903] 1994.

Floyd-Thomas, Juan M. *Liberating Black Church History: Making It Plain.* Nashville: Abingdon Press, 2014.

Foner, Eric. *Freedom's Lawmakers: A Directory of Black Officeholders During Reconstruction.* New York: Oxford University Press, 1993.

_____. *Reconstruction: America's Unfinished Revolution, 1863–1877.* The New American Nation Series. Edited by Henry Steele Commager and Richard B. Morris. New York: Perennial Classics, 1988.

Giggie, John. "'Disband Him from the Church': African Americans and the Spiritual Politics of Disfranchisement in Post-Reconstruction Arkansas." *The Arkansas Historical Quarterly* 60, no. 3 (Autumn 2001): 245–264.

Glaude, Eddie. *Exodus!: Religion, Race and Nation in Early Nineteenth-Century America.* Chicago: University of Chicago Press, 2000.

GlaudeJr. Eddie S. *African American Religion: A Very Short Introduction.* Oxford: Oxford University Press, 2014.

Green, Hilary. *Educational Reconstruction: African American Schools in the Urban South, 1865–1890.* Reconstructing America. Edited by Andrew Slapp. New York: Fordham University Press, 2016.

Harper, Matthew. *The End of Days: African American Religion and Politics in the Age of Emancipation.* Chapel Hill: University of North Carolina Press, 2016.

Harris, Michael W. The Mist Amidst Them: Narrative Tradition and Enslaved Religious Thought. Presentation. Union Theological Seminary, 1999.

Harvey, Paul. *Redeeming the South: Religious Cultures and Racial Identities among Southern Baptists, 1865–1925.* The Fred W. Morrison Series in Southern Studies. Chapel Hill: University of North Carolina Press, 1997.

Hayden, J. Carleton. "After the War: The Mission and Growth of the Episcopal Church among Blacks in the South, 1865–1877." *Historical Magazine of the Protestant Episcopal Church* 42 (December 1973): 403–27.

Henderson, William D. *The Unredeemed City: Reconstruction in Petersburg, Virginia: 1865–1874.* Washington, DC: University Press of America, 1977.

Heyrman, Christine Leigh. *Southern Cross: The Beginnings of the Bible Belt.* Chapel Hill: University of North Carolina Press, 1997.

Hildebrand, Reginald F. *The Times Were Strange and Stirring: Methodist Preachers and the Crisis of Emancipation. Durham:* Duke University Press, 1995.

Irons, Charles F. *The Origins of Proslavery Christianity: White and Black Evangelicals in Colonial and Antebellum Virginia.* Kindle ed. Chapel Hill: University of North Carolina Press, 2008.

Jemison, Elizabeth. "Proslavery Christianity after the Emancipation." *Tennessee Historical Quarterly* 72, no. 4 (Winter 2013): 255–268.

Johnson, William H. *A Sketch of the Life of Rev. Henry Williams, D. D., Late Pastor of the Gilfield Baptist Church.* Petersburg: Fenn & Owen Printers and Binders, 1901.

Jones, Martha S. *All Bound up Together: The Woman Question in African American Public Culture, 1830–1900.* Chapel Hill: University of North Carolina Press, 2007.

_____. *Birthright Citizens: A History of Race and Rights in Antebellum America*. Cambridge: Cambridge University Press, 2018.

Lewis, Harold T. *Yet with a Steady Beat: The African American Struggle for Recognition in the Episcopal Church*. Valley Forge: Trinity Press International, 1996.

Mamiya, Lawrence H. "African American Religion: From the Civil War to Civil Rights." In *Encyclopedia of Religion in America*, edited by Charles H. Lippy and Peter W. Williams, 34–43. Washington, DC: CQ Press, 2010. doi: 10.4135/9781608712427.n11.

Martin, Sandy Dwayne. "Vindicated Faith, Not a Lost Cause: African American Baptist Identity and Vision in the Civil War and Postwar Eras, 1850–1900." In *Between Freedom and Fetters: African American Baptists since Emancipation*, edited by Edward R. Crowther and Keith Harper, 9–26. Macon: Mercer University Press, 2015.

Masur, Kate. *An Example for All the Land: Emancipation and the Struggle over Equality in Washington, D.C.* Chapel Hill: University of North Carolina Press, 2010.

"Minutes of the Fifteenth Annual Session of the Hasadiah Baptist Association Held with the Mount Obed Baptist Church, of Appomattox County, Va, September 5th, 6th, and 7th, 1888."

Montgomery, William E. *Under Their Own Vine and Fig Tree: The African-American Church in the South, 1865–1900*. Baton Rouge: Louisiana State University Press, 1993.

Newman, Richard S. *Freedom's Prophet: Bishop Richard Allen, the AME Church and the Black Founding Fathers*. New York: New York University Press, 2008.

Rosen, Hannah. *Terror in the Heart of Freedom: Citizenship, Sexual Violence, and the Meaning of Race in the Postemancipation South. Gender and American Culture*. Chapel Hill: University of North Carolina Press, 2009.

Shattuck, Gardiner H., *Jr. Episcopalians and Race: Civil War to Civil Rights*. Lexington: The University Press of Kentucky, 2000.

Testimony Taken by the Joint Select Committee to Inquire into the Condition of Affairs in the Late Insurrectionary States. North Carolina. Washingtong DC: Government Printing Office, 1872.

ThompsonJr., H. *Paul. A Most Stirring and Significant Episode: Religion and the Rise and Fall of Prohibition in Black Atlanta, 1866–1877*. DeKalb: Northern Illinois University Press, 2013.

Turner, Nicole Myers. *Soul Liberty: The Evolution of Black Religious Politics in Postemancipation Virginia*. Chapel Hill: University of North Carolina Press, 2020.

Walker, Corey D. B. A *Noble Fight: African American Freemasonry and the Struggle for Democracy in America*. Urbana and Chicago: University of Illinois Press, 2008.

Warnock, Raphael G. *The Divided Mind of the Black Church: Theology, Piety & Public Witness*. Religion, Race, and Ethnicity. Edited by Peter J. Paris. New York: New York University Press, 2013.

Washington, James Melvin. *Frustrated Fellowship: The Black Baptist Quest for Social Power*. Macon: Mercer University Press, 1986.

Wells-Oghoghomeh, Alexis S. "'She Come Like a Nightmare': Hags, Witches and the Gendered Trans-Sense among the Enslaved in the Lower South." *Journal of Africana Religions* 5, no. 2 (2017): 239–274.

Williams, Heather Andrea. *Self-Taught: African American Education in Slavery and Freedom*. The John Hope Franklin Series in African American History and Culture. Chapel Hill: University of North Carolina Press, 2005.

Williams, Kidada. *They Left Great Marks on Me: African American Testimonies of Racial Violence from Emancipation to World War I*. New York: New York University Press, 2012.

Woodson, Carter G. *The History of the Negro Church*. Third ed. Washington DC: The Associated Publishers, 1921, 1945, 1972.

Young, Jason. "African Religions in the Early South." *The Journal of Southern Religion* 14 (2012): http://jsr.fsu.edu/issues/vol14/young.html.

NOTES

1   Carrie Bragg Campbell, "An accurate early history of St. Stephen's Church," Carrie Bragg Campbell Papers, Box 1, Acc.#1991–66, Special Collections/Archives, Johnston Memorial Library, Virginia State University Library, Petersburg, Virginia.

2   Quoted in William E. Montgomery, *Under Their Own Vine and Fig Tree: The African-American Church in the South, 1865–1900* (Baton Rouge: Louisiana State University Press, 1993), 163.

3   Elsa Barkley Brown, "Negotiating and Transforming the Public Sphere: African American Political Life in the Transition from Slavery to Freedom," in *The Black Public Sphere: A Public Culture Book*, edited by Houstan A. Baker, Jr. Black Literature and Culture (Chicago: The University of Chicago Press, 1995).

4   Michael W. Harris, The Mist Amidst Them: Narrative Tradition and Enslaved Religious Thought, Presentation, Union Theological Seminary, 1999; Stephanie M. H. Camp, *Closer to Freedom: Enslaved Women and Everyday Resistance in the Plantation South* (Chapel Hill: The University of North Carolina Press, 2004), 24–25.

5   Melissa L. Cooper, *Making Gullah: A History of Sapelo Islanders, Race, and the American Imagination* (Chapel Hill: The University of North Carolina Press, 2017), 75; Alexis S. Wells-Oghoghomeh, "'She Come Like a Nightmare': Hags, Witches and the Gendered Trans-Sense among the Enslaved in the Lower South," *Journal of Africana Religions* 5, no. 2 (2017): 240, 50; Jason Young, "African Religions in the Early South," *The Journal of Southern Religion* 14 (2012): http://jsr.fsu.edu/issues/vol14/young.html; Yvonne Chireau, "The Uses of the Supernatural: Toward a History of Black Women's Magical Practices," in *A Mighty Baptist: Race, Gender, and the Creation of American Protestantism*, edited by Susan Juster and Lisa MacFarlane (Ithaca: Cornell University Press, 1996).

6   W. E. B. Du Bois, *The Negro Church: report of a social study made under the direction of Atlanta University; together with the proceedings of the eighth conference for the study of Negro problems, held at Atlanta University, May 26th, 1903*, Reprint ed. (Walnut Creek, Lanham, New York and Oxford: Altamira Press, 1903, 2003), chapter 6; Montgomery, *Under Their Own Vine and Fig Tree*, 5.

7   Julius H. Bailey, *Down in the Valley: An Introduction to African American Religious History* (Minneapolis: Fortress Press, 2016), 59; Eddie S. Glaude, *African American Religion: A Very Short Introduction* (Oxford: Oxford University Press, 2014), 39.

8   Glaude, *African American Religion*, chapter 3.

9   Bailey, *Down in the Valley*, 57.

10 Elizabeth Jemison, "Proslavery Christianity after the Emancipation," *Tennessee Historical Quarterly* 72, no. 4 (Winter 2013): 255, 60, 62; Charles F. Irons, *The Origins of Proslavery Christianity: White and Black Evangelicals in Colonial and Antebellum Virginia*, Kindle ed. (Chapel Hill: University of North Carolina Press, 2008), 10; Christine Leigh Heyrman, *Southern Cross: The Beginnings of the Bible Belt* (Chapel Hill: The University of North Carolina Press, 1997), 24–25.

11 Montgomery, *Under Their Own Vine and Fig Tree*, 7–11.

12 George F. Bragg, *The Story of the First of the Blacks, the Pathfinder Absalom Jones, 1746–1818* (Baltimore, MD, 1929).

13 Richard Newman uses the date 1787 in accordance with Allen's writings, because Newman believes this was the day Allen conceived the plan. Milton Sernett has argued that the date of the exodus was actually 1792. See Richard S. Newman, *Freedom's Prophet: Bishop Richard Allen, the AME Church and the Black Founding Fathers* (New York: New York University Press, 2008), 63–68.

14 Matthew Harper, *The End of Days: African American Religion and Politics in the Age of Emancipation* (Chapel Hill: University of North Carolina Press, 2016), 23.

15 Juan M. Floyd-Thomas, *Liberating Black Church History: Making it Plain* (Nashville: Abingdon Press, 2014), 52.

16 Harper, *The End of Days*, 25; Eddie Glaude, *Exodus!: Religion, Race and Nation in Early Nineteenth-century America* (Chicago: University of Chicago Press, 2000), chapter 3.

17 On vindication: Sandy Dwayne Martin, "Vindicated Faith, not a Lost Cause: African American Baptist Identity and Vision in the Civil War and Postwar Eras, 1850–1900," in *Between Freedom and Fetters: African American Baptists since Emancipation*, edited by Edward R. Crowther and Keith Harper (Macon: Mercer University Press, 2015).

18 Nicole Myers Turner, *Soul Liberty: The Evolution of Black Religious Politics in Postemancipation Virginia* (Chapel Hill: University of North Carolina Press); Corey D. B. Walker, *A Noble Fight: African American Freemasonry and the Struggle for Democracy in America* (Urbana and Chicago: University of Illinois Press, 2008); Glaude, *Exodus!*, 80. Walker argues for democratic roots in associational culture.

19 James Melvin Washington, *Frustrated Fellowship: The Black Baptist Quest for Social Power* (Macon: Mercer University Press, 1986), 108–111.

20 Washington, *Frustrated Fellowship*, 111.
21 Floyd-Thomas, *Liberating Black Church History*, 68. Montgomery, *Under Their Own Vine and Fig Tree*, chapter 1.
22 Foner highlights white racism as a primary cause of black separation. See Eric Foner, *Reconstruction: America's Unfinished Revolution, 1863–1877* (New York: Perennial Classics, 1988), 88; Glaude, *African American Religion*.
23 Harper, *The End of Days*, 28–29.
24 Montgomery, *Under Their Own Vine and Fig Tree*, 106.
25 General Education Board of the R.Z.U.A. Church, *History of the Reformed Zion Union Apostolic Churches of America* (Lawrenceville: Brunswick Publishing, 1998), 3–4, 8.
26 Glaude, *African American Religion*, 49; Lawrence H. Mamiya, "African American Religion: From the Civil War to Civil Rights," in *Encyclopdia of Religion in America*, ed. Chalres H. Lippy and Peter W. Williams, 34–43 (Washington, DC: CQ Press, 2010).
27 Foner, *Reconstruction*, 91, Bennett, *Religion and the Rise*, 2005.
28 Turner, *Soul Liberty*, chapter 1; Foner, *Reconstruction*, 88, 90, 91; Martha S. Jones, *Birthright Citizens: A History of Race and Rights in Antebellum America* (Cambridge: Cambridge University Press, 2018).
29 Brown, "Negotiating and Transforming the Public Sphere," 142–143. Walker, *A Noble Fight*.
30 Collier-Thomas asserts that slave communities were communal, while patriarchy existed in the churches and benevolent societies. Bettye Collier-Thomas, *Jesus, Jobs and Justice: African American Women and Religion* (New York: Alfred A. Knopf, 2010), 56.
31 Bailey, *Down in the Valley*, 73.
32 Turner, *Soul Liberty*.
33 Anna Julia Cooper, *A Voice from the South*, edited by Henry Louis Gates, Jr. The Schomburg Library of Nineteenth-Century Black Women Writers (New York: Oxford University Press, 1892, 1988), 44.
34 Cooper, *A Voice*, 76–78.
35 Martha S. Jones, *All Bound Up Together: The Woman Question in African American Public Culture, 1830–1900* (Chapel Hill: The University of North Carolina Press, 2007), 163–64. Jones differs, suggesting that there was more power for women in the Baptist denomination.
36 Turner, *Soul Liberty*.
37 Carter G. Woodson, *The History of the Negro Church*, 3rd ed. (Washington DC: The Associated Publishers, 1921, 1945, 1972).
38 Montgomery, *Under Their Own Vine and Fig Tree*, 95.
39 Turner, *Soul Liberty*. chapter 2
40 Collier-Thomas, *Jesus, Jobs and Justice*, 33. 2010
41 Turner, *Soul Liberty*.
42 William H. Johnson, *A Sketch of the Life of Rev. Henry Williams, D. D., Late Pastor of the Gilfield Baptist Church* (Petersburg: Fenn & Owen Printers and Binders, 1901).
43 Reginald F. Hildebrand, *The Times Were Strange and Stirring: Methodist Preachers and the Crisis of Emancipation* (Durha: Duke University Press, 1995), 69.
44 Elsa Barkley Brown, "To Catch the Vision of Freedom: Reconstructing Southern Black Women's Political History, 1865–1880," in *African American Women and the Vote, 1837–1965*, edited by Ann D. Gordon (Amherst: University of Massachusetts, 1997).
45 Stephen W. Angell, *Bishop Henry McNeal Turner and African-American Religion in the South* (Knoxville: University of Tennessee Press, 1992), 181; Jones, *All Bound Up Together*, 183–186.
46 Collier-Thomas, *Jesus, Jobs and Justice*, 106–107.
47 Heather Andrea Williams, *Self-Taught: African American Education in Slavery and Freedom* (Chapel Hill: University of North Carolina Press, 2005), 73–74.
48 Eric Foner, *Freedom's Lawmakers: A Directory of Black Officeholders During Reconstruction* (New York: Oxford University Press, 1993); Luis-Alejandro Dinnella-Borrego, *The Risen Phoenix: Black Politics in the Post-Civil War South* (Charlottesville: University of Virginia Press, 2016); W. E. B. Du Bois, *The Souls of Black Folk*, Dover Thrift ed. (New York: Dover Publications, Inc., [1903] 1994), chapter 3.

49   Paul Harvey, *Redeeming the South: Religious Cultures and Racial Identities among Southern Baptists, 1865–1925* (Chapel Hill: The University of North Carolina Press, 1997), 56.

50   Julius H. Bailey, *Around the Family Altar: Domesticity in the African Methodist Episcopal Church, 1865–1900* (Gainesville: University Press of Florida, 2005), 39–41.

51   Ronald E. Butchart, *Schooling the Freed People: Teaching, Learning, and the Struggle for Black Freedom, 1861–1876* (Chapel Hill: University of North Carolina Press, 2010), 123.

52   On post-emancipation violence and black people's responses to it, see: Hannah Rosen, *Terror in the Heart of Freedom: Citizenship, Sexual Violence, and the Meaning of Race in the Postemancipation South*, Gender and American culture (Chapel Hill: University of North Carolina Press, 2009); Kidada Williams, *They Left Great Marks on Me: African American Testimonies of Racial Violence from Emancipation to World War I* (New York: New York University Press, 2012).

53   William D. Henderson, *The Unredeemed City: Reconstruction in Petersburg, Virginia: 1865–1874* (Washington DC: University Press of America, 1977), 67; J. Carleton Hayden, After the War: The Mission and Growth of the Episcopal Church among Blacks in the South, 1865–1877," *Historical Magazine of the Protestant Episcopal Church* 42 (December 1973): 416. See also, Testimony taken by the Joint Select Committee to inquire into the condition of affairs in the late insurrectionary states. North Carolina, (Washingtong DC: Government Printing Office, 1872).

54   Williams, *Self-taught*, 73–74; Hilary Green, *Educational Reconstruction: African American Schools in the Urban South, 1865–1890*, edited by Andrew Slapp, Reconstructing America (New York: Fordham University Press, 2016).

55   Hahn, *A Nation Under Their Feet*, 145.

56   Eric Foner documents 237 ministers among the 1465 black officeholders during Reconstruction. Foner, *Freedom's Lawmakers*; Foner, *Reconstruction*, 111.

57   Foner, *Reconstruction*, 92–93.

58   Harvey, *Redeeming the South*, 169. On the broad responsibilities of ministers, see: Woodson, *The History of the Negro Church*, 220–221.

59   Turner, *Soul Liberty*. On influence church members exerted, see: John Giggie, " 'Disband Him from the Church': African Americans and the Spiritual Politics of Disfranchisement in Post-Reconstruction Arkansas," secondary, *The Arkansas Historical Quarterly* 60, no. 3 (autumn 2001): 256–257.

60   Hildebrand, *The Times Were Strange and Stirring*, 67.

61   Giggie, " 'Disband Him from the Church.' "

62   Hildebrand, *The times were strange and stirring*, 70.

63   „Minutes of the fifteenth annual session of the Hasadiah Baptist Association held with the Mount Obed Baptist Church, of Appomattox County, VA, September 5th, 6th, and 7th, 1888".

64   Foner, *Freedom's Lawmakers*.

65   Montgomery, *Under Their Own Vine and Fig Tree*, 178.

66   Montgomery, *Under Their Own Vine and Fig Tree*, chapter 4. Hildebrand, *The Times Were Strange and Stirring*, chapter 2.

67   Harper, *The End of Days*; H. Paul Thompson, Jr., *A Most Stirring and Significant Episode: Religion and the Rise and Fall of Prohibition in Black Atlanta, 1866–1877* (DeKalb: Northern Illinois University Press, 2013); Raphael G. Warnock, *The Divided Mind of the Black Church: Theology, Piety & Public Witness*, (New York: New York University Press, 2013).

68   Jane Dailey, *Before Jim Crow: The Politics of Race in Postemancipation Virginia* (Chapel Hill: University of North Carolina Press, 2000).

69   Harold T. Lewis, *Yet with a Steady Beat: The African American Struggle for Recognition in the Episcopal Church* (Valley Forge: Trinity Press International, 1996); Gardiner H. Shattuck, Jr., *Episcopalians and Race: Civil War to Civil Rights* (Lexington: The University Press of Kentucky, 2000). On claims for social equality in the political sphere, see: Kate Masur, *An Example for all the Land: Emancipation and the Struggle over Equality in Washington, D.C.* (Chapel Hill: University of North Carolina Press, 2010).

70   Turner, *Soul Liberty*.

Part IV

IMPERIALISM

Chapter Seventeen

IN SEARCH OF A "WORKING CLASS RELIGION": RELIGION, ECONOMIC REFORM, AND SOCIAL JUSTICE

Janine Giordano Drake
Indiana University, Bloomington, Indiana

"Disestablishment" is a bit of a myth. Precisely because the United States has no official, tax-funded religion, religious groups have always depended upon the largesse of the wealthy for their very existence. As a result, business owners, professionals, and their heirs have always offered outsized social and political influence over the religious communities they have patronized. Hence, while the Christianity most celebrated in churches has always technically stood independent from the nation, it has rarely trespassed their cultural and political authority.

We see this pattern throughout American religious history. From the earliest days of the industrial revolution in the United States, Protestant pastors, financed by the wealthy, preached on the virtues of entrepreneurialism and the vices of laziness and disobedience. When the poor remained poor despite long hours of work under desperate circumstances, they were told to look to their false religion, a poor work ethic, unnecessary spending, and alcohol as the root causes of their poverty. "Christian" unions rarely gained much traction in the public square. When a small number of Irish Americans began to rise in social class in the early nineteenth century, their religious beliefs were declared outside the boundaries of good citizenship and they were prohibited from attending some of the most elite institutions of higher education. When "Christian" journeymen's associations suggested that they deserved the value of their labor, they received little to no support from most churches. The Knights of Labor, a union that required you to believe in "God, The Creator and Universal Father of all" was largely rejected by both churches and Christian leaders for their secret rituals.[1] After the Knights dropped their secret society status and entered the public square as a Christian workers organization, distanced themselves from striking, united in the middle class condemnation of alcohol, and pleaded that they only wanted the just fruits of their own labor, they were still rejected by most churches as guilty by association with the "heresy" of socialism. Throughout most of the nineteenth century, most churches, and their patrons, rejected critiques of capitalism as assaults on American Christianity.

Yet, this wholesale rejection of has never stopped wage earners from having spiritual encounters with Jesus. To the extent working men and women became visible to merchant-class church authorities as fellow Christians, they often themselves adopted the dispositions

A Companion to American Religious History, First Edition. Edited by Benjamin E. Park.
© 2021 John Wiley & Sons, Inc. Published 2021 by John Wiley & Sons, Inc.

and attitudes of the wealthy classes. As Paul Johnson has profoundly observed, the "social betters" sometimes accepted Anglo-Protestant workers into their churches as fellow Christians.[2] Not surprisingly, as these Anglo-Protestants experienced a modicum of social mobility relative to their peers, especially people of color, they also became less likely to agitate for the rights of laborers as a class.

How did wage earners navigate the official dictum, sanctioned by nearly all the churches, that Christianity affirmed the doctrine of free enterprise? How did black and white, Catholic and Protestant wage earners respond to the Anglo-Protestant cultural expectations of respectability? How did they handle the relentless efforts of business leaders to segment them by race, religion and ethnicity in order to thwart labor organizing? There were moments when large numbers of workers successfully mobilized their faith to resist the hegemony of business leaders and the well-resourced churches they propped up. However, most of the working-class religious history of the nineteenth and twentieth centuries is composed of a struggle among workers to define a politically useful "working class religion," especially a working-class Christianity.[3] This chapter considers four moments when social factors fragmented workers but a politically-potent, working class Christianity was useful in coalition building. It considers what these moments, and their unmaking, tell us about the history of religion, class, and economic justice in the United States.

The Industrial Revolution and the Eight Hour Day

The Industrial Revolution brought great wealth to merchants but untold poverty to a growing class of wage laborers. In Britain, the birthplace of mills and factories, the children of peasants found themselves working ten or twelve hours per day in order to keep themselves out of public poor houses. Soon, the same was happening in mills along the east coast of North America. In both Britain and the US, writers observed capitalism as the fundamental problem. According to critics like Robert Owen, Charles Fourier, and Karl Marx, workers created the wealth that company owners took in as profit. Journeymen artisans throughout the English-speaking world insisted on their human equality with employers before God as they evangelized what they called the "labor theory of value." This doctrine maintained that since workers were the true creators of wealth in the industrial economy, their work should be compensated in proportion to value they added to the commodity's sale price. Several workingmen's societies noted the extent to which the "iron law of wages," the assumption that workers should be paid according to market conditions, was out of accord with Christian economic principles.

Many framed their critiques within a Christian context. These reformers cited scripture, especially the maxim from Hebrew Law that "a worker is worthy of his wages" (Lev 19:13, 1 Timothy 5:18 and Matthew 10:10). The Noble and Holy Order of the Knights of Labor, a union founded as a spoof off a medieval guild, opened membership in the 1880s to anyone who legitimately earned their wealth. This included industrial wage workers and tenant farmers, women, and African Americans. All were invited to membership except those who claimed wealth by "rent, profit or interest."[4] The guild prayed together and upheld scripture in their newspaper masthead. The organization held that it was possible to establish a just and Christian distribution of wealth through a greater respect for the value of labor.

The "labor theory of value" formed the foundation for several related nineteenth century movements for economic justice. Robert Owen, a Christian Socialist and Chartist political organizer in England, was the first to coin the message, "Eight Hours Labor, Eight Hours Recreation, Eight Hours Rest." The message moved quickly across the Atlantic and became an organizing principle within early American craft unions. In 1867, for instance, the Illinois legislature passed a law declaring an eight hour limit on the workday within "all mechanical trades, arts and employments" and all day labor. Two rather large loopholes, however, came after that. First, all agricultural labor was excused, which meant that sharecroppers and farmhands across the South could still be worked at conditions bordering on slavery. Second, the law held that exceptions could also be made for any "special contracts or agreements to the contrary," which virtually all employers claimed.[5] The failure of Illinois to enforce their own law demonstrated to workers the great limitations of legislation as an avenue for effecting real labor reform.

As a result, social action, alongside a cultural and religious publicity movement, arose as the forefront of the late nineteenth century labor movement. As William Mirola and Heath Carter have articulated, the labor movement continued to organize in the late nineteenth century around the Christian principle that workers were worthy of being paid the full value they offered their employers.[6] When we consider the popularity of the "labor theory of value" within craft unions and the Knights of Labor, one might observe this as an emergence of a distinct strain of working class Christianity.

However, these ideas were also mirrored within the best-selling works of literature of the day. If this was a working class Christianity, it had appeal far beyond the labor movement. Journalists and economists like Henry George, Laurence Gronlund, and Henry Demarest Lloyd offered plain-spoken critiques of free market capitalism and hopeful suggestions of the possibility of creating a cooperative and even "Christian" commonwealth. American novelists like Francis Bellamy, Charlotte Perkins Gilman, and Upton Sinclair wrote didactic novels — a popular genre of the time — intended to help the American public imagine real alternatives to the system of unrestrained capitalism that they experienced. Both ordained and public theologians also gained widespread popularity.

Within popular books, magazines, and public lectures, Americans researched and debated who Jesus *really* was, what he *really* meant within the Sermon on the Mount, and to what extent the ancient Jew, son of a carpenter, would be welcomed if he entered American churches which professed his name. As the historian Dave Burns has ably noted, some of this discussion and debate emerged from European debates resulting from the historical analysis, and critique, of Scripture. Skeptical Bible scholars, known by the scholarly movement for "Higher Criticism," began to separate the historical Jesus — salvageable from the scientific, historical and textual evidence — from the Jesus of faith. Within the United States, journalists and popular orators like Robert Ingersoll popularized these ideas as they publicly critiqued the churches.[7]

Before long, a number of orthodox and heterodox public theologians took center stage in a national debate over the proper role of Christian churches in the public sphere. Some of these called themselves ministers, such as Bouck White, a radical whose New York City church sought to unite Jewish and Gentile immigrants under a common movement for Christian redemption from the sins of late industrial capitalism. Others, like Walter Rauschenbush, were ordained ministers within well-resourced, national churches who offered solidarity, and Christian sanction, for the goals of the labor movement. But, perhaps most telling of the fact that this really was a mass movement, was the popularity of books on the subject by writers with no credentials, official or unofficial, for their extensive commentary on the *real* intentions of the historical Jesus and the *real* intentions of the early Church.[8]

Labor and socialist leaders like Eugene Debs and George Herron had a great deal to say about Jesus' solidarity with the poor. They spoke with confidence in part because of the real tradition of socialist Christian theology. Cyrenus Osborne Ward, an ancient historian and member of the International Workingmen's Party (the party of Karl Marx), wrote several volumes of historical scholarship on the working class history of the early church. He emphasized the early Christian purpose of guilds and their parallels in modern labor unions. When labor leaders like Debs and Herron spoke of Jesus and the Christianity that was practiced in the early church, they did so by reference to real scholarship, and saw themselves proclaiming an incontrovertible and scientific truth about Christianity.[9]

Investigative journalists, including Lyman Abbott, Upton Sinclair, Charles Sheldon, and Mary Heaton Vorse, also entered this conversation. They spent less time on the historic church but offered reflections on the dissonance between the Early Church and the contemporary churches. Radicals, clerics, and everyone in between intensely debated how they imagined the early church to have looked. Lyman Abbott, for example, was much less convinced that Jesus was a radical than writers like Sinclair and Vorse.[10] Nonetheless, the national conversation continued in no small part because these ideas kept selling books, magazines and newspaper subscriptions.

Christian demands about the "labor theory of value" had purchase in large part because of their location within this vast American conversation on the *real* teachings of Jesus. However, efforts to organize for a shorter workday and higher pay still faltered. Judges, pastors, and politicians stood indignant before the claims that the Christianity preached in their churches was incorrect or incomplete. Police, usually Irish Americans, were paid like wage laborers and were often union members. However, public employees in the Gilded Age were famously indebted to party bosses for the opportunity to keep their jobs. In May, 1886, radicals and labor leaders convened a large rally for the Eight Hour Day in Haymarket Square in Chicago. Police encroached on the event and instigated conflict with the protesters. Journalists claimed that the ideas behind the labor rally promoted violence. Before anyone knew it, a bomb exploded in the square and dozens were killed or injured. The State of Illinois turned the Labor Day protest into a cautionary tale for future union members. They decided to publicly execute the "radical" perpetrators behind the event — magazine editors and organizers — even while there was no evidence that these men who organized the Eight Hour protest had any role in the bombing.[11]

The Haymarket movement for the eight-hour day may not have been possible without the support it found in the national conversation on Christian justice. However, if the public execution of the Haymarket "spies" is any indication, a popular, mass movement — even coupled with friendly legislation and wide support in the labor news media — was still not enough to effect real economic change. Strikes were failing, and the mass labor protest in Chicago did nothing to reverse the exploitation of American workers within American mines, farms, and factories. After the humiliation of the labor movement in the jailing and public execution of Haymarket martyrs, the membership of the Knights of Labor tanked precipitously, anarchist discussions dove deeper underground, and the various strands of the labor movement regrouped and rearranged themselves. The eight-hour day remained an important rallying cry of the labor movement up through the 1930s, but it receded from primacy in the next decade.[12] In its place emerged a concept developed within 1880s Christian and socialist discussions: the ideal of a Christian, "Cooperative Commonwealth."

Social Fragmentation and the Cooperative Commonwealth

In the early years of industrialization following the Civil War, both farmers and industrial workers began to toss around the dream of a "Farmer-Labor Alliance." The idea was as simple as it was seductive. The vast majority of Americans were, after all, poor. Moreover, this majority of Americans believed in the labor theory of value; they also believed that agricultural laborers and industrial workers were underpaid in comparison to the value they added to the final prices of the commodities they helped produce. Meanwhile, they observed, a small handful of Americans were rising to extraordinary riches and profligately spending a tremendous excess of wealth. According to some, this was wealth that workers had legitimately earned.

The dream of a Farmer-Labor Alliance was to find common points of solidarity among the poor, including farmers, agricultural wage workers (farmhands), sharecroppers, miners, factory workers, and service workers. Toward that end, leaders from the Knights of Labor, the

Populist Party (a coalition of farmers) and the Central Labor Union united on several occasions to draft platforms of common agreement and lists of legislative proposals that they shared in common.[13] The big tenets of the platform, however, were not the biggest challenge. It was not hard to agree that the railroads needed regulation, that Congressmen should be more accountable to the people, that large banks were extorting the poor with high interest rates, and that workers should have the right to strike.

The hardest part, rather, was in selling the value of this coalition to their various constituencies. Karl Marx predicted that workers who were disgruntled and alienated from their work would gravitate toward some kind of radical "working class consciousness," and that this common consciousness would drive social change. But for various reasons, such a thing did not materialize in the United States. On one level, social rank intervened. Many farmers in the Populist movement were cash poor because they bought farming implements on credit and waited the entire growing season in order to earn back their initial investment. They were upset with railroads and banks for the high, fixed costs of farming: shipping fees on hauling and interest rates for buying farming supplies. For many, these high fixed costs meant their profit margin was so meager that they had to take on additional wage jobs in order to keep their land. However, the fact that these farmers were landowners — even if they had acquired that land cheaply by homesteading — meant that they often saw themselves at a higher social rank from non-landowners. By the 1880s, hardly a generation had passed since property qualifications receded from voting requirements in most states. What many farmers feared, and wanted to protect, was their status which set them apart from the tenant farmers, farmhands, and sharecroppers who also called themselves "farmers."[14] The Knights had organized heavily among this latter group, but their national leadership faltered by the 1890s. In order to maintain some unity within their coalition, they needed a vision that transcended these serious social divisions.

In cities, social rank interrupted hopes of "working class consciousness" just as abruptly. No division was more powerful than the chasm between those who called themselves "skilled," and those whom these "tradesmen" labeled as "unskilled" wage workers. The American Federation of Labor, the largest national union by the 1880s, defined their purpose in defending the monetary value of workers' skills. They organized nationally by trade and refused to align with any political party. This approach may have protected mid-nineteenth century workers' trade secrets, and with it their pay and dignity as tradespeople.[15] But, it was powerless against the onslaught of engineers who rapidly sought to observe and atomize the work of skilled tradespeople in order to create much lower-paying jobs for workers without previous training. More and less skilled workers could agree on the value of an eight-hour day, the right to strike, and safer working conditions. But, trades unionists' indifference at the low wages and extraordinary discipline imposed on de-skilled workers threatened to fracture the labor movement.

It is difficult to overstate the ways that racial and religious differences overlaid and exacerbated these tensions in social station. The white farmers who squeezed out modest profits made a living because they underpaid their field hands. In the rural West and South, these congregations slowly raised the funds — with great help from Northern and Eastern brethren — to plant churches in the period following the Civil War.[16] Yet, the Southern, middle class evangelicalism that surfaced was largely a "Religion of the Lost Cause." It was a faith that centered Southerners as martyrs in a tragic struggle for sovereignty over their region; they hoped and prayed that the South would "rise again." Many Southern evangelicals becames members of the Ku Klux Klan and defended the virtues of the racial order.[17] Nostalgia for "Old Time Religion" within early twentieth-century Fundamentalism not only hearkened memories of the Old South for white Southerners who had begun to migrate far and wide. It also built real and imagined ties among white former Southerners, ties which celebrated white entrepreneurialism and left the white supremacist racial order intact.[18]

Poorer farmers, and particularly tenant farmers and sharecroppers, were more likely to connect with the Holiness tradition, a charismatic offshoot of Methodism, than the middle class churches of the landowning classes. Charismatic evangelicals most often congregated in open-air summer encampments and along the sporadic gatherings of traveling speakers.[19] Church edifices, after all, cost money and tenant farmers had little to no cash. When wealthy members of Eastern congregations donated money for the building of these churches, they often imagined that their churches would serve a cross-class constituency. However, as Charles Sheldon illustrated so vividly in his best-selling *In His Steps*, the very poor were usually rejected from church membership in the churches of their bosses — even and especially as the poor were a substantial and growing fraction of the American population.[20] Some of these impoverished, usually migratory workers and their families self-identified as *real*, Bible-believing Christians who rejected the Higher Critics and believed in the plainspoken Word of God.[21] This emphasis perhaps came across stronger because they were so ostracized from the "legitimate" houses of worship within their own communities. For many migratory workers, then, critiques of the Jesus of the wealthy offered a common foundation of protest. The popular music of the Industrial Workers of the World frequently critiqued the ministers who preached "pie in the sky when you die," but were unwilling to make labor reforms.[22]

Within cities, a larger fraction of immigrants and a growing number of African Americans further exacerbated social fragmentation. Large, ornate Protestant churches were commissioned by wealthy Anglo-Americans in order to illustrate their mark on the urban landscape.[23] The working-class, Anglo transplants who found themselves in cities were sometimes invited into these ornate churches, but they often adhered to the Charismatic or Holiness traditions and found traditional liturgies alienating.[24] Other urban migrants fled the war-torn regions of Russia, Italy, Poland, Germany, and Eastern Europe, and carried Eastern Orthodox, Catholic, Protestant, and Jewish traditions with them. Indeed, many migrated as religious and political refugees, especially Russsian Jews. However, despite their large numbers, before the first decade of the twentieth century, there was no single and united Roman Catholic Church in the United States. Instead, there were multiple missionary churches, sent from every Catholic nation to serve the migrants in the New World who hailed from their "national parish."

As a result, even though Catholics outnumbered Protestants, the Roman Catholic Church in the United States hardly acted as a monolith. The hierarchy officially dismissed socialism as heresy because of its dogged focus on justice in the material world, but they endorsed trade unions as valuable avenues for achieving justice. Irish Americans led both the churches and the trade union movement, but this leadership did not make unionization easy. Migrants from Southern and Eastern Europe, already faced with less desirable jobs than trade unionists, sometimes resented Irish leadership within these multiple spheres.

However, despite the fact that some Irish Americans were coming into power within their churches, city government, public service, and even nursing, many Anglo Protestants still harbored old critiques of Catholics' abilities to participate in the nation as independent citizens.[25] Moreover, Anglo Protestants often harbored centuries-old mistrust of Jews as sly moneychangers and Christ-killers. To complicate matters further, many immigrant groups resented one another in their struggle for scarce resources such as good jobs, decent housing, and union leadership.[26] The American Federation of Labor, as a federation of skilled tradesmen, included Anglo Protestants, Catholics (especially Irish Americans), and Jews, but the stated goals of the coalition were merely to protect the value of their skills. They offered little to no critique on the ways businesses profiteered off the creation of low-skill jobs made for poor immigrants. The radical labor movement, including the Industrial Workers of the World and the Western Federation of Miners, also included a variety of cultures and took no official position on religion.

How did Americans, otherwise culturally at odds with one another, build solidarity in their efforts to resist low wages, regulate the railroads, restrain interest rates, regulate food and industrial safety, and take back control over their ostensibly representative government? In many respects, this effort failed. William Jennings Bryan, the joint nominee of the Populist Party and the Democratic Party, and orator whose discourse was filled with religious symbolism, still lost to William McKinley, a staid Protestant and a Republican. McKinley raised tariffs to protect American industry, and invaded both the Philippines and Cuba to secure larger markets for American manufacturers. While he was succeeded by Republicans Roosevelt and Taft, who broke up some trusts and secured small union victories, attempts at a strident Farmer-Labor coalition mostly failed until the passage of the New Deal.

However, a more generous judge would identify the William Jennings Bryan presidential campaign in 1896 as a moment that galvanized a politically potent, working class Christianity. Bryan won the Democratic nomination based on his ideological support for Farmer-Labor solidarity, especially in his hopes of benefitting all workers by moving off the gold standard. The Populist Party, which had membership in the millions and a growing number of locals across the Midwest and South, threw their weight behind him as their nominee as well. If we devalued the currency, Bryan argued, interest rates could fall, credit would loosen, and land ownership would be more attainable for all. In his tour of the United States during the summer of 1896, Bryan celebrated a hardscrabble everyman Jesus who stood behind farmers and other laborers in their toil. He spoke of a future "Cooperative Commonwealth," an old Populist phrase which hearkened to the prospect that small communities could share resources and govern themselves, and thus cease relying upon the whims of Eastern banks, business interests, and distant politicians. He spoke of the moral obligation of the people to restrain industrial tycoons and their drive toward internal and overseas empire.

Within Bryan's rhetorical coalition, the tenant farmers and agricultural laborers who were not rich enough to be ushered into fancy churches found a religious and political home.[27] His political coalition united several socioeconomic strata of poor white farmers behind a semi-religious, moral coalition. Though Bryan's presidential campaign ended in defeat, the former union leader Eugene Debs built his Social Democratic Party on a very similar rhetorical foundation. Debs had less to say about monetary policy and much more to say about the war between "labor and capital." But their short-term goals — to put underemployed people to work, regulate or nationalize the railroads, and empower unions — were strikingly similar. Both sought to unite urban and rural laborers under a common umbrella, and both celebrated a Jesus who was the son of a carpenter and an enthusiastic believer that the poor should inherit the earth because wealth was inherently corrupting. Both spoke of a "Cooperative Commonwealth," supported women's rights to vote, and identified racism as a problem that only further fragmented the working classes.[28] Debs picked up many of Bryan's followers as he traversed the nation himself and stumped for the Socialist Party of America. Debs also lost several contests for the American presidency, but he sustained and extended a politically potent working-class Christianity that no church denomination or revival movement could catalyze on their own.

There are important reasons, however, that both Bryan and Debs failed in their party's efforts to win the presidency, or even take Congress. First and foremost was the fact that large numbers of farm hands and sharecroppers were people of color with no voting rights. African Americans technically won their freedom and suffrage at the end of the Civil War, but Southern states almost immediately passed laws which prevented former slaves from registering to vote. Poll taxes required that African Americans register far in advance of elections with a sum of cash. "Grandfather" clauses held that one was unable to register to vote unless one's grandfather had the right to vote. "Literacy tests" ostensibly tested literacy, but in fact required former slaves to interpret sections of the Constitution to the fancy of the voting registrar. Combined, laws like this made it impossible for a large fraction of working people to exercise their right to the ballot. They also discouraged poor whites and immigrants from trust that their votes mattered.

By the 1910s, a politicized working-class Christianity might have been a logical foundation for a national campaign, but the Socialist Party officially secularized its goals. For years, socialists had fought among themselves over the extent to which Christianity was America's greatest problem. Priests and pastors, after all, continually attacked socialists for their "atheism" and for their efforts to disrupt patriarchal gender and family norms. Meanwhile, self-styled "Christian Socialists" insisted that the problem was with corrupt religious leaders but not the Christian faith itself. Christian Socialists even had their own national magazine, *The Christian Socialist,* edited by a minister and officially linked to the Socialist Party. Through the newspaper's messages that Jesus was a socialist and called for a socialist revolution, socialists liked to organize among evangelicals. In 1908, and again in 1912, however, the official delegates to the Socialist Party of America decided to table the issue of religion from any further debate. Christian Socialists were not prohibited from membership in the party, but many officials did not want religion to be used in organizing. In 1919, the party had to revisit the question again, a fact that reveals the persistent popularity of religious ideas among socialists.[29] However, the party's official secular bent meant that religion had officially receded from prominence in leftist visions of the Cooperative Commonwealth.

In the 1920s and 1930s, testimonies of personal faith grew through revivals and the rise of Fundamentalism. However, while Fundamentalism would later translate into formal politics, the start of the movement emphasized other-worldly faith and trust in a new set of religious authorities. It was not really until the post-war period that Fundamentalism would structure a conservative, political revolution.[30] By that time, however, a new set of working class Christianities, founded in Roman Catholic and African American traditions, was growing.

Working Class Religiosity and the New Deal

The Great Depression was, at least initially, a great social leveler. A series of droughts and the overuse of the plow meant that rural white and African American tenant farmers, not to mention Native Americans, experienced poverty together. Starting in the 1920s, poor rainfall and overused soil led to poverty throughout the South and West. While charities were the first line of support for the poor, they were founded to serve particular populations, and these were deeply segmented by race and religion. As the 1930s approached, many charities began to go bankrupt. Those that were able to stay afloat created policies to further ration aide. Catholics, to everyone's surprise, had the most money but they prioritized their own members. At these policies, the poor — a group now comprising both white and blacks — stood together in petitioning help from the federal government.[31] Meanwhile, in Northern and urban centers, purchasing products and stocks on credit led to a massive run on banks and the economic collapse of cities like Detroit. Faced with destitution and a scarcity of good work, immigrant and second-generation Catholics, African Americans, and native-born white Protestants, stood together in demanding that the federal government ensure that the jobs which did exist offered high wages, safe working conditions, and limited work hours.[32]

Was it a "working class religion" that brought workers together in the Congress of Industrial Organizations or other working-class political campaigns? A number of historians have pointed out the striking interracial solidarities that were forged on the common ground of religion during this era. Organizations such as the Southern Tenant Farmers Union, the Fellowship of Reconciliation, the Catholic Worker, the National Catholic Welfare Council, the Federal Council of Churches, the CIO, and the Association of Catholic Trade Unionists all preached a language of Christian justice. Their broad Christian message elevated the importance of a living wage for the poor, opportunities for sustainable farming, the end of Jim Crow segregation, and the necessity of an expanded social safety net.[33] For decades, working class Christians had been preaching on the value of social programs such as old age pensions, workmen's compensation, unemployment benefits, and higher income taxes on the wealthy. The CIO was instrumental in putting pressure on the Democratic Party to pass such reforms.

However, critics of the New Deal remind us that many of its jobs programs were targeted at the white working classes and did little to help destitute people of color, especially African Americans in the Deep South and Mexican Americans in the Southwest. Both the Agricultural Adjustment Act and the National Industrial Recovery Act disproportionately helped large business owners and large landowners, and did little to help farmers and businesses which had gone bankrupt during the Depression. Nevertheless, it is very unlikely that the Second New Deal — the social safety net — would have passed and remained in place so long if not for the decades of grassroots organizing among working class Christian and Jewish religious groups, unions, charities, and political groups. The New Deal was a victory for interracial Christian organizing, but its long-term effects largely put white people back in power.

Race and Religion in the Postwar Era

Movements in the name of interracial solidarity would not move to the center of public discussions until during and after World War II. The March on Washington for Jobs and Freedom, held on the national mall in 1963, marked both the end of the quiet interracial solidarities of the New Deal Coalition, and the start of a public alliance between the labor movement and the Civil Rights Movement. It was at this event that Martin Luther King gave his signature "I Have a Dream" speech, a jeremiad on the ways the United States fell short of its democratic promise. More than 200,000 people were estimated to have attended this gathering, and most were recruited through labor union and church connections.

A. Phillip Randolph and Bayard Rustin, co-organizers of the movement and close comrades to King, had deep roots in both labor and religious communities. Since the 1920s, Randolph had organized and led the Brotherhood of Sleeping Car Porters, the first predominantly African American labor union. He was the first director of the National Negro Congress (NNC), a Depression-era organization, connected to the CIO. As a labor and civil rights coalition, the NNC sought to build relationships among communists, socialists, and liberals organizing against racial and economic equality.[34] Rustin, too, was a socialist with long connections to the labor movement. However, his entry into the national political world derived from his roots in the black church and Wilberforce University, communities steeped in what scholars have called the "Black Social Gospel."[35] A decade earlier, he had connected with A. J. Muste and other labor-connected activists in the Fellowship of Reconciliation (FOR), a pacifist organization which opposed the Great War and committed itself to nonviolence and racial justice.[36] In 1942, he helped found the Congress on Racial Equality, a similar group which committed itself to nonviolent change.

It was neither Martin Luther King, nor Rustin or Randolph, who made the March on Washington a turning point. Rather, the event brought together labor unions, pacifist organizations, the Black and White Social Gospel movements, and the several movements for racial reconciliation under support for the new era in Social Christianity.[37] White support meant that the national newsmedia covered the sit-ins, freedom rides, and voter registration campaigns of the 1960s. Moreover, while the Red Scares of early twentieth century had driven many left-leaning and pacifist organizations underground, activists in the 1960s were able to use Presidents Kennedy and Johnson's words on the US commitment to "democracy" in defense of their public commitment to social justice.[38]

Lyndon Johnson's War on Poverty, an extension of the early Civil Rights movement, indicated the fusion of a set of early-twentieth-century working-class Christianities. The passage of Medicare, Medicaid, and expansions to the Social Security administration also came with strong support from the National Council of Churches, the union of mainline Protestant denominations, and the Roman Catholic Church.[39] In fact, several encyclicals which came out of Vatican II, especially *Gaudium et Spes* (1965) and *Populorum Progressio* (1967), articulated the systematic factors leading to poverty; these factors included colonialism and neo-colonialism, resource deprivation, and racism. Several scholars have described the late 1960s as a grassroots commitment to a "Catholic War on Poverty."[40] Not all lay Catholics supported the work of their churches, but many used Vatican language to support efforts to desegregate communities and alleviate poverty.[41]

By the time Richard Nixon came to office in 1969, the working-class Christian coalition that had supported the Civil Rights Movement and the War on Poverty was already beginning to fall apart. Evangelical fundamentalism had grown very popular among whites, and with it a sense that national values should be aligned with evangelical cultural imperatives. They lamented Supreme Court decisions which updated the legal relationships among children, parents, and the state. They also offered criticism for sex education in schools, the decline in school-supported prayer, and — worst of all — easier access to divorce, birth control, and abortions. Pundits described all these changes as attacks on "the family."[42] Meanwhile, by the late 1970s, most American cities had lost a large fraction of their population, and with it their jobs and their tax base. The soaring cost of housing made it even harder for the urban poor, especially people of color, to move to the suburbs and experience similar social mobility to that of their white counterparts.[43]

Catholic anti-abortion activism further contributed to the unraveling of support for the Great Society. The 1973 Supreme Court decision *Roe v. Wade* legalized abortion as a right to privacy between a woman and her doctor. American Catholics took this legalization of "murder" as an attack on their values; some invested themselves in campaigns for the "consistent ethic of human life," which they saw as an extension of their activism against the Vietnam War.[44] For a while in the 1970s, this anti-abortion activism did not fit neatly into one political party or the other. After all, the post-Vatican councils had enumerated threats to human flourishing which included neo-colonialism, war, racism, social and economic inequality, euthanasia, and capital punishment. The Catholic Church was not supportive of efforts to be "tough on crime" or to roll back the welfare state.

However, starting in the 1980s, Jerry Fallwell's Moral Majority, a lobbying group representing evangelical "family values," began to build a substantial partnership with Catholics. American Catholics had rarely aligned politically with evangelicals in the past, but many joined the Moral Majority, primarily out of resistance to abortion. The coalition not only helped put Ronald Reagan in the presidency, but the flood of cultural conservatism also rolled back the high graduated income taxes which had helped fund Johnson-Era social programs. However, Reagan did nothing to stop abortion. He invested more heavily in the military (including nuclear weapons) than his predecessors. While some spoke out about the ethics of such policies, the Republican Party had built a relationship with these churches that would last several more decades.[45]

Why is Working-Class Religion so Elusive?

In some respects, it is remarkable that religious movements in the name of the working classes have been so fleeting within the United States. The country has among the highest rates of religious affiliation in the world. However, as the history of the nineteenth and twentieth century suggests, race, ethnicity, religion, and class have served to fragment religious movements for social justice. While generalizations always have exceptions, it is fair to note a pattern with regards to race: in moments of economic crisis, when working class whites and African Americans have struggled together in poverty, whites have often resisted measures which would enable Blacks and whites equal opportunities for social mobility. White supremacy has proven resilient, even and especially within the religion of white Protestantism. Patterns of housing discrimination and voter suppression along the lines of race continue to vex working class movements in the twenty-first century. Labeling socialism as "un-American" has also proven a durable method of suppressing interracial social movements. Because of the endurance of white supremacy in the United States, immigrants have consistently sought white identities, a pattern that has only reinforced the nation's racial caste system.[46]

One might observe that Protestantism has more often functioned as a social network for sustaining white supremacy than it has functioned as a tool in building resistance to oppression. Moreover, the expectation of justice and prosperity in an afterlife sometimes distracts from attention to leveling social and economic inequalities. However, rhetorics of Judeo-Christian resistance to inequality and injustice have proven just as enduring as doctrines of white supremacy and meritocracy. Spotlights on those who have achieved their goals through prayer, evangelism, and earnest effort have served as a double-edged sword. While these testimonoials have sometimes obscured the preponderance of evidence which shows that capitalism is an engine of social and economic inequality, they have also built "beloved communities" and emboldened them to well-organized, social action.[47] Doctrines of justice rooted in Scripture may distract communities of faith, but they also to knit together groups of believers who might never have united on the basis of "working class consciousness" alone.

FURTHER READING

Burns, David. *Life and Death of the Radical Historical Jesus.* New York: Oxford University Press, 2013.

Carter, Heath. *Union Made: Working People and the Rise of Social Christianity in Chicago.* New York: Oxford University Press, 2017.

Chapell, David. *A Stone of Hope: Prophetic Religion and the Death of Jim Crow.* Chapel Hill: University of North Carolina Press, 2005.

Greene, Alison Collis. *No Depression in Heaven: The Great Depression, the New Deal, and the Transformation of Religion in the Delta.* New York: Oxford University Press, 2017.

Johnson, Paul. *Shopkeeper's Millennium: Society and Revivals in Rochester, New York, 1815–1837.* Repr. New York: Hill and Wang, 2004.

Roll, Jarod. *Spirit of Rebellion: Labor and Religion in the New Cotton South.* Urbana: University of Illinois Press, 2010.

NOTES

1   Edward Blum, " 'By the Sweat of Your Brow': The Knights of Labor, the Book of Genesis and the Christian Spirit of the Gilded Age," *Labor: Studies in Working-Class History of the Americas* 11, no. 2 (May 2014): 29–34.

2   Paul Johnson, *Shopkeeper's Millennium: Society and Revivals in Rochester, New York, 1815–1837,* repr. (New York: Hill and Wang, 2004).

3   I take the concept of "working class religion" from Dan McKanan, *Prophetic Encounters: Religion and the American Radical Tradition* (Boston: Beacon Press, 2011).

4   For more on the religious dimensions nineteenth century labor unions, see: Jama Lazerow, *Religion and the Working Class in Antebellum America* (Washington, DC: Smithsonian, 1995); William Sutton, *Journeymen for Jesus* (University Park: Pennsylvania State University Press, 1998); Robert Weir, *Beyond Labor's Veil: The Culture of the Knights of Labor* (University Park: Penn State University Press, 2006).

5   Illinois General Assembly, 1867, 820 ILCS 145/ Eight Hour Work Day Act. http://www.ilga.gov/legislation/ilcs/ilcs3.asp?ActID=2408&ChapterID=68.

6   William Mirola, "Asking for Bread, Receiving a Stone: The Rise and Fall of Religious Ideologies in Chicago's Eight-Hour Movement," *Social Problems* 50, no. 2 (2003): 273–293; Heath Carter, "Scab Ministers, Striking Saints: Christianity and Class Conflict in 1894 Chicago, "*American*

Nineteenth Century History 11, no. 3 (2010): 321–349; Heath Carter, *Union Made: Working People and the Rise of Social Christianity in Chicago* (New York: Oxford University Press, 2015).

7   David Burns, *The Life and Death of the Radical Historical Jesus* (New York: Oxford University Press, 2013).

8   On the Social Gospel movement as a broad spectrum of ideas on Christianity and social justice, see: Henry May, *Protestant Churches and Industrial America* (New York: Octagon Books, 1963); Robert Crunden, *Ministers of Reform: The Progressives' Acheivement in American Civilization, 1889–1920* (New York: Basic Books, 1982).

9   Burns, *Life and Death*.

10 Janine Giordano Drake, "Between Religion and Politics: The Working-Class Religious Left, 1880–1920," (PhD diss, University of Illinois, 2014).

11 For more on Haymarket, see: James Green, *Death in the Haymarket: A Story of Chicago, The First Labor Movement and the Bombing that Divided Gilded Age America* (New York: Anchor Books, 2007).

12 On the quest for working class leisure, see: Roy Rosensweig, *Eight Hours for What We Will: Workers and Leisure in An Industrial City, 1870–1920* (New York: Cambridge University Press, 1983).

13 On the history of a farmer-labor alliance, see: Elizabeth Sanders, *Roots of Reform: Farmers, Workers, and the American State, 1877–1917* (Chicago: University of Chicago Press, 1999); Robert McMath, *American Populism: A Social History, 1877–1898* (New York: Farrar, Straus and Giroux, 1993); Edward O'Donnell, *Henry George and the Crisis of Inequality: Progress and Poverty in the Gilded Age* (New York: Columbia University Press, 2017).

14 For more on this, see Nell Irvin Painter, *Standing at Armageddon: A Grassroots History of the Progressive Era* (New York: W. W. Norton, 2008); David Montgomery, *Beyond Equality: Labor and the Radical Republicans, 1862–1872* (Urbana: University of Illinois Press, 1981).

15 Julie Greene, *Pure and Simple Politics: The American Federation of Labor and Political Activism, 1881–1917* (New York: Cambridge University Press, 1999).

16 Ferenc Morton Szasz, *The Protestant Clergy in the Great Plains and Mountain West, 1865–1915* (Albuquerque: University of New Mexico Press, 1988).

17 Kelly Baker, *Gospel According to the Klan: The KKK's Appeal to Protestant America, 1915–1930* (Lawrence: University Press of Kansas, 2011); Charles Reagan Wilson, *Baptized in Blood: The Religion of the Lost Cause, 1865–1920* (Athens: University of Georgia Press, 1980); Gaines Foster, *Ghosts of the Confederacy: Defeat, the Lost Cause, and the Emergence of the New South, 1865–1913* (New York: Oxford University Press, 1988); Ralph Luker, *The Social Gospel in Black and White: American Racial Reform, 1885–1912* (Chapel Hill: University of North Carolina Press, 1991).

18 Gloege, *Guaranteed Pure*; Dochuk, *Bible Belt*.

19 Darren Dochuk, *From Bible Belt to Sunbelt: Plain-Folk Religion, Grassroots Politics, and the Rise of Evangelical Conservatism* (New York: W. W. Norton, 2010); James Green, *Grass-Roots Socialism: Radical Movements in the Southwest, 1895–1943* (Baton Rouge: Louisiana State University Press, 1978).

20 For more on migratory work, see Tobias Higbie, *Indispensable Outcasts: Hobo Workers and Community in the American Midwest, 1880–1930* (Urbana: University of Illinois Press, 2003).

21 On the rise of common-sense Bible interpretations among middling classes, see: Mark Noll, *The Civil War as a Theological Crisis* (Chapel Hill: University of North Carolina Press, 2006).

22 On critiques of religion within IWW literature, see: Archie Green, David Roediger, et al, *Big Red Songbook: 250+ IWW Songs* (Chicago: Charles Kerr, 2007); Donald Winters, *The Soul of the Wobblies: IWW, Religion and American Culture in the Progressive Era, 1905–1917* (Westport: Greenwood Press, 1985); Anne Tripp, *The IWW and the Patterson Silk Strike of 1913* (Urbana: University of Illinois Press, 1987).

23 On churches and social class, see: Tom Rzeznik, *Church and Estate: Religion and Wealth in Industrial-Era Philadelphia* (State College: Penn State Press, 2013); Matthew Bowman, *The Urban Pulpit: New York City and the Fate of Liberal Evangelicalism* (New York: Oxford University Press, 2014); Timothy Gloege, *Guaranteed Pure: The Moody Bible Institute, Business, and the Making of Modern Evangelicalism* (Chapel Hill: University of North Carolina Press, 2017).

24 Herbert Gutman, "Protestantism and the American Labor Movement: The Christian Spirit in the Gilded Age" *American Historical Review* 72, no. 1 (October 1966): 74–101.

25 On Irish/Catholic leadership in American urban centers, see James Barrett, *The Irish Way: Becoming American in the Multiethnic City* (New York: Penguin Press, 2012).

26 Daniel Katz, *All Together Different: Yiddish Socialists, Garment Workers, and The Labor Roots of Multiculturalism* (New York: New York University Press, 2011); Jennifer Guglielmo, *Living the Revolution: Italian Women's Resistance and Radicalism in New York City, 1880–1945* (Chapel Hill: University of North Carolina Press, 2010); Tony Michels, *A Fire in their Hearts: Yiddish Socialists in New York* (Cambridge, MA: Harvard University Press, 2005).

27 For more on Bryan and his coalition see: Michael Kazin, *A Godly Hero: The Life of William Jennings Bryan* (New York: Anchor Books, 2006).

28 On Debs, see: Nick Salvatore, *Eugene V. Debs: Citizen and Socialist* (Urbana: University of Illinois Press, 1982); Dave Burns, *Life and Death.*

29 Jacob Dorn, *Socialism and Christianity in Early 20ᵗʰ Century America* (New York: Praeger, 1998); Drake, "Between Religion and Politics."

30 See Dochuk, *Bible Belt*; William Trollinger, *God's Empire: William Ben Riley and Midwestern Fundamentalism* (Madison: University of Wisconsin Press, 1991); Kevin Kruse, *One Nation Under God: How Corporate America Invented Christian America* (New York: Basic Books, 2016); Bethany Moreton, *To Serve God and Walmart: The Making of Christian Free Enterprise* (Boston: Harvard University Press, 2009).

31 Alison Greene, *No Depression in Heaven: The Great Depression, the New Deal, and the Transformaiton of Religion in the Delta* (New York: Oxford University Press, 2015).

32 Matthew Pehl, *The Making of Working-Class Religion* (Urbana: University of Illinois Press, 2016).

33 Kip Kosek, *Acts of Conscience: Chrisitan Nonviolence and Modern American Democracy* (New York: Columbia University Press, 2011); Kenneth Heinemann, *A Catholic New Deal: Religion and Reform in Depression Pittsburgh* (State College: Penn State University Press, 1999); Erik Gellman and Jarod Roll, *The Gospel of the Working Class: Labor's Southern Prophets in New Deal America* (Urbana: University of Illinois Press, 2011); Jarod Roll, *Spirit of Rebellion: Labor and Religion in the New Cotton South* (Urbana: University of Illinois Press, 2010); Steve Rosswurm, *The CIO's Left-Led Unions* (New Brunswick: Rutgers University Press, 1992); Francis Broderick, *Right Reverend New Dealer, John Ryan* (New York: Macmillan, 1963).

34 Jeffrey Hegelson, "American Labor and Working-Class History," *Oxford Research Encyclopedias*, https://oxfordre.com/americanhistory/view/10.1093/acrefore/9780199329175.001.0001/acrefore-9780199329175-e-330.

35 Edward Blum, *WEB DuBois, American Prophet: Politics and Culture in Modern America* (Philadelphia: University of Pennsylvania Press, 2009); Gary Dorrien, *The New Abolition: WEB DuBois and the Black Social Gospel* (New Haven: Yale University Press, 2015); Gary Dorrien, *Breaking White Supremacy: Martin Luther King and the Black Social Gospel* (New Haven: Yale University Press, 2019); Barbara Savage, *Your Spirits Walk Beside Us: The Politics of Black Religion* (New York: Belknap Press, 2012); Wallace Best, *Langston's Salvation: American Religion and the Bard of Harlem* (New York: New York University Press, 2019).

36 John D'Emlio, *Lost Prophet: The Life and Times of Bayard Rustin* (New York: Free Press, 2003); Joseph Kip Kosek, *Acts of Conscience: Christian Nonviolence and Modern American Democracy* (New York: Columbia University Press, 2009).

37 Martin Luther King, "I Have a Dream," Address Delivered at the March on Washington for Jobs and Freedom, 28 August 1963. https://kinginstitute.stanford.edu/king-papers/documents/i-have-dream-address-delivered-march-washington-jobs-and-freedom.

38 Mary Dudziak, *Cold War Civil Rights: Race and the Image of American Democracy* (Princeton: Princeton University Press, 2011); Thomas Borstelmann, *The Cold War and the Color Line: American Race Relations in the Global Arena* (Cambridge, MA: Harvard University Press, 2003).

39 Jill Gill, *Embattled Ecumenism: The National Council of Churches, the Vietnam War, and the Trials of the Protestant Left* (Dekalb: Northern Illinois University), 2011; David Swartz, *Moral Minority: The Evangelical Left in an Age of Conservatism* (Philadelphia: University of Pennsylvania Press, 2012); Carolyn Dupont, *Mississippi Praying: Southern White Evangelicals and the Civil Rights Movement, 1945–1975* (New York: New York University Press, 2015).

40 Bauman, Robert. ""Kind of a Secular Sacrament": Father Geno Baroni, Monsignor John J. Egan, and the Catholic War on Poverty" *The Catholic Historical Review* 99, no. 2 (2013): 298–317; Pehl, *Making.*

41 Karen Johnson, *One in Christ: Chicago Catholics and the Quest for Interracial Justice* (New York: Oxford University Press, 2018); Mark Newman, *Desegregating Dixie: The Catholic Church in the South and Desegregation, 1945–1992* (Jackson: University Press of Mississippi, 2018).

42 William Martin, *With God on our Side: The Rise of the Religious Right in America* (New York: Broadway, 1996); Preston Shires, *Hippies of the Religious Right: From the Countercultures of Jerry Garcia to the Subculture of Jerry Fallwell* (Waco: Baylor University Press, 2007); Kruse, *One Nation Under God*; Frances Fitzgerald, *The Evangelicals: The Struggle to Shape America* (New York: Simon and Schuster, 2018).

43 Rick Perlstein, *Nixonland: The Rise of a President and the Fracturing of America* (New York: Scribner, 2007); Kevin Kruse, *White Flight: Atlanta and the Making of Modern Conservatism* (Princeton: Princeton University Press, 2005); Jason Sokol, *There Goes my Everything: White Southerners in the Age of Civil Rights, 1945–1975* (New York: Vintage, 2007).

44 Daniel K Williams, *Defenders of the Unborn: The Pro-Life Movement Before Roe v. Wade* (New York: Oxford University Press, 2016); Kathleen Tobin, *The American Religious Debate Over Birth Control, 1907–1937* (Jefferson: McFarland and Company, 2001).

45 Swartz, *Moral Minority*.

46 Roediger, *Working Toward Whiteness: How America's Immigrants Became White* (New York: Basic Books, 2005); Matthew Frye Jacobson, *Whiteness of a Different Color* (Cambridge, MA: Harvard University Press, 1998).

47 Kate Bowler, *Blessed: A History of the American Prosperity Gospel* (New York: Oxford University Press, 2015); Philip Sinitiere, *Salvation with a Smile: Joel Osteen, Lakewood Church, and American Christianity* (New York: New York University Press, 2015); Johnson, *Shopkeeper's Millennium*; Evelyn Brooks Higginbotham, *Righteous Discontent: The Women's Movement in the Black Baptist Church, 1880–1920* (Cambridge, MA: Harvard University Press, 1994); Glenda Gilmore, *Gender and Jim Crow: Women and the Politics of White Supremacy in North Carolina, 1896–1920* (Durham: University of North Carolina Press, 1996).

Chapter Eighteen

THE BUSINESSMAN'S GOSPEL: MAKING BUSINESS CHRISTIAN

Nicole C. Kirk

Meadville Lombard Theological School, Chicago, Illinois

Introduction

The gates for the Centennial Exhibition opened in Philadelphia on May 10, 1876, to a waiting crowd. It was the first world's fair in the United States.[1] Sprawled across seventy-five acres of Fairmount Park, the exhibition offered an impressive panorama: an open green space divided by wide promenades, woods, streams, lakes, and five monumental buildings constructed for the occasion. Dozens of smaller buildings peppered the landscape — beer gardens, restaurants, photography studios, nine buildings representing an array of foreign countries, and a Women's Pavilion, among others.[2] The fair hummed with thousands of visitors from across the United States and around the world. The steady buzz of machines, powered by the gargantuan Corliss steam engine, transformed the once-pastoral park into a thriving, albeit temporary, metropolis. Barely a decade after the Civil War and in a period of economic turmoil, the fair advanced a reshaping of the American story and envisioned the future.

The Centennial displayed more than the latest machinery, fine art, and cultural artifacts.[3] Religion was also on display. The opening ceremonies featured speeches that promoted the story of a unified United States with a special destiny as God's chosen nation.[4] The activities began with a long prayer by a Lutheran minister, the Reverend Joseph Seiss. Ulysses S. Grant, the former Civil War general and now president of the United States, gave a hopeful speech emphasizing progress and possibility. And finally, following Grant's speech, a large choir christened the occasion with a performance of George Frideric Handel's "Hallelujah" chorus.[5]

The presence of religion at the Centennial Exhibition extended well beyond the fair's inaugural speeches and prayers; it appeared in multiple guises on the fairgrounds. Perhaps most prominent, the Centennial's centerpiece fountain featured a story from the Bible. Formally titled "The Catholic Total Abstinence Union Fountain," the fountain stood near the Machinery Building at the intersection of two major pedestrian thoroughfares; it was designed and paid for by the Catholic Temperance Union to promote abstinence from alcohol, while celebrating contributions of American Catholicism and Irish immigrants.[6] The eye-catching fountain presented a towering Moses holding in the crook of one arm a tablet with the Ten Commandments and a staff, and standing on a mountain of granite where water

A Companion to American Religious History, First Edition. Edited by Benjamin E. Park.
© 2021 John Wiley & Sons, Inc. Published 2021 by John Wiley & Sons, Inc.

poured out beneath his feet into a small pool below. The statue depicted a biblical passage from the Book of Exodus where God instructed Moses to strike a rock at Horeb with his staff to bring forth water for the thirsty Israelites, who had been wandering in the desert after their emancipation from slavery.[7]

The story of Moses at Horeb was a familiar and beloved tale to many fairgoers in the late-nineteenth-century; the biblical story became popular through its frequent depiction in literature and visual imagery.[8] For Christians, the fountain's symbolism referenced the popular idea that Moses striking the rock foretold the death of Jesus, as well as how his death brought life-giving salvation.[9] Ringing the pool with Moses at its center were four statues: they each honored significant American Irish Catholics, among them Commodore John Berry, a revolutionary war hero and Navy officer, and Archbishop John Carroll, a leader against religious intolerance who served as the first bishop in the United States and became archbishop of Baltimore.[10] At the base of the four statues, sixteen water fountains offered fairgoers an alternative to alcohol by providing refreshing drinking water. For the sponsors, the fountain actively promoted abstinence and linked temperance with Christian salvation.[11]

Additional statues continued the religious connections: American Presbyterians erected a large statue of the cleric John Witherspoon, signatory of the Declaration of Independence and former president of the College of New Jersey (now Princeton University). B'nai B'rith, a Jewish charitable organization, commissioned a marble statue of an eight-foot-tall woman wearing a crown of thirteen golden stars and holding the American Constitution, allegorically representing the republic and "religious liberty."[12] Next to her, an eagle crushes in its talons a serpent representing the power of the republic to overcome oppression, and a young boy stands next to her holding a lamp representing religion and faith under her protection.[13] The statue was not finished in time for the fair, but was installed in Fairmount Park on Thanksgiving Day of that same year.[14]

Inside the exhibition buildings, religion was on display as an exhibit and for purchase alongside textiles, machines, and handicrafts. Many of the goods brought by visiting foreign nations were religious in nature. Belgium transported an elaborately carved wooden pulpit for display, while Germany brought dozens of statues of the saints, Madonnas, and "Christ on the Cross."[15] England, Russia, and other countries similarly brought an assortment of luxurious ecclesiastical goods, from sumptuous altar cloths to finely engraved altar pieces depicting Jesus.[16] The French shop of Froc, Robert, & Son displayed the gothic-styled golden altar that had been commissioned for the Basilica of the Sacred Heart, the University of Notre Dame's new campus chapel.[17] One of the more popular presentations in the French section was by Raffl & Co., with its painted plaster statues of the "Adoration of the Infant Saviour by the Shepherds and the Wise Men" staged in a wooden stable surrounded by fresh hay.[18] An exhibit from Palestine sold "Holy Land" goods in "bazaars" named "Jerusalem" and "Bethlehem." The Bible Pavilion, one of two major displays of Bibles at the fair, held a number of historical volumes for viewing, including Bibles in twenty-nine languages, and the newest Bibles for sale.[19]

Running for six months and open twelve hours a day, the exhibition attracted nearly ten million visitors. The fair displayed American ingenuity, technology, industrialization, and art, and it projected an imperialistic vision for economic and territorial growth.[20] As one of the major events in the United States during the nineteenth century, it was a cultural and financial triumph.

An extraordinary event, the Philadelphia's Centennial Exhibition served as the backdrop and a muse for another astonishing development — the birth of the American department store. Four days before the Centennial Fair began, Philadelphia merchant, John Wanamaker, opened a new experimental store near the Fairmount Park fairgrounds in an old freight train depot he had purchased the year before. Within a year, Wanamaker's "New Kind of Store" would become one of the first American department stores.[21]

An illustrious businessman, Wanamaker had made his fortune in retail. He was also a prominent Protestant Christian who started a Sunday school and a church, and contributed to the growth of Sunday school curriculum. From his youth in the 1850s until his death in 1922, Wanamaker participated in many of the major Protestant moral reform movements that gained momentum during the second half of the nineteenth century, tackling Protestant concerns over the perceived decline of Christianity, the decay of morality, the impact of massive immigration, and the rapid growth of cities.[22]

For the six decades, Wanamaker led his thriving retail business and brought together his religious commitments and his business ingenuity. He made his department store an extension of his moral reform work and, by doing so, transformed them both. Wanamaker's efforts to build a new retail experience and promote his religious moral beliefs presents the context for understanding the interaction of religion, culture, and business in the late nineteenth century and early twentieth centuries. Wanamaker's department store demonstrates how religion frequently appeared outside the confines of homes, churches, synagogues, and other religious institutions. This essay explores how and why John Wanamaker, a leading American retailer, intertwined commerce, business, and religion in the public space of his Philadelphia department store.

"A New Kind of Store"

Wanamaker saw his new store as an opportunity to experiment with a large volume of merchandise and greater variety, combining in one place what several individual shops might offer. The large open floor space lit from above by natural light flowing through the glass train shed, as well as rows of gas lights, allowed Wanamaker to play with organization and display in a way that echoed the exhibition's massive displays. Wanamaker hoped the store would introduce his store and his innovative retail practices to a national audience. He advertised the store as a "fair annex" — an additional Philadelphia attraction to visit as a part of the Centennial Fair.

Before Wanamaker opened the doors for his new store, he brought religion into his depot building. Mere weeks prior to the beginning of the Centennial Fair, the train depot had hosted another monumental event in Philadelphia — a Christian revival. Starting in November 1875, evangelists Dwight L. Moody and Ira Sankey held 250 worship services over several months. They attracted thousands to sit under the glass roof of the depot to hear the sermons and music of the famous revivalist duo.

Moody and Sankey arrived in Philadelphia on the heels of their successful revival tours in England and New York City. To promote the revival, Moody's advertising machine plastered the city with posters, encouraged news stories, and offered promotions.[23] Special streetcars were commissioned to give easy access to the revival site. Tickets were issued for crowd control and to make the revival feel like a special event. Breathless press coverage recounted the sermons, music, and crowds. A dais placed behind Moody's pulpit allowed nearly 300 business leaders and dignitaries to get close to the action — they were also on display to the revival audience, creating a visual link between the wealthy business and political leaders and Moody's Christian message. Business marketing and advertising techniques made the Moody and Sankey revivals a great success.[24] By the end of the religious spectacle, nearly one million people had attended.[25] Wanamaker's property was now well-known to nearly all Philadelphians. Within hours of the last worship service, construction workers scrambled to convert the revival space into a retail store in time for the Centennial Fair's opening day.

Business and Religion

American religion and business have been intertwined since the beginning of the United States, long before Wanamaker turned the site of Moody's revival into a monument to American commerce and the Centennial Fair mixed religion with technology, art, and culture.[26] However, until the end of the twentieth century, historians had, according to one scholar, "regularly neglected" religion in American historical studies.[27] When they did turn their attention toward religion, they often treated religion and business as separate, distinct categories, relegating religion to the private sphere while placing business in the public sphere.

Part of this neglect was due to the fact that many historians embraced the secularization thesis proposed by Max Weber in *The Protestant Ethic and the Spirit of Capitalism*, which claimed religion was eroded by secularization and the modernization of society.[28] Arguing against this thesis, however, Laurence Moore's *Selling God: American Religion in the Marketplace of Culture* claimed American religious organizations embraced commerce starting in the colonial period when they entered "the cultural marketplace," adapting technologies of business and commerce to attract adherents.[29] Moore and other scholars writing more recently have shown the creative and inventive ways American religion has changed and adapted through its complex relationship with business and commerce.[30] For example, historian Kate Carté has shown how the Moravians, settlers to Pennsylvania in the mid-1700s from a small Protestant sect founded in Germany, brought together a religious mission and economic endeavors for mutual support and benefit.[31] Mark Valeri has traced the mutual influence and shaping of Puritanism and the development of American commerce.[32] By the nineteenth century, the connections between religion and commerce developed in new and remarkable ways. Religious leaders and organizations freely borrowed business practices and techniques to further their religious goals, although not without criticism. In some cases, business leaders promoted their religious and moral agendas through financial contributions and leadership in religious organizations. Some business leaders even incorporated their religious beliefs and values into their businesses.

Wanamaker's retail business and religious commitments were not compartmentalized in his life. Rather, the two mixed freely: his Protestantism and concerns for morality shaped his business practices. The wealth he made from his stores funded churches, the YMCA, the temperance movement, the development of religious education materials, foreign Christian missions, the Salvation Army, and a host of other social reform efforts. He hosted Moody's multimonth revival and contributed to it financially. Wanamaker lodged Moody's family in his home during the revival. In addition, Wanamaker supplied over 300 ushers for the revival from the ranks of his stores' staff, and he himself attended the revival most nights. After the revival meetings ended, Wanamaker gathered new converts at a nearby Methodist church for postrevival prayer services. Years later, Wanamaker bought property for Moody to start the Northfield Seminary in Massachusetts. Yet his blending of business and religion started long before the Centennial Fair and the Moody Revival.

Wanamaker was raised in a religious household. His grandfather was a lay Methodist minister, and he attended a Sunday school. When he was eighteen years old, he stumbled upon an evening church meeting where he fully embraced Christianity. The meeting featured a man who worked as a hatmaker; the man spoke of the "practical" side of Christianity and how Christianity need not be separate from one's work life and business. Following this event, Wanamaker threw himself into church work, leading prayer meetings, attending church regularly, and promoting temperance at the shop where he worked.

Wanamaker also joined the local chapter of the YMCA, an organization created in 1844 by a London store clerk, George Williams, and eleven of his friends.[33] Creative in its approach, the YMCA focused on the "spiritual, mental, and social condition of young men" from rural areas arriving in cities looking for work.[34] The "Y" aimed to help its members combat the temptations of city life and develop their character through educational programs, drawing on a Protestant Christian framework. Wanamaker's earnest enthusiasm led the president of the YMCA branch in Philadelphia to hire him as a paid secretary — the first such administrative position in North America. Wanamaker increased Y membership, raised money to fund the chapter, and when a revival swept down the eastern seaboard in response to a financial collapse on Wall Street in 1857, he led revival prayer meetings at the Y.

The same year Wanamaker led Philadelphia's YMCA, he also started a Presbyterian mission Sunday school in his old working-class neighborhood. The school grew quickly, and by the end of its first year its members had named the school Bethany and, after meeting in a tent for many months, had constructed a modest building. At the end of Bethany's fifth year, the school became a church and called its first minister. The church continued to grow, and by 1876 Bethany had become a megachurch for its time, boasting more than five thousand members and an array of neighborhood social programs supported by the church and funded by Wanamaker. Some of Bethany's services included men's and boys' clubs, a penny savings bank, a vocational school, and a retirement home. Throughout his life, Wanamaker made it a priority to attend church at Bethany and to lead the Sunday school classes as its superintendent.

The money Wanamaker earned for his work at the Y provided the seed money to open his first store. By 1860, he was married to Mary Brown, who had helped him establish his Sunday school, and he entered a partnership with her brother, Nathan Brown. The new store rented space and opened Wanamaker & Brown's "Oak Hall" as a men's and boys' ready-to-wear clothing merchant at Sixth and Market Streets in Philadelphia in 1861, days before the beginning of the Civil War.

The war made the early days of the store challenging. But Wanamaker had kept a role at the YMCA, where he now served as president of the branch and participated in national meetings. His prominence as a Christian and his religious network benefited the store's reputation and allowed the young men to secure credit and other resources that made the difference between success and failure.[35] In addition, a contract for Union uniforms provided enough income to keep the store open during the war years.[36] Three years after the war, Nathan Brown died. Wanamaker then purchased Brown's business shares and continued to expand the business from a small dry goods retailer focusing on men's and boys' clothing to a purveyor of luxury men's wear by opening additional stores. By 1878, Wanamaker's was the largest retail business in Philadelphia and a full-fledged department store.[37]

Wanamaker's success and increasing wealth were not without critique. A year after the revival, Moody wrote to Wanamaker encouraging him to sell his business and join him in ministry. He warned Wanamaker that his salvation was at risk. Business and retail, according to Moody, suffered from bad reputations. He feared that Wanamaker's growing wealth in a business criticized for dishonesty threatened his religious commitments.[38] Wanamaker, however, met Moody's pleas with silence and continued to grow his business.

By the second half of the nineteenth century, criticism of business had increased. Rapid industrialization, the development of massive, impersonal corporations, and a series of major economic collapses fueled a negative perception of business, a view that continued into the twentieth century.[39] A history of well-known unseemly business practices made retail particularly problematic, leading to accusations of greed, trickery, and duplicitousness. The press regularly lampooned merchants in cartoons and questioned their motives.[40]

Several popular books outlined these critiques of American businesses in religious and moral terms. One bestseller imagined Jesus visiting the city of Chicago and critiquing the city's wealthy business leaders. Written by journalist William T. Stead, *If Christ Came to Chicago!* depicted Chicago's most powerful businessmen — in particular, meat-packing tycoon Philip Armour, luxury railroad-car producer George Pullman, and department-store merchant prince Marshall Field. Stead described their cutthroat business practices and compared the wealthy businessmen's opulent lifestyles to the lives of their struggling workers.[41]

To make sense of his growing wealth, Wanamaker actively sought ways to make his business and religion mutually supportive. He used his store profits to fund Bethany Church and its numerous programs. He used his money to finance a wide assortment of religious organizations and endeavors in the United States and abroad, including the Salvation Army. Through these efforts, Wanamaker strove to prove his commitments to Christianity and capitalism were not in conflict and were mutually beneficial.

Perhaps most importantly, Wanamaker became a proponent of a "prosperity gospel." During this time, he became close friends with local Baptist minister Russell Conwell, another prominent spokesperson for this movement. Before Conwell arrived in Philadelphia, he had traveled the country delivering a lecture called "Acres of Diamonds" in churches and along the Chautauqua circuit, and he continued to preach the message in his pulpit at Grace Baptist Church in Philadelphia. Conwell, like Wanamaker, provided a way to reconcile Protestant Christianity with the growing affluence of many Americans. In "Acres," he told his listeners that money was not the root of evil; rather, it was a godly pursuit if done in a moral and honest way. Money, Conwell suggested, fueled the spread of the gospel and supported the church. An individual's success was a sign of God's approval and blessing.[42] Other ministers and businessmen took up the refrain. Wanamaker, fueled by these ideas, believed he could use his business to change the nature of retail by aligning it with his Christian values and making it an instrument of moral reform.

Wanamaker's Christianity shaped many of his stores' practices. A devout member of the temperance movement, Wanamaker never allowed alcohol to be sold in his stores. As a Sabbatarian, he believed Sundays were reserved for worship, and despite the loss of profit and outside pressures, he closed his stores on Sundays. An innovator in the world of newspaper advertising, Wanamaker placed full-page ads every day of the week, except Sundays. During the holidays, Wanamaker reminded shoppers of the purpose of Christmas through his extravagant holiday displays, musical programs, and Christmas carol singing where the baby Jesus, lit from above by a beam of light, was a central part of the decorations. He rejected the harsh criticism he received from outsiders, especially after he became involved in national politics when he was appointed by President Benjamin Harrison to be postmaster general.[43] Political cartoonists poked fun at Wanamaker's religiosity — especially his return home every weekend so he could teach Sunday school at Bethany. Critics made fun of Wanamaker by calling him "Holy John."

In the earliest years of his business, Wanamaker and Brown had decided to forgo the usual retail business practices and offer a new way of doing business that reflected their religious beliefs. In the nineteenth century, price haggling was the norm and placed the burden of securing a good price on the customer's ability to negotiate down the price. Shoppers entering a store were expected to make a purchase — browsing was not allowed. Customers were also generally not permitted to return or exchange merchandise. And in some stores, the "sample" goods on display were of a better quality than the goods wrapped up for the customer to take home. To combat retail's poor reputation, Wanamaker and his partner implemented a one-price system for all; customers no longer haggled, and all paid the same price, which was clearly visible on a new invention: the price tag. They also offered a limited money-back guarantee. These new practices proved enormously popular. By the time of the Centennial Fair, Wanamaker advertised "one price; cash payment (no credit); full guarantee; money refunded" as the four cardinal principles of his store with a compass as his symbol.[44]

Wanamaker wanted to share his system, which he called "The Golden Rule of Business," with other retailers. He produced a number of booklets promoting the approach and delivered a number of speeches on the topic, as did his managers. Significantly, he believed his system was Christian and moral, declaring "the Golden Rule of the New Testament has become the Golden Rule of business."[45] He thought his golden rule had the potential to reform retail and the mercantile reputation.[46] What began as four cardinal principles quickly proliferated into a series of rules and regulations Wanamaker imposed on his stores and employees.

A central part of his Golden Rule of Business centered on training and shaping his employees. For Wanamaker, everything from employee decorum to the way employees dressed and carried themselves reflected on the store and his reputation. In the early days of his business, Wanamaker opened a school for his youngest employees, many of them starting work around age twelve to help support their families. Stores employed children in stockrooms and on the sales floor as cleaners and as couriers between the sales desks and a central cash register.[47] Starting with a school for young boys, Wanamaker later expanded his school to include men and later girls and women, albeit with a different curriculum. The school covered more than arithmetic, writing, spelling, and business courses. While the employees were paid to attend the school, their grades impacted their employment and advancement in the store. It was a paternalistic program that focused on teaching Protestant and middle-class values and behavior to his workers to better serve the white middle-class and upper-middle-class store clientele.[48]

Borrowing from his experiences with the YMCA, Wanamaker's education programs similarly focused on moral and physical education. To bolster physical training, he opened a seaside summer camp, created sports teams, and adopted a military-style framework for the school that included uniforms and marching drills. He called his students the "Wanamaker Cadets." Intensive music programs not only benefited the employees with free instruments and music lessons, but they also provided the store with orchestras, bands, and choirs to draw in customers with special performances. Wanamaker saw the school as training future workers for his business and as emissaries of his moral business model. Although many department stores did not employ African Americans, Wanamaker employed around three hundred black workers in service positions and offered a selection of vocational classes and music programs separate from his school program for white employees. However, African Americans were not hired as store clerks and did not receive the same treatment as white employees.

As Wanamaker sought to transform his workers, he looked at ways to influence the urban environment. After the Centennial Fair, Wanamaker renovated the train shed to make it a permanent store location and, over time, closed his other locations to focus on the growing megastore. He broadened the lines of merchandise to five departments and brought in girls', women's, and household goods. The store proved so successful after its first year that Wanamaker continued adding more departments, purchased neighboring properties to enlarge the institution, and installed the latest technologies both to support the business and to draw customers. Soon other retailers had also moved to Market Street, making it the central shopping district. By 1890, Wanamaker owned an entire city block in what was now becoming the center of Philadelphia with the completion of the new city hall across the street.

Through multiple additions that added height and width to the store, the Grand Depot had become a rambling structure with a hodgepodge appearance inside and out. But Wanamaker dreamed of something more: constructing a state-of-the-art, purpose-built retail building, like the department stores he saw in Paris, to replace the adapted depot. He wanted a new store building to add more sales floor space and to serve as a positive moral influence on the city and his customers.

Wanamaker believed there was a direct link between "a city's physical appearance and its moral state," as one historian explained.[49] In doing so, he was a part of a popular movement among nineteenth-century Protestant moral reformers that believed in the moral influence of architecture.[50] Inspired by minister and theologian Horace Bushnell's concept of "Christian nurture," the movement emphasized the idea that character formation occurred slowly over time by direct instruction and unconscious nurturing through the home and church.[51] Architects, art critics, and moral reform leaders picked up the idea and popularized it. The settlement house movement, tenement reform, the Sunday school movement, the City Beautiful movement, and the YMCA all felt that the architectural and aesthetic design of public buildings, parks, churches, and civic spaces helped counter the ill effects of the urban environment and bettered the behavior of its inhabitants. Wanamaker's Sunday school and church, Bethany, had already been an experiment in this vein. Mission Sunday schools were opened in impoverished neighborhoods to provide basic reading and writing along with religious education steeped in middle-class values.

Just as Wanamaker borrowed from the YMCA for his employee education programs, the Y also shaped his perspective on the power of architecture. Historian Paula Lupkin has argued, "From the beginning, the YMCA was invested in defining class, race, and ethnicity as well as gender through its buildings."[52] A YMCA building gave physical form to the organization's values by providing multiple defined spaces for wholesome leisure, learning, and, later, physical activity. Wanamaker felt that a new building for his Philadelphia store could do more than house his successful business; it would also foster a physical environment that would gently cultivate morally responsible citizens. He had attributed part of Bethany's success to its positive influence on the surrounding area of the church, making the neighborhood "a desirable place for residence."[53]

During Wanamaker's visit to the Columbian Exhibition in 1893, he visited the construction site of Marshall Field's new department building in Chicago. Impressed by the exhibition's architecture and Field's new store, Wanamaker hired the man connected to both architectural feats, Daniel Burnham. Construction on Wanamaker's new store began in 1902, though it proceeded in three phases so as not to interrupt store business. Finally, in December 1911 the store was ready for its dedication. Burnham created an enormous granite building — covering an entire city block and rising twelve stories — in a Renaissance palazzo style with columns framing the four entrances. Burnham proclaimed, "The building as a whole, both inside and outside, is the most monumental commercial structure ever erected anywhere in the world."[54] It was impressive.[55]

Promotional materials celebrating the completion of the new building and the store's anniversary explained that Wanamaker wanted a "sincere," "simple," and "suitable" building that expressed the "soul" of his business.[56] He wanted a monumental building on the scale of other public buildings, courthouses, libraries, and museums serving the city. He desired a store that was "noble," "classic," "a work of art," and "a monument for all time."[57] He also wanted the mechanics of the building to be state of the art to promote safety but also demonstrate modernity. On top of the building, Wanamaker installed a Marconi wireless station that connected him with his New York store and allowed customers to send messages. Later, he added a radio station that broadcast the sermons from the minister at Bethany on Sundays. For Wanamaker, his store building symbolized the character of his business.

Burnham adapted his department store design to Wanamaker's needs, including adding a massive sky-lit atrium in the center of the store, anchored by a three-story golden organ topped off by an angel blowing a horn. Although most department stores were moving beyond store organs by 1911, Wanamaker made it a central feature of his store and scheduled organ concerts daily. Wanamaker named the atrium "The Grand Court of Honor" and used it as a backdrop for his holiday festivals and music concerts. At Christmastime, the Grand Court became an ornate gothic Christian cathedral, with the Great Organ at its center.

In addition to the Grand Court, the store offered customers several restaurants and multiple concert spaces outfitted with extravagant decorations. For his employees, the building offered classrooms, exercise rooms, health facilities, and an outdoor running track on the roof of the building. Wanamaker's art gallery offered shoppers a respite on the upper floors of the store with hundreds of paintings with several depicting Jesus, Madonna, and stories from the Bible as well as other themes. In one of the galleries, he placed his two favorite and most famous paintings by Hungarian artist Mihály Munkáscy, *Christ before Pilate* and *Christ at Calvary*. The two gigantic paintings were hung in such a way that it felt possible to walk into the paintings' versions of the gospels.[58] Store materials encouraged shoppers to visit the paintings to educate themselves.

During Christmas and Easter the building featured ornate displays and musical performances, like other department stores, but remained focused on the Christian message. Wanamaker saw his department store as an extension of his religious work. Writing in response to a letter he received in 1896 asking about his vocation as a Christian and a business man, Wanamaker explained,

> I have tried to be in one sense a preacher of at least good business habits, and hope I have not failed in training a great many people whose lives are better after having spent them with me in our business. I would like to use my store as a pulpit on week days, just as much as my desk at Bethany on Sundays, to lift people up that they may better lift themselves up.[59]

Conclusion

For sixty-one years, John Wanamaker shaped American retail and created an enormously successful department store.[60] But Wanamaker understood his Philadelphia department store as more than a money-making business. A deeply religious man, he simultaneously put his time and money into starting a church, leading the YMCA, assisting religious revivals, and supporting moral reform. Wanamaker saw his business as an instrument for moral reform and as a way to share his Protestant Christian sensibilities through his store's architecture, religious and patriotic holiday decorations and events, art gallery, and employee training programs. The creation and propagation of his "Golden Rule of Business" attempted to bridge the divide between retail and Christianity.[61] While Wanamaker's adoption of Russell Conwell's prosperity gospel helped him make sense of his growing wealth in light of his Christian values, he understood his tremendous success as a blessing from God.

John Wanamaker's department store demonstrates how business leaders blended religion in the late nineteenth and early twentieth centuries. Unquestionably, not all business leaders shared Wanamaker's approach. Some business leaders paid little attention to religion while others used religion to improve their reputations. Previously overlooked by scholars or dismissed as insincere, John Wanamaker illustrates some of the ways business leaders brought together their religious faith with business.

FURTHER READING

Giggie, John M. *After Redemption: Jim Crow and the Transformation of African American Religion in the Delta, 1875–1915*. New York: Oxford University Press, 2008.

Kirk, Nicole C. *Wanamaker's Temple: The Business of Religion in an Iconic Department Store*. New York: New York University Press, 2018.

Lofton, Kathryn. *Consuming Religion*. Chicago: University of Chicago Press, 2017.

Martin, Lerone A. *Preaching on Wax: The Phonograph and the Shaping of Modern African American Religion*. New York: New York University Press, 2014.

Porterfield, Amanda, Darren E. Grem, and John Corrigan. *The Business Turn in American Religious History*. New York: Oxford University Press, 2017.

Stievermann, Jan, Philip Goff, and Detlef Junker, eds. *Religion and the Marketplace in the United States*. New York: Oxford University Press, 2015.

Watts, Jill. *God, Harlem U.S.A.: The Father Divine Story*. Berkeley: University of California Press, 1992.

BIBLIOGRAPHY

Baptist, Edward E. *The Half Has Never Been Told: Slavery and the Making of American Capitalism.* New York: Basic Books, 2014.

Benson, Susan. "The Cinderella of Occupations: Managing the Work of Department Store Saleswomen, 1900–1940." *Business History Review* 55, no. 1 (Spring 1981): 1–25.

———. *Counter Cultures: Saleswomen, Managers, and Customers in American Department Stores, 1890–1940.* Champaign: University of Illinois Press, 1988.

Bowler, Kate. *Blessed: A History of the American Prosperity Gospel.* New York: Oxford University Press, 2013.

Carté Engel, Katherine. *Religion and Profit: Moravians in Early America.* Philadelphia: University of Pennsylvania Press, 2009.

Corrigan, John. *Business of the Heart: Religion and Emotion in the Nineteenth Century.* Berkeley: University of California Press, 2002.

Dochuk, Darren. *Anointed with Oil: How Christianity and Crude Made Modern America.* New York: Basic Books, 2019.

Ershkowitz, Herbert. *John Wanamaker: Philadelphia Merchant.* Conshohocken: Combined Publishing, 1999.

Evensen, Bruce. *God's Man for the Gilded Age: D. L. Moody and the Rise of Modern Mass Evangelism.* New York: Oxford University Press, 2003.

———. "It's Harder Getting into the Depot than Heaven: Moody, Mass Media and the Philadelphia Revival of 1875–76." *Pennsylvania History* 69, no. 2 (Spring 2002): 149–178.

Gasparini, Daria. "A Celebration of Moral Force: The Catholic Total Abstinence Union of American Centennial Fountain." MA thesis, University of Pennsylvania, Philadelphia, 2002.

Glass, William R. "Liberal Means to Conservative Ends: Bethany Presbyterian Church, John Wanamaker, and the Institutional Church Movement." *American Presbyterians* 68, no. 3 (Fall 1990): 181–192.

Gloege, Timothy E. W. *Guaranteed Pure: The Moody Bible Institute, Business, and the Making of Modern Evangelicalism.* Chapel Hill: University of North Carolina Press, 2015.

Grem, Darren E. *The Blessings of Business: How Corporations Shaped Conservative Christianity.* New York: Oxford University Press, 2016.

Hammond, Sarah R., and Darren Dochuk. *God's Businessmen: Entrepreneurial Evangelicals in Depression and War.* Chicago: University of Chicago Press, 2017.

Harris, Neil. *Cultural Excursions: Marketing Appetites and Cultural Tastes in Modern America.* Chicago: University of Chicago Press, 1990.

Hines, Thomas S. *Burnham of Chicago: Architect and Planner.* Chicago: University of Chicago Press, 1979.

Hopkins, C. Howard. *History of the YMCA in North America.* New York: National Board of Young Men's Christian Associations Press, 1951.

Hudnut-Beumler, James D. *In Pursuit of the Almighty's Dollar: A History of Money and American Protestantism.* Chapel Hill: University of North Carolina Press, 2007.

Kirshenblatt-Gimblett, Barbara. *Destination Culture: Tourism, Museums, and Heritage.* Berkeley: University of California Press, 1998.

McCabe, James D. *The illustrated history of the Centennial exhibition: held in commemoration of the one hundredth anniversary of American independence; with a full description of the great buildings and all the objects of interest exhibited in them ... to which is added a complete description of the city of Philadelphia.* Philadelphia: National Publishing Company, 1877.

Moore, R. Laurence. *Selling God: American Religion in the Marketplace of Culture.* New York: Oxford University Press, 1994.

Nasaw, David. *Children of the City: At Work and at Play.* New York: Anchor, 2012.

Noll, Mark A. *God and Mammon: Protestants, Money, and the Market, 1790–1860.* New York: Oxford University Press, 2002.

Orsi, Robert. *Gods of the City: Religion and the American Urban Landscape.* Bloomington: Indiana University Press, 1999.

Porterfield, Amanda, Darren E. Grem, and John Corrigan. *The Business Turn in American Religious History.* New York: Oxford University Press, 2017.

Rydell, Robert W. *All the World's a Fair: Visions of Empire at American International Expositions, 1876–1916.* Chicago: University of Chicago Press, 1984.

Schmidt, Leigh Eric. *Consumer Rites: The Buying and Selling of American Holidays.* Princeton: Princeton University Press, 1995.

Smith, Gary Scott. *The Search for Social Salvation: Social Christianity in America, 1880–1925.* Lanham: Lexington Books, 2000.

Stead, William Thomas. *If Christ Came to Chicago! A Plea for the Union of All Who Love in the Service of All Who Suffer.* Chicago: Laird & Lee, 1894.

Stievermann, Jan, Philip Goff, and Detlef Junker, eds. *Religion and the Marketplace in the United States.* New York: Oxford University Press, 2015.

Valeri, Mark R. *Heavenly Merchandize: How Religion Shaped Commerce in Puritan America.* Princeton: Princeton University Press, 2010.

Wayland-Smith, Ellen. *Oneida: From Free Love Utopia to the Well-Set Table.* New York: Picador, 2016.

Weber, Max. *The Protestant Ethic and the Spirit of Capitalism.* New York: Scribner, 1976.

Weisenfeld, Judith. *Hollywood Be Thy Name: African American Religion in American Film, 1929–1949.* Berkeley: University of California Press, 2007.

NOTES

1   An earlier fair in New York City failed to garner the national support and attention that the Centennial did. Other fairs had elements of the global exhibitions, but the sheer size and scale of the Centennial Fair made it notable. The Fair was also the first in a series of world's fairs that opened across the United States.

2   Robert W. Rydell, *All the World's a Fair: Visions of Empire at American International Expositions, 1876–1916* (Chicago: University of Chicago Press, 1984), 11.

3   For an introduction to the great exhibitions and religious display see Barbara Kirshenblatt-Gimblett, *Destination Culture: Tourism, Museums, and Heritage* (Berkeley: University of California Press, 1998). For a history of the exhibitions and their links to the development of American museums and department stores, see Neil Harris, *Cultural Excursions: Marketing Appetites and Cultural Tastes in Modern America* (Chicago: University of Chicago Press, 1990).

4   Rydell, *All the World's a Fair*, 14–15.

5   Rydell, *All the World's a Fair*, Kindle ed.

6   Catholics and Irish immigrants faced discrimination during the nineteenth century, with several notable tragic events happening in Philadelphia. For a detailed description and history of the fountain, see Daria Gasparini, "A Celebration of Moral Force: The Catholic Total Abstinence Union of American Centennial Fountain" (MA thesis, University of Pennsylvania, Philadelphia, 2002), https://repository.upenn.edu/cgi/viewcontent.cgi?article=1361&context=hp_theses.   Frank's Illustrated Guide to the Fair lists the fountain as the "Roman Catholic Fountain."

7   Gasparini, "Celebration of Moral Force," 8.

8   Gasparini, "Celebration of Moral Force," 8.

9   Gasparini, "Celebration of Moral Force," 8–9.

10   For a detailed description and history of the fountain, see Gasparini, "Celebration of Moral Force," 13.

11   Gasparini, "Celebration of Moral Force," 8–9.

12   "Religious Liberty (1876), by Sir Moses Jacob Ezekiel (1844–1917)," Association for Public Art, https://www.associationforpublicart.org/artwork/religious-liberty/.

13   "Religious Liberty (1876)."

14   "Religious Liberty (1876)." The statues has been moved twice and now sits outside of the National Museum of Jewish History in Philadelphia.

15   James D. McCabe, *The illustrated history of the Centennial exhibition: held in commemoration of the one hundredth anniversary of American independence; with a full description of the great buildings and all the objects of interest exhibited in them … to which is added a complete description of the city of Philadelphia* (Philadelphia: National Publishing Company, 1877), 415.

16   McCabe, *The illustrated history of the Centennial exhibition*, 461.

17   "Froc Robert's Exhibit — Main Building," Free Library of Philadelphia, https://libwww.freelibrary.org/digital/item/1286; and "Basilica of the Sacred Heart Is the Heart of Indiana's University of Notre Dame Campus," Midwest Guest, December 21, 2010, https://www.midwestguest.com/2010/12/basilica-of-the-sacred-heart-is-the-heart-of-indianas-university-of-notre-dame-campus.html.

18   McCabe, *The illustrated history of the Centennial exhibition*, 405. The figures were estimated to be two-thirds life-size.

19   McCabe, *The illustrated history of the Centennial exhibition*, 356, 710.

20   Rydell, *All the World's a Fair*, 7–8.

21   Wanamaker never called his stores "department stores," while his customers and competition did so. I use the term "department store" in this essay because it describes his retail model. The department store lacks a clear point of origin, although many stores lay claim to the title. The first department store was likely Le Bon Marché in Paris, France.

22   Nicole C. Kirk, *Wanamaker's Temple: The Business of Religion in an Iconic Department Store* (New York: New York University Press, 2018); Robert Orsi, *Gods of the City: Religion and the American Urban Landscape* (Bloomington: Indiana University Press, 1999), 15–16.

23   Bruce Evensen, "It's Harder Getting into the Depot than Heaven: Moody, Mass Media and the Philadelphia Revival of 1875–76," *Pennsylvania History* 69, no. 2 (Spring 2002): 167–169, passim.

24   Evensen, "It's Harder Getting into the Depot"; Bruce Evensen, *God's Man for the Gilded Age: D. L. Moody and the Rise of Modern Mass Evangelism* (New York: Oxford University Press, 2003).

25   Evensen, "It's Harder Getting into the Depot"; Evensen, *God's Man.*

26   Amanda Porterfield, Darren E. Grem, and John Corrigan, *The Business Turn in American Religious History* (Oxford: Oxford University Press, 2017), 2.

27   R. Laurence Moore, *Selling God: American Religion in the Marketplace of Culture* (New York: Oxford University Press, 1994), 9; and Porterfield, Grem, and Corrigan, *Business Turn in American Religious History.*

28   Max Weber, *The Protestant Ethic and the Spirit of Capitalism* (New York: Scribner, 1976).

29   Moore, *Selling God*, 6.

30   Mark Noll, *God and Mammon: Protestants, Money, and the Market, 1790–1860* (New York: Oxford University Press, 2002), 3.

31   Katherine Carté Engel, *Religion and Profit: Moravians in Early America* (Philadelphia: University of Pennsylvania Press, 2009).

32   Mark Valeri, *Heavenly Merchandize: How Religion Shaped Commerce in Puritan America* (Princeton: Princeton University Press, 2010).

33   C. Howard Hopkins, *History of the YMCA in North America* (New York: National Board of Young Men's Christian Associations Press, 1951), 5–6.

34   Hopkins, *History of the YMCA*, 36.

35   Hopkins, *History of the YMCA*, 45.

36   Herbert Ershkowitz, *John Wanamaker: Philadelphia Merchant* (Conshohocken: Combined Publishing, 1999), 39.

37   Macy's started in 1858 and became a department store in 1877. Bloomingdale's was founded in 1872. Gimbels started in Milwaukee in 1887, opening branches in Philadelphia in 1894 and in New York City, directly across the street from Macy's, in 1910. By the 1890s, department stores appeared across the United States. See Jan Whitaker, *World of Department Stores* (New York: Vendome, 2011), 270.

38   Letters from Dwight L. Moody to John Wanamaker, Box 1, Folder 2, Wanamaker Papers, Pennsylvania Historical Society (hereafter, WP). See also Kirk, *Wanamaker's Temple*; and Timothy Gloege, *Guaranteed Pure: The Moody Bible Institute, Business, and the Making of Modern Evangelicalism* (Chapel Hill: University of North Carolina Press, 2015).

39   Johns Corrigan, *Business of the Heart: Religion and Emotion in the Nineteenth Century* (Berkeley: University of California Press, 2002), 80.

40   Corrigan, *Business of the Heart*, 79.

41   William Thomas Stead, *If Christ Came to Chicago! A Plea for the Union of All Who Love in the Service of All Who Suffer* (Chicago: Laird & Lee, 1894), 75. See also Gary Scott Smith, *The Search for Social Salvation: Social Christianity in America, 1880–1925* (Lanham: Lexington Books, 2000), 73, 78. For a history of Protestants and money, see James D. Hudnut-Beumler, *In Pursuit of the Almighty's Dollar: A History of Money and American Protestantism* (Chapel Hill: University of North Carolina Press. 2007).

42 Russell Conwell, *Acres of Diamonds* Reprinted by BN Online Publishing, 2007), 16. For more on the prosperity gospel then and now, see Kate Bowler, *Blessed: A History of the American Prosperity Gospel* (New York: Oxford University Press, 2013); and Darren Dochuk, *Anointed with Oil: How Christianity and Crude Made Modern America* (New York: Basic Books, 2019).

43 Wanamaker was also criticized for donating a large amount of money to Harrison's campaign. He was accused of buying his cabinet seat. Later, scandal clouded his relationship with the president again when Wanamaker and some friends bought a vacation home on Cape May near Wanamaker's summer residence as a gift for Harrison's wife. The upheaval over the gift resulted in the Harrisons returning the house.

44 "Oak Hall," Gibbons Drawer 1, WP.

45 "Oak Hall (1861) Founder's Aim," Gibbons Drawer 1, WP. Other retailers, such as J. C. Penny, shared Wanamaker's concerns and created their own business reform programs and retail practices.

46 "Oak Hall (1861) Founder's Aim," Gibbons Drawer 1, WP.

47 David Nasaw, *Children of the City: At Work and at Play* (New York: Anchor, 2012), 43–44; and Brewer, "Child Labor in the Department Store," *Annals of the American Academy of Political and Social Science* 20 (1902): 167–177; 167.

48 Susan Benson, *Counter Cultures: Saleswomen, Managers, and Customers in American Department Stores, 1890–1940* (Champaign: University of Illinois Press, 1988), 6, 22; and Benson, "The Cinderella of Occupations: Managing the Work of Department Store Saleswomen, 1900–1940," *Business History Review* 55, no. 1 (Spring 1981): 1–25.

49 Paul Boyer, *Urban Masses and Moral Order: 1820–1920 (Cambridge, MA: Harvard University Press, 1978)*, 252, 262.

50 Richard Bushman, *Refinement of America: Persons, Houses, Cities (New York: Vintage, 1993)*, passim; Boyer, *Urban Masses and Moral Order*, 162–187.

51 Colleen McDannell, *Christian Home in Victorian America: 1840–1900 (Bloomington: Indiana University Press, 1986)*, 48.

52 Paula Lupkin, *Manhood Factories: YMCA Architecture and the Making of Modern Urban Culture (Minneapolis: University of Minnesota Press, 2010)*, xxi.

53 William R. Glass, "Liberal Means to Conservative Ends: Bethany Presbyterian Church, John Wanamaker, and the Institutional Church Movement," *American Presbyterians* 68, no. 3 (Fall 1990): 185, 190.

54 Thomas S. Hines, *Burnham of Chicago: Architect and Planner* (Chicago: University of Chicago Press, 1979), 303.

55 The Wanamaker Building is still in use today. It has been adapted for office space; however, the central part of the store around the atrium and several adjacent floors remain a department store, now Macy's (as of 2020). Macy's continues the tradition of playing the Great Organ everyday.

56 Joseph H. Appel and Leigh M. Hodges, *Golden Book of Wanamaker Stores: Jubilee Year, 1861–1911 (Philadelphia: Self-published by John Wanamaker, 1911)*, 246.

57 Appel and Hodges, *Golden Book, 246*.

58 "Christ Before Pilate Sold," *New York Times*, February 10, 1887. Wanamaker purchased *Christ before Pilate* in 1877 and *Christ at Calvary* in 1888 and befriended the artist. He paid the highest price ever recorded for a painting in the United States at the time.

59 JW to R. M. Luther, December 31, 1896, WP.

60 Wanamaker opened a branch in New York City in 1896 when he purchased A. T. Stewart's former store. The store also had a very successful mail order business that extended the reach of the store across the country. After Wanamaker's death, the store expanded to local malls in addition to its center city Philadelphia and New York locations.

61 "The Wanamaker System: Its Place in Applied Economics," Box 75, Folder 3, WP. Also see Appel and Hodges, *Golden Book of Wanamaker Stores*, 160–177.

Chapter Nineteen

THE PROHIBITION CRUSADE AND AMERICAN MORAL POLITICS

Joseph L. Locke
University of Houston-Victoria, Victoria, Texas

January 17, 1920, was a day of funerals. John Barleycorn, the popular personification of alcohol, had died at the stroke of midnight and, later that morning, celebratory elegies sounded in thousands of churches and tabernacles all across the United States. In Norfolk, Virginia, ten-thousand revelers helped the professional baseball player turned celebrity evangelist Billy Sunday bury him in a mock grave. Twenty singing pallbearers — trailed by a man in a devil's mask melodramatically weeping and moaning — carried an empty, twenty-foot empty casket to Sunday, who smiled over it in triumph. "Good-bye John," Sunday shouted. "You were God's worst enemy; you were hell's best friend." Sunday nailed the casket shut, climbed back into his pulpit and, waving an American flag, shouted the Doxology — "Praise Father, Son, and Holy Ghost" — together with the ten thousand.[1]

Sunday wasn't alone. Religious leaders buried their own John Barleycorns all across the country. In Fort Worth, the proto-fundamentalist J. Frank Norris buried him in a pine casket full of empty whiskey bottles.[2] The Ku Klux Klan and the Anti-Saloon League paraded him down Atlanta's Peachtree Street together and burned him in effigy over an alcohol-fueled bonfire. A man dressed as Uncle Sam carried him to Boston's Morgan Memorial Methodist Church in a hearse.[3] William Jennings Bryan had celebrated at the stroke of midnight with politicians and Anti-Saloon League leaders at the First Congregational Church in Washington, DC. "Let the world rejoice," he said, for "the greatest moral reform of the generation has been accomplished."[4] Local chapters of the Women's Christian Temperance Union and the Anti-Saloon League also celebrated throughout the country. Church doors were thrown open to celebratory services. The whole machinery of American Protestantism had dedicated itself to the eradication of alcohol and, on that January day, pastors, evangelists, reformers, crusaders, women's leaders, and professional lobbyists all reveled in their victory. John Barleycorn was dead. Prohibition had come.

Prohibition was the culmination of years of labor, first by antebellum "temperance" activists and then by turn-of-the-century prohibitionists. It represented the high-water mark of American religion's raw political power, the moment when America's Protestant churches could take a pen to the Constitution and write in their own morality clause. Although the Eighteenth Amendment would be repealed, the relationship between religion and politics — and not just between church and state — would never again be the same.

A Companion to American Religious History, First Edition. Edited by Benjamin E. Park.
© 2021 John Wiley & Sons, Inc. Published 2021 by John Wiley & Sons, Inc.

Prohibition politicized Protestant America. It injected morality into national politics and national politics into morality. The antiliquor crusade taught American Protestants to incorporate politics as an essential component of their theology. The prohibition crusade offered a training ground for fundamentalists who would spend another century fighting America's culture wars, for women who found their entryway into American public life, and for religious lobbyists who finally learned how to steer the nation's political machinery toward religious ends. It brought southern religion into American life, heralding the political maturation of the Bible Belt and the explosive political emergence of southern evangelicalism. Prohibition united white Protestant America: liberal and conservative churches, evangelical and mainline denominations, northern and southern faiths, political progressives and conservatives, and urban and rural congregations put aside their differences to battle for a national moral awakening. Although it would not last, prohibition's triumph, however temporary and however compromised it would be in practice, testified more than anything else for all time to the raw political power of American Protestantism in national life.

The religious struggle for prohibition stretched back to the antebellum temperance movement, when, in the afterglow of the Second Great Awakening, a newly aroused American evangelicalism, flush with millennial visions of a "Benevolent Empire," threw itself into public life to dry out the United States. Leading American religious leaders, including Lyman Beecher and Charles Grandison Finney, denounced the evils of intemperance. Churchmen and churchwomen personally pledged themselves to temperance — moderation — and then, increasingly, to complete abstention from alcohol.[5] Temperance became a marker of moral respectability. In 1826, Beecher and Dr. Justin Edwards organized the American Temperance Society (ATS). Within a few short years, it claimed over a million members. And as the movement grew, reformers widened their ambitions. Buoyed increasingly by the reformist energies of the antebellum women's movement and the abolitionist crusade — early temperance activism was concentrated primarily in the North — and by nativist suspicions of not only surging Irish and German immigration but the associated growth of American Catholicism, Protestant temperance activists waged war on alcohol in the United States. At first, they employed the soft tools of moral suasion. They published literature and deployed lecturers. But a growing movement demanded stronger measures. Reformers turned to politics. They organized and they pressured and they won a string of victories at the state and local levels. The 1851 "Maine Law" outlawed the production and consumption of alcohol there and a dozen northern states soon followed.[6] Most of these laws, however, were short-lived. The problems of enforcement and the vagaries of politics, particularly the turmoil of the growing sectional crisis, led to the quick repeal of most. Nevertheless, their passage testified to the growing power of religion in public life and provided a foundation for future endeavors.[7]

Although temperance reform flickered in the years during and immediately after the Civil War, the collapse of Reconstruction softened the division between North and South and allowed moral reformers across the country to reunite behind prohibition and others moral reform movements. Beginning in the 1870s, activists culled the remnants of the antebellum temperance movement, condemned anew the evils of alcohol, and launched one of the greatest political movements in American religious history.

America was busy growing up in the decades around the turn of the twentieth century. An antebellum world of small farms and small towns driven by horse power and steam power gave way to electricity and the automobile and skyscrapers and steel. Industrial America's insatiable hunger for cheap labor pulled into its cities a new working class. Millions of immigrants came from China, Mexico, and, most especially, from every corner of Europe, bringing with them their foreign languages and their Catholicism and their Judaism. That was already enough to rile native-born Protestant Americans. But the immigrants brought their saloons, too. Immigrant and working-class male culture revolved around saloons, many of them located amid sprawling red light districts awash with prostitution and gambling and jazz and dancing and other urban vices.

The nation's white middle class revolted. Amid the luxuries and the turmoil of the industrial conquest, native-born Protestants comprehended a world lost to greed and corruption and ambition and callousness and cosmopolitanism and sin and disorder. But there was hope. An older America had passed but lived on in the nostalgic longings of Protestant America who believed they could accomplish what one historian called a national "moral reconstruction."[8] Anxious religious leaders turned to moral reform. They attacked gambling, prostitution, obscenity, Sabbath-breaking, and a host of other alleged moral outrages. But nothing so moved Protestant America as the decades-long fight against alcohol. "Prohibition," wrote historian Norman H. Clark, "was to many people the *most* important reform, indeed, the *most* important question in American life."[9] Alcohol bred crime, critics said. Drunkards produced disorder. The pestilential reach of saloons — alleged breeding grounds for crime, disease, poverty, political corruption, and sexual violence — polluted the moral climate of entire neighborhoods, even entire towns and cities. And so American Protestants organized against it.

After the Civil War, organizations such as the National Temperance Society, the Prohibition Party, and the Woman's Christian Temperance Union — the latter especially under the leadership of Frances Willard — pushed the antiliquor reform movement beyond "temperance" and toward prohibition. Like their forebears, these early groups emerged from within northern churches, enmeshed themselves with millennial theologies, and embraced a broad host of social reforms. But unlike their temperance forebears, they eschewed the traditional tactics of moral suasion — relying upon sermons and speeches and printed material and public shame — and committed themselves instead to sustained political action.

Progress was slow. The prohibition movement had yet to achieve sufficient organizational strength, many religious leaders had yet to embrace the politics of moral reform, the women's movement had not yet achieved the power and prominence that it would later leverage on behalf of prohibition, the nation had yet to surrender itself to the Progressive Era's mania of "reform," too few yet saw the American state as a proper engine for moral legislation, and southern evangelicalism still slumbered in a Bible Belt that had to realize its full political power. But all of that would soon change. The churning of industrial capitalism and labor of various social reformers convinced Americans of the need for reform legislation, the women's movement matured and threw itself behind prohibition, the organizational maturation of the prohibition movement offered financial and logistical paths to achieve legal prohibition, and the political awakening of southern evangelicals catapulted prohibition onto its path to the United States constitution.

Protestant women were always the backbone of the prohibition crusade. A number of local campaigns in the Northeast and Midwest cohered in Ohio in 1874 with the official founding of the Woman's Christian Temperance Union (WCTU), a league of locally organized and largely autonomous women's groups committed to "the entire prohibition of the manufacture and sale of intoxicating liquors as a beverage."[10] Their church work had brought them out of their homes, and their commitment to prohibition thrust them into the WCTU. Local chapters organized picnics and marches, petitioned politicians, and spoke forcefully against the evils of alcohol. And their aims grew.[11]

Religious work for prohibition was, for many women, an entrée into a broader engagement in politics and public life, just as abolition had been before the Civil War. Under the leadership of Frances Willard, the Woman's Christian Temperance Union adopted a "do everything" policy to aid American women in their battles not just against liquor but against gambling, prostitution, urban poverty, and, eventually, for the ballot.[12] By 1890, the WCTU had 200,00 members. It was the largest women's organization in the country. One historian called the WCTU "the major vehicle through which women developed a changing role for themselves in American society."[13] Although its members may not yet have been able to vote, they learned to organize, petition, lobby, educate, speak, and campaign. Prohibition and the women's suffrage movement overlapped almost completely. A suffragist was almost certainly a prohibitionist; a prohibitionist was almost certainly a suffragist. "Put the ballot in the hands of woman," a Los Angeles Methodist preached, "and she will send the saloons to the damnation of hell."[14]

Not all women relied upon the vote or the respectable tactics of pressure politics. In Kansas, Carrie Nation took a hatchet to illegal saloons and became a national sensation. Nation, a WCTU member who had suffered through two abusive, alcoholic husbands, received a "Baptism of the Holy Ghost" and felt called by God to destroy the state's illicit saloons.[15] Her "hatchetations" turned her into a national celebrity and she toured the country selling small souvenir hatchets and preaching the gospel of prohibition. She described herself as "a bulldog running along at the feet of Jesus, barking at what He doesn't like."[16] Although a flamboyant spectacle who largely operated apart from the movement's sober and respectable crusaders, she nevertheless embodied for many the fiery passion of the American women who fought for prohibition.

Men also organized, of course. Male preachers and pastors mobilized their congregations and worked to achieve prohibition at the local and state levels. Recognizing the need for coordinated action, Rev. Howard Hyde Russell founded the Anti-Saloon League (ASL) as an Ohio-based pressure group in 1893. Two years later, flush with funds and declaring itself "the church in action against the saloon," the organization went national.[17] It largely pioneered single-issue American lobbying and mastered the art of fund-raising, drawing particular support from larger donors such as John D. Rockefeller and Andrew Carnegie. It quickly yoked a nationwide grassroots organization to a Washington, DC-based campaign eager to dry out all of America. Wayne Wheeler became superintendent in 1903 and, under his leadership, the ASL put the full weight of its millions of members against any politician — Democrat, Republican, or anything else — who opposed antiliquor policies.[18] That flexibility allowed what was often seen as a northern reform to flourish in the American South.[19]

When northern evangelicals fought for various reforms before the Civil War, southerners balked.[20] The imperatives of a slave society largely constrained them. Their social outlook was defensive and reactionary: they said slavery was biblical, the South was a Christian Nation, and Reconstruction necessitated southern "redemption."[21] But anything else was "politics." And so, when they weren't busy sacralizing the southern social order, they looked inward. Their theology emphasized a soul-centered faith of personal salvation. But then slavery died and Reconstruction collapsed. Fears of activist religion finally abated and southern evangelicals were freed to inject themselves as a proactive force in American life. They quickly learned to incorporate a new political gospel into their theology. The "Bible Belt" was busy being born.[22]

Still, the southern crusade faced obstacles. A generation who had come to associate religious activism with abolitionism still looked warily upon religious reformers. "The world had long suffered from the oppressions of government under the pretext of ruling by divine right," the aging president of the Confederacy, Jefferson Davis, warned amid a statewide prohibition campaign in Texas in 1887. "In this," Davis said, "I see the forbidden union of Church and State. My grief is real and relates to both."[23] That particular campaign collapsed amid a chorus of similar anticlerical rhetoric. Voters beat it back handily, as they would in a multitude of southern states in the latter years of the nineteenth century.

But southern evangelicals were stirring. The political awakening of the Bible Belt had many roots: the influx of wealth into denominations from New South merchants, the rising influence of pastorates in new urban "First Churches," the construction of vast denominational bureaucracies, the proliferation of denominational newspapers and well-endowed religious universities, and the persistent activism of charismatic religious leaders.[24] But still the religious South needed a lever. They needed an excuse to get into politics and public life. They needed cause to dethrone political leaders. They needed prohibition.

Northern Protestants continued to fight hard for prohibition — southerners, for instance, long identified the WCTU and ASL as "northern" institutions — but it was the Bible Belt that devoted itself fully and uncompromisingly to the prohibition crusade. By turning religious leaders into politicians and politicians into religious leaders, prohibition redefined what it meant for white southerners to be religious. Anticlerical political barriers crumbled across the South. Texas Senator Morris Sheppard, a Methodist who would later author the Eighteenth Amendment, said "there can be no society and no citizenship disassociated from the idea of God."[25] In Virginia, Methodist Bishop James Cannon leveraged his leadership roles in the Anti-Saloon League and the Methodist Church to become not only a veritable political boss in his own state, but one of America's most powerful political voices.[26] (H. L. Mencken said he was, at the peak of his influence, "the undisputed boss of the United States."[27]) Revivalists such as Sam Jones and Mordecai Hamm, meanwhile, barnstormed the South saving souls by preaching prohibition, muddying the distinction between traditional politics and religious identity.[28]

Prohibition marked an unprecedented religious triumph in the South. In many ways, it birthed the modern Bible Belt.[29] One historian argued that prohibition "gauged the distance that postwar congregations and ministers had traveled over the course of the nineteenth century."[30] Another called prohibition the "most important effort to enforce evangelical values in the South."[31] Regardless, Protestant churches locked arms across the South to dry up their communities in so-called "local option" elections and, soon, their states through legislation and constitutional referenda. And they won. By 1907, New York City had more saloons than the entire American South.[32]

Protestant America united behind prohibition. Political and theological divisions gave way. Northern Republicans and southern Democrats rallied together. Liberal Social Gospelers and rigid theological conservatives entered the fray arm in arm. The Anti-Saloon League, for instance, declared itself "the union of churches so long hoped for, a union brought about not by discussion of doctrine or dogma, which intensifies differences, but a real fellowship developing out of co-operation against a common enemy."[33] By the late-nineteenth century, religious reformers cohered into a national movement — what one historian called the "Christian lobby"[34] — that believed morality could best be adjudicated by national policy.

Crusading Protestants threw themselves and their faith directly into national politics. The Eighteenth Amendment was the movement's crowning achievement, but religious activists championed a host of reforms — anti-polygamy laws, anti-gambling laws, anti-prostitution laws, obscenity laws, Sabbath laws, and much other moral legislation. In 1873, for instance, Congress passed the Comstock Law, barring the dissemination of "Every obscene, lewd, or lascivious, and every filthy book, pamphlet, picture, paper, letter, writing, print, or other publication of an indecent character" through the US mail, and in 1909 the Mann Act, barring the transportation of prostitutes across state lines. Many pushed for a so-called "Christian amendment," a constitutional declaration of the United States as a Christian nation.[35]

The flowering of moral reform movement also coincided with, and comprised a key element of, that period of reform known as the Progressive Era.[36] Awakening to the reality of America's powerfully corrupting interests and reimaging the possibilities for an expanded, activist national state, Americans embraced all manner of political reforms. Although liberal-minded critics such as the mid-century American historian Richard Hofstadter — who dismissed prohibition as a "pseudo-reform, a pinched, parochial substitute for reform which had a widespread appeal to a certain type of crusading mind"[37] — later associated prohibition primarily with prudishness and intolerance, prohibition and progressivism largely overlapped for most contemporaries.[38] Both sought to use government to reshape society; both sought to remake the nation in the image of middle-class white Protestantism. Religious energy, moreover, certainly fueled much of the progressive impulse in the United States, and the Social Gospel brought a number of religious leaders, theologians, and social activists together in pursuit of social justice. Nevertheless, while Protestant leaders embraced much of progressive reform — especially women's suffrage — prohibitionists and other moral reformers spoke more often of "morality" than "justice" and the politicization of American Protestantism in pursuit of moral reform depended as much upon an aversion to individual sin as it did on the promise of social salvation.

The white middle-class who pushed for prohibition believed, championed, and reinforced the racial and ethnic prejudices endemic to their class. Prohibition emerged from white Protestants, and the prohibition movement therefore reflected the racial and ethnic imperatives of white Protestants. White southerners, for instance, not only saw no contradiction between support for prohibition and support for Jim Crow, they saw a tremendous overlap. Although many religious leaders in South refrained from the absolute worst of southern race-baiting, the politics of prohibition nevertheless flowed easily with the politics of white supremacy. In Georgia, for instance, Rebecca Latimer Felton was a potent ally of poor white women and a powerful enemy of African American men. She emerged as a major public figure first as an advocate for her husband, a Methodist minister turned state and national congressman, and, after he retired from public life, as a leading voice for reform in her own stead. In 1907, she not only helped dismantle the state's convict leasing system, she successfully pushed Georgia to pass one of the nation's first statewide prohibition laws. Felton argued that prohibition and lynching would protect white women from black rapists. "If it takes lynching to protect women's dearest possession from drunken, ravening beasts," she said, "then I say lynch a thousand a week."[39] Her version of progressive politics and her ruthless racial politics were intertwined. She unabashedly defended women's suffrage *and* lynching as protections for white women against black men. In 1922, she was appointed briefly to the senate, becoming America's first woman senator.[40]

Some African Americans, especially those who conceived of themselves as part of a middle- and upper-class "better sort," hoped that overt support for prohibition might ingratiate themselves with southern white society and stake a claim for themselves as respectable citizens.[41] But it wasn't enough to unravel the tangled knot of prohibition and white supremacy. Even northerners trafficked in toxic racial notions. Frances Willard toured the South in the 1880s and actively courted white southern support for prohibition. She was notably silent on lynching and the violence of Jim Crow, hinting even at times that prohibition might profit southern white women. Soon after the WCTU held its annual convention in Atlanta in 1890, Willard declared herself "a true lover of the southern people" and, complaining about black voters in America, acknowledged that "The Anglo-Saxon race will never submit to be dominated by the Negro so long as his altitude reaches no higher than the personal liberty of the saloon, and the power of appreciating the amount of liquor that a dollar will buy."[42] When antilynching activist Ida B. Wells was asked about Willard's interview, she scoffed. "It is," she complained, "a matter of keen regret that a Christian organization, so large and influential as the Woman's Christian Temperance Union, should refuse to give its sympathy and support to our oppressed people."[43]

But if the prohibition movement largely accommodated itself to the politics of white supremacy, it wholeheartedly demonized immigrant Americans. Beer was widely associated with German-born immigrants — Busch, Miller, Coors, Anheuser, Schlitz, Pabst — who founded the nation's largest breweries and saloons were forever linked in the minds of prohibitionists with the first- and second-generation immigrants who populated much of America's urban working class. In his seminal 1890 expose of America's urban poverty, *How the Other Half Lives,* Jacob Riis, for instance, lamented that saloons outnumbered churches forty to one in New York's Lower East Side. Many American Protestants feared immigrants. They associated them with crime, ignorance, and vice. Frances Willard, for instance, warned against the "scum of the Old World" and decried the "alien illiterates [who] rule our cities today."[44] For prohibitionists, a blow against alcohol and the saloons would be a blow against an immigrant lifestyle they dreaded, a lifestyle that, if they couldn't yet prevent its practitioners from entering the country, at least they could remake into the image of middle-class Protestant culture. Nativist attacks repelled American immigrants, but they attracted increasing support for prohibition.

The prohibition crusade was on the path to victory by the early twentieth century. The WCTU and ASL mobilized, organized, and empowered Protestant churchgoers who subsequently convulsed local and state governments all across the country. Prohibitionists pressed their case wherever they could. If they could not achieve national prohibition, they would work for state bans, and if states could not be won, then local-option elections, and if that failed, then Sunday closing laws, or tighter licensing, or exclusion zones around schools and churches, or limitations on the types and amounts of liquor sold. Evangelists such as Sam Porter Jones, Mordecai Hamm, and the famed Billy Sunday rallied thousands around the nation behind such campaigns. The Anti-Saloon League, meanwhile, pushed for local-option elections as well as statewide bans and adapted itself to local, regional, state, and national conditions. The prohibition movement was not one movement but a thousand.[45]

Once prohibitionists had dried up large swaths of the nation, entire states began to fall. Georgia passed prohibition in 1907 in the aftermath of the Atlanta Race Riot. Oklahoma entered the union that same year with a dry constitution. Alabama, Mississippi, and North Carolina voted out liquor in 1908. Tennessee followed in 1909. Twenty-three states were dry when the United States entered World War I, and America's churchgoers had done it. As a Boston settlement house worker put it in 1916, "It is the plain church-going people of the towns and the countryside who by their inherent moral force are bringing about this stupendous achievement."[46] In Washington, DC, Secretary of State William Jennings Bryan served grape juice at state dinners. Secretary of the Navy Josephus Daniels barred alcohol from the Navy and discouraged nonessential work on the Sabbath.

As prohibition marched across the country, activists, in a radical departure from antebellum temperance ambitions, set their sights on the United States Constitution. On December 10, 1913, several thousand members of the Anti- Saloon League and the Women's Christian Temperance Union marched in Washington, DC and, on the steps of the US Capitol, delivered petitions for a prohibition amendment to Texas Senator Morris Sheppard and Alabama Representative Richard Hobson. Speeches were made and the assembly sang "Onward Christian Soldiers" together.[47] Legislative success would have to wait: Sheppard's proposal for an amendment died in committee, and Hobson's on the floor of the House. But a national movement was born. "From that December day in 1913," Anti-Saloon League president Wayne Wheeler later recalled, "letters, telegrams, and petitions … rolled in by tens of thousands, burying Congress like an avalanche."[48] Sheppard would introduce the amendment every year for the next four years until, in 1917, the "Sheppard Dry Amendment" made it through Congress and on to the states for ratification.

When the US entered World War I, a contagious, hyper-nationalistic "one-hundred-percent-Americanism" melded so seamlessly with the moral crusade that national prohibition swept through the political system. Congress sent the Eighteenth Amendment to the states for ratification on December 18, 1917. Statewide ratifications rolled in over the next thirteen months until, on January 16, 1919, Nebraska became the thirty-sixth state to ratify the amendment, giving it the required three-fourths of states. Prohibition had been put into the constitution.[49] When news reached the Senate, senators broke decorum and loudly applauded Senator Sheppard, the "Father of National Prohibition." "The mothers and Christian citizenship of the Nation," said Senator William Kenyon of Iowa, "are thanking God that there came to Congress a man with courage, persistency, devotion, and love of humanity."[50] The Eighteenth Amendment had been ratified.

Ratification marked a high-water point in the relationship between religion and politics. "The Eighteenth Amendment," critic H. L. Mencken put it, "was fastened upon the Constitution, not as a political measure and by political devices, nor even as a moral measure and by moral devices, but as an almost purely theological measure and by devices borrowed from the camp-meeting."[51] Never before and never again would a united Protestant America employ pressure politics so successfully in pursuit of such a clearly specified and ambitious goal. Although national prohibition was short-lived, its accomplishment revealed the transformed relationship between religion and American public life. Religion revealed itself fully as a potent force in national politics. Government now seemed to American Protestants the proper and logical mechanism to ensure morality. Politicians, such as Senator Morris Sheppard of Texas, for instance, openly promoted a "Christian nation." Religious leaders, such as the Methodist Bishop James Cannon of Virginia, swayed presidential elections.[52]

The passage of the Eighteenth Amendment marked the triumph of American political Christianity, but the battle against alcohol wasn't won. The nation was supposed to go dry a year later, at the stroke of midnight on January 17, 1920. But it didn't. And as bootleggers and moonshiners and speakeasies made a mockery of federal enforcement, the alliance of American Protestants that had united to bury John Barleycorn broke apart. Historian Gaines Foster wrote that "Prohibition, the crowning achievement of moral reconstruction, became its culmination as well."[53] American religion — and American culture more broadly — came undone in the 1920s. Many liberal Protestants lost their vigor for the fight against alcohol at the same time that flagrant disregard for the Volstead Act — the enforcement mechanism for the Eighteenth Amendment — fueled the rise of a fundamentalist movement and the Klan and the culture wars of the 1920s.

The pursuit of prohibition had rewarded the political pugilism of religious leaders, a militance that continued to work its logic long after the accomplishment of the Eighteenth Amendment. A militant wing of "fundamentalists" continued to fight and targeted not just saloons but evolution and jazz and ever-loosening controls over female sexuality.[54] Robert Shuler was a Tennessee-born Methodist pastor who cut his teeth on the prohibition crusades in Texas during the 1910s before winning fame in Southern California during the 1920s and 1930s as the fundamentalist "Fighting Bob" Shuler. J. Frank Norris, who had joined in the national burials of John Barleycorn, leveraged his reputation figting for prohibition and other popular cultural causes into a national reputation. His Fort Worth Baptist church became the largest church in the country and he would spend the next several decades battling bootleggers, evolution, the New Deal, Catholicism, communism, and civil rights.

The impossibility of enforcement, meanwhile, transformed erstwhile social reformers into advocates for aggressive policing. Enforcing the Volstead Act demanded an expanded police state, and many prohibitionists pivoted from the reformation of society to the punishment of individuals in an ever-expanding criminal justice system.[55] Moreover, prohibition brought suspicion of a largely unregulated southern border, prompting the establishment in 1924 of the US Border Patrol, designed to stop not just immigrants but liquor smugglers.

Prohibition remained a potent political issue into the 1920s. In 1928, it helped break, if only temporarily, the Democrat's stranglehold over the American South. Five states of the old Confederacy turned to Herbert Hoover, a dry Republican Protestant, rather than vote for Al Smith, a wet Democratic Catholic. "Whether for good or for ill," the caustic southern critic H. L. Mencken wrote, "the old sharp separation of church and state has been definitely abandoned."

Many prohibitionists channeled their frustrations with enforcement through the Ku Klux Klan. The so-called "Second" Klan attracted millions of Americans into its ranks in the 1920s. While many Protestants certainly recoiled at the extremes of the organization, many others joined, attracted not only to the Klan's racial and ethnic hatreds but by what one historian called its "moral authoritarianism." The Second Klan had many roots, and prohibition was one of them. "The father and mother of the Ku Klux is the Anti-Saloon League," the famed American agnostic Clarence Darrow argued in 1924. "I would not say every Anti-Saloon Leaguer is a Ku Kluxer, but every Ku Kluxer is an Anti-Saloon Leaguer."[56] Bootleggers stood alongside Catholics, immigrants, and African Americans as objects of the Second Klan's hooded bigotry.

As the 1920s progressed, a backlash to the Klan, increasing negative coverage of religious fundamentalism, widespread assumptions about the impossibility of prohibition's enforcement, and the onset of the Great Depression all conspired to undermine prohibition. "Here we are in the midst of the greatest crisis since the Civil War," John Dewey complained in 1932, "and the only thing the two national parties seem to want to debate is booze."[57] The Twenty-first Amendment, repealing the Eighteenth, was ratified in 1933. Although prohibition lingered on in several states, and still today in scattered counties, the prohibition era was over.

Repeal washed away the life's work of Senator Morris Sheppard, author of the Amendment and a tireless defender of prohibition. Sheppard had been widely quoted as saying "there's as much chance of repealing the 18th Amendment as there is for a hummingbird to fly to Mars with the Washington Monument tied to its tail." But Sheppard did not despair when prohibition fell and John Barleycorn rose from the grave. "The victories of righteousness must be perpetually repeated," Sheppard said.[58] He was ready to continue the work. "What we must do," he told a Methodist congregation in 1934, "is to labor for the placement of God and religion at the head of all human activity."[59] He had spent his career doing just that, and generations of politically active American Protestants followed him, travelling along a well-worn path blazed not just by Sheppard but by Billy Sunday, Carrie Nation, J. Frank Norris, and the countless other Protestants who took up the prohibition crusade in the early twentieth century.

Prohibition remade American religion. It mobilized politically minded Protestants behind charismatic crusaders and organizations such as the Anti-Saloon League, it brought women further into public life through churchwork and organizations such as the Women's Christian Temperance League, and it unleashed the full power of the Bible Belt upon national life. Moral reformers march united behind a political crusade that rewrote the American constitution and redefined the parameters of what it meant to be religious in the United States. Although the cause itself would fail — John Barleycorn would rise from the grave that so many Protestants had worked to bury him in — the transformations wrought in American religious life would not be so easily undone.

FURTHER READING

Coker, Joe L. *Liquor in the Land of the Lost Cause: Southern White Evangelicals and the Prohibition Movement.* Lexington: University Press of Kentucky, 2007.

Foster, Gaines. *Moral Reconstruction, Christian Lobbyists and the Federal Legislation of Morality, 1865–1920.* Chapel Hill: University of North Carolina Press, 2002.

McGirr, Lisa. *The War on Alcohol: Prohibition and the Rise of the American State.* New York: W. W. Norton, 2016.

Okrent, Daniel. *Last Call: The Rise and Fall of Prohibition.* New York: Simon and Schuster, 2010.

Szymanski, Ann-Marie. *Pathways to Prohibition: Radicals, Moderates, and Social Movement Outcomes.* Durham: Duke University Press, 2003.

Tyrrell, Ian. *Reforming the World: The Creation of America's Moral Empire.* Princeton: Princeton University Press, 2010.

BIBLIOGRAPHY

Abzug, Robert H. *Cosmos Crumbling: American Reform and the Religious Imagination.* New York: Oxford University Press, 1994.

Blocker, Jack S. *American Temperance Movements: Cycles of Reform.* Boston: Twayne Publishers, 1989.

_____. *Retreat from Reform: The Prohibition Movement in the in the United States, 1890–1913.* Westport: Greenwood Press, 1976.

Blum, Edward J. *Reforging the White Republic: Race, Religion, and American Nationalism, 1865–1898.* Baton Rouge: Louisiana State University Press, 2005.

Bordin, Ruth. *Frances Willard: A Biography*. Chapel Hill: University of North Carolina Press, 1986.

_____. *Woman and Temperance: The Quest for Power and Liberty, 1873–1900*. Philadelphia: Temple University Press, 1981.

Carwardine, Richard J. *Evangelicals and Politics in Antebellum America*. New Haven: Yale University Press, 1993.

Clark, Norman H. *Deliver Us from Evil: An Interpretation of American Prohibition*. New York: Norton, 1976.

Coker, Joe L. *Liquor in the Land of the Lost Cause*. Lexington: University Press of Kentucky, 2007.

Crunden, Robert Morse. *Ministers of Reform: the Progressives' Achievement in American Civilization, 1889–1920*. New York: Basic Books, 1982.

Dorr, Lisa Lindquist. *White Women, Rape, and the Power of Race in Virginia, 1900–1960*. Chapel Hill: University of North Carolina Press, 2004.

Faust, Drew Gilpin. *The Creation of Confederate Nationalism: Ideology and Identity in the Civil War South*. Baton Rouge: Louisiana State University Press, 1988.

Foster, Gaines. *Moral Reconstruction, Christian Lobbyists and the Federal Legislation of Morality, 1865–1920*. Chapel Hill: University of North Carolina Press, 2002.

Funderburg, J. Anne. *Bootleggers and Beer Barons of the Prohibition Era*. Jefferson: McFarland, 2014.

Gilmore, Glenda. *Gender & Jim Crow: Women and the Politics of White Supremacy in North Carolina, 1896–1920*. Chapel Hill: University of North Carolina Press, 1996.

Gordon, Linda. *The Second Coming of the KKK: The Ku Klux Klan of the 1920s and the American Political Tradition*. New York: Liveright, 2018.

Gould, Lewis L. *Progressives and Prohibitionists: Texas Democrats in the Wilson Era*. Austin: University of Texas Press, 1973.

Greenwood, Janette Thomas. *Bittersweet Legacy: The Black and White "Better Classes" in Charlotte, 1850–1910*. Chapel Hill: University of North Carolina Press, 1994.

Griffith, R. Marie. *Moral Combat: How Sex Divided American Christians and Fractured American Politics*. New York: Basic, 2017.

Hamm, Richard F. *Shaping the Eighteenth Amendment: Temperance Reform, Legal Culture, and the Polity, 1880–1920*. Chapel Hill: University of North Carolina Press, 1995.

Harvey, Paul. *Redeeming the South: Religious Cultures and Racial Identities among Southern Baptists, 1865–1925*. Chapel Hill: University of North Carolina Press, 1997.

Hofstadter, Richard. *The Age of Reform: From Bryan to FDR*. New York: Knopf, 1955.

Hohner, Robert A. *Prohibition and Politics: The Life of Bishop James Cannon, Jr.* Columbia: University of South Carolina Press, 1999.

Howe, Daniel Walker. *What Hath God Wrought: The Transformation of America, 1815–1848*. New York: Oxford University Press, 2007.

Irons, Charles, *The Origins of Proslavery Christianity: White and Black Evangelicals in Colonial and Antebellum Virginia*. Chapel Hill: University of North Carolina Press, 2008.

Kobler, John. *Ardent Spirits: The Rise and Fall of Prohibition*. New York: Putnam, 1973.

Leuchtenburg, William E. *The Perils of Prosperity, 1914–1932*. Chicago: University of Chicago Press, 1958.

Link, William A. *The Paradox of Southern Progressivism, 1880–1930*. Chapel Hill: University of North Carolina Press, 1992.

Locke, Joseph L. *Making the Bible Belt: Texas Prohibitionists and the Politicization of Southern Religion*. New York: Oxford University Press, 2017.

Marty, Martin E. *Pilgrims in Their Own Land: 500 years of Religion in America*. Boston: Little, Brown, 1984.

McGirr, Lisa. *The War on Alcohol: Prohibition and the Rise of the American State*. New York: Norton, 2015.

Okrent, Daniel. *Last Call: The Rise and Fall of Prohibition*. New York: Simon and Schuster, 2010.

Ownby, Ted. *Subduing Satan: Religion, Recreation, and Manhood in the Rural South, 1865–1920*. Chapel Hill: University of North Carolina Press, 1990.

Patterson, Michael S. "The Fall of a Bishop: James Cannon Jr. Versus Carter Glass, 1909–1934." *The Journal of Southern History* 39 (November 1973): 493–518.

Pegram, Thomas R. *Battling Demon Rum: The Struggle for a Dry America, 1800–1933*. Chicago: Ivan R. Dee, 1998.

Rorabaugh, W. J. *Prohibition: A Concise History*. New York: Oxford University Press, 2018.

Russell, C. Allyn. "J. Frank Norris: Violent Fundamentalist." *Southwestern Historical Quarterly* 75 (January 1972): 271–302.

Schweiger, Beth Barton. *The Gospel Working Up: Progress and the Pulpit in Nineteenth-Century Virginia.* New York: Oxford University Press, 2000.

Szymanski, Ann-Marie. *Pathways to Prohibition: Radicals, Moderates, and Social Movement Outcomes.* Durham: Duke University Press, 2003.

Thompson, Jr., Paul H. *A Most Stirring and Significant Episode: Religion and the Rise and Fall of Prohibition in Black Atlanta, 1865–1887.* DeKalb: Northern Illinois University Press, 2013.

Timberlake, James H. *Prohibition and the Progressive Movement, 1900–1920.* Cambridge: Harvard University Press, 1963.

Tyrrell, Ian R. Sobering Up: From Temperance to Prohibition in Antebellum America, 1800–1860. Westport, Conn.: Greenwood Press, 1979.

_____. *Woman's World/Woman's Empire: The Woman's Christian Temperance Union in International Perspective 1880–1930.* Chapel Hill: University of North Carolina Press, 1991.

Wilson, Charles Reagan. *Baptized in Blood: The Religion of the Lost Cause, 1865–1920.* Athens: University of Georgia Press, 1980.

NOTES

1 "Billy Sunday Greets 'Old J.B.' With a Grin; Preaches His Funeral," *New York Tribune*, January 17, 1920, 3; "Billy Sunday Conducts 'Funeral,'" *New York Herald,* January 17, 1920, 4; "Billy Sunday Preaches John Barleycorns Funeral," *Christian Advocate,* January 22, 1920, 124.

2 C. Allyn Russell, "J. Frank Norris: Violent Fundamentalist," *Southwestern Historical Quarterly* 75 (January 1972): 282.

3 J. Anne Funderburg, *Bootleggers and Beer Barons of the Prohibition Era* (Jefferson: McFarland, 2014), 5–7.

4 Martin E. Marty, *Pilgrims in Their Own Land: 500 years of Religion in America* (Boston: Little, Brown, 1984), 376.

5 "Teetotaler" derives from the commitment to total abstinence. Daniel Walker Howe, *What Hath God Wrought: The Transformation of America, 1815–1848* (New York: Oxford University Press, 2007), 167–168.

6 Unlike the later prohibition movement, southerners remained largely aloof from antebellum temperance efforts: the defensive imperatives of a slave society stunted an such an interventionist faith.

7 Robert H. Abzug, *Cosmos Crumbling: American Reform and the Religious Imagination* (New York: Oxford University Press, 1994); Ian R. Tyrrell, *Sobering Up: From Temperance to Prohibition in Antebellum America, 1800–1860* (Westport: Greenwood Press, 1979); W. J. Rorabaugh, *Prohibition: A Concise History* (New York: Oxford University Press, 2018).

8 Gaines Foster, *Moral Reconstruction, Christian Lobbyists and the Federal Legislation of Morality, 1865–1920* (Chapel Hill: University of North Carolina Press, 2002).

9 Norman H. Clark, *Deliver Us from Evil: An Interpretation of American Prohibition* (New York: Norton, 1976), 5.

10 *Constitution, By-Laws, and Order of Business of the Women's Christian Temperance Union, 1876* (Toronto: The Guardian Office, 1876), 1.

11 Ruth Bordin, *Woman and Temperance: The Quest for Power and Liberty, 1873–1900* (Philadelphia: Temple University Press, 1981); Ian Tyrrell, *Woman's World/Woman's Empire: The Woman's Christian Temperance Union in International Perspective 1880–1930* (Chapel Hill: University of North Carolina Press, 1991).

12 Ruth Bordin, *Frances Willard: A Biography* (Chapel Hill: University of North Carolina Press, 1986).

13 Bordin, *Woman and Temperance,* xviii.

14 Rorabaugh, *Prohibition,* 42.

15 Carry A. Nation, *The Use and Need of the Life of Carry A. Nation* (Topeka: Steves & Sons, 1908), 91.

16 Quoted in Daniel Okrent, *Last Call: The Rise and Fall of Prohibition* (New York: Simon and Schuster, 2010), 24.

17 William Hamilton Anderson, *The Church in Action Against the Saloon: Being an Authoritative Statement of the Movement Known as the Anti-Saloon League* (Westerville: American Issue, 1906).

18 Jack S. Blocker, *American Temperance Movements: Cycles of Reform* (Boston: Twayne Publishers, 1989); Thomas R. Pegram, *Battling Demon Rum: The Struggle for a Dry America, 1800–1933* (Chicago: Ivan R. Dee, 1998).

19 Joe Coker, *Liquor in the Land of the Lost Cause: Southern White Evangelicals and the Prohibition Movement* (Lexington: University Press of Kentucky, 2007).

20 Carwardine, *Evangelicals and Politics in Antebellum America* (1993).

21 Charles Irons, *The Origins of Proslavery Christianity: White and Black Evangelicals in Colonial and Antebellum Virginia* (Chapel Hill: University of North Carolina Press, 2008); Drew Gilpin Faust, *The Creation of Confederate Nationalism: Ideology and Identity in the Civil War South* (Baton Rouge: Louisiana State University Press, 1988); Charles Reagan Wilson, *Baptized in Blood: The Religion of the Lost Cause, 1865–1920* (Athens: The University of Georgia Press, 1980).

22 For southern religion in this period, see especially Beth Barton Schweiger, *The Gospel Working Up: Progress and the Pulpit in Nineteenth-Century Virginia* (New York: Oxford University Press, 2000); Paul Harvey, *Redeeming the South: Religious Cultures and Racial Identities among Southern Baptists, 1865–1925* (Chapel Hill: University of North Carolina Press, 1997); and Ted Ownby, *Subduing Satan: Religion, Recreation, and Manhood in the Rural South, 1865–1920* (Chapel Hill: University of North Carolina Press, 1990).

23 Varina Davis, *Jefferson Davis: Ex-President of the Confederate States of America*, 890–892; Partially quoted in William J. Cooper, *Jefferson Davis, American*, 694–695; See also Coker, *Liquor in the Land of the Lost Cause*, 80–82.

24 Schweiger, *Gospel Working Up*.

25 Morris Sheppard, *Fraternal and Oher Addresses* (Omaha: Beacon Press, 1910), 284.

26 Robert A. Hohner, *Prohibition and Politics: The Life of Bishop James Cannon, Jr.* (Columbia: University of South Carolina Press, 1999).

27 Michael S. Patterson, "The Fall of a Bishop: James Cannon Jr. Versus Carter Glass, 1909–1934," *The Journal of Southern History* 39, no. 4 (Nov. 1973) 493.

28 Jones preached to as many as three million Americans over the course of his career. Hamm would convert Billy Graham, the most notable figure in postwar evangelical history.

29 Joseph L. Locke, *Making the Bible Belt: Texas Prohibitionist and the Politicization of Southern Religion* (New York: Oxford University Press, 2016). In addition, Beth Barton Schweiger, Paul Harvey, Ted Ownby, and Gaines Foster have all specifically identified the embrace of prohibition as a revolutionary moment. Schweiger, *The Gospel Working Up*, 193; Ownby, *Subduing Satan*, 170; and Foster, *Moral Reconstruction*, 6, 46, 221, 224.

30 Schweiger, *Gospel Working Up*, 193.

31 Ownby, *Subduing Satan*, 170.

32 William A. Link, *The Paradox of Southern Progressivism, 1880–1930* (Chapel Hill: University of North Carolina Press, 1992), 96.

33 Anderson, *The Church in Action Against the Saloon*, 64.

34 Foster, *Moral Reconstruction*, 1.

35 Foster, *Moral Reconstruction*, 27–46.

36 Robert Morse Crunden, *Ministers of Reform: the Progressives' Achievement in American Civilization, 1889–1920* (New York: Basic Books, 1982); James H. Timberlake, *Prohibition and the Progressive Movement, 1900–1920* (Cambridge: Harvard University Press, 1963).

37 Richard Hofstadter, *The Age of Reform: From Bryan to F. D. R.* (New York: Knopf 1955), 289.

38 Timberlake, *Prohibition and the Progressive Movement*; Lewis L. Gould, *Progressives and Prohibitionists: Texas Democrats in the Wilson Era* (Austin: University of Texas Press, 1973). For criticism, see especially Jack S. Blocker Jr., *Retreat from Reform: The Prohibition Movement in the in the United States, 1890–1913* (Westport: Greenwood Press, 1976).

39 Lisa Lindquist Dorr, *White Women, Rape, and the Power of Race in Virginia, 1900–1960* (Chapel Hill: University of North Carolina Press, 2004), 22.

40 On Rebecca Latimer Felton, prohibition, and the South, see Coker, 153–154.

41 See especially Glenda Gilmore, *Gender & Jim Crow: Women and the Politics of White Supremacy in North Carolina, 1896–1920* (Chapel Hill: University of North Carolina Press, 1996); Janette Thomas Greenwood, *Bittersweet Legacy: The Black and White "Better Classes" in Charlotte, 1850–1910* (Chapel Hill: University of North Carolina Press, 1994); and Paul H. Thompson, Jr., *A Most*

Stirring and Significant Episode: Religion and the Rise and Fall of Prohibition in Black Atlanta, 1865–1887 (DeKal: Northern Illinois University Press, 2013).

42 "The Race Problem: Miss Willard on the Political Puzzle of the South," *The Voice*, October 23, 1890, quoted in Edward J. Blum, *Reforging the White Republic: Race, Religion, and American Nationalism, 1865–1898* (Baton Rouge: Louisiana State University Press, 2005), 202.

43 Jacqueline Jones Royster, ed., *Southern Horrors and Other Writings: The Anti-Lynching Campaign of Ida B. Wells, 1892–1900* (Boston: Bedford/St. Martin's, 1997) 138.

44 Daniel Okrent, *Last Call: The Rise and Fall of Prohibition* (New York: Simon and Schuster, 2010), 26; Rorabaugh, *Prohibition*, 33.

45 Ann-Marie E. Szymanski, *Pathways to Prohibition: Radicals, Moderates, and Social Movement Outcomes* (Raleigh: Duke University Press, 2003); Blocker, *American Temperance Movements*.

46 Robert Woods, "Winning the Other Half," *Survey*, December 30, 1916, 352, Quoted in Szymanski, *Pathways to Prohibition*, 192.

47 "Anti-Rum Army at Capitol," *New York Times*, December 11, 1913, 5; Foster, *Moral Reconstruction*, 193–194.

48 John Kobler, *Ardent Spirits: The Rise and Fall of Prohibition* (New York: Putnam, 1973), 201.

49 Richard F. Hamm, *Shaping the Eighteenth Amendment: Temperance Reform, Legal Culture, and the Polity, 1880–1920* (Chapel Hill: University of North Carolina Press, 1995).

50 *Dallas Morning News*, January 17, 1919; *Fort Worth Star-Telegram*, January 17–18, 1919.

51 H. L. Mencken, "Overture to a Melodrama," *Baltimore Evening Sun*, January 28, 1929, quoted in S. T. Joshi, *The Unbelievers: The Evolution of Modern Atheism* (New York: Prometheus, 2011), 129.

52 Hohner, *Prohibition and Politics*.

53 Foster, 221.

54 R. Marie Griffith, *Moral Combat: How Sex Divided American Christians and Fractured American Politics* (New York: Basic, 2017).

55 Lisa McGirr, *The War on Alcohol: Prohibition and the Rise of the American State* (New York: Norton, 2015).

56 Linda Gordon, *The Second Coming of the KKK: The Ku Klux Klan of the 1920s and the American Political Tradition* (New York: Liveright, 2018), 29.

57 William E. Leuchtenburg, *The Perils of Prosperity, 1914–1932* (Chicago: University of Chicago Press, 1958), 266.

58 Morris Sheppard, "Introduction," in Atticus Webb, *Dry America: A Study for the Use of Churches, Sunday Schools, Young People's Societies, Women's Organizations, Etc.* (Nashville: Cokesbury Press, 1931).

59 Morris Sheppard, "Religion and the American Republic," Address, State Line Methodist Church, South, Texarkana September 2, 1934, Morris Sheppard Papers, 1894–1953, Center for American History, The University of Texas at Austin.

Chapter Twenty

RACE, ETHNICITY, AND GENDER AMONG EARLY PENTECOSTALS

Arlene M. Sánchez-Walsh
Azusa Pacific University, Azusa, California

When one speaks of Pentecostalism in the US, one has to speak of Pentecostalisms. Pentecostalisms are movements within Christianity that are evangelical in theological outlook, but unlike other branches of evangelicalism, they emphasize the active role of the Holy Spirit in everyday life. When the New Testament mentions healings, speaking in tongues, prophecy, shoo-ing away snakes, and perhaps most amazingly, raising people from the dead, Pentecostals, historically and today, believe they are imbued with that same spiritual power to perform those actions. Not all Pentecostal groups, however, emphasize the same miraculous actions: some focus on healing, others focus on prophecy, some on the prosperity gospel, still others focus on downplaying miraculous activity and prefer to focus on things like evangelism. While there were Pentecostal revivals in Europe, Asia, and North America around the same time as the 1906 Azusa Street Revival, Azusa Street has become the most well-known and significant event.[1]

The early years of American Pentecostalism (1906–1940), began with the 1906 Azusa Street revival in Los Angeles and concluded with the creation of dozens of different denominations. Out of the Los Angeles mission, groups that focused on maintaining holiness as a standard and groups that rejected the Trinitarian formula for baptism came two schisms born of theological differences. The purpose of this chapter is to explore not only the theological differences of the early Pentecostal movement, but also to examine the role of race, ethnicity, and gender in the early years. Pentecostal pioneers were very aware of the theological divisions chipping away at the fragile unity of their movement, but rarely, if ever, wrote about their lives as people of color and women. Taking a look at two pioneers, Florence L. Crawford and Garfield T. Haywood allows us to examine two of the theological issues responsible for schisms as well as examine how both of them occupied subservient roles within the movement as a woman and an African American man. Crawford, a twice-divorced woman who struggled with the veneration of marriage as the apex of a woman's life, and Haywood, who, despite growing up the son of former slaves and living in segregated Indianapolis, rarely, if ever wrote about race as an issue despite it being the major reason why his movement split up in 1924. Exploring issues of race, ethnicity, and gender through the lives of these two pioneers allows us to not only look at those issues, but also examine the theological issues that divided the movement given that, for Pentecostals, theology was key to nearly every

A Companion to American Religious History, First Edition. Edited by Benjamin E. Park.
© 2021 John Wiley & Sons, Inc. Published 2021 by John Wiley & Sons, Inc.

schism since its early years. Before discussing Crawford and Haywood in some depth, how-ever, we should define some theological terms and set the stage for how a movement, con-vinced it was part of the "last wave" of Christianity before the Second Coming of Jesus, became so divided so fast.

Early Pentecostal magazines are filled with descriptions of miraculous events and healings. Yet while illnesses due to physical ailments and diseases are healed, other healings were related to some perceived moral failing. Converts described healing from smoking, drinking, drug abuse, being freed of the desire to dance, and being freed of heresy. Healing from things like drinking and dancing were typical not only of Pentecostal testimonies, but they were also part of the movement's roots in the nineteenth-century Holiness movement. Holiness was a Protestant movement that believed there was an experience after conversion that prepared followers to lead lives of near sinless perfection. This experience, called sanctification, was not something one received magically, but one had to put in the work of sanctification, which was abstaining from things like drinking, dancing, gambling, and all manner of worldly amusements. One also had to ask and receive sanctification. Many Holiness advocates who described this experience, described being overcome by emotion, crying, and feeling as if they were imbued by the Holy Spirit to live a life without sin. Pentecostalism's genius then was to harness the desire of Holiness advocates' drive to be perfect, but also to have a tangi-ble physical experience measure it. Pentecostals then would argue that you could know whether or not you were sanctified because there was another baptism that followers should actively seek in order to strengthen themselves for the eternal fight against sin.

The baptism of the Holy Spirit, for Holiness advocates, was the reception of sanctification, and the baptism of the Holy Spirit for Pentecostals was evidenced by an ability to speak in other tongues. The reasons why this physical act was attached to Spirit Baptism are compli-cated and beyond the scope of the chapter; suffice to say, speaking in tongues was a way that Pentecostals would be prepared to evangelize the world before the Second Coming. Pentecostalism's conviction that it was the last movement before the end of the world there-fore necessitated different sets of theological tools to assist this evangelization. These tools, particularly Spirit baptism and healing, convinced converts that sanctification, Spirit baptism, and healing were all part of a post-conversion life. Displacing the primary role of sanctification as the key post-conversion experience, as some Pentecostals did, then, marked one of the first schisms of the movement.Those Pentecostals who continued to support the primacy of sanc-tification soon found themselves in opposition to others who advocated the "Finished Work" theology that Spirit Baptism was an all-inclusive experience that included sanctification.

The other theological issue was the spread of a doctrine that insisted the Trinitarian for-mula for baptizing was incorrect, because its definition of God was wrong. Christian belief holds that there are three separate people in one God: Father, Son, and Holy Spirit. Some Christians, however, have challenged that definition and suggest that there are not separate people, but there is only one God with three different names. The Trinitarian formula for baptizing followers then needed to be re-done since the whole idea of the Trinity, for Oneness Pentecostals, was either a misreading of the Bible, a Catholic creation, or both. Both Oneness and Trinitarian Pentecostals were deeply anti-Catholic and convinced of their own proper reading of the Bible. Oneness captured enough Trinitarian Pentecostals' attention, then, that within the largest Trinitarian denomination, the Assemblies of God (AG), many of their lead-ers were re-baptized and this "New Issue" became something that AG evangelists and mis-sionaries were warned about. Oneness was as spiritually dangerous as other "heresies" such as Mormonism, Christian Science, Catholicism, and Spiritualism.

Still, the magazines described a movement that was unified and simply ridding itself of theo-logical stragglers — those who could not follow the clear path to the Second Coming. That clear path for many Pentecostals was to convince people to convert and, once that was accom-plished, to pray for them to receive Spirit Baptism with evidence of speaking in tongues. When magazines mentioned that some people received Spirit Baptism first and converted later, then, it caused theological tensions in the movement, since Protestantism at large, especially evangelical movements, privileged conversion above all else, and it had to happen first. Pentecostalism was different, diverse, and did not follow the rules. Despite Pentecostalism's theological and performative diversity, Pentecostals still wished to define themselves as a unified global phenomenon, beginning in Los Angeles, but soon branching out to Africa, Asia, and Latin America within mere months after the revival began in April 1906. Unity was important because any Christian movement that was going to be the last one before Jesus came back had to be unified, but expansion often caused schism. Within a couple of years following Azusa Street, Pentecostalism had broken up into several denominations and within those denominations there were further problems that limited the extent of Pentecostal unity: the realities of racial and ethnic bias that relegated African Americans, Latinos, Asians, and Native Americans to subservient status.[2]

It is perhaps tragically ironic that those who attended Azusa Street thought that the multicultural and multiracial make-up of the crowds would somehow translate to societal harmony. As we will see when looking at the case of Garfield Haywood, the best of intentions to unify churches was simply not good enough to ensure that Pentecostals would want to continue to attend church together. Though the examples of how African American and Latino Pentecostals were treated as they entered these various denominations is quite different, they do have one thing in common — both groups were viewed as incapable of running their own affairs in church and were soon either subjected to supervision by white overseers or, left to create their own denominations.

For example, the well-known Mexican evangelist, Francisco Olazábal, a Methodist convert to Pentecostalism, soon went to work as a healing evangelist on behalf the Assemblies of God (AG), who ordained him in 1916. Settling in Texas, Olazábal began to work on getting out the Pentecostal message to the Mexican and Mexican American communities in South Texas. By all accounts, he was very successful — almost too successful. AG overseers Henry C. Ball and Alice E. Luce, both of whom had been working with Mexican population in the borderlands since 1915, grew concerned that Olazábal was becoming too powerful. Olazábal had not only become the most revered healing evangelist in the AG, traveling extensively and preaching the Pentecostal message across the US, Mexico, and Puerto Rico, he also secured a printing press to continue the practice of promoting Pentecostalism through the distribution of tracts. The question with the AG at the time, then, was not whether Mexicans could worship with whites, since they usually did not due to the language difference, and Spanish-language services were therefore conducted separately. The question for the AG when it came to Olazábal was whether he was capable of leadership, could handle finances, and whether they would allow him to keep his printing press.

What seemed to alarm the overseers most was that Olazábal opened up a bible college in El Paso in 1922, which appeared to compete with the bible college that Ball began in South Texas. The overseers, along with other leadership of the AG, therefore decided that Olazábal had accumulated too much power and stripped him of his leadership, financial independence, and printing press. Olazábal then left the AG and founded his own denomination in 1923, known as the Concilio Latino Americano de Iglesias Cristianas or the Latin American Council of Christian Churches. At one point he claimed that the AG would allow "El Ruso, El Griego ... pero nunca El Mexicano," which meant that the AG trusted a Russian and a Greek person to be in leadership, but they would never trust a Mexican.

At the heart of these debates was a cultual suspicion. The pages of early AG magazines demonstrate a two-fold suspicion of Mexicans. First, they were suspect because they were seen as barely civilized and still in the grasp of "Romanism," and therefore needed lots of supervision to make sure they were freed of their Catholicism. The other suspicion was that, because they were overwhelmingly Spanish-speaking with little formal education (most of the early converts came from the farm worker class), they could not be trusted to carry on their own theological education, and therefore Luce and Ball continued to supervise Mexican converts well into the 1940s.[3]

One does not have to dig too deeply, of course, to see that the issue with the AG was one of white superiority. That same sense is evident in the history of the PAW and the breakup of the interracial experiment in Indianapolis. Before we discuss the PAW, we should go back to 1906, where the American iteration of Pentecostalism received its biggest boost, and the story of William J. Seymour, whose vision of an interracial church was way ahead of its time. Indeed, the Azusa Street revival began in April 1906 when William Seymour, an African American from Louisiana, having finally received Spirit Baptism, began preaching the necessity of this experience for all followers. To understand both Crawford and Haywood, a detour to explaining the significance of Seymour's Azusa Street church is necessary.

Azusa Street meant everything to Crawford, as she was converted there and was part of the leadership, but she also felt alienated and left Los Angeles to go back to Portland. There are many explanations for her alienation at Azusa Street. Whatever the reason, though, Seymour's outsized personality and leadership rubbed Crawford the wrong way. Depending on which sources one chooses to accept, Crawford left Azusa Street because she did not want to be subservient to Seymour because she was either racist, or upset at his theological divergence, or disappointed at Seymour's decision to marry, or all of the above. Regardless the specifics, Seymour's leadership at Azusa Street had something to do with Crawford's decision to leave.

Seymour was born in Centerville, Louisiana, in 1870, where he was also baptized Catholic. He moved to Indianapolis when he was twenty-five years old and joined a black congregation of mostly white Methodists. Seymour was interested in racial integration and sought out churches that promoted that idea. In 1900, noted Holiness preacher Martin Wells Knapp in Cincinnati, Ohio, who also believed in racial integration, healing, and had a millennialist streak, began teaching Seymour. Seymour later joined the interracial Evening Light Saints, who promoted holiness, healing, and racial integration. Seymour returned to the south in 1903, first with relatives in Houston, Texas, and then two years later, moving to Jackson, Mississippi, where he joined a Holiness church. By 1905, Seymour had enrolled in Charles Parham's bible school in Houston, Texas, where he had to learn by sitting outside the classroom, because Parham would not allow him inside. Despite Parham's overt racism and his later attempts to usurp Seymour's leadership at Azusa Street, Seymour received the Pentecostal message and when invited to Los Angeles to preach, began preaching about this new experience.[4]

One of the original six female members of Azusa Street was Florence L. Crawford, who was born in 1872 in Oregon. She was raised in a secular home. She moved from Portland to Los Angeles in 1890 for health reasons, though she was also seeking a way out of her first marriage to a rancher. She married again in 1891, this time to a real estate businessman, Frank Crawford. The Crawford's were firmly established within LA's economic and social life as they lived a rather average middle-class life. Frank worked as a realtor and Florence busied herself with the city's many social events.[5] She became part of the Women's Christian Temperance Union (WCTU), as well as the National Congress of Mothers (later known as the PTA), and worked in jails with the poor in LA.[6] But Crawford grew tired of the Protestant reform ethos of her LA church and sought a new religious experience at Seymour's church, where she soon converted to Pentecostalism.

Crawford's testimony reads like hundreds if not thousands of testimonies that converts shared in churches, revivals, and in the pages of Pentecostal magazines that were meant not only to be shared with the faithful as proof of the certainty of their faith, but with the faithless as a sign that they too could rid themselves of all the dance halls, saloons, and jewelry that ensnared them to the world. Crawford testified that "the jewelry went off my hands and the flowers in the feathers out of my hat. I began to dress in modest apparel and live the life."[7]

She thrived in her new Pentecostal ministry. Like many new converts, the vibrancy of the worship along with the emphasis on healing and the steadfastness of Holiness message attracted at first hundreds, then thousands of new converts. Crawford became an itinerant evangelist on behalf of the Azusa Street mission, and Seymour named her State Overseer for California.[8] But for various reasons, Crawford became dissatisfied with Azusa Street leadership and her personal life began to suffer. According to Historian Vivian Deno, Pentecostalism presented Crawford's family life with a tremendous strain.[9]

Crawford envisioned Pentecostalism as the perfect medium for the "remoralizing" of men and the redemption of fathers, yet her marriage crumbled under the weight of the demands of her new faith. Crawford's ministry affected her second marriage because she spent so much time at work at a time when married women stayed home and viewed that sphere as their sole responsibility. She then decided to ignore those conventions and work as a minister full-time, and when her marriage became a hindrance to her ministry, she got out of it. Over the objection of her husband and male ministers, she left Los Angeles and moved back to Portland in late 1906. According to Deno, this decision "was grounded not only in her ... spiritual authority but also cloaked in divine authority. It exemplified her defiance of male power and negotiation of patriarchal social and religious expectations."[10] She had chosen her own way.

Another scholar, Margaret Alminana, believes that Crawford left Azusa Street due to a theological dispute with Seymour, who, Crawford believed, was backing away from his support of full inclusion of women in ministry, and there was some belief that Seymour was about to support the "Finished Work" theology that Crawford found offensive.[11] Another possible reason explaining why Crawford left Azusa Street, however, is simpler. Crawford and her friend, Clara Lum, left Los Angeles and moved to Portland to start a new ministry, and they took two of the Azusa Street mailing lists with them. In a newsletter dated summer 1908, Crawford made an announcement: "We have moved the paper, which the Lord laid on us to begin at Los Angeles to Portland, Oregon, which will now be its headquarters." This was done without Seymour's approval.[12] These mailing lists were valuable to Azusa Street's financial health, since mail was how the leadership kept supporters apprised of what was happening at the church. Without mailing lists, it would be difficult for the leadership to send out its magazine and make pleas for money to support the ministry. Crawford's Portland start-up ministry would therefore have a great start with those lists. Not everyone is convinced that Crawford absconded with those mailing lists, however, and the official church history of the AFC does not mention these mailing lists. What is clear from all these competing stories is that Crawford's religious authority, already problematic due to her status as a divorced woman, would have been bolstered if she had left Azusa Street out of principle, and it would have been diminished if the roots of her Portland ministry were to be found in the pettiness and ego of church politics.

Crawford's religious authority, then, had to be won by diminishing her personal history as a twice-divorced woman, which she did with a deft handling of marriage. Marriage was the aspirational ideal for traditional families, but, like her, it was also to be shunned by those truly dedicated to the ministry. Because few, if any, questioned Crawford's dedication to the ministry, those who followed her in ministry, like her son Raymond, made it a point not to blame his mother for the divorces, but to rather blame his father, Frank, whose refusal to allow Florence freedom to ministry was a worse sin than divorce.[13]

Crawford, twice divorced, founder of a denomination, is not unique in terms of the pioneer generation of women who decided that their ministries were more important than their marriages. Church of God, Cleveland, Tennessee evangelist to Mexico, Maria Atkinson, who received little to no support for her ministry from her husband, left him and continued her ministry, becoming one of the most successful evangelists for the fledgling denominations in the early twentieth century. Probably the most famous Pentecostal divorcee though is Aimee

Semple McPherson. McPherson, whose first husband died, later re-married, and divorced him when he failed to support her ministry. McPherson, like Crawford, was a single mother, and also founded a denomination, the International Church of the Foursquare Gospel. By re-drawing the very traditional lines of marriage, Pentecostal women managed to lead denominations, evangelize, pastor, and assume roles that were normally closed to them as married women. While divorce would have normally been viewed as a serious breach of an infallible marriage contract, because the women made the case that husbands were hindering the preaching of the Gospel, they were forgiven for their divorced status.[14]

Crawford's Portland ministry focused on working-class men, particularly sailors, lumber-jacks, bricklayers, and storekeepers. Men, according to Crawford, needed redemption to save themselves. Women, conversely, needed men to be redeemed because that would ensure the continuance of traditional homes where women stayed home and men were the head of the household. Male remoralization meant the return of working-class men to the folds of the faith. Crawford created a space for women to be empowered by insisting on rigid moralism of her working women followers and this allowed them to navigate the worldly city of Portland and the often-tenuous lives in their homes.[15] Crawford, like many other pioneering Pentecostal women operated in a religious system that privileged a tradi-tional family hierarchy that demanded men morally redeem themselves and resume their family obligations. Which is why when it came to her own denomination, the Apostolic Faith Church (AFC), rather than having a lenient policy on divorce, Crawford instituted one of the strictest policies against the practice. Divorce was forbidden, along with any sec-ond marriages if either party had former spouses. If they did leave their first spouse, in other words, they were encouraged to go back to them.

Crawford's complicated relationship with marriage may have been rooted in her personal experience, but it was enhanced by her conversion. The millennial character of Pentecostalism affected Crawford's views on the necessity of marriage. Because the Second Coming of Jesus was imminent, marriage was a waste of time, particularly Azusa Street leader Seymour's mar-riage to Jennie Moore, because Pentecostals should be spending their time evangelizing non-believers. Historian Charles Barfoot quotes Ernest Williams, who was an eyewitness and participant at the Azusa Street revival and knew of Crawford's views on marriage: "she was opposed to marriage ... she boards and trains promising young Apostolic ministers. When they marry, iron-willed "Mother" Crawford turns them out. She advocates celibacy, recom-mends continent among married folk, was chagrined when her two children married."[16] Asking her charges to be celibate is not unusual, but it did say a lot about her views on mar-riage that she expected her married followers to abstain.

It is difficult to ascertain how much of Crawford's hostility to marriage is because of her own bad experiences, and how much is theological, because she rarely, if ever, discussed her divorces; even when she did, she would inevitably explain her views on marriage in theological terms. What we can determine is Crawford married young, divorced, moved to Los Angeles, married again, had a child, and got another divorce because her ministry came first; thus, Crawford, the single mom, began raising her daughter Mildred in her Pentecostal faith.

Crawford's move back to Portland to start her own church experienced a major setback when the Portland *Evening Telegram* reported this story, "Color Line Obliterated: White and Negro Fanatics Hold Services," which claimed that little girls were taking part in those "fanatical" services." Local law authorities tried to take Crawford's daughter, Mildred, away because she was at the integrated Pentecostal service. Crawford was then taken to court and branded an unfit mother in early 1907. Because of this episode, Crawford was labeled "The Los Angeles Fanatic" by the same paper. The case eventually went to court, with the police chief acting as a witness against Crawford. When Crawford lost, the judge ordered her to send Mildred to school immediately or risk jail. Crawford refused to comply, skipped the jurisdiction, and moved back to LA.[17]

This episode is a good place to stop and examine the racial issues that similarly affected the early years of Pentecostalism. While Crawford's desire was to have control over her daughter's religious upbringing, there is little evidence that Crawford's motives stemmed from a desire for racial reconciliation. In fact, it may be that Crawford exhibited the same racial animus that plagued many white Americans in the early twentieth century. Historian Charles Barfoot, quoting Ernest Williams again, wrote that Crawford did not expect to work for Seymour because she saw African Americans as "servants."[18] This, along with a host of other issues, including the desire to go back to Portland and begin her own denomination, complicates the picture that many sympathetic scholars have painted of Crawford as being driven by purely theological concerns, concerns that promoted her unwavering convictions, but diminished her views on gender roles, marriage and race.

* * *

The thread of race was interwoven with the Pentecostal movement from the beginning. Pentecostalism, scholar Iain MacRobert wrote, "was born at a time when fundamentalist Christians were anticipating the Second Advent and blacks were seeking a solution to the inequalities in American society. For many, the Pentecostal movement appeared to promise the impending fulfillment of both dreams."[19] Some in attendance at Azusa Street certainly believed that Pentecostalism was the fulfillment of some kind of post-racial utopia. Indeed, the idea of the "color line being washed away in the Blood," made famous by Azusa Street pioneer Frank Bartleman, was a response to the integrated nature of the revival and hope that the same religious fervor that gave rise to the revival would somehow continue to diminish the segregated reality for most African Americans. Unfortunately, Bartleman's utopia lasted about as long as Azusa Street did. For some scholars who have never been sanguine about the influence of Azusa Street on race relations, the idea that the color line was removed in any capacity was wishful thinking on the part of well-intentioned followers who perhaps put more faith in what Pentecostalism could do to erase America's most intractable problem.

The problem of black/white relations in Pentecostalism was a lot like the problem many people had with race in general. Blacks and whites should worship, just not together. When it came to the specifics of church politics, the issue often came back to white supremacy. As such, whenever blacks were even perceived to have authority over whites, those churches usually made moves to ensure that blacks were separated from the majority white groups, and that they had no authority over white ministers. What happened to Haywood's church, the Pentecostal Assemblies of the World (PAW), had been done before, when the black members of the AG left to join the Church of God in Christ after controversy over ministerial credentials and interracial churches, or when the Pentecostal Holiness Church voted blacks out of the church rather than accept them as full-fledged members of an interracial denomination.[20] This, indeed, was a common theme.

Seymour's Azusa Street did have racial integration as one of the main theological tenets, though, and did indeed break some rules for who can worship with whom. Racially integrated services were unique, and in many parts of the United States, illegal. It was quite a feat for the three years that Azusa Street was up and running that it attempted to be a racial oasis in Los Angeles, as the city, in 1906, was already racially segregated, mostly due to the influence of real estate agents and land developers, who redlined and restricted racial minorities from living in certain parts of the city. Seymour, though, had vision for an integrated movement, as he had seen what integrated churches could be due to his involvement in two groups that promoted racial unity, the Methodist Episcopal Church and the Evening Light Saints.[21] Seymour would learn a lesson he no doubt had experienced already, however, that division over race, theology, the role of women, and a myriad of other issues, meant that trying to keep his church together would be nearly impossible.

Whether it was inability to weather the racism of the times, or too many theological and ego disputes to overcome or both, Azusa Street's experiment with racial integration was over by 1909. In Indianapolis, though, it was about to start once again in a Oneness church led by Garfield T. Haywood. Haywood, as an African American man in Indianapolis in the 1910s, knew all too well the city's racial past and indeed the state's reputation as a hotbed of KKK activity.

Haywood was born in Greencastle, Indiana in 1880. His parents, Ben and Ann Haywood, were slaves in Raleigh, North Carolina. Haywood grew up in the black Baptist tradition. Despite his parent's slave past, his life in segregated Indianapolis, and his life navigating the racial politics of church life, Haywood rarely, if ever, mentioned race in his early writings.[22] This choice to not mention race continued into Haywood's life as a minister, where his writing included books and booklets on theology and hymns, most of which, were free of any mention of racial issues.

Before becoming a minister, Haywood made a living as a day laborer and eventually, he became an illustrator for black newspapers *The Freeman and The Recorder*. Similar to Azusa Street, Indianapolis was known for its racial integration. The Indianapolis revival of 1907 received visitors from Azusa Street including Seymour and Oneness pioneer, Glenn Cook. Cook, a supporter of Seymour's racially inclusive vision, even worked with Seymour at Azusa Street. In Indianapolis, he preached at an interracial church of 110 persons, and he preached at Charles Mason's Church of God In Christ in Memphis. When Haywood attended a revival in Indianapolis in 1908, he converted after hearing hearing Cook preach.[23] Haywood then shopped around for a Pentecostal church, and apparently even considered joining the mostly white Assemblies of God. Though Haywood was never credentialed by the AG, he was a part of the denomination's debate over the Oneness controversy, and he ended his affiliation with them by 1916, probably because he had become convinced of the Oneness message.[24] The AG was also not a denomination that Haywood would have wanted to join, though, if racial integration was central to his theology, and Haywood would have probably known of the AG's history with African American Pentecostals, who left the denomination early in its formation and created the African American dominant Church of God in Christ.

Before exploring the brief interracial era of the Pentecostal Assemblies of the World (PAW), it would be helpful to untangle the theological issues that caused Haywood to leave trinitarian Pentecostalism and become a zealous Oneness evangelist.

The roots of PAW are difficult to uncover. Some date the denomination's beginnings to 1906, while others to different dates in the 1910s. Regardless of the starting dates, the PAW began as a trinitarian Pentecostal group and later became part of the Oneness movement. Oneness, again, depending on different Pentecostal groups, does not have an origin date at all, but rather is something begun in biblical times. The 1913 Arroyo Seco Revival in Pasadena, California, where Canadian minister Robert E. McAlister is said to have received a vision of the proper way to baptize people, in the name of Jesus only, is still the flash point for the new iteration of Oneness. The movement grew so fast that within a year, the newly formed Pentecostal denomination, the Assemblies of God (AG) experienced a schism as many of their converts decided to get re-baptized and left to join the PAW and other assorted associations promoting the non-Trinitarian baptismal formula. In 1914, then, the PAW experienced a schism as well when the Trinitarian members left, many of them joining the AG. As PAW went through its split, it had moved from Los Angeles to Portland, Oregon, and eventually, it moved to Indianapolis in 1919 where it was led by Haywood and white minister E. W. Doak, creating an interracial leadership group that lasted till 1924.

Like many early Pentecostal groups, the PAW was involved in several theological controversies that would eventually lead to a schism within the group. One of the controversies was the extent to which the PAW was going to follow Holiness teachings, policies about marriage and divorce, and the role of women in ministry. Haywood, who wrote several books, pamphlets, and hymns, did not use those vehicles to discuss race matters, and mostly used them to write about Oneness theology; he seemed bogged down in an intradenominational squabble with one of his most prominent converts, Robert C. Lawson. For Lawson, couples had to dissolve their marriage and return to their first spouse, if possible, or else, they should remain unmarried. Haywood did not believe that divorce, especially if it was completed before the person converted to Oneness, was a problem, however, so he did allow divorced people to participate in church. Haywood also supported roles for women in ministry.[25] Unable to come to a compromise, Lawson left in 1919 and began his own denomination called the Church of Our Lord Jesus Christ. Eventually, Lawson's denomination broke apart into several other groups.

In the early 1920s, black ministers began joining the PAW in greater numbers, which resulted in whites leaving.[26] While PAW was led by Doak and Haywood, an interracial leadership, the Indianapolis church of about 450 people was about 60 percent black and 40 percent white members. By 1924, though, in an action brought by the Texas district of the PAW, white ministers voted to segregate the churches into black and white members. The white group then renamed itself the Pentecostal Assemblies of Jesus Christ.[27] The interracial experiment was over. What is unclear is whether PAW members viewed their experiment as part of God's divine plan to integrate churches or whether it was a harse reminder that despite any hint of a divine plan, integration was something white church members and especially leaders, did not find worthy of investment.

To try to understand what happened with PAW, it may be helpful to see this as a part of a historic trajectory of segregation in churches, which, even today, is still the norm. Early Pentecostals were convinced that they were living in the last days. The message Pentecostals took from interracial Azusa Street was not about making American society more just, but a way to signal to unbelievers what heaven would look like. Working for an end to segregation, then, was not what Azusa Street was about, despite the visions of Seymour and Haywood. In reality, an interracial utopia was not how most early Pentecostals viewed their faith.

In the aftermath of the break-up of PAW in 1924, Haywood attempted to ease the concerns of those who believed that divisions in PAW would cast aspersions on the Pentecostal movement as a whole. Haywood wrote, "the Pentecostals Assemblies of the World is not divided, those who have reorganized themselves are supposed to have done so in order that the Southern brethren might not be hindered in reaching the public with their message. It should have been called the southern branch of the PAW."[28] This statement, while obviously not factual, was made to make it appear that the division of PAW was not potentially harming evangelism. The rationale for southern churches was precipitated by two overtly racist actions — one by the Texas district, and the other by white church members unwilling to have their ministerial certifications signed by African American ministers. Considering the realities for most African Americans in Jim Crow America, it may be simple survival that influenced Haywood's generous description of what happened to PAW. Or it may be, as Iain MacRobert and other have noted, that black churches operated on very different political levels, not all of them took interest in the liberative projects of the historic black church, but instead, conformed to a "white middle-class conservative evangelicalism."[29]

Regardless, by the 1940s, most of the early strains of Pentecostalism had been molded into some kind of denomination, mostly segregated along race and ethnicity and reinforcing traditional gender values. Pentecostalism was into its fourth decade and institutionalization meant that the movement looked very much like any other Protestant movement. Pentecostals opened bible colleges, trained missionaries, ordained their own clergy, and established layer upon layer of organized bureaucracy to run their far flung denominations. The 1950s would pose many more challenges to people of color in Pentecostalism. There was a burgeoning civil rights movement that remained out of sight of white members of most Pentecostal groups, but it did not go unnoticed by African American denominations. Perhaps the most challenging times for Pentecostalism were just beginning, not only with the Civil Rights movement, but with the advent of television and popular culture, keeping their flocks away from the influence of entertainment viewed as "ungodly" would soon become nearly impossible. For women in Pentecostalism, who today comprise over half of the world's 500 million Pentecostals, the quest for ordination and for full equality in the church is still a challenge, but the openness that denominations have toward divorce and re-marriage has changed, even if their doctrinal statements have not changed, Pentecostals have as many divorced members within their churches as other Protestant churches do.[30] Over a hundred years after its emergence, the various strands of Pentecostalism in the US are mostly theologically conservative, many still have limited pastoral roles for women and mirror other Protestant denominations in their racial segregation. One might say that as Pentecostals have been able to overcome theological issues such as whether there is a Trinity or not, they have not been able to overcome historic resistance to women in the pastorate or the social realities of racial and ethnic segregation.

FURTHER READING

Butler, Anthea. *Women in the Church of God in Christ: Making a Sanctified World*. Chapel Hill: University of North Carolina Press, 2007.
Payne, Leah. *Gender and Revivalism: Making a Female Ministry in the Early 20th Century*. New York: Palgrave MacMillan, 2015.
Ramírez, Daniel. *Migrating Faiths*. Chapel Hill: University of North Carolina Press, 2015.
Sánchez-Walsh, Arlene M. *Pentecostals in America*. New York: Columbia University Press, 2018.
Tarango, Angela. *Choosing the Jesus Way: American Indian Pentecostals and the Fight for the Indigenous Principle*. Chapel Hill: University of North Carolina Press, 2014.

BIBLIOGRAPHY

Alminana, Margaret English de. "Florence Crawford and Egalitarian Precedents in Early Pentecostalism." In *Women in Pentecosal and Charismatic Ministry*, edited by Margaret English de Alminana and Lois E. Olena, 103–193. Leiden: Brill, 2016.
Barfoot, Charles H. *Aimee Semple Mcpherson and the Making of Modern Pentecostalism, 1890–1926*. New York: Routledge, 2014.
Butler, Anthea. *Women in the Church of God in Christ: Making a Sanctified World*. Chapel Hill: University of North Carolina Press, 2007.
Center, Pew Research. "Religious Landscape Study: Divorced or Separated Aduits." Pew Research Center. https://www.pewforum.org/religious-landscape-study/marital-status/divorcedseparated/.
Deno, Vivian. "God, Authority, and the Home: Gender, Race, and U.S. Pentecostals, 1906–1926." *Journal of Women's History* 16, no. 3 (2004): 83–105, 221.
French, Talmadge L. "Early Oneness Pentecostalism, Garfield Thomas Haywood, and the Interracial Pentecostal Assemblies of the World (1906–1931)." PhD diss., University of Birmingham, 2011.
Hjalmeby, Erik J. "A Rhetorical History of Race Relations in the Early Pentecostal Movement, 1906–1916." MA thesis, Baylor University, 2007.
MacRobert, Iain. *The Black Roots and White Racism of Early Pentecostalism in the USA*. New York: Palgrave MacMillan, 1988.
Sánchez-Walsh, Arlene M. *Pentecostals in America*. New York: Columbia University Press, 2018.
Tarango, Angela. *Choosing the Jesus Way: American Indian Pentecostals and the Fight for the Indigenous Principle*. Chapel Hill: Univerity of North Carolina, 2014.

NOTES

1   Arlene M. Sánchez-Walsh, *Pentecostals in America* (New York: Columbia University Press, 2018). See especially chapter 1, "Pentecostal Faith and Practice."
2   This is true for the early years of the movement, by the time Pentecostalism entered its institutional/denomination building era around the early 1940s, Native Americans had already begun to use their Pentecostalism to their advantage and shed the subservient role. For African Americans,

who had their own denominations since the 1910s, the solution was self-governance and usually, self-segregation. For more on Native Americans and African Americans, especially those in the Church of God in Christ, please see the following: Angela Tarango, *Choosing the Jesus Way: American Indian Pentecostals and the Fight for the Indigenous Principle* (Chapel Hill: University of North Carolina Press, 2014); Anthea Butler, *Women in the Church of God in Christ: Making a Sanctified World* (Chapel Hill: University of North Carolina Press, 2007).

3   For more information on the Latino Pentecostal work, please see my *Latino Pentecostal Identity*, especially chapter 2 "Workers for the Harvest: LABI and the Institutionalizing of a Latino Pentecostal Identity." Arlene M. Sánchez-Walsh, *Latino Pentecostal Identity* (New York: Columbia University Press, 2003).

4   Charles H. Barfoot, *Aimee Semple Mcpherson and the Making of Modern Pentecostalism, 1890–1926.* (New York: Routledge, 2014), 193–140.

5   Vivian Deno, "God, Authority, and the Home: Gender, Race, and U.S. Pentecostals, 1906–1926," *Journal of Women's History* 16, no. 3 (2004): 87.

6   Margaret English de Alminana, "Florence Crawford and Egalitarian Precedents in Early Pentecostalism," in *Women in Pentecosal and Charismatic Ministry*, ed. Margaret English de Alminana and Lois E. Olena (Leiden: Brill, 2016), 103.

7   Deno, "God, Authority, and the Home: Gender, Race, and U.S. Pentecostals, 1906–1926," 87.

8   Erik J. Hjalmeby, "A Rhetorical History of Race Relations in the Early Pentecostal Movement, 1906–1916" (MA thesis, Baylor University, 2007), 74.

9   Deno, "God, Authority, and the Home: Gender, Race, and U.S. Pentecostals, 1906–1926," 88.

10   Ibid.

11   Alminana, "Florence Crawford and Egalitarian Precedents in Early Pentecostalism," 120.

12   Hjalmeby, "A Rhetorical History of Race Relations in the Early Pentecostal Movement, 1906–1916," 74–75.

13   Deno, "God, Authority, and the Home: Gender, Race, and U.S. Pentecostals, 1906–1926," 88.

14   Sánchez-Walsh, *Pentecostals in America*. See especially chapter 3, "Gender, Sexualities and Pentecostalism."

15   Ibid.

16   Barfoot, *Aimee Semple Mcpherson and the Making of Modern Pentecostalism, 1890–1926*, 141–142.

17   Deno, "God, Authority, and the Home: Gender, Race, and U.S. Pentecostals, 1906–1926," 80. Unless otherwise noted, the quotations from this section are all from this source.

18   Barfoot, *Aimee Semple Mcpherson and the Making of Modern Pentecostalism, 1890–1926*, 139–140.

19   Iain MacRobert, *The Black Roots and White Racism of Early Pentecostalism in the USA* (New York: Palgrave MacMillan, 1988), 34.

20   Ibid., 66.

21   Hjalmeby, "A Rhetorical History of Race Relations in the Early Pentecostal Movement, 1906–1916," 44–45.

22   Talmadge L. French, "Early Oneness Pentecostalism, Garfield Thomas Haywood, and the Interracial Pentecostal Assemblies of the World (1906–1931)," (PhD diss., University of Birmingham, 2011), 67.

23   Hjalmeby, "A Rhetorical History of Race Relations in the Early Pentecostal Movement, 1906–1916," 109.

24   Ibid., 131–132.

25   Ibid., 199–200.

26   MacRobert, *The Black Roots and White Racism of Early Pentecostalism in the USA*, 73.

27   Ibid., 74

28   French, "Early Oneness Pentecostalism, Garfield Thomas Haywood, and the Interracial Pentecostal Assemblies of the World (1906–1931)," 250.

29   MacRobert, *The Black Roots and White Racism of Early Pentecostalism in the USA*, 34.

30   The Pew Forum on Religion did not separate out Pentecostals in this survey, but they are included in the evangelical Protestant group. For more see: Pew Research Center, "Divorced or Separated Adults: Religious Composition of Divorced or Separated Adults," Religious Landscape Study, https://www.pewforum.org/religious-landscape-study/marital-status/divorcedseparated/.

Chapter Twenty-One

RELIGION AND US FEDERAL INDIAN POLICY

Sarah Dees
Iowa State University, Ames, Iowa

In 1978, the US Congress passed the American Indian Religious Freedom Act (AIRFA). The act outlined a federal policy of protecting Native American and Indigenous beliefs and practices:

> Henceforth it shall be the policy of the United States to protect and preserve for American Indians their inherent right of freedom to believe, express, and exercise the traditional religions of the American Indian, Eskimo, Aleut, and Native Hawaiians, including but not limited to access to sites, use and possession of sacred objects, and the freedom to worship through ceremonials and traditional rites.[1]

Many Indigenous activists and religious practitioners celebrated the passage of this act. Reflecting on its importance forty years later, a Kiowa religious leader explained in 2018, "this law allowed us to openly dance, sing, and mostly pray as our grandfathers did. ... To be able to do these things without outside interference is what makes the American Indian Religious Freedom Act significant."[2]

The First Amendment of the United States' Bill of Rights ostensibly ensures its citizens' free exercise of religion, but, as AIRFA makes clear, Native American traditions have not always benefitted from constitutional protections. Answering the question of why Native Americans' religious practices have required additional legal protections, beyond those already granted to its citizens, implicates the US government itself. Furthermore, it requires chronicling Native Americans' changing relationships to the US body politic and tracing seismic shifts in ideas about religion, race, culture, society, and sovereignty.

Ultimately, Native religions have faced a long history of discrimination, with complex roots and an enduring legacy. While some US laws and policies have been enacted to protect and preserve Native religions, others have served to manage, contain, and constrain them. This chapter compares AIRFA's account of the history of Native American religious discrimination to scholarly work on the topic. It focuses on the period leading up to the Assimilation Era from the 1880s to the 1930s. Federal policies in this era — perhaps more so than in any other era in US history — specifically and systematically targeted Native American religions.

A Companion to American Religious History, First Edition. Edited by Benjamin E. Park.
© 2021 John Wiley & Sons, Inc. Published 2021 by John Wiley & Sons, Inc.

Pushback against assimilation policies eventually led to AIRFA and other legal measures to protect Native religions. The gaps between AIRFA's historical narrative and critical scholarship on the same topic illuminate how the law, religious freedom, and the category of religion have themselves been implicated in violence toward Native American religions. Legal mechanisms such as AIRFA are offered as solutions to complex problems that federal Indian policies played a role in creating.

* * *

The text of AIRFA underscores the importance of religion for Native Americans and emphasizes the ideal of religious freedom in the United States. It also signals the reality of historic and ongoing discriminatory treatment of Native American traditions. AIRFA declares freedom of conscience to be a central US value and affirms that "the United States has traditionally rejected the concept of a government denying individuals the right to practice their religion." Further, it states that the United States "has benefitted from a rich variety of religious heritages," extolling religious diversity as a key feature of American life and identity. Finally, AIRFA notes that religion is a key feature of Native cultures, stating that "the religious practices of the American Indian (as well as Native Alaskan and Hawaiian) are an integral part of their culture, tradition, and heritage, such practices forming the basis of Indian identity and value systems." While the act does not directly define the category of religion, it does indicate that religious beliefs, expressions, and activities qualify for protection. It gestures to the significance of land and nature for Indigenous communities by highlighting the need for practitioners to access sacred sites. It also mentions the importance of sacred objects. Taken together, the act refers to religious beliefs, practices, sacred space, and material religion as key elements of religious traditions worthy of and requiring protection.

Yet despite these lofty claims of American ideals, the AIRFA was necessary because of a long history of discrimination against Native traditions. Indeed, the act explicitly outlines some of the reasons for its creation, noting that "traditional American Indian ceremonies have been intruded upon, interfered with, and in a few instances banned." It does not go into detail about the nature of these intrusions — nor does it identify specific perpetrators or targets — but it does hint at the government's role in limiting Native religious practices.

The text of AIRFA identifies two primary causes of these infringements: the absence of clearly articulated federal Indian policies and insensitivity to the effects of laws on Native religions and cultures. The act cites "the lack of a clear, comprehensive, and consistent Federal policy" regarding the regulation or protection of Native practices. Indeed, federal Indian law and policy unfolded unsystematically over time.[3] In addition, AIRFA mentions "the lack of knowledge of the insensitive and inflexible enforcement of Federal policies and regulations" that were "designed for such worthwhile purposes as conservation and preservation of natural species and resources" but unduly affected Native religious practices.[4] For example, the statement alludes to laws such as the 1940 Bald and Golden Eagle Protection Act (16 U.S.C. 668-668c), which prohibited individuals from possessing eagle feathers, objects that are sacred to numerous Native nations. It was passed to protect endangered species that are culturally significant for the United States but has created difficulties for Native communities seeking to obtain feathers for ceremonial purposes. A process allows Native people to apply for a permit to obtain feathers, but it has been described as slow, restrictive, and burdensome on those who seek to maintain their traditions.[5]

While religious practitioners, activists, lawmakers, and scholars praised the passage of AIRFA, many have noted its limitations. In particular, they have criticized the act for "lacking teeth" — in other words, they argue it offers little in the way of enforcement.[6] The act required the President to direct federal agencies to study their impact on Native religions. Agencies were to "evaluate their policies and procedures with Native traditional religious leaders to determine appropriate changes necessary to protect and preserve Native American religious cultural rights and practices."[7] The President was expected to then report back to Congress the following year with a full report. In 1979, a task force, under the direction Secretary of the Interior Cecil D. Andrus, provided an overview of issues affecting Native traditions. The task force identified barriers to the free exercise of Native religious practices, worked with federal agencies and Native nations to identify specific problems, and offered recommendations.[8] Subsequent laws, including the 1990 Native American Graves Protection and Repatriation Act (NAGPRA), the 1993 Religious Freedom Restoration Act (RFRA), and 1994 amendments to AIRFA, were enacted to remedy some of the earlier act's shortcomings. Critics of the original 1978 act itself described it as not being concerned with results but with processes.[9]

Discrimination against Native American religions has taken many forms, including legal forms. This creates a challenge when seeking to identify legal solutions to discrimination. In describing the need for the protection of Native religions, the American Indian Religious Freedom Act of 1978 does not fully account for the intricacies of the problems that it was enacted to redress. Discrimination has been due in part to changing ideas about religion and the shifting status of Native peoples vis-à-vis US government. Longstanding ideologies regarding Euro-American cultural superiority and Christian supremacy have led to social and political biases against Native traditions. These underlying ideologies led to the implementation of a series of assimilation efforts that sought to change Native practices. 1978's AIRFA, while significant in signaling a change in federal policies and affirming the rights of Native religious practitioners within the US legal system, only accounts for limited aspects of the greater problem. The text of the act omits noteworthy information and generally oversimplifies the causes of discrimination against Native religions.

AIRFA intimates that the US government has banned practices and infringed upon Native traditions. However, when explaining the reasons for these infringements, the act cites only a lack of foresight about the repercussions of regulations that were deemed "not related." Further, the act fails to explicitly convey that Native traditions have been the primary *targets* of federal policies — not merely collateral damage. Federal regulations during the Assimilation Era specifically singled out Native beliefs and practices, and the US government has knowingly authorized actions that have damaged Native sacred sites and material culture.

There is a long backstory to this tension. In the past, non-Natives have not always recognized Native traditions as valid types of "religions." Part of this may be due to issues of translation. Religion as a parallel term and concept might not exist in original languages and cultures. But another issue has been assumptions of Euro-American cultural and religious superiority. While a primary premise of US politics is that a strict "wall of separation" exists between church and state, religious values — specifically, Christian values — have formed the basis of some aspects of US law. Further, Americans, building on European traditions, have viewed Christianity as a marker of "civilized" culture, and efforts to assimilate Native Americans to mainstream American society assumed the superiority of Christianity and required Native people's conversion. In addition, the expansive nature of many Indigenous religions exceed historic definitions of religion developed out of and pertaining largely to monotheistic religions. Rather than focusing on individual beliefs and being limited to worship in purpose-built structures, Indigenous religious traditions are often connected to special ceremonies as well as everyday practice, legal structures, relationships and protocols. This has led to some difficulties in protecting Indigenous religions under the law.[10]

* * *

The unique and changing status of Native American individuals and nations with respect to the United States helps to explain both the causes of religious discrimination against Native people and the development of AIRFA. As of March 2020, there are 574 federally recognized Native nations, and at least sixty-six tribes that are recognized by state governments.[11] As sovereign sociopolitical entities predating the formation of the United States, Native nations have held the original cultural and religious claims to the land on which the United States developed. Through the process of settler colonialism, Europeans and Euro-Americans have sought to displace Native Americans from their original homelands and appropriate their territories and resources. As the United States took root and gained increasingly more expansive landholdings — through treaty, purchase, war, or seizure — Native communities were eventually partially subsumed into the jurisdiction of the United States as "domestic dependent nations." While they are subject to the US government, many groups have retained rights as sovereign Native nations.[12] However, during the Assimilation Era, Native Americans had not yet been granted US citizenship. In other words, Native Americans were subject to federal policies *before* they were US citizens.

When identifying the causes of the infringement of Native religions, AIRFA places some blame on the lack of a clear federal Indian policy. Indeed, federal Indian laws and policies developed unevenly over time, and often did so in response to US — not Indigenous — objectives. Regulations were often contradictory, with different branches of the government holding different ideas about US relations with Native Americans. While the 1978 act sought to protect Native practices, in preceding eras the US government used laws and policies to exert power and control over Native lands, resources, and lifeways. Legal scholars have argued that US law "did not just *declare* and *enforce* the preeminent role of the United States over the states and the tribes ... it *provided justifications* for subordinating the tribes to the federal sovereign and asserting rights to tribal lands."[13] In other words, federal Indian law and policy has claimed federal US power over Native nations, enforced its own rules through available means — which includes police and the military — and justified these policies and practices through a frame of reference that places the needs and goals of the United States over those of Native nations.

While different branches of the federal government have had different goals and policies with respect to Native nations, it is possible to discern an overarching shift in the federal treatment of Native nations. When the United States was founded, the federal government treated Native nations as sovereign foreign nations. Over the course of the nineteenth century, policies increasingly devalued Native sovereignty, and the US government made decisions limiting the rights of Native communities without their input. By the mid- to late-twentieth century, the federal government began to shift back toward recognizing the inherent rights of Native self-governance.[14] The US government's treatment of Native American religions has often roughly paralleled these shifts: in eras when the US government has not recognized Native sovereignty, it has undermined the free exercise of Native traditions; over the course of the twentieth century, protections of Native religions, such as the passage of AIRFA, have been granted as government recognition of Native sovereignty has grown.

At the broadest level, *US federal Indian policy* refers to an official set of principles governing political relations between the US federal government and Native American polities. One of the first chroniclers of Indian policy defined it as "a course of action pursued by any government and adopted as expedient by that government in its relations with any of the Indians of the Americas." "Expedient" actions are those considered to be "advantageous or advisable under the particular circumstances or during a specific time span."[15] Federal Indian policy, then, is rooted in and privileges the United States' goals and interests — which, over time, have often conflicted with the needs and desires of Native nations. A related concept and system, *US federal Indian law* refers more specifically to the body of rules and laws, subject to enforcement, that regulate the relationships between Native nations and the government and outline the rights and restrictions of Native people and nations. *Tribal law* is a distinct category that refers to the specific, unique laws and policies that each Native nation develops and that apply to its members under its own jurisdiction.

Federal Indian law draws on a wide array of sources and precedents: treaties between the US government and Native nations; the US Constitution; legislation (federal acts, codes, or statutes); court case judgments; executive orders; and administrative policies determined by relevant agencies such the Bureau of Indian Affairs. US federal Indian laws and policies did not emerge as coherent systems but have developed over time. To complicate matters further, many US policies were inherited from earlier European practices.[16] As legal scholars have noted, broad policies goals have changed, and different branches of the government have pursued inconsistent goals during the same era.[17]

Religion has played a significant role federal Indian law and policy in five key ways: as a justification, method, target, challenge, and refutation. That is, European and Euro-American forms of Christianity have served as an ideological basis and method of settler colonial assimilation practices. In the context of settler colonialism, Indigenous religions have been a target of as well as a form of resistance to destructive US federal Indian policies. Today, Native religious traditions serve as evidence of the ultimate failure of destructive US federal Indian policies to eliminate Indigenous cultures. Native cultures have survived and thrived in the face of settler colonialism and assimilation. The passing of AIRFA and the ongoing presence of Native religious practices demonstrate that, while assimilation policies may continue to impact Native religious practitioners, efforts on the part of the United States to eliminate Native traditions were never wholly successful. Today, many Native communities are working to recover, restore, and reimagine traditions and practices that were once targeted by federal assimilation policies.

A brief survey of federal policies is useful in highlighting these interactions, as well as the culmination of these various policies and laws seeking to manage Native religions in the late nineteenth century. The roots of US Indian policy lie in ideas and practices inherited from earlier European policies. The foundation for European interactions with Native Americans was formed even before Columbus first sailed to the Caribbean. Between 1085 and 1492, the Crusades and the *Reconquista* provided an ideological basis and practical model for interactions between Europeans and Indigenous inhabitants of the Americas. During these periodic episodes of religiously and politically motivated warring, which were initially authorized by the Pope, European (Catholic) Christians fought Muslims for control of sacred sites and landholdings in the Middle East and Europe. Centuries of conflict cultivated animosity between Christians and Muslims, shaping Christian ideas of religious and racial "others" that would serve as a blueprint for interactions between Natives and newcomers in the Americas.[18]

As European powers led expeditions around the African continent and into the Indian Ocean in the fifteenth century, the Pope granted them the authority to convert or conquer non-Christians and take their land and resources. In 1454, the Pope conferred upon Portuguese King Alfonso license to "invade, conquer, and subjugate any and all Saracens [Muslims or Arabs] and pagans, enemies of Christ, their lands and their possessions, to reduce all to servitude and to keep everything for his own use and that of his descendants."[19] During this era, religious and racial categories overlapped and "exploration" was inextricably tied to the conquest of non-European or non-Christian peoples. While Spain and Portugal were the only nations that drew directly on divine authority to justify their conquest of Native people and lands, Spanish modes of justification would later be adopted by the US government. In 1594, the Treaty of Tordesillas had divided newly "discovered" lands outside of Europe between the Spanish and the Portuguese. This was the right of land ownership via "discovery" — despite the fact that Native Americans already inhabited, used, and cared for the lands. In the early decades of the United States, Native communities were treated as foreign nations, as they had been described in the Constitution. However, the doctrine of discovery re-emerged in 1823 in the case of Johnson v. M'Intosh. This famous case upheld the idea that, as the inheritors of European Christian rule, the US held title to Indian lands the Europeans had "discovered."[20]

In some instances, Europeans treated Native communities as independent nations; in others, as inferior societies that needed to assimilate. Spanish theologians argued that Native Americans were "natural slaves" and proto-Christians who would benefit from the violent *encomienda* system, similar to plantation slavery, that Spain instituted in the Caribbean. In contrast, French entrepreneurs formed networks with Native hunters and traded for pelts in the Great Lakes region, relying more on partnership with than subjugation of Native inhabitants. Eventually, French Jesuits introduced the goal of assimilating Native people, establishing colonies in which Native Americans would live, work, and worship. Though short-lived, Dutch colonies formed a basis for modes of engagement that the British would later adopt. The Dutch recognized Native titles for land and purchased lands with bills of sales documenting the agreement. This is in contrast to earlier assumptions about the divine right of Europeans to claim Native lands. In addition, the Dutch formed alliances with nations, particularly the Iroquois, with whom they traded for protection. The British established colonies with the intent of fully taking control over new lands. Some British recognized Native sovereignty, engaging in trade and forming alliances. However, others sought to assimilate Native people using "praying towns." Most notably, the missionary John Eliot encouraged Native people to live in British-style homes and engage in British forms of culture and industry in addition to trainings in Christian faith and practice.[21] US policies were later modeled off of these forms of interactions. Similar to European nations, US states and governments at different times fought, formed alliances, engaged in trade with and sought to assimilate Native Americans.

Over the course of the nineteenth century, federal Indian policies transitioned from interacting with Native nations as sovereign foreign entities to seeking to incorporate Natives into Euro-American society. As the United States moved enacted policies to assimilate Native people to mainstream society, Christianity was a tool, and Native religions were targets. The Civilization Fund Act of 1819, "An Act Making Provision for the Civilization of the Indian Tribes Adjoining the Frontier Settlements," marked a turning point toward US efforts to assimilate Native Americans. This act mentioned the possibility of and concern for the "extinction" of Native American people. The act authorized the President to "employ capable persons of good moral character" to instruct Native adults and children in a variety of subjects, from agriculture to reading, writing, and math. $10,000 per year was directed to Christian missionaries for their work educating, and ultimately assimilating, Native communities. Christians of many denominations were eager to take up this work. Their goals of conversion were all-encompassing: Native Americans were expected to give up aspects of their individual and communal identity, from languages to societal structures. American missionaries viewed labor as necessary for Natives' spiritual development.

Assimilation policies were ostensibly enacted in order to reduce tensions between Euro-Americans and Native people, who would be incorporated into the folds of mainstream society. However, racial animosity coupled with Euro-American desire for Native land and resources persisted. This is clearly illustrated by the US treatment of the "Five Civilized Tribes." By the nineteenth century, the Cherokee, Choctaw, Creek, Chickasaw and Seminole nations in the Southeast were known as the "Five Civilized Tribes" due to their acceptance of Christianity and selective adoption of features of Euro-American culture and society. White settlers set their eyes on Native lands in Alabama, Florida, Georgia, North Carolina, and Tennessee, and began attacking Natives' homesteads. States began agitating for the removal of Native Americans to lands further west, away from Euro-Americans. In 1830, President Andrew Jackson signed the Indian Removal Act, which authorized him to negotiate with Native nations for lands further west. Despite the 1832 decision in Worcester v. Georgia that Native Americans were entitled to their land, the federal government sent troops to enforce removals in the 1830s.[22] These removals wrenched thousands of Southeastern Natives from their ancestral homelands. In this case, the fact that Native nations had selectively incorporated features of Euro-American technology, religion, and culture into their societies was not enough to grant them legitimacy in the eyes of white settlers who wanted their lands.

By 1850, US government leaders looked to the establishment of reservations, which are lands set aside for Native nations, as a way maintain distance between Native Americans and non-Natives. These reservations were administered by the Office of Indian Affairs. During this period, Christian leaders advocated for policies that would prioritize reform of Native individuals and societies. In 1868, President Ulysses S. Grant was concerned about the corruption of federal Indian agents who ran many of the reservations. He proposed a new policy that entrusted care of reservations to missionary organizations. Missionaries, who saw themselves as advocates for Native people, oversaw strict policies that limited features of Native religion and culture. At times they coordinated with US military to keep Native Americans on reservations.[23] In this way, missionaries often functioned as para-governmental entities that policed Native communities and enforced federal Indian policies.

After a series of engagements between the US military and Native nations in the west after the Civil War, politicians and the broader American public called for a comprehensive set of policies to manage Indian affairs. By the 1880s, senators and concerned advocates advocated for assimilation policies that would entail religious conversion, education, and new forms of landholding. Together, non-Natives hoped that these policies would "civilize" Native Americans.

* * *

During the Assimilation Era, policies specifically targeted Native American religious traditions. An 1883 list of punishable "Indian offenses" included participation in traditional dances and healing rituals. In effect, this policy banned key features of communal practice and attacked the authority of religious leaders. Individuals who broke these rules risked having essential rations withheld by local Bureau of Indian Affairs officials. In 1890, government concerns about a new dance were at least partially responsible for the massacre of Miniconjou Lakota at Wounded Knee, South Dakota.[24]

Additional policies during this era were destructive to Native religions on multiple fronts. Boarding schools affected the transmission of traditions from elders to young adults and children. Policymakers and advocates envisioned boarding and day schools as institutions that would assimilate Native children to Euro-American society. Initially these schools were administered by missionaries on or near reservations. In 1879, the government established the Carlisle Indian Industrial School, the most well-known of the federal boarding schools. In their attempts to assimilate children, school policies attacked features of Native religion and culture. Children were expected to adopt Christian practices and not allowed to speak their Native languages or maintain aspects of their culture. While some students valued aspects of the education they received, these schools damaged family connections and removed children from the ceremonial cycles of their communities.[25]

Another significant policy during this era involved Indigenous landholdings. The Dawes Act of 1887 was meant to re-fashion Native forms of land ownership. The Act stipulated that communally held lands on reservations would be divided up and assigned to Native individuals. "Excess" lands would then be sold to Euro-Americans. These policies resulted in the loss or splintering of lands significant to Native culture and traditions.[26] Many subsequent court cases related to Native religious practice have taken up the issue of access to sacred sites, which the allotment process exacerbated.[27]

Destructive federal Indian assimilation policies continued to target Native cultures through the first two decades of the twentieth century. In 1924 the Indian Citizenship Act was passed, which granted full US citizenship to Native American. Up to this point, Native American were not subject to constitutional protections. Policies began to change in the 1930s with the publication of a report entitled "The Problem of Indian Administration." Prepared under the direction of Lewis Meriam, this document, often known as the "Merriam Report," outlined the many ways federal Indian policies were ineffectual and damaging to Native communities. Armed with this data, John Collier, who became the head of the Commissioner of Indian Affairs in 1933, advocated for a reversal of many of the assimilation policies that had directly targeted or indirectly affected Native religious traditions. The federal government backtracked in the 1940s and 1950s during the Termination and Relocation Era, seeking to sever nation-to-nation relationships and enacting relocation programs. Under these programs, adults living on reservations were incentivized to move to cities where they were expected to find jobs and assimilate into the local population. Inadvertently, these policies led to the development of pan-Indian communities. New traditions began to flourish in this urban setting among Indigenous people from many nations who were searching for a sense of community. This, in turn, helped to create political alliances.[28]

Since the 1960s, federal Indian policies have slowly turned toward the recognition of Native sovereignty and the value of Native cultures. In 1968, the Indian Civil Rights Act was passed. Participants in the Red Power movement agitated for rights and recognition. Activists drew attention to the ways that the US government has failed to uphold treaties through efforts including the occupation of Alcatraz, which began in 1969, and the 1971 Trail of Broken Treaties. Native Americans sought to re-claim traditions that had previously been targeted. With its passage, the First Amendment's Free Exercise Clause was finally applied to Native Americans. Finally, in 1978, the passage of the American Indian Religious Freedom Act (AIRFA) seemed like a victory for practitioners of Native religions. AIRFA promised to remedy to the historical discrimination of Native religious traditions.

But the legal redemption of Native religions would not be automatic. A number of court cases revealed the limits of the protections for Native traditions — both individual forms of practice and communal access to sacred lands. In the infamous 1990 case Employment Division v. Smith, the Supreme Court ruled against members of a misunderstood Native practice. Alfred Smith and Galen Black were fired after ingesting peyote, a sacrament in Native American Church. They were denied unemployment benefits because of their participation. The court decided that because laws restricting the use of peyote applied to all citizens, this outcome did not result in a substantial burden for practitioners of Native religions. 1994 amendments to the American Indian Religious Freedom Act updated legal protections to account for the religious use of peyote. Cases related to Native sacred sites have also been unsuccessful. The 1998 case Lyng v. Northwest Indian Cemetery Protective Association ruled against the Yurok, Karuk, and Tolowa nations who sought to prevent the US Forest Service from constructing of a road through sacred lands. The Supreme Courts ruled against the Native nations, allowing the construction of the road to proceed, by changing the redefining the requirements that Natives would need to prove an action placed a "substantial burden" on their practices.[29]

Challenges remain for practitioners of Native religions. Their traditions are often incommensurable with laws that were created with monotheistic, belief-based traditions in mind. In some cases new policies are created with particular Native nations in mind that have, nonetheless, applied to many groups whose contexts and structures may not suit all communities. However, practitioners have been successful on a number of other fronts. The 1990 Native American Graves Protection and Repatriation Act called for museums and universities to return of tens of thousands of significant objects and human remains that had been collected by anthropologists and were housed in federally funded institutions. Increasingly, policies have been developed and implemented to return these objects to Native communities. At the global level, the UN Declaration of the Rights of Indigenous People was adopted in 2007, which outlines the significance of Indigenous religious practices. This document articulates the importance of traditions for Native cultures, and Native communities in the US has drawn on it to authorize their efforts to protect and preserve their traditions. Finally, Indigenous supporters from around the world made their way to North Dakota in the fall of 2016 to support members of the Standing Rock Sioux Tribe who sought to prevent the construction of the Dakota Access Pipeline. These global Indigenous solidarity movements have raised public consciousness about the significance of Native traditions. Protest itself has become a way for Native communities to exercise and expand their religious practices.[30] And, indeed, the ongoing persistence of Native traditions today stands as evidence that policies meant to stamp out Native American religions were never wholly successful.

Further Reading

Adams, David Wallace. *Education for Extinction: American Indians and the Boarding School Experience, 1875–1928*. Lawrence: University Press of Kansas, 1995.
Deloria, Vine. *God is Red: A Native View of Religion, 3rd ed*. Golden: Fulcrum, 2003.
_____. *The Gods of Indian Country: Religion and the Struggle for the American West*. Oxford: Oxford University Press, 2018.
Holm, Tom. *The Great Confusion in Indian Affairs: Native Americans and Whites in the Progressive Era*. Austin: University of Texas Press, 2005.
Niezen, Ronald. *Spirit Wars: Native North American Religions in an Age of Nation Building*. Berkeley: University of California Press, 2000.
Wenger, Tisa. *We Have a Religion: The 1920s Pueblo Indian Dance Controversy and American Religious Freedom*. Chapel Hill: University of North Carolina Press, 2009.

Bibliography

Adams, David Wallace. *Education for Extinction: American Indians and the Boarding School Experience, 1875–1928*. Lawrence: University Press of Kansas, 1995.
Adams, William Y. *Indian Policies in the Americas from Columbus to Collier and Beyond*. Santa Fe: School for Advanced Research Press, 2014.
Berger, Benjamin. *Law's Religion: Religious Difference and the Claims of Constitutionalism*. Toronto: University of Toronto Press, 2015.
Bowden, Henry Warner. *American Indians and Christian Missions: Studies in Cultural Conflict*. Chicago: University of Chicago Press, 1981.
Boyarin, Jonathan. *The Unconverted Self: Jews, Indians, and the Identity of Christian Europe*. Chicago: University of Chicago Press, 2009.
Coulthard, Glen. *Red Skin, White Masks: Rejecting the Colonial Politics of Recognition*. Minneapolis: University of Minnesota Press, 2014.
Deloria, Vine, Jr. and Clifford M. Lytle, *American Indians, American Justice*. Austin: University of Texas Press, 1984.
De Meo, Antonia M. "Access to Eagles and Eagle Parts: Environmental Protection v. Native American Free Exercise of Religion." *Hastings Constitutional Law Quarterly* 22, no. 3 (Spring 1995): 771–814.
Duthu, N. Bruce. *American Indians and the Law*. New York: Penguin, 2008.
_____. "Federal Indian Law." *Oxford Research Encyclopedia of American History*. 2014. Accessed March 2020. DOI: 10.1093/acrefore/9780199329175.013.18.
Estes, Nick. *Our History is the Future: Standing Rock versus the Dakota Access Pipeline, and the Long Tradition of Indigenous Resistance*. New York: Verso, 2019.
Fletcher, Matthew L. M. "The Supreme Court and Federal Indian Policy." *Nebraska Law Review* 85, no. 121 (2006): 121–185.
Goldberg, Carole and Kevin K. Washburn. "The Indian Law Canon as Narrative: Stories of Legal Strategy and Native Persistence." In *Indian Law Stories*, edited by Carole Goldberg, Kevin K. Washburn, and Philip Frickey, 1–29. New York: Foundation Press, 2001.
Goldberg, Carole, Kevin K. Washburn, and Philip Frickey, eds. *Indian Law Stories*. New York: Foundation Press, 2011.
Graber, Jennifer. "'If a War it May be Called': The Peace Policy with American Indians." *Religion and American Culture* 41, no. 1 (2014): 36–69.

_____. *The Gods of Indian Country: Religion and the Struggle for the American West*. Oxford: Oxford University Press, 2018.

Harjo, Suzan Shown. "American Indian Religious Freedom Act after Twenty-five Years." *Wicazo Sa Review* 19, no. 2 (2004): 129–136.

Hoxie, Frederick. *A Final Promise: The Campaign to Assimilate the Indians, 1880–1920*. Lincoln: University of Nebraska Press, 1984.

Johnson, Greg, and Siv Ellen Kraft. "Standing on the Sacred: Ceremony, Discourse, and Resistance in the Fight against the Black Snake." *Journal for the Society of Religion, Nature, and Culture* 11, no. 1 (2017): 131–147.

Loesch, Martin C. "The First Americans and the 'Free' Exercise of Religion." In *Native American Cultural and Religious Freedoms*, edited by John R. Wunder, 19–84. New York: Garland Publishing, 1999.

McNally, Michael. "Native American Religious Freedom Beyond the First Amendment." In *After Pluralism: Reimagining Religious Engagement*, edited by Courtney Bender and Pamela Klassen, 225–251. New York: Columbia University Press, 2010.

Morman, Todd. *Many Nations under Many Gods: Public Land Management and American Indian Sacred Sites*. Norman: University of Oklahoma Press, 2018.

Newcomb, Steven. *Pagans in the Promised Land: Decoding the Doctrine of Christian Discovery*. Golden: Fulcrum Press, 2008.

Niezen, Ronald. *Spirit Wars: Native North American Religions in an Age of Nation Building*. Berkeley: University of California Press, 2000.

Sullivan, Winnifred Fallers. *The Impossibility of Religious Freedom*. Princeton: Princeton University Press, 2005.

Talbot, Steve. "Spiritual Genocide: The Denial of American Indian Religious Freedom, from Conquest to 1934." *Wicazo Sa Review* (Fall 2006): 7–39.

Tyler, S. Lyman. A *History of Indian Policy*. Washington, DC: Government Printing Office, 1973.

US Federal Agencies Task Force. American Indian Religious Freedom Act Report. PL 95-341(1979).

Vecsey, Christopher, ed. *Handbook of American Indian Religious Freedom*. New York: Crossroad, 1991.

Wenger, Tisa. *We Have a Religion: The 1920s Pueblo Indian Dance Controversy and American Religious Freedom*. Chapel Hill: University of North Carolina Press, 2009.

Wilkins, David E. and K. Tsianina Lomawaima. *Uneven Ground: American Indian Sovereignty and Federal Law*. Norman: University of Oklahoma Press, 2001.

Wolfe, Patrick. "Settler Colonialism and the Elimination of the Native." *Journal of Genocide Research* 8, no. 4 (2006): 387–409.

Wunder, John R., ed. *Native American Cultural and Religious Freedoms*. New York: Garland Publishing, 1999.

Zotigh, Dennis. "Native Perspectives on the 40th Anniversary of the American Indian Religious Freedom Act." *Smithsonian Magazine Blog, November* 30, 2018. https://www.smithsonianmag. com/blogs/national-museum-american-indian/2018/11/30/native-perspectives-american-indian-religious-freedom-act/.

NOTES

1   The act was passed as a joint resolution on August 11, 1978 as Public Law 95-341 and was amended in 1994 as Public Law 103-344.

2   Tim Tsoodle in an interview with Dennis Zotigh. Zotigh, "Native Perspectives on the 40th Anniversary of the American Indian Religious Freedom Act," *Smithsonian Magazine Blog*, November 30, 2018, https://www.smithsonianmag.com/blogs/national-museum-american-indian/2018/11/30/native-perspectives-american-indian-religious-freedom-act/. Tsoodle is a Headsman of the Kiowa Gourd Clan, a society formed in 1957 that sponsors a yearly ceremonial gathering in Oklahoma.

3   See N. Bruce Duthu, *American Indians and the Law* (New York: Penguin, 2008).

4   The American Indian Religious Freedom Act (Public Law 95-311).

5   Antonia M. De Meo, "Access to Eagles and Eagle Parts: Environmental Protection v. Native American Free Exercise of Religion," *Hastings Constitutional Law Quarterly* 22, no. 3 (Spring 1995): 771–814.

6   Christopher Vecsey, "Prologue," *Handbook of American Indian Religious Freedom* (New York: Crossroad, 1991), 9.

7   The American Indian Religious Freedom Act, (Public Law 95-311).

8   US Federal Agencies Task Force, *American Indian Religious Freedom Act Report*, PL 95-341(1979).

9   Vernon Masayevsa, "Epilogue," *Handbook of American Indian Religious Freedom*, edited by Chris Vecsey (New York: Crossroad, 1995), 135.

10   Michael McNally, "Native American Religious Freedom Beyond the First Amendment," in *After Pluralism: Reimagining Religious Engagement*, edited by Courtney Bender and Pamela Klassen (New York: Columbia University Press, 2010), 227–228.

11   "Federal and State Recognized Tribes," National Council of State Legislatures, https://www.ncsl.org/research/state-tribal-institute/list-of-federal-and-state-recognized-tribes.aspx#State, updated March 2020. This designation refers to federal or state governments' recognition of Native nations as sovereign entities. Indigenous studies scholar Glen Coulthard discusses the implications of federal recognition, particularly for Canadian First Nations, in *Red Skin, White Masks: Rejecting the Colonial Politics of Recognition* (Minneapolis: University of Minnesota Press, 2014).

12   The category of "domestic dependent nations" has been used to describe Native nations' status as sovereign nations within the bounds of the United States. See Adams, *Indian Policies in the Americas: From Columbus to Collier and Beyond* (Santa Fe: School for Advanced Research Press, 2014), 296–300.

13   Carole Goldberg and Kevin K. Washburn, "The Indian Law Canon as Narrative: Stories of Legal Strategy and Native Persistence," in *Indian Law Stories,* edited by Carole Goldberg, Kevin K. Washburn, and Philip Frickey (New York: Foundation Press, 2011), 4 (emphasis added).

14   Adams, *Indian Policies in the Americas*, 237–261.

15   S. Lyman Tyler, *A History of Indian Policy* (Washington, DC: Government Printing Office, 1973), 2.

16   For a broad overview and comparison of European and US policies, see Adams, *Indian Policies in the Americas.*

17   See Duthu, *American Indians and the Law* and Goldberg, et al. *Indian Law Stories.*

18   Jonathan Boyarin, *The Unconverted Self: Jews, Indians, and the Identity of Christian Europe* (Chicago: University of Chicago Press, 2009).

19   Adams, *Indian Policies in the Americas*, 21–22.

20   Steven Newcomb, *Pagans in the Promised Land: Decoding the Doctrine of Christian Discovery* (Golden: Fulcrum Press, 2008).

21   Henry Warner Bowden, *American Indians and Christian Missions: Studies in Cultural Conflict* (Chicago: University of Chicago Press, 1981), 96–133.

22   Tyler, *A History of Indian Policy*, 54–69.

23   Jennifer Graber, "'If a War it May be Called': The Peace Policy with American Indians," *Religion and American Culture* 41, no. 1 (2014): 36–69.

24   Steve Talbot, "Spiritual Genocide: The Denial of American Indian Religious Freedom, from Conquest to 1934," *Wicazo Sa Review* (Fall 2006): 7–39.

25   David Wallace Adams, *Education for Extinction: American Indians and the Boarding School Experience, 1875–1928* (Lawrence: University Press of Kansas, 1995).

26   Frederick Hoxie, *A Final Promise: The Campaign to Assimilate the Indians, 1880–1920* (Lincoln: University of Nebraska Press, 1984).

27   Todd Morman, *Many Nations under Many Gods: Public Land Management and American Indian Sacred Sites* (Norman: University of Oklahoma Press, 2018).

28   For a history of Native activism, see Nick Estes, *Our History is the Future: Standing Rock versus the Dakota Access Pipeline, and the Long Tradition of Indigenous Resistance* (New York: Verso, 2019).

29   Suzan Shown Harjo, "American Indian Religious Freedom Act after Twenty-five Years," *Wicazo Sa Review* 19, no. 2 (2004): 129–136.

30   Greg Johnson and Siv Ellen Kraft, "Standing on the Sacred: Ceremony, Discourse, and Resistance in the Fight against the Black Snake," *Journal for the Society of Religion, Nature, and Culture* 11, no. 1 (2017): 131–147.

Chapter Twenty-Two

"For the Good of Mankind": Atomic Exceptionalism, Religion, and United States Empire in the Postwar Pacific

Carleigh Beriont
Harvard University, Cambridge, Massachusetts

On March 6, 1946, one hundred and sixty-seven Bikinian Marshallese gathered for their final church service on Bikini, a low-lying atoll in the northern Pacific Ocean that today is part of the Republic of the Marshall Islands.[1] This religious tradition dated back to 1908, when a Marshallese Congregational missionary from a southern atoll arrived on Bikini to convert the people to Christianity. Every week since — throughout the German occupation of the Marshall Islands, during the subsequent Japanese occupation, and to this point in the American occupation — the Bikinians assembled together to worship God.[2] On this particular Sunday, they held the service outside. Navy Seabees had already dismantled their church.

Under the glaring sun, as palm fronds rustled in the breeze coming off the turquoise lagoon, Josiah, the minister, gave his last sermon. As the cameras rolled, an American yelled "cut," and asked Josiah to repeat his remarks. Once the Americans were satisfied with the footage, they asked the Bikinians to gather in a grove of coconut trees close to the beach. Ben Wyatt, the American Military Governor of the Marshall Islands, perched on the sloped trunk of a palm tree as James Milne, the Navy's Marshallese translator, spoke to the Bikinians, who were seated on the grass in front of Wyatt.

Through Milne, Wyatt explained the destructive power of America's atomic weapons and reminded the Bikinians that the Americans had vanquished the Japanese, the former occupiers of the Marshall Islands. As Wyatt spoke to the Bikinians, he compared them "to the children of Israel whom the Lord saved from their enemy and led into the Promised Land."[3] Then Wyatt asked the Bikinians to leave their homeland so that the Americans could conduct a series of atomic tests in order to "turn this great destructive force into something good for mankind." Juda, a Bikinian elder and leader stood and spoke on behalf of the community: "Emman. Men otemjej rej ilo bein Anij (Everything is in God's hands)." After repeating this back-and-forth several times for the cameras, Wyatt asked Milne to "tell [the Bikinians] everything being in God's hands, it cannot be other than good." In archival footage of the encounter, a voice off camera can be heard saying, "Ok. All set."

After the filmed exchange with Wyatt, the Bikinians were removed from their island home, setting the stage for the demonstration of unprecedented destructive power. Over

A Companion to American Religious History, First Edition. Edited by Benjamin E. Park.

the course of the next decade, the United States detonated sixty-seven nuclear weapons in the Marshall Islands. Twenty-three of the tests took place at Bikini Atoll. The most powerful nuclear device ever detonated by the United States, code named Castle Bravo, was set off on March 1, 1954. The fifteen-megaton Bravo blast created a fireball hotter than the surface of the sun.[4] The tests obliterated entire islands and irradiated Bikini, Enewetak, and neighboring atolls. Ultimately, the radioactive fallout from the tests poisoned generations of Marshallese, hundreds of American service personnel, and twenty-three Japanese fishermen.[5] The removal of the Bikinians from their homeland enabled the United States to test atomic bombs on a fleet of ships, scores of animals, and the land and lagoon of Bikini Atoll. The 1946 tests, code named Operation Crossroads, and subsequent nuclear testing in the Marshall Islands also enabled the United States to study the short and long-term impact of radiation on Marshallese people.

As the events that took place on Bikini were reported back to the continental United States in the spring and summer of 1946, the Bikinians were routinely held up by the American military and media as paragons of Christian virtue for sacrificing their atoll "for the good of mankind." The film crews and journalists who descended on Bikini alongside military personnel portrayed the Bikinians as models of the Christian values that many American political and religious leaders saw as important in the immediate postwar period and early days of the Cold War.

However, the recollections of many of the Bikinians who lived through this dislocation tell a different story. Their recollections emphasize the sense of profound loss that was often obscured in the religiously romanticized accounts generated by the United States government. Since 1946, the Bikinians and their descendants have been unable to return to live on their home(is)land. The United States government has failed to provide meaningful compensation and has also repeatedly given misleading or false information to the community about the condition of Bikini. In the wake of the nuclear testing, some Bikinians have invoked the Americans' own paternalistic and laudatory language of Christian sacrifice and chosenness to confront the United States for its abuses in the islands and to demand reparations and repatriation. In doing so, they have articulated their own vision for the religious and political relationship between the Marshall Islands and the United States.

In 1946, Operation Crossroads became the most documented event in history.[6] Because of this, the events that took place at Bikini provide an illuminating site for reflection on the diverse ways that significant events in the history of United States Empire have been shaped and informed by the faith of those involved, including those who occupied positions of power and those who were subjected to American imperial control. At the time of Operation Crossroads, Americans were steeped in a discourse of what I term "atomic exceptionalism." Articulated by political and religious leaders alike in the aftermath of the bombings of the Japanese cities of Hiroshima and Nagasaki, atomic exceptionalism was the belief that the United States' unique atomic power was a divine providence. That is, evidence of God's favor. As a result of this belief, many Americans articulated and justified their nation's actions during and after World War II through the lens of atomic exceptionalism. In the context of Bikini, American military personnel and reporters highlighted the Christian identity of the Marshallese and portrayed the Bikinians and Americans alike as key actors in the divine drama of history.

Some Bikinians also offered their own theologically inflected narratives. Drawing from their Marshallese Christian faith and, at times, the rhetoric of Wyatt and other Americans, Bikinians' understandings of their history and their shared identity as Christians helped them to make sense of the experience of dislocation and destruction during the 1940s and 1950s. Later on, they continued to draw from these narratives in an effort to hold the United States accountable for its actions in the Marshall Islands. That is, the Bikinians' Christian identity did not simply make them pawns of American imperialism, but also shaped and informed their critique of it. Following from Edward Said's important observation in *Culture and*

Imperialism that "the power to narrate or to block other narratives from forming and emerging" is an essential form of imperialism, this chapter focuses on the American military's removal of the Bikinians in 1946 and explores the ways in which Bikinian counternarratives — informed by the Bikinians' beliefs and experiences — cast into sharp relief the discourse of atomic exceptionalism that underpinned the United States government's actions and their political, historical, and ethical consequences.[7]

"God's — and Man's — Miracle": The Birth of American Atomic Exceptionalism

The Republic of the Marshall Islands is located about halfway between Hawai'i and Australia. It consists of twenty-nine coral atolls and five islands spread across almost one million square miles of ocean. The total combined landmass is about seventy square miles, making it slightly larger than Washington, DC if all of the islands were compressed together. The history of the Marshall Islands is a history of competing colonialisms. First settled by Micronesians as early as the second millennium BCE, the Marshall Islands was later colonized by Spain (1529–1885) and then Germany (1885–1919) before it became part of the Japanese Nan'yo, or League of Nations South Seas Mandate, following World War I. The islands remained under Japanese control until 1944, when the United States invaded and occupied the islands during a series of bloody battles and skirmishes that devastated many Marshallese communities. During the decade of nuclear testing that followed World War II, the Marshall Islands and Marshallese people remained under US control: first, as an occupied territory and later as part of the United Nations-sanctioned United States Trust Territory of the Pacific.

From the earliest days of the Atomic Age, the United States understood itself and its military power in terms of atomic exceptionalism. On August 9, 1945, the United States dropped an atomic bomb on the Japanese city of Nagasaki. It was the third atomic bomb explosion in history, coming three days after the United States dropped an atomic bomb on Hiroshima and three weeks after the United States tested the first nuclear device in New Mexico. In a speech that evening, President Truman explained the decision to use atomic weapons in Japan, which resulted in the deaths of between 130,000 and 226,000 people. In his speech, Truman asserted that the United States was a "peace-loving nation." He attributed his choice to use nuclear weapons to a desire to "shorten the agony of war" and "save the lives of thousands and thousands of young Americans."[8] Although scholars have debated whether the United States' decision to use nuclear weapons in Japan ultimately shortened the war or saved lives, one thing is clear: at the time, the United States was the only nation that possessed nuclear weapons.[9] Reflecting on this atomic exceptionalism, Truman thanked "God that [the bomb] has come to us, instead of to our enemies," and prayed that God "may guide us to use it in His ways and for His purposes." The President promised that the United States would serve as a "trustee" of the bomb, "prevent its misuse" and ensure that it be used in "service to mankind" and "world peace."

Truman's speech expressed a popular belief about atomic power.[10] For many Americans, the bomb represented what one *Life* magazine reader described as God's "intervention ... in human affairs" on behalf of the United States.[11] A number of religious leaders shared this understanding. In a letter to the editor of *The Christian Century*, for instance, Thomas Opie, an Episcopalian minister, stated his conviction that the American advent of atomic weapons was evidence of divine favor. As Opie saw it, God was clearly working through the United States. He described "the atomic bomb" as "God's — and man's — miracle."[12] In contrast to the official position of organizations such as the Federal Council of Churches, which was more critical of the United States government's decision to use atomic weapons in Japan, Opie asserted that violence was a necessary part of American Christianity and should guide

American foreign policy. Indeed, he viewed the President's decision to use the atomic bomb in Japan as the godly thing to do. After all, Opie insisted, "Christ's religion is not all heart and no guts ... God is no pink-tea grandmother." Edgar Guest, a popular poet and writer for the *Detroit Free Press*, expressed a similar sentiment in his poem, "Atomic Bomb": "The power to blow all things to dust / was kept for people God could trust / and granted to them alone/that evil might be overthrown."[13] The statements of writers like Opie and Guest offer important examples of how atomic exceptionalism was justified and popularized through the use of Christian theology. It was up to American officials, however, to turn this theology of American atomic exceptionalism into American foreign policy.

In the wake of World War II, a number of American politicians considered American foreign policy and God's will to be one and the same. They viewed the atomic bomb as the key to carrying out this providential agenda and solidifying American power in the postwar period. In spite of the fact that the bombings of Hiroshima and Nagasaki caused hundreds of thousands of deaths, injuries, and cases of radiation sickness, United States officials maintained that the atomic bomb was a weapon of peace. In a November 1945 editorial titled "Flaunting Providence?" Edwin Johnson, a United States Senator from Colorado and the chairman of the Senate Military Affairs Committee, explained how the United States would use the weapon of war to prevent future wars from occurring. Like Opie, Johnson believed that "peace requires brute force to make it endure" because humans were naturally "cruel, selfish, and savage animal[s]." Johnson, a Lutheran, wrote that possessing nuclear weapons would enable the United States to "compel mankind to adopt the policy of lasting peace ... or be burned to a crisp." The United States would either save humanity or bring it to a fiery end. Although the stakes were high, Johnson remained optimistic that the United States would prevail. After all, he declared, "Divine Providence has placed in the hands of this nation the instrument to establish lasting peace throughout the world." Rather than sharing the technology with the rest of the world or ceding control of atomic power to an international body in the form of a United Nations panel consisting of civilians, Johnson argued that the United States military should maintain "exclusive control" over atomic energy.[14]

In addition to using the bomb to promote peace and compliance with the United States' aims abroad, some within the government sought to use atomic exceptionalism to combat the rising tide of atheism and advance what they believed were American Christian and democratic values abroad. During a Congressional hearing on Operation Crossroads in the spring of 1946, John Rankin, a member of the House of Representatives from Mississippi and noted racist and anti-Semite, testified to his own understanding of America's atomic exceptionalism.[15] Rankin considered the United States to be the "leading Christian nation in the world." As such, he told Congress, God had chosen the United States for a special task: to advance "Christian civilization" and world peace. In order to carry out this plan, God provided the United States with the atomic bomb. He exclaimed: "Almighty God has placed this great weapon in our hands at a time when atheistic barbarism is threatening to wipe Christianity from the face of the earth" so that the United States could stem this tide while advancing "the cause of our Christian civilization" and "maintain[ing] peace" around the globe. For Rankin, American atomic exceptionalism could be used to promote a white and Christian supremacist American agenda in the postwar era.

Rankin, to be sure, was not alone in his desire to connect the development of atomic weapons with what he understood to be the United States' divine role on the world stage. President Truman also spoke of the need for a religious revival in the wake of World War II and at the beginning of the atomic age. In a nationally broadcast speech to the Federal Council of Churches on March 6, 1946 — amidst the United States government's removal of the Bikinians from their atoll — Truman called for "a genuine renewal of religious faith" and a postwar religious "revival."[16] He declared that "if the civilized world as we know it today is to survive, the gigantic power which man has acquired through atomic energy must be matched by spiritual strength of greater magnitude." Remarking on the "awesome" scientific "discoveries" made during the first half of the 1940s, Truman asserted that the "greatest discoveries of the future will be in the realm of the spirit." He testified to the power of religion, declaring, "there is no problem on this earth tough enough to withstand the flame of a genuine renewal of religious faith. And some of the problems of today will yield to nothing less than that kind of revival."

Many American public officials joined Truman in interpreting the newfound atomic power as evidence of the righteousness of American policy during World War II and in the war's immediate aftermath. They argued that the discovery of atomic fission by scientists in the United States was divine sanction for their political agenda, which included spreading American democratic, capitalist, and Christian values and administering the former Japanese mandate in the Pacific. In particular, the assertion of divine sanction for American policy also functioned as a way to counter criticism of nuclear testing as well as to naturalize the American occupation of the Marshall Islands, a politically fraught undertaking during a period of postwar decolonization globally.

Choosing Bikini: Atomic Testing "For the Good of Mankind"

Less than a week after the United States bombed Nagasaki, American civilian and military leaders argued that the United States needed to further explore the devastating power of the atomic bomb. These discussions took place against the backdrop of internecine fighting within the United States military, particularly the Army Air Force and the Navy, about the future and funding of those organizations.[17] While the Army and the Navy agreed that the atomic bomb would define the future of warfare, neither branch of the military was sure of how it would impact their relative status going forward. If an atomic bomb had to be dropped on its target by an airplane, did that mean that the Army Air Force would play a critical role in the future of American warfare? Or did it mean that the United States had no use for a large squadron of bombers and only needed a few planes? Did the bomb's devastating power mean that a single bomb could sink an entire navy? Did that mean there was no place for the Navy in modern warfare?

To answer such questions, the Secretary of the Navy, James Forrestal, established the Office of Special Weapons and appointed Vice Admiral William Blandy as its director.[18] Bringing together the Army Air Force and the Navy, Blandy assembled a Joint Task Force to assess "the military implications of atomic energy" for the stated "purposes of national defense."[19]

On January 11, 1946, Blandy began the search for a suitable site for further atomic testing.[20] The military decided that the tests needed to take place in a location under United States control but away from heavily populated areas, in a climate with predictable winds and water currents, and in a geographic region with a protected anchorage for the test ships and support ships.[21] Blandy believed that if they chose an inhabited locale, "it was important that the local population be small and co-operative so that they could be moved to a new location with a minimum of trouble."[22] Two men in the Office of Special Weapons eventually chose Bikini Atoll.[23] According to their reasoning, it "just popped up as the one atoll that made all sorts of sense."[24] Admiral Blandy announced the plan, "Operation Crossroads" — so named, he explained, because warfare and "civilization itself literally stands at the Crossroads" — to Congress on January 24, 1946.[25]

The Marshall Islands and neighboring archipelagos were fresh on the minds of many Americans for having been the site of a number of bloody battles as the United States military "island hopped" to Japan. Although James Michener's widely circulated *Tales of the South Pacific* would not be released until the following winter, Americans had also been constructing a romanticized and exoticized vision of the South Pacific for the past half-century. This idealized image was fueled by the 1898 annexation of Hawai'i and hula circuits that toured the United States during the first half of the twentieth century, a burgeoning "tiki" culture sparked by the end of Prohibition and the opening of Polynesian-themed restaurants and clubs like Don the Beachcomber and Hinky Dink's (later Trader Vic's) in cities across the United States, as well as hit films like *Bird of Paradise* (1932), *Hei Tiki* (1935), and *Waikiki Wedding* (1937).[26] Although the geographical reality is quite different — the Marshall Islands is in fact located in the north Pacific Ocean — much of the coverage of Operation Crossroads subsumed Bikini and the Marshall Islands into this conceit of the "South Pacific." It was also known, particularly within New England Congregational communities, as the site of one of the most successful Christian missionizing efforts of the nineteenth and twentieth centuries.

When Wyatt first arrived at Bikini on February 10, 1946, the Bikinians knew none of what had transpired in the Office of Special Weapons in Washington, DC. They were, however, familiar with United States military personnel who had regularly visited their atoll since the beginning of the occupation in order to trade with the Bikinians for handicrafts, provide medical treatment, re-establish schools, and encourage "law and order."[27] As Jonathan Weisgall explains in *Operation Crossroads*, United States involvement in Bikini after the war "dramatically" improved living conditions and the Bikinians' perceptions of the Americans: "the United States provided for many of the Bikinians needs, and the islanders thought highly of their American friends."[28] In addition, the United States Navy "introduced" the Bikinians to a new form of democratic local government.[29] The surviving accounts of what happened at the February meeting come directly from Wyatt, later Navy reports about the interaction based on his telling of the events, newspaper articles based on interviews with Wyatt, and noncontemporary Bikinian recollections.[30] The Associated Press published one of the earliest descriptions of the meeting on Bikini twelve days later. It reported that Wyatt, speaking on behalf of the United States, had not "gone in and ordered [the Bikinians] off the islands without explanation and arbitrarily set them up on another island." Rather, the Associated Press claimed that Wyatt had approached the task of relating the news about Operation Crossroads to the Bikinians with "sympathy and understanding." The story, directed at a rapt American and international audience, described the Bikinians as both democratic and Christian. The Bikinians were represented as "gentle" and "intelligent" people who unanimously "voted' to leave their island because they believed their "sacrifice [would] be a contribution to world peace and the advancement of science."[31]

Reporters and colleagues frequently described Wyatt, a white Protestant former navy pilot from Kentucky, as "a student of the Bible."[32] During his time serving as the Military Governor of the Marshall Islands, Wyatt's biblical fluency made him an asset to the Navy. As one reporter explained, it "helped him immeasurably in winning the cooperation, respect and affection of the Marshallese people." According to the official history of the United States Naval Administration of the Trust Territory, Wyatt's faith and knowledge of the Bible enabled him to "translate the stark language" of the Navy's decision to remove the Bikinians "into gentle words."[33] When explaining nuclear weapons and the United States' aims to the Bikinians, Wyatt reportedly drew on the Bible as "the common denominator of the Americans and the Marshallese" and "compared the Bikinians to the children of Israel whom the Lord saved from their enemy and led into the Promised Land."[34]

The Bikinians were also avid students of the Bible, and they understood Wyatt's references to Exodus. Yet, if the Bikinians were the "children of Israel," what did that make the United States? Would the United States government watch over and provide for the Bikinians? Had the Bikinians been chosen by God for this task? If the Americans truly controlled the very elements of nature, this "great destructive force," and they had chosen Bikini "for the good of mankind," what choice did the Bikinians have except to leave?

"Manit" — indigenous knowledge and practice — is underpinned by and centers on the Marshallese people's relationship to their land. The Marshallese consider their islands to be their "jolet jen anij," their "sacred inheritance from god."[35] Given this, it seems likely that at least some of the Bikinians believed the sacrifice of their home(is)land to be a holy act. Whether or not the majority of Bikinians viewed Wyatt as a prophet of atomic exceptionalism or an imperial bearer of bad tidings, they surely recognized that their atoll's fate was out of their hands for the time being.

Although Wyatt's superiors warned him not to promise anything in the way of compensation, he assured the Bikinians that "God, in his infinite wisdom, has always provided ... for people who truly worship him." According to Wyatt's recollection of the meeting, Juda had replied: "if the United States government and the scientists of the world want to use our island ... for furthering a development which, with God's blessing will result in kindness and benefit to all mankind, my people will be pleased to go elsewhere."[36] From Wyatt's accounts, the Bikinians appeared to have willingly sacrificed their home(is)land and joined the United States military in their crusade to rid the world of warfare and advance the United States' agenda. Some Bikinians understood Wyatt's promise to the Bikinians as a covenant, or a sacred agreement about the continuing relationship between the Bikinians and the United States.

In later interviews, however, some Bikinians challenged Wyatt's depiction of them as willing participants in the United States' crusade. Kilon Bauno was present at the 1946 meeting. A child at the time, Bauno later recalled that although many Bikinians "really didn't understand what was going on," they nevertheless came away from the meeting with a sense that Wyatt "was the most powerful man in the world."[37] The Bikinians were told they had to leave because the US needed to use Bikini to test "juon baam (one bomb)." A few short weeks after Wyatt's first visit, the Bikinians packed up their belongings and were moved by the United States military. As they sailed away from Bikini on a United States Navy landing vessel, Bauno watched as the American military personnel began "burning all of our houses" and everything that the Bikinians were unable pack up and take with them. A profound sadness settled over the Bikinians: many were too distraught to eat during the voyage to Rongerik.[38] On the ship, the Bikinian poet Lore Kessibuki composed a song expressing this sadness that has since become the Bikinian Anthem. In it, Kessibuki compares leaving Bikini to leaving his spirit, rendering him "helpless and in great despair."[39]

"We Have Sacrificed for Them": MORIBA and the Legacy of Nuclear Testing

After the American occupation of the Marshall Islands ended in 1979, Marshallese Senator Tomaki Juda explained that the Bikinians did not feel as though they had a choice in leaving Bikini.[40] He described members of the community as feeling powerless to oppose the Americans: "We felt that [Wyatt] had to be listened to because the Americans had just beaten the Japanese in the war." Like his father Juda, who stood up at the 1946 meeting and told Wyatt that everything was in God's hands, Tomaki also expressed a belief that God was ultimately in control of the Bikinians' destiny. He considered the Bikinians' sacrifice of their islands to have been "a great service to mankind." After all, Tomaki reasoned, there had not been another world war since that time. For Tomaki, the "Cold War was ... fought and won on the beaches of Bikini Atoll, and the world is a better place because of it." Although the Bikinians had not wanted to leave their atoll, he explained that he nevertheless believed "this has all been part of God's plan for us."[41]

After the Bikinians were removed from Bikini in 1946, the islanders were resettled on a series of environmentally and spiritually inhospitable atolls and islands — Rongerik Atoll, Kwajalein Atoll, and finally Kili Island and tiny Ejit in Majuro Atoll. Finally, in 1968, the United States government under President Johnson promised the Bikinians that their island was safe enough for them to return. A couple of years later, a handful of families returned only to have to leave again when scientists reported that the levels of radiation were still too high to be safe for human habitation.

Unsurprisingly, many Bikinians lost faith in the United States after decades of both misinformation and outright lies about the habitability of Bikini, as well as the United States government's refusals to adequately acknowledge or compensate the Marshallese for damages caused by American nuclear testing. Other Bikinians continued to insist that the United States government uphold the promises Wyatt made in 1946 when he compared the people there to the children of Israel and told them, "everything being in God's hands, it must be good."

For example, Kelen Joash was sixteen when the United States military removed the Bikinians. In a 2004 interview, he insisted that the United States find the Bikinians somewhere permanent to live, even if it is not Bikini, because, as he emphasized, "We're the children of America."[42] Similarly, Dretin Jokdru, a Bikinian elder, argued that the Bikinian's "relationship with America should never end — Never."[43] He vowed that the Bikinians will continue to "remind [the Americans] of how we have sacrificed for them," and "we will ask them to continue to take care of us. That was their promise and we will hold them to it."[44] Before his death in 1992, Kilon Bauno also insisted on continuing the Bikinians' relationship with the United States. He explained, "We want the Americans to continue taking care of us, and we want them to be part of our future."[45]

Many Bikinians believed that they would be able to return to their home(is)land soon after the nuclear testing. They were unaware of the long-term effects of radiation and could not have anticipated that the United States would refuse to adequately decontaminate their atoll. Bauno wished for the United States to continue its relationship with the Bikinians. This meant returning Bikini to the Bikinians and returning the Bikinians to Bikini. As he explained, "I want to go back to my paradise where God intended us to be. I am asking the Americans to take us home."[46] Decades after nuclear testing and independence, Bikinians reiterate Wyatt's characterization of their community as the children of Israel in sermons on the island where many Bikinians now reside. At a church service on Ejit in the mid-2000s, for instance, the pastor, Lannij Johnson reminded the congregation, "we are like the children of Israel."[47] In the Marshall Islands, this identity of being "like the children of Israel" conveys a sense of chosenness and proximity to God as well as recognition of the Bikinian's sacrifice of their home(is)land. But as the former Mayor of Bikini-Kili-Ejit, Alson Kelen, also pointed out, over time the metaphor has become less appropriate: "the children of Israel wandered in the desert for only 40 years," while the Bikinians have now been away from Bikini, their promised land, for over seven decades.[48]

Outside of the courtroom, one powerful reminder to the United States of the sacrifice the Bikinians made "for the good of mankind" is the Bikinian flag, which closely resembles the American flag. It has the same red and white stripes and blue box in the top left corner. Unlike the American flag, which has fifty stars, the Bikinian flag has twenty-three stars — representing the twenty-three islands in Bikini Atoll — in the top left corner. In addition, the flag has three black stars on the top right corner, which represent the three islands that were completely destroyed during later nuclear testing. The flag also has two black stars on the bottom right side, which represent the two islands where the majority of the Bikinians now live: Kili and Ejit. These two stars are on the opposite side of the flag from the stars representing the islands in Bikini Atoll in order to emphasize how far away the islands where the Bikinians live today are from their home atoll. On the bottom of the flag, next to the stars for Kili and Ejit, appear the words: "MEN OTEMJEJ REJ ILO BEIN ANIJ" ("Everything is in God's hands"). According to the Bikinians' official website, their flag closely resembles the American flag in order to "remind the people and government of America that a great debt is still owed ... to the people of Bikini."[49]

As the Bikinians have attested since 1946, losing their islands to nuclear testing and radiation poisoning was deeply traumatic. In losing their islands they lost their livelihoods, the place where their history has unfolded and where their ancestors are buried, and their way of life. The leaders of the Marshall Islands explained the devastating impact of American nuclear testing on the land and, by extension, on their identities in a 1956 petition to the United Nations. There, they attested to the fact that land is "more than just a place where you can … build your houses; or a place where you can bury your dead. It is the very life of the people. Take away their land and their spirits go also."[50] It is telling that Juda's 1946 response to Wyatt (translated as "Everything is in God's hands") remains salient in the contemporary Marshall Islands. The Marshallese shorthand for the phrase, M-O-R-I-B-A, is written on the sides of buildings and tattooed across people's knuckles. It graces the front of the Bikinian children's school uniforms and often concludes online discussions about how to deal with the effects of the newest anthropogenic challenge facing the Marshallese: climate change. It remains, in other words, at the center of historical and ethical debates about American imperialism and its legacy for future generations.

FURTHER READING

Hau'ofa, Epeli. "Our Sea of Islands." In *A New Oceania: Rediscovering Our Sea of Islands*, edited by Eric Waddell, Vijay Naidu, and Epeli Hau'ofa, 2–16. Suva: Fiji, 1993.

Immerwahr, Daniel. *How to Hide an Empire: A History of the Greater United States.* New York: Farrar, Straus and Giroux, 2019.

Kiste, Robert. *The Bikinians: A Study in Forced Migration.* Menlo Park: Cummings Publishing Co., 1974.

Maffly-Kipp, Laurie. "Eastward Ho!: American Religion from the Perspective of the Pacific Rim." In *Re-telling U.S. Religious History*, edited by Thomas Tweed, 127–148. Berkeley: University of California Press, 1997.

Matsuda, Matt K. "The Pacific." *The American Historical Review* 111, no. 3 (June 2006): 758–780.

Teaiwa, Teresia. "Bikinis and Other S/Pacific N/Oceans." *The Contemporary Pacific* 6, no. 1 (Spring 1994): 87–109.

BIBLIOGRAPHY

Barker, Holly. *Bravo for the Marshallese: Regaining Control in a Post-Nuclear, Post-Colonial World.* Belmont: Wadsworth, 2004.

"Bikini Natives Vote to Yield Home to Aid Atomic Science." *The Morning News* (Delaware), February 22, 1946.

Boyer, Paul S. *By the Bomb's Early Light: American Thought and Culture at the Dawn of the Atomic Age.* Chapel Hill: University of North Carolina Press, 1994.

Doulatram, Desmond. "The Lolelaplap (Marshall Islands) in Us: Sailing West to East (Ralik→Ratak) to These Our Atolls (Aelon Kein Ad) Ad Jolet Jen Anij (Our Blessed Inheritance from God)." MA thesis, University of San Francisco, 2018.

Drake, Waldo. "Work of U.S. Chief in Islands Lauded." *Los Angeles Times*, July 14, 1946.

Graybar, Lloyd. "Bikini Revisited." *Military Affairs* 44, no. 3 (October 1980): 118–123.

Guest, Edgar. "Atomic Bomb." *Detroit Free Press*, September 17, 1945.

Hanley, Charles. "Bikini and the Hydrogen Bomb: A Fifty Year Perspective." *The Asia-Pacific Journal* 2 no. 7. (July 13, 2004): https://apjjf.org/-Senator-Tomaki-Juda/1868/article.html.

Hanley, Charles. "Islanders Yearn to Return to Bikini Atoll." *Los Angeles Times*, May 16, 2004. https://www.latimes.com/archives/la-xpm-2004-may-16–adfg-bikini16–story.html.

Imada, Adria L. *Aloha America: Hula Circuits Through the U.S. Empire.* Durham: Duke University Press, 2012.

Johnson, Edwin. "Flaunting Providence?" *The News-Palladium*, November 13, 1945.

Johnson, Giff. "Back to Bikini." *New Internationalist Magazine*, June 1997. http://newint.org/features/1997/06/05/bikini/.

Johnson, Giff. *Nuclear Past, Unclear Future.* Majuro, Marshall Islands: Micronitor, 2009.

Kessibuki, Lore. "Bikinian Anthem." March 1946. https://www.bikiniatoll.com/anthem.html.

Laurence, William. "Bikini's King Juda Receives Official Thanks from Truman." *Honolulu Advertiser*, July 19, 1946.

Lindley, Ernest. "Marshall Islanders Expected to be Wards of U.S. for Long Time." *Des Moines Register*, July 15, 1946.

Mason, Leonard. "Relocation of the Bikini Marshallese: A Study in Group Migration." PhD diss., Yale University, 1954.

Niedenthal, Jack. *For the Good of Mankind: A History of the People of Bikini and their Islands.* Majuro, Marshall Islands: Bravo Publishers, 2001. PDF.

Office of the Historian, Joint Task Force One. *Operation Crossroads: The Official Pictorial Record.* New York: Wm. H. Wise & Co., 1946.

Opie, Thomas F. "Letter to the Editor: So Hiroshima was Sodom!" *Christian Century* 63, March 27, 1946.

Richard, Dorothy. *The United States Naval Administration of the Trust Territory of the Pacific Islands.* 3 vols. Washington, DC: Office of the Chief of Naval Operations, 1957.

Said, Edward. *Culture and Imperialism.* New York: Random House, 1993.

Shurcliff, W. A. *Bombs at Bikini: The Official Report of Operation Crossroads.* New York: Wm. H. Wise & Co., 1947.

Stone, Robert, dir. *Radio Bikini.* 1987; Los Angeles, CA: New Dimension Films, 2003. DVD.

Truman, Harry. "Address in Columbus at a Conference of the Federal Council of Churches, March 6, 1946." Harry S. Truman Public Papers. National Archives. https://www.trumanlibrary.gov/library/public-papers/52/address-columbus-conference-federal-council-churches.

———. "Radio Report to the American People on the Potsdam Conference, August 9, 1945." The American Presidency Project. UCSB. https://www.presidency.ucsb.edu/documents/radio-report-the-american-people-the-potsdam-conference.

Weisgall, Jonathan. *Operation Crossroads: The Atomic Tests at Bikini Atoll.* Annapolis: Naval Institute Press, 1994.

NOTES

1 The bikini bathing suit derives its name from Bikini Atoll. Louis Reard, a French designer named the new two-piece swimsuit the "bikini" in 1946 after the nuclear explosions in the Marshall Islands. See "Louis Reard, Engineer, Dies; Designed the Bikini in 1946," *New York Times*, Sept. 18, 1984, https://www.nytimes.com/1984/09/18/obituaries/louis-reard-engineer-dies-designed-the-bikini-in-1946.html.

2 The Marshall Islands is presently an independent country in Free Association with the United States. This enables Marshallese people to travel to the United States and live, study, and work indefinitely without a visa. It also enables Marshallese to serve in the US military. And it enables the US to operate a military base in the Marshall Islands and to test Intercontinental Ballistic Missiles in the waters of the Marshall Islands. However, unless they are born in the US, Marshallese are ineligible for US citizenship. In many places, they are also barred from receiving public services including healthcare. Since the passage of the Personal Responsibility and Work Opportunity Act in 1996, Marshallese in the United States have been classified as "lawful nonimmigrant aliens."

3 It's worth noting that as Wyatt was comparing the Bikinians to the "children of Israel" the State of Israel was being created on the other side of the globe. The imagery of the Promised Land is also commonly found in Jewish, Palestinian, colonial American, and African American history. See, for instance, Albert Raboteau, "African Americans, Exodus, and the American Israel," in *Religion and American Culture: A Reader*, 2nd ed., edited by David G. Hackett (New York: Routledge, 2003), 73–87.

4 For additional details on the bomb and fallout see Holly Barker, *Bravo for the Marshallese: Regaining Control in a Post-Nuclear, Post-Colonial World* (Belmont: Wadsworth, 2004).

5 Giff Johnson, *Nuclear Past, Unclear Future* (Majuro, Marshall Islands: Micronitor, 2009).

6 The US reported that Operation Crossroads was the "the *best*-reported as well as *most*-reported technical experiment of all time" (W. A. Shurcliff, *Bombs at Bikini: The Official Report of Operation Crossroads* [New York: Wm. H. Wise & Co., 1947], 38). In footage from preparations for Operation Crossroads one of the men who filmed the tests explained, "There'll be a hundred-n-4 still cameras, 208 motion picture cameras … some of our statisticians have computed that we're going to make as many pictures in the first, uh, several seconds as are made in 11 … Hollywood

productions. … we brought over 18 tons" of film (*Radio Bikini,* directed by Robert Stone [1987; New Dimension Films, 2003], DVD).

7 Edward Said, *Culture and Imperialism* (New York: Random House, 1993), xiii.

8 Harry Truman, "Radio Report to the American People on the Potsdam Conference, August 9, 1945," in The American Presidency Project, UCSB, https://www.presidency.ucsb.edu/documents/radio-report-the-american-people-the-potsdam-conference.

9 Government censorship generally prevented the public from learning about atomic scientists' own misgivings in great detail and that other nations were not as close to developing an atomic bomb as the US was in 1945. The US did share some information regarding the bomb with the governments of Canada and Great Britain.

10 Paul S. Boyer, *By the Bomb's Early Light: American Thought and Culture at the Dawn of the Atomic Age* (Chapel Hill: University of North Carolina Press, 1994), 211. Boyer's text provides an excellent study of the cultural impact of atomic weapons.

11 Quoted in Boyer, *By the Bomb's Early Light,* 211.

12 Thomas F. Opie, "Letter to the Editor: So Hiroshima was Sodom!" *Christian Century* 63 (March 27, 1946): 400. Opie was commenting on the Federal Council of Churches' 1946 Calhoun Commission Report, which retracted their earlier sanctioning of "wholesale obliteration" bombing, decrying it as immoral. Note that the Calhoun Commission Report was not officially endorsed by the Federal Council of Churches.

13 Edgar Guest, "Atomic Bomb," *Detroit Free Press,* September 17, 1945.

14 Edwin Johnson, "Flaunting Providence?" *The News-Palladium,* November 13, 1945, 1. See also Jonathan Weisgall, *Operation Crossroads: The Atomic Tests at Bikini Atoll* (Annapolis: Naval Institute Press, 1994), 80. Johnson was also the sponsor of the May-Johnson Bill, which sought to give the US government exclusive control over the development of atomic energy.

15 79 Cong. Rec. S2128 (statement of Sen. Rankin), quoted in Lloyd Graybar, "Bikini Revisited" *Military Affairs* 44, no. 3 (October 1980): 120.

16 Harry Truman, "Address in Columbus at a Conference of the Federal Council of Churches, March 6, 1946," in Harry S. Truman Public Papers, National Archives, https://www.trumanlibrary.gov/library/public-papers/52/address-columbus-conference-federal-council-churches.

17 For a detailed discussion of the Army Air Force-Navy debate at the end of World War II see Weisgall, *Operation Crossroads,* 1–23.

18 Weisgall, *Operation Crossroads,* 14–15. James Forrestal was the Secretary of the Navy from 1944–1947. He became the first United States Secretary of Defense when the position was created in 1947.

19 Shurcliff, *Bombs at Bikini,* ix.

20 In addition to the atomic bombs dropped on Hiroshima and Nagasaki, the United States exploded an atomic weapon in New Mexico in July 1945.

21 Shurcliff, *Bombs at Bikini,* 16–17. See also Dorothy Richard, *The United States Naval Administration of the Trust Territory of the Pacific Islands,* vol. 3 (Washington, DC: Office of the Chief of Naval Operations, 1957), 507.

22 William H. P. Blandy, "Atomic Test Case," *Colliers* 117 (June 8, 1946): 39 quoted in Weisgall, *Operation Crossroads,* 31.

23 Vice Adm. Frederick L. Ashworth, interview by Albert B. Christman, Naval Weapons Center, China Lake, CA, April 1969 (NWC-75201-S61) quoted in Weisgall, *Operation Crossroads,* 33.

24 Weisgall, *Operation Crossroads,* 33.

25 Office of the Historian, Joint Task Force One. *Operation Crossroads: The Official Pictorial Record* (New York: Wm. H. Wise & Co., 1946), 6.

26 For further discussion, see Adria L. Imada, *Aloha America: Hula Circuits Through the U.S. Empire* (Duke University Press, 2012).

27 Leonard Mason, "Relocation of the Bikini Marshallese: A Study in Group Migration" (PhD diss., Yale University, 1954), 30.

28 Weisgall, *Operation Crossroads,* 104–105.

29 Ibid., 105.

30 Ibid., 107.

31 "Bikini Natives Vote to Yield Home to Aid Atomic Science," *The Morning News* (Wilmington, Delaware), February 22, 1946, 10.

32 Ernest Lindley, "Marshall Islanders Expected to be Wards of U.S. for Long Time," *Des Moines Register*, July 15, 1946; Waldo Drake, "Work of U.S. Chief in Islands Lauded," *Los Angeles Times*, July 14, 1946, 4; William Laurence, "Bikini's King Juda Receives Official Thanks from Truman," *Honolulu Advertiser*, July 19, 1946, 7.

33 Richard, *United States Naval Administration of the Trust Territory*, 509.

34 Ibid.

35 Desmond Doulatram, "The Lolelaplap (Marshall Islands) in US: Sailing West to East (Ralik→Ratak) to These Our Atolls (Aelon Kein Ad) Ad Jolet Jen Anij (Our Blessed Inheritance from God)" (MA thesis, University of San Francisco, 2018), http://repository.usfca.edu/capstone/725; RMI Const. preamble. 1979. https://rmiparliament.org/cms/constitution.html.

36 "Bikini Natives Vote to Yield Home to Aid Atomic Science," *The Morning News* (Delaware) February 22, 1946, 10.

37 Kilon Bauno in *Radio Bikini*, 5:59, 5:05.

38 Ibid., 8:59.

39 Lore Kessibuki, 1914–1994, "Bikinian Anthem," 1946, https://www.bikiniatoll.com/anthem.html.

40 Jack Niedenthal, *For the Good of Mankind: A History of the People of Bikini and their Islands* (Majuro, Marshall Islands: Bravo Publishers, 2001), 159.

41 Ibid.

42 Charles Hanley, "Bikini and the Hydrogen Bomb: A Fifty Year Perspective," *The Asia-Pacific Journal* 2, no. 7 (July 13, 2004): 5.

43 Niedenthal, *For the Good of Mankind*, 146.

44 Ibid., 147.

45 Ibid., 163.

46 Kilon Bauno in *Radio Bikini*, 49:54.

47 Charles Hanley, "Islanders Yearn to Return to Bikini Atoll," *Los Angeles Times*, May 16, 2004, https://www.latimes.com/archives/la-xpm-2004-may-16-adfg-bikini16-story.html.

48 Ibid.

49 Niedenthal, *For the Good of Mankind*, 183.

50 Quoted in Giff Johnson, "Back to Bikini," *New Internationalist Magazine*, June 1997, http://newint.org/features/1997/06/05/bikini/.

Part V

MODERNITY

Chapter Twenty-Three

THE HATE THAT HATE PRODUCED: REPRESENTING BLACK RELIGION IN THE TWENTIETH CENTURY

Vaughn A. Booker

Dartmouth College, Hanover, New Hampshire

Introduction

In the words of journalist Mike Wallace, *The Hate That Hate Produced* was "a study of the rise of black racism, of a call for black supremacy among a small but growing segment of the American Negro population." The controversial five-part series featured interviews between journalist Louis Lomax and controversial black religious and political leaders, including Elijah Muhammad (1897–1975) and el-Hajj Malik el-Shabazz, also known as Malcolm X (1925–1965), so that they would contextualize their religious teachings and footage of their public speeches that captivated urban black America at mid-century. The program juxtaposes black Muslim rhetoric with responses from respected local and national African American leaders. Among these black public intellectuals is Anna Arnold Hedgeman (1899–1990), the only woman interviewed to provide context for the black religious movement that was "the most powerful of the black supremacist groups," in Wallace's language.

After listing Hedgeman's resume, Wallace describes her as "liv[ing] among her fellow Negroes" to capture her status as a race representative. In her interview with Lomax, Hedgeman declares that a "bottled up" African American population, whose civil rights white America has denied, is now responding with reactionary rhetoric deemed anti-white and anti-Semitic. She emphasizes that the reason for such discourse is not its justification. To explain reactionary religious rhetoric, Lomax attempts to quote a recent speech in which Hedgeman declared that "God may not be black, but he certainly isn't white." Hedgeman corrects Lomax to insist she was speaking of Jesus, referring to the historical person apart from the supreme deity. Hedgeman explains the importance of this statement: "I think maybe some of us like to say, as Christians, that there's no picture of Jesus in the Bible because everybody then could claim him. And you see, you claim when pressure has been put

---

NOTE: This chapter is intended to accompany the viewing of the 1959 television program *The Hate That Hate Produced*, a multimedia primary source for studying African American religion in the twentieth century (available: https://archive.org/details/PBSTheHateThatHateProduced)

upon you to claim things in terms of color, as it has in this country. You want a piece of this guy who was a terrific prophet." For African Americans to desire and declare a physical likeness to Jesus is, according to Hedgeman, as important as claiming spiritual and mental likeness to him, "because America has made this important, you see. We've made this important everywhere. One goes down the streets in Bombay and sees the models — not brown, Indian girls, but Anglo-Saxon girls, because the British then were in control." Lomax retorts that religious teachings which associate divine figures with the colors of racial groups represent a "tribalistic" social reversion for African Americans. Hedgeman agrees, but she states that "America is about at the tribalistic stage, yes" on the issue of color, a fact so pronounced in the racial superiority of those with white skin, "blue eyes and blonde hair."

Without directly engaging or reflecting upon Hedgeman's analysis, Wallace laments the current radical direction of black religious discourse, evidence that "a growing segment of the Negro population is losing faith in the American dream." A second segment of Lomax's interview with Hedgeman offers her explanation of the nationalistic movements among African Americans. Hedgeman declares that African Americans worked to identify with the American nation because they are "the most American of any group here," but "America has never permitted it" with its Jim Crow system of oppression.

Wallace summarizes Hedgeman's segment as "tragic and irrefutable evidence that a small but growing segment of the American Negro population is giving ear to a flagrant doctrine of black supremacy."[1] As this chapter demonstrates, however, black Protestant religious discourse in the 1920s and 1930s contextualizes the progressive theological expressions that Hedgeman offered in her 1959 interview. Many black intellectual religious leaders influenced and were shaped by these modes of public religious engagement in the middle decades of the twentieth century, including Bethune-Cookman College president and activist Mary McLeod-Bethune (1875–1955), Howard University School of Religion Dean and Morehouse

Figure 23.1 Black religious activists Martin Luther King, Jr. (left) and Anna Arnold Hedgeman (right) meeting with unidentified students (center), April 9, 1958. Photo by Afro American Newspapers/Gado/Getty Images.

College President Benjamin Elijah Mays (1894–1984), theologian and Church for the Fellowship of All Peoples co-pastor Howard Thurman (1899–1981), Abyssinian Baptist Church pastor and Congressman Adam Clayton Powell, Jr. (1908–1972), and a younger generation of prominent nonviolent civil rights activists that included Martin Luther King, Jr. (1929–1968), Coretta Scott King (1927–2006), and James M. Lawson, Jr. (b. 1928). Importantly, this public black religious engagement helps us to understand the progressive religious voices of Powell and Hedgeman, who appear in *The Hate That Hate Produced* to contextualize the rhetoric about race and religion that the Black Muslims, also known as the Nation of Islam (NOI), preached.

The journalists consulted Hedgeman for contextualization of racialized religious rhetoric because of her decades of professional experience as a racial and religious liaison to white America on behalf of African Americans. It was Hedgeman's early life, religious career, activism, and experience with Jim Crow segregation that shaped her public intellectual voice as she explained race and religion to a national audience.

The Journey of a Black Protestant Activist and Public Intellectual

Anna Arnold Hedgeman was an African American who, like many, grew up outside the context of communities of black people. After attending college in South Carolina, her parents raised their family in the Midwest, ultimately in Anoka, Minnesota, a town with white Americans of Norwegian, Swedish, Irish, and German descent. Members of her family could "pass" racially — one of her sisters had blue eyes and blonde hair, and townspeople were often unsure of her father's racial identity because of his light skin and features. It was when a younger girl on Hedgeman's route to school asked her, "Anna, are you really a nigger?" that she became aware of the difference of her identity. Hedgeman's mother offered her daughter a Christian response to receiving this epithet: "I hope you will never use such un-Christian words yourself, for all races must be respected. If anyone calls you a name of this kind, you must realize he is not an intelligent person. Ask the Lord to forgive him and then forget about it."[2]

Hedgeman did not have her first experience in an African American church until she was in high school, during a visit to St. Paul, MN with her aunt: "When we arrived in St. Paul, Aunt Mayme took us to church and we were amazed to see only brown people. ... The church service was a curiously dismaying experience. It was an emotional shock to hear shouting during a service. At some point in the minister's sermon a voice from the rear cried out, 'Preach it, Master.' In amazement I turned to my aunt who whispered quickly, 'Don't look back, I'll explain later.'" It was after this service that Hedgeman met other young African Americans her age who would later become noteworthy, including Roy Wilkins, future executive of the National Association for the Advancement of Colored People (NAACP) throughout the civil rights movement.[3]

Hedgeman attended Hamline University, a Methodist college in St. Paul, and she was the school's first African American student.[4] While in college in 1919, Hedgeman heard a lecture by W. E. B. Du Bois, then-head of the NAACP, as he lectured to the Hamline audience on African leaders working toward independence from colonial rule.[5] Following college, Hedgeman was racialized — truly made aware of her identity as black, and black as subordinated to white — when she traveled South to take a teaching job in Mississippi. She became more aware of her non-whiteness by being placed in the Jim Crow system that heavily policed/circumscribed her in accordance with strict racial boundaries and the perceived sexual availability of African American women to white men. She experienced segregated travel and dining conditions, both of which lacked cleanliness for black patrons and offered lower-quality food options. And she was very candid about her discomfort around black people while traveling, revealing her own middle-class status of relative privilege that made her dismissive of laboring black folks whose worn clothes, noisiness, and lack of propriety struck her negatively.[6]

Hedgeman taught at the Methodist-affiliated Rust College in Holly Springs, Mississippi, whose dean was Dr. J. Leonard Farmer, father of CORE founder James Farmer.[7] But she grew angry with the South after teaching at Rust for two years, asking "How could conditions like this be tolerated in the United States? How dared such people call themselves Christians? Why were Negroes denied the ordinary human freedoms? What could I do about it?" Hedgeman recognized that she was a Northerner, and she decided to "return North and organize the Midwest to help eliminate the cruelty of the southern part of my country. Courageous southern Negroes had to be rescued from the kind of white people I had seen in the South."[8]

Hedgeman accepted a position with the Young Women's Christian Association (YWCA) in Springfield, Ohio, in 1924. This was four years after the YWCA "officially shifted its focus to interracialism" as it remained a segregated organization. With greater financial support of black YWCA branches, the organization "enabled black women's leadership" and women like Hedgeman "saw that even a segregated Y[WCA] provided them with rare opportunities for professional development and for forging meaningful alliances with middle-class white women."[9] In Springfield, Hedgeman experienced northern segregation in this context. She encountered segregated facilities for YWCA youth (the gymnasium, swimming pools, and cafeteria of the YWCA's Central Association building were off-limits for African Americans). The Midwest lacked the signs "black" and "white" but held the same segregated practices. Hedgeman wrote: "During the first week [of her position] a Negro minister walked into a drug store of [Springfield], bought some aspirin, and then asked the clerk at the soda fountain for a glass of water with which to take the tablet. The clerk handed him the water, watched him drink it with the pill, and then, in the minister's presence, broke the glass." Hedgeman reflected frequently on the exhausting labor of anti-racist education, Hedgeman's laborious experience over decades to explain racism to white audiences, and particularly white Christian audiences, beginning with her YWCA work:

> As executive of the YWCA Negro branch in Springfield, I was much in demand for lectures on race relations, but I found such lectures difficult, for there WERE no relations. The adults to whom I spoke were usually good Christian white people, who thought of themselves as "liberal" if they invited a Negro speaker to their meetings. It was difficult for me to know how and where to begin for it was obvious that they did not understand this Jesus whom they quoted so lavishly in the prayers preceding my speech. Their image of the Negro always emerged clearly in the question period following my speech and their questions gave me nightmares. The first was always "What do Negroes want?" It did not occur to them that the question itself was an insult. I lashed out at them with the bitterness and venom born of Mississippi, and, now, the Midwest and they loved it, in a way, for it relieved them of their shame for a moment, even as it purged me.[10]

Hedgeman worked for YWCA branches in Jersey City, NJ and New York City during the 1920s. She moved to Harlem during the period that its black ministers began to view churches as socially responsible agents that must "[lead] community activities toward jobs, housing, education and political and governmental opportunity." Under her leadership, the Harlem YWCA prepared "nurses, domestics, stenographers, secretaries, bookkeepers, dressmakers and designers, and power-machine operators. We battled the garment industry, the trade union movement, the employment services, the department stores and other private industries to produce openings for the [African American] people we were training and for the already trained."[11] Hedgeman became executive director of the black YWCA's Philadelphia branch in 1933, addressing issues of housing discrimination. In November 1933, she married Merritt Hedgeman. With the rise of WWII, Hedgeman worked with A. Philip Randolph on the March on Washington Movement and to establish a permanent Fair Employment Practices Commission.[12]

This was Hedgeman's experience as a black Protestant public intellectual before becoming involved in New York state politics and then the civil rights activism of the 1950s and 1960s. But what accounts for Hedgeman's defense of the prominent discourses of race and religion that Malcolm X also offered in New York City? To understand Hedgeman's public intellectual role — a black Protestant who elected to contextualize non-Christian religious thought — it is necessary to examine Afro-Protestant Christianity through the aims of its "modernist" leadership in the early decades of the twentieth century. The next section focuses on these black Protestants as they produced public discourses about the lived complexities of race and religion that often resulted in interreligious engagements.

A Modernist Trajectory for Black Protestant Christianity

Before the Great War, an *A. M. E. Church Review* editorial declared the status for African American clergy as race representatives to be "a mission to American [read: white] Christianity." Among the many charges of the black male minister, the editorial declared that he was "to combat the dehumanizing influence of Jim Crowism, awaken the American conscience against the crime of lynching, [and] to uphold political justice and civic righteousness."[13] The African Methodist Episcopal Zion (AMEZ) church's publication *The Star of Zion* often reprinted articles from the NAACP's official magazine *The Crisis*, providing its readership with national news of progressive racial politics alongside the denomination's theological teachings, AMEZ women's writings on education, and editorials frequently addressing national social, racial, and political matters. One early editorial by William J. Walls, future head bishop of the AMEZ church, responded to a black evangelist who criticized a meeting of ministers responding to the Chicago race riot of 1919 and supporting a memorial for African American soldiers who fought in France in the Great War. According to Walls, this evangelist wanted "the cause of evangelism" and "the souls of men" to be the sole concerns for these ministers. Walls characterized this argument as out of step with modern black ministers ("We are glad that this is not the rule of the race ministry any more"), a "fallacious teaching" that missed Christianity's prescriptive potential to address matters like racial violence: "Our religion is suited to all living matters. ... It is good religion to know the cause of outbreaks between the races and how to stop them. The man or set of men who would discover the solvent to this and other momentous evils in society will go a long stride in applying Christianity to real life." Furthermore, Walls supported the vision of black Protestant religious leadership that encouraged the presence of other race representatives to create a division of labor in addressing racial inequality: "We should preach business, profession, and economy, and encourage education, race spirit and a Christian vision for invention, discovery and independent manhood. Christ came that we might have abundant life. ... What sense is there in the Christian leadership of such a striving people as ours remaining a one track leadership in the midst of conditions such as we face?"[14]

Prominent African American historians lauded the aspirations of black Protestant clergy for extending a tradition of race representation into the modern era. In 1921, Carter G. Woodson's *The History of the Negro Church* covered an early history of missionary encounter to African slaves, the development of the free black Protestant denominations (National Baptist Convention [NBC], African Methodist Episcopal [AME], AMEZ, Colored Methodist Episcopal [CME]), and the political efforts of their respective clergymen. Woodson highlighted the importance of these denominational institutions for their ability to bring forward politically-minded leaders interested in the progress of the race. He distinguished these "progressive" churchmen, who valued education (religious and secular) in addition to valorizing white American notions of religious worship, church structure, and moral propriety, from the "conservatives" who appreciated the institution of African American Christianity as they had experienced it before Emancipation, given that it was then the sole social institution operated by African Americans. In his move to the contemporary period of the early twentieth century with "The Negro Church of Today," Woodson focused on defending black Christian denominational institutions in the face of "a few radical members of the race" who viewed them collectively as a conservative force impeding black social progress.[15] Woodson argued, "The church then is no longer the voice of one man crying in the wilderness, but a spiritual organization at last becoming alive to the needs of a people handicapped by social distinctions of which the race must gradually free itself to do here in this life that which will assure the larger life to come." Social improvement must take precedence over divine reward, and black Protestant churches were practical in their efforts to fight segregation and in funding the NAACP.[16]

The civil rights activist Channing H. Tobias and the Congregational minister Jesse E. Moorland asked Woodson to produce a book for the Young Men's Christian Association (YMCA) press to counter W. D. Weatherford's 1912 work, *Present Forces in Negro Progress*. Woodson's unpublished 1921 manuscript, initially titled "The Case of the Negro," was his attempt to respond to the racism of Weatherford, a prominent YMCA figure and supporter of African Americans who also promoted white superiority. However, Woodson criticized African American ministers in his book, prompting Tobias and Moorland to cease supporting it.[17] "The Case of the Negro" expressed Woodson's optimism in the early years following World War I for progressive black elites' potential to advance African Americans through "creating schools, establishing opportunity, and proper leadership." And this optimism extended to black religious leaders, the best of whom headed "institutional" churches that addressed community social needs.[18]

While Woodson was critical of African American Protestants who had not embraced a more engaged social presence, he also criticized white Americans for appearing to abandon literal conceptions of ultimate paradise and judgment and, instead, deifying whiteness through the institution of Jim Crow.[19] "The Case of the Negro" framed black Protestant religiosity alongside what Woodson considered the absence of genuine religion among whites. "The blacks are superior to whites in that they are more religious," Woodson wrote. "It must be admitted that many Negroes are more superstitious than religious, but in holding on to religion until a more forceful factor for inhibition can be developed, the Negroes have thereby maintained a system which serves them as a moral police force." Woodson's generalizations about African American religiosity in this manuscript reveal his ambivalence about the ultimate value of religion as a "factor" for the race's advancement, serving practically, to him, as a system of restraint. Woodson stated there was a general, literalist embrace of the Bible "in word and spirit" by African Americans, and he conjectured that many African Americans were "wisely conservative in dealing with their oppressors" because they believed in Christian doctrines of eternal punishment after death.[20] Despite their perceived religious superiority, Woodson also characterized African Americans as increasing in infidelity "[b]ecause of the incongruity between the white man's profession and practice" of Christianity. He concluded:

> The Negro, therefore, has little faith in the [Western world's] so-called Christian civilization. He is not inclined to ascribe to this religion in its corrupted form the credit which it has received as the supreme and absolute in bringing the world to its present advanced stage. The Negro, a Christian himself, does not doubt the power of the principles enunciated by Jesus of Nazareth. He contends that this religion has not yet been tried. The Negro agrees with that writer who says that whites nailed Christianity to the cross. There is much doubt that actual Christianity ever existed in Europe and even if it did, it suffered an untimely death in transit across the Atlantic.[21]

As historian of African American religion Barbara Savage has written, Woodson continued to develop and articulate his criticisms and prescriptions for African American Protestantism in the 1930s. Most notably, he argued for a "United Negro Church" and aligned himself with black religious "modernists" against both the "fundamentalists" of the race and those "extremists" who advocated African Americans dismissing churches wholesale as effective social institutions.[22] Although unpublished, Woodson's "The Case of the Negro" reveals a set of critical attitudes about African American Protestantism that he and other black social and intellectual leaders, alongside progressive educated black clergy, sought to reform or improve upon as they forged a modern black Protestantism for the new era.

Black Protestant Christianity: Race Representation and Interreligious Dialogue

As evident in Hedgeman's interracial religious engagements, black mainline Protestants worked to forge and maintain social and theological ties with other white American Protestant denominations to benefit African American social and political progress. When Howard University scholar Kelly Miller (1863–1939) asserted that "[t]he Christian ministry offers the best field for the outlet of Negro capacity and genius," he saw the prospect that modern theologies, which were gaining prominence among white seminarians, would also entice a younger generation of educated African Americans to become religious race leaders: "The theological opinion of the world is becoming more and more liberalized. The college man need no longer hesitate concerning the ministry because of old theological exactions which compromised his intellectual integrity." Miller charged African American colleges with "infus[ing] into the rising generation of educated youth the wisdom and necessity of dedicating their lives to the great task of moral and spiritual leadership, in the name of God, humanity and race."[23]

In line with Miller's endorsement of modern theologies, some mainline black Protestant denominations expressed their reception of contemporary biblical scholarship. For instance, *The Star of Zion* printed a story discussing the scholarly consensus on the theological evolution of the Hebrew Bible: "Scholars now recognize that the Hebrew people began as polytheists (believers in many gods), then became henotheists (worshippers of a national deity) and finally were converted to monotheism, which teaches that there is one sovereign being, the creator and ruler of the universe. Their great prophets attributed to Him outstanding characteristics of His nature."[24] However, the conversations that African American religious modernists shared in the black religious press may not have easily comported with the attitudes of African American church parishioners, especially older ones. In 1927, Miller lamented the balancing act that black ministers must perform to assuage older congregants and keep younger ones from dismissing the religious institution: "There is not an avowed Negro modernist in America. If so, he must needs keep his modernity in the back part of his mind; for the good and sufficient reason that the older half of his congregation would repudiate him utterly. But the younger generation is shot through with the newer interpretation." For Miller, African American clergy deserved "great sympathy in the dual task of such great spiritual complexity" that balanced the theological and liturgical desires of both younger and elder churchgoers between pulpit and press.[25]

While faced with the shifting rhetorical terrain of the era's religious modernism, black Protestant public intellectuals also navigated representing their race as religiously modern to likeminded middle-class black Protestants and to white Protestant religious practitioners. In the 1920s, the NBC, USA Inc.'s newspaper *The National Baptist Voice* reprinted editorials from the white liberal Presbyterian magazine *Christian Work*.[26] In 1921, a piece titled "The

Evil Heart of Unbelief" argued not only that unbelief was a position relative to different religious traditions ("To Mohammedans, Buddhists and Christians are unbelievers; to Christians, non-Christians are unbelievers"), but that skepticism was inherent to evolving religious beliefs:

> Belief here is the acceptance of certain specific tenets. The moment these appear to be untrue or unreasonable to a man he is at once to those who hold them an unbeliever. Thru unbelief of this kind, all progress has come; every progressive must be more or less an unbeliever in the *status quo*; certain abandonments must always be made at every stage of an onward movement. Wycliffe, Luther, Paul, and Jesus were all great unbelievers by the religious standards of their own time, and through their unbelief came enlargement and salvation. Such belief is only faith in larger truth.

The "evil heart" of such unbelief, however, was humanity's potential "desire to get rid of any sense of supreme rulership in the universe, to deny the existence of a universal moral order that should be obeyed, to get rid of the feeling of duty and obligation to a higher will than our own, and to live without regulative principles." The article's author persuaded the reader to scrutinize all religious tenets, certain that a universal morality withstands such examination. "Whatever the risk," the author wrote, "I claim for every man the sacred right of asking questions and of exploring the foundations of unbelief however sacred and however old, there must be no sphere artificially shielded from the investigator. There is no doubt that an admission of the evolutionary view of life gives new point to such questions as, What is sin? What is freedom? What is conscience? What is morality? What is religion? I do not propose to discuss these questions now, but only to say that no well-informed theory of evolution, no well-established science, diminishes by one iota our obligation to be and to do the very highest and best that we possibly can be and do." An attachment to belief in a supreme being and its systems of morality resonated with *The National Baptist Voice*'s editors. The author stated further, "Personally I have long recognized that the framework of orthodox theology has been damaged beyond repair by the arrival of new knowledge. It is impossible for educated men to believe that the human race began its career with two perfect human beings, or with any number of perfect human beings, and the whole scheme of redemption based upon that supposition, so far as its formal doctrines are concerned, is undermined. But this does not mean that sin is not a fact in human life and that the greatest need of man is to be saved from it, and that we can only be so saved by the living God." The author contended that the concept of sin persisted because of humanity's behaviors and despite the plausibility of new evolutionary knowledge.[27]

"The Evil Heart of Unbelief" stood alongside other articles in 1921, such as S. N. Vass's "Is There A Burning Hell," which denied the presence of such a fiery destination in the Hebrew Bible but promised its fate for unredeemed sinners according to Jesus's words in New Testament passages. Vass, an African American educator, minister, and district secretary of the American Baptist Publication Society, framed biblical scholarship to afford black Baptists a conservative evangelical foundation to continue preaching against personal immorality in concert with their white Baptist contemporaries.[28] Another 1921 article, titled "Negroes to Pray that God Trouble the Conscience of White America," announced a call from the NAACP to "colored ministers throughout the United States" to use Sunday, April 24 to preach sermons on the theme "Justice to the Negro — the Test of Christianity in America," which the ministers were to follow with an offering of prayer, in support of the civil rights organization's membership drive.[29]

Later in the decade, *The Star of Zion* editor Rev. William H. Davenport (1868–1936), who assumed the position following Walls's promotion to bishop, voiced his own dependence on a concept of "supreme rulership" as he also made known his support for evolutionary theory.

Davenport endorsed a concept of theistic evolution: "To our mind, evolution is a serious fact. ... As the world grows older and men think more clearly[,] the supposed chasm between evolution and religion is bridged, and no one is injured thereby."[30] In light of the Scopes controversy, the white Protestant magazine *The Christian Century* lauded Davenport's defense of evolutionary theory: "It will be remembered that North Carolina, in which [*The Star of Zion*] is published, is adjacent to the state of Tennessee; and that the Negro race is supposed by some to be intellectually inferior and backward."[31]

A June 1929 article from Davenport responded to "the brutal lynching of a Negro a few days ago in the Fundamentalist State of Tennessee — a State which bitterly resisted the teaching of evolution in its schools"; "What relation lynching bears to fundamentalism, or what relation fundamentalism bears to lynching is not clear, but it is notorious that the [*sic*] most of the lynchings take place in the States where fundamentalism is a fetish." For Davenport, collective white racial violence against African Americans had likely roots in literal interpretations of scripture that he felt were untenable for modern Christians.[32] With another more direct response to the anti-evolutionists concerned with Tennessee's Scopes trial, AMEZ Bishop E. D. W. Jones addressed the NAACP's 22nd Annual Conference in Pittsburgh in 1931. He stated that African Americans were "as far removed from the Scopes trial in Tennessee and the religious and educational enactments of legislatures against evolution and discoveries of science as the enlightened Englishman is far removed from the cave man." The more pressing matter, for Jones, was to address white Americans' "Christianity of injustice, prejudice, hate, cold indifferent brotherhood, war, slaughter and armed missionary invasion" that was morally deficient in comparison to "the Christianity of the Negro." Jones also resonated with black intellectuals and Social Gospel proponents, who criticized African American Protestants for focusing on the hereafter while neglecting commitments to social and political change in America. He declared his (and his denomination's) modern concept of a "heaven" that had evolved beyond the heaven of enslaved generations of African Americans who sought eternal deliverance from earthly oppression: "Heaven and a desire to get there ... grew out of our hellish condition from inhumane tortures we hoped to be relieved from. But now our heaven is in service, duty, fighting for fellowship, manhood, honest courageous citizenship, right acting toward one another, reverence for personality."[33]

In 1925, the *Africo-American Presbyterian* reprinted an article celebrating the gathering of 15,000 people in New York City's Madison Square Garden to launch a drive to raise $15 million for the Episcopal Cathedral of St. John the Divine. The article claimed that "the alarm raised by radical ministers of the Gospel, that the country, led by the younger generation, has cast religion definitely in the discard" was unwarranted in light of this evidence of modern religious vitality. Similarly, the announcement from the University of Michigan that it intended to found the Michigan School of Religion for comparative religious studies provided enough evidence that "[t]here is life in the old truth yet, but each age requires its restatement in valid and comprehensible terms." Of the Michigan School of Religion, the article stated, "This institution is nonsectarian in its point of view and established on the belief that 'the facts of life and the world, as they come to be known and appreciated, instead of betraying its spiritual values, can only enhance these, and that Christianity itself, like any other religion even greater in its spirit and purpose than in its letter, can only gain as it studies other religions sympathetically and responds honestly to new knowledge about men and things.'" For these black and white Presbyterians, religion was "[w]orking its way slowly and tortuously out of the concepts and definitions untenable in the light of science" and "press[ing] on to new concepts and definitions which shall satisfy the ever-hungry soul of the man in the new order."[34]

Similarly, progressive ministers worked to foster interracial ties in the 1920s by taking initial, symbolic steps like exchanging pulpits on Abraham Lincoln's birthday. The Chicago Church Federation's race relations committee arranged for such exchanges for a sequence of Sundays in 1925, including having Dr. Robert Clements, white pastor of Austin's First

Presbyterian Church, exchange pulpits with Dr. W. Edward Williams, black pastor of Chicago's Hope Presbyterian Church.[35] It is important to note, however, that an embrace of modernism did not capture the entire Presbyterian church, and a few months later the denomination approached a General Assembly meeting contesting the place of fundamentalists, modernists and rationalists, and moderates.[36]

Black Protestant Christianity: Religious Tolerance and Criticisms of Oppression

Among AMEZ ministers, there was also promise in the early years of the decade to articulate religious tolerance that paralleled white ministers and academics long invested in comparative religious appreciation of different traditions — although ultimately claiming Christianity's relative religious superiority. A minister in the Methodist Conference of Detroit preached that "no man or woman who is sincerely trying to find God should refer to another's religion as false," and if other religions are inadequate, "in each are found persons who are conscientious of their belief." *The Star of Zion* affirmed this sentiment, calling it "the true spirit of Christian love and tolerance" and positing an ideal world benefitting from worshippers truly committed to their ancestral traditions or the new religions they embraced: "It were better for the world if the followers of one sect or creed would permit other sects and creeds go on their way worshipping God according to the forms that their mothers and fathers followed, or that were of their own conscientious adoption. The person who believes his own religion the only one and who is disposed to make quarrel with his neighbors because their religion is of a different kind, might as well contend that no one can get to heaven by any religion other than that of his particular kind. It is the doctrine of this paper that people find [it and plan to get to heaven first]."[37]

In the 1930s, black Protestants' religious engagements with Mohandas K. Gandhi and his nonviolent campaigns included press coverage and editorial debates, resulting in Sunday School lessons comparing Gandhi to Jesus[38] as well as "international travel and interreligious exchanges" that "influenced a community of black Christian intellectuals and activists who were developing theological blueprints for an American racial justice movement."[39] *The Star of Zion* maintained that this sentiment existed among the denomination's leadership in the 1930s, including Bishop Cameron Chesterfield Alleyne. When the bishop presided over an AMEZ conference in 1938, his ecumenical stance was on display in his praise for Gandhi: "One man's religion, whether it be Hindu, Mohammedanism [*sic*] or Christianity, was as good as another man's, if it disciplined his life and produced good character." The paper noted that following Alleyne's tribute to Gandhi, "his colleagues cried shame at him. But whether Gandhi worshipped a cow or any other thing, he prayed that the world would have more Gandhis."[40]

And as African American social and religious leaders focused on British India as a model for anticolonial resistance, leaders like Gandhi and Rabindranath Tagore — with the former regarded as a modern religious and political exemplar for his race — produced discourses of Christianity that resonated with the Protestant Christianities that an oppressed American racial minority both embraced and forged. When the poet Tagore addressed an English missionary by letter, he wrote, "Do not be always trying to preach your doctrine, but give yourself in love. Your western mind is too much obsessed with the idea of conquest. Your inveterate habit of proselytism is another form of it. Christ never preached himself, or any dogma or doctrine. He preached the love of God." This letter circulated in several black and white Protestant publications, and *The Star of Zion*'s editorial response declared, "Tagore strikes the conceit out of the English imperialistic Christian and calls him to his need in this letter. It will help us all to read this from a Mohammedan to see what to others we are seen to be."[41]

In a 1927 *Star of Zion* editorial, Davenport reminded readers that "the bayonets of the Western powers have followed the Bible." The suspicion of "Western Christianity" by non-Western peoples was not a surprise to black Christians who had experienced its oppressive racial consequences, for "... wherever Western Christianity has penetrated, racial experiences, racial culture and nationalism have been suppressed or superseded by the indoctrination of foreign ideas and methods. The exclusiveness, the superiority complex of the missionary has stirred up nationalistic prejudices, and instigated anti-Christian resistance in China, Japan, India; and there are mutterings in Africa." Davenport urged the adoption of Christian missionary work that "combats assumptions of [racial] superiority.[42] In their work to forge a common worldview with white Protestants, black Protestants shared a missionary project. However, they qualified this mission by recognizing the ever-present prospect of conversions that served larger colonizing projects.

The black religious press also captured the social and political activism of denominational leaders. Rev. George Frazier Miller, the African American rector of Brooklyn's St. Augustine's Protestant Episcopal Church, was also a socialist, founding member of the Niagara Movement, and president of the National Equal Rights League. Miller urged black Protestants "to adopt incessant individual prayer and group prayer as a measure of relief from proscription" in addition to pursuing "independent voting for men and measures, union of all kinds of race bodies to use the political and economical resources to compel relief from segregation, disfranchisement, lynching and proscription, [and] membership in one or more civil rights organizations."[43] Miller even composed a "Race Prayer" for black Protestant churches and individuals to model "in their devotion on Thanksgiving Day, or other days of prayer and religious devotions[.]"[44]

Additionally, the black religious press frequently highlighted the work of white religious allies in the fight against racial violence. One ally was the Presbyterian Rev. James Myers, Industrial Relations Secretary of the Federal Council of Churches of Christ in America. In 1934, Myers composed a "Penitential Prayer for the Sin of Lynching" in his book, *Prayers for Self and Society*.[45] *The Star of Zion* welcomed any opportunity to promote white Christian voices in opposition to the nation's lynching crisis, and the paper reprinted the text of Myers's prayer for its audience.[46]

The 1945 edition of Woodson's *The History of the Negro Church* concluded with a short chapter on the rise of "New Temples for Strange Prophets," a brief assessment of the failings of the conventional black Protestant Christian denominations and the rise of "cults" with autocratic leadership. Woodson claimed that the departure of black intellectuals from Christianity — based on their view of Christian hypocrisy in the sanction of American slavery — left the "mentally underdeveloped Negroes at the mercy of the ignorant ministry and unprincipled cult leaders" and that they kept alive the "old time religion of the emotional, shouting fathers ... greatly influenced by the African war dances," this time in a "war on sin."[47] These so-called cults were flourishing in urban centers that black migrants populated, namely, "Washington, Baltimore, Philadelphia, New York, Boston, Pittsburgh, Cleveland, Detroit, Chicago, and St. Louis." Woodson identified them as the Mount Sinai Holy Church of America, Inc., the United House of Prayer for All People, the Church of God, the Church of God in Christ, the Church of God and Saints in Christ, the Moorish Science Temple of America, the Father Divine Peace Mission Movement, and the "Mohammedans" later known as the NOI.[48] Although Woodson expressed his hope that educated Afro-Protestants would lead their race and make enterprising religious minorities unnecessary or uncompelling to the masses, these progressive black Protestant public intellectuals forged, and were influenced by, interreligious environments. In turn, this interreligious atmosphere often resulted in respectful dialogues to comprehend the historical contexts, motivations, and shared social and political concerns across black theological differences. Armed with this exposure and knowledge of their religious neighbors, black Protestant public intellectuals like Anna Arnold Hedgeman also worked to represent their non-Christian theological expressions as plausible developments within the world of black thought and expression — expected developments, even, in contexts of racial oppression.

Conclusion: Black Protestant Public Intellectuals, Representation, and Activism

The Hate That Hate Produced sought to explain why "black racism" was spreading so effectively in the late 1950s, a claim based upon the perceived widespread interest in NOI teachings. In historian Manning Marable's analysis, it was "a covert appeal to white liberals, which reflected Mike Wallace's politics."[49] The program represented black public speech as problematic at best, threatening at worst. Racialized talk of God is problematic, whether it is the NOI's suspect theology or it is the identification of God with black skin among some African American Christians. Wallace's constant editorializing served to distance the NOI both from the African American Protestant mainstream as well as from "orthodox" Muslims. The program's producers likely anticipated that Protestant religious race leaders like Powell and Hedgeman would aid the contrast between the black mainstream and the NOI, given its racialized theology. Because they did not, and because they expressed deep sentiments with the failings of American Christianity and the idea that whiteness has become the norm of the religion, Wallace was able to render their thinking partially responsible for the NOI's rhetorical persuasiveness among African Americans — he noted that Malcolm X preached vespers in Powell's church, and he showcased Hedgeman's exchange with Louis Lomax on her statement that Jesus was "certainly not white."

In the tradition of many black Protestant public intellectuals, activism and organizing accompanied Hedgeman's national visibility and discursive authority. With the emergence of sit-in demonstrations in 1960, Hedgeman organized for the National Council of Churches (NCC) and traveled to Atlanta to encounter students involved in nonviolent demonstrations. As the Coordinator of Special Events for the NCC's Commission on Religion and Race, Hedgeman's responsibility was "getting involved in the [March on Washington's] leadership and getting white people, particularly Protestants, to participate." She was responsible for making religious activism present and visible at the 1963 March on Washington and in nonviolent direct action demonstrations.[50] To get white Midwesterners to put pressure on their legislators to pass the 1964 Civil Rights bill, Hedgeman implemented the "Midwest Strategy" by embarking upon a midwestern speaking tour and bringing student demonstrators from the Southern Christian Leadership Conference (SCLC) and the Student Nonviolent Coordinating Committee (SNCC) to testify in white churches to their efforts and experiences. "She asked people to pray for the bill — and then to organize, to mobilize, to act." This resulted in letter writing campaigns of support, buses of delegates traveling from the Midwest to Capitol Hill to keep the bill from stalling in the House and Senate, and prayer demonstrations at nearby churches for ministers, lay leaders, and volunteer seminary students to conduct a "preaching mission" by leading constituents in an ecumenical service.[51]

In addition to her civil rights activism to mobilize white support for student nonviolent activism, Hedgeman continued her public intellectual role of explaining to white Americans the outcries of African Americans as they pursued the end of Jim Crow. The 1966 "Black Power" position statement by the National Committee of Negro Churchmen (later the National Conference of Black Christians), with Hedgeman as secretary of the organization, represented leading black religious voices as they worked to theologically justify and clarify the emergence of Black Power language. This discourse would soon thereafter inform the language of black liberation theology, a progressive black Protestant religious movement to wed race and religion in the minds of American Christians by defining God as black and declaring that the alleviation of oppression is the central Christian mission. And as a

Figure 23.2 Brotherhood of Sleeping Car Porters President A. Philip Randolph (left), NAACP Executive Secretary Roy Wilkins (center), and Commission on Religion and Race Special Events Coordinator Anna Arnold Hedgeman (right) meeting in Harlem on August 3, 1963 to plan the August 28, 1963 March on Washington. Photo by Bettmann/Getty Images.

testament to the enduring significance of interreligious engagement to progressive black Protestant discourses, the 1991 book *Martin & Malcolm & America: A Dream or a Nightmare* by the leading black liberation theologian James H. Cone (1938–2018) represented a religious endeavor to valorize both civil rights figures' ideologies and activism.

For Anna Arnold Hedgeman and other likeminded, activist black Protestants, bettering the lives of African Americans required multiracial and multireligious coalition work founded upon the appreciation of religious difference and the insistence that white Americans were capable of working against their phenotypic social privileges. As she wrote in her memoir, *The Trumpet Sounds*:

> We are grateful for the thunder of the rebels. It is important and I would not for one moment limit the sound of it. We have heard it from William Stringfellow, a white Christian layman, who says "My people is the enemy." We have heard it from James Baldwin whose vigorous exposure of our sins has moved many Christians. We have heard it from Malcolm X, when he castigates the Christian record. We have heard it from Louis Lomax when he speaks of the revolt against Negro leadership.
>
> We are grateful for such angry voices as these and for the thunder which comes from picket lines, sit-ins, stall-ins, and jails. There is, however, another sound in the air. It is a trumpet sound within the souls of some white men. It is heard by many white Protestants across this nation. It is heard in the synagogues and Catholic churches. It is a trumpet sound which grows louder each day as white men and women join us in living with hostility, with the deprivation and agony of the Crucifixion.
>
> It can be the trumpet sound which precedes the Resurrection. It echoes in the prophet's ancient cry that "Justice roll down like rivers."[52]

The oppressed who lived in perpetual states of crucifixion must comprehend what animated theologies of "hate" to render these teachings as intelligible criticisms of historical injustice. And when joined by religious and racial others, there was hope that their shared experiences of hostility, deprivation, and agony — the risks of allying with Jim Crow America's marginalized populations — would revive the biblical mandate for justice, which progressive Christians declared was manifest in the life of the historical Jesus. With reference to the words of Amos 5:24 and the Christian resurrection, Anna Arnold Hedgeman reframed the "hate" that hate produced as rebellious thunder against injustice, an interracial and interreligious collective's productive recasting of American society through public rhetoric and civil rights activism.

FURTHER READING

Azaransky, Sarah. *This Worldwide Struggle: Religion and the International Roots of the Civil Rights Movement.* New York: Oxford University Press, 2017.

Evans, Curtis J. *The Burden of Black Religion.* New York: Oxford University Press, 2008.

Marable, Manning. *Malcolm X: A Life of Reinvention.* New York: Viking, 2011.

Mathews, Mary Beth Swetnam. *Doctrine and Race: African American Evangelicals and Fundamentalism between the Wars.* Tuscaloosa: University of Alabama Press, 2017.

Savage, Barbara. *Your Spirits Walk Beside Us: The Politics of Black Religion.* Cambridge, MA: Belknap, 2008.

Scanlon, Jennifer. *Until There Is Justice: The Life of Anna Arnold Hedgeman.* New York: Oxford University Press, 2016.

Weisenfeld, Judith. *New World A-Coming: Black Religion and Racial Identity during the Great Migration.* New York: New York University Press, 2016.

BIBLIOGRAPHY

Books

Azaransky, Sarah. *This Worldwide Struggle: Religion and the International Roots of the Civil Rights Movement.* New York: Oxford University Press, 2017.

Coffman, Elesha J. *The Christian Century and the Rise of Mainline Protestantism.* New York: Oxford University Press, 2013.

Hedgeman, Anna Arnold. *The Trumpet Sounds: A Memoir of Negro Leadership.* New York: Holt, Rinehart and Winston, 1964.

Marable, Manning. Malcolm X: *A Life of Reinvention.* New York: Viking, 2011.

Pipkin, James Jefferson. *The Story of a Rising Race: The Negro in Revelation, in History, and in Citizenship.* St. Louis and New York: N. D. Thompson Publishing Company, 1902.

Savage, Barbara D. "Biblical and Historical Imperatives: Toward a History of Ideas about the Political Role of Black Churches." In *African Americans and the Bible: Sacred Texts and Social Textures,* edited by Vincent L. Wimbush, 367–388. New York: The Continuum International Publishing Group, Inc., 2000.

_____. *Your Spirits Walk Beside Us: The Politics of Black Religion.* Cambridge, MA: Belknap, 2008.

Scanlon, Jennifer. *Until There Is Justice: The Life of Anna Arnold Hedgeman.* New York: Oxford University Press, 2016.

Taylor, Clarence *The Black Churches of Brooklyn.* New York: Columbia University Press, 1994.

Woodson, Carter G. *Carter G. Woodson's Appeal.* Edited by Daryl Michael Scott. Washington, DC: The Association for the Study of African American Life and History Press, 2008.

_____. *The History of the Negro Church.* Washington, DC: The Associated Publishers, 1921.

Collections

Alexander Gumby Collection of Negroiana. Rare Book and Manuscript Library, Columbia University.

Multimedia

Lomax, Louis E., Mike Wallace, and Ted Yates, Jr. "The Hate That Hate Produced." *News Beat,* WNTA-TV. New York City, NY: July 23, 1959.

Periodicals

The Africo-American Presbyterian
The National Baptist Voice
The Pittsburgh Press
The Star of Zion

NOTES

1   Louis E. Lomax, Mike Wallace, and Ted Yates, Jr. "The Hate That Hate Produced," *News Beat*, WNTA-TV, New York City, NY: July 23, 1959.

2   Anna Arnold Hedgeman, *The Trumpet Sounds: A Memoir of Negro Leadership* (New York: Holt, Rinehart and Winston, 1964), 7–10.

3   *The Trumpet Sounds*, 12.

4   *The Trumpet Sounds*, 13.

5   *The Trumpet Sounds*, 16.

6   *The Trumpet Sounds*, 18–22.

7   *The Trumpet Sounds*, 23.

8   *The Trumpet Sounds*, 27–28.

9   Sarah Azaransky, *This Worldwide Struggle: Religion and the International Roots of the Civil Rights Movement* (New York: Oxford University Press, 2017), 27.

10 *The Trumpet Sounds*, 30–32.

11 *The Trumpet Sounds*, 49–50.

12 *The Trumpet Sounds*, 86.

13 "The Ministry of the Negro Minister," in *The Negro on the American Stage in the Higher Altitudes of Music, Literature and Religion: Reprints from the A. M. E.* Review (Philadelphia: The A. M. E. Book Concern, 1913), 14; located in the Alexander Gumby Collection of Negroiana; reel 13, vol. 69, Rare Book and Manuscript Library, Columbia University.

14 William J. Walls, "The Preacher's Range," *The Star of Zion*, June 24, 1920, 4.

15 Carter G. Woodson, *The History of the Negro Church* (Washington, DC: The Associated Publishers, 1921), 278.

16 Woodson, 280.

17 Carter G. Woodson, *Carter G. Woodson's Appeal*, ed. Daryl Michael Scott (Washington, DC: The Association for the Study of African American Life and History Press, 2008), xiv-xv.

18 *Carter G. Woodson's Appeal*, xxxiii, xxxv-xxxvi.

19 Woodson wrote, "This failure to look out for a man in this life is an unfortunate situation in the Negro church at the very time when the white man has an entirely different attitude toward religion. Few white people now think of a hereafter in the sense of men living on a beautiful island of by-and-by or being doomed to torment in a lake that burns with fire and brimstone. They no longer have the former conception of God, the indulgent Father, which they engrafted upon the minds of the Negroes first brought to this country. God in the mind of the white man is his race. His race is supreme and absolute among the other races of the world. One would inquire: Where is their Christianity? Where is their regard for the brotherhood of man and fatherhood of God? These principles with them are things of the past. The white people believe in a new theology, which has for its main tenet the principle that, if there is a conflict between the interests of the white race and the teachings of Christ, the interests of the white race must stand first. The Negro unfortunately knows too little of the social revolution which has taken place in the world, if he fails to understand this situation and to conduct himself accordingly" (*Carter G. Woodson's Appeal*, 87–88).

20 Woodson added, "It would be difficult to imagine exactly how the racial conflict would have worked out in this country if the Negro, like the white man, had abandoned this sort of religion without accepting some other system to secure restraint" (*Carter G. Woodson's Appeal*, 112–113).

21 *Carter G. Woodson's Appeal*, 145–146.

22 Woodson's arguments appeared primarily in his columns for the *New York Age*. See Barbara D. Savage, "Biblical and Historical Imperatives: Toward a History of Ideas about the Political Role of Black Churches," in *African Americans and the Bible: Sacred Texts and Social Textures*, ed. Vincent L. Wimbush (New York: The Continuum International Publishing Group, Inc., 2000), 367–388.

23   Kelly Miller, "The College Bred Negro and the Church," *The Star of Zion*, December 7, 1922, 1.

24   See "World News — The Hebrew People," *The Star of Zion*, March 1, 1928, 5.

25   See Miller, "Is the Negro Church Deteriorating?" *The Star of Zion*, March 3, 1927, 8.

26   Elesha J. Coffman, *The Christian Century and the Rise of Mainline Protestantism* (New York: Oxford University Press, 2013) 62, 93.

27   "The Evil Heart of Unbelief," *The Christian Worker*, reprinted in *The National Baptist Voice*, January 29, 1921, 9, 12.

28   James Jefferson Pipkin, *The Story of a Rising Race: The Negro in Revelation, in History, and in Citizenship* (St. Louis and New York: N. D. Thompson Publishing Company, 1902), 100. Vass discussed the uses of Sheol, Gehenna, and Hades in the Hebrew Bible and Christian New Testament. See S. N. Vass, "Is There A Burning Hell," *The National Baptist Voice*, March 26, 1921, 4.

29   See J. W. Bailey, "Negroes to Pray that God Trouble the Conscience of White America," *The National Baptist Voice*, April 23, 1921, 10.

30   "A Psalm of the Evolutionist," *The Star of Zion*, October 28, 1926, 4.

31   See "Negro Editor Speaks a Kind Word for Evolution," *The Christian Century*, reprinted in *The Star of Zion*, November 25, 1926, 5.

32   "Crossroads," *The Star of Zion*, June 6, 1929, 4.

33   "Anti-Evolutionists Lag Behind Negroes Declares Bishop Jones In Pittsburgh," *The Star of Zion*, July 9, 1931, 4.

34   "Religious Signs of the Times," *The Independent*, reprinted in *The Africo-American Presbyterian*, February 19, 1925, 2.

35   This article also states that Dr. J. H. Carstens, white pastor of the Austin Baptist Church, exchanged pulpits with Rev. F. S. Maliney, pastor of Chicago's Wayman African Methodist Episcopal Church ("White and Negro Pastors Exchange," *The Africo-American Presbyterian*, March 5, 1925, 2).

36   See "Facing the Issue," *The Presbyterian*, reprinted in *The Africo-American Presbyterian*, May 14, 1925, 2.

37   "A Tolerant Preacher," *The Star of Zion*, December 8, 1921, 5 (last line of text obscured).

38   See Barbara Savage, *Your Spirits Walk Beside Us: The Politics of Black Religion* (Cambridge, MA: Belknap, 2008), 87–89.

39   Azaransky, *This Worldwide Struggle*, 17.

40   "Bishop Alleyne at the AME Zion Church," *The Star of Zion*, January 20, 1938, 7.

41   William J. Walls, "Rabindranath Tagore's Advice to the Missionaries," *The Star of Zion*, June 22, 1922, 4.

42   "Why the Anti Christian Fight," *The Star of Zion*, April 7, 1927, 4.

43   Clarence Taylor, *The Black Churches of Brooklyn* (New York: Columbia University Press, 1994), 122.

44   "November Twenty-Fifth As Prayer Day. Entire Race Urged to Adopt Prayer Relief from Oppression — President of League Offers a Form of Prayer for Nation Wide Use," *The Africo-American Presbyterian*, November 18, 1926, 4.

45   "New Prayers Ask Social Aid — Modern Versions Include Slums, Lynching, Unemployed, Capital, Labor," *The Pittsburgh Press*, August 11, 1934, 5.

46   See "Penitential Prayer For The Sin of Lynching," *The Star of Zion*, February 22, 1934, 1.

47   Woodson, 301.

48   Woodson, 301–303. For a study of black Protestant opposition to these religio-racial movements, see Judith Weisenfeld, Ch. 7, "Community, Conflict, and the Boundaries of Black Religion," in *New World A-Coming: Black Religion and Racial Identity during the Great Migration* (New York: New York University Press, 2016).

49   Manning Marable, *Malcolm X: A Life of Reinvention* (New York: Viking, 2011), 161.

50   Jennifer Scanlon, *Until There Is Justice: The Life of Anna Arnold Hedgeman* (New York: Oxford University Press, 2016), 158.

51   *Until There Is Justice*, 177–182.

52   *The Trumpet Sounds*, 201–202.

Chapter Twenty-Four

THE PENTAGON EXORCISM: 1960S COUNTER-CULTURE AND THE OCCULT REVIVAL

Joseph P. Laycock

Texas State University, San Marcos, Texas

On 21 October 1967, 3,500 protesters gathered at the Pentagon to perform an exorcism of the building. Led by such figures as Beat poet Allen Ginsberg, anarchist Abbie Hoffman, and Ed Sanders of the band The Fugs, the protesters planned to surround the building and perform a magical ritual that would cause it to levitate 300 feet in the air, turn orange, and spin. This, it was claimed, would expel the demons of violence that resided in the building, bringing an end to the Vietnam War.[1] In practice, the exorcism was a chaotic and eclectic event that incorporated Asian religious traditions, ancient magical formulae, Wiccan ritual, and magical practices drawn from occultist Aleister Crowley. Journalist Norman Mailer, who witnessed the ritual, wrote that, "The March on the Pentagon was an ambiguous event whose essential value or absurdity may not be established for ten or twenty years, or indeed ever."[2]

Today, conservative pundits still cite the exorcism of the Pentagon as an example of liberal insanity, while those who defend the event often frame it as "political theater" or even "a prank." But the event was more complicated than either of these narratives. Some participants, such as Hoffman, wanted the exorcism to be an absurd spectacle. However, the use of absurdity was part of a larger strategy to manipulate the media and draw attention to the protest. Other participants, such as Ginsberg and Sanders, took the event more seriously as a "magical" ritual. "Magic," for these thinkers, was the use of language to manipulate reality by changing the way people see the world. Finally, there were some people involved in the ritual, such as filmmaker and occultist Kenneth Anger, who saw the exorcism as the literal manipulation of supernatural powers.

Whether prankish, metaphorical, or literal, the exorcism of the Pentagon was a watershed moment in what sociologists sometimes refer to as "the occult revival" of the 1960s.[3] This was a period when the counter-culture sought out and experimented with alternative religious practices, including Western esotericism, Paganism, and Asian religions. The Pentagon Exorcism drew from and blended together many of these traditions in a pattern that historian Catherine Albanese describes as religious "combinativity."[4]

Some historians have argued that the occult revival in general, and the Pentagon exorcism specifically, demonstrate that young people in the 1960s had taken a narcissistic turn, abdicating their duty to be mature, politically active citizens. Others, however, have argued that young protesters turned to "magic" as an act of desperation when the standard institutions

A Companion to American Religious History, First Edition. Edited by Benjamin E. Park.
© 2021 John Wiley & Sons, Inc. Published 2021 by John Wiley & Sons, Inc.

of civic engagement seemed to have failed them. At stake in these interpretations is a larger sociological theory called "the secularization narrative." In the 1960s, sociologists assumed that as civilization advanced in science and technology, society would become more secular: education would cause people to stop believing in the supernatural and religion would decrease in importance. The sight of hundreds of college-educated, middle-class people using occult rituals against the Pentagon was a serious problem for this theory. Today, few sociologists still argue for the secularization narrative and "magic" — while it can be defined many ways — is alive and well in the American religious landscape.

October 1967

In 1965, the United States began deploying troops in Vietnam. By 1967, there had been thousands of American casualties and an enormous protest movement had formed against the war. The Pentagon exorcism was only a small part of a much larger protest called "Stop the Draft Week" during which some 1100 men burned their draft cards.[5] On 21 October, there were as many as 100,000 protesters in Washington, although only 35,000 actually marched on the Pentagon. The Pentagon had brought in 2,400 soldiers to protect the building and installed tear gas launchers on the roof.[6] By the end of the day, 647 demonstrators had been arrested and forty-seven hospitalized.[7]

It is unclear who exactly came up with the idea to exorcise the Pentagon. Bill Ellis has suggested there were two separate ideas — one to levitate the Pentagon, and one to exorcise it — which blended together.[8] What is certain is that the idea emerged during a "Human Be-In," a gathering held on 14 January 1967 in San Francisco's Golden Gate Park. The Be-In brought together numerous figures from "The New Left" — a loosely organized movement, consisting largely of white, college students, that advocated democracy, civil rights, university reform, and opposed the Vietnam War.[9] There were poets from the "Beat" movement such as Allen Ginsberg and Gary Snyder, the painter Michael Bowen, and Allen Cohen, the editor of the underground paper *The Oracle*. Also present was activist Jerry Rubin, who had been asked to give a speech.[10]

A protest organization called the National Mobilization Committee to End the War in Vietnam ("the Mobe") had recruited Jerry Rubin to lead a march on Washington. Rubin was already known for stunts such as visiting the New York Stock Exchange with Abbie Hoffman, where they threw dollar bills at stockbrokers and set money on fire in order to critique capitalism and generally sow chaos. The Mobe hoped that by recruiting Rubin, an alliance could be formed between committed "old left" activists, and the hippies.[11] It was Rubin's idea to target the Pentagon, rather than Congress, commenting, "The Pentagon would be seen as the enemy, whereas Congress is kind of neutral. It would be the wrong message to march on Congress."[12] Various people — some allegedly under the influence of LSD — suggested using a magic ritual to levitate/exorcise the Pentagon and the idea took hold.

Rubin immediately tapped his friend Hoffman, who excelled in playful, innovative forms of protest.[13] Hoffman began preparing with a series of public stunts designed to draw media attention to the event. His explanation was simple: "Media is free. Use it. Don't pay for it. Don't buy ads. Make news."[14] First, Hoffman arrived at the Pentagon with a friend and the two began measuring it to determine how many protestors would be needed to completely surround the building. He determined that one side of the Pentagon was approximately 240 people wide, and calculated that 1200 people would be needed to surround all five sides. While taking these measurements, Hoffman was arrested by a national guardsman who told him it is illegal to measure the Pentagon.

Hoffman calmly told Pentagon authorities that he was measuring the Pentagon so that hippies could surround the building and levitate it. Authorities explained he would need a permit for such a protest, so he requested one. The General Services Administrator granted him the permit on two conditions: First, the Pentagon could be raised only three feet so as not to damage the foundations. Second, participants would be allowed to gather in front of the building but not to surround it. Hoffman found the offer acceptable: He and the administrator shook on it.[15] Activist Sal Gianetta commented on this discussion, "It was unbelievable. That meeting was like 2 1/2 hours or so and probably 20% of that meeting was devoted to this serious talk about levitating the Pentagon. And this is our military, right?"[16]

Next, Hoffman travelled to New York City where he announced the levitation in a press conference. He was quoted in *The East Village Other*:

> We will dye the Potomac red, burn the cherry trees ... sorcerers, swamis, witches, voodoo, warlocks, medicine men and speed freaks will hurl their magic at the faded brown walls. ... We will fuck on the grass and beat ourselves against the doors. Everyone will scream "VOTE FOR ME." We shall raise the flag of nothingness over the Pentagon and a mighty cheer of liberation will echo through the land.[17]

He also recruited the Diggers — an activist and street theater group — to scavenge thrift stores for "witch costumes" that protestors could wear. They readied two van-loads of the oddest clothing they could find for the trip to Washington.

On 13 October, Hoffman organized a ritual and benefit concert at the Village Theater to raise funds for the protest. Ed Sanders of The Fugs presided over this ritual in which a photo of the Pentagon was burned. The ashes were then gathered into a bottle, which would be buried in Washington and then cast on the Pentagon itself. According to newspaper accounts, the ritual lasted over an hour and was attended by some 200 people. Performers wore green paint in order to offset red, the color of Mars, god of war.[18] A Native American shaman consecrated the ceremony by throwing down cornmeal.[19] As the performance climaxed, participants joined hands around a table-sized plywood model of the Pentagon and chanted "Up, demon! Up, demon!," as the model was pulled by piano wires toward the ceiling. The Associated Press covered the event and several newspapers ran headlines like "Hippie magic Readied to Destroy Pentagon."

Ed Sanders was tasked with designing the exorcism ritual. According to Sanders, the ritual was originally to be modeled on the "Catholic or Episcopalian" rite of exorcism.[20] Sanders recalls contacting his friend the occultist Harry Smith, who was a regular at his New York bookstore, The Peace Eye. According to Sanders:

> So I went to Harry and asked him what happened in an exorcism and he gave me some advice. So he filled me in on what his view was. He told me about consecrating the four directions, surrounding it, circling it, using elements of earth, air, fire and water, alchemical symbols to purify the place, to invoke certain deities, and so on. So I sing-songed a whole retinue of deities past and present, imaginary and real, to summon the strength to exorcise this place. It was part real, part symbolic, part wolf ticket, part spiritual, part secular, part wishful thinking and part anger. And it had humor. You gotta have the universal humor. And since I knew Indo-European languages, I learned this Hittite exorcism ritual. I actually put together a decent exorcism.[21]

Sander's "decent exorcism" was then made into a mimeographed sheet with the liturgical structure for the ritual. A formula appeared at the top of the text taken from the Greek magical papyri — a corpus of ancient texts discovered in the nineteenth century that describe rituals for manipulating supernatural forces. The formula Sanders chose is part of a spell for conjuring a supernatural servant.[22] At the bottom of the page was transliterated Hittite, presumably an exorcism. The actual ritual consists of ten steps including such ritual acts as praying for the bad karma of American soldiers, consecrating the four directions, encircling the Pentagon in cornmeal, and the use of a "sacred Grope relic." These preparations are followed by the actual "ceremony of exorcism" with ritual steps corresponding to the four elements, "the rising of the Pentagon," and something called "the EXORGASM." The ritual concludes with a peace mantra.

There also were many plans for the ritual that never saw fruition, such as finding a Native American to circle the Pentagon with a trail of cornmeal and acquiring a live cow to symbolize Hathor, the Egyptian cow-goddess and patroness of arts and schools.[23] Journalist Paul Krassner was scheduled to speak at a literary conference at the University of Iowa. Abbie Hoffman tapped him to purchase organic Iowa cornmeal — enough to encircle the Pentagon. But the morning before the exorcism, Krassner and some friends decided to "test" the cornmeal by encircling the Washington Monument and were detained by law enforcement. After explaining that they were conducting a religious ritual, the activists were released. Their cornmeal, however, was confiscated.[24] As for the goddess Hathor, plans had been made with Harry Smith to bring in a cow from Virginia, painted with occult symbols, but the cow was intercepted by police and never made it to Washington.

Finally, daisies had been purchased with the intention of chartering a small plane that would be used to rain flowers onto the Pentagon. Activists were stopped at the airport by the FBI, but allowed to keep the daisies. These were taken to the march and some were placed by activists in the barrels of M-16s held by guards defending the Pentagon.[25] This unintended chain of events led to famous photographs of peace activists placing flowers into gun barrels. Some argued that these photos were the real propaganda victory of the march. Military analyst Daniel Ellsberg commented, "Once the kid put his flower in the barrel of the kid looking just like himself but tense and nervous, the authority of the Pentagon psychologically was dissolved."[26] In 1971, Ellsberg leaked documents known as "The Pentagon Papers" to *The New York Times*. The documents revealed that four presidential administrations had misled the public about their intentions in Vietnam and their leak furthered opposition to the war.

The exorcism itself was less organized than Sanders's mimeograph would suggest and lasted approximately fifteen minutes. The Fugs performed the ritual from a flatbed truck equipped with a gas-powered generator and a canvas backdrop painted with a Day-Glo image of the "Eye of Providence." Handfuls of colored cornmeal were sprinkled to the four directions.[27] Ed Sanders's ritual was circulated through the crowd. It included a spell that read in part:

> October 21, 1967, Washington, D.C., U.S.A., Planet Earth
> We Freemen, of all colors of the spectrum, in the name of God, Ra Jehovah, Anubis, Osiris, Tlaloc, Quetzalcoatl, Thoth, Ptah, Allah, Krishna. ... We are demanding that the pentacle of power once again be used to serve the interests of GOD manifest in the world as man. We are embarking on a motion which is millennial in scope. Let this day, October 21, 1967, mark the beginning of suprapolitics.
> By act of reading this paper you are engaged in the Holy Ritual of Exorcism. To further participate focus your thought on the casting out of evil through the grace of GOD which is all (ours). A billion stars in a billion galaxies of space and time is the form of your power, and limitless is your name.[28]

The crowd responded with refrains of "Out Demons! Out!" and "Burn the money!" Mailer recalls that the ritual ended with a sustained chant of the Hindu syllable "Om."[29] Beneath the truck, filmmaker and occultist Kenneth Anger was performing his own ritual against the Pentagon. Anger's films were meant to portray his philosophy of magic in which old values must be destroyed to make way for a new age. *Scorpio Rising* (1963) featured bikers entering a church and trampling Bibles and urinating on the altar. Anger's approach to the occult was seen as both sincere and sinister by other collaborators on the Pentagon exorcism. Allen Ginsberg recalled, "While Ed was trying to un-hex the Pentagon, Kenneth Anger was underneath his wagon trying to hex him."[30]

Counter-Culture and Combinativeness

Whatever else it was, The Pentagon exorcism revealed the new landscape of alternative religions that was shaping the counter-culture of the 1960s. The ritual Sanders cobbled together from a hodge-podge of different religions and mythologies demonstrates combinativeness in which elements are drawn from different religions to create new forms of belief and practice. While combinativeness has been evident throughout American history, it was especially prominent in the 1960s as the baby-boomer generation responded to a greatly expanded range of religious options that included religions of Asia, a newfound interest in Native American religion, and esoteric traditions such as Paganism and ritual magic.

One of the seminal events of American religion in the 1960s was the Hart-Cellar Act of 1965, which abolished the old system in which immigration was restricted by a quota system. The quota system had largely excluded immigrants from Asia. Now, immigrants were arriving from such places as India and Korea. They brought their religions with them and attracted the curiosity of the counter-culture. One of the most striking examples of this pattern was the International Society for Krishna Consciousness (ISKCON) founded in 1966 by A.C. Bhaktivedanta Swami Prabhupada. ISKCON teaches a form of Hinduism that emphasizes ecstatic devotion to the god Krishna, frequently expressed through a chant called the Maha Mantra. (The group is popularly referred to as "the Hare Krishnas" after their chant.) A mantra is a sacred chant found in Hinduism and Buddhism and the counter-culture found mantras fascinating. In cities such as San Francisco, ISKCON successfully recruited members of the American counter-culture to their particular form of Hinduism. Many more never formally joined ISKCON but were intrigued by its beliefs and practices. Witnesses of the Pentagon exorcism reported that some protestors began to spontaneously chant the Maha Mantra.

Buddhism was another arrival from Asia. In the late 1950s, a group of San Francisco writers and artists began promoting a form of Buddhism that came to be called "Beat Zen." Writers such as Jack Kerouak and Alan Watts helped to popularize Zen and other religions — at least as they understood them from their study of Asian religious texts. Two figures associated with Beat Zen were involved with the exorcism: Gary Snyder and Allen Ginsberg.

In the summer of 1967, Gary Snyder wrote his poem, "Curse on the Men in Washington, Pentagon." The poem is a brutal indictment of "the white man" as the enemy of both Vietnamese civilians and Native Americans. It ends with the lines, "This magic I work, this loving I give / that my children may flourish / And yours won't live."[31] (Snyder 1967). When it was written, Snyder's poem was considered too inflammatory even for underground publications like the San Francisco *Oracle*. However, it was eventually distributed as a mimeographed broadside by the Diggers.[32]

The mimeograph demonstrates Snyder's interest in both Native American religion and Tibetan Buddhism. The body of the poem is preceded by the Buddhist mantra, "om a ka ca ta ta pa ya sa svaha." This is a Tibetan mantra, "for causing cities to tremble."[33] At the bottom of the page is the phrase "hi'alawa' vita'ki'ai," which Snyder claimed to be the chorus of a Cheyenne ghost dance song meaning "We shall live again."[34] This poem likely inspired the format for Ed Sander's exorcism ritual, which also sandwiched English between words of power from other cultures and religions.

Allen Ginsberg also drew on Buddhist mantras in poems like "Wichita Vortex Sutra," where he declared:

> I call on all Powers of imagination
> make Mantra of American language now
> I here declare the end of the War![35]

Much like the chant performed by The Fugs, on which it was certainly an influence, this poem invokes a litany of gods and supernatural beings — both Asian and Western — to aid the poet in declaring an end to the war. In September 1967 Ginsberg wrote, "Pentagon Exorcism," which may have been intended as a more positive version of Snyder's, "Curse on the Men in Washington, Pentagon." Like Snyder's poem, it incorporates Tibetan mantras against rakshas (demons) and calls the Pentagon to apocatostasis — the reconciliation of good and evil.[36]

Another influence on the ritual was an interest in the indigenous religions of the Americas. The hippies sought to emulate "Native American culture" — at least as they understood it. The 1967 "Be-in" in San Francisco was described as "a gathering of the tribes" in reference to Native American culture.[37] Beat poets, including Ginsberg, experimented with the hallucinogen peyote, imitating Native American religious rituals. According to some accounts, the idea to levitate the Pentagon was proposed by Michael Bowen after consulting with Mexican shamans.[38] Gary Lachman reports that the idea to encircle monuments in corneal was proposed by Rolling Thunder — an activist and self-proclaimed Native American shaman — who suggested that, "among his people the surest way to contain evil emanations is to encircle them."[39]

In addition to borrowing beliefs and practices from other cultures, the counter-culture was also interested in Western magical and occult traditions. One such tradition was Wicca, a modern form of ancient European Pagan religion. The history of modern Wicca begins with Gerald Gardner, a retired British civil servant who claimed he was initiated into witchcraft in the 1930s. In 1954 he published *Witchcraft Today*, which launched a revival of Paganism. "Gardnerian Wicca" attracted a following and soon many other traditions of Wicca emerged as well. For Gardner, witchcraft was actually an ancient fertility cult and many of its rituals are performed nude or sexual in nature. This emphasis on open sexuality likely attracted the Fugs, who performed raunchy songs with titles like "Boobs a Lot" and "Coca Cola Douche." Bill Ellis notes that the structure of Ed Sanders's exorcism ritual shares much of the format of a Wiccan ceremony and the sexual elements of the ritual (the Grope relic, the Exorgasm) are reminiscent of Gardnerian sexual magic. Gardner also wrote about a ritual to "raise of cone of power," which Ellis notes is similar to step eight of Sander's ritual, "the rising of the Pentagon."

Since the 1970s, Wicca has become increasingly mainstream and Wiccan activists have continued to use magic in political protests. For example, during protests of the World Trade Organization in Portland, Oregon, in 1999, witch activist Starhawk conducted a "WTO spell." This was a public ritual that featured an ice sculpture, the melting of which symbolized WTO's power "dissolving."[40] In 2018, witches in New York City began holding regular public meetings to "hex" president Donald Trump and controversial Supreme Court appointee Brett Kavanaugh.[41]

The 1960s also saw the emergence of more transgressive forms of religious ritual such as Satanism. In 1966, Anton LaVey founded the Church of Satan in San Francisco, creating the first open and organized Satanic religion. In his home (called "The Black House") LaVey hosted black masses that used nude women as an altar as well as other Satanic rituals. However, LaVey described himself as an atheist and described his rituals as a therapeutic "decompression chamber" that undid the damage of a stifling Christian upbringing. LaVey expressed scorn for the hippies and their values of love and egalitarianism. However, his ideas about sexuality were not so different from those of The Fugs.

Kenneth Anger was a close friend of LaVey, although he described himself as a "Pagan" rather than a Satanist. Both men had studied the writings of magician Aleister Crowley — whom the Beatles helped popularize in 1967 by putting his face on the cover "Sgt. Pepper's Lonely Hearts Club Band." LaVey dismissed Crowley and often claimed magic was only a form of psychotherapy. But Anger expressed that his magical rituals actually manipulated supernatural forces. Regarding his film *Lucifer Rising* (1972), Anger stated, "I'm a pagan and the film is a real invocation of Lucifer."[42] While Anger brought a certain degree of "occult authenticity" to the Pentagon exorcism, he shared LaVey's contempt for the hippies, describing the other protestors as "idiots." Anger claimed that he actually infiltrated the Pentagon and left magical talismans in ninety-three men's rooms. (The Pentagon was built with an unusually high number of restrooms due to segregation laws that required people of color to use separate rooms). Anger explained that this was a magical attack on Mars, the god of war and ruling deity of America.[43]

Whether or not this infiltration actually occurred, Anger was observed performing a magical ritual beneath the Fug's flatbed truck. Ed Sanders described the scene:

> Anger, bare from the waist up, revealing what appeared to be a tattoo of Lucifer on his chest, burned a picture of the devil within a consecrated pentagram, shouting oaths and hissing as he flashed a magic ring at inquiring reporters thrusting microphones at him hunched down the gravel.[44]

Elsewhere, Sanders recalled, "In other words the thing we were doing above him, he viewed that as the exoteric thing and he was doing the esoteric, serious, zero-bullshit exorcism. So I went along with that."[45]

Making Sense of it All

The exorcism of the Pentagon was a complicated event that is difficult to characterize. Why did the participants do this? Did they really believe their ritual would harness supernatural forces? And if not, was this all a big joke? Some concluded that resorting to magic — especially the ironic performances of magic promoted by Abbie Hoffman and Ed Sanders — was indicative of a generation who lacked the maturity for serious political engagement. Historian Christopher Lasch described Hoffman's antics as, "The degeneration of politics into spectacle."[46]

In the years following the Pentagon exorcism, scholars attempted to make sense of the occult revival. Sociologists of religion noted that the newfound popularity of witchcraft, Satanism, and psychic abilities directly contradicted the secularization narrative.[47] In a decade where science was allegedly killing off Christianity, people were not *supposed* to be dredging up ancient magical traditions. Furthermore, the occult revival was being spearheaded by middle-class (and mostly white) college students. These were the very people who were expected to no longer need religion or the supernatural due to their modern education. One reason people were so quick to dismiss the exorcism as "a colossal put on" was that this interpretation allowed the secularization narrative to go unchallenged.[48]

From its very inception, those involved in the exorcism had different ideas of what they were doing and why they were doing it. While everyone agreed performing a magical ritual in public would be a good way to protest the Vietnam War, they demonstrated different understandings about what "magic" is and how it could be harnessed for their cause. It is reasonable to conclude that for Kenneth Anger, occult forces such as "the power of Mars" were real and could be harnessed by magicians. Because Anger believed they were real, it was irrelevant whether or not anyone saw him perform his ritual. Similarly, activist Ponderosa

Pine reports that Michael Bowen believed the Pentagon would literally levitate. He recalled, "We didn't expect the building to actually leave terra firma, but this fellow arrived with ideas on how to make it happen and I began to see there was an interesting difference between East Coast and West Coast."[49]

Conversely, for Abbie Hoffman creating a public spectacle was the entire point. Hoffman saw "magic" as a source of shock value that could be used to rattle the establishment, generate media attention, and perhaps make his opponents seem ridiculous in the process. While preparing for the Pentagon exorcism, he wrote, "The magic is beginning to work, but the media must be convinced."[50] But beneath Hoffman's jokes and antics was a more serious theory of political change informed by the Dada movement of the early twentieth century, which shared Hoffman's rejection of capitalism. Hoffman believed shocking spectacles had the power to change the way people saw the world, especially the status of powerful and "sacred" institutions such as the New York stock exchange or the Pentagon. If magic meant anything to Hoffman, it was a metaphor for changing people's minds by appealing to the imagination. Hoffman commented on the exorcism, "Never for a moment did I believe guerrilla theater or 'monkey warfare,' as I had come to call it, could alone stop the war in Vietnam. But it did extend the possibilities of involving the senses and penetrating the symbolic world of fantasy."[51] Or as Daniel Ellsberg put it, "Removing deference from any of these institutions is very, very important, and this is of course the kind of thing that Abbie understood very instinctively.[52]

Ed Sanders, along with Beat poets such as Allen Ginsberg, seemed to espouse a third approach to magic that was neither as literal as Angers nor as purely political as Hoffman's. After all, if Sanders described Anger's ritual as a "serious zero-bullshit exorcism," this implies his own exorcism contained only some bullshit. So what about Sanders's exorcism was not bullshit? If magical ritual was not powered by literal gods and spirits, how did it work?

By 1967 Allen Ginsberg's study of Buddhist mantras had led him to conclude that reality is constructed through language. In 1965, Ginsberg successfully disarmed a conflict between hippies and Hell's Angels by leading a chant of the Prajnaparamita Sutra. (The Hell's Angels began chanting too). In 1966, he wrote in his poem "Wichita Vortex Sutra" that, "the war is language." Accordingly, he believed that ritual utterances could be a powerful tool for social change. In what Alex Houen called Ginsberg's theory of "potentialism," language and imagination offered the possibility for a new reality apart from the one created by mass media. By contrast, Ginsberg described the language of Lyndon Johnson and the State Department as "black mantras," that were creating a false reality.[53] Ginsberg commented on the Pentagon exorcism, "I think we demystified the authority of the Pentagon, and in that sense we *did* levitate it." Ginsberg felt the Pentagon exorcism was successful and pointed out that four months later, a Gallup poll showed that 52 percent of Americans were opposed to the war.[54]

Jesuit sociologist Andrew Greeley noted that interest in the occult in the 1960s correlated closely with both political protesting and "Woodstock syndrome" in which people checked out of modern society, seeking solace in alternative lifestyles and psychedelic drugs.[55] Perhaps the best interpretation of why white middle-class protestors turned to magic in the 1960s comes from sociologist Edward Tiryakian, who noted that occult revivals often occur when there is a "loss of confidence" in the established way of doing things. He argues that occult beliefs and practices become more popular during historical periods of transition, such as the end of the Roman Empire and the Renaissance.[56] Norman Mailer suggests that the youth who participated in the exorcism were keenly aware that they lacked real political agency, in part because their college educations had caused them to be suspicious of their ability to influence government through normal democratic means.[57] Hoffman and Sanders both described frustration with the more sober wing of the anti-war movement, whose methods appeared ineffective. Theodore Roszak commented on the radical strategies of the New Left:

If violence and injustice could be eliminated from our society by heavy intellectual research and ideological analysis, by impassioned oratory and sober street rallies, by the organization of bigger unions ... then we should long since have been living in the new Jerusalem.[58]

This was a scenario in which "the occult" — shorthand for a whole range of religious traditions that had recently appeared in America's spiritual marketplace — held out the promise of both a better world and a new way of changing the world. In his spell, Sanders referred to this idea of some power beyond the conventional political apparatus as "suprapolitics." In a candid moment, Sanders said of the exorcism, "It was a bunch of people trying to be creative when there was nothing we could actually do to stop the war."[59] Perhaps it is unsurprising, then, that in a political age defined by hyper-partisanship, gerrymandering, and the interference in our elections by hostile foreign powers, we are once again seeing young people include hexes and other public displays of magic into their political repertoires.

FURTHER READING

Kaplan, Jeffrey, and Heléne Lööw, eds. *The Cultic Milieu: Oppositional Subcultures in an Age of Globalization*. Walnut Creek: AltaMira Press, 2002.
Lachman, Gary. *Turn Off Your Mind: The Mystic Sixties and the Dark Side of the Age of Aquarius*. New York: Disinformation, 2003.
Mailer, Norman. *The Armies of the Night. History as a Novel. The Novel as History*. Harmondsworth: Penguin Books, 1971.
Miller, Timothy. *The 60s Communes: Hippies and Beyond*. Syracuse: Syracuse University Press, 2002.
Partridge, Christopher. "Occulture is Ordinary." In *Contemporary Esotericism*, edited by Egil Asprem and Kennet Granholm, 113–133. Hoboken: Taylor and Francis, 2014.

BIBLIOGRAPHY

Albanese, Catherine. *America: Religion and Religions*. Belmont: Thomson Wadsworth, 2012.
Betz, Hans Dieter. *The Greek Magical Papyri in Translation, Including the Demotic Spells*. Chicago: University of Chicago Press, 1996.
David, Sara. "Ritual to Hex Kavanaugh Is So Popular That Witches Organized Another One." *Vice News*, 16 October 2018, https://www.vice.com/en_us/article/mbdwnp/witch-hex-brett-kavanaugh.
Ellis, Bill. *Raising the Devil: Satanism, New Religions, and the Media*. Lexington: University Press of Kentucky, 2000.
Ginsberg, Allen. *Collected Poems*. London: Penguin, 1987.
Gosse, Van. *Rethinking the New Left: An Interpretative History*. New York: Palgrave Macmillan, 2005.
Greeley, Andrew. "Implications for the Sociology of Religion of Occult Behavior in the Youth Culture." *Youth and Society* 2, no. 2 (1970): 131–140.
Houen, Alex. "'Back! Back! Back! Central Mind-Machine Pentagon ...' Allen Ginsberg and the Vietnam War." *Cultural Politics: An International Journal* 4, no. 3 (November 2008): 351–373.
Hoffman, Abbie. *Soon to Be a Major Motion Picture*. New York: Putnam, 1980.
_____. *Revolution for the Hell of It*. New York: Thunder's Mouth Press, 2005.
Jenkins, Philip. *Dream Catchers: How Mainstream America Discovered Native Spirituality*. New York: Oxford University Press, 2004.
Lachman, Gary. *Turn Off Your Mind: The Mystic Sixties and the Dark Side of the Age of Aquarius*. New York: Disinformation, 2003.
Landis, Bill. *Anger: The Unauthorized Biography of Kenneth Anger*. New York: HarperCollins, 1995.
Lasch, Christopher. *The Culture of Narcissism: American Life in an Age of Diminishing Expectations*. New York: W.W. Norton & Company, 1971.
Mailer, Norman. *The Armies of the Night. History as a Novel. The Novel as History*. Harmondsworth: Penguin Books, 1971.
Marty, Martin. "The Occult Establishment." *Social Research* 37 (1970): 212–230.
McMillian, John and Paul Buhle, editors. *The New Left Revisited*. Philadelphia: Temple University Press, 2003.

Miller, Timothy. *The 60s Communes: Hippies and Beyond*. Syracuse: Syracuse University Press, 2002.

Raskin, Jonah. *For the Hell of It: The Life and Times of Abbie Hoffman*. Berkeley: University of California Press, 1996.

Roszak, Theodore. *The Making of a Counter Culture: Reflections on the Technocratic Society and its Youthful Opposition*. Garden City: Doubleday, 1969.

Sanders, Ed. *The Family: The Manson Group and its Aftermath*. London: Nemesis Books, 1993.

Sloman, Larry, Michael Simmons, and Jay Babcock. "Out Demons Out." *Arthur* 13 (November 2004): 22–62.

Snellgrove, David L. *The Hevajra Tantra: A Critical Study, Part I: Introduction and Translation*. London: Oxford University Press, 1971.

Snyder, Gary. "A Curse on the Men in Washington, Pentagon." 1967. http://www.diggers.org/digpaps68/images/d68_02_l.jpg.

Starhawk. "An Open Letter to the Pagan Community." 1999. http://www.starhawk.org/activism/activism-writings/openletter.html.

Stone, Geoffrey R. *Perilous Times: Free Speech in Wartime from the Sedition Act of 1798 to the War on Terrorism*. New York: W. W. Norton & Co., 2004.

Sullivan, James D. *On the Walls and in the Streets*. Urbana: University of Illinois Press, 1997.

Taylor, Derek. *It Was Twenty Years Ago Today*. New York: Bantam, 1987.

Tiryakian, Edward A. "Toward the Sociology of Esoteric Culture." *American Journal of Sociology* 78, no. 3 (1972): 491–512.

Vogel, Steve. *The Pentagon: A History: The Untold Story of the Wartime Race to Build the Pentagon — and to Restore it Sixty Years Later*. New York: Random House, 2008.

NOTES

1   Abbie Hoffman, *Revolution for the Hell of It* (New York: Thunder's Mouth Press, 2005), 3.

2   Norman Mailer, *The Armies of the Night. History as a Novel. The Novel as History* (Harmondsworth: Penguin Books, 1971), 53.

3   Edward A. Tiryakian, "Toward the Sociology of Esoteric Culture," *American Journal of Sociology* 78, no. 3 (1972): 491–512.

4   Catherine Albanese, *America: Religion and Religions* (Belmont: Thomson Wadsworth, 2012), 234.

5   Van Gosse, *Rethinking the New Left: An Interpretive History* (New York: Palgrave Macmillan, 2005), 93.

6   Steve Vogel, *The Pentagon: A History: The Untold Story of the Wartime Race to Build the Pentagon — and to Restore it Sixty Years Later* (New York: Random House, 2008), 367–374.

7   Geoffrey R. Stone, *Perilous Times: Free Speech in Wartime from the Sedition Act of 1798 to the War on Terrorism* (New York: W. W. Norton & Co., 2004), 430.

8   Bill Ellis, *Raising the Devil: Satanism, New Religions, and the Media* (Lexington: University Press of Kentucky, 2000), 175.

9   McMillian, John and Paul Buhle, eds., *The New Left Revisited* (Philadelphia: Temple University Press, 2003), 5.

10 Sloman, Larry, Michael Simmons, and Jay Babcock. "Out Demons Out." *Arthur* 13 (November 2004): 22.

11 Stone, *Perilous Times*, 448.

12 Sloman et al., "Out Demons Out," 12.

13 Stone, *Perilous Times*, 449.

14 Hoffman, *Revolution for the Hell of it*, 44.

15 Sloman et al., "Out Demons Out," 30.

16 Ibid.

17 Hoffman, *Revolution for the Hell of It*, 39.

18 Timothy Miller, *The 60s Communes: Hippies and Beyond* (Syracuse: Syracuse University Press, 2002), 7.

19 Sloman et al., "Out Demons Out," 30.

20 Derek Taylor, *It Was Twenty Years Ago Today* (New York: Bantam, 1987), 241.

21 Sloman et al., "Out Demons Out," 30.

22 Hans Dieter Betz, *The Greek Magical Papyri in Translation, Including the Demotic Spells* (Chicago: University of Chicago Press, 1996), 6.

23 Taylor, *It Was Twenty Years Ago Today*, 241–242.

24 Sloman et al., "Out Demons Out," 30–32.

25 Ibid., 32.

26 Ibid., 38.

27 Ibid., 33.

28 Mailer, *The Armies of the Night*, 120–121.

29 Mailer, *The Armies of the Night*, 122.

30 Sloman et al., "Out Demons Out," 33.

31 Gary Snyder, "A Curse on the Men in Washington, Pentagon," 1967, http://www.diggers.org/digpaps68/images/d68_02_l.jpg.

32 James D. Sullivan, *On the Walls and in the Streets* (Urbana: University of Illinois Press, 1997), 76–77.

33 This mantra appears in Snellgrove's translation of the Tibetan Hevajra Tantra, published in 1959 and again in 1964. Snyder most likely found the mantra from Snellgrove's translation. See David L. Snellgrove, *The Hevajra Tantra: A Critical Study, Part I: Introduction and Translation* (London: Oxford University Press, 1971), 50.

34 Sullivan, *On the Walls*, 79.

35 Allen Ginsberg, *Collected Poems* (London: Penguin, 1987), 407.

36 Ibid., 483.

37 Philip Jenkins, *Dream Catchers: How Mainstream America Discovered Native Spirituality* (New York: Oxford University Press, 2004), 156.

38 Taylor, *It Was Twenty Years Ago*, 240–241.

39 Gary Lachman, *Turn Off Your Mind: The Mystic Sixties and the Dark Side of the Age of Aquarius* (New York: Disinformation, 2003), 356.

40 Starhawk, "An Open Letter to the Pagan Community," 1999, http://www.starhawk.org/activism/activism-writings/openletter.html.

41 Sara David, "Ritual to Hex Kavanaugh Is So Popular That Witches Organized Another One," *Vice News*, 16 October 2018, https://www.vice.com/en_us/article/mbdwnp/witch-hex-brett-kavanaugh.

42 Bill Landis, *Anger: The Unauthorized Biography of Kenneth Anger* (New York: Harper Collins, 1995), 237.

43 Sloman et al., "Out Demons Out," 33–34.

44 Ed Sanders, *The Family: The Manson Group and its Aftermath* (London: Nemesis Books, 1993), 24–25.

45 Sloman et al., "Out Demons Out," 34.

46 Christopher Lasch, *The Culture of Narcissism: American Life in an Age of Diminishing Expectations* (New York: W.W. Norton & Company, 1971), 81.

47 Andrew Greeley, "Implications for the Sociology of Religion of Occult Behavior in the Youth Culture," *Youth and Society* 2, no. 2 (1970): 131–140; Martin Marty, "The Occult Establishment," *Social Research* 37 (1970): 212–230; Tiryakian, "Toward the Sociology of Esoteric Culture."

48 Jonah Raskin, *For the Hell of It: The Life and Times of Abbie Hoffman* (Berkeley: University of California Press, 1996), 120.

49 Taylor, *It Was Twenty Years Ago Today*, 240–241.

50 Abbie Hoffman, *Soon to Be a Major Motion Picture* (New York: Putnam, 1980), 44.

51 Ibid., 126.

52 Sloman et al., "Out Demons Out," 30.

53 Alex Houen, "'Back! Back! Back! Central Mind-Machine Pentagon …' Allen Ginsberg and the Vietnam War," *Cultural Politics: An International Journal* 4, no. 3 (November 2008): 360.

54 Ginsberg's interpretation does not consider that between the Pentagon Exorcism and this poll was the Ten Offensive of January 1968, which made it far more difficult for the Johnson administration to convince Americans they were winning the war. See Taylor, *It Was Twenty Years Ago Today*, 251.

55   Greeley, "Implications for the Sociology of Religion of Occult Behavior," 131.

56   Tiryakian, "Toward the Sociology of Esoteric Culture," 510.

57   Mailer, *The Armies of the Night*, 257.

58   Theodore Roszak, *The Making of a Counter Culture: Reflections on the Technocratic Society and its Youthful Opposition* (Garden City: Doubleday, 1969), 154.

59   Taylor, *It Was Twenty Years Ago Today*, 248–249.

Chapter Twenty-Five

Native American Christians and the Varieties of Modern Pentecostalism

Angela Tarango
Trinity University, San Antonio, Texas

A desire to go into the ministry seized Brother Cree, and he enrolled at a French-Canadian Bible college, despite his hatred of the French. There, through the power of the Holy Spirit he said that he learned to overcome his own racial prejudice. He recounted: "I remember going to school and walking and I heard someone say (in French) 'the savage has come.' The Holy Spirit kept me from turning around … I learned how to deal with those people."[1]

Introduction

When Mohawk evangelist Rodger Cree told me his Pentecostal conversion narrative, he was in his late seventies, his memories sharpened by years of giving regular testimony. I first encountered him at the Assemblies of God archives in Springfield, Missouri, where he sought me out to tell the story of his remarkable life on a hot August afternoon. His hatred of French-Canadians was fed by their own colonialist and racist attitude toward him — until his conversion to Pentecostal Christianity. Brother Cree admitted to me that it wasn't instantaneous, but that the Holy Spirit was constantly "working" on him and that that intercession was what allowed him to become a successful Assemblies of God evangelist and leader. Cree's advocacy for Native leadership came from his life-long suspicion of white missionaries. The Holy Spirit may have cured him of his hatred of French-Canadians, but he also understood that indigenous leadership was crucial to making Pentecostalism a form of *indigenous* Christianity outside of white structures of power.

Traditionally, the history of Native American Christianity is associated with missionary history and in the popular imagination ends at the end of the nineteenth century. In the standard US history survey, Native people disappear from the textbooks at this moment, only to perhaps reappear during the American Indian Movement's protests in the late 1960s and early 1970s. Little is widely known about modern Native lives, especially about modern Native Christians who created their own forms of indigenous Christianity. New scholarship in the last decade shows that there is a small, but important subculture of both Pentecostal and independent non-denominational Christian Native Americans that continue to engage Christianity in a variety of ways, and in doing so, shift how these two movements are understood in the American imagination.

A Companion to American Religious History, First Edition. Edited by Benjamin E. Park.
© 2021 John Wiley & Sons, Inc. Published 2021 by John Wiley & Sons, Inc.

This essay will specifically cover Native Americans who are a part of the Pentecostal and charismatic movements in the twentieth century, as well as those who are in conversation with them in the contextualization movements that have spread beyond Pentecostalism into some aspects of non-denominational Christianity. These are groups that are understudied in the field of Native religious history and that have recently grown and expanded among Native peoples. Modern (Protestant) Native Christians come in a dizzying variety — from those who are connected to traditional institutions such as the Assemblies of God or the Southern Baptist Convention, to those affiliated with independent churches, and still others who are closely allied to Mainline Protestantism but who have evangelical leanings or charismatic practices. For the sake of clarity, I will note that some of the authors whose work I draw from use the term Pentecostal loosely, while other distinguish between different kinds of Pentecostal groups or also use the term neo-Pentecostal.

Traditionally, Pentecostalism is a term identified with the denominations that grew out of the early twentieth century revivals and emphasizes baptism in the Holy Spirit, speaking in tongues and faith healing (for example, the Assemblies of God or the Church of the Foursquare Gospel). Neo-Pentecostalism tends to be non-denominational and comes out of the charismatic revivals in the 1950s and 1960s and emphasizes prophesy, exorcism or spiritual deliverance, as well as faith healing. There is no hard line between the two, as they are fluid and the traditions tend to mix together and share significant similarities and roots. The essay will pull from recent scholarship and focus on Pentecostal Natives affiliated with the Assemblies of God, non-denominational neo-Pentecostals among the Navajo and Crow tribes, Pentecostal Natives in the Church of God (Cleveland) and non-denominational Christian Native Americans.

What stands out in the history of Native American Pentecostals, Charismatics, and non-denominational Christians are two interconnected themes. The first is that both groups create religious innovation, spaces of indigeneity, and innovative re-imaginings of culture out of the problem of exclusion. Many Native believers and Native clergy are excluded by white leadership in their larger religious affiliations and denominations and out of their exclusion they created theological push back such as the push for indigenous leadership within a Pentecostal context in the Assemblies of God, or the movement to incorporate aspects of Native culture into Christianity (known as the contextualization movement) among certain North American Native churches. The fruit of this indigenous engagement with exclusion is the development of Native leadership, both within and outside of existing denominational structures.

The second theme is that there remains a complicated relationship with the incorporation of traditional beliefs into Christianity among Native Christians. Some groups openly embrace and endorse religious flexibility in terms of incorporating traditional beliefs (contextualization), which is contrasted by a studied and decided inflexibility among certain Native groups who view traditionalism as problematic at best, and demonic at worst. This approach also comes out of the politics of exclusion — some groups want to embrace the stricter stance of the religious groups that they belong to in order to fit in, or to create their own re-imagining of their culture, while other groups embrace certain indigenous traditions as a way to push back against exclusion and to claim an indigenous Christian space on their own terms, in order to acknowledge important aspects of their culture.

These politics of exclusion are what have profoundly shaped Native Christianity in the twentieth century and have created a liminal space for Native Christians: a space that allows them to develop their own leadership, indigenous theology, and rules for incorporation or separation of traditional rituals. In the space of exclusion, Native Christians carved out their own religious identities and voices that uplift a wide variety of Native Christian practices. This was the case for Rodger Cree, who spent his entire life trying to boost his people into places of power and influence within North American Pentecostalism's biggest denomination.

Native American Pentecostals and Religious Leadership

Despite Pentecostalism's early multicultural beginnings, which included African Americans and Latino leadership at the early twentieth century revivals, the movement inevitably fractured upon racial lines. The Assemblies of God (AG), for instance, is traditionally understood to be the largest of the white Pentecostal denominations that emerged out of the early twentieth century Pentecostal revivals. In 1914, white Midwestern and Southern Pentecostals attended the first council composed of Pentecostal leader in Hot Springs, Arkansas, and notably did not invite any African-American evangelists. Excluded because of segregationist attitudes, African-American Pentecostals organized mainly under the Church of God in Christ (COGIC), while Latinos and Native Americans were placed under the category of "home missions" by the AG.[2] Although missions to Native Americans in the lower forty-eight states and Alaska began early in the history of the AG, and Native leadership developed within the AG by the middle of the twentieth century, Native leaders were excluded from positions of power by the AG's white leadership throughout the twentieth century. This led to pushback against the racism and ethnocentrism of the denomination and the Native development of what they called the indigenous principle.

AG missionaries initially targeted Native Americans in order to save them from the "darkness" of traditional religion, peyote (also known as the Native American Church), or Catholicism. The missionaries viewed all three competitors as demonic. In the early decades of missionary work (1930–1950), white missionaries went to reservations on faith missions with no money, no training, little education, and minimal knowledge of Native cultures, aside from what they may have seen in the movies. During this era, white Pentecostals sent reports to the *Pentecostal Evangel* (the AG's weekly newspaper) noting the poverty of the reservations, how Native people "lived in darkness," and used ethnocentric language by referring to drums as "tom toms" and noting the "savage dances" of the traditional believers.[3] These early descriptions of Native Americans by white Pentecostals are deeply problematic — and display at best, ignorance, and at worst, racism towards the people they were supposed to be serving as missionaries.

Despite the inauspicious and haphazard beginnings of missionary work to Native Americans, indigenous leadership emerged from these early Pentecostal encounters with white missionaries. A major factor in this is the inherent flexibility and egalitarian ethos of Pentecostalism. One did not need to attend seminary or even Bible school in those days — Pentecostals believed that anyone who could testify to a life-changing conversion and experience of the Holy Spirit, who could read the Bible and preach clearly, could become a missionary or a pastor. This applied to Native American converts, even if some early white leaders believed they could be nothing more than "missionary helpers." On remote reservations across the country, away from the watchful eye of the AG leadership in Springfield, Missouri, Native leaders emerged and flourished.[4]

The early Native American leadership was mainly composed of men, many who began their careers evangelizing their own tribe or among neighboring tribes. One such example is the Navajo evangelist Charlie Lee. Reared in a traditional Navajo sheep-farming family, Lee grew up in a traditional family until an Apache friend invited him to a revival. The Holy Spirit came upon Lee at the revival and he became a Pentecostal. Already a recognized talent as a traditional Navajo artist, Lee attended Central Bible Institute in Springfield, Missouri. Upon his graduation, Lee became the first official appointed home missionary within the AG.[5] Fluent in Navajo, Lee conducted his early missionary work in the language of his people, something a white missionary would have never been able to do. Traditionally, white missionaries preached through translators when working among tribes that retained their traditional language. Lee's home region included the Shiprock-Farmington area, which is a remote part of the Navajo reservation. Preaching in a remote part of the state, and generally not noticed by the AG authorities in Springfield, Lee put into motion the ideas that he learned while at Central Bible Institute, including what came to be called the indigenous principle.

Originally espoused by Melvin Hodges in his books *The Indigenous Church* and *The Indigenous Church and the Missionary*, the ideas behind the indigenous principle are not unique to Pentecostalism. Simply put, Hodges argued that Christians needed to emulate the ideals of Paul the Apostle — that churches should be rooted in the culture of the converted and cultivate local leadership that recognized and celebrated their particular culture.[6] Hodges simply articulates this vision in a Pentecostal context, stressing the power of the Holy Spirit to move indigenous believers into positions of leadership. Having been trained by Hodges at Central Bible Institute, Lee took the ideas for the indigenous principle and argued for a particularly Native version of it — that AG churches among Native peoples needed to be rooted in local, tribal cultures, and must encourage the perpetuation of those cultures, along with spirit-filled Christianity.

Despite the fact that early white Pentecostals praised themselves for not being involved in the creation of the reservation system, the plains wars, or the development of boarding schools and forced assimilation — moments in history that heavily implicated American Christianity — they still carried ethnocentric and imperialist ideas with them onto the reservations they evangelized. Lee's leadership encouraged the movement to train more Native American missionaries and leaders within the AG, and to start creating self-supporting Native churches, not missions dependent on white Pentecostal funding. In fact, Lee's church, then called Mesa View Assembly of God, became the first self-supporting district-affiliated AG church among Native Americans in 1976.

Along with Lee, other Native evangelists also helped to break new ground regarding the indigenous principle including Rodger Cree (Mohawk), John Maracle (Mohawk), George Effman (Klamath), Jimmie Dan (Shoshone), and John McPherson (Cherokee). These men were active in the AG from the 1930s–1970s and made up the vanguard of early Native leadership. Alta Washburn, a white missionary in Arizona among the Pima-Maricopa tribe, who later defied the AG leadership in Springfield to develop a Bible college especially to cultivate Native leadership, tirelessly worked on the behalf of Native American Pentecostals and fervently argued for the indigenous principle alongside her friend and colleague Brother Lee.[7]

Native Pentecostals demanded that white Pentecostals live up to the ideals of their denomination — that the Holy Spirit could really fall on anyone and select anyone for leadership, including Native peoples. But the fact remained that white Pentecostals fell well short of the ideal and were suspicious of Native culture. They saw traditional Native religion as demonic. Rather than argue about this viewpoint, the first generation of early Native leaders tended to side-step it by emphasizing that Native language, styles of dress and jewelry, food and familial customs should be preserved by Native Pentecostals. Lee even argued that traditional beliefs simply didn't work anymore because the social structures that created and upheld them no longer existed. To him, the future lay in an indigenous form of Christianity. The fact is, early Native Pentecostals were careful to tread a middle ground — they refused to denounce Native culture in its entirety, but they emphasized the aspects of Native culture that were seen as least-threatening to Pentecostals. In the end, we don't really know how much of traditional Native culture that the first generation of indigenous members of the AG brought or did not bring into their worship services.[8]

Native AG innovation came from two main factors — the embrace of and the authority of the indigenous principle, and out of the politics of exclusion. It's no surprise that the most successful indigenous missionaries were well-removed from the watchful eyes of the AG leadership in Springfield and located out in the deserts of the Southwest or the rural parts of the Northeast. Excluded from having a national voice until the twenty-first century, and left to cope with little funding or recognition, Native Pentecostals filled the void with a forcefully articulated vision of Native Pentecostalism within the AG.

Independent Pentecostalism and Traditionalism Among the Navajo and Crow

At the same time that Charlie Lee built the foundations of his AG ministry to the Navajo, competition sprung up in the form of neo-Pentecostalism. Characterized by independent Native leadership, an emphasis on spirit-filled tent revivals, no denominational control and the exclusion of traditional Navajo religion as demonic, the Oodlání (as they call themselves in Navajo) emerged as a different kind of Christian experience for Navajo Christians. In this way, they positioned themselves away from denominationally affiliated Native Pentecostals like Lee. They found power in their independence from white Christianity. In the case of the Oodlání, their exclusion from white controlled denominations, including traditional Pentecostal denominations such as the AG, allowed them space to articulate their own identities as Navajo and charismatic Christians.[9]

The beginnings of neo-Pentecostalism among the Navajo can be traced to the ministry of the Pentecostal evangelist A. A. Allen. Allen began his ministry initially within the AG and, after being inspired by the Pentecostal healing revivalist Oral Roberts, created his own camp meeting circuit. His meetings tended to be racially integrated and focused on the poor and his detractors often criticized him for being too brash and outspoken. Allen emphasized miraculous healings and resurrections of the dead in his tent revivals and was by all accounts, a tremendous showman. In 1955, he experienced a falling out with the AG and struck out on his own. He started a series of tent meetings known as "Miracle Revivals" in the Phoenix, AZ area, where urban Navajos experienced his particular flavor of Pentecostalism. They then took his ideas back to the reservation, which was visited by a string of charismatic Native evangelists, including Navajos and those from other tribes. Allen and other neo-Pentecostal revivalists were products of the 1950s independent charismatic revivals that spread across North America.[10] They were also in direct competition for souls with the AG evangelists, including Lee and Alta Washburn, who seems to hint at Allen's ministry as a form of religious competition in her autobiography multiple times.[11]

The Oodlání acknowledge the power of traditional Navajo beliefs. Although the Oodlání no longer believe *in* traditional religion they still believe it can *do* harm. In one recollection Ma Beverly, an Oodlání, noted a terrifying skinwalker attack that targeted her. Traditionally seen as malevolent creatures, skinwalkers are shapeshifters who in traditional Navajo culture can curse or "witch" a person. Upon encountering the skinwalker where she slept, Ma Beverly prayed with her son, and engaged in spiritual warfare. The spell of the skinwalker loosened and Ma Beverly noted that a weird little beetle came off her and ran away. She attributed her salvation to her neo-Pentecostal beliefs, and the power of the skinwalker to the Devil. Some might view that Ma Beverly's belief both in neo-Pentecostalism and skinwalkers makes her an "incomplete" Christian.[12]

But the anthropologist Kimberly Jenkins Marshall rightfully points out that Native religions has always lived with the inherent "tension between continuity and rupture."[13] She notes that the belief in skinwalkers "suggests that feelingful attachment to expressive form persists, but that the inherent ambiguity of these forms allows for the attachment of drastically different meanings."[14] In this case, the skinwalker isn't a traditional shapeshifter that needed to be dealt with in a traditional way. Instead, it is understood as a demonic being, under the possession of the Devil (which is a Christian, not Navajo term) and combatted by the power of Christian prayer and belief. This, Marshall calls "resonant rupture." The skinwalker's power is not denied, instead it is countered in a particularity Christian way. Marshall notes that

Pentecostal rupture is neither wholly assimilative nor wholly traditional but is a type of rupture enriched by "feelingfully" familiar aesthetic forms. Because of their feelingful connection to the past, these expressive forms (skinwalker stories, cardinal direction symbols) can suggest a type of cultural continuity ... Their apparent similarity actually masks fundamental denial of similarity happening at the level of asserted meaning.[15]

Spiritual warfare or deliverance is a common feature of neo-Pentecostalism around the globe, but Marshall argues here that resonant rupture is more than just aligning traditionalism with the Devil. That instead, it can act as a cultural continuity of key Navajo beliefs through Pentecostal re-interpretation.

Another example that Marshall gives of this resonant rupture is the burning of jish. Jish is a Navajo word that means medicine bundle, which is usually a small buckskin bag filled with a collection of ritual items such as fetishes, rattles, arrowheads, and herbs that are used in curing ceremonies. Traditionally, Jish are passed down in families and are considered a powerful, living being that need to be properly cared for. If well-treated, the jish will serve as protection for a person and their family. When Navajos convert to neo-Pentecostalism and become Oodlání, they often destroy their jish because it is powerful — you cannot just give away the jish to a family member. The jish's power, however, is re-interpreted by Christian believers to mean a power that opposes Christianity (demonic) rather than just traditional Navajo power. Unlike other Christians (Catholics, mainline Protestants), who would urge believers to just set aside the medicine bundle because it has no power, it is understood to still have power that must be destroyed. Therefore, to some of the Oodlání, Jish must be burned, which is a controversial stance on the reservation. The Oodlání define for themselves what is demonic or not and draw the lines at what they see as good and evil. Their exclusion from the traditional denominational centers of power, and their status as non-denominational and indigenous-run gives them room to indigenize their controversial stance towards traditionalism. Resonant rupture in Oodlání hands is a deeply indigenous stance.[16]

The reinterpretation of the traditional as demonic is not unique to Navajo neo-Pentecostalism. Similar attitudes have been found towards traditional religions on the modern Crow reservation in Montana. There is a variety of religious affiliations among the Crow, with the most dominant being Pentecostal and neo-Pentecostal believers — the Pentecostals attending the AG and Foursquare churches and the neo-Pentecostals attending the independent charismatic churches. Those who belong to the non-denominational Pentecostal churches have a much stronger stance against traditionalism compared to those who belong to a denomination. In one example, the Crows who are a part of the Church of the Foursquare Gospel tend to not condone traditionalism, but also don't openly preach against it.[17] Once again, exclusion from major denominational centers of power means that Pentecostal Crows get to decide how they will contend with their traditionalist competitors. Non-denominational Pentecostal Crows react to traditional religion much in the way as their Oodlání cousins, while those who belong to Pentecostal denominations tend to temper their condemnation of traditional beliefs in a way that the denomination likely would not approve. But their physical and mental distance from the center of the institution that they belong to also means that they have the space to chart their own course in how to address the situation.

Similar to the Oodlání, many neo-Pentecostal Crows also see traditional Crow religion as demonic or evil. One such example is that of Rhea Goes Ahead. Although neo-Pentecostal beliefs formed a rich part of Goes Ahead's family history, she converted as a young woman after a period of rejection of Christian belief. Like many neo-Pentecostals, Goes Ahead recalls a detailed conversion narrative in her interview, and details how Pentecostal belief changed her life trajectory. She then describes the problems of traditional Crow religion.

A lot of Indians don't realize how medicine attracts evil spirits. There was an aunt I used to visit all the time. When I went in that home as a child there was a medicine chest there. And her family would say, "Don't sit on that! That's sacred!" And they were forever seeing things looking at them in the windows. That house always had an eerie feeling. But at our home, because my mom as Holy Ghost-filled, praying all the time, we never noticed nothing in our house.[18]

Goes Ahead notes that medicine bundles were in the chest, and that is what she felt attracted evil spirits. She states that smudging also attracts evil spirits, and that traditional Crow medicine will seek a person out unless it is rebuked in the name of Jesus. Goes Ahead recounts another piece of family lore: after Pentecostal conversion, her grandmother went into the hills to fast and pray. An owl came to her and asked her what she was doing there and her grandmother told the owl to leave her alone in the name of Jesus. The owl flew away, and "her prayer was not intercepted because she knew the true and living God. She knew Jesus. Otherwise owl would have become her Indian medicine."[19] Since in Crow culture, an owl means death, it was an unwelcome form of medicine according to Looks Ahead.

Crow neo-Pentecostals also change how they interact with their familial structures as part of the rejection of traditional beliefs. In traditional Crow culture, clan aunts and uncles play an important spiritual role for people; when someone sees a bad omen, it is usually clan aunts and uncles who are given gifts to come to the family house to pray it away. But Goes Ahead describes her family as one that doesn't take part in those beliefs anymore. Instead, if there was a need, her Holy Ghost believing family members would go into a room together and pray in a Christian manner. Now that she is a Christian, Goes Ahead says she no longer needs the misunderstanding of traditional belief.

I believe our traditional ancestors before Christianity had a form of religion and in their fasting that animal would come in and intercept their prayers. So then the animal became their god. But when you look at Genesis 1:26, God gave dominion over the fowl of the air, over the things underwater, over things on land. We're not to worship eagles … But we make it [the eagle] spiritual. Then the devil works on your superstition. He feeds on that superstition, He really likes that. You know, he's been around a long time too.[20]

Like the Oodláni, Goes Ahead experienced a resonant rupture from the traditional culture of the Crow and reinterprets her culture now through the lens of Pentecostal belief.

Goes Ahead is not the only Crow neo-Pentecostal who saw traditionalism as demonic. Neo-Pentecostal believer Fannie Plain Feather Ward also described two times that she encountered an evil spirit. First, when observing a traditional Crow hand game tournament, and secondly when she went to a Peyote ceremony. Both times she saw a black demon, lurking nearby and reported it to her mother who warned her it was because she was visiting places where evil was present. Later in life, when she was working as a youth pastor, Ward experienced spiritual warfare. She recalls in the middle of the night, the pastor's wife (she was living with the pastor's family who led the church she worked for) came to her as they heard drums from a distance. The pastor's wife implored Ward to pray and they did for some time. When they felt a breakthrough and went back to bed, the pastor's wife reported seeing angels at their beds, protecting them. Later they found out that four traditional men tried to drive them out of town because of their work with the church and had placed a type of curse on them. Ward later reported that the curse rebounded and all four men became sick in some way.[21]

Not all Crow Pentecostals emphasize all of traditionalism as demonic. Some counseled patience and tolerance, although they reject some aspects of traditional religion. Kenneth Pretty on Top Sr. pastored the large Foursquare church on the reservation. Even though Pretty on Top drew the line at his parishioners using medicine bundles or smudging, he is also careful to emphasize God's love more than the demonic aspect of traditionalism. While its clear he does not encourage traditionalist beliefs, Pretty on Top seems to believe that being better, more loving Christians, will be what encourages others convert. "As Christians we can be so judgmental. We can be judgmental about everything around us, but what does that do? That just brings people down."[22] While he rejects medicine bundles and smudging, Pretty on Top allows people to use the sweat lodge so long as they don't worship the sweat lodge. He states "I see it as a medicinal thing, just like a good cleansing, a good bath, that tales the soreness out. But some turn around and worship it."[23] Like some other Crow Christians, certain aspects of culture can be embraced by Pentecostals so long as it has a practical purpose that does not conflict with Pentecostal beliefs. Also, as a member of the older Pentecostal Foursquare denomination, Pretty on Top is less likely to hold the stricter views towards traditionalism compared to neo-Pentecostal Crows drawing parallels with how Native believers in the AG approached issues around traditionalism.

The final important theme to note is that some Crows are not religious exclusives. Meaning that some go between two faiths, say for example Catholicism and traditionalism, while many have family members from a variety of traditions. Many Pentecostal Crowns recalled family members who are Catholics, traditionalists and members of the Native America Church. Some others work across traditions — Fanny Plain Feather Ward is a devout Pentecostal but also worked as a teacher in a Catholic school.[24] Despite that fact that some Pentecostals certainly saw traditionalism as demonic, the majority of Crow believers move between faiths fairly regularly and often many have multiple religious affiliations, thus complicating and enriching Crow religious identity.

Moving to the Margins: The Contextualization Movement

There are only a few Pentecostal and non-denominational voices that advocate for contextualization of Native practices with Christianity, the most famous being the non-denominational Lakota evangelical Christian Richard Twiss. There is also a small, but slowly growing contextualization movement within the Church of God in Christ (Cleveland), a Pentecostal denomination. Both Twiss's leadership within the North American Institute for Indigenous Theological Studies (NAIITS), and the COG (Cleveland)'s contextualization movement, are situated well outside mainstream Christian power structures. Twiss preferred it that way, believing his work was best when situated indigenously and away from white Christians that he viewed as harmful. This also seems to be the case of the COG Cleveland practitioners, some who did not allow white scholars to witness their practice. One Seminole practitioner stated to scholar Corky Alexander, "Not only do I not want you to come, I do not want you to see pictures of the observance, for everything the white man has looked at he has ruined."[25] While other contextualization practitioners did allow Alexander to observe and interview them their numbers were small, indicating some distrust among Native Christians. Those who are a part of the contextualization movement tend to be on the margins of Native Christianity, and they find autonomy and leadership within that space of exclusion. In fact, Twiss intentionally set himself up to be excluded by white denominations and other Christians, in an effort to make his argument for contextualization.

Among the Native members of the COG (Cleveland), some embraced contextualization and incorporated five Native practices into their Pentecostal rituals — Native language, smudging, drums and rattles, dance, and talking circles. Among Navajos there is also an adaptation of the Enemy Way ceremony, which is a ceremony traditional and specific to their tribe. Of these Native practices the only one that crosses all Native Christian groups is language. Native Christians as a whole tend to be protective of their traditional languages, retain them and encourage their children to learn them. The other practices tend to be seen as demonic, or at least problematic by Native Christians who are not in the contextualization movement, and in fact many Native believers maintain that the contextualization movement is syncretic.[26]

The practitioners of the contextualization movement tended to both look to scripture and tradition in order to defend their practices. For one example, smudging is usually considered deeply problematic by many Native Pentecostals and evangelicals, as it is seen as attracting the demonic. But Native practitioners in the COG (Cleveland) defend it as a sacramental action and by pointing out that incense has been used for a long time in Christianity, "You know, tell the people that it's not actually smoke that cleanses you, it's only a symbol, the same way that the waters of immersion baptism don't actually cleanse or wash away your sins, but its symbolic. It's only an outward sign of an inward experience."[27] Others point to how references to smudging are found in the Old Testament, and therefore there is scriptural justification for it.

In the case of the use of the drum in worship services, Native members of the COG (Cleveland) note the important role the drum set takes in traditional Pentecostal services — some megachurch drummers could give arena rock band drummers a run for their money — but also that drumming itself is a ministry that can transform people. Although the banning of drums remains one of the longest-held taboos in Christian worship around the world (white missionaries are skeptical of indigenous drumming world-wide as it is believed in many traditional cultures that the drum has a soul of its own), Native contextual believers defend their use of the drum as something distinct from traditional uses. The Cherokee/Creek pastor Larry "Grizz" Brown defended the drum in this way: "We are not a powwow drum, we are not a traditional drum, we are a worship drum. It is a new tradition among born again Native people who walk in the freedom of Worshiping God with the beauty of our dance and song and actions."[28] For COG contextualization practitioners, the drum could be re-made into a new form of religious practice, a religious innovation that incorporated their culture with their new beliefs. Some, however, would say this is syncretism.

Syncretism, or the mixing of certain elements of religions, is viewed suspiciously by white evangelical and Pentecostals. Native theologian Richard Twiss (Twiss retained no denominational affiliation by the end of his life, he is considered an indigenous Christian who was trying to create an indigenous form of evangelical Christianity) pointed out that syncretism is defined by Western culture and therefore might not be applicable to Native culture in his book *Rescuing the Gospel from the Cowboys*. "While theologians and church leaders attempt to define syncretism with "relative objectivity," I don't see this being possible because the conversation is situated within, thus prejudiced by, Western reductionist categories."[29] He goes on to note that "Native North American ministry leaders have never seriously studied its meaning outside these Western categories and are thus predisposed to consider syncretism to be synonymous with biblical heresy."[30] Thus, syncretism is reduced to being a "dirty word" by the very western thinkers who came up with it and that prejudice is passed on to the missionized. Twiss proposes that syncretism "be rescued from 'the Cowboys' or 'Western cultural captivity.'"[31] Twiss sees "syncretism" as a form of religious mixing that is a work in progress: "Rather than creating categories of true and false, I think we would be better served if we considered syncretism to be the exploration of the synthesis of faith, belief, and practice in a dynamic process of blending, adding, subtracting, changing, testing and working things out."[32] When understanding syncretism as a process that is informed by a community, rather than an individual, Twiss believed balance can be achieved, and faithfulness towards Jesus will remain.

Twiss moves to a place where few indigenous Christians will publically go: he points out that whiteness tends to be conflated with American Christianity and that American nationalism is a form of counteractive syncretism that is destructive to Christianity. Twiss notes that this "presupposes an idealized national exceptionalism of God's chosenness [sic], blessing and approval of America. The result is a unique Americanized version of Christianity that directs attention away from identity in Christ and his kingdom."[33] Twiss turns the tables on those who would accuse him of syncretism in his contextualizing movement by instead nothing that American Christianity is syncretic at its very core: it is enmeshed in nationalism and whiteness. White accusations that contextualized indigenous Christianity is syncretic is only to Twiss a false assertion of their own syncretic power.

Twiss's work raises a salient point. How do you decouple Christianity from Western categories and identities in order to make it truly indigenous? Also, what does contextualization look like? Twiss struggled with this himself noting "How are we negotiating our own colonial theological oppression and contextualizing the gospel amongst ourselves as we resist assimilation and struggle for survival within a neo-colonial reality?"[34] Twiss was still a work in progress in articulating a need for indigenous Christianity when he died tragically young, but his defense of the various aspects of contextualization show how he understood how Christianity could become truly indigenous. His goal was to de-couple Christianity from its ugly settler colonial history, and his work lives on through the other leaders of the NAIITS, and the students who continue to argue for a contextualized gospel. Twiss's goal was to remove the whiteness of American Christianity and to make it relevant to his own people. He was able to make this argument because he stood in that void created by exclusion. Free from any denominational controls, Twiss could criticize the colonialist-settler discourse that pervades Christianity in the United States and develop his own form of indigenous Christianity, as well as merge Native traditions with western traditions to create a new form of Christianity.

Conclusion

Native American Christians remain excluded from the centers of white religious power in the United States. Out of that exclusion they created their own space, their own voices and their own theologies and grappled with what it means to be a Native American and a Christian. For some this meant taking traditional Christian theologies such as the indigenous principle and using them to force powerful white denominations such as the AG to acknowledge that Native American believers could be leaders and innovators too. For others, exclusion meant separation and departure from the traditional centers of power for locally-run, non-denominational churches, places where Native believers could decide how to run their own worship services, and which traditional practices to reject or re-frame in their own world-view. Finally, distance from power allowed Native contextual thinkers to re-incorporate traditional rituals into their forms of Pentecostal and evangelical worship on their own terms justified by their understanding of Scripture and culture. In short, exclusion from the centers of white power allowed Native Pentecostals and Evangelicals to create their own centers of indigenous power, as well as their own forms of indigenous Christianity.

The issue of what is an indigenous Christianity is also not uniquely Native American. It is one that is on the minds of Christians around the world. If you manage to de-couple Christianity from Western ideas, then whole new forms of it will flourish and bloom in places like Africa, Latin America and Asia, where the native people of those lands re-interpret Christianity through their own cultures. If anything, this short overview of modern Native American Pentecostalism, neo-Pentecostalism and non-denominational Christianity shows the myriad of ways that indigenous peoples in general reshape Christianity in their own image — how they create their own rules, practices and beliefs depending on how much of their own traditional cultures they want to includes, or reject. Thus, how Native American Christians come to understand their own indigenous Christianity is a barometer for global Christianity in general.

FURTHER READING

Alexander, Corky. *Native American Pentecost: Praxis, Contextualization and Transformation.* Cleveland: Cherohala Press, 2012.

Clatterbuck, Mark. *Crow Jesus: Personal Stories of Native Religious Belonging.* Norman: University of Oklahoma Press, 2017.

Kracht, Benjamin R. *Religious Revitalization Among the Kiowas: The Ghost Dance, Peyote, and Christianity.* Lincoln: University of Nebraska Press, 2018.

Marshall, Kimberly Jenkins. *Upward, Not Sunwise: Resonant Rupture in Navajo Neo-Pentecostalism.* Lincoln: University of Nebraska Press, 2016.

Smith, Andrea. *Native Americans and the Christian Right: The Gendered Politics of Unlikely Alliances.* Durham: Duke University Press, 2008.

Tarango, Angela. *Choosing the Jesus Way: American Indian Pentecostals and the Fight for the Indigenous Principle.* Chapel Hill: University of North Carolina Press, 2014.

Treat, James, ed. *Native and Christian: Indigenous Voices on Religious Identity in the United Stated and Canada.* New York: Routledge, 1996.

Twiss, Richard. *Rescuing the Gospel from the Cowboys: A Native American Expression of the Jesus Way.* Downers Grove: Intervarsity Press, 2015.

NOTES

1 Angela Tarango, *Choosing the Jesus Way: American Indian Pentecostals and the Fight for the Indigenous Principle* (Chapel Hill: University of North Carolina Press, 2014), 85. © 2014 The University of North Carolina Press.

2 See Tarango, chapter 1.

3 Ibid., 84.

4 See Ibid., chapter 3.

5 Home missionaries (versus world, or international missionaries) had always existed within the AG. But the appointment process wasn't made formal until the early 1950s, which is how Lee became the first *appointed* home missionary. The previous missionaries simply set off by themselves without a formal appointment from the denomination and with no funding or support. These are what is known as faith missions.

6 Melvin L. Hodges, *The Indigenous Church* (including *The Indigenous Church and the Missionary*) (Springfield: The Gospel Publishing House, 1976 and 1978).

7 See Tarango, chapters 3 and 4.

8 Tarango, 89–95.

9 Anthropologist Kimberly Jenkins Marshall notes that the term Oodláni only refers to neo-Pentecostal, non-denominational indigenous believers. These are specifically not affiliated with the older Pentecostal denominations such as the AG, Nazarene, or Foursquare. See Kimberly Jenkins Marshall, *Upward Not Sunwise: Resonant Rupture in Navajo Neo-Pentecostalism* (Lincoln: The University of Nebraska Press, 2016), 44.

10 Ibid., 62–63.

11 Tarango, 115.

12 Marshall, 1.

13 Ibid., 3.

14 Ibid., 15.

15 Ibid.

16 Ibid., 71–78.

17 Clatterbuck, Mark, ed., *Crow Jesus: Personal Stories of Native Belonging.* Norman, OK: University of Oklahoma Press, pg 116.

18 Clatterbuck, 102.

19 Ibid., 93.

20 Ibid., 104.

21 Ibid., 107–114.

22 Ibid., 118.

23   Ibid., 125.

24   Ibid., 107.

25   Corky Alexander, *Native American Pentecost: Praxis, Contextualization, Transformation* (Cleveland: Cherohala Press, 2012), 105.

26   See Alexander, chapter 2.

27   Ibid., 59.

28   Ibid., 64.

29   Richard Twiss, *Rescuing the Gospel from the Cowboys: A Native American Expression of the Jesus Way* (Downers Grove: Intervarsity Press, 2015), 29.

30   Ibid.

31   Ibid., 31.

32   Ibid., 33.

33   Ibid., 37.

34   Ibid., 195.

Chapter Twenty-Six

SEX, POLITICS, AND THE RISE OF THE NEW CHRISTIAN RIGHT

Emily Suzanne Johnson
Ball State University, Muncie, Indiana

In many ways, Ronald Reagan defined the 1980s. A charismatic populist conservative, he stood in sharp contrast to the left-wing movements that so many people associated with the 1960s and 1970s.[1] These decades had witnessed rapid social and cultural change, a sexual revolution, and the proliferation of social movements demanding civil rights for minorities of all kinds. Reagan successfully courted voters who felt alienated by these changes, and produced a conservative turn that became known as the "Reagan Revolution." A key component of this revolution was the groundswell of support from a newly mobilized group of mostly white, conservative Christians — a movement that would soon be known as the New Christian Right.

Of course, conservative (and progressive) Christians have been influential in US politics since the nation's beginnings. However, the New Christian Right was different for four key reasons. First, this movement galvanized millions of conservative Christians who had previously been profoundly ambivalent about the idea of political engagement. Second, and relatedly, many of those who became active in this movement first encountered its fundamental ideas not by seeking out activist groups or political publications, but instead through their involvement in a growing conservative Christian subculture that included things like inspirational conferences, self-help books, and Christian pop music. Third, this movement put issues of sex and gender at its center. Leaders vocally opposed abortion, feminism, and homosexuality, and defined their goals around preserving a particular vision of traditional gender and family roles. Earlier movements had sometimes addressed similar issues, but for the New Christian Right, they were at the heart of the movement. Finally, unlike earlier conservative Protestant movements that had been deeply hostile to Catholics, Mormons, and other non-Protestant groups, the New Christian Right thrived by creating alliances between diverse groups of Christians.

This chapter examines the history of this movement and its emergence in the 1970s by focusing on these unique characteristics. Specifically, it asks: why were a majority of conservative Christians ambivalent about political engagement for much of the twentieth century? How did so many go from a belief that "religion and politics don't mix," to the idea that political engagement was a core component of their religious duty? How did a supposedly

A Companion to American Religious History, First Edition. Edited by Benjamin E. Park.
© 2021 John Wiley & Sons, Inc. Published 2021 by John Wiley & Sons, Inc.

apolitical subculture help to facilitate that transition? And finally, did it really bridge centuries-old rifts between disparate Christian groups?

The answers to each of these questions are more complex than they may first seem. Though many conservative Christians were not particularly politically engaged through much of the twentieth century, a long history of conservative Christian activism and lobbying efforts undergirded the emergence of the New Christian Right in the late 1970s. From the perspective of many who became active in this later movement, the sexual revolution of the 1960s was the source of multiple problems now facing the nation, including a growing acceptance of homosexuality, abortion, and feminist critiques of the suburban nuclear family ideal. Yet, these same believers also embraced certain aspects of the sexual revolution in their own flourishing genre of sexual advice manuals by and for conservative Christians. These manuals — along with other seemingly apolitical products of a growing conservative Christian subculture — played an enormous role in developing and disseminating the political assumptions and ideas that would eventually form the basis of the New Christian Right. This included an ongoing negotiation of conservative Protestants' complicated feelings about non-Protestant Christians, even those who largely shared their views on family and politics.

It is essential to understand the nuances of this complicated movement because it changed the political landscape of the United States in fundamental and long-lasting ways. It is the direct precursor of the modern religious right, which continues to have an enormous impact on local and national politics, particularly within the Republican Party. Further, conservative Christian activists and lobbying groups have been some of the most influential forces in legislative debates over education, abortion, and LGBTQ rights over the past several decades. Studying this movement is therefore an essential part of learning about US politics in the past and the present.

Historical Precedents, 1910–1960

When the New Christian Right emerged in the late 1970s, it seemed to many observers to have come out of nowhere. During the preceding decades, there had been Christian influences in American political culture, but there was no widely recognized mass movement that defined its political aims in terms of a mandate from God, as the New Christian Right did. Yet the precedents for this movement stretched back at least a hundred years.

The period between the 1880s and 1920s is known as the Progressive Era because of its overwhelming optimism. Americans in these decades faced issues related to rapid industrialization, urbanization, and unprecedented immigration, but the Progressives believed that they could solve any problem by applying science and expertise. During this time, the "progressive" label was not limited to the leftmost side of the political spectrum. In fact, most Americans identified with Progressive ideals to a certain extent even though they often disagreed about the specifics. For American Protestants, the Progressive fervor was crystallized in the Social Gospel, a theology that tied social reform to religious duty. Social Gospelers were among the nation's most vocal advocates for labor laws, prison reform, and welfare programs for the poor.[2]

But not all Protestants were impressed with the Social Gospel. Between 1910 and 1915, a group of conservative evangelical pastors and theologians published a series of essays called *The Fundamentals*, which decried Progressive reform as a distraction from the "fundamentals" of the faith. They preached that the Bible should be interpreted literally and that Christians should reject any modern ideas that seemed to contradict biblical accounts.[3] In contrast to the more interdenominational movement that emerged in the 1970s, fundamentalists also forcefully condemned non-Protestant Christians, including Catholics and Mormons.[4]

These conservative Protestants were especially troubled by Darwin's theory of evolution, which was then gaining widespread acceptance among scientists and popular audiences. At the time, most Christians accepted the theory as compatible with their belief in a divine creator. Fundamentalists, on the other hand, did not. For them, a literal interpretation of the Bible meant that the world and its contents had to have been fully formed within six days. More than that, they worried that the widespread acceptance of Darwinian evolution indicated a broader cultural turn away from Christianity. They lobbied state legislators to outlaw the teaching of evolution and won some early political victories; by 1925, twenty-one states had considered antievolution bills and five had made it illegal to teach evolution in public schools.[5]

This fight culminated in the 1925 Scopes "Monkey" Trial, in which Tennessee substitute teacher John Scopes was tried for the crime of teaching evolution. The trial was a test case to see whether anti-evolution laws would stand up in court. Two of the nation's most famous lawyers tried the case, which captured unprecedented national media attention. The fundamentalists won in court — Scopes was found guilty and fined — but they were embarrassed in the media. The most famous journalist of the time covered the trial extensively, and described fundamentalists in one instance as, "poor clod[s] ... deluded by childish theology, full of an almost pathological hatred of all learning, all human dignity, all beauty, all fine and noble things."[6] It seemed like fundamentalists had won the court battle but lost the culture war.

However, the fundamentalist movement continued to thrive in the decades that followed, and their preachers continued to decry evolution, communism, and the moral decline that they believed would bring about the apocalypse.[7] After the Second World War, the conservative theologies that had found especially fertile ground in southern states began to gain national influence. In these years, white southerners migrated in large numbers to thriving Sunbelt cities in Texas and Southern California. There, according to historian Darren Dochuk, they congregated in fundamentalist and evangelical churches that mixed familiar social conservatism with a free-market economic philosophy that matched their new upward mobility.[8]

Over the next five decades, fundamentalists and conservative evangelicals also redoubled their efforts toward building a subculture that stretched beyond the churches to include a growing selection of conferences, books, magazines, music, radio programs, schools, and interdenominational networks built by and for like-minded believers.[9] Many of them continued to lobby for political change, but for others, this subcultural cocoon produced a world in which conservative ideas could be taken for granted, not as a hard-fought political ideology but as the basic assumptions that everyone shared. Though they maintained a conservative worldview and were fairly reliable Republican voters between the 1930s and 1960s, fundamentalists were not yet widely recognized as a political movement to be reckoned with.[10] Most did not even regard themselves as political activists.

Indeed, conservative preachers during these decades were as likely to preach a strict separation between religion and politics as they were to encourage their flock to take up political activism. For example, the Baptist pastor Jerry Falwell became one of the leading figures in the New Christian Right in the late 1970s. He helped to found one of the movement's leading organizations — the Moral Majority — and he was always ready with a soundbite when media outlets wanted to report on conservative Christian activism. But in 1965, he preached against the black and white pastors active in the African American civil rights movement. "Nowhere are we commissioned to reform the externals," he argued in a sermon that was also widely distributed as a pamphlet; "We are not told to wage wars against bootleggers, liquor stores, gamblers, murderers, prostitutes, racketeers, prejudiced persons or institutions or any existing evils as such." Instead of taking up political activism, he told his followers, Christians "need to get off the streets and back into the pulpits and into our prayer rooms."[11] For Falwell and many other fundamentalists, however, this perspective would soon begin to shift.

Political Mobilization, 1970s–1980s

For many conservative Christians, political mobilization seemed unnecessary in the 1940s and 1950s because they already saw their values reflected in mainstream American culture. The Cold War began just as the Second World War ended in 1945, and the combination of postwar prosperity and aggressive anticommunism during this period ushered in a particularly conservative moment in American culture and society. Cold War rhetoric was deeply patriotic and often explicitly Christian. Both the Soviet Union and the United States characterized communism as incompatible with religion. American politicians and preachers, therefore, emphasized freedom of religion as a feature of capitalist societies. Most often, they used Christianity as their frame of reference. It was in this context, for example, that Congress added "In God We Trust" to American money and the words "under God" to the pledge of allegiance.[12]

This was also an unusually conservative period when it came to the politics of family and gender. Americans had suffered through a decade of economic depression in the 1930s followed immediately by a massive war effort in the 1940s, and many had put their families on hold. Postwar prosperity and stability made it possible for many white Americans to move out of crowded cities and into suburban homes. During the war, white, married, middle-class women had entered the workforce in unprecedented numbers. After the war, they faced enormous pressure to return to their roles as wives and homemakers. Between 1945 and 1960, Americans got married younger, had more children, and sought divorce less often, on average, than in any other period in the twentieth century.[13] The ideal of the suburban nuclear family with a male breadwinner and happy homemaker became a symbol for the American Way of Life. In the context of the emerging Cold War, the dream of the modern home with a new car in the driveway and all the latest appliances also represented the promise of capitalism and a bulwark against the threat of communism. For conservative Christians, these ideals corresponded with their core belief that the nuclear family had been devised by God as the essential building block of a healthy and righteous nation.

However influential the suburban nuclear family ideal was, though, it was never a universal reality. Soon, it came under fire from several fronts. Throughout the 1950s and 1960s, civil rights leaders pointed out the ways in which people of color had been systematically excluded from the suburbs. Federal policies and private banking practices deliberately made it extraordinarily difficult for black and Latinx people to get home loans. In many suburbs, homeowners signed neighborhood covenants promising never to sell their houses to people of color. In the 1950s and 1960s, landmark Supreme Court cases chipped away at legal segregation, and the Civil Rights Act of 1964 made most forms of public discrimination illegal. Patterns of neighborhood segregation remained entrenched, however, having been cemented in place by generations of racist policies and practices.[14]

Supreme Court rulings on education helped to spur the explosive growth of the conservative Christian school movement in the 1970s. In addition to ordering school desegregation, the Supreme Court in the 1950s and 1960s prohibited mandatory prayer and Bible reading in public schools. Since private schools did not have to observe these rules, many white Christian parents began to send their children to private religious academies. Christian education also appealed to parents who wanted to shield their children from progressive influences in public school curricula, including evolution and sex education. Ultimately, these schools extended the reach of conservative Christian ideology in the lives of believers and helped to produce new national networks of Christian educators and students.[15]

In this context, the 1970 Supreme Court decision in *Green v. Connally* seemed to many conservative Christians like a direct attack on their religious autonomy. The Court ruled that nonprofit organizations that discriminated on the basis of race could lose their tax-exempt status. In theory, this would include most Christian schools, whose students were overwhelmingly white. For many conservative Christians, the issue was not only segregation but also the federal government's apparent effort to interfere in church business. Across the country, sermons, pamphlets, and newsletters warned that *Green* was just the first step in establishing government control over Christian school curricula and even church teachings. These predictions did not materialize, and very few schools lost their tax-exempt status; but for many, this decision added to a growing sense that conservative Christian values were not only falling out of the mainstream but were actually under attack.[16]

Another apparent source of this onslaught was the feminist movement, which was reinvigorated in the 1960s in part through opposition to the postwar suburban family ideal. Betty Friedan's 1963 book, *The Feminine Mystique* — which is often credited with mobilizing a new generation of feminists — centrally criticized this domestic model as a source of "aching dissatisfaction" for many women.[17] Friedan did not directly address church teachings — she was Jewish, after all — but this critique cut to the core of conservative Protestant ideas about the family and its fundamental role in society.

The suburban family ideal was also the target of the 1960s counterculture, which shunned middle-class conformity in favor of radical politics as well as sex, drugs, and rock n' roll. Young people in this decade launched a "sexual revolution" that was also propelled by technological and legal developments. In 1960, the first birth control pill came on the market, making it easier to separate sex from reproduction. Over the next twelve years, a series of Supreme Court cases made it easier for people to get "the Pill" by striking down earlier laws against birth control and sexual education. In 1973, the Court's decision in *Roe v. Wade* decriminalized abortion. Over this same period, the Supreme Court also eased existing obscenity laws, a move which both reflected and contributed to a pattern of more explicit content in popular media. The gay rights movement, which had been quietly active since the 1950s, also experienced a moment of generational change in the 1960s.[18] Gay, lesbian, and trans activists "came out of the closet" *en masse* and vocally advocated for equal rights and protection from discrimination.

No single event led directly to the mass mobilization of conservative Christians, but as a whole, these trends proved deeply troubling for them. Different leaders of the New Christian Right would later point to different moments as the inspiration for the movement. Catholic activist Phyllis Schlafly, for example, began her political career in the 1950s, but it was the 1972 proposal of a gender-based Equal Rights Amendment that helped her to mobilize conservative women nationwide against the feminist movement.[19] Beverly LaHaye, who founded the lobbying group Concerned Women for America in 1979, was similarly drawn into politics through her opposition to feminism, but for her, the crystallizing event was the federally funded, feminist-led International Women's Year Conference in Houston in 1977.[20] Many leaders, including Jerry Falwell, would later say that it was *Roe v. Wade* that convinced them of the need for conservative Christian political action, although many Protestants did not get involved in the anti-abortion movement until years later.[21]

By the mid-1970s, then, the political, cultural, and legal changes that had piled up over the past decade combined to produce a sense of cultural alienation among many conservative Christians. Values that they had once taken for granted were no longer the overwhelming norm in mainstream culture. In fact, many of those values were now the subject of intense controversy.

The Total Woman and a Changing Culture

Sex and gender were hot topics as conservative Christian subculture continued to grow in the 1960s and 1970s, and Christian publishers — who had previously focused on publishing Bibles, Sunday School materials, and books for missionaries — expanded their catalogs to include books for general audiences. Publishers knew that women had long been their most valuable customers, and they began to hire more female authors to write books for women. Following the traditions of conservative ministries, women were generally not allowed to "preach" to mixed-gender audiences, but it was perfectly acceptable for them to teach other women, especially if they focused on issues related to gender, family, and childrearing.[22]

Christian publishers also expanded their offerings by producing conservative Christian versions of popular trends in secular culture. In the 1970s, self-help was one of the bestselling genres of non-fiction; sex advice was especially profitable. The sexual revolution made it more permissible to talk openly about having great sex; it also made people wonder what they could do to improve their own sex lives.[23]

Conservative Christian marriage manuals written during this time mixed conservative messages about gender and family with influences from the sexual revolution. Most audiences that sought out these books were not looking for political messages, but they were seeking marriage advice that would affirm their socially conservative worldviews. The bestselling Christian marital advice manuals of the 1970s are therefore useful sources for understanding the New Christian Right for three reasons. First, they offer crucial insights into how political ideas circulated in the supposedly apolitical spaces of conservative Christian subculture in the years before this movement emerged. Second, they demonstrate how that subculture wrestled with contemporary debates about sex and gender in complicated ways. Third, they demonstrate how the political landscape shifted in the 1970s, such that ideas that might have seemed uncontroversial a decade earlier were now drawn to the center of national cultural and political debates.

When Marabel Morgan published her evangelical marriage manual *The Total Woman* in 1973, she did not think that it had anything to do with politics. The short, peppy book merely offered marital and sexual advice based on Morgan's own experiences. Morgan told readers that she had assumed marriage would be easy — "strawberries for breakfast and lovin' all the time" — but she had found the reality to be much different. Within months of her wedding, the spark had gone out of her relationship; she and her husband were merely "polite" to one another. "Being mediocre in any aspect of life never appealed to me," she wrote, "least of all in marriage." So she read marital advice alongside the Bible and came up with a program that she believed could revive any marriage. It combined a modified version of a patriarchal family ideal with some surprisingly spicy sex advice, including erotic costumes and instructions like: "Tonight is your night for super sex. Prepare, anticipate, and enjoy!"[24]

Morgan's program was based in part on the "doctrine of wifely submission," which had been the basis of marriage ideals in many conservative churches for generations. It comes from a verse from the New Testament, in which the apostle Paul instructed a new church in the city of Ephesus: "Wives, submit yourselves to your own husbands as you do to the Lord. For the husband is the head of the wife as Christ is the head of the church."[25] Over the centuries, different churches have interpreted this verse and its contexts in different ways, but a core tenet of fundamentalism is that the Bible speaks for itself, with no need to consider historical or cultural contexts. Most conservative Protestants in the twentieth-century United States took this verse at face value, preaching that wives should treat their husbands' wills with the same deference that they would pay to God.

Morgan's doctrine of submission, however, was slightly modified. For one thing, she never used the word "submission." Instead, she counseled women to "adapt" to their husbands' needs and desires. She also emphasized that these actions had to spring from a woman's willing and enthusiastic choice rather than an attitude of subservience. Further, she told readers that although God designed husbands to take charge in the home, this did not mean that women were inferior to men or that they could not take on leadership roles in other realms.[26] Compared to the strictest interpretations of submission doctrine, these were significant changes. As evangelical publishers began to hire more female writers in the 1970s, these writers still upheld conservative ideas about gender but also modified and negotiated them in ways that substantially impacted church teaching on these subjects.[27]

Morgan's book became a runaway success. It was one of the first books of Christian marriage advice written by a woman and released by a major evangelical publisher. Even so, it was not expected to do as well as it did, and the publisher only printed five thousand copies initially. Within two years, they had sold over three million. *Total Woman* became a cultural phenomenon. Marabel Morgan was featured on the cover of *Time* magazine and regularly appeared on the major daytime talk shows of the era.[28]

Almost immediately, the book became a touchstone in contemporary political debates about family and gender. Critics called it "out-of-style dogma" and accused Morgan of "setting back the Women's Liberation movement."[29] Morgan has always maintained that she did not intend for the book to engage in politics in any way. "I was stunned that people were angry at me because Charlie and I were finally getting it together and loving each other," she told me in a 2012 interview.[30] Morgan's fans were split on the issue; some agreed with Morgan that the book did not deserve to be embroiled in politics while others saw it as a welcome alternative to feminism. Speaking to the *New York Times* in 1975, one reader insisted: "all the Total Woman course is about is happiness in marriage; it is not opposed to and is not a reaction against women's liberation." Another reader countered, arguing that "women's liberation has cut men to ribbons" and that feminists "don't want to nurture anybody — husbands or children."[31] The wide variety of reactions to Morgan's book are an indication of the cultural fracture that was underway at this time.

From a twenty-first-century perspective, there are aspects of Morgan's book that seem clearly political. Her insistence on a gendered hierarchy within marriage is the most obvious example, but not the only one. Morgan also counseled readers that they should maintain happy marriages not only for their own sakes but also to prevent their children from growing up to be gay. She warned that in a "household off balance," in which "the family leadership was upside down," a son could be at risk to "identify with his mother and begin to develop certain feminine qualities on a subconscious level." In such a case, Morgan wrote, "the door is open to homosexuality."[32]

Yet, as she wrote *Total Woman*, Morgan had good reason to believe that these ideas would not be controversial. Throughout the postwar period and into the 1970s, this was standard fare in pop psychology, women's magazines, and popular culture writ large. The specter of overbearing mothers who produced gay sons even had a name — "momism" — coined by author Philip Wylie in his 1942 bestseller *A Generation of Vipers*.[33]

By the time that *Total Woman* was published in 1973, these ideas were in flux. Feminist critiques of mainstream ideas about gender and family were beginning to gain widespread attention. One key feminist insight was the idea that the "personal is political." In other words, feminists argued that "politics" were not limited to the realm of elections and activism, but were also embedded in the assumptions, oppressions, and power imbalances that make up everyday life. For feminists, this was an exciting new frontier. For many conservatives, it felt like an incursion that brought controversy and condemnation into a realm that should have been a refuge from the stresses of the outside world.

For Morgan and many of her readers, the critical reaction to *Total Woman* crystallized a sense of cultural alienation that had already been percolating. In response to feminist critiques of her book, Morgan told a reporter, "I'm not anti-feminist. I'm pro-happiness in marriage." But she lamented that "feminists have set up a nine-to-five as an ideal for women and have made the woman at home feel like a dodo."[34] As contemporary feminists criticized patriarchal family relationships and emphasized women's work outside of the home, they often assumed that all women were either on board with feminist ideas, or at least would be if they were properly educated in gender politics. For women who wanted to be stay-at-home wives and mothers, feminism sometimes seemed less liberating and more like an unwelcome attack on their lives and values.

Over the following decades, other supposedly apolitical texts like marriage manuals continued to introduce conservative Christians to the political assumptions of a growing movement. In some cases — like Morgan's — this may have been unintentional. In other cases, it was part of a deliberate strategy. In the 1970s to the early 2000s, political organizer Beverly LaHaye purposefully used evangelical subculture to mobilize new political activists. Like Morgan, she began her career as a writer of Christian marital advice, but both she and her husband went on to be leading figures in the New Christian Right. In 1979, she founded the lobbying group Concerned Women for America (CWA), which quickly became the largest political group for conservative Christian women nationwide. She continued to publish advice manuals for evangelical women that followed the patterns of apolitical books like Morgan's, but she also began to incorporate overt political messages and calls to action, including explicitly antifeminist messages and information about how to join CWA.[35]

Another popular genre of Christian writing during this time was apocalyptic nonfiction, which applied biblical prophecy to contemporary events. One of the most popular books of the 1970s — on both Christian and secular bestseller lists — was Hal Lindsey's *The Late Great Planet Earth* (1970). In it, Lindsey spoke about the nuclear bomb and developments in the Middle East as the fulfillment of biblical prophecies about the end of time. The book was not partisan, but its interpretations of modern global events helped to shape conservative Protestant perspectives on foreign affairs. For example, Israel and Jerusalem play central roles in evangelical apocalypticism, which has influenced conservative Christians' strong support for the modern Israeli state.[36]

Not all conservative Christians who came to identify themselves as political activists during this period shared this same experience of political mobilization. Many came to political activism through single-issue campaigns that drew them into participation in the broader movement. Others were mobilized through the National Association of Evangelicals, the main conservative Christian lobbying group of the postwar decades. However, books like Morgan's, LaHaye's, and Lindsey's were part of a growing subculture that shaped the underlying politics of the movement and helped to circulate its core beliefs. Because the books, magazines, conferences, televangelist networks, and other media of this subculture were mostly at least superficially apolitical, they reached wide audiences of people not yet willing to identify as political activists nor likely to seek out explicitly political publications or groups. To a certain extent, this subculture also insulated believers from the social and political changes of the 1960s and therefore contributed to a more severe experience of cultural alienation in the 1970s.

The Rise of the New Christian Right

When the New Christian Right emerged as a powerful political force in the late 1970s, it was built on a political and cultural foundation that had developed over several decades. But for much of the mid-twentieth century, conservative Christians expressed a profound aversion toward direct political engagement. Even Billy Graham, the nation's most famous evangelist and a spiritual advisor to several presidents, warned churches to "stay out of straight politics."[37]

This characteristic political ambivalence eroded over the course of the 1970s. Conservative evangelicals and their beliefs came to mainstream attention in part through the election of Southern Baptist president Jimmy Carter. Though many were initially enthusiastic about the prospect of one of their own in the White House, Carter soon disappointed them in his approach to issues that mattered most. For many conservative Christian leaders, this experience with the Carter presidency was a turning point, convincing them that it was both necessary and possible for their movement to begin to wield real influence in the nation's politics.

In 1976, when Jimmy Carter ran for president for the first time, most Americans were not familiar with the term "evangelical," and Carter's frequent self-identification as evangelical helped to bring the term into the public consciousness. Reflecting this new public awareness, a *Newsweek* cover story even declared 1976 "the year of the evangelical." Carter's relationship with fundamentalists and other conservative Protestants was often complicated — especially after Carter agreed to sit down for an interview with *Playboy* magazine — but many were sufficiently impressed by his Southern Baptist credentials and his frequent professions of faith in order to vote for him that year.[38]

Carter was a Democrat, but he ran as a political outsider. Just two years earlier, Republican president Richard Nixon had been forced to resign under the weight of the Watergate scandal. Carter's campaign represented him as a folksy alternative to the corruption in Washington. In 1976, the party lines were also not quite the same as they are today. During the Civil War in the 1860s, and for several decades afterward, the Democrats were the party of white supremacist confederates. During the twentieth century, Southern Democrats continued to advocate for segregation and other socially conservative policies, but Democrats in the north moved to the left on issues including race, gender, and labor. This growing split in the Democratic Party intensified when Democratic president Lyndon B. Johnson signed the sweeping Civil Rights Act in 1964. That same year, far-right Republican presidential candidate Barry Goldwater campaigned on a populist platform that appealed to many conservatives who were beginning to feel alienated within the Democratic Party. Goldwater lost the election, but subsequent Republican candidates, including Richard Nixon, continued to court conservative Christian voters. When Jimmy Carter ran for president in 1976, this transition was still underway. Many of the "culture war" issues that would define the political divide of the 1980s — including feminism, abortion, and gay rights — were therefore not yet clearly split along party lines.

Very quickly, though, Carter disappointed conservative Christians who had voted for him. His presidency was marked by economic, political, and diplomatic crises. Many Americans were unimpressed with Carter's performance, but conservative Christians were especially disillusioned with his approach to the politics of gender and family. Although Carter personally opposed homosexuality and abortion, he did not believe that it was the government's role to regulate these issues.[39] During his term, he sponsored the UN-backed International Women's Year Conference in Houston in 1977 and promoted the organization of a White House Conference on Families in 1979. In both cases, conservative evangelicals were outraged at Carter's apparent willingness to work with feminists and gay-rights advocates, even as he tried to appease all sides.

By the time Carter ran for re-election in 1980, he had lost the support of most conservative Christian voters. However, his presidency had helped to build new networks of conservative Christian powerbrokers and to convince them that they could — and should — build a movement that could more effectively shape political developments moving forward.[40]

In the year leading up to the election, Christian Right luminaries Jerry Falwell, Pat Robertson, Tim LaHaye, and Paul Weyrich formed the Moral Majority, an organization that would become the leading voice of the movement over the next several years. Their goal was to transform conservative Christians' concerns about issues like abortion, homosexuality, obscenity, and feminism from sporadic single-issue campaigns into a broadbased and sustained movement that could influence public policy in the long term. They mobilized grassroots support by reaching through existing church and activist networks to publicize specific issues and events, and the *Moral Majority* newsletter disseminated information to supporters. Even more important, the organization articulated a framework for conservative Christian activism that brought together a wide range of longstanding concerns using the rhetoric of cultural alienation, national moral decline, and apocalyptic urgency.

The Moral Majority proved to be short-lived, lasting less than a decade, but the New Christian Right was never a movement with a single leader or organizational hierarchy. During the late 1970s and 1980s, conservative Christian groups proliferated, forming new networks that sustained conservative Christian activism and influence. For preachers, these organizations also created a space for direct political engagement without threatening the tax-exempt status of their churcghes.[41]

One of the defining characteristics of this new movement was its embrace of interdenominational cooperation between previously antagonistic groups of Protestants as well as Catholics, Mormons, and other religious conservatives. Anticatholicism and antimormonism had been core concerns for conservative evangelicals for decades. One of the National Evangelical Association's biggest campaigns, for instance, had centered around their opposition to the election of a Catholic president (John F. Kennedy) in 1960.[42] For evangelicals, however, the belief that contemporary moral decline was literally apocalyptic helped to justify at least temporary interdenominational cooperation.

In the late 1970s, influential evangelical writer Francis Schaeffer promoted the idea of "co-belligerency" to define this approach to interdenominational cooperation. Schaeffer wanted to encourage evangelical Protestants to join the anti-abortion movement, which was then overwhelmingly Catholic. He argued that Catholics and other non-Protestant conservatives were "co-belligerents," which he defined as "a person with whom I do not agree on all sorts of vital issues, but who, for whatever reason of their own, is on the same side in a fight for some specific issue of public justice."[43] Unlike the early twentieth-century fundamentalists who saw Catholicism and Mormonism as dire threats, Schaeffer argued that non-Protestants could be provisional allies in more urgent political battles.

Another major organization founded in 1979 exemplifies this trend. Concerned Women for America (CWA) was founded by Beverly LaHaye to organize conservative women in opposition to a feminist movement that they believed worked against their interests. Within a few years, the organization claimed its place as the largest conservative women's lobbying group in the nation, with its headquarters in Washington, DC and local chapters in nearly every state. Yet, from the beginning, LaHaye consistently claimed that CWA was the *only* conservative Christian women's organization in the country, even though she was well aware of Catholic activist Phyllis Schlafly, whose groups STOP ERA and the Eagle Forum had played a major role in defeating the feminist-backed Equal Rights Amendment. For Catholic women, LaHaye's oversight may have seemed like a simple mistake, but for fundamentalist women who had grown up hearing that Catholicism was not "real" Christianity, it sent the message that CWA was still committed to fundamentalist Protestantism regardless of any alliances with non-fundamentalist groups.

The New Christian Right quickly gained national recognition in part thanks to the mobilization of grassroots supporters across the country. Their strength in numbers was underscored by the April 1980 Washington for Jesus rally, which attracted hundreds of thousands of conservative Christian activists to the national mall just seven months before that year's presidential election.

The eagerness of the Reagan campaign and subsequent Republican Party candidates to court conservative evangelical voters also contributed to the movement's rapid rise. Campaigning for the presidency in 1980, Reagan famously told a group of conservative Christian leaders, "I know you can't endorse me, but I want you to know that I endorse you and what you are doing."[44] Though he did not adopt New Christian Right positions wholesale, he aligned with this movement on key issues and frequently deployed a language of religious nationalism that appealed to these voters. In return, they helped to deliver him the presidency in 1980 and again in 1984.

Conclusion

In the decades that followed, this conservative Christian coalition continued to develop new networks and new strategies. Conservative Christian candidates ran for office at the local, state, and national levels. They litigated cases before state and federal Supreme Courts. They organized grassroots groups and founded sophisticated professional lobbying firms. They pursued ballot measures and organized get-out-the-vote campaigns. And they continued to connect through a growing subculture of political and purportedly apolitical books, music, conferences, and television.

They also expanded their influence within the Republican Party through professional lobbying and reliable voting. By the early twenty-first century, many pundits and political organizers defined the Republican base in terms of conservative Christian concerns. Outside of the party, they played an outsized role in directing the national conversation on the moral issues that concerned them most. The Culture Wars of the 1980s and 1990s were shaped by political fracture over issues like abortion, feminism, and gay rights. In the twenty-first century, conservative Christian activists have continued to organize around these issues, spending millions of dollars and untold volunteer hours to protect their vision for the nation.

Understanding this movement is therefore essential for anyone who wants to understand the politics of the United States, now or in the recent past. The apparently meteoric rise of the religious right was based on political and cultural trends that stretch back to the beginning of the twentieth century. In the 1960s and 1970s, rapid cultural change and a shifting political landscape contributed to a widespread sense of alienation and profound concern among many conservative Christians. Party politics also underwent a fundamental shift during this period, prompting the Republican Party and conservative Christian leaders to forge a relationship that helped to bring both into power. The defining characteristics of this movement — including its core theological identity, its relationship to politics, and its perspective on sex and gender — are all products of a surprisingly complex history that offers important insight into a group that continues to wield extraordinary influence in American politics and society.

FURTHER READING

Dochuk, Darren. *From Bible Belt to Sunbelt: Plain Folk Religion, Grassroots Conservatism, and the Rise of Evangelical Conservatism*. New York: W. W. Norton, 2010.

Dowland, Seth. "'Family Values' and the Formation of a Christian Right Agenda," *Church History* 78, no. 3 (September 2009): 606–631.

Lienesch, Michael. *Redeeming America: Piety & Politics in the New Christian Right*. Chapel Hill: University of North Carolina Press, 1993.

McGirr, Lisa. *Suburban Warriors: The Origins of the New American Right*. Rev. ed. Princeton: Princeton University Press, 2015.

Nickerson, Michelle. *Mothers of Conservatism: Women and the Postwar Right*. Princeton: Princeton University Press, 2012.

Petro, Anthony. *After the Wrath of God: AIDS, Sexuality, and American Religion*. Oxford: Oxford University Press, 2015.

Vaca, Daniel. *Evangelicals Incorporated: Books and the Business of Religion in America*. Cambridge, MA: Harvard University Press, 2019.

BIBLIOGRAPHY

Amstutz, Mark. *Evangelicals and American Foreign Policy*. New York: Oxford University Press, 2014.

Boyer, Paul. *When Time Shall Be No More: Prophecy Belief in Modern American Culture*. Cambridge, MA: The Belknap Press of Harvard University Press, 1992.

Carpenter, Joel. *Revive Us Again: The Reawakening of American Fundamentalism*. New York: Oxford University Press, 1997.

Critchlow, Donald T. *Phyllis Schlafly and Grassroots Conservatism: A Woman's Crusade.* Princeton: Princeton University Press, 2005.

D'Emilio, John. *Sexual Politics, Sexual Communities: The Making of a Homosexual Minority in the United States, 1940–1970.* 2nd ed. Chicago: University of Chicago Press, 1998.

Davis, Rebecca L. *More Perfect Unions: The American Search for Marital Bliss.* Cambridge, MA: Harvard University Press, 2010.

DeRogatis, Amy. "What Would Jesus Do? Sexuality and Salvation in Protestant Evangelical Sex Manuals, 1950s to Present." *Church History* 74, no. 1 (May 2005): 97–137.

Dochuk, Darren. *From Bible Belt to Sunbelt: Plain Folk Religion, Grassroots Conservatism, and the Rise of Evangelical Conservatism.* New York: W. W. Norton, 2010.

Dowland, Seth. *Family Values and the Rise of the New Christian Right.* Philadelphia: University of Pennsylvania Press, 2017.

Evans, Christopher H. *The Social Gospel in American Religion: A History.* New York: New York University Press, 2017.

Flippen, J. Brooks. *Jimmy Carter, the Politics of Family, and the Rise of the New Christian Right.* Athens: University of Georgia Press, 2011.

Friedan, Betty. *The Feminine Mystique.* Revised and updated. New York: W. W. Norton, 2001.

Griffith, R. Marie. *God's Daughter's: Evangelical Women and the Power of Submission.* Berkeley: University of California Press, 2000.

Harding, Susan Friend. *The Book of Jerry Falwell: Fundamentalist Language and Politics.* Princeton: Princeton University Press, 2000.

Johnson, Emily Suzanne. *This Is Our Message: Women's Leadership in the New Christian Right.* New York: Oxford University Press, 2019.

Kleiman, Carol. "Only room for one boss in the 'Total Woman's' home." *Chicago Tribune*, March 23, 1975.

Kruse, Kevin M. *One Nation Under God: How Corporate America Invented Christian America.* New York: Hachette Book Group, 2015.

LaHaye, Beverly. *The Restless Woman.* Grand Rapids: Zondervan, 1984.

_____. *I Am a Woman by God's Design.* Old Tappan: Fleming H. Revell, 1980.

Levine, Jo Ann. "Housewife a dodo? Not at all." *The Christian Science Monitor*, March 24, 1975.

Lienesch, Michael. *In the Beginning: Fundamentalism, the Scopes Trial, and the Making of the Antievolution Movement.* Chapel Hill: University of North Carolina Press, 2007.

Marsden, George M. *Fundamentalism and American Culture.* 2nd ed. Oxford: Oxford University Press, 2006.

May, Elaine Tyler. *Homeward Bound: American Families in the Cold War Era.* New York: Perseus Group, 2011.

Mencken, H. L. "In Memoriam: William Jennings Bryan." *Baltimore Sun*, July 27, 1925.

Meyerowitz, Joanne. "Women and Gender in Postwar America, 1945–1960." In *Not June Cleaver: Women and Gender in Postwar America, 1945–1960.* Philadelphia: Temple University Press, 1994.

Morgan, Marabel (author of *Total Woman*), interview with author, September 11, 2012.

_____. *Total Woman.* Old Tappan: Fleming H. Revell, 1973.

Plant, Rebecca Jo. *Mom: The Transformation of Motherhood in Modern America.* Chicago: University of Chicago Press, 2010.

Schaeffer, Francis A. *The Complete Works of Francis A. Schaffer: A Christian Worldview.* 2nd ed. Vol. 7. Westchester: Crosswar Books, 1985.

Sugrue, Thomas J. *The Origins of the Urban Crisis: Race and Inequality in Postwar Detroit.* Rev. ed. Princeton: Princeton University Press, 2005.

Sutton, Matthew Avery. *American Apocalypse: A History of Modern Evangelicalism.* Cambridge, MA: Harvard University Press, 2017.

Time. "Fighting the Housewife Blues." March 14, 1977.

Troy, Gil. *The Reagan Revolution: A Very Short Introduction.* Oxford: Oxford University Press, 2009.

Warren, Virginia Lee. "In This Day of Liberation, They Study How to Please Their Men." *New York Times*, June 28, 1975.

Williams, Daniel K. *God's Own Party: The Making of the Christian Right.* New York: Oxford University Press, 2010.

Young, Neil J. *We Gather Together: The Religious Right and the Problem of Interfaith Politics.* New York: Oxford University Press, 2016.

NOTES

1   Gil Troy, *The Reagan Revolution: A Very Short Introduction* (Oxford: Oxford University Press, 2009).

2   Christopher H. Evans, *The Social Gospel in American Religion: A History* (New York: New York University Press, 2017), 2.

3   "Evangelical" and "fundamentalist" are both tricky terms to define, because neither is confined to a single denomination. Generally speaking, evangelicalism is a type of Protestant Christianity that emphasizes an emotional conversion experience, a personal relationship with God, and the practice of trying to convert others (also known as evangelizing). It has its roots in the early 1700s. Fundmentalism is a subset of evangelicalism, which emphasizes biblical literalism. Most conservative Protestants in the United States have been influenced by both of these theologies.

4   George M. Marsden, *Fundamentalism and American Culture*, 2nd ed. (Oxford: Oxford University Press, 2006), 118–120.

5   Michael Lienesch, *In the Beginning: Fundamentalism, the Scopes Trial, and the Making of the Antievolution Movement* (Chapel Hill: The University of North Carolina Press, 2007), 115.

6   H. L. Mencken, "In Memoriam: William Jennings Bryan," *Baltimore Sun*, July 27, 1925.

7   Matthew Avery Sutton, *American Apocalypse: A History of Modern Evangelicalism* (Cambridge, MA: Harvard University Press, 2014), 177.

8   Darren Dochuk, *From Bible Belt to Sun Belt: Plain Folk Religion, Grassroots Conservatism, and the Rise of Evangelical Conservatism* (New York: W. W. Norton, 2010).

9   Joel Carpenter, *Revive Us Again: The Reawakening of American Fundamentalism* (New York: Oxford University Press), 3–4.

10 Sutton, *American Apocalypse*, 352.

11 Jerry Falwell, "Ministers and Marchers," (1965), quoted in: Susan Friend Harding, *The Book of Jerry Falwell: Fundamentalist Language and Politics* (Princeton: Princeton University Press, 2000), 22.

12 Kevin M. Kruse, *One Nation Under God: How Corporate America Invented Christian America* (New York: Hachette Book Group, 2015), xiii. As Kruse argues, these developments had roots in the 1930s and 1940s, but it was no accident that they emerged with such force in the Cold War era.

13 Elaine Tyler May, *Homeward Bound: American Families in the Cold War Era* (New York: Perseus Group, 2011), 1–8. Of course, postwar culture was not monolithic and many women remained in the workforce and maintained other public roles; see Joanne Meyerowitz, ed., *Not June Cleaver: Women and Gender in Postwar America, 1945–1960* (Philadelphia: Temple University Press, 1994).

14 Thomas J. Sugrue, *The Origins of the Urban Crisis: Race and Inequality in Postwar Detroit*, rev. ed. (Princeton: Princeton University Press, 2005).

15 Seth Dowland, *Family Values and the Rise of the New Christian Right* (Philadelphia: University of Pennsylvania Press, 2017), 25–38.

16 Dowland, *Family Values*, 46.

17 Betty Friedan, *The Feminine Mystique*, revised and updated (New York: W.W. Norton, 2001 [1963]), 33.

18 John D'Emilio, *Sexual Politics, Sexual Communities: The Making of a Homosexual Minority in the United States, 1940–1970*, 2nd ed. (Chicago: University of Chicago Press, 1998).

19 Donald T. Critchlow, *Phyllis Schlafly and Grassroots Conservatism: A Woman's Crusade* (Princeton: Princeton University Press, 2005).

20 Emily Suzanne Johnson, *This Is Our Message: Women's Leadership in the New Christian Right* (New York: Oxford University Press, 2019), 79.

21 Susan Friend Harding, *The Book of Jerry Falwell*, 189–190, 195.

22 Johnson, *This Is Our Message*, 25–31.

23 See also: Rebecca L. Davis, *More Perfect Unions: The American Search for Marital Bliss* (Cambridge, MA: Harvard University Press, 2010), 204–211; Amy DeRogatis, "What Would Jesus Do? Sexuality and Salvation in Protestant Evangelical Sex Manuals, 1950s to the Present," *Church History* 74, no. 1 (March 2005): 97–137.

24 Marabel Morgan, *Total Woman* (Old Tappan: Fleming H. Revell, 1973), 15–16, 22–27, 126. "Adapt to him" was part of Morgan's central four-step program, which also included "admire Him," "accept him," and "appreciate him."

25   Ephesians 5:22–23 (New International Version).

26   Marabel Morgan, *Total Woman* (Old Tappan: Fleming H. Revell, 1973), 70–71.

27   Johnson, *This Is Our Message*, 22; R. Marie Griffith, *God's Daughter's: Evangelical Women and the Power of Submission* (Berkeley: University of California Press, 2000).

28   Johnson, *This Is Our Message*, 21.

29   "Fighting the Housewife Blues," *Time*, March 14, 1977, 62–70; Carol Kleiman, "Only room for one boss in the 'Total Woman's' home," *Chicago Tribune*, March 23, 1975, D3.

30   Marabel Morgan, interview with author, September 11, 2012.

31   Virginia Lee Warren, "In This Day of Liberation, They Study How to Please Their Men," *New York Times*, June 28, 1975, 14.

32   Morgan, *Total Woman*, 147–148.

33   Rebecca Jo Plant, *Mom: The Transformation of Motherhood in Modern America* (Chicago: University of Chicago Press, 2010), 19–54.

34   Jo Ann Levine, "Housewife a dodo? Not at all," *The Christian Science Monitor*, March 24, 1975, 13.

35   Beverly LaHaye, *I Am a Woman by God's Design* (Old Tappan: Fleming H. Revell, 1980); Beverly LaHaye, *The Restless Woman* (Grand Rapids: Zondervan, 1984).

36   Paul Boyer, *When Time Shall Be No More: Prophecy Belief in Modern American Culture* (Cambridge, MA: The Belknap Press of Harvard University Press, 1992), 212–213; Mark Amstutz, *Evangelicals and American Foreign Policy* (New York: Oxford University Press, 2014), 118–119, 237.

37   Daniel K. Williams, *God's Own Party: The Making of the Christian Right* (New York: Oxford University Press, 2010), 69.

38   J. Brooks Flippen, *Jimmy Carter, the Politics of Family, and the Rise of the New Christian Right* (Athens: University of Georgia Press, 2011).

39   Flippen, *Carter*, 21.

40   Williams, *God's Own Party*, 159.

41   Williams, *God's Own Party*, 177.

42   Williams, *God's Own Party*, 50–52.

43   Neil J. Young, *We Gather Together: The Religious Right and the Problem of Interfaith Politics* (New York: Oxford University Press, 2016), 172–173; Francis A. Schaeffer, *The Complete Works of Francis A. Schaeffer: A Christian Worldview*, 2nd ed., vol. 4 (Westchester: Crosswar Books, 1985), 30.

44   Williams, *God's Own Party*, 187.

Chapter Twenty-Seven

IMMIGRATION AND RELIGION AMONG CHINESE AMERICANS, 1965 TO THE PRESENT

Melissa May Borja
University of Michigan, Ann Arbor, Michigan

Chinatown in lower Manhattan is well known as one of New York City's densest ethnic enclaves and busiest commercial hubs, but less appreciated is the significance of the neighborhood as a center of spiritual and religious life. A stroll through Chinatown's streets reveals a rich array of beliefs, practices, identities, and institutions. There is the majestic Mahayana Buddhist temple, which houses a sixteen-foot Buddha statue, the tallest in city. On Mott Street, the historic heart of Chinatown, there is a more modest Eastern States Buddhist Temple. Further down Mott lies the Church of Transfiguration; once serving Irish and Italian Catholics, it now ministers to Chinese Catholics and celebrates Mass in both English and Mandarin. Around the corner, on Bowery, is the Huang Da Xian Taoist Temple, and throughout the neighborhood are Baptist, Lutheran, Methodist, and Presbyterian Chinese churches. And, finally, there are thousands of Chinese homes, restaurants, and shops where families conduct rituals to show respect to their ancestors, to honor gods and spirits, and to ensure prosperity, health, and good luck.

The vibrancy of religious life in Chinatown makes clear that religion remains important in the lives of immigrants starting life anew in the United States. Historians of American immigration — including Oscar Handlin, the great mid-century scholar who wrote one of the first major histories of American immigration — made this observation over half a century ago. Writing about "the uprooted" immigrants from Europe in the nineteenth and twentieth century, Handlin observed that "[a] man holds dear what little is left. When much is lost, there is no risking the remainder."[1] Historians of European immigration to the United States have long paid attention to religion and its significance to the preservation of ethnic identity — how, for example, popular religious rituals were central to the life of urban Italian American communities early in the twentieth century.[2] Historians of Asian American religious history — a more recent field of study — have found a similar pattern: that Asian immigrants have also held fast to religious and cultural traditions, a fact evidenced by the many shrines, temples, and churches in Chinatown.

Importantly, the religious life of immigrants is not simply a story about preservation, but also of transformation. Recreating religious communities and continuing religious beliefs and practices have required immigrants to adjust and adapt to the specific social, cultural, legal, and economic conditions of the United States. At the same time, immigration has

A Companion to American Religious History, First Edition. Edited by Benjamin E. Park.
© 2021 John Wiley & Sons, Inc. Published 2021 by John Wiley & Sons, Inc.

changed the religious lives of not just immigrants, but all Americans who have had to adjust and adapt as their neighborhoods — and their nation more generally — have become more religiously diverse. Focusing on the religious lives of Chinese Americans throughout the past half century, this essay explores the intertwined histories of religion and immigration in the United States, and it uses the case of Chinese Americans to illustrate how new immigration laws and new immigrant communities have created a more complex religious America in the post-World War II era.

This essay argues that immigration has changed religious life in four main ways. To begin, immigration has played a significant role in changing the religious composition of American society. Beginning in the nineteenth century, state and federal immigration laws excluded particular racial and religious groups — the 1882 Chinese Exclusion Act, for instance, owed in part to white Christian hostility toward Chinese people whom they perceived as godless, immoral "heathens." However, immigration reforms in the middle of the twentieth century, most notably the 1965 Hart-Celler Act, opened the door to new immigrant populations that have contributed to growing numbers of non-Christian groups in the United States as well as greater diversity within American Christianity. Reflecting these trends are the religious demographics of the Chinese American community, which includes Christians of all denominations; practitioners of Buddhism, Daoism, Confucianism, and folk religions; and many people who, for various reasons, fall under the category of religious "nones." In the face of all of these changes, the white Christian American population has often responded with ambivalence. While some people have embraced religious diversity as a symbol of American exceptionalism, religious hostility has also remained central to xenophobic and nativist movements in the United States.

In addition to changing the religious demographics of the United States, immigration has also changed the institutional landscape of American religion. Like those who arrived earlier, recent immigrants have valued their religious beliefs, practices, identities, and institutions and have gone to great efforts to transplant them in the United States. They have done so for several reasons. For one, religious beliefs, practices, and identities have provided strength and support for immigrants, and religious institutions have been an important means for immigrants to gain greater security as they build new lives in America. These religious institutions, especially the Protestant-style congregations that have attracted most of the attention of social science research, have been significant sites of immigrant integration and mutual aid.

The activities at these religious institutions extend beyond what is obviously religious. Churches and temples have functioned as community centers where immigrants provide material support to one another, develop connections with members of their ethnic group, and even become activists who advocate for more just immigration policies. Again, white Christian Americans have offered only a lukewarm welcome to these new religious institutions, but immigrant communities have persisted in establishing their own religious institutions, despite the barriers and opposition.

The determination of immigrants to claim their own place in the American religious landscape is part of a broader effort to claim their own place in American public life, which raises the third theme of this essay: that immigration has changed the public square, including how Americans put ideals of freedom, tolerance, and pluralism into practice. As immigrant communities adhering to minority religious traditions have become more established, they have also become more vocal and assertive in insisting on rights, respect, recognition, and representation. From changing local educational policies to bringing First Amendment cases before the Supreme Court, they have argued that they, too, belong in the United States and should be free to practice their religion unencumbered by legal restriction or personal prejudice. At the same time, immigration and its associated religious diversity have given rise to ongoing debates about what it means to be "American" and how American people should make good on their commitment to religious freedom and religious pluralism.

These are not easy issues to resolve, in part because while Americans generally agree that there should be no prohibition on the free exercise of religion, there is no universal understanding of what defines "religion." This matter highlights the final issue of this essay, which is that immigration has broadened the category of religion and changed what it means to be religious. Historically, Americans defined religion primarily on Protestant terms. However, immigrants, especially those coming from predominantly non-Christian countries like China, often adhere to beliefs and practices that do not easily fit the Protestant template for religion. As a result, their efforts to secure rights, recognition, respect, and representation have involved challenging Protestant norms of belief and practice — in courtrooms and in classrooms, and even in how scholars have studied religion. In numerous ways, Chinese American religious life reveals important shifts in how Americans are understanding and governing religion in the United States today.

Immigration and the Changing Religious Composition of American Society

The religious diversity for which the United States is famous has always owed, at least in part, to immigration. Before the United States had even been founded as a nation, migration — whether forced or voluntary — brought to North America people with different religious beliefs, practices, and institutional affiliations, adding to the rich array of spiritual traditions of Native people. Indeed, one of the most powerful founding stories that continues to shape American self-imagining today is that of the English Pilgrims, a religious community that migrated to North America with a distinctively religious vision for their new life in America. The Pilgrims' vision, of course, was ultimately complicated by the presence of other groups of people who had a different religion and their own vision for America — Native Americans, most obviously, as well as non-Protestant migrants. The enduring power of this founding Pilgrim narrative, however, reveals that Americans have always understood religion and migration as intertwined and have long cherished the idea of America as a place that draws people of faith in search of great religious possibility.

While the migration of religious people has been source of national pride, it has also been a source of anxiety and animosity. Indeed, the story of migration to the United States is not only one of welcome but also of restriction and exclusion. Immigration historians have offered detailed accounts about how white efforts to uphold racial hierarchies have propelled local, state, and federal efforts to limit both immigration and access to citizenship.[3] Immigration restrictionists have often intentionally crafted immigration laws to keep out people who are poor and deemed a threat to public health and morality.[4] However, the development of immigration laws intended to restrict and exclude have also played a critical role in limiting religious diversity and shaping the religious composition of the United States. In the formation of these laws, religion and race operated in tandem: ideas about religious difference were central to ideas about racial difference.

Throughout American history, immigration restrictions have functioned as powerful instruments of reproducing the racial and religious homogeneity of the nation. The first restrictions developed during the antebellum period at the state and local level, with the intention of keeping out poor Irish Catholics, whom Protestant Americans feared were too loyal to the Pope and the Catholic Church to be loyal to the United States.[5] Later, federal laws such as the Chinese Exclusion Act of 1882 further protected the Protestant majority. White Americans behind the push for Chinese Exclusion considered the Chinese a racially inferior group that damaged the prospects of free white laborers and a heathen, vice-ridden population that endangered the morality of Christian America.[6] And though the Chinese Exclusion Act targeted the Chinese, its impact reached more broadly, by facilitating the shift of the United States into a gate-keeping nation and helping establish the bureaucratic infra-structure for enforcing immigration laws, controlling borders, and regulating citizenship.[7]

The racial and religious nativism of the pre-World War II period culminated in the Johnson-Reed Act of 1924. Among other things, this legislation created a set of discriminatory national origins quotas that favored immigrants from Northern and Western Europe and limited immi-grants from Southern and Eastern Europe. In addition, the Johnson-Reed Act also excluded all people who were ineligible for citizenship — including Asian people who were racially ineli-gible for citizenship because of Supreme Court decisions that had determined that Asian people are not white.[8] Although the Johnson-Reed Act focused most explicitly on the catego-ries of nation and race, there were also religious causes and consequences of this landmark legislation. The virulent nativism that produced the Johnson-Reed Act was animated in part by religious animosity directed toward the large numbers of Catholics and Jews who had immigrated to the United States in the four decades preceding 1924, and the discriminatory national origins quotas and the exclusion of people who were racially ineligible for citizenship together effectively shut out many non-Protestant immigrants.

However, the middle of the twentieth century brought new social and political circum-stances that paved the way for new immigration laws. Immigration reforms arose in part from international concerns — in particular, the foreign policy imperative of maintaining amicable relations with allies during the Second World War and the Cold War. In addition, the domes-tic Civil Rights politics of the postwar period contributed to efforts to similarly challenge immigration laws. During the decades after the Second World War, Americans grappled with the "American dilemma" of enduring racism and prejudice, and Black Americans led efforts to end racial discrimination and secure equal rights. In a similar vein, the children of Eastern and Southern European immigrants who had arrived earlier in the twentieth century began to advocate for fairer laws and equal treatment. Having proven their Americanness during the war and ascended to the middle class, this second generation used their new influence to push for the end of the national origins quotas that discriminated against their co-ethnics.

The middle of the twentieth century thus saw the door open gradually wider to immi-grants, especially immigrants from Asia. First, in 1943, the U.S. government ended its policy of Chinese Exclusion, which was primarily a symbolic gesture intended to ensure good rela-tions with China, the United States' wartime ally. In practice, however, this one particular policy change did not mean much, as the number of Chinese people who could immigrate to the United States was capped at a paltry 105 people per year. The end of Chinese Exclusion heralded a series of other critical reforms that facilitated increased Pacific migration. The McCarran-Walter Act of 1952, for example, ended policies that had excluded other Asian immigrants and laws that had prevented Asian people from becoming naturalized citizens. Most significantly, the Hart-Celler Act of 1965 ended the discriminatory national origins quotas that had been designed to keep out Asians and Southern and Eastern Europeans. To be clear, the Hart-Celler Act also closed the door on some immigrants — it imposed the first numerical restrictions on Western Hemisphere migration and thus helped produce the prob-lem of unauthorized migration. However, it facilitated higher levels of immigration from elsewhere in the world, including Asia, and the number of Asian immigrants skyrocketed in the last three decades of the twentieth century.[9]

The Hart-Celler Act had an important impact on the ethnic, racial, and religious composi-tion of immigrants coming to the United States and on American religious life overall. For one, these new immigrants have changed the racial demographics of Christian churches in the United States, a phenomenon that Stephen Warner described as "the de-Europeanization of American Christianity."[10] The majority of the immigrants who arrived in the United States during this period were, like the American population, Christian. Even among Asian Americans — the racial group with the highest level of religious diversity and the largest proportion of people who are religiously unaffiliated, or religious "nones" — Christians are the largest group and comprise a plurality, as they accounted for about 42 percent in a 2012

Pew survey.[11] Christians, in other words, are often overrepresented among the incoming immigrant population. For example, Indian Christians comprise a larger percentage of the migrating population (approximately 11 percent, as of 2015) than they do in the general population of their home country (about 2 percent).[12] The demographics of Chinese Americans offer another useful illustration of the presence of Christians. According to the 2012 Pew survey, approximately 22 percent identified as Protestant, and 8 percent identified as Catholic.[13]

In addition, the immigrants who arrived after 1965 brought unprecedented religious diversity to the United States. Asian immigrants have been the primary drivers of this new religious diversity. Asian Americans, as a group, are unusually religiously diverse: as of 2012, 14 percent identified as Buddhist, 10 percent as Hindu, 4 percent as Muslim, 1 percent as Sikh, 2 percent as an "other religion," and 26 percent as religiously unaffiliated. Chinese Americans have exemplified this diversity — as of 2012, 31 percent identified as Christian, 15 percent identified as Buddhist, and 52 percent identified as religiously unaffiliated.[14] The religious diversity of immigrants coming to the United States has only accelerated in recent decades. Pew found, for example, that between 1992 and 2012, the share of Muslim immigrants who arrived in the United States grew from 5 percent to 10 percent, and the share of Hindu immigrants increased from 3 percent to 7 percent.[15]

Immigration and the Changing Institutional Landscape of American Religious Life

In addition to changing the religious demographics of the United States, immigrants have transformed the institutional landscape of American religious life. Across the country, immigrants have established their own churches, temples, and other sites of worship, the building of which has been a source of pride and a public expression of their commitment to preserving their distinctive ethnic and religious traditions in the United States.[16] At the same time, these institutions reflect the influence of American life, as many immigrant religious groups, including those that are non-Christian, follow the Protestant congregational model in the United States.[17] Even for Asian immigrants who might not have organized their spiritual and religious lives in congregational form in their countries of origin, establishing religious institutions in the United States has been critical for "building faith communities," and Asian immigrants have created their own churches, temples, and religious organizations since their first arrival in America.[18] Pious Chinese immigrants, for example, established their first temple in San Francisco in 1853, and by 1900 there were over 400 Chinese sites of worship in the western region of the United States. Sinophobic critics warned of the danger of Chinese "joss houses," which both fascinated and horrified Christian Americans. However, the mere existence of these sites of ritual practice attested to the spiritual commitment of Chinese Americans.[19]

These new religious institutions are significant for several reasons. For one, they reflect how immigrants have prioritized maintaining their religious beliefs and practices and transplanting their religious communities to a new American setting. For many immigrants, religion has been central to ethnic identity, and holding onto their religious traditions has provided immigrants an important connection to their home community and native culture. Will Herberg, the mid-century sociologist of religion, noted the importance of preserving religious traditions in his landmark book, *Protestant, Catholic, Jew: An Essay in American Religious Sociology*, published in 1955:

> Of the immigrant who came to this country it was expected that, sooner or later, either in his own person or through his children, he would give up virtually everything he had brought with him from the "old country" — his language, his nationality, his manner of life—and would adopt

the ways of his new home. Within broad limits, however, his becoming an American did not involve his abandoning the old religion. ... Quite the contrary, not only was he expected to retain his old religion, as he was not expected to retain his old language or nationality, but such was the shape of America that it was largely in and through religion that he, or rather his children and grandchildren, found an identifiable place in American life.[20]

Post-1965 immigrants have valued the maintenance of religious traditions much like the early-twentieth-century European immigrants at the center of Herberg's research. For recently arrived immigrants from Asia, the Middle East, and Latin America, religion has remained vital, in part because religion is a significant medium for reproducing culture and because religious institutions are unique spaces where immigrants are free to speak their own language and adhere to the traditions of their home country.[21] Indeed, scholars have observed that immigrants become even more religious in the United States. For example, the sociologist Carolyn Chen found that migration to the United States served to revitalize the religious lives of Taiwanese Buddhists, for whom Buddhism changed from being an "embedded religion" to an "explicit religion." In other words, Buddhism was no longer "a taken-for-granted tradition," but in an American context became "an articulated set of religious practices and beliefs that is a significant source of social identity."[22]

Religious institutions have allowed immigrants to attend to the specific ritual needs of their ethnic communities. Some immigrant religious groups have chosen to rent space from other churches, an arrangement that has worked adequately for those groups that have enough in common such that a shared space can accommodate the religious needs of both communities. However, for religious groups with distinct ritual requirements and specifications for sacred space — non-Christian groups, in particular — the establishment of a temple or church has been an important way to ensure that the space is suitable for their practices. For instance, Chinese Americans have found it useful to build their own funeral homes, which accommodate Buddhist and Confucian families that want to make offerings of food and fruit, burn incense and paper money, and obtain specialty items such as "long-life" clothing and paper versions of horses, cars, and houses to burn during funeral ceremonies.[23]

In addition, immigrant religious institutions have been valuable sites of mutual aid, especially for immigrants who are economically, socially, and politically vulnerable during the difficult first few years in the United States. As the sociologists Helen Ebaugh and Janet Chafetz observed, immigrant churches often follow what they call "the Community Center Model."[24] For example, in Chinatown in Manhattan, the anthropologist Kenneth Guest found that temples and churches help recently arrived immigrants find housing, employment, and healthcare. Some religious institutions even provide financial services by providing credit through informal revolving loan funds and facilitating remittances sent to families and communities back in China.[25]

These religious communities have also been an important way for immigrants to solve the problem of undocumented status. Religious leaders have been involved in connecting unauthorized immigrants with immigration lawyers and assisting in asylum claims involving religious persecution.[26] Churches have even served as places where immigrants have gathered to organize and advocate for more just and compassionate immigration policies.[27] Importantly, there is a long and rich history of religion playing a central role in activism and justice work for immigrants. As Stephanie Hinnershitz argued in her study of Asian American civil rights activists in the early twentieth century, Chinese, Japanese, and Filipino Christian students drew on their shared religious commitments to organize coalitions and resist unequal treatment.[28]

Religious institutions have also functioned as pillar organizations of the ethnic community, places where members of the ethnic community gather and participate in activities that pass down cultural traditions and reinforce ethnic identity. In his study of Chinese Christians, the sociologist Fenggang Yang found that Chinese Christian churches in the United States have helped to continue the observance of traditional Chinese celebrations, such as Chinese New Year and Mid-Autumn Festival. Chinese language schools have also ensured that American-born Chinese learn Mandarin.[29] Chinese religious institutions, whether Christian churches or Buddhist temples, have therefore served as important centers of community-building even in situations when the ethnic Chinese community does not have an identifiable Chinatown and Chinese Americans are more geographically dispersed. In these cases, religious institutions have been less significant as sites of mutual aid and economic networking and more important as sites of cultural connection.[30]

While religious institutions have helped to preserve ethnic traditions and reinforce both cultural and religious identities, they have also served as places that help immigrants become American. Religion has helped immigrants find hope, resilience, and meaning as they experience the economic, political, social, and cultural dislocations of migration. In his study of Chinese religious life in New York City, Guest found that recent Fuzhounese immigrants coped with the challenges of migration by choosing to "frame their experiences in religious terms." He found that religious communities do more than facilitate immigrant incorporation — rather, they function as "important locations for constructing alternative associational networks, identities, and systems of meaning that place value on their faith, responsibility, and morality."[31] Chen observed a similar phenomenon in her study of Taiwanese Americans who converted to Buddhism and evangelical Christianity in the United States. "Christianity and Buddhism provide Taiwanese immigrants with new narratives, practices, and habits for remaking themselves as Americans in the United States," she wrote. "In important, but often overlooked ways, Taiwanese immigrants become American by becoming religious."[32]

Importantly, the religions, like the people who practice them, have become American, too. In their efforts to transplant their religious traditions to American soil, immigrants have adjusted their beliefs and practices to meet the needs of a different legal, cultural, and political setting and have created new, hybrid American versions of their religious traditions in the process. Funerals in San Francisco's Chinatown, for instance, reveal how urban, middle-class Chinese Americans have combined elements of Chinese and Western religion and culture. The involvement of a Western marching band during funeral processions through Chinatown reveal how Chinese Americans have forged their own distinctive, syncretic rituals.[33] This hybridity has characterized not only religious practices, but also religious beliefs. For example, Chinese Americans who belong to conservative Protestant churches in the United States have often found creative ways to merge their evangelical Christianity with Chinese Confucian values.[34]

Immigration, the Public Square, and the Changing Politics and Practices of Pluralism

As is the case with attitudes about immigration, the American public has greeted the arrival and growth of new religious groups with ambivalence. On one hand, Americans in the twenty-first century have demonstrated remarkable openness — even enthusiasm for — a multicultural, multireligious America. In 2017, the Pew Research Center found, for example, that Americans viewed different religious groups more favorably than they had just three years previous. Using a "feeling thermometer" on a scale of 1 to 100, Pew asked respondents to register the degree of positive feelings they directed toward members of different religious groups. Pew found that American adults felt more positively about nearly every religious group. Ratings of Buddhists, for instance, climbed from fifty-three to sixty between 2014 and 2017.[35]

Favorable opinions about new religious diversity have owed in part to the fact that many Americans have relationships with people of different religious beliefs, practices, and identities. In their book *American Grace: How Religion Divides and Unites Us*, the political scientists Robert Putnam and David Campbell explored how "America peacefully combines a high degree of religious devotion with tremendous religious diversity." At the center of their work is a puzzle: "How can religious pluralism coexist with religious polarization?" They argued that religious tolerance in the United States owes to what they called the "Aunt Susan Principle":

> We all have an Aunt Susan in our lives, the sort of person who epitomizes what it means to be a saint, but whose religious background is different from our own. Maybe you are Jewish and she is Methodist. Or perhaps you are Catholic and Aunt Susan is not religious at all. But whatever her religious background (or lack thereof), you know that Aunt Susan is destined for heaven. And if she is going to heaven, what does that say about other people who share her religion or lack of religion? Maybe they can go to heaven too. To put the Aunt Susan Principle in more technical terms: We are suggesting that having a religiously diverse social network leads to a more positive assessment of specific religious groups, particularly those with low thermometer scores.[36]

Survey findings have supported the "Aunt Susan Principle." In the same survey that revealed that Americans' feelings about religious groups have become generally more positive in recent years, Pew found that personal relationships with somebody in a different religious group correlated with more favorable opinions of that particular religious group. To use the case of Buddhists again: people who did not have a personal relationship with a Buddhist rated Buddhists, on average, a fifty-six on the feeling thermometer. In contrast, survey respondents who did have a personal relationship with a Buddhist viewed Buddhists more positively, with a much higher average rating of seventy-five.[37]

This spirit of tolerance and acceptance only goes so far, however. In reality, the relationships that Putnam and Campbell identified as a critical force for promoting religious tolerance have been somewhat limited. Part of the problem is that Christian Americans have had relatively few relationships with Buddhist Americans and other members of religious minority groups. For instance, as of 2017, only 45 percent of Americans said that they had a personal relationship with a Muslim. The statistics were even worse for adherents of other Asian religions: only 23 percent had a relationship with a Buddhist, and only 22 percent had a relationship with a Hindu.[38]

The rarity of relationships between Christians and Muslims, Buddhists, and Hindus is not an accident, but the direct consequence of long-standing and intentional efforts to exclude non-Christian people at all levels, from the nation to the neighborhood. The white Protestant majority has long used immigration policies to shut the door on religious groups it deems a threat, and these efforts have continued into the twenty-first century, a putatively more "liberal" era of immigration policy. The most famous recent example of this exclusionary approach at the federal level is the Trump Administration's controversial Executive Order 13769, known popularly as the "travel ban" and "Muslim Ban." However, just as important have been local efforts at exclusion and restriction. In cities and towns across the United States, neighbors and local governments have lobbied against the building of temples and mosques and used zoning regulations and other means to preserve the religious homogeneity of their communities.

The sociologist Robert Wuthnow, who conducted a national survey about American opinions about religious diversity, found that one in five respondents said that they were in favor of outlawing the ability of Buddhists and Hindus to meet in the United States.[39] And while four in ten Americans said that they would not be bothered by plans for a mosque to be built in their town, an equal number said that it would bother them, and only one in six Americans would actually welcome the mosque. The reception for a Hindu temple was slightly warmer, but only by a little: over one in three Americans said they would be bothered by the temple, and, as with attitudes about the mosque, only one in six Americans said that they would welcome the Hindu temple.[40]

Wuthnow's survey findings echo real-life examples of how Americans have actively worked to prevent the presence of non-Christian communities in their neighborhoods and cities. Across the country, people have used zoning laws and lobbied local governments to prevent the building of new houses of worship, as was the case when Sikhs in North Hills, California, tried to transform a home into a gurdwara and when Vietnamese Buddhists tried to establish Chua Quan Am, a "home temple" in Garden Grove, California. Plans for mosques have caused controversies all across the country — for example, in Murfreesboro, Tennessee; St. Anthony, Minnesota; Quincy, Massachusetts; and Edmond, Oklahoma. Even when groups have secured local government approval for building a house of worship, religious groups have faced intimidation from their neighbors. In Sayreville, New Jersey, for instance, efforts by the local Hindu community to transform a former YMCA into a temple caused opponents to spray paint "Get out Hindoos" and "KKK" on the proposed temple site.[41]

Despite these hostile attitudes, these new religious groups have claimed their place in the United States and asserted that their religions are *American* religions. The most important illustration of the Americanness of these immigrant religious communities is the fact that as these groups have become more established, they have also become more vocal and active in using American laws and public institutions to insist on equal rights, respect, recognition, and representation in the United States. These efforts have changed the policies and practices of public institutions such as schools, hospitals, and the military. In addition, the public conversation has changed. The advocacy and activism on behalf of immigrant religious groups have been part of broader debate about who belongs in America, what it means to be "American," and how Americans should adapt to new religious diversity, put ideals of religious pluralism into practice, and get along with people who are religiously different.

The religious and cultural activities of Chinese Americans, especially around Lunar New Year, usefully illustrate how new immigrants have claimed a place at America's multifaith and multicultural table. According to the folklorist Juwen Zhang, Lunar New Year is a syncretic holiday, with celebrations often combining Chinese folk beliefs and practices, American cultural traditions, and sometimes even Christian religious traditions. But despite the varied origins of the holiday's rituals and the internal diversity of Chinese Americans themselves, Lunar New Year functions as a central community event and core identity marker for Chinese Americans. These celebrations, which have long been important to Chinese Americans, have become increasingly popular in recent years, engaging not only Chinese and other Asian ethnic groups in the United States, but also non-Asian groups. As Zhang argued, Lunar New Year "demonstrates a positive development of multicultural interaction between the insiders and the outsiders in the public sphere."[42]

Recent years have witnessed the growing presence of Lunar New Year celebrations in the public sphere. While Lunar New Year has continued to be celebrated primarily in the domain of family homes and ethnic enclaves, Lunar New Year is also now recognized and celebrated by non-Chinese people living far from Chinatown. For example, in 2015, New York Department of Education added three new holidays to the public school calendar — Eid al-Adha, Eid al-Fitr, and Lunar New Year. The addition of the latter was a response to an important demographic reality in New York City: the fact that a large and growing portion of its population is Asian American, with 15 percent of the city's public school children celebrating Lunar New Year.[43] American politicians, in recognition of their Asian constituents, have also begun to recognize Lunar New Year. The same year that the date was added as a New York City public school holiday, the White House hosted its first Lunar New Year celebration, which involved a greeting from President Barack Obama, speeches about community engagement by Asian American government officials, and cultural performances by various Asian ethnic groups, including a Chinese Lion Dance, a Korean Poongmulnori, a Twelve Meter Hat Ribbon Dance, and a Vietnamese Ao Dai performance.[44] Finally, Lunar New Year has even become an event in consumer culture, with Lego now selling a "Chinese New Year's Eve Dinner" set, which features three generations of a family gathering to feast and exchange red envelopes in their brightly decorated living room.

Immigration and the Changing Definition of "Religion"

The growing frequency with which local, state, and national governments have recognized Lunar New Year illuminates a final way that immigration has changed American religious life, and it hints to how new religious communities have broadened how Americans have understood the very definition of "religious." Chinese Americans have followed the template established by Christians, Jews, and Muslims by focusing efforts on securing accommodations for a major holiday. However, unlike Eid Al-Adha and Eid Al-Fitr, the two Muslim holidays that the New York City Department of Education also added to its school calendar in 2015, Lunar New Year is not typically recognized as a religious holiday per se. In general, Chinese Americans, along with other Asian Americans who celebrate this holiday, have described Lunar New Year as "a deeply important cultural observance," to use the words of New York City Councilwoman Margaret Chin.[45] At the same time, Chinese Americans have often conducted rituals with religious origins and meanings during Lunar New Year. For example, celebrants often burn incense or make offerings to ancestral spirits, both of which are practices that have enough non-Christian religious significance that Chinese Americans who hold conservative Protestant beliefs typically avoid those customs.[46]

Lunar New Year thus raises an important issue: what counts as "religion"? Indeed, whether a belief, practice, or holiday counts as religious matters because the category of religion carries significant legal, cultural, and political weight in the United States. The First Amendment explicitly protects the free exercise of religion, and for some minority groups, securing rights, protections, and accommodations has required that they make the case that their beliefs and practices are legitimately religious. The past half century has thus witnessed important developments in First Amendment jurisprudence as adherents of non-Christian traditions have used the courts to claim religion and, more broadly, to challenge narrow, Protestant-centric definitions of religion.[47] However, many Asian groups have found that their traditions do not easily conform to the Western category of religion, and as a result, their beliefs and practices have been neither recognized as religion nor accommodated as such.[48] Fundamentally, the issue of religious recognition has been a matter of power and resources.[49] If claiming religion has been a means of securing rights and recognition, then denying a claim of religion and categorizing beliefs and practices as "culture" or "superstition" can function as a means of controlling and marginalizing minority groups and reinforcing unequal relations of power.[50]

The beliefs and practices of Chinese Americans exemplify how Asian traditions confound the Western category of religion. That Chinese beliefs and practices are not commensurable to Protestant standards of religious life have meant that they are often overlooked and invisible to most Americans, including those who study religious life. For example, scholars have traditionally focused on congregations as sites of religious life. This approach is not unreasonable; as Stephen Warner and other scholars have pointed out, many immigrant religious groups have chosen to reorganize themselves into Protestant-like congregations in the United States.[51] However, immigrants have not universally conformed to the congregational template. Chinese Americans, for example, have continued to conduct many of their rituals at recognizably religious sites such as temples, monasteries, and meditation centers, but they have also made ritual offerings, set up altars, and celebrated religious festivals in seemingly secular places, including homes, restaurants, stores, and city streets. Because so much of

Chinese American religious life occurs outside of houses of worship, scholars who have focused on religious congregations have failed to appreciate the vibrancy of Chinese American religious life.[52]

The incommensurability of Chinese traditions with the Western category of religion has caused many Americans to overlook not only the religiousness of Chinese American places, but also the religiousness of Chinese American people. A 2012 Pew survey of Asian American religious life found that Asian Americans are the racial group in the United States with the largest percentage of religiously unaffiliated people, and among Asian Americans, Chinese American have the largest percentage of religiously unaffiliated people, with over half (52 percent) identified as religious nones.[53] However, as Kenneth Guest argued in his study of the religious lives of Fuzhounese immigrants in New York City, social scientists have underestimated the religiosity of Chinese Americans because surveys have been shaped by a Western analytical framework that fails to adequately reflect the spiritual lives of Chinese Americans. Historically, Chinese religious life has centered on family and village customs that combine Buddhism, Daoism, and Chinese popular religious beliefs, and Chinese immigrants have continued to practice these intertwined traditions in the United States. Typical religion survey questions that rely on a Western paradigm of religion are thus not appropriate for Chinese Americans. "Asking Chinese New Yorkers by telephone to place their religious beliefs within the framework of world religious systems such as Protestant Christianity, Catholicism, or Buddhism miscalculates the complexity and diversity of Chinese religious expression," Guest wrote. "In this regard it should come as no surprise that the majority of respondents claim no religious affiliation."[54]

Aware of the limitations of the Western framework, social scientists have strived to find other ways to study the religious and spiritual lives of Chinese Americans. One strategy that Pew adopted in its 2012 survey of Asian Americans was to inquire not only about religious belief and identity, but about specific practices, such as whether respondents meditate, keep a home altar, or put up a Christmas tree.[55] More significantly, scholars have rejected the Western paradigm altogether and worked to develop alternative frameworks more firmly rooted in native Chinese beliefs and practices. For example, Russell Jeung, Helen Kim, and Seanan Fong studied the religious lives of Chinese Americans and found that even though surveys show that Chinese Americans are the most non-religious group in the United States, they nevertheless hold deeply-held values and practice regular rituals that they consider ethical. Jeung, Kim, and Fong described these values and rituals as Chinese American familism because the family is the primary narrative by which Chinese Americans derive meaning and purpose.

Moreover, Jeung, Kim, and Fong argued that religious nones should not be understood in terms of the absence of beliefs and religious affiliations. Instead, they proposed using a Chinese term, *liyi*, to describe the values and rituals of religious nones held by Chinese Americans. As Jeung, Kim, and Fong showed, scholars must consider alternative kinds of spirituality than the Western paradigm of religion presupposes.[56] The work of these scholars offers new possibilities for how to study and understand the religious and spiritual lives of Chinese Americans and, more broadly, all people who fall under the category of religious "nones."

Conclusion

As the case of Chinese American religious life shows, the history of immigration and religion is intertwined, and an understanding how American religious life has changed, especially over the course of the past half century, requires consideration of the impact of new immigration policies and new immigrant populations. The arrival of significant numbers of people from Asia, Latin America, Africa, and the Middle East has transformed the United States in numerous ways: by changing its religious demographics, by diversifying its religious institutions, by reshaping the public square and the practices of religious pluralism, and, indeed, by challenging even the very meaning of being religious.

Americans in the white Christian majority have been ambivalent about these new immigrants and the religious changes they have introduced. Some Americans have welcomed the fact that the United States is an increasingly multiracial, multicultural, and multireligious nation, while others have been anxious about and even hostile towards those who threaten the longstanding ascendency of white Christians. Recent proposals to change immigration laws and reduce the number of both legal and unauthorized immigrants arise in part from concerns about labor, economics, and national security, but also from anxieties about the changing ethnic, racial, and religious composition of the United States. However, even if immigration restrictionists succeed in enacting their policies and decreasing the number of immigrants in the future, the fact remains that the immigrants who arrived in the past half century have already made an indelible impact on religious life in the United States. The changes in public institutions and the policies and practices of governing religious difference cannot easily be undone.

Most significantly, the religiously diverse people who have come to the United States are here and unlikely to go away. They have established their communities, they have built their temples and churches, and they have made the United States their home. Chinatown — which has expanded over the years to claim portions of Manhattan that were once home to Irish, German, Italian, and Jewish immigrants — is an example of how thriving neighborhoods, like thriving nations, change over time.

FURTHER READING

Chen, Carolyn. *Getting Saved in America: Taiwanese Immigration and Religious Experience*. Princeton: Princeton University Press, 2008.

Guest, Kenneth. *God in Chinatown: Religion and Survival in New York's Evolving Immigrant Community*. New York: New York University Press, 2003.

Jeung, Russell, Seanan S. Fong, and Helen Jin Kim. *Family Sacrifices: The Worldviews and Ethics of Chinese Americans*. New York: Oxford University Press, 2019.

Lew-Williams, Beth. *The Chinese Must Go: Violence, Exclusion, and the Making of the Alien in America*. Cambridge, MA: Harvard University Press, 2018.

Pew Research Center. "Asian Americans: A Mosaic of Faiths." Pew Research Center, August 2012.

Yang, Fenggang. *Chinese Christians in America: Conversion, Assimilation, and Adhesive Identities*. University Park: Pennsylvania State University Press, 1999.

BIBLIOGRAPHY

Bender, Courtney, and Pamela Klassen, eds. *After Pluralism: Reimagining Religious Engagement*. New York: Columbia University Press, 2010.

Bender, Courtney, and Jennifer Snow. "From Alleged Buddhists to Unreasonable Hindus: First Amendment Jurisprudence after 1965." In *A Nation of Religions*, edited by Stephen Prothero, 181–208. Chapel Hill: University of North Carolina Press, 2006.

Carnes, Tony, and Fenggang Yang. *Asian American Religions: The Making and Remaking of Borders and Boundaries*. New York: New York University Press, 2004.

Chen, Carolyn. *Getting Saved in America: Taiwanese Immigration and Religious Experience*. Princeton: Princeton University Press, 2008.

Crowder, Linda Sun. "Chinese Funerals in San Francisco Chinatown: American Chinese Expressions in Mortuary Ritual Performance." *The Journal of American Folklore* 113, no. 450 (Autumn 2000): 451–463.

Ebaugh, Helen Rose Fuchs, and Janet Saltzman Chafetz, eds. *Religion and the New Immigrants: Continuities and Adaptations in Immigrant Congregations*. Walnut Creek: AltaMira Press, 2000.

Eck, Diana. *A New Religious America: How a "Christian Country" Has Now Become the World's Most Religiously Diverse Nation*. New York: HarperSanFrancisco, 2001.

Galvez, Alyshia. *Guadalupe in New York: Devotion and the Struggle for Citizenship Rights among Mexican Immigrants*. New York: New York University Press, 2009.

Grynbaum, Michael M., and Sharon Otterman. "New York City Adds 2 Muslim Holy Days to Public School Calendar." *The New York Times*, March 4, 2015, sec. New York. https://www.nytimes.com/2015/03/05/nyregion/new-york-to-add-two-muslim-holy-days-to-public-school-calendar.html.

Guest, Kenneth. *God in Chinatown: Religion and Survival in New York's Evolving Immigrant Community*. New York: New York University Press, 2003.

Handlin, Oscar. *The Uprooted*. 2nd ed. Boston: Little, Brown and Company, 1973.

Hardikar, Aditi. "Celebrating Lunar New Year at the White House," February 20, 2015. https://obamawhitehouse.archives.gov/blog/2015/02/20/celebrating-lunar-new-year-white-house.

Harris, Elizabeth A., and Michael M. Grynbaum. "Mayor de Blasio to Make Lunar New Year a School Holiday." *The New York Times*, June 22, 2015, sec. New York. https://www.nytimes.com/2015/06/23/nyregion/mayor-de-blasio-to-make-lunar-new-year-a-school-holiday.html.

Herberg, Will. *Protestant, Catholic, Jew; an Essay in American Religious Sociology*. Garden City: Doubleday, 1955.

Hinnershitz, Stephanie. *Race, Religion, and Civil Rights: Asian Students on the West Coast, 1900–1968*. New Brunswick: Rutgers University Press, 2015.

Hirota, Hidetaka. *Expelling the Poor: Atlantic Seaboard States and the Nineteenth-Century Origins of American Immigration Policy*. Oxford: Oxford University Press, 2017.

Jeung, Russell, Seanan S. Fong, and Helen Jin Kim. *Family Sacrifices: The Worldviews and Ethics of Chinese Americans*. New York: Oxford University Press, 2019.

Josephson-Storm, Jason Ananda. "The Superstition, Secularism, and Religion Trinary: Or Re-Theorizing Secularism." *Method and Theory in the Study of Religion* 30, no. 1 (2017): 1–20.

Lee, Erika. *At America's Gates: Chinese Immigration During the Exclusion Era, 1882–1943*. Chapel Hill: University of North Carolina Press, 2003.

_____. *The Making of Asian America: A History*. New York City: Simon & Schuster, 2016.

Lew-Williams, Beth. *The Chinese Must Go: Violence, Exclusion, and the Making of the Alien in America*. Cambridge, MA: Harvard University Press, 2018.

Ling, Huping. "Reconceptualizing Chinese American Community in St. Louis: From Chinatown to Cultural Community." *Journal of American Ethnic History* 24, no. 2 (Winter 2005): 65–101.

Masters, Frederick. "Pagan Temples in San Francisco." In *Asian Religions in America: A Documentary History*, edited by Thomas Tweed and Stephen Prothero, 75–78. New York: Oxford University Press, 1999.

Min, Pyon Gap, and Sou Hyun Jang. "The Diversity of Asian Immigrants' Participation in Religious Institutions in the United States." *Sociology of Religion* 76, no. 3 (Autumn 2015): 253–274.

Min, Pyong Gap, and Jung Ha Kim, eds. *Religions in Asian America: Building Faith Communities*. Walnut Creek: AltaMira Press, 2002.

Ngai, Mae M. *Impossible Subjects: Illegal Aliens and the Making of Modern America*. Princeton: Princeton University Press, 2004.

Orsi, Robert. *The Madonna of 115th Street: Faith and Community in Italian Harlem, 1880–1950*. 2nd ed. New Haven: Yale University Press, 2002.

Pew Research Center. "Americans Express Increasingly Warm Feelings Toward Religious Groups," February 15, 2017. https://www.pewforum.org/2017/02/15/americans-express-increasingly-warm-feelings-toward-religious-groups/.

_____. "Asian Americans: A Mosaic of Faiths." Pew Research Center, August 2012. https://www.pewforum.org/2012/07/19/asian-americans-a-mosaic-of-faiths-overview/.

_____. "Asian Americans: A Mosaic of Faiths." Pew Research Center,. "The Religious Affiliation of U.S. Immigrants: Majority Christian, Rising Share of Other Faiths," May 17, 2013. https://www.pewforum.org/2013/05/17/the-religious-affiliation-of-us-immigrants/.

Prothero, Stephen, ed. *A Nation of Religions: The Politics of Pluralism in Multireligious America*. New ed. Chapel Hill: University of North Carolina Press, 2006.

Putnam, Robert D., and David E. Campbell. *American Grace: How Religion Divides and Unites Us*. New York: Simon & Schuster, 2010.

Sullivan, Winnifred Fallers. *The Impossibility of Religious Freedom*. Princeton: Princeton University Press, 2005.

The Pluralism Project. "Not in This Neighborhood! Zoning Battles." Accessed December 16, 2019. http://pluralism.org/encounter/todays-challenges/not-in-this-neighborhood-zoning-battles/.

Warner, R. Stephen. *A Church of Our Own: Disestablishment and Diversity in American Religion*. New Brunswick: Rutgers University Press, 2005.

_____. "The De-Europeanization of American Christianity." In *A Church of Our Own: Disestablishment and Diversity in American Religion*, 257–262. New Brunswick: Rutgers University Press, 2005.

Warner, R. Stephen, and Judith Wittner, eds. *Gatherings in Diaspora Religious Communities and the New Immigration*. Philadelphia: Temple University Press, 1998.

Wenger, Tisa. *We Have a Religion: The 1920s Pueblo Indian Dance Controversy and American Religious Freedom*. Chapel Hill: University of North Carolina Press, 2009.

Wuthnow, Robert. *America and the Challenges of Religious Diversity*. Princeton: Princeton University Press, 2005.

Yang, Fenggang. *Chinese Christians in America: Conversion, Assimilation, and Adhesive Identities*. University Park: Pennsylvania State University Press, 1999.

Yoo, David, *ed. New Spiritual Homes: Religion and Asian Americans*. Honolulu: University of Hawai'i Press, in association with UCLA Asian American Studies Center, Los Angeles, 1999.

Zhang, Juwen. "Chinese American Culture in the Making: Perspectives and Reflections on Diasporic Folklore and Identity." *Journal of American Folklore* 128, no. 510 (Fall 2015): 449–475.

_____. "Falling Seeds Take Root: Ritualizing Chinese American Identity Through Funerals." PhD diss., University of Pennsylvania, 2001.

NOTES

1 Oscar Handlin, *The Uprooted*, 2nd ed. (Boston: Little, Brown and Company, 1973), 105.

2 Robert Orsi, *The Madonna of 115th Street: Faith and Community in Italian Harlem, 1880–1950*, 2nd ed. (New Haven: Yale University Press, 2002).

3 Mae M Ngai, *Impossible Subjects: Illegal Aliens and the Making of Modern America* (Princeton: Princeton University Press, 2004).

4 Beth Lew-Williams, *The Chinese Must Go: Violence, Exclusion, and the Making of the Alien in America* (Cambridge, MA: Harvard University Press, 2018); Hidetaka Hirota, *Expelling the Poor: Atlantic Seaboard States and the Nineteenth-Century Origins of American Immigration Policy* (Oxford: Oxford University Press, 2017).

5 Hirota, *Expelling the Poor*.

6 Lew-Williams, *The Chinese Must Go*.

7 Erika Lee, *At America's Gates: Chinese Immigration During the Exclusion Era, 1882–1943* (Chapel Hill: University of North Carolina Press, 2003).

8 Ngai, *Impossible Subjects*.

9 Erika Lee, *The Making of Asian America: A History* (New York City: Simon & Schuster, 2016).

10 R. Stephen Warner, "The De-Europeanization of American Christianity," in *A Church of Our Own: Disestablishment and Diversity in American Religion* (New Brunswick: Rutgers University Press, 2005), 257–262.

11 Pew Research Center, "Asian Americans: A Mosaic of Faiths" (Pew Research Center, August 2012).

12 Pyon Gap Min and Sou Hyun Jang, "The Diversity of Asian Immigrants' Participation in Religious Institutions in the United States," *Sociology of Religion* 76, no. 3 (Autumn 2015): 260.

13 Pew Research Center, "Asian Americans: A Mosaic of Faiths."

14 Ibid.

15 Pew Research Center, "The Religious Affiliation of U.S. Immigrants: Majority Christian, Rising Share of Other Faiths," May 17, 2013, https://www.pewforum.org/2013/05/17/the-religious-affiliation-of-us-immigrants/.

16 Diana Eck, *A New Religious America: How a "Christian Country" Has Now Become the World's Most Religiously Diverse Nation* (New York: HarperSanFrancisco, 2001).

17 R. Stephen Warner, *A Church of Our Own: Disestablishment and Diversity in American Religion* (New Brunswick: Rutgers University Press, 2005); R. Stephen Warner and Judith Wittner, eds.,

Gatherings in Diaspora Religious Communities and the New Immigration (Philadelphia: Temple University Press, 1998).

18 For useful studies of different Asian American religious communities, see Stephen Prothero, ed., *A Nation of Religions: The Politics of Pluralism in Multireligious America*, new edition (Chapel Hill: University of North Carolina Press, 2006); Tony Carnes and Fenggang Yang, *Asian American Religions: The Making and Remaking of Borders and Boundaries* (New York: New York University Press, 2004); Pyong Gap Min and Jung Ha Kim, eds., *Religions in Asian America: Building Faith Communities* (Walnut Creek: AltaMira Press, 2002); David Yoo, ed., *New Spiritual Homes: Religion and Asian Americans* (Honolulu: University of Hawai'i Press, in association with UCLA Asian American Studies Center, Los Angeles, 1999).

19 Frederick Masters, "Pagan Temples in San Francisco," in *Asian Religions in America: A Documentary History*, edited by Thomas Tweed and Stephen Prothero (New York: Oxford University Press, 1999), 75–78.

20 Will Herberg, *Protestant, Catholic, Jew; an Essay in American Religious Sociology* (Garden City, New York: Doubleday, 1955), 27-28.

21 Warner, *A Church of Our Own*, 236.

22 Carolyn Chen, *Getting Saved in America: Taiwanese Immigration and Religious Experience* (Princeton: Princeton University Press, 2008), 79.

23 Juwen Zhang, "Falling Seeds Take Root: Ritualizing Chinese American Identity Through Funerals" (PhD diss., University of Pennsylvania, 2001).

24 Helen Rose Fuchs Ebaugh and Janet Saltzman Chafetz, eds., *Religion and the New Immigrants: Continuities and Adaptations in Immigrant Congregations* (Walnut Creek: AltaMira Press, 2000), 354.

25 Kenneth Guest, *God in Chinatown: Religion and Survival in New York's Evolving Immigrant Community* (New York: New York University Press, 2003), 131, 138.

26 Guest, 188.

27 Alyshia Galvez, *Guadalupe in New York: Devotion and the Struggle for Citizenship Rights among Mexican Immigrants* (New York: New York University Press, 2009).

28 Stephanie Hinnershitz, *Race, Religion, and Civil Rights: Asian Students on the West Coast, 1900– 1968* (New Brunswick: Rutgers University Press, 2015).

29 Fenggang Yang, *Chinese Christians in America: Conversion, Assimilation, and Adhesive Identities* (University Park: Pennsylvania State University Press, 1999).

30 Huping Ling, "Reconceptualizing Chinese American Community in St. Louis: From Chinatown to CulturalCommunity," *Journal of American Ethnic History* 24, no. 2 (Winter 2005): 65–101.

31 Guest, *God in Chinatown*, 8–9.

32 Chen, *Getting Saved in America*, 5.

33 Linda Sun Crowder, "Chinese Funerals in San Francisco Chinatown: American Chinese Expressions in Mortuary Ritual Performance," *The Journal of American Folklore* 113, no. 450 (Autumn 2000): 451–463.

34 Yang, *Chinese Christians in America*.

35 Pew Research Center, "Americans Express Increasingly Warm Feelings Toward Religious Groups," February 15, 2017, https://www.pewforum.org/2017/02/15/americans-express-increasingly-warm-feelings-toward-religious-groups/.

36 Robert D. Putnam and David E. Campbell, *American Grace: How Religion Divides and Unites Us* (New York: Simon & Schuster, 2010), 526-527.

37 Pew Research Center, "Americans Express Increasingly Warm Feelings Toward Religious Groups."

38 Ibid.

39 Robert Wuthnow, *America and the Challenges of Religious Diversity* (Princeton: Princeton University Press, 2005), 80.

40 Wuthnow, *America and the Challenges of Religious Diversity*.

41 The Pluralism Project, "Not in This Neighborhood! Zoning Battles," accessed December 16, 2019, http://pluralism.org/encounter/todays-challenges/not-in-this-neighborhood-zoning-battles/.

42 Juwen Zhang, "Chinese American Culture in the Making: Perspectives and Reflections on Diasporic Folklore and Identity," *Journal of American Folklore* 128, no. 510 (Fall 2015): 457.

43 Elizabeth A. Harris and Michael M. Grynbaum, "Mayor de Blasio to Make Lunar New Year a School Holiday," *The New York Times*, June 22, 2015, sec. New York, https://www.nytimes.

com/2015/06/23/nyregion/mayor-de-blasio-to-make-lunar-new-year-a-school-holiday.html; Michael M. Grynbaum and Sharon Otterman, "New York City Adds 2 Muslim Holy Days to Public School Calendar," *The New York Times*, March 4, 2015, sec. New York, https://www. nytimes.com/2015/03/05/nyregion/new-york-to-add-two-muslim-holy-days-to-public-school-calendar.html.

44 Aditi Hardikar, "Celebrating Lunar New Year at the White House," February 20, 2015, https:// obamawhitehouse.archives.gov/blog/2015/02/20/celebrating-lunar-new-year-white-house.

45 Harris and Grynbaum, "Mayor de Blasio to Make Lunar New Year a School Holiday."

46 Yang, *Chinese Christians in America*, 132–133.

47 Courtney Bender and Jennifer Snow, "From Alleged Buddhists to Unreasonable Hindus: First Amendment Jurisprudence after 1965," in *A Nation of Religions*, edited by Stephen Prothero (Chapel Hill: University of North Carolina Press, 2006), 181–208.

48 Winnifred Fallers Sullivan, *The Impossibility of Religious Freedom* (Princeton: Princeton University Press, 2005); Tisa Wenger, *We Have a Religion: The 1920s Pueblo Indian Dance Controversy and American Religious Freedom* (Chapel Hill: University of North Carolina Press, 2009).

49 Courtney Bender and Pamela Klassen, eds., *After Pluralism: Reimagining Religious Engagement* (New York: Columbia University Press, 2010).

50 Jason Ananda Josephson-Storm, "The Superstition, Secularism, and Religion Trinary: Or Re-Theorizing Secularism," *Method and Theory in the Study of Religion* 30, no. 1 (2017): 1–20.

51 Warner, *A Church of Our Own*; Min and Jang, "The Diversity of Asian Immigrants' Participation in Religious Institutions in the United States."

52 Guest, *God in Chinatown*, 125–126.

53 Pew Research Center, "Asian Americans: A Mosaic of Faiths."

54 Guest, *God in Chinatown*, 124–125.

55 Pew Research Center, "Asian Americans: A Mosaic of Faiths."

56 Russell Jeung, Seanan S. Fong, and Helen Jin Kim, *Family Sacrifices: The Worldviews and Ethics of Chinese Americans* (New York: Oxford University Press, 2019).

Chapter Twenty-Eight

MODERN JUDAISM AND THE GOLDEN AGE OF TELEVISION

Jennifer Caplan
Towson University, Towson, Maryland

Introduction

Television watchers today have an unprecedented amount of choice in terms of where, and how, they find content. Although some people still have traditional cable subscriptions, millions of people "cut the cord" every year, and by 2018 the average TV viewer used at least three different services to watch their chosen shows.[1] Services like Netflix, Hulu, Amazon Prime, HBO Max, and Apple TV+ all vie for subscribers and so they are all trying to find ways to carve out their share of the audience. Traditional TV networks have responded by upping their game as well, meaning the quality, quantity, and diversity of available programs is at an all-time high. Now is the time when networks and television producers can take risks and greenlight shows that highlight diverse groups and cultures, and that has led to greater representation of many minority groups, including Jews.

Jews have always occupied a statistically disproportionate place in American culture. As a group of religious outsiders, they have never constituted more than 3 perent of the American population, and according to the *World Population Review*, Jews account for at least 1 percent of the population in only sixteen out of fifty states.[2] There are many complicated and inter-connected reasons why such a small population have retained such a prominent place in the fabric of America. Certainly, part of it has to do with East Coast, particularly New York, chauvinism. The massive wave of Eastern European Jewish immigration to the United States that took place from the late nineteenth century, up to the immigration reforms of 1924, brought an estimated 2 million Jewish immigrants. The majority of them settled in New York City, which was considered by many to be the greatest city in the world at that moment in time. A focus on New York as the cultural center of the United States, therefore, carried with it a focus on these new Jewish immigrants as an important group of new Americans, despite their very small numbers in the rest of the country.

Other reasons for the ongoing prominence of Jews in public discourse include publications like Will Herberg's 1955 book *Protestant, Catholic, Jew*. In this influential text, Herberg identified Jews as one-third of the American "Triple Melting Pot."[3] When Herberg published his book, an estimated 90 percent of the American population was Christian (Protestant or Catholic), yet he included Jews as the third part of his study of American religious life.

A Companion to American Religious History, First Edition. Edited by Benjamin E. Park.
© 2021 John Wiley & Sons, Inc. Published 2021 by John Wiley & Sons, Inc.

Many Christians, especially Protestants, similarly hold on to the notion of the "Judeo-Christian" lineage and therefore see Judaism as an important part of the ethical and moral structures of the United States. The longevity of the "Judeo-Christian" construct, therefore, is certainly another part of this puzzle. In the end there is not one single reason why Jews remain a highly visible minority, but there are many partial reasons which all offer answers which are simultaneously satisfying, and not.

In this chapter I will address the place of Jews in America in the first quarter of the twenty-first century --what French television scholar Alexis Pichard dubbed "the New Golden Age of American Television" --by looking at television shows with Jewish characters and significant Jewish content.[4] This Golden Age is marked by several features, notably the production quality that comes from increased original programming from streaming services, which in turn pushes both cable and standard networks to produce bigger budget shows in order to stay competitive. In addition to bigger budgets and higher production values, however, this Golden Age also offers viewers unprecedented choice. And as there are more series than ever before available, production companies seem more willing to take risks in shows that speak to minority or "niche" communities in the hopes that they will find an audience. Previously, it was assumed that there was enough audience to only support one well-written show about a minority group at a time — whether it be African American, Hispanic, or Asian American — but the market now appears to broaden its gaze.

This dynamic had been especially noticeable as it related to Judaism Even though all major networks were led by Jewish owners there was a paucity of Jewish characters on television. According to David Zurawik, from 1954–1972 there was not a single show on television with a Jewish leading character.[5] This happened again from 1978–1987. For decades there were fears of what Zurawik calls "surplus visibility," which led the Jewish executives at the networks to fear putting Jewish characters on the air.

That changed in the late 1980s, however, because the networks transitioned from being owned by Jewish families to being owned by corporations who had no fear of exposure. Vincent Brook argues that this ushered in the "rise of the Jewish sitcom," but the series he highlights are largely focused on "perceptually Jewish" characters, meaning the audience reads them as Jewish (often simply because they are from New York), but the characters rarely, if ever, mention being Jewish or engage in Jewish activities.[6] Series like *Mad About You*, *Anything But Love*, and of course *Seinfeld* are all emblematic of this trend to put Jewish performers in shows and let the audience infer their characters' Jewishness.

The series outlined in this chapter, however, are different, because this Golden Age of Television is different. Simply putting Jewish bodies on the air may have seemed risky in 1989, but that ship has sailed and the mere presence of most minorities on the air is now *de rigeur*. (Sadly, we are not yet to the same place with LGBTQ representation). In fact, a major trend in Jewish television today is that it is increasingly common to cast non-Jewish performers in Jewish roles. While some may see that as a step backwards in terms of opportunities for Jewish performers, it is nonetheless a clear indication that the mainstreaming of American Jews has been so successful that it is not seen as odd when non-Jewish performers play Jewish characters.

Below, I will analyze three case studies: *Crazy Ex-Girlfriend*, *Transparent*, and *The Marvelous Mrs. Maisel*. I selected these three for their notoriety, frequent use of Jewish themes and ideas, and the way they illustrate these trends around casting. Although they all overlap on many points, with each I will focus on one element of contemporary American Jewish life: *Crazy Ex-Girlfriend* depicts a young Jewish woman wrestling with many elements of her identity, including her Jewish identity; *Transparent* depicts a twenty-first century Jewish family that conforms to current trends in affiliation with Jewish life; and finally, *The Marvelous Mrs. Maisel* is a period piece, which means that while it does is not show us an image of contemporary Jewish life, it instead allows us to engage with the larger conversations involving Jewish mainstreaming and how that is reflected in casting choices.

Crazy Ex-Girlfriend

Crazy Ex-Girlfriend is a difficult series to define. It is the brainchild of two Jewish women: Aline Brosh McKenna, a film-writer known mainly for romantic comedies, and Rachel Bloom, a singer and comedic performer who was building her career posting YouTube videos. Brosh McKenna stumbled across Bloom's videos and reached out to her about collaborating on a vehicle for Bloom's talents. For the first two seasons, the show was easy to classify as a wacky, zany, and musical romantic comedy with biting wit and extremely clever songs. But in season three the show turned much darker, and the audience was made to question their perceptions of reality as we discovered that everything we thought was fun and happy may have been artifacts of an unwell mind, and that nothing was as it seemed to be. The show concluded in April 2019 after its fourth season.

Bloom plays Rebecca Bunch, a lawyer who suddenly leaves her high-powered job in New York City because she runs into Josh Chan, a childhood fling from summer camp who tells her he is moving back to his hometown of West Covina, CA. She impulsively decides to follow him there and win him back, thus setting into motion most of the action of the series. The show establishes Rebecca's character, including her Jewishness, in the first episode, while simultaneously addressing casual anti-semitism. She takes a job with a small firm in West Covina and her new boss, Darryl, reveals that he is getting a divorce and is concerned that his wife is going to win full custody of their daughter because her lawyer is "one of those real smart Jewish guys." When Rebecca says she is Jewish, Darryl's response is, "I had no idea! That is a TINY nose, it's like a button."[7]

Although Rebecca does not immediately respond to Darryl's blatantly anti-semitic assumption about Jewish noses, her facial expressions show that she is becoming uncomfortable with the direction the conversation is taking. Darryl then asks Rebecca to represent him, and continues to blunder through increasingly offensive statements like, "I just want to see my wife's face. I mean, her Jew went to CSU Long Beach. My Jew? Harvard and Yale." But while it seems as though Rebecca is just going to let the comments slide, as she rushes out of the office to go track down Josh, she turns to her boss and says, "let's circle back about the 'Jew' thing, because that's a conversation we're going to need to have." The matter was not going to be dropped.

The show, of course, is a comedy, and Darry's oblivious anti-semitism is being played for laughs, but Rebecca's assertion that they need to have that conversation is already a more affirmative statement of Jewish identity than most previous Jewish television characters have exhibited. Rebecca could have just mugged for the camera and let Darryl's comments go, but instead she asserts herself and tells him that is not the type of comment she is going to allow. Bloom and Brosh McKenna lean further into Rebecca's Jewish identity throughout the first season, with the strongest expression coming in the musical number "JAP Battle."[8] In this number, widely ranked as one of the top ten songs of the entire series, Rebecca and her long-time rival Audra Levine battle it out as two "Shebrews from Scarsdale."[9] In the song, Audra and Rebecca happily adopt all sorts of Jewish stereotypes, both good and bad, from being politically liberal to being wealthy to being high-achieving academically. Although the stereotypes they reclaim are not necessarily those traditionally associated with Jewish American Princesses, however, they are Jewish stereotypes more broadly speaking.[10]

From the pilot, Bloom and Brosh McKenna set the tone for the way they would treat Jewish themes and ideas. Whenever Tova Feldshuh guest stars as Rebecca's mother, Naomi, the off-hand Jewish references to what is happening at her synagogue, or what her rabbi recently said, are plentiful. Feldshuh sings the show-stoppers "Where's the Bathroom" during her first visit to West Covina in season 1, and "Remember that We Suffered" in season 2, and in both she runs through rapid fire Jewish stereotypes. In season two, Rebecca brings Josh home to New York to attend a bar mitzvah, which is as close as the show ever comes to depicting Jewish ritual practice. Across the show's four seasons, Rebecca is shown to be a woman who is not engaged with her local Jewish community, but is very attached to her identity as a Jew who is wrestling with what that identity even means. In fact, as the series goes on, Rebecca's references to her own Jewishness increase, indicating that as the character matures she also begins to more frequently think of herself in Jewish terms. By the final season there are running jokes about Rebecca's Jewishness affecting everything from her mental health to her alcohol consumption. In fact, her Jewishness is one of the only stable things in Rebecca's life; she stops being a lawyer, she stops being a girlfriend, she changes almost everything about her life, and the more things change the more she makes references to being Jewish, as though that is the constant in her otherwise chaotic life.

Rebecca's relationship to her own Jewishness is representative of trends in American Judaism in the twenty-first century. Rebecca is a Millennial, and according to the Pew Foundation's most recent portrait of American Jews, Millennials are the most likely generation to both identify as Jewish as well as claim no religion.[11] Nearly a third of Millennial Jews surveyed chose that option, compared to the Greatest Generation who had the lowest rate of Jews of no religion, at 7 percent. Furthermore, across all Jews surveyed, a nearly identical number said that "having a sense of humor" (42 percent) was as important to a Jewish identity as "attachment to the state of Israel" (43 percent), while 68 percent thought that not believing in God was compatible with being Jewish. All signs indicate that American Jews in the twenty-first century have shifted the narrative of what it means to be Jewish, and Rebecca is very much in line with those shifts. Although we see her in Jewish spaces, such as synagogues, rarely, and only for special occasions, we see her as someone who proudly proclaims her Jewishness, even in situations where that is awkward or difficult.

While the musical-fantasy format of *Crazy Ex-Girlfriend* is uncommon, in many other ways it is the most traditional show of the three case studies in this analysis. It is the only one to air on a traditional television network, although The CW is the smallest of the five networks (ABC, CBS, Fox, NBC, and The CW). Because it aired on a network, then, it was subject to more stringent censorship than shows that first air on premium cable or streaming services. Despite that, the show was often vulgar or obscene, and several of the musical numbers also had "explicit" or "unedited" versions available online.[12] The primary Jewish characters, Rebecca and her mother Naomi, are both played by Jewish actors. Although Rebecca is much more vocally Jewish than someone like (the character) Jerry Seinfeld, she nonetheless still conforms to many of the traditional tropes of network television, and the show does occasionally (though not always) use Jewishness as more of a punchline than a character trait. Nevertheless, *Crazy Ex-Girlfriend* is emblematic of the changing ways in which Jews are depicted on television. Rebecca's journey of self-discovery includes coming to terms with her mental health, her job, her mother, and ultimately her self-perception, and the increase in her references to her Jewishness in the fourth season indicate that she, like most American Jews of her generation, is figuring out what being Jewish in America means to her.

Transparent

Transparent has been called "the Most Profoundly Jewish Show in Television History."[13] It is an Amazon Original series, available exclusively with their Amazon Prime streaming service, or for purchase through Amazon.com. As a streaming original, it is part of this new wave of programming that denotes the New Golden Age of American Television. Because it is created for a streaming service, it is subject to minimal censorship and oversight, which means that it can include both language and topics that would be impossible to air on a network show.

The show follows the life of the Pfefferman family, focused especially on Maura Pfefferman, played by Jeffrey Tambor. Maura comes out as transgender in the first season, finally revealing to her adult children and her ex-wife what she has known for much of her life. The series is semi-autobiographic as creator Joey Soloway's parent came out as transgender late in life, just as Maura did. While Maura is the protagonist, the show also follows the lives of the three Pfefferman children, Sarah, Josh, and Ali, and to a lesser extent their mother Shelly.

The Judaism of the Pfefferman family is both constant and insecure. As one review put it, "everyone refers to 'Jewy' stuff all the time, as if vaguely confused by their identification with a religion."[14] The family occasionally celebrates Shabbat at home, although the implication is that it is not common. They have a Passover Seder even when they are on a cruise, but they do not make any effort to perform any of the actual rituals. The synagogue is a place of safety and belonging, but they all seem to use it in different ways at different times, and with different degrees of religious sincerity. Although many people identify the Pfeffermans as "certainly culturally Jewish ... but not particularly observant," that is, perhaps, misunderstanding what contemporary Judaism looks like in America.[15]

Another of the findings of the aforementioned 2013 Pew study is that 30 percent of American Jews report not being affiliated with any denomination. The three major denominational movements in Judaism still retain the majority of American Jews, with 35 percent claiming Reform affiliation, 18 percent Conservative, and 10 percent Orthodox. But that makes Jews of no affiliation effectively the second largest population after Reform Jews. And although the Pfefferman family does not show a high degree of observance, they do appear to be loosely affiliated with a synagogue. An episode in season 2 follows the various members of the family as they observe Yom Kippur in their own way.[16] Shelly and Josh have the most traditional observance as they are fasting and attending synagogue services. As they reach the front of the line, however, Shelly mentions to the usher that she has tickets set aside that she hasn't paid for yet, which is an indication that they are not dues-paying members of this synagogue despite Josh being engaged to the rabbi.

This all continues to align the Pfeffermans with the Pew findings. Although one-third of American Jews do not report having a denominational affiliation, more than half (53 percent) report that they fast all or part of Yom Kippur. And a whopping 70 percent report participating in a Seder. Furthermore, of the 78 percent of American Jews who describe themselves as religiously Jewish (as opposed to those Jews of "no religion" we mentioned above) only 39 percent belong (i.e. pay dues) to a synagogue. So while it may be correct to call the Pfeffermans "not particularly observant," that description does not tell the full story. This family seems to be, statistically and practically speaking, a close simulacrum of the average American Jewish family in the 2010s. If more American Jews are unaffiliated than belong to Conservative and Orthodox synagogues combined, it stands to reason that we need to rethink our rubric for describing American Jewish practice. If "not particularly observant" is so statistically common, then is that still a valuable way of describing deviation from an imagined norm?

Judaism on *Transparent* functions as more than just a mirror held up to the American Jewish family's practices. Unlike *Crazy Ex-Girlfriend*, *Transparent* is a dramedy. Although the show has very funny moments, it is also allowed to be quite serious, and religion is often what the show uses to be serious. In a season 1 episode called "The Wilderness," Judaism is the vehicle several characters use to show the ways in which they are changing as people.[17] Sarah and her new girlfriend Tammy have begun doing Shabbat dinners at their home, and on this Friday they invite Maura. This is momentous because Maura has not yet seen Sarah's children, her grandchildren, since coming out, so this will be their first chance to meet their grandparent on her own terms. To begin the meal they light the Shabbat candles and say the accompanying blessings. This is a ritual performed by the women of the family, so Sarah invites Maura up to light the candles with her. What is notable is that, although Maura has spent a lifetime engaging in Jewish rituals on some level or another, this is the first time she has ever performed this woman-centered ritual. She begins to chant the blessing, but Sarah corrects her that she is using the Hanukkah melody, not the Shabbat melody. Men and women light the candles together at Hanukkah so that is the haptic memory Maura has for performing this ritual. She is, both symbolically and practically, becoming the matriarch of the family through the learning of Jewish rituals that are new to her.

In this same episode, Josh is going through a bit of an existential crisis. He has lived his life as a hedonistic man-child, but for the first time he is facing that the "relationship" he had with his babysitter when he was a child was really statutory rape, and his longstanding pride in "bagging" a much older woman is giving way to decades of bottled-up feelings. In the midst of this crisis he attends Shabbat services at the synagogue the Pfeffermans attend, (when they attend services). He is shown sitting alone in the back of the sanctuary, listening to Rabbi Raquel speak about finding your way out of the wilderness. Maura's Shabbat dinner is intercut with Josh's synagogue experience, and what we see is both Josh and Maura coming to terms with who they are now, and how that person differs from who they have long believed themselves to be. The fact that the series uses Judaism as the mechanism for their personal growth is further proof that simply describing the Pfefferman family as "culturally Jewish" both denies the important role Judaism plays in their lives, and mischaracterizes the relationship a very large percentage of American Jews have to Judaism as somehow less than.

Transparent ended sort of abruptly in September 2019. Jeffrey Tambor was accused of serious, though apparently not criminal, misconduct with women associated with the show, in particular Trace Lysette. Tambor left the show, and Joey Solloway decided to end with one feature-length episode instead of an entire Maura-less season. The episode began with Maura being found dead by her friend and roommate Devina, although Maura's body is never shown as Tambor was not involved in the finale at all. The finale follows the reactions of Maura's friends and family to the loss of such an important part of their lives. It may be an understatement to say that the episode was polarizing. Headlines in the days following the finale's premiere ranges from "*Transparent's* Excruciating Musical Finale Hits One False Note After the Next"[18] and "Amazon's Musical Finale Strikes the Wrong Chord, Too Many Times,"[19] on one side to "The *Transparent Musicale Finale* is the show at its best, worst, and everything in between,"[20] in the middle, to "Gloriously Close to the Bone,"[21] and "Transparent's musical finale lays out the series' intent and its legacy"[22] on the other side.

Most of the controversy seems to be around the show's final number, called "Joyocaust." "Joyocaust" takes the language and imagery around Holocaust remembrance and argues that instead of dwelling on the sad and tragic, what "we" (and it seems that we is directed to Jews, but also meant for all people) need is a Joyocaust, and upwelling of joy and positivity. Many people thought the number crossed a line from edgy to offensive, while others thought it embodied the show's slightly odd relationship to Judaism perfectly. Overlooked in all the debate about the Joyocaust is the much quieter journey that Maura's youngest child has been on. The second half of season 4 followed the Pfeffermans to Israel. Maura had long believed her mother's story that her father was dead, but it turns out he was alive in Israel, so Maura and the family go to find him. The characters all had different reactions to visiting "The Promised Land," but Ali's was the most transformative. Ali announces at the end of the season that they are now using they/them pronouns and identifying as non-binary (another semi-autobiographical element as Joey Soloway also identifies this way). In the finale, Ali has begun to use the name Ari and has returned from Israel with a much deeper interest in Jewish practice than they or their siblings had in the past.

Ari, like many American Jews, apparently associates Israel with a level of Jewish "authenticity" that their American Jewish life lacks. Ari is now interested in becoming a rabbi and insists that the Pfefferman siblings should say Kaddish for Maura, which is the Jewish prayer for the dead. Additionally, Ari's song in the finale, "Father's House" is the most universally-praised song of the finale. It uses the biblical text of Genesis 12 in which God directs Abram (later to be known as Abraham) to leave his home, his father's house, and go to a new land where God will bless him. Part of the Torah portion known as "Lech Lecha," which literally means "go!" — this passage is seen by Jews as being the moment when the Jewish people are born. Ari's use of this motif is a final reminder by the show that American Jewish identity is a complicated thing and the apparent juxtaposition between the "authentic" Judaism Ari finds in Israel and the "cultural" Judaism Sarah and Josh live in the United States is exposed as really just a matter of approach, and not a fundamental difference in upbringing or socialization.

The Marvelous Mrs. Maisel

The final case study in this essay is also the most recent, and the only one still running as of 2021. *The Marvelous Mrs. Maisel*, like *Transparent*, is an Amazon Studios original series and was created by Amy Sherman-Palladino. The series follows Midge Maisel, initially an upper-middle class Jewish housewife, who suddenly discovers her gift for stand-up comedy when her husband leaves her. Sherman-Palladino is best known for creating *The Gilmore Girls*, a long running series that aired on the WB/CW (*Crazy Ex-Girlfriend's* network).

Sherman-Palladino was raised, in her own words, as "Jewish. Sort of."[23] Her father was Jewish and her mother was a Southern Baptist who "never considered actually converting to Judaism."[24] Her upbringing was therefore even less Jewishly-affiliated than the Pfeffermans': "It was the kind of Jewish that included Hanukkah, Star of David paraphernalia, and the occasional trip to temple, usually on high holidays or when someone my parents cared about died, which wasn't often 'cause my parents didn't really care about anybody."[25] She did not attend Hebrew school because it conflicted with her dance classes, and dance was the priority for her. It may have come as a surprise to some when Sherman-Palladino traded the extremely WASPy world of the Gilmore family's southern Connecticut for the very Jewish Upper West Side of the Maisels. But Sherman-Palladino speaks of her own Jewishness in terms of comedians. "If my mother would not convert, if I could not have a bat mitzvah, if I could never truly learn the rituals, the words, the point of leaving a chair open at Passover, at least I had them. I had Mel [Brooks]. I had Carl [Reiner]. I had found my inner Jew."[26] For Sherman-Palladino, Jewish humor was much more important than Jewish practice, and we can see that in the choices she has made with *Mrs. Maisel*.

The response to *Mrs. Maisel* has been mixed, especially within Jewish circles. Some publications, such as *The Times of Israel* and *The Forward*, herald the show with similar accolades to those heaped on *Transparent* a few years earlier. They call it "The Most Marvelously Jewish Show on Television" or proclaim its "Marvelous Jewishness."[27] At the same time, Rachel King, in an interview on the Jewish Women's Archive, said the show is "problematic when it came to portraying Jewish life at the time. I think this show is Amy Sherman Palladino's chance to finally inhabit a Jewish world (something the WASP-y storyline of *Gilmore Girls* didn't allow!), but rather than this feeling like a fond, winky portrait for a Jewish audience, I felt like the show is overly broad and full of cheap shots and stereotypes."[28] So while the sheer quantity of Jewish life on *Mrs. Maisel* is much higher than on *Transparent* or *Crazy Ex-Girlfriend*, the critics of the show seem to be responding to something more qualitative about the show's Jewishness.

This certainly comes, in part, from the fact that *Mrs. Maisel* is a period piece. It takes place in the late 1950s, so where *Crazy Ex-Girlfriend* and *Transparent* are trying to tap into elements of American Jewish life today, *Mrs. Maisel* is trying to recreate the Jewish world of sixty years ago. In doing so it relies much more heavily on, as King said, "overly broad … cheap shots and stereotypes." For example, a plotline in both season one and season two revolves around the Weissmans (Midge's parents) hosting the rabbi for Yom Kippur break-fast. In both seasons, extraordinary catastrophes occur, causing the rabbi to leave their house in horror. These dinner table scenes involve the family shouting at each other, each one trying to be louder than the rest, and failing to communicate with each other in any meaningful way. It is reminiscent of the famous "Easter dinner scene" from Annie Hall, in which Woody Allen contrasts the staid, polite holiday dinner of the (WASP) Hall family with a split-screen view of a holiday table from his childhood, in which his (Jewish) family screamed and shouted and grabbed at food in a scene of total chaos.[29] Sherman-Palladino is revisiting these same stereotypes about Jewish family dinners, but in 2019 they came across as dated or hackneyed to some viewers.

Other elements of the show are more refreshing, including how the entire series decamps to the Catskills for much of season 2. The Jewish resorts of the Catskills Mountains were an important part of the Americanization process for Jews. Before World War II Jews were excluded from many popular resorts, so if they wanted to escape the summer heat of the city it was necessary for them to have a place of their own. But even after the War, when most of those other resorts desegregated, Jews hung on to the Catskills as a place where they could vacation like other Americans, but still keep the option of Jewish holiday observances or kosher food. Most contemporary depictions of the Jewish Catskills resorts of the 1950s and 1960s rely on broad jokes about over-eating, matchmaking, and Jews lacking athletic prowess. These are all present in *Mrs. Maisel*, but they are not nearly as over-the-top as the Yom Kippur dinner scenes. Instead of the Catskills just being non-stop gluttony and spouse-hunting, then, the vacationers are shown stargazing, playing silly games like Simon Says, and doing sunrise calisthenics. With the exception of Shirley Maisel (Midge's former mother-in-law), who fares extremely poorly at Sherman-Palladino's hands no matter where she is, the other primary characters are much more human in the Catskills than they are in New York City. Midge's father Abe, especially, has a life and interests of which we saw no hints in the city, while Midge's misanthropic manager Susie actually makes friends and participates in a group talent show.

That the show is being well-received by some Jewish and most non-Jewish audiences, while being criticized by other Jewish groups, speaks to the way the series is situated as an artifact of contemporary American Judaism. The first season won both the Emmy and Golden Globe for outstanding comedy series. (*Transparent* also won the Golden Globe for Best Musical/Comedy, while only being nominated for the Emmy, and *Crazy Ex-Girlfriend* was never even nominated for any of the major series awards.) *Mrs. Maisel* can therefore safely claim to be the most critically-acclaimed of the three series, although all three have been recognized and appreciated. At the same time, however, *Mrs. Maisel*'s success demonstrates the ways in which Jews in America in the 2010s and 2020s are no longer a group whose experience is so unique that only Jews can understand it.

The strongest evidence for this transition comes from casting choices. As mentioned above, *Crazy Ex-Girlfriend* is traditional in its casting, as Rachel Bloom and Tova Feldshuh, who play the two primary Jewish characters, are both Jewish. *Transparent* is a mixture; while the older generation, Maura and Shelly, are played by Jeffrey Tambor and Judith Light, both of whom are Jewish, none of the actors playing the Pfefferman children are Jewish, and even fan-favorite Rabbi Raquel is played by Kathryn Hahn, who is, in her own words, "a nice Catholic girl from Cleveland."[30] In *Mrs. Maisel*, however, identity-based casting has disappeared completely. Neither Rachel Brosnahan, who plays Midge, nor Tony Shaloub or Marin Hinkle, who play her parents, are Jewish. And while many of the supporting actors are Jewish, including those playing Midge's ex-husband and his parents, those characters are also given the least depth and the most unrealistically stereotyped characterizations. To complicate things even further, Alex Borstein, who plays Susie, *is* Jewish, although her character, inexplicably, is not.[31]

So with *Mrs. Maisel* we have the fulfillment of "the Jewish vision of the American Dream," as "Jewish" has become an American identity that any actor can play, and the Jewish experience is one that any demographic can understand.[32] Although the series certainly still contains some inside jokes that a Jewishly-literate audience are more likely to appreciate, it relies more heavily on jokes that a New York City-literate audience will appreciate. (And, to be sure, it is frequently difficult to separate "Jewish" from "New York," as discussed above.) Sherman-Palladino is making a clear statement that to her Jewishness is religious and cultural, but not ethnic. In the same way any actor could play a Catholic priest, or someone from anywhere in the world could learn a Southern accent to play a Mississippi farmer, anyone can pick up the accent and mannerisms to play a New York Jew. This is certainly not an attitude that is shared by all American Jews, but it is increasingly aligned with what studies tell us younger American Jews believe.

Conclusion

Doing something new in television is always a risk. Television shows have to find an audience willing to return week after week — or for the streaming services binge season after season — in order to remain on the air. Given this context, the traditional fears that a population as small as American Jews could only really support one Jewish television show at a time make sense. But the quantity, quality, and diversity of new television platforms and services have proven that that it was shortsighted to assume either that Jews could only support one show, or that only Jews would be interested in shows about very Jewish characters and themes. One need only look to the phenomenon of *Shtisel* for proof that there is an audience for Jewish stories on television, even ones that depict much less popular or well-known types of Judaism. *Shtisel* is an Israeli television show about a Haredi (very traditionally Orthodox) community that was an overnight sensation with American audiences when it was picked up by Netflix in 2019. Suddenly a show that appeared to end in 2016 after two seasons got a third Israeli season, while an American adaptation set in Williamsburg, Brooklyn began development. So while the shows I have highlighted here align with and demonstrate what is true for a large portion of American Jews, it is always important to remember that Judaism — especially in America — is a complex and multi-faceted thing that defies any attempts to reduce it to simple, linear, or monolithic terms.

Observing the trends in representations of Jews on television, from expressions of Jewish identity to depictions of Jewish ritual and communal affiliation to issues of identity-based casting, is a helpful way to think about the place of Jews in contemporary America. All three shows discussed above indicate a move away from Jewishness being primarily about religious practice, and toward Jewishness being aligned to social or behavioral practices. Rebecca Bunch identifies strongly as Jewish, and speaks of herself in Jewish terms, despite the fact that we almost never see her engage with Jewish ritual or holiday practices. The Pfefferman family does not appear to belong to a synagogue, but they do return to the synagogue and to their Jewish communities to help them through difficult times; they seem to believe in the power of Jewish connectivity regardless of whether they believe in anything more traditionally "religious." The behaviors on *Mrs. Maisel* are different, since it depicts a fantasy of the Jewish past instead of a vision of the Jewish present. But through the choices of the creator and the reception to the show, we can nevertheless understand it as another piece of the contemporary American Jewish puzzle.

To return to the Pew profile of American Jews one more time, one of the overall trends it found is a movement away from Jewishly specific associations and toward generic American principles. The only things a majority (or near majority) of American Jews believed were "an essential part of what being Jewish means" were: remembering the Holocaust (73 percent), leading an ethical/moral life (69 percent), working for justice/equality (56 percent), and being intellectually curious (49 percent). Those are certainly all things many Jews value, but none of them are unique to Jews. Things like caring about Israel, being part of a Jewish community, observing Jewish law, or eating traditional Jewish foods all came in well below 50 percent. At the same time, 94 percent said working on the Sabbath was compatible with being Jewish, while 89 percent said the same of being highly critical of Israel and 68 percent agreed about belief in God. While these findings in no way speak for all American Jews, and there is a great deal of variation and nuance that such a survey cannot contain or convey, the trends do tell us that what we're seeing on television is in line with what is happening with certain segments of the American Jewish population.

There will always be trends and realities that exist outside of the mainstream and do not show up in either popular television shows or broadly conducted surveys. Unaffiliated Jews and Jews of no religion continue to grow while the traditional movements, especially the Conservative movement shrink, but Orthodoxy in America is growing, particularly in Haredi communities. Some of that comes from high birthrate (Orthodox Jews have a birthrate twice as high as the American or Jewish American average), but a lot of it comes from people, mainly Jews raised in a less traditional manner, being attracted to the strength and routine of those communities. The data, both sociological and media-based, all indicate that Jews have a robust and dynamic future in America, and on the airwaves.

Further Reading

Bernardi, Daniel, Murray Pomerance, and Hava Tirosh-Samuelson, eds. *Hollywood's Chosen People: The Jewish Experience in American Cinema*. Detroit: Wayne State University Press, 2017.

Diner, Hasia. *The Jews of the United States, 1654–2000*. Berkeley: University of California Press, 2006.

Kranson, Rachel. *Ambivalent Embrace: Jewish Upward Mobility in Postwar America*. Chapel Hill: University of North Carolina Press, 2017.

Wertheimer, Jack. *The New American Judaism: How Jews Practice Their Religion Today*. Princeton: Princeton University Press, 2018.

Bibliography

Annie Hall. Directed by Woody Allen. New York: United Artists, 1977.

Berman, Judy. "Transparent's Excruciating Musical Finale Hits One False Note After the Next." *Time*, September 25, 2019.

Brook, Vincent. *Something Ain't Kosher Here: The Rise of the "Jewish" Sitcom*. New Brunswick: Rutgers University Press, 2003.

Butler, Isaac. "*Transparent* Is the Most Profoundly Jewish Show in TV History." *Slate*, September 27, 2017.

Caplan, Jennifer. "Rachel Bloom's Gaping MAAW: Jewish Women, Stereotypes, and the Boundary Bending of *Crazy Ex-Girlfriend*." *The Journal of Modern Jewish Studies* 19, no. 1 (2020): 93–109.

Chavez, Danette. "The *Transparent Musicale Finale* is the show at its best, worst, and everything in between." *AV Club*, September 27, 2019.

Cohen, Sascha. "The Marvelous Jewishness of Mrs. Maisel." *The Forward*, December 4, 2017.

Crazy Ex-Girlfriend. "Josh and I Go to Los Angeles." Episode 1.13. Directed by Michael Patrick Jann. Written by Aline Brosh McKenna. The CW, February 29, 2016.

_____. "Josh Just Happens to Live Here." Episode 1.1. Directed by Marc Webb. Written by Rachel Bloom and Aline Brosh McKenna. The CW, October 12, 2015.

Heilman, Uri. "Kathryn Hahn Opens Up About Playing a Rabbi on *Transparent*." *Canadian Jewish News*, February 21, 2020.

Herberg, Will. *Protestant, Catholic, Jew: An Essay in American Religious Sociology*. Chicago: University of Chicago Press, 1960.

Hoffman, Jordan. "The Most Marvelously Jewish Show on Television is Back, and It's Just as Funny." *The Times of Israel*, December 5, 2018.

King, Rachel and Larisa Klebe. "A Tale of Two Maisels." *Jewish Women's Archive*, December 7, 2017.

Loofbourow, Lili. "How *The Marvelous Mrs. Maisel* Re-imagines the Stand-up Show." *The Week*, November 29, 2017.

Murray, Noel. "Transparent's Musical Finale Lays Out the Series' Intent and Its Legacy." *The Verge. com*, October 1, 2019.

Pew Research Center. "A Portrait of Jewish Americans." *Pewresearch.org.* October 1, 2013.

Pichard, Alexis. *Le nouvel âge d'or des séries américaines.* Paris: Editions Le Manuscrit, 2011.

Ramaswamy, Chitra. "Transparent: Musicale Finale Review — Gloriously Close to the Bone." *The Guardian*, September 27, 2019.

Sherman-Palladino, Amy. "How the 2,000-Year-Old Man Taught Amy Sherman-Palladino That She Was a Real Jew." *New York Magazine*, February 25, 2013.

Thurm, Eric. *"Transparent* Is the Most Jewish Show on Television." *Esquire*, October 6, 2016.

Transparent. "The Book of Life." Episode 2.7. Directed by Jim Fronha. Written by Ethan Kuperberg. Amazon Studios, December 11, 2015.

———. "The Wilderness." Episode 1.6. Directed by Joey Soloway. Written by Ethan Kuperberg. Amazon Studios, September 26, 2014.

———. "Transparent Musicale Finale." Episode 5.1. Directed by Joey Soloway. Written by Joey Soloway and Faith Soloway. Amazon Studios, September 27, 2019.

Travers, Ben. "'Transparent' Review: Amazon's Musical Finale Strikes the Wrong Chord, Too Many Times." *IndieWire.com*, September 28, 2019.

Watson, Amy. "Average Number of TV Services Used by Viewers in North America in 2017 and 2018." *Statista.com.* https://www.statista.com/statistics/798106/number-streaming-services-used-pay-tv-subscriber/.

World Population Review. "Jewish Population by State 2020." *World Population Review.com.* http://worldpopulationreview.com/states/jewish-population-by-state/.

Zurawik, David. *The Jews of Prime Time.* Lebanon: Brandeis University Press, 2003.

Notes

1. https://www.statista.com/statistics/798106/number-streaming-services-used-pay-tv-subscriber/.
2. http://worldpopulationreview.com/states/jewish-population-by-state/.
3. Will Herberg, *Protestant, Catholic, Jew: An Essay in American Religious Sociology* (Chicago: University of Chicago Press, 1960).
4. Alexis Pichard, *Le nouvel âge d'or des séries américaines* (Paris: Editions Le Manuscrit, 2011).
5. David Zurawik, *The Jews of Prime Time* (Lebanon: Brandeis University Press, 2003), 7–9.
6. Vincent Book, *Something Ain't Kosher Here: The Rise of the "Jewish" Sitcom* (New Brunswick: Rutgers University Press, 2003).
7. *Crazy Ex-Girlfriend*, "Josh Just Happens to Live Here," episode 1.1, directed by Marc Webb, written by Rachel Bloom and Aline Brosh McKenna, The CW, October 12, 2015.
8. *Crazy Ex-Girlfriend*, "Josh and I Go to Los Angeles," episode 1.13, directed by Michael Patrick Jann, written by Aline Brosh McKenna, The CW, February 29, 2016.
9. See, for example, https://www.vulture.com/2018/02/crazy-ex-girlfriend-best-songs-ranked.html, https://www.npr.org/2019/04/08/709062466/the-top-27-songs-of-crazy-ex-girlfriend-ranked-ruthlessly-and-dispassionately, or https://www.vox.com/culture/2018/1/19/16885806/crazy-ex-girlfriend-songs-ranked-list.
10. For a longer discussion of the depictions of the JAP and the Jewish Mother on this show, see "Rachel Bloom's Gaping MAAW: Jewish Women, Stereotypes, and the Boundary Bending of *Crazy Ex-Girlfriend*," *The Journal of Modern Jewish Studies* 19, no. 1 (2020): 93–109.
11. https://www.pewresearch.org/wp-content/uploads/sites/7/2013/10/jewish-american-beliefs-attitudes-culture-survey-overview.pdf.
12. The explicit version of "JAP Battle," for example, is far superior to the version that aired on the show.
13. https://slate.com/culture/2017/09/transparent-is-a-profoundly-jewish-tv-show.html.
14. https://www.esquire.com/entertainment/tv/a49295/judaism-on-transparent-jill-soloway/.

15   Ibid.
16   *Transparent*, "The Book of Life," episode 2.7, directed by Jim Fronha, written by Ethan Kuperberg, Amazon Studios, December 11, 2015.
17   *Transparent*, "The Wilderness," episode 1.6, directed by Joey Soloway, written by Ethan Kuperberg, Amazon Studios, September 26, 2014.
18   https://time.com/5682200/transparent-musicale-finale-review/.
19   https://www.indiewire.com/2019/09/transparent-finale-review-musical-ending-amazon-1202177103/.
20   https://tv.avclub.com/transparent-musicale-finale-is-the-show-at-its-best-wo-1838508933.
21   https://www.theguardian.com/tv-and-radio/2019/sep/27/transparent-musicale-finale-review-even-its-flaws-are-perfect.
22   https://www.theverge.com/2019/10/1/20892228/transparent-musical-finale-amazon-series-tv-review-legacy-history-jill-soloway-jeffrey-tambor.
23   https://www.vulture.com/2013/02/amy-sherman-palladino-2000-year-old-man.html.
24   Ibid.
25   Ibid.
26   Source: Amy Sherman-Palladino, "How the 2,000-Year-Old Man Taught Amy Sherman-Palladino That She Was a Real Jew" 2013. https://www.vulture.com/2013/02/amy-sherman-palladino-2000-year-old-man.html.
27   https://www.timesofisrael.com/the-most-marvelously-jewish-show-on-television-is-back-and-its-just-as-funny/, https://forward.com/schmooze/388943/the-marvelous-jewishness-of-mrs-maisel/.
28   https://jwa.org/blog/tale-of-two-maisels.
29   *Annie Hall*, directed by Woody Allen, New York: United Artists, 1977.
30   https://www.cjnews.com/culture/entertainment/kathryn-hahn-opens-up-about-playing-a-rabbi-on-transparent.
31   Susie's identity is actually a major problem for the show. Audiences assumed in season 1 that Susie was both Jewish, and gay. Season 2 revealed decisively that Susie is not Jewish, and the show seems very hesitant to confirm that she is a lesbian, much to the frustration of many critics. See for example, https://www.autostraddle.com/make-susie-gay-you-cowards-on-the-marvelous-mrs-maisels-lesbian-problem-443802/.
32   https://theweek.com/articles/740088/how-marvelous-mrs-maisel-reimagines-standup-show.

Index

Note: *Italics* refers to figure.

A Companion to American Religious History, First Edition. Edited by Benjamin E. Park.
© 2021 John Wiley & Sons, Inc. Published 2021 by John Wiley & Sons, Inc.